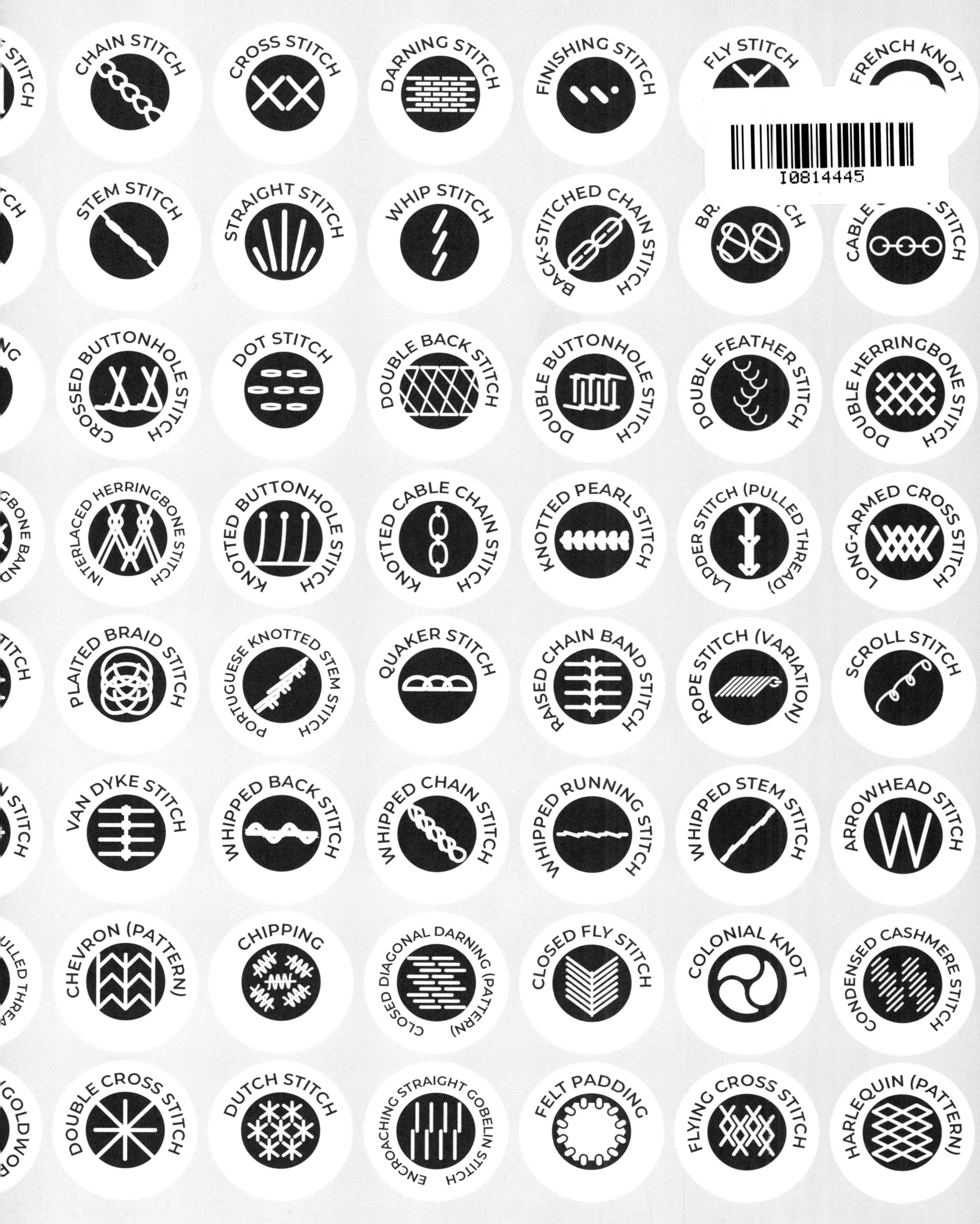
CHAIN STITCH
CROSS STITCH
DARNING STITCH
FINISHING STITCH
FLY STITCH
FRENCH KNOT
I0814445
STEM STITCH
STRAIGHT STITCH
WHIP STITCH
BACK-STITCHED CHAIN STITCH
CROSSED BUTTONHOLE STITCH
DOT STITCH
DOUBLE BACK STITCH
DOUBLE BUTTONHOLE STITCH
DOUBLE FEATHER STITCH
DOUBLE HERRINGBONE STITCH
INTERLACED HERRINGBONE STITCH
KNOTTED BUTTONHOLE STITCH
KNOTTED CABLE CHAIN STITCH
KNOTTED PEARL STITCH
LADDER STITCH (PULLED THREAD)
LONG-ARMED CROSS STITCH
PLAITED BRAID STITCH
PORTUGUESE KNOTTED STEM STITCH
QUAKER STITCH
RAISED CHAIN BAND STITCH
ROPE STITCH (VARIATION)
SCROLL STITCH
VAN DYKE STITCH
WHIPPED BACK STITCH
WHIPPED CHAIN STITCH
WHIPPED RUNNING STITCH
WHIPPED STEM STITCH
ARROWHEAD STITCH
CHEVRON (PATTERN)
CHIPPING
CLOSED DIAGONAL DARNING (PATTERN)
CLOSED FLY STITCH
COLONIAL KNOT
CONDENSED CASHMERE STITCH
DOUBLE CROSS STITCH
DUTCH STITCH
ENCROACHING STRAIGHT GOBELIN STITCH
FELT PADDING
FLYING CROSS STITCH
HARLEQUIN (PATTERN)

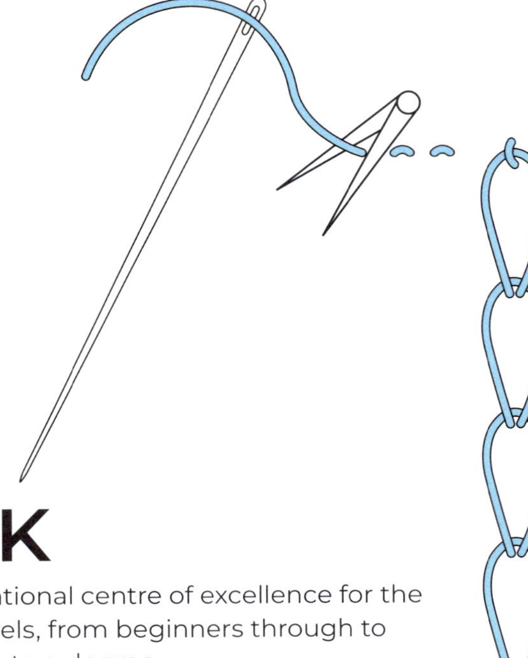

ROYAL SCHOOL OF NEEDLEWORK

The Royal School of Needlework (RSN) is the international centre of excellence for the art of hand embroidery and offers courses for all levels, from beginners through to advanced stitchers. These range from short courses to a degree.

The RSN teaches at the magnificent Hampton Court Palace in south-west London; across the UK; internationally in North America and Japan; and online, opening its doors to stitch lovers around the world. In addition, the Royal School of Needlework offers embroidery services at its studio in Hampton Court Palace, creating beautiful bespoke commissions for the future as well as restoring historical textiles and bringing heirlooms back to life. It also offers online talks and exhibitions at its headquarters that are open to all.

RSN Stitch Bank, a free online world directory of stitches, launched in September 2021 by revealing the first 150 stitches as the official opening of the renowned organization's 150th anniversary celebrations. More and more stitches continue to be added as part of the aim to digitally conserve and preserve every stitch from around the globe.

Dr Susan Kay-Williams has been Chief Executive of the RSN since 2007. During her time with the RSN, Susan has introduced the Degree in Hand Embroidery; the Professional Embroidery Tutor programme; the Diploma in Technical Hand Embroidery, regular onsite exhibitions and in particular, in response to lockdown, teaching online and the incredible resource, RSN Stitch Bank.

Susan curated the RSN's 150th anniversary exhibition at the Fashion and Textile Museum and is also author of *An Unbroken Thread – Celebrating 150 Years of the Royal School of Needlework* and *The Story of Colour in Textiles*.

200 Essential Embroidery Stitches

RSN
ROYAL SCHOOL OF NEEDLEWORK
Founded 1872

RSN
ROYAL SCHOOL
OF NEEDLEWORK
Founded 1872

RSN STITCHBANK

200 Essential Embroidery Stitches

SEARCH PRESS

CONTENTS

▲▲ Details from tambour work jacket, RSN Collection COL.46

This unusual garment combines Indian-style embroidery with European fashion. It is difficult to ascertain how this object came to be; perhaps it was made in the Indian subcontinent for the European export market or, more likely, someone cut up a piece of Indian embroidery and sewed it onto a plain jacket. This is suggested by the fact that the embroidery has been seamed together in some spots. Though the embellished toggles remain a mystery, the cords and tassels are typically Victorian.

It is made of cream buff silk with a cream silk satin interior. It is embroidered down the centre front, along the neck, and along all of the borders with pink, red, purple and blue flowers and green leaves. Chain stitch (see page 22) is used extensively. Some of the flowers can be identified as roses, and some have centres of silver passing threads. The embroidery is worked on linen which has been cut out and sewn onto the buff silk.

INTRODUCTION

RSN Stitch Bank was devised as the stitching equivalent of the Kew Millennium Seed Bank – a way to conserve and preserve every stitch in the world for future reference for stitchers, curators, historians and students. This was needed because embroidery and the textiles it adorns are some of the most fragile of items; they can be destroyed and damaged and stitches are lost.

The Royal School of Needlework (RSN) recognized that we should undertake this initiative because we are the international centre of excellence in hand embroidery and maintaining the art of hand embroidery is a fundamental principle of our founding. As a charity, the RSN had to raise the funds for this special project and did so by asking foundations and people to sponsor the early stitches. Today people can continue to support RSN Stitch Bank by giving annual support. As a result, we can keep access to RSN Stitch Bank free to all.

RSN Stitch Bank was considered such an important initiative that we launched it as the opening activity to our 150th anniversary on 5 November 2021 and continued to add to it throughout the anniversary year. We did not stop there, and at the time of publication, RSN Stitch Bank details more than 500 stitches.

Stitching brings many people and cultures together and it is fascinating to see some stitches which have literally gone round the world. Chain stitch, for example, started in China and is now found everywhere. Other stitches may seem to be the same as one another, yet the working of them may differ. What became clear was that there are a good number of stitches which are known in many cultures, and it is from these that we have selected the 200 in this volume.

We will continue our quest to find both these common stitches and more unusual ones, until we have found every stitch we can.

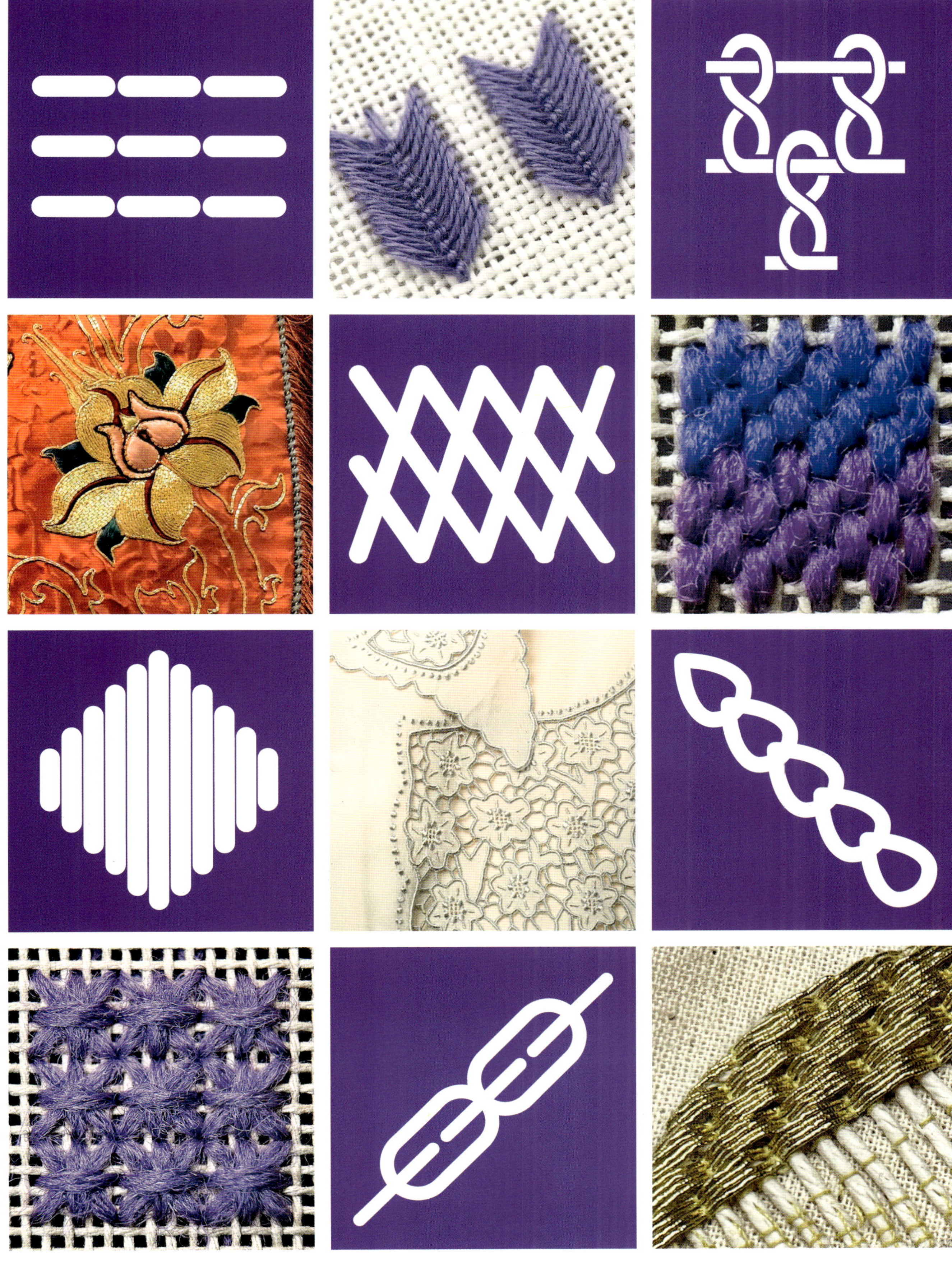

RSN:

ROYAL SCHOOL OF NEEDLEWORK

Founded in 1872, the Royal School of Needlework is the international centre of excellence for the art of hand embroidery. It is based at Hampton Court Place in west London and offers courses across the UK, in the USA, Japan, Australia and worldwide via its online programme. Today it is a thriving dynamic centre of teaching and learning, and believes that hand embroidery is a vital art form that impacts on many aspects of our lives from clothes to ceremonial outfits, and from home furnishings to textile art.

To enable and encourage people to learn the skill of hand embroidery, the RSN offers courses from one-day beginner classes to full-time professional qualifications. The wide range of short courses includes introductions to each of the stitch techniques the RSN uses, beginning with Introduction to Embroidery. The RSN's Certificate and Diploma in Technical Hand Embroidery offers students the opportunity to learn a range of techniques to a very high technical standard. The Professional Embroidery Tutor Programme is specifically designed for those pursuing a career in teaching hand embroidery. The RSN's BA (Hons) Hand Embroidery is the only UK degree course solely focused on hand embroidery and offers students opportunities to learn core stitch techniques, which they are then encouraged to apply in contemporary and conceptual directions. RSN Degree Graduates can go on to find careers in embroidery relating to fashion, couture, costume; to interiors and soft furnishings; or in the area of textile art, including jewellery and millinery.

At its main base in Hampton Court Palace, the RSN welcomes people for all kinds of classes and events, including bespoke classes, International Summer School, intensive Certificate and Diploma studies and exhibitions which showcase pieces from the unique RSN Collection & Archive as well as students' work. The RSN also has bases across the UK, teaching in Bristol, Rugby, Durham and Scotland. In addition, for those who live further afield, online classes and talks are available throughout the year.

The RSN Collection & Archive comprises more than 10,000 unique and priceless pieces that capture the passion for embroidery throughout history. It includes intricate hand-embroidered artwork on both clothes and textiles; beautiful designs; and also the RSN's development, documented through papers, books and photographs. The items have been collected and donated from all over the world, and illustrate many different techniques and approaches to stitch.

The RSN Embroidery Studio, based at Hampton Court Palace, undertakes new commissions, conservation and restoration work for many different clients, including public institutions, places of worship, stately homes and private individuals. Again, this illustrates the wide variety of roles embroidery can play, from altar frontals and vestments for churches to curtains, hangings and chair covers for homes and embroidered pictures as works of art. The experts in the Embroidery Studio also worked on nine different pieces for the Coronation of King Charles III and Queen Camilla.

HOW TO USE THIS BOOK

Embroidery is a living art. The aim of RSN Stitch Bank is to ensure hand embroidery is not just kept alive, but flourishes into the future. The 200 stitches in this book are a mix of practical and purely decorative stitches, carefully selected to provide a broad and varied basis for any embroiderer. Our aim is for RSN Stitch Bank to empower you to create contemporary works informed and supported by centuries of experience.

STITCH USE AND TECHNIQUES

The 200 stitches have been divided across seven chapters, each covering a particular usage, such as shading or edging, rather than by technique like many books. We have taken this approach as many stitches are used across multiple techniques such as whitework or crewel embroidery.

These chapters are colour coded (see below) to make it easy to find the right stitches while you work. This book also includes a number of historical pieces to highlight how stitches from across the whole book were traditionally used. These appear throughout the book, on the pages with purple bars – see page 14 for an example.

The pieces are mostly drawn from the RSN Collection, which is housed at Hampton Court Palace. The pieces are offered as inspiration, and range from samplers to clothing to devotional art. They are a showcase of the skill of embroiderers throughout history – and also show how stitches from across the whole range can be combined.

▲▲ Sampler, RSN Collection No. 475

This whitework technical sampler showcases different pulled and drawn stitches. Each petal and space between the petals features a different stitch.

Pulled thread is where threads are pulled together to make regular holes, while drawn thread is where threads are withdrawn to leave regular, patterned gaps in the warp or weft. This was worked in the 20th century by Mrs D Mitchell; the use of the ecru colour would suggest the first half of the century.

KEY TO CHAPTER COLOURS

- Basic stitches
- Outline and border stitches
- Filling stitches
- Shading stitches
- Open and powdered filling stitches
- Edging stitches
- Embellishment stitches

STITCH NAMES

The names given to the stitches in this book are those which are most commonly used by British embroiderers. We have consulted a variety of publications, largely from the last 100 years, to establish the primary name. Where necessary, a clarification is given in brackets: *buttonhole bars (cutwork)* differentiates it from *detached buttonhole bars*, which are worked as a surface stitch.

Stitchers from other traditions use different names, and some names have changed over time. To make things as clear as possible, any such alternative names are included alongside each stitch, as shown in the anatomy of a stitch, below. Foreign names are included only if the stitch is, or has been, commonly known by that name in the UK. You will notice that some stitches share their name with one or more other stitches: the name 'cushion stitch' can be used for cross stitch, burden stitch, Florentine stitch, long and short stitch and Scottish squares – not to forget the entry for cushion stitch itself.

Some names give an insight into the evolution or structure of the stitch. Fly stitch, for example, is also known as open loop stitch which makes sense if you know that detached chain stitch is also known as loop stitch. Likewise, cross bar with link trellis is sometimes called link powdering stitch, which is another of detached chain stitch's many names, as it describes a trellis embellished with chain stitches.

If a stitch is listed with 'variation' after its name – such as rope stitch (variation) on pages 108–109 – go to www.rsnstitchbank.org to see other alternatives. We would love to have included all of the stitches from RSN Stitch Bank in this book, but as it is ever-growing, this is sadly impossible!

ANATOMY OF A STITCH

This shows how each stitch appears on the page, to help you quickly find the key details of a particular stitch. Below this information are step-by-step instructions accompanied by diagrams and photographs.

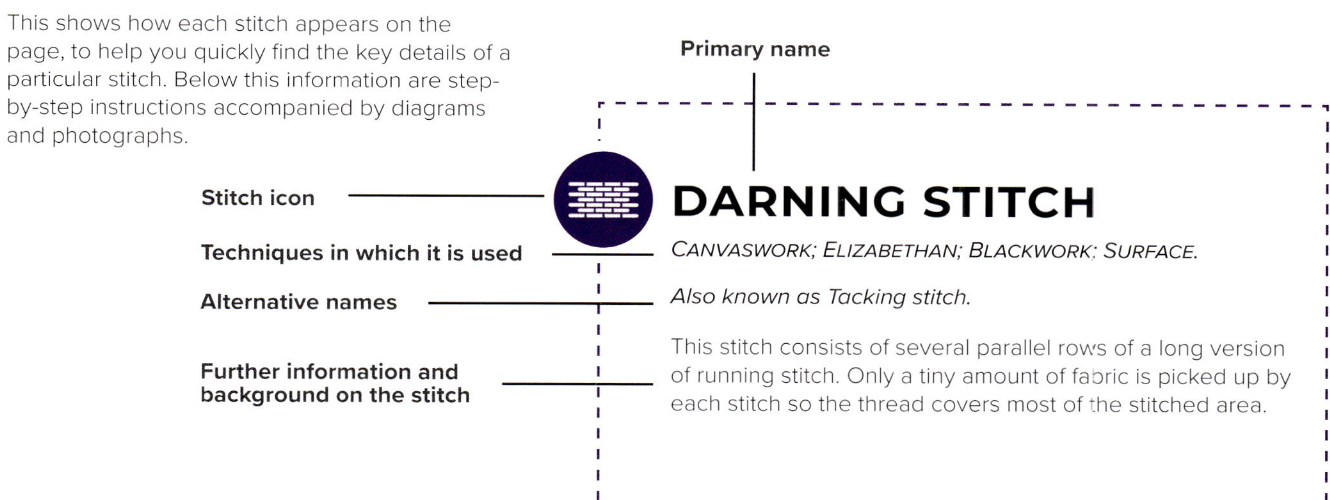

STITCH DIAGRAMS

The diagrams are shown step-by-step, and are designed to be as easy to follow as possible. Stitches are shown in blue, with integrated directional arrows (A) where this is relevant.

Stitches from earlier steps are sometimes shown in grey (C), in order to help distinguish them from those being described in the current step.

Large blue arrows (B) indicate where the needle will be brought up in the following step.

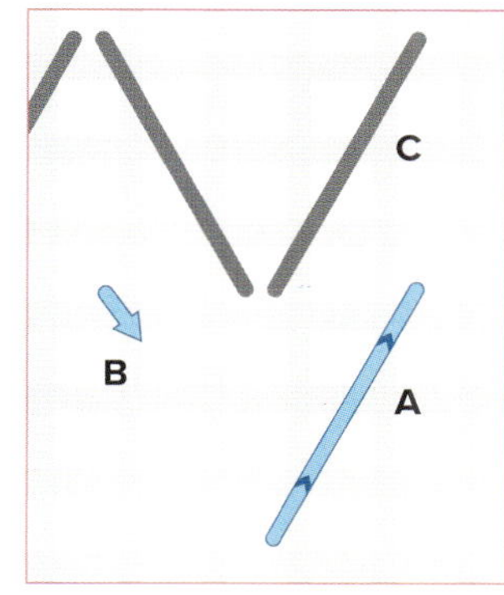

BASIC STITCHES

These stitches form the basis of most stitchers' repertoire, and are essential for all embroiderers to master, whatever you aim to produce.

Some of the stitches in this chapter, such as holding stitch or finishing stitch, are used literally every time we pick up a needle and thread. Others are ornamental as well as being practical – back stitch and herringbone stitch, for example, are used by tailors and dressmakers for many different purposes.

You may have learnt some of these stitches as a child, but do not dismiss their importance: buttonhole and chain stitch are used both in their own right and also as the basis for many other stitches; running stitch and cross stitch are used as the sole stitch in entire pieces of embroidery in traditions from around the world, proving just how versatile a single stitch can be.

PAGE 16

PAGE 18

PAGE 20

PAGE 22

PAGE 24

PAGE 26

PAGE 27

PAGE 28

PAGE 29

PAGE 30

PAGE 31

PAGE 32

PAGE 34

PAGE 36

PAGE 37

PAGE 39

PAGE 40

PAGE 42

PAGE 43

EMBROIDERY TECHNIQUE: CREWELWORK

Also known as Jacobean work, Jacobean crewelwork, or crewel work.

Crewelwork is a style of surface embroidery using crewel wool thread, which was particularly popular in early 17th-century Britain during the reign of King James VI of Scotland and I of England. In Latin, 'James' was rendered as *Jacobus*, hence the period is referred to as Jacobean; and hence this embroidery technique is often termed Jacobean work or Jacobean crewelwork. Its popularity spread with the early settlers to the United States.

Designs from this period are often based on a tree of life motif which consists of a central tree emerging from stylized hillocks. The tree features flowing branches embellished with stylized leaves, flowers, fruit and animals, often chosen for their symbolism. The tree of life motif was almost certainly influenced by its use on *palampores* (bedcovers) which were being imported from India, and the increase in botanical illustrations prompted by the discovery of previously unknown plants from the New World.

Original Jacobean crewelwork pieces were often created as large hangings or other items for domestic houses. Colour palettes are normally greens, blues, bright yellows and browns with some red, worked on an off-white or beige tightly woven linen twill fabric. Pieces often feature a wide variety of embroidery stitches which create a richly textured surface.

▸▸ Four-panel screen, RSN Collection

This four-panel screen in Jacobean Crewelwork was made by one woman in the 1920s. It exhibits a very high level of technique and consistency with excellent ranges of colour. When the stitcher passed away, her family donated this screen to the Royal School of Needlework. It is now a source of inspiration for both RSN Students and Tutors.

▴▴ Detail of French knots – page 29

▴▴ Detail of outline stitch – pages 32–33

BACK STITCH

Blackwork; Crewelwork; Wessex stitchery; Canvaswork; Basic; Surface; Counted thread; Cross stitch; Mountmellick; Berlin wool work.

Also known as Hem stitch.

Back stitch is a basic flat stitch in which the visible element of the stitch is worked backwards to the general direction of sewing to create a continuous solid line.

Back stitch's history is hard to ascertain: the earliest examples which we can be confident of dating are seen in English Jacobean crewelwork (from the 16th century) but it is most probably considerably older.

Portuguese Guimarães whitework dates back to the 10th century, and now employs back stitch as one of its many stitches but it is unclear whether it was one of the original stitches. Similarly, the Indian techniques of Chikan embroidery (a whitework technique from northern India popularized during the 19th century, but originating much earlier) and Rabari embroidery (done by the Rabari nomadic people to decorate the seams of garments) both use back stitch, but the origins of both techniques are obscure.

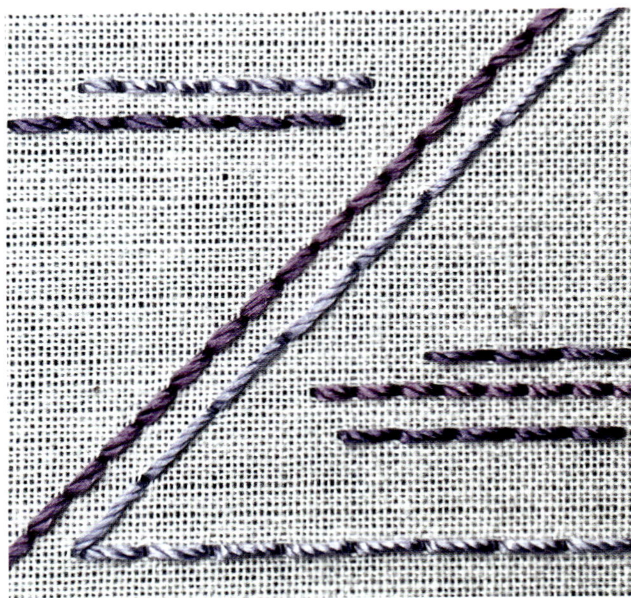

METHOD

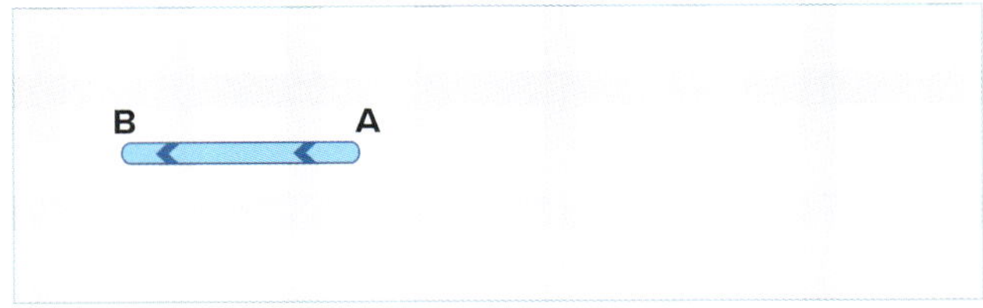

1 Decide how long you want the stitches to be and bring the needle up on the design line that distance from the start. Insert the needle through the fabric at the start of the line to make the first stitch.

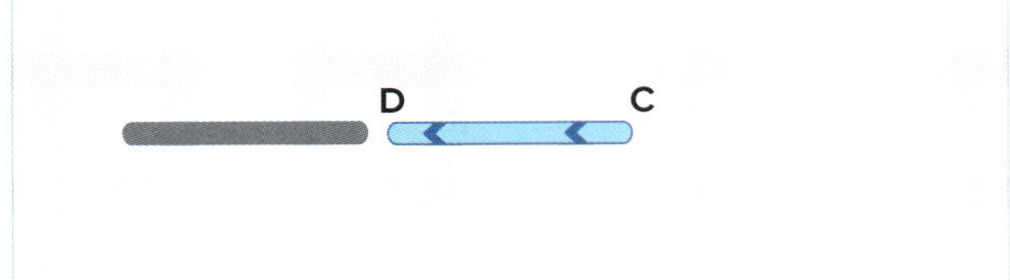

2 Continue along the line, bringing the needle up at the desired stitch length from the first stitch.

3 Take the needle down into the fabric at the end of the previous stitch.

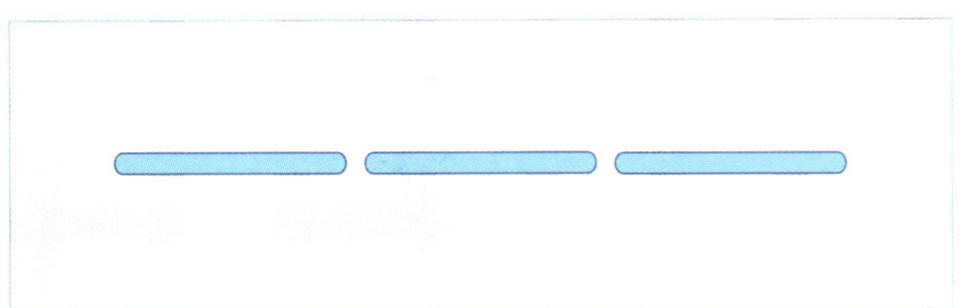

4 Continue along the line to the end.

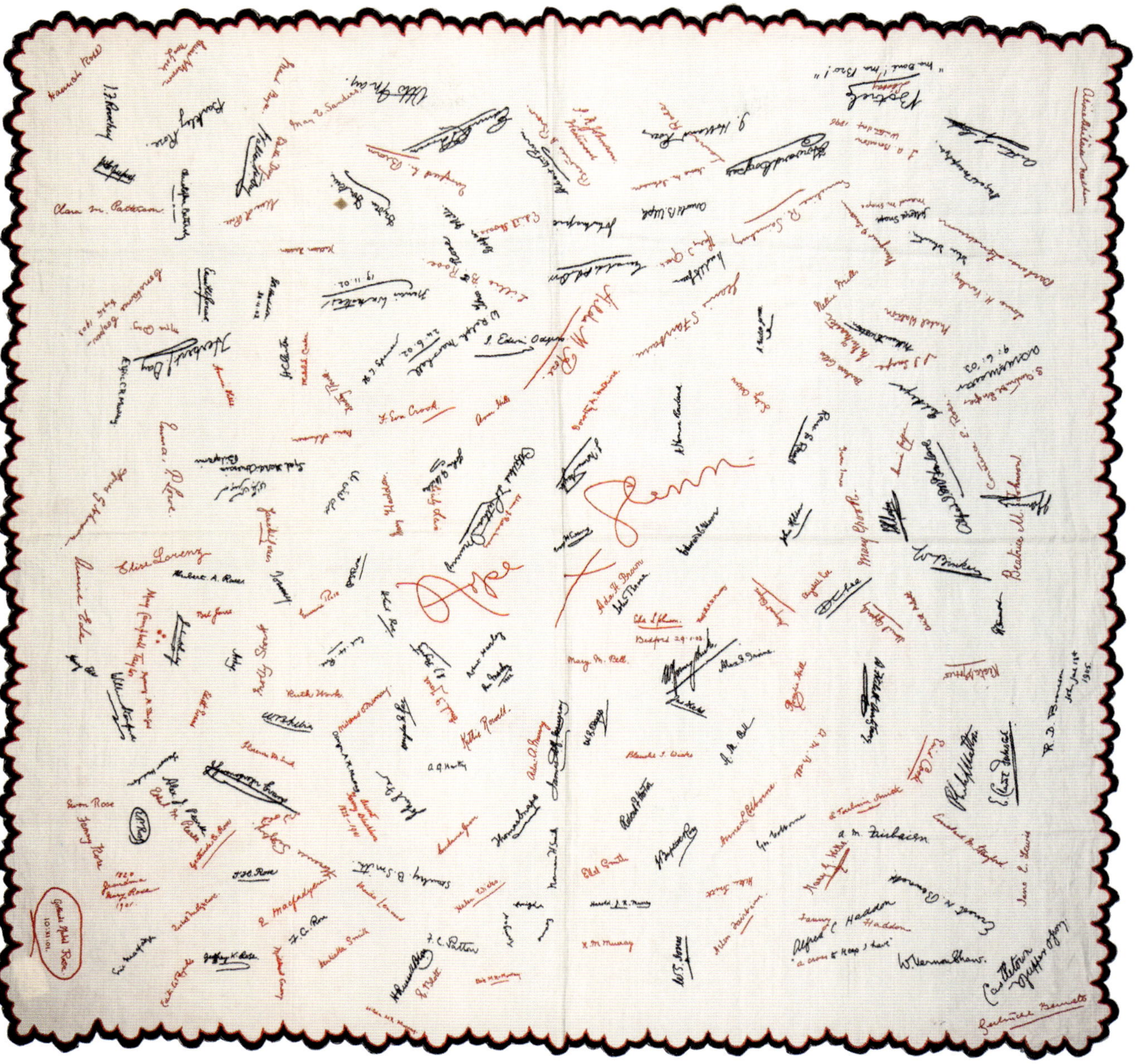

▲▲ Tablecloth, RSN Collection COL.2009.26

An almost square tablecloth in fine white linen with scalloped embroidered edging in black silk buttonhole stitch and red silk whipped chain stitch, scattered with 215 embroidered signatures in red or black silk back stitch. The back stitch is a variation involving forwards and backwards movement, resulting in a smooth line on the front.

Some of the signatures are accompanied by dates between 1896 and 1905; of these, 212 are in English and the remaining three are in Urdu, Arabic, or Farsi.

It is likely that this object was embroidered by Gertrude Mabel Rose, whose name and a date, 10 November 1901, are enclosed in red stem stitch in one corner – as shown in the detail to the right. It is likely that 10 November 1901 is either when she began or finished this tablecloth.

BLANKET STITCH

BASIC; SURFACE; BLACKWORK.

Also known as Blanket edge, or Open buttonhole stitch.

Blanket stitch consists of a row of loops each anchored by the following stitch to form an L-shape. It is stitched in a similar way to buttonhole stitch (see page 20): the only difference is the spacing.

The earliest evidence we have of blanket stitch is from excavations of 4th-century AD artefacts in Kellis, Egypt, where a child's tunic has been found with multicoloured blocks of blanket stitch around the edge of the hood.

Blanket stitch has continued to be used in various embroidery traditions such as within Guimarães embroidery from Portugal; and by embroiderers from the Siwa Oasis, Egypt.

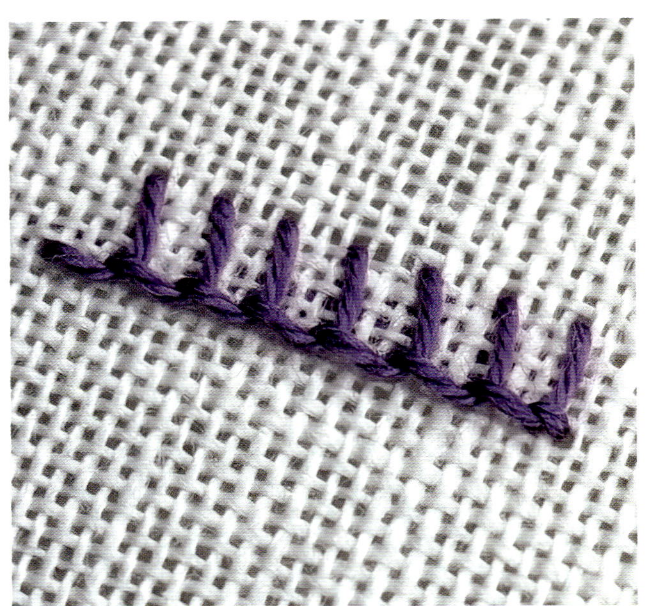

METHOD

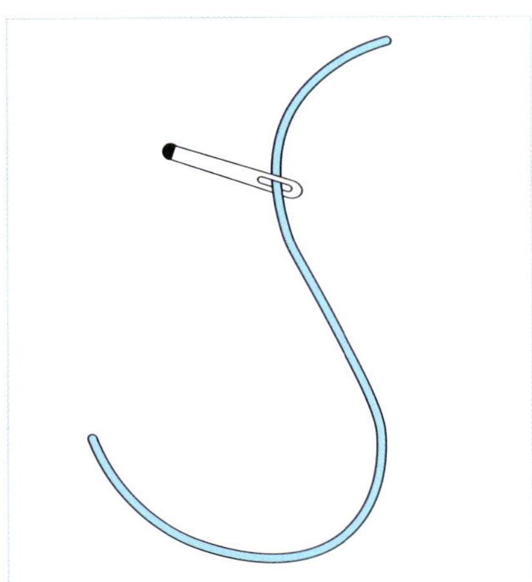

1 Come up on the outside edge of the shape and take the needle down on the inside of the shape, a little further in the direction of travel.

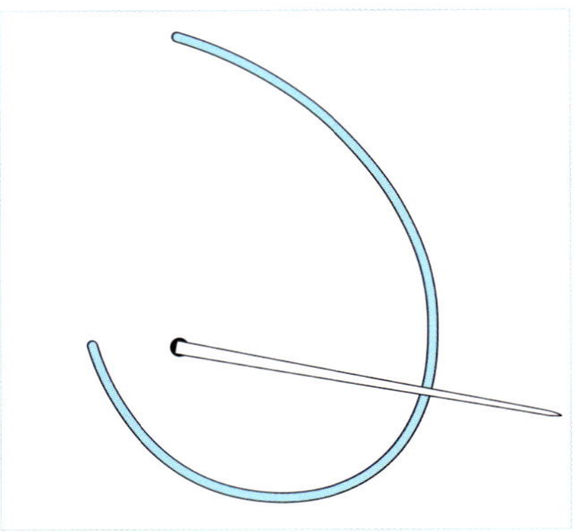

2 Assuming you are working left to right, hold the surface thread in a loop to the right, then bring the needle up directly below, on the outside edge, ensuring the needle is inside the loop.

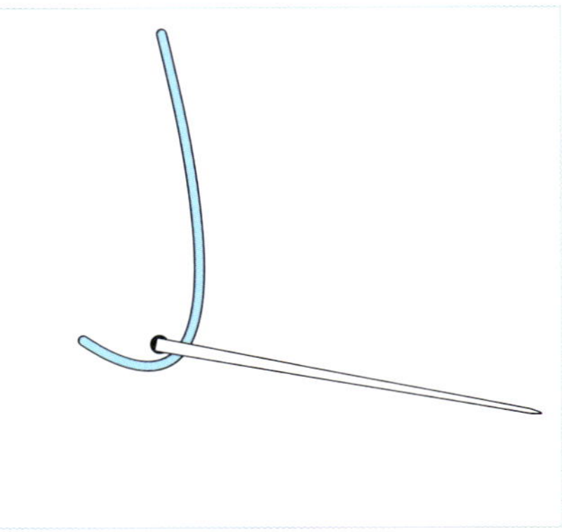

3 Hold the needle in the fabric securely with your surface hand while you pull the thread from the underside to tighten the slack against the loop.

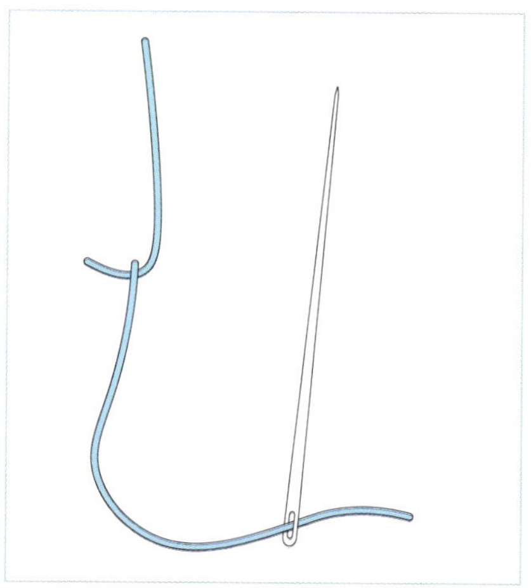

4 Pull the needle through and bring the thread up to the surface.

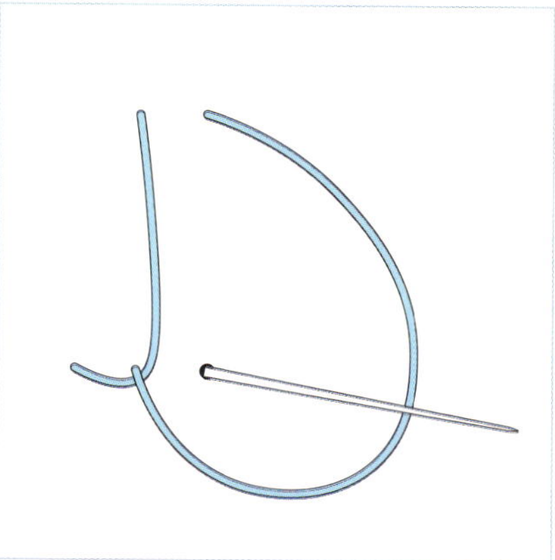

5 For the next stitch, take the needle down through the fabric on the inside edge of the shape, leaving a gap to the right of the first stitch. Again, leave a loop to the right and bring the needle up on the outside edge within the loop.

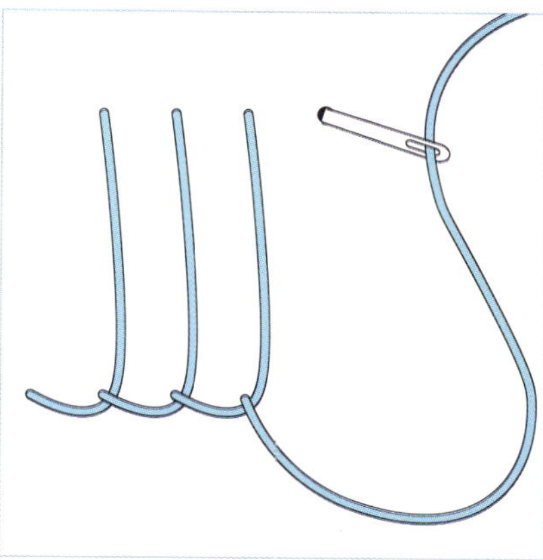

6 Tighten the slack while holding the needle in the fabric, then pull the needle through and bring the thread to the surface. Repeat these stitches until the shape is filled.

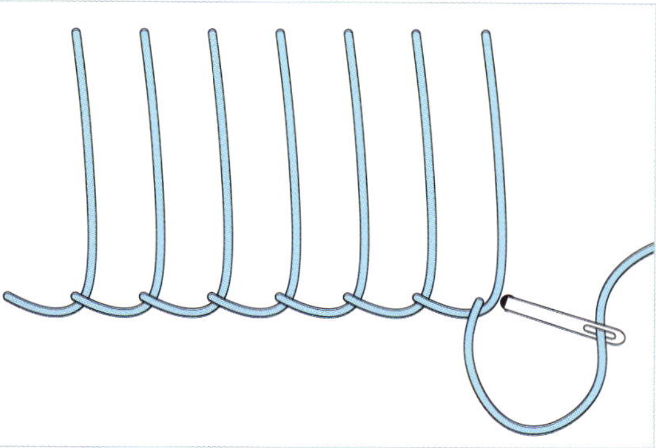

7 The final stitch needs a holding stitch on the outside edge to secure the last loop.

▲▲ Detail from cushion cover, RSN Collection COL.2005.3

Blanket stitch is used here for edging some of the design elements, alongside heavy chain stitch, stem stitch and seeding stitch (see pages 76, 40–41 and 265 respectively). The full piece can be seen on page 77.

BUTTONHOLE STITCH

Whitework; Hardanger; Crewelwork; Surface; Stumpwork; Appliqué; Basic; Mountmellick; Elizabethan; Blackwork.

Also known as Point Mexico stitch, Point noné stitch, Close stitch, Double overcast stitch, or Buttonholed satin stitch.

As the name suggests, this stitch was originally used to reinforce the slots cut for buttons. It produces a neat outline of its own and can be worked with vertical threads or shaped and angled to fit a space (when used in this way, particularly in whitework techniques, it is sometimes called buttonholed satin stitch). You can work the stitches more closely together for a dense appearance or slightly spread out for a less dense appearance. It is very similar to blanket stitch – the only distinction is the spacing between the stitches.

Buttonhole stitch has been in use since at least the 16th century; in Italian cutwork, in English Jacobean embroidery and in German/Swiss ecclesiastical embroidery. By the 19th century it was a notable feature of Broderie Anglaise in the UK and Rococo embroidery in northern Europe.

More widely, buttonhole is a popular stitch in parts of Asia: Pakko and Rebari work in Kutch, north-western India; Chikan work from Lucknow in Uttar Pradesh, Kashmir embroidery from the Jammu and Kashmir region in north-western India; and in Hazarajat, Afghanistan.

Further west, it is used in Dresden and Schwalm embroidery, Germany; on traditional *aska takwas* shirts in Nigeria and on traditional *huipiles* (tunics) in Mexico; finally it is a particular feature of Wallachian whitework from the USA (distinct from the original Romanian Wallachian embroidery).

METHOD

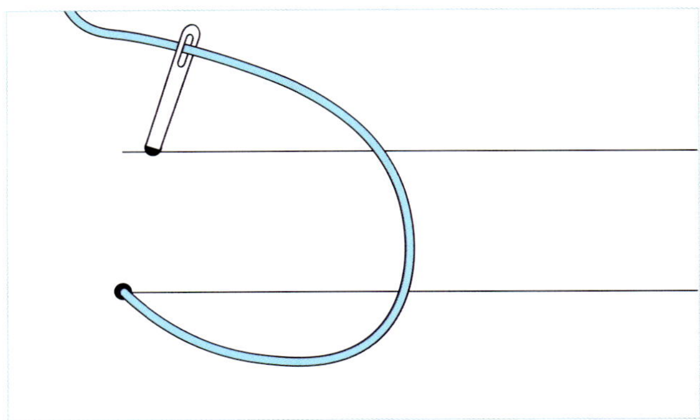

1 Come up on the outside edge of the shape and take the needle down on the inside of the shape.

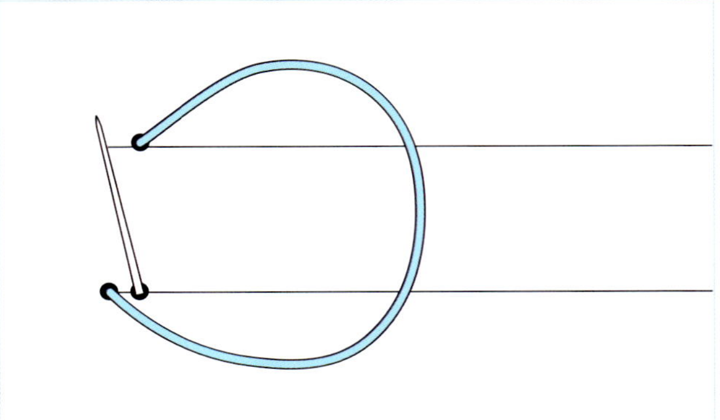

2 Assuming you are working left to right, hold the surface thread in a loop to the right, then bring the needle up on the outside edge, ensuring the needle is inside the loop.

3 Hold the needle in the fabric securely with your surface hand while you pull the thread from the underside to tighten the slack on the loop.

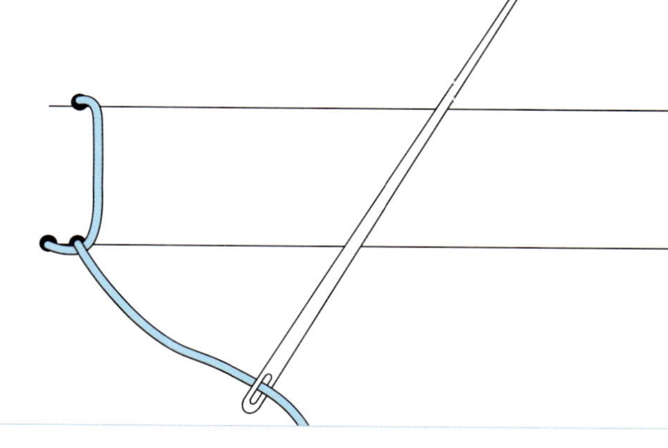

4 Pull the needle through and bring the thread up to the surface.

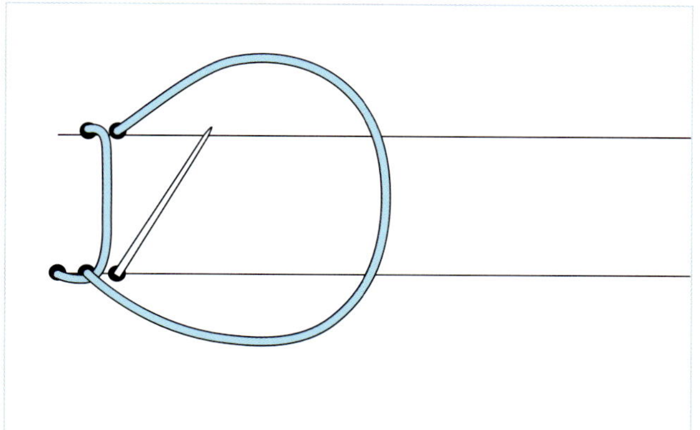

5 For the next stitch, take the needle down through the fabric on the inside edge of the shape, slightly to the right of the first stitch. Again, leave a loop to the right and bring the needle up on the outside edge within the loop.

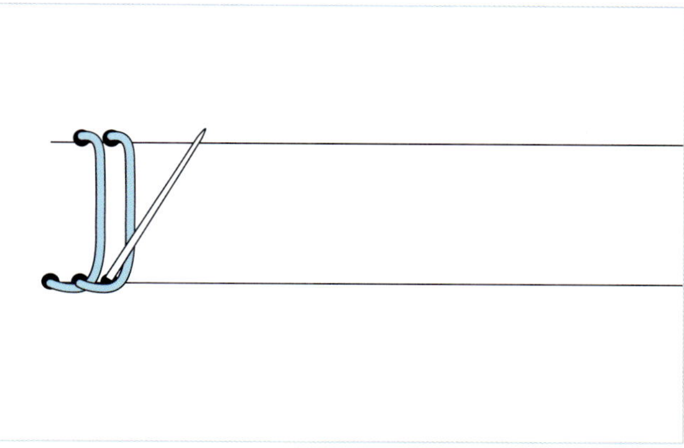

6 Tighten the slack while holding the needle in the fabric, then pull the needle through and bring the thread to the surface. Repeat these stitches until the shape is filled.

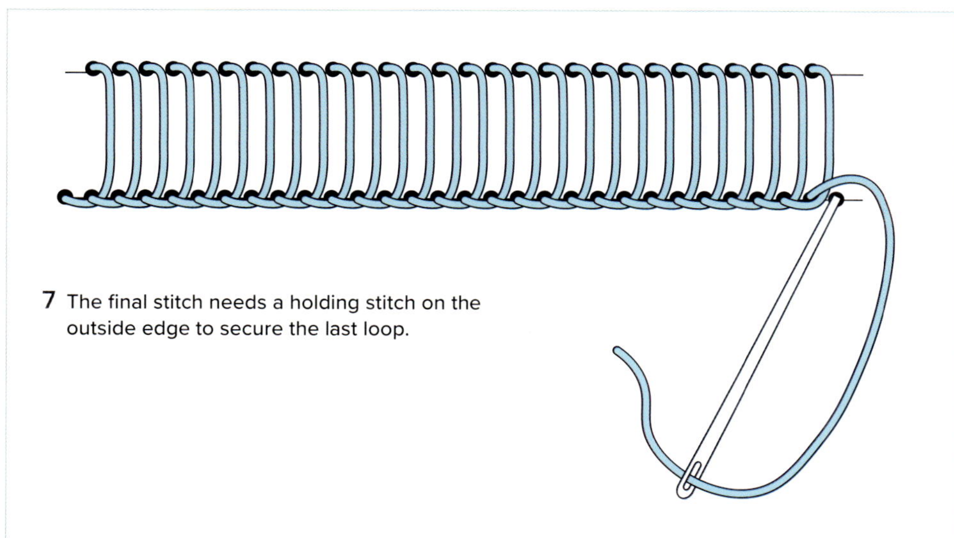

7 The final stitch needs a holding stitch on the outside edge to secure the last loop.

CHAIN STITCH

BLACKWORK; CREWELWORK; BASIC; MOUNTMELLICK; SURFACE; STUMPWORK; ELIZABETHAN.

Chain stitch consists of a series of interlocking loops, each held in place by the next.

Chain stitch is one of the oldest and most widely known stitches in existence. Examples have been found in Egypt on textiles from Tutankhamun's tomb, dated to the 14th century BC; on embroideries found in Pazyryk tombs dating from the 4th to the 3rd centuries BC (excavated in southern Siberia but probably originating in China). Later evidence from China indicates the stitch was the most prevalent stitch there until the T'ang dynasty towards the end of the first millennium AD.

METHOD

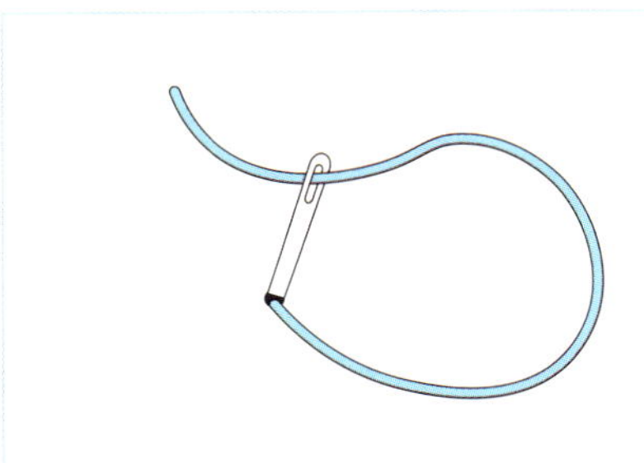

1 Bring the needle up and down in the same hole, leaving a large loop on the surface of the fabric.

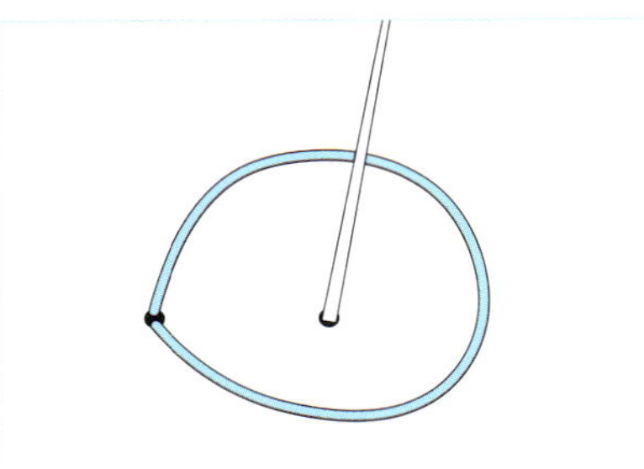

2 Bring the needle up again at the point you wish to anchor the loop, making sure you bring the needle up inside the loop.

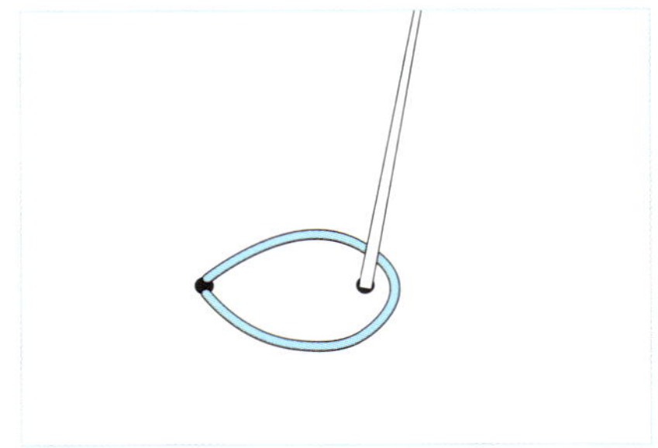

3 Hold the needle in the fabric with your surface hand while you use your underside hand to pull through the slack of the loop by tightening against the needle.

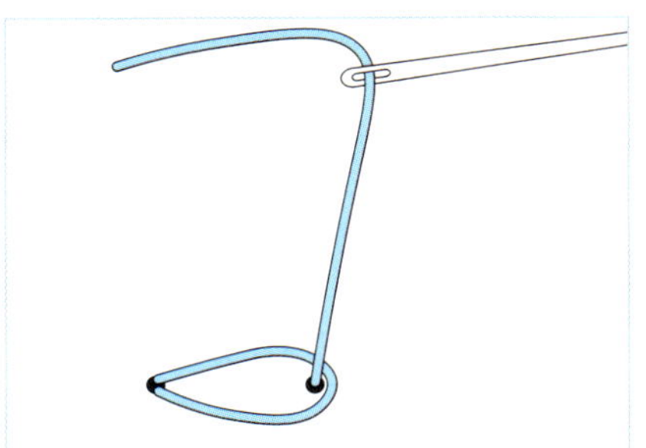

4 Bring the needle and thread all the way through to the surface.

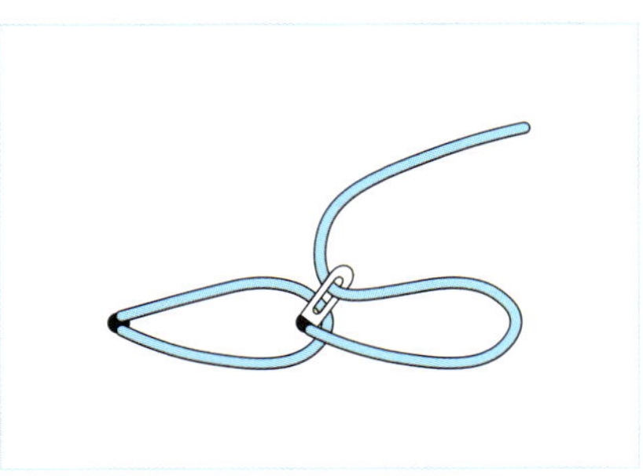

5 Form the second chain by taking the needle back through the same hole.

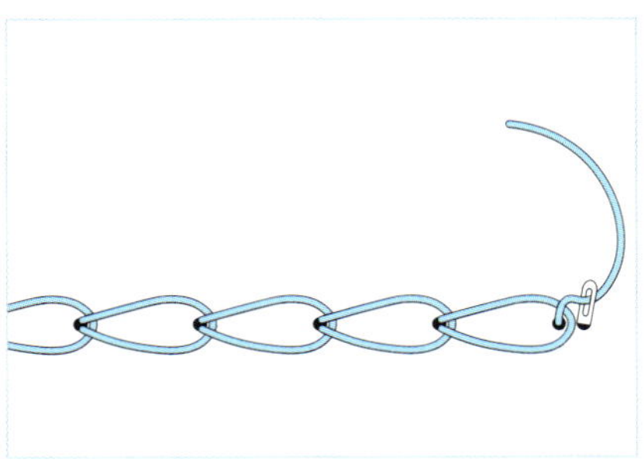

6 Continue along the design line to the end, then secure the last loop with a holding stitch.

▲▲ Detail from Juno, Venus, Minerva and Proserpine screen, RSN Collection No. 2707

A section of a large, four-panel screen designed by Selwyn Image and worked by the RSN. Using one colour and one stitch – chain stitch, in this example – was one of the approaches of art embroidery to make the working of large items quicker, such as screens.

CROSS STITCH

Counted thread; Canvaswork; Cross stitch; Surface; Berlin wool work; Stumpwork.

Also known as Sampler stitch, Gros point, Cushion stitch, Point de croix stitch, Point de marque stitch, or Simple cross stitch.

Cross stitch consists of two straight, crossing stitches which can be worked individually or in rows. The direction of the top stitch should always be in the same direction (unless variation of the shade is required). When used for marking, it is often worked in a way that the stitching is identical on both sides (two-sided cross stitch) or so it forms a neat square at the back of the linen (marking cross stitch).

Cross stitch is mainly used as a counted thread technique on aida fabric and in canvaswork, but it is also found in free embroidery on evenweave fabric. Both are commonly worked from a gridded pattern called a chart.

The stitch directions could be reversed (i.e. bottom left to top right as the underneath stitch, and bottom right to top left as the top stitch); it does not matter as long as the top diagonal stitch is consistent across all stitches.

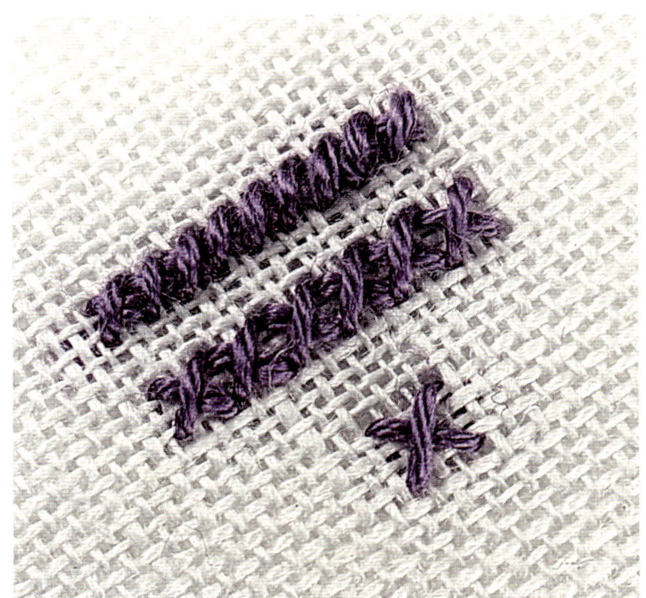

INDIVIDUALLY WORKED

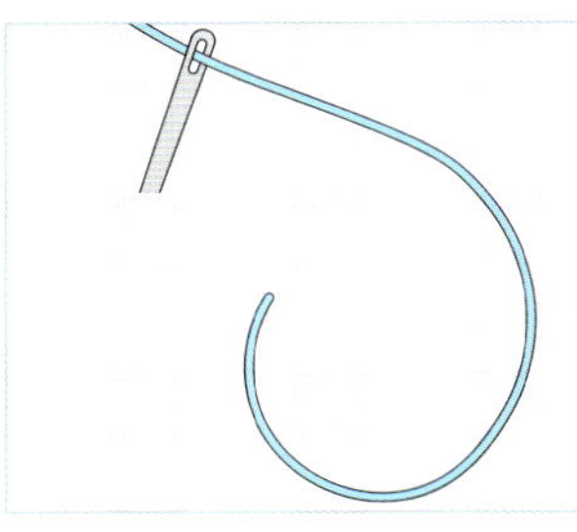

1 Take the first part of the stitch from the right-hand bottom side of the square across to the left-hand top side.

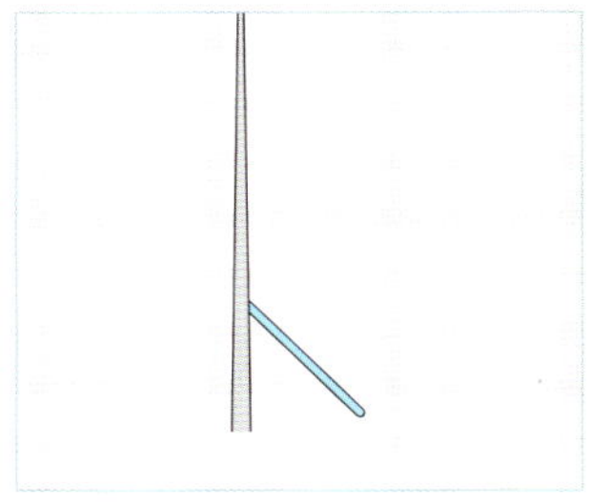

2 Bring the needle up at the left-hand bottom side of the square.

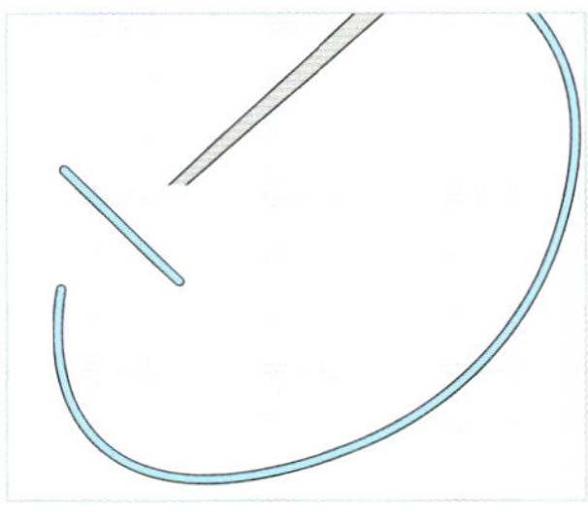

3 Work the second stitch from the left-hand bottom side of the square across to the right-hand top side.

A complete cross stitch, worked individually.

WORKED IN A ROW

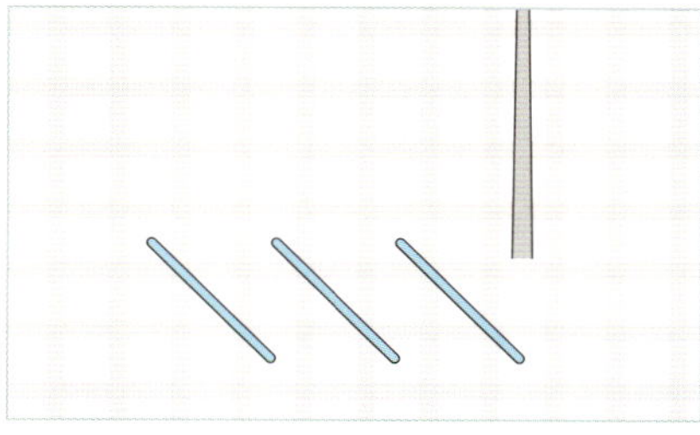

1 Work the first part of each stitch from top left to bottom right.

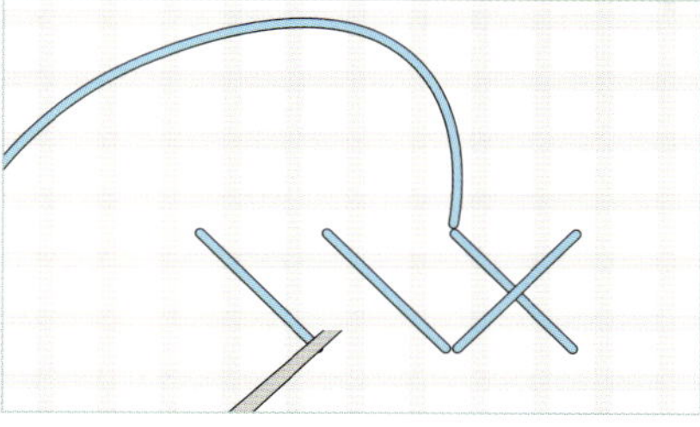

2 On the way back, work the second part of each stitch from top right to bottom left.

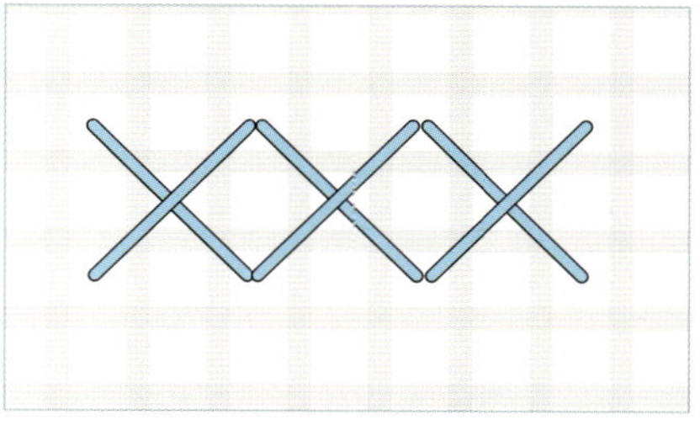

A completed row of cross stitch.

▲▲ Berlin wool work Border, RSN Collection COL.8

The image shows a small piece of border worked in cross stitch and the vibrant coloured wools associated with this style of embroidery.

Berlin wool work is a canvaswork technique which originated in Berlin in the early 19th century. Pattern books with coloured symbols were published with various designs, from motifs of flora and fauna to copies of famous paintings. It is characterized by the use of brightly-coloured wool, often attributed to the advent of synthetic aniline dyes in the 1850s.

The formulaic nature and the bold colour choices of Berlin wool work led to it falling out of favour. This in turn led to the rise of the art needlework movement, and ultimately the creation of the Royal School of Needlework.

DARNING STITCH

CANVASWORK; ELIZABETHAN; BLACKWORK; SURFACE.

Also known as Tacking stitch.

This stitch consists of several parallel rows of a long version of running stitch (see page 36). Only a tiny amount of fabric is picked up by each stitch so the thread covers most of the stitched area. Geometric patterns can be built up by varying the arrangement of the stitches. In this example, a simple brick pattern arrangement is formed by offsetting the stitches.

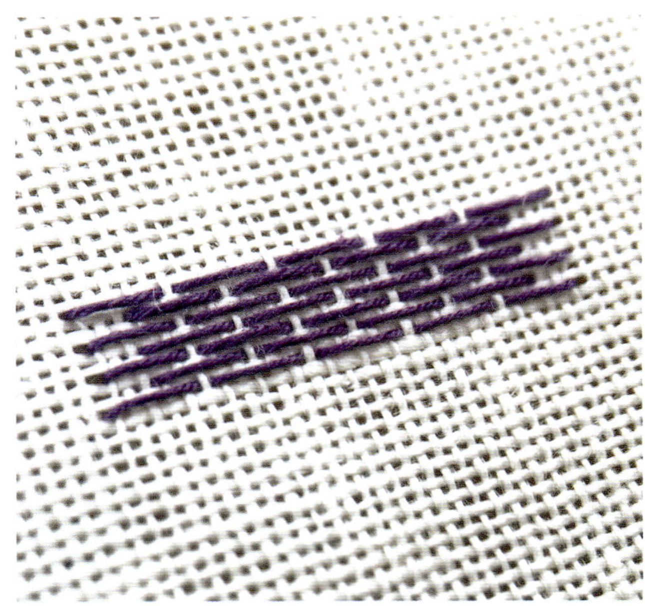

METHOD

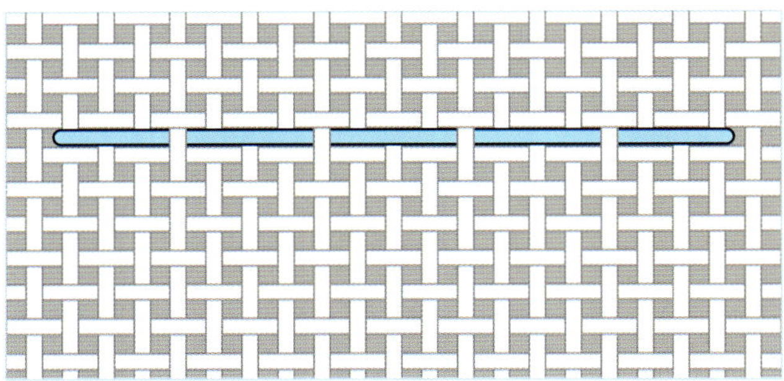

1 Work a long running stitch picking up only a small amount of fabric in between the stitches.

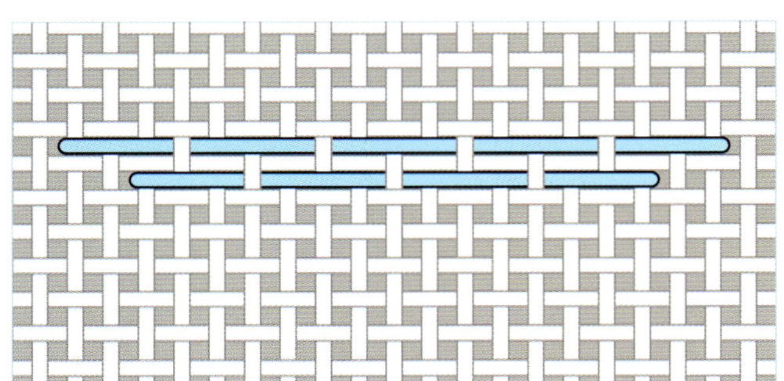

2 Work the second row in the same way, but arranging the stitches to make a simple brick pattern as shown.

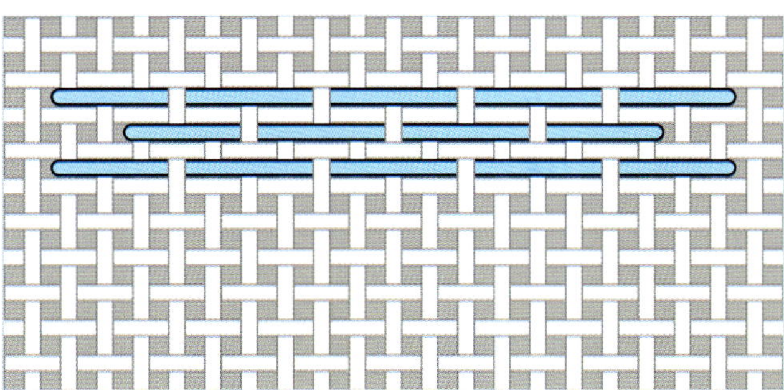

3 Work the third row in line with the first so that the brick pattern is being built up.

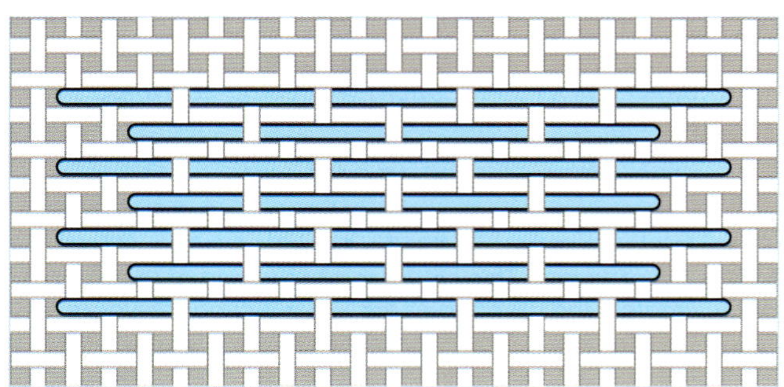

4 Continue in the same way to fill the area.

FINISHING STITCH

APPLIQUÉ; AYRSHIRE; BASIC; BEAD EMBROIDERY; CREWELWORK; CUTWORK; GOLDWORK; HARDANGER; MOUNTMELLICK; OPUS ANGLICANUM; SILK SHADING; STUMPWORK; SURFACE; WESSEX STITCHERY; WHITEWORK.

Finishing stitches are used to securely end a piece of thread by anchoring it to the fabric.

See holding stitch on page 31 for how to use this method to finish your thread.

METHOD

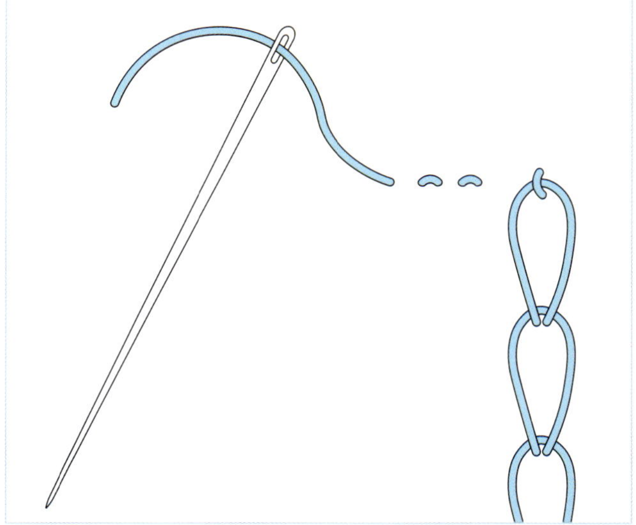

1 Working in an area that will subsequently be hidden beneath stitching, make two tiny stitches. Alternatively (if this is the last stitching in this area), carefully angle the needle and bring it up between previous stitches and make two tiny stitches, hiding them under your existing stitches.

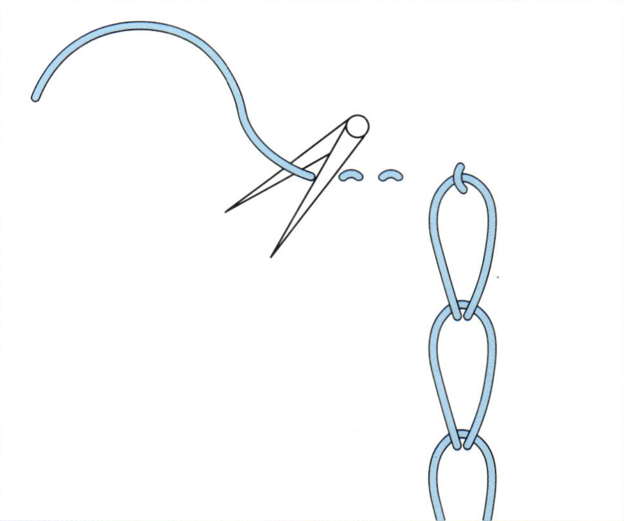

2 Bring the needle through to the top of the fabric and cut it off close to the fabric surface.

FLY STITCH

WESSEX STITCHERY; MOUNTMELLICK; RIBBONWORK; SURFACE.

Also known as Open loop stitch, or Y-stitch.

Fly stitch consists of a straight stitch pulled down into a 'V' shape by an anchoring stitch. Elongating the anchoring stitch transforms the stitch into a 'Y' shape.

For a solid line version of this stitch, see closed fly stitch on page 147.

Fly stitch is cited as one of the range of historic stitches used by May Morris and the other embroiderers employed by Morris & Co., the iconic Arts and Crafts company. Try varying the length of the stitches and the angle of the 'V' to achieve different looks.

METHOD

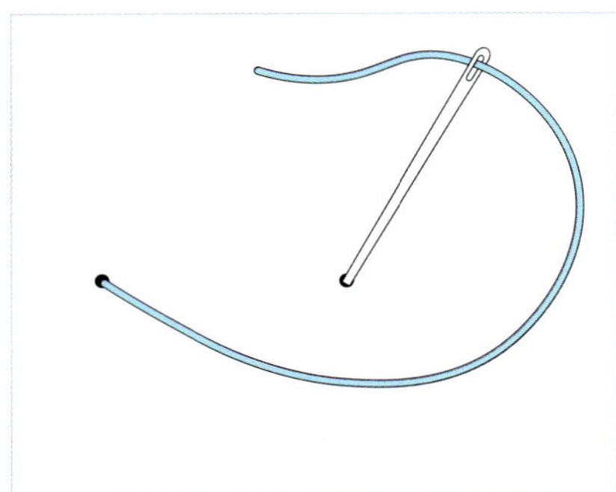

1 Bring the needle and thread up and down through the fabric, a short distance apart.

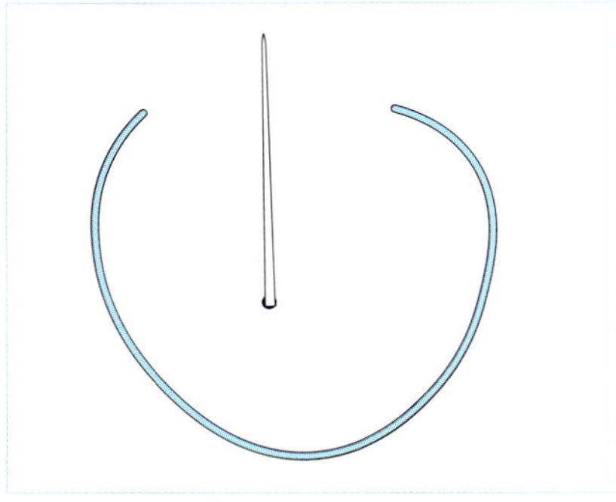

2 Leaving a loop on the surface, bring the needle up inside the loop, between its two ends.

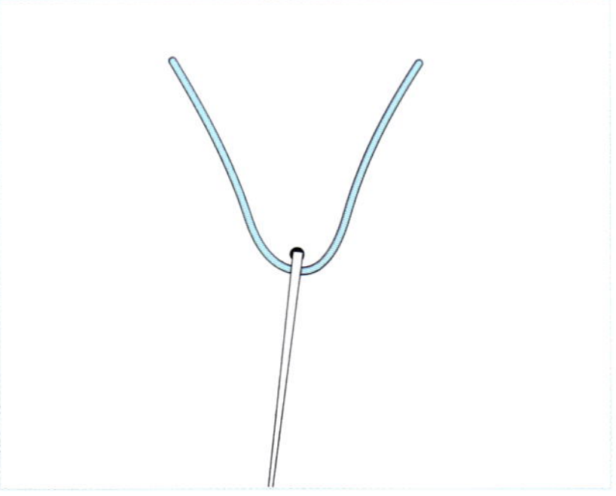

3 Pull the slack through to tighten the loop against the needle.

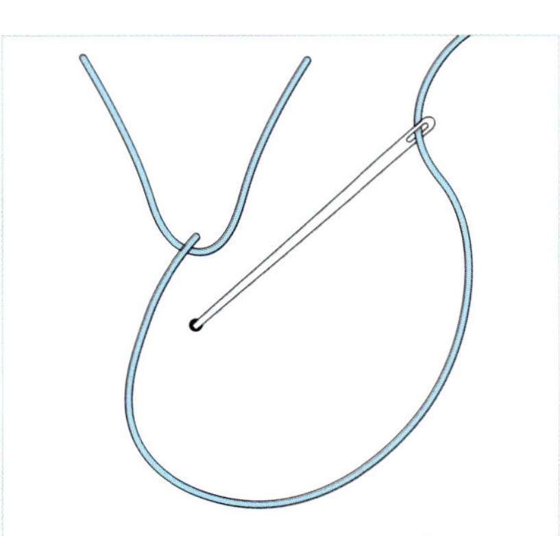

4 Pull the thread to the surface and take the needle down the other side to secure the loop.

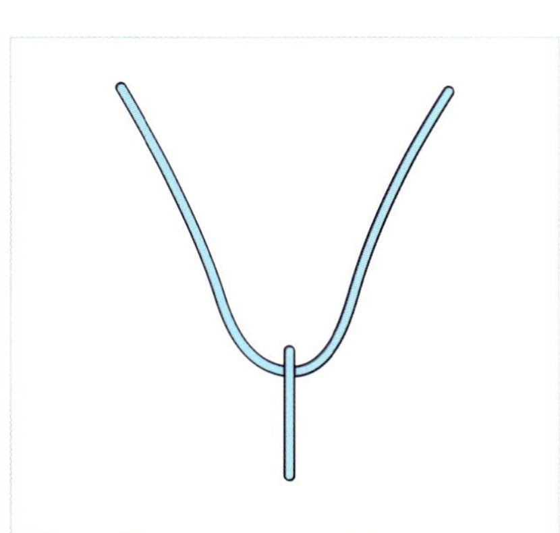

5 Pull through to complete the stitch, then secure.

FRENCH KNOT

CREWELWORK; OPUS ANGLICANUM; STUMPWORK; SILK SHADING; WHITEWORK; BASIC; MOUNTMELLICK; RIBBONWORK; SURFACE; ELIZABETHAN.

Also known as French knots, French dot, Knotted stitch, Twisted knot stitch, Point noué stitch, or Wound stitch.

A bold raised knotted dot used for decorative purposes, giving texture to the surface of the material. They can be used singly or in closely packed groups or scattered.

French knots appear as one of the stitches on the Butler-Bowdon Cope, a piece of Opus Anglicanum from the 14th century (although they were not a particularly common stitch in this tradition). They were also used on a notable piece of Swiss/south German ecclesiastical embroidery from the 16th century and by the following century were certainly in common usage in both Jacobean crewelwork and in raised work (frequently used to depict foliage or hair).

By the 19th century French knots were being used across different embroidery traditions and regions.

METHOD

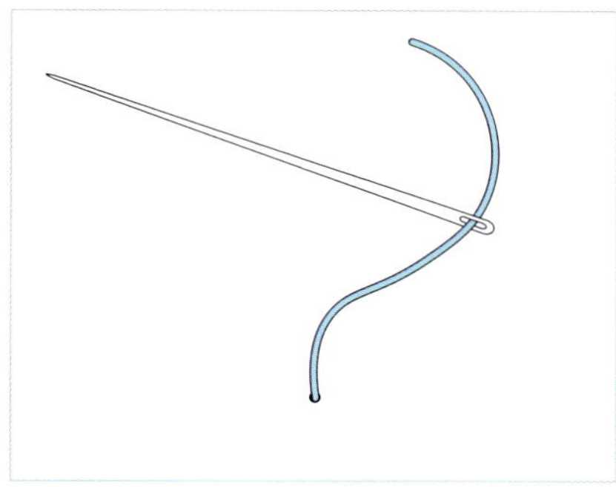

1 Bring the needle up through the fabric where you want the knot to sit.

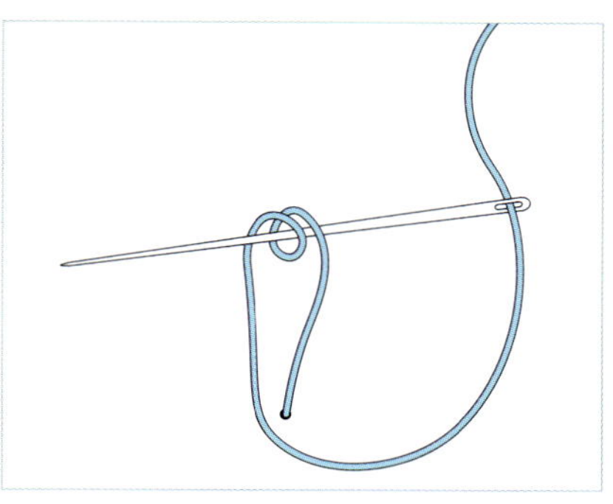

2 Take the thread around the needle once or twice to form a spiral.

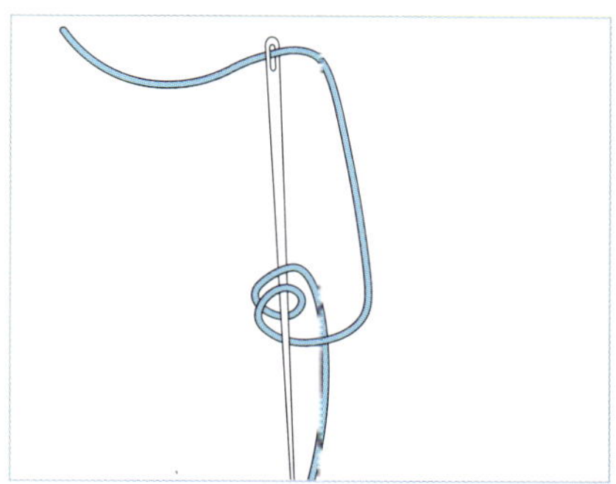

3 Place the needle into the fabric, very close to where it emerged.

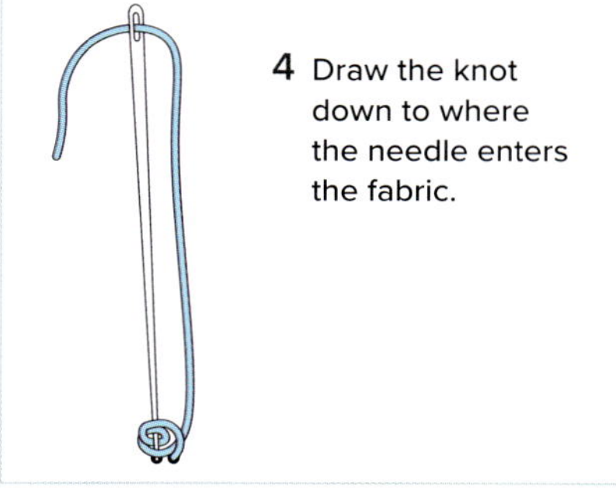

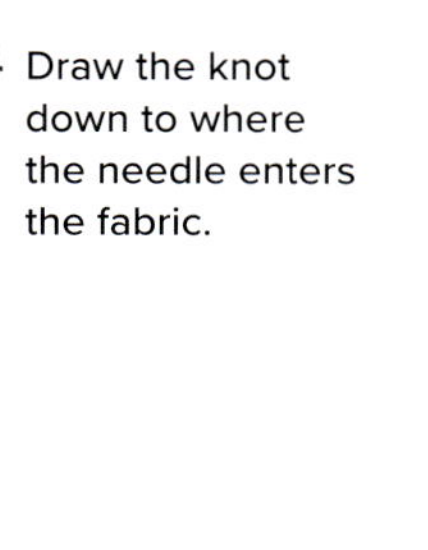

4 Draw the knot down to where the needle enters the fabric.

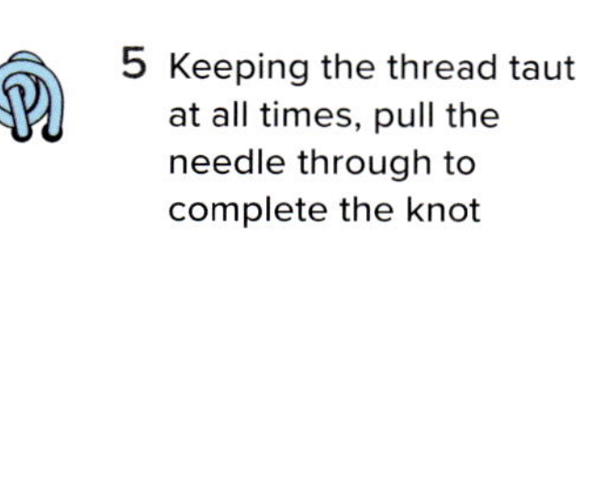

5 Keeping the thread taut at all times, pull the needle through to complete the knot

HERRINGBONE STITCH

CREWELWORK; WESSEX STITCHERY; APPLIQUÉ; MOUNTMELLICK; SHADOW WORK; SURFACE; BLACKWORK.

Also known as Plaited stitch, Catch stitch, Russian cross stitch, Russian stitch, Barred witch stitch, Witch stitch, Mossoul stitch, Point croise, or Cat stitch.

This stitch consists of a two rows of slanted, parallel stitches which cross each other near their ends. The reverse of the stitch produces two parallel rows of what looks like running stitch (see page 36). Also see the entry for closed herringbone stitch (see pages 58–59) which produces two parallel rows of back stitch on the reverse. These reversible traits mean these stitches lend themselves well to shadow work.

Much in evidence from the Elizabethan era through to the Jacobean, Herringbone was frequently used in curling foliage stems. Across the world, it is used in Assisi embroidery; in Chefchaouen embroidery; in Telli; by the Bedouin of Jordan, Syria, Palestine and Israel; by women in the oases of western Egypt; in Rabari embroidery from northwest India and in Kashmir embroidery from Pakistan.

METHOD

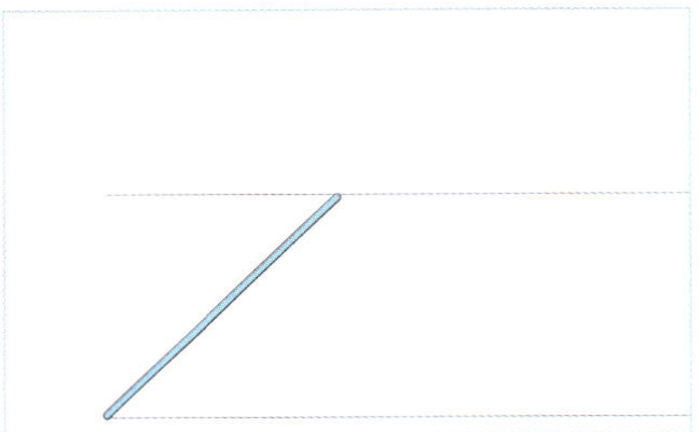

1 Draw two parallel design lines. Bring the needle up at the left edge of the bottom design line, and take it down on the opposite line to create a diagonal stitch.

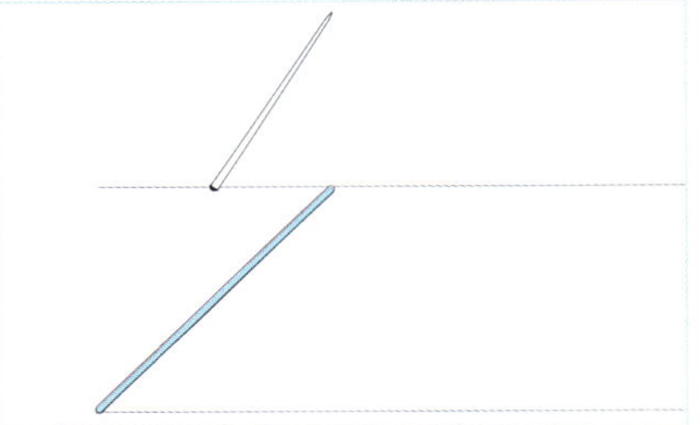

2 Bring the needle up a little way behind where you took it down, staying on the design line.

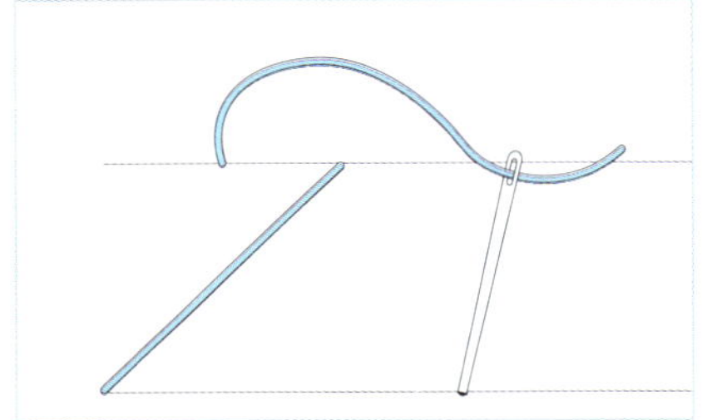

3 Take the needle diagonally across the initial stitch, as shown, then down. The stitch should be a similar length to your first diagonal stitch.

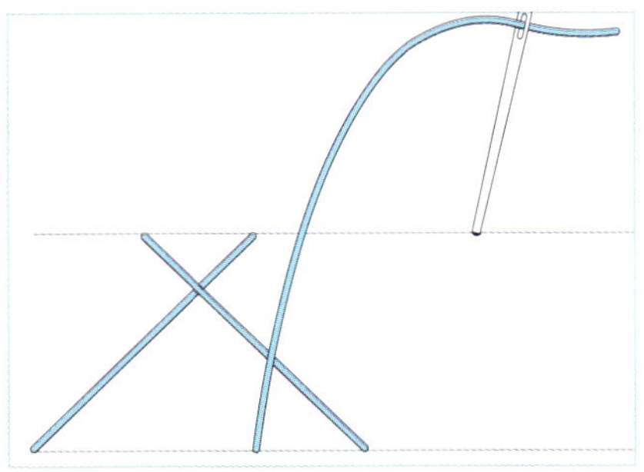

4 Pull the thread through, then bring the needle up behind where you took it down. Form another diagonal stitch, as before.

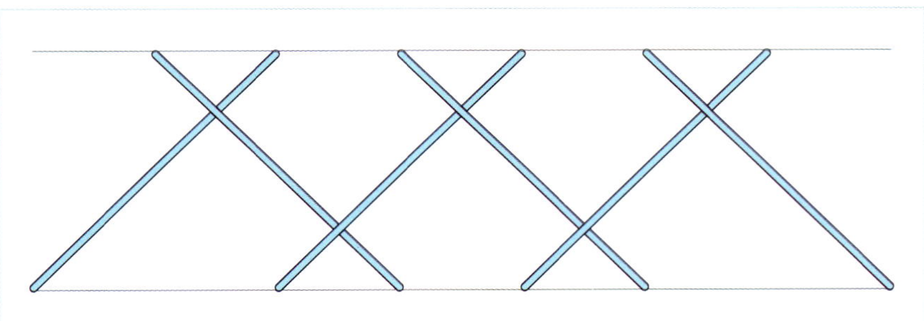

5 Continue in this way until the shape is filled.

HOLDING STITCH

Appliqué; Ayrshire; Basic; Bead embroidery; Crewelwork; Cutwork; Goldwork; Hardanger; Mountmellick; Opus Anglicanum; Silk shading; Stumpwork; Surface; Wessex stitchery; Whitework.

Also known as Stab stitch, or Waste knot.

Although rarely seen, this is your most important stitch. Using these when starting each thread will keep your stitches secured to your fabric. A waste knot is so-called as it is a temporary way of holding the thread which is then cut off and 'wasted'.

Also see finishing stitch on page 27 for how to use this method to finish your thread.

METHOD

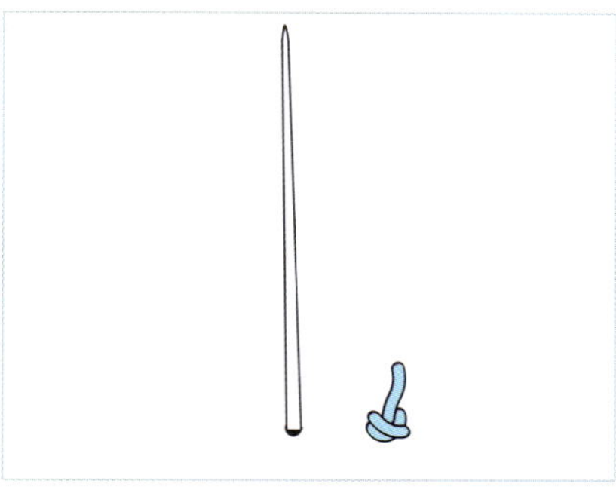

1 Knot the end of the thread and take the thread down through the fabric from the top (this is known as a waste knot). Pull the thread through, then bring the needle up just behind the knot, either on the line or within the shape you are filling, so that it will lie under the stitching.

2 Pull the thread through, then make a tiny stitch close by.

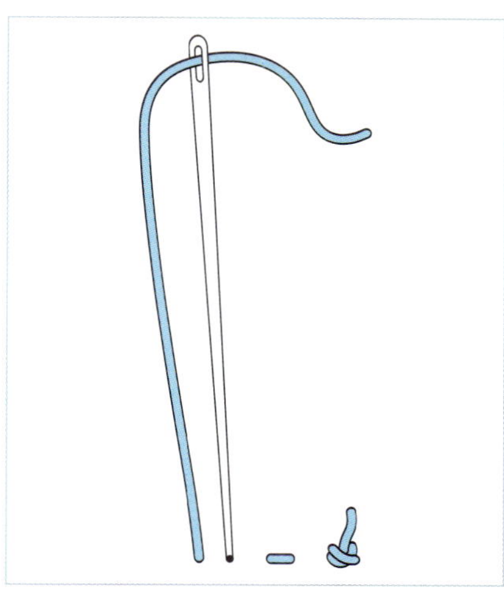

3 Make a tiny back stitch next to the first stitch.

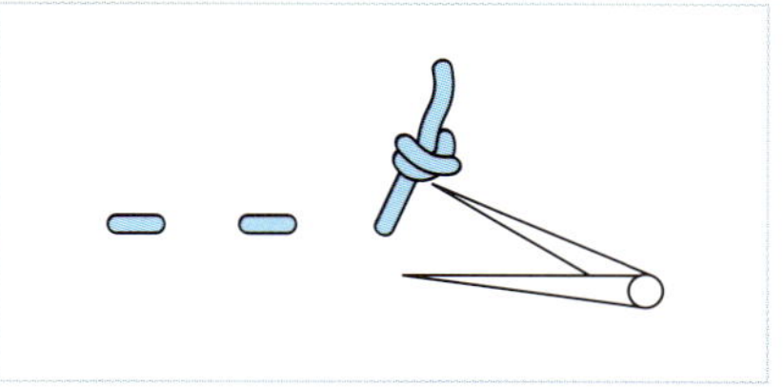

4 Bring the needle up where you wish to start the first stitch and cut off the knot close to the fabric surface.

OUTLINE STITCH

Basic; Crewelwork; Surface; Whitework; Blackwork; Stumpwork.

Also known as Rope stitch.

Outline stitch is very similar to stem stitch (see pages 40–41), the only difference is that it is stitched by holding the loop to the left instead of the right. This results in a slightly more jagged stitch.

Outline stitch features in various embroidery techniques: such as in 17th and 18th century Chinese embroidery. Elsewhere, it has been a feature of Baldyring embroidery, part of the Hedebo tradition in Denmark, and also of Deerfield embroidery, a tradition from Massachusetts, USA, which started at the end of the 19th century.

METHOD

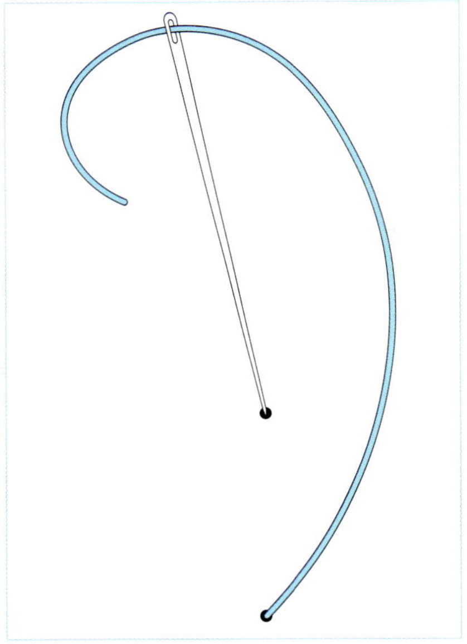

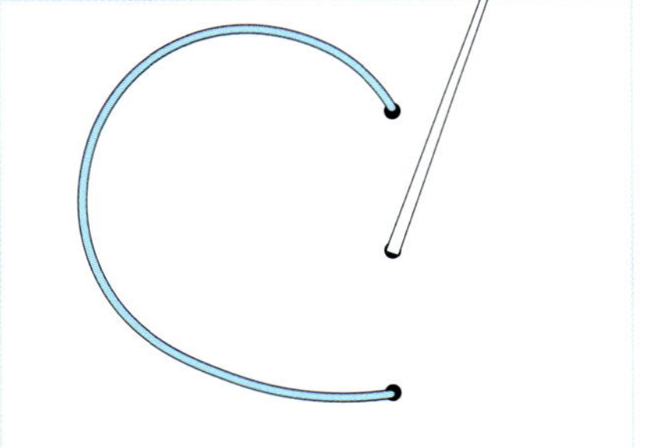

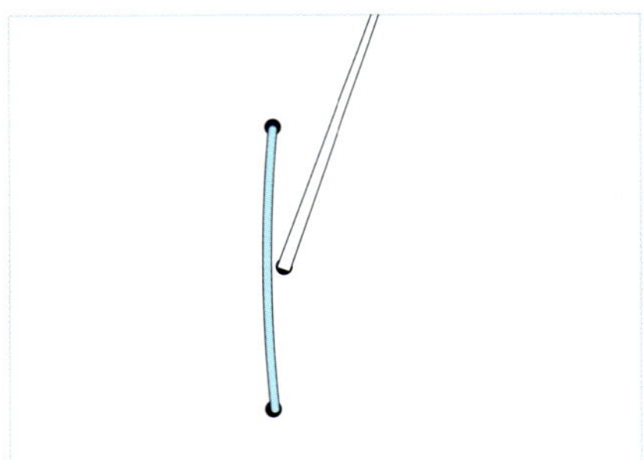

1 Start at the base of your line. Decide on the stitch length and take the needle down through the fabric at that point. Leave a loop on the fabric's surface.

2 Hold the loop to the left as you bring the needle up to the surface halfway between the stitch length.

3 Leave the needle in the fabric while you tighten the slack on the loop against the needle.

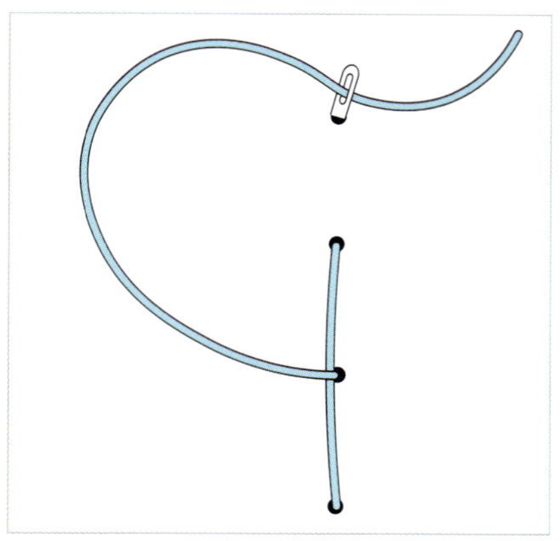

4 Pull the needle through the fabric and bring the thread all the way through. Make another looped stitch, equal in length to the first.

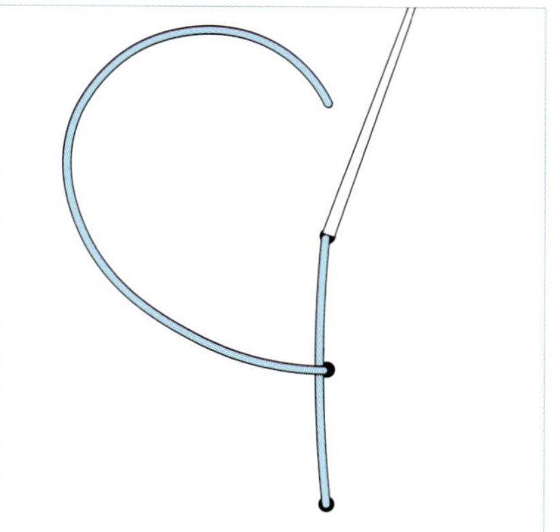

5 Leaving a loop on the surface of the fabric, Repeat step four by bringing the needle up halfway between the stitch length, again holding the loop to the left.

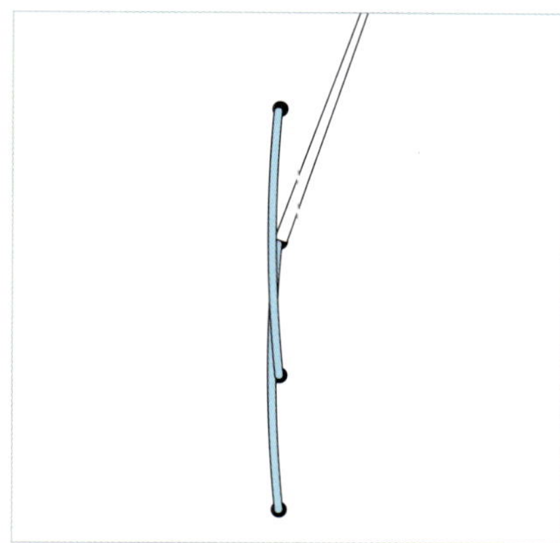

6 Again, leave the needle in the fabric while you tighten the slack on the loop against the needle.

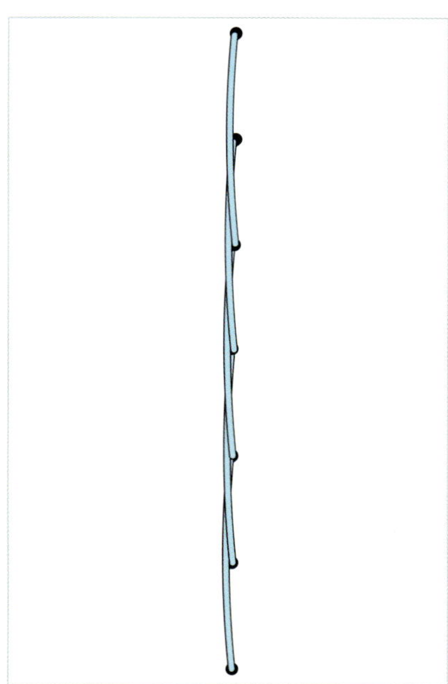

7 Repeat to the end of the line. Each stitch should be equal in length and begin halfway along the previous stitch.

▲▲ Detail from tea cosy, RSN Collection COL.24

This detail, from a padded and embroidered tea cosy made in the late 19th or early 20th century, features a bird on one side and butterflies on the other. Outline stitch is used here to provide a strong outline to these flowers stems.

The full piece can be seen on page 38.

PLUNGING

Goldwork; Surface.

Plunging is the method used to take couched threads through to the reverse of the fabric where they are secured in place. It is predominantly used for metal threads but can be used for any thick thread which does not readily pass through to the reverse of the fabric. This entry also demonstrates how to tie back the plunged threads: this means securing them on the reverse of the fabric.

The alternative to plunging is to cut the thread off and secure it with a double couching stitch near the end. This is less secure than plunging it and some threads will fray over time but it is a less time-consuming method of finishing thread.

The use of plunging certainly dates to the 19th century, as the 1867 text *Church Embroidery, Ancient and Modern* describes its use, including the type of needle used to pierce the fabric. Metal threads were in common use at various points prior to this, but there is little documentary evidence to indicate whether the ends were cut or plunged. The term 'plunging' is first used in print in the 1970s.

METHOD

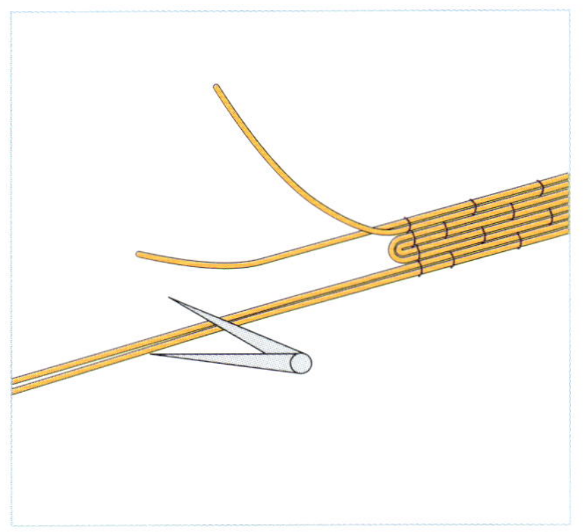

1 Leave a tail of the couched thread to be plunged, it should be at least 3cm (1⅛in) long.

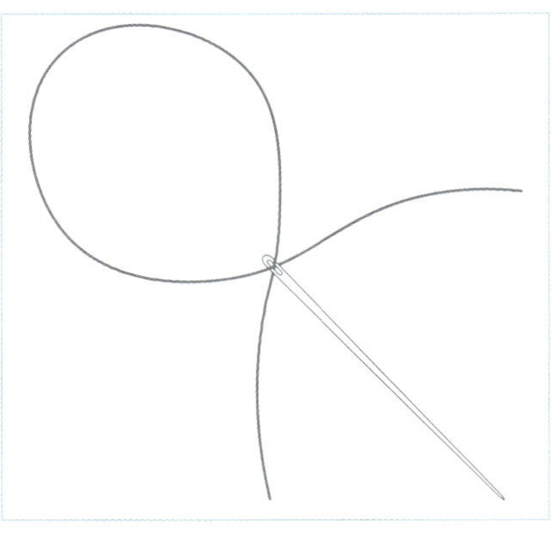

2 Create a lasso by cutting a short length of strong thread, then thread each end into opposite sides of the eye of a chenille needle.

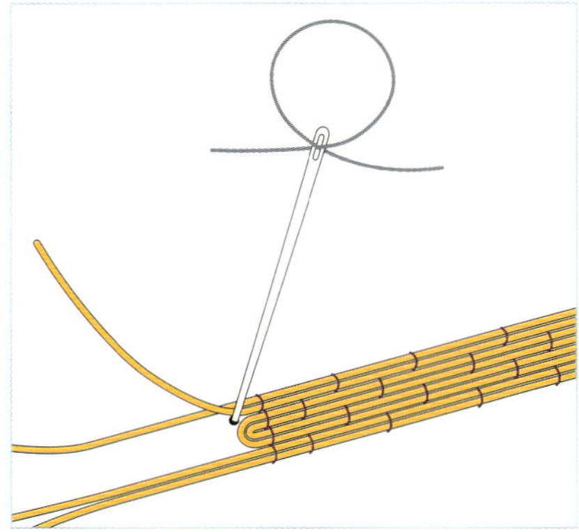

3 With the point of the needle, locate the point you wish to plunge the couched thread. This should be in line with the couched thread.

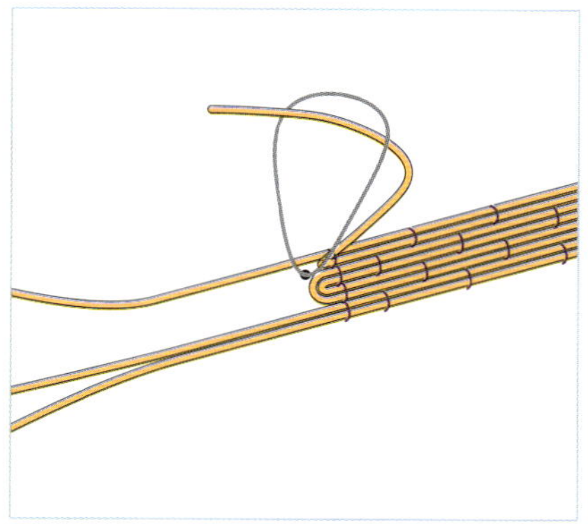

4 Take the needle down through the fabric, leaving the loop of the lasso or eye of the needle visible. Thread in the tail end of the couched thread.

5 Support the fabric either side of the needle with your index and middle fingers, then pull the needle down and force the couched thread below the surface.

6 Repeat to take all the desired threads to the back of the fabric. Plunge each couching thread separately, even if stitched in pairs on the surface.

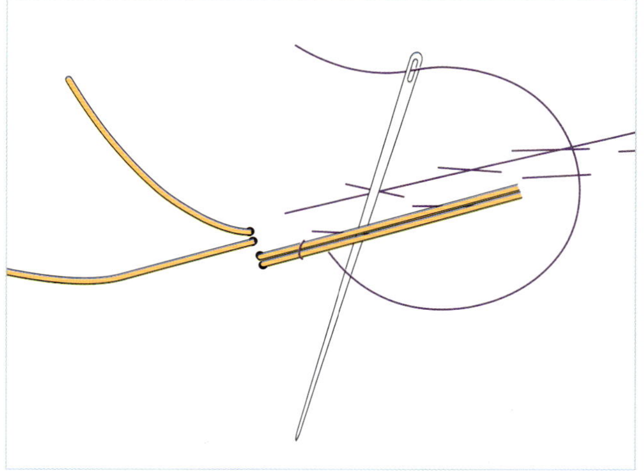

7 Now tie back the plunged threads. Bend the plunged threads back so that they lie directly under where they were couched (this can be done in pairs). Fasten on a length of sewing machine thread in a curved needle and bring your needle up at the point where the gold was plunged. Use a whipping motion of small stitches underneath the gold to catch the backing fabric and angled stitches on the surface; pull your thread taut to secure the gold threads. Continue for approximately 1cm (½in), then whip back in the opposite direction. Finish off the sewing machine thread securely and trim the tail end of the gold.

TIP

Where there is a gap in the design which is being couched, plunging can be used to take a thread through to the back at the end of one area, and then brought through to the front (in effect plunged from the back of the fabric to the front) to start a new area.

Historically, threads were sometimes pasted onto the back of the fabric. This is obviously quicker than stitching them in place, but runs the risk of the glue bleeding through to the front of the fabric or the chemicals within it adversely affecting the fabric.

RUNNING STITCH

Crewelwork; Surface; Whitework; Bead embroidery; Blackwork; Basic; Mountmellick; Ribbonwork; Shadow work.

Also known as Basting stitch.

Made up of equally-sized straight surface stitches spaced at regular intervals to produce a simple line, running stitch has many uses, such as gathering, quilting, outlining, reinforcement for cutwork as well as the base for other stitches.

Basting stitch is a specific type of temporary running stitch used to hold two pieces of fabric together or to indicate an outline. The stitches are normally longer than for running stitch so that they are more easily removed. Sometimes the stitches on the surface are longer than those underneath. An early reference to basting stitch features in the *Academy of Amory*, a late 17th-century publication.

Running stitch has been employed as a decorative stitch across the world for centuries: in 5th century Egypt; in Buratto evenweave embroidery in 16th century Europe; Kantha in Bangladesh and eastern India; Sashiko in Japan; Huckaback embroidery in 17th century Europe; and Kashmir embroidery in 19th century northern India.

Some of these traditions blur the line between embroidery and quilting as they use multiple layers of cloth, and the running stitch has a dual purpose of holding the layers together and a decorative function.

METHOD

1 Decide on the length of your first stitch then bring the needle up, estimating the same stitch length for the gap.

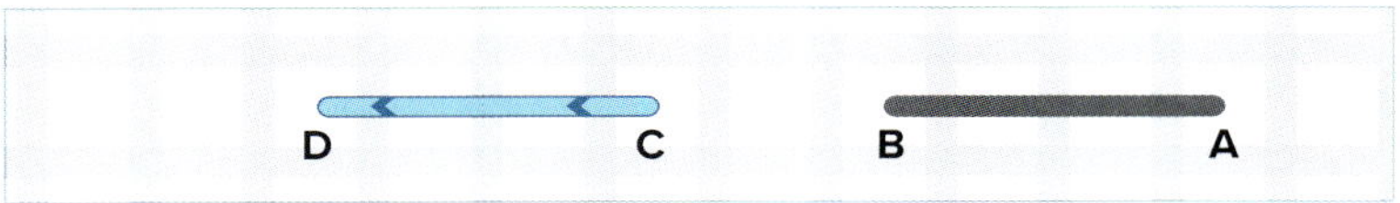

2 Continue along your line, producing stitches of the same length.

3 Ensure the under stitches are also of equal length so that stitches are equally spaced.

SATIN STITCH

WHITEWORK; OPUS ANGLICANUM; CREWELWORK; HARDANGER; AYRSHIRE; SURFACE; APPLIQUÉ; MOUNTMELLICK; TAMBOUR; STUMPWORK; BERLIN WOOL WORK; ELIZABETHAN.

Also known as Damask stitch, French plumetis stitch, Point passé stitch, Point perlé stitch, Au passé stitch, Long stitch, Passé stitch, or Flat stitch.

A series of straight stitches worked parallel to one another to produce a smooth solid filling. It is typically used in monogramming, leaves and petals.

The earliest evidence of satin stitch is from Dunhuang in China, 1st century AD. It has also been part of the tradition of whitework since at least the 12th century.

METHOD

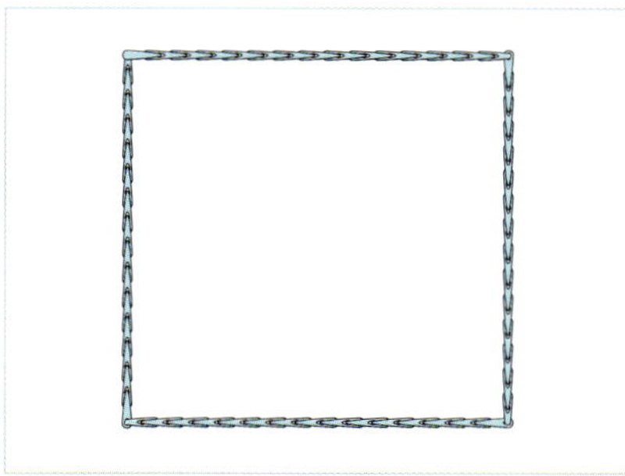

1 To achieve a crisp neat edge, complete a split stitch outline to the shape to be filled (optional). Your stitches should be approximately 3mm (⅛in) long.

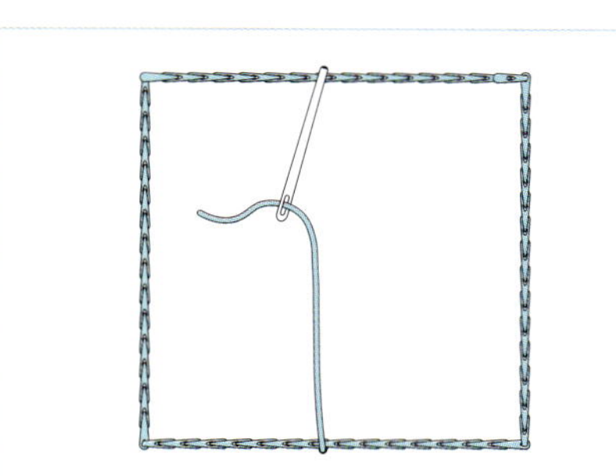

2 Beginning halfway along one side, bring the needle up just outside the split stitch outline. Hold the thread to set the angle of the first stitch and take the needle down accordingly, just outside the split stitch.

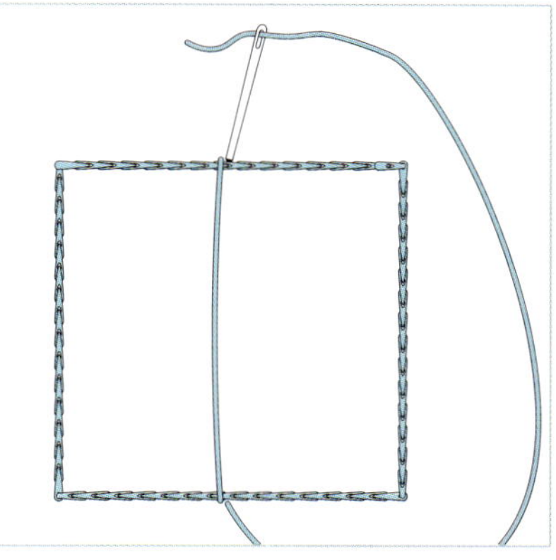

3 Bring the needle up, very close on one side of the first stitch. Make a second stitch, angling the needle towards the previous stitch and towards the split stitch. Repeat to complete one side of the shape.

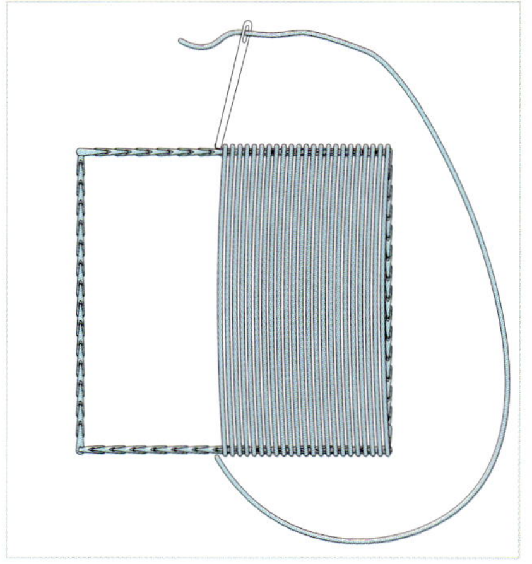

4 Then begin again in the middle. This time bring the needle up on the other side of the shape, and angle the needle towards the previous stitch as before.

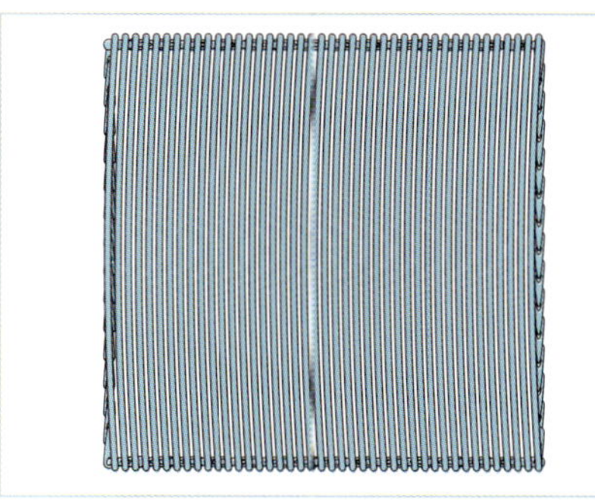

5 Continue to fill the other side of the shape.

▲▲ Tea cosy, RSN Collection COL.24

The head and the chest of the bird are worked in long and short stitches, resulting in skilful silk shading. The wings and tail feathers are wrought in satin and fishbone stitches. The stems, flowers, and cherries are outlined and infilled with different stitches including buttonhole, French knots, long and short, split, chain, Burden, and running.

The butterfly shown in the detail appears on the other side of the tea cosy. Its wings are outlined in split stitch (see opposite) and infilled with both long and short stitch (see pages 224–225) and more split stitches.

SPLIT STITCH

Opus Anglicanum; Silk shading; Whitework; Crewelwork; Basic; Mountmellick; Surface; Stumpwork; Elizabethan.

Also known as Kensington outline stitch.

This is a form of back stitch (see page 16), with the needle splitting the centre of the previous stitch rather than coming up in the same hole. This results in what looks like a mini chain stitch.

The earliest notable use of split stitch is within Opus Anglicanum where it was used extensively as a filling stitch to provide fine details such as faces. It was used in a similar manner in 14th-century Byzantine embroidery, and continued to be used in traditions across the world from Medieval Iceland to China during the Ming dynasty. In the 19th century, Arts and Crafts embroidery frequently used split stitch as filling stitch for flesh.

METHOD

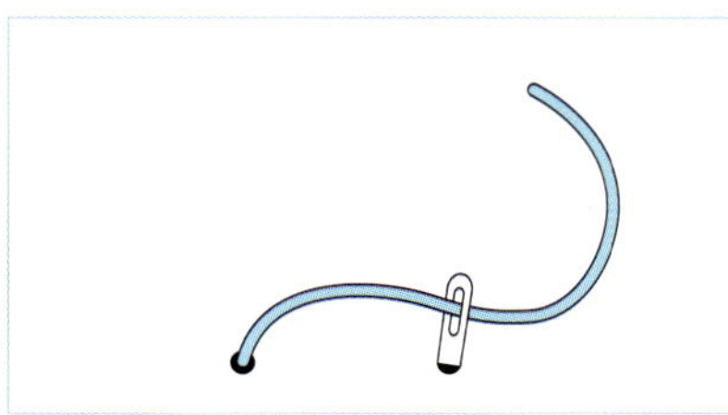

1 Bring the needle up at the start of the design line. Decide on the length of your stitch and take the needle down through the fabric, on the line at the desired length. Pull the thread through to the underside.

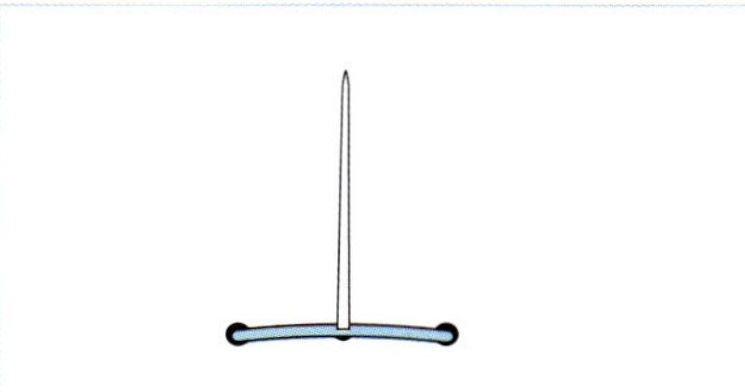

2 Push the needle up through the fabric in the centre of your first stitch, splitting the thread with the needle on the way to the surface.

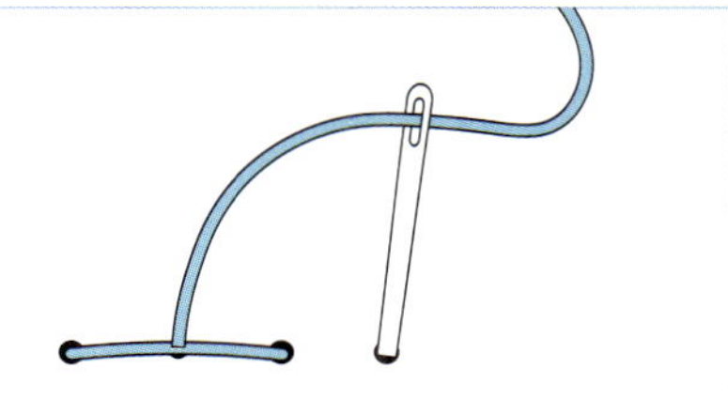

3 Each stitch should be equal in length to the first stitch but halfway back along the previous stitch. Continue along the painted line.

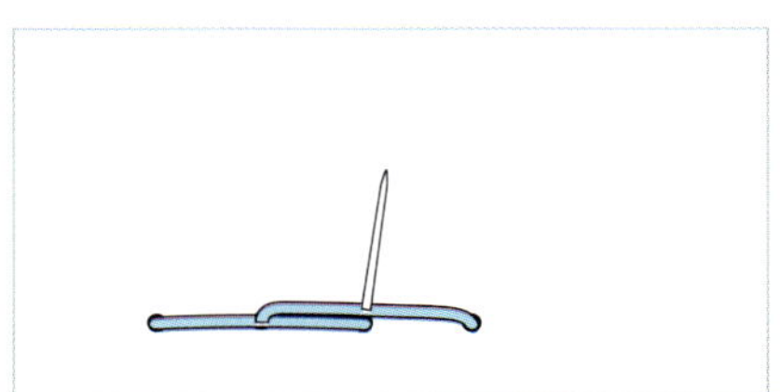

4 Pull the thread through to finish the second stitch. Start the third stitch at the end of the first, halfway along the second.

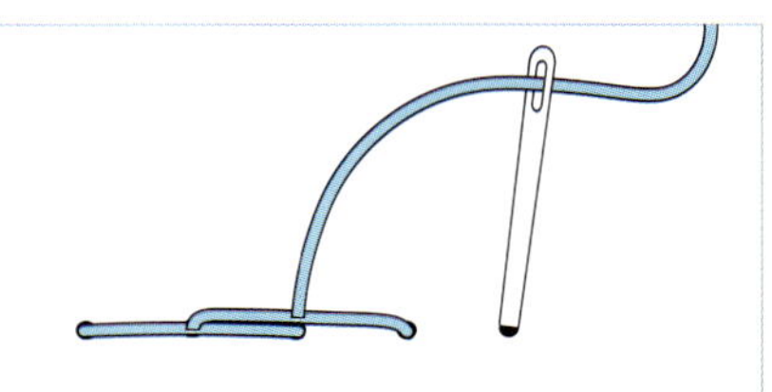

5 Finish the third stitch in the same way as before.

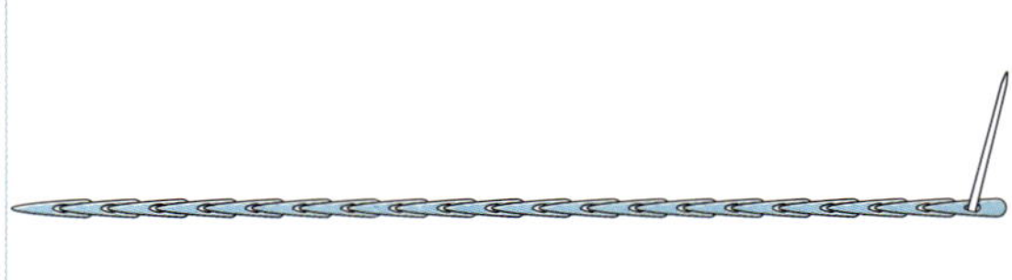

6 Continue to work along the design to the end.

STEM STITCH

CREWELWORK; SILK SHADING; WHITEWORK; OPUS ANGLICANUM; BASIC; MOUNTMELLICK; RIBBONWORK; SURFACE.

Also known as Crewel stitch, South Kensington stitch, Arrow stitch, Rope stitch, Stalk stitch, or Outline stitch.

Stem stitch uses repeated straight stitches with each stitch coming up beside the previous stitch to form a rope-like line, curved or straight.

Evidence of stem stitch has been found in both Egyptian and Peruvian grave artefacts from 14th century BC and between 600BC and 200BC, respectively. Later excavations at Kellis in Egypt (1st–5th centuries AD) and Mammen in Denmark (970AD) also show the use of stem stitch. From a slightly later period in Peru, Chancay open weave darning used a long stem stitch to embellish an open weave gauze fabric.

It was used in the Bayeux Tapestry (11th century), in Icelandic ecclesiastical works from approximately the 15th century and in 17th century English Jacobean work. In the 18th century it was being used in China on Mandarin squares, in the USA as one of the main stitches in candlewick embroidery, and within shadow work. By the following century it was being used in whitework (for muslin embroidery at the start of the century and then later for Broderie Anglaise), by William Morris in his recreation of 17th-century embroidery, and in Kashmir to outline motifs. More generally it was used in Chinai (on the coast of India), and in Meknes, Morocco.

METHOD

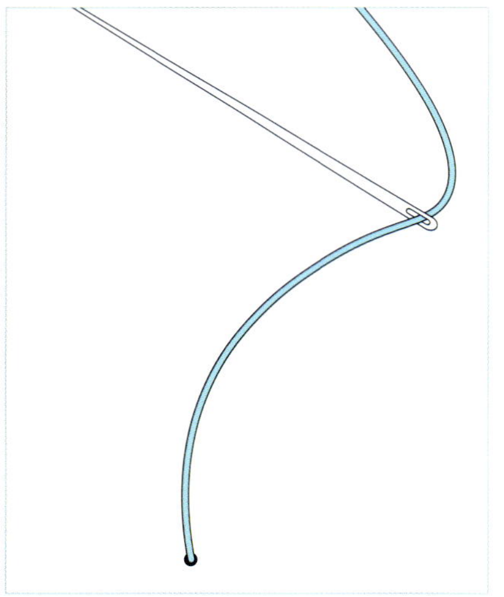

1 Push the needle up through the fabric at the base of your stitching area. Pull the thread through to the surface.

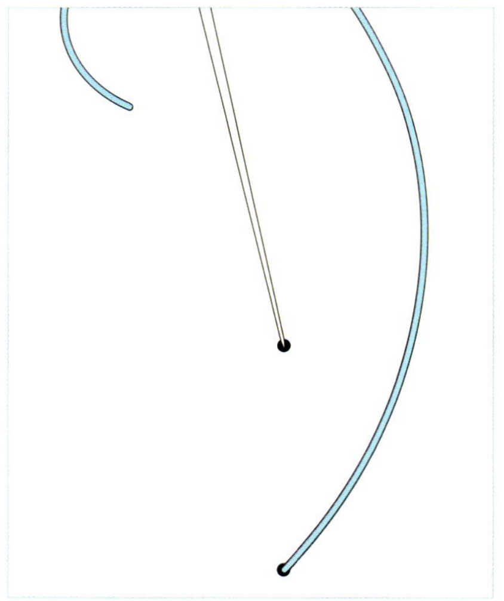

2 Decide on the stitch length and take the needle down through the fabric at that point.

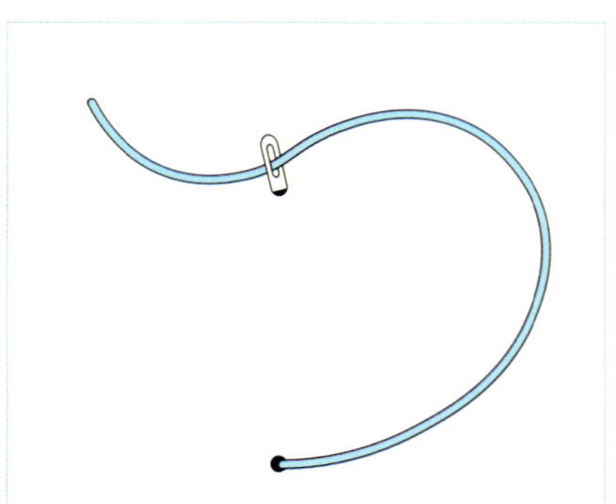

3 Pull the thread through the fabric, leaving a loop on the surface of the fabric.

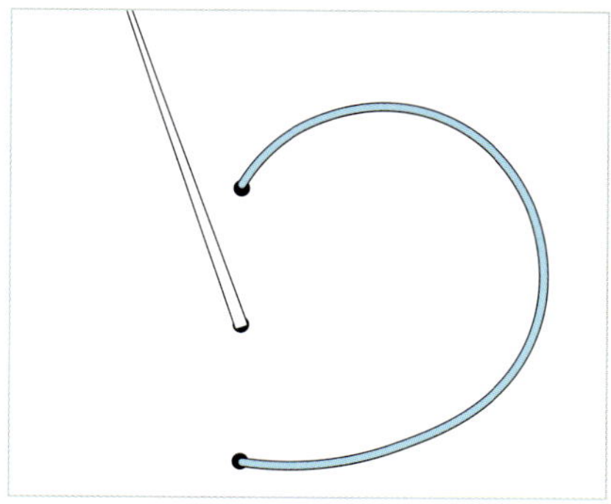

4 Hold the loop out of the way to the right as you bring the needle up to the surface halfway between the stitch length.

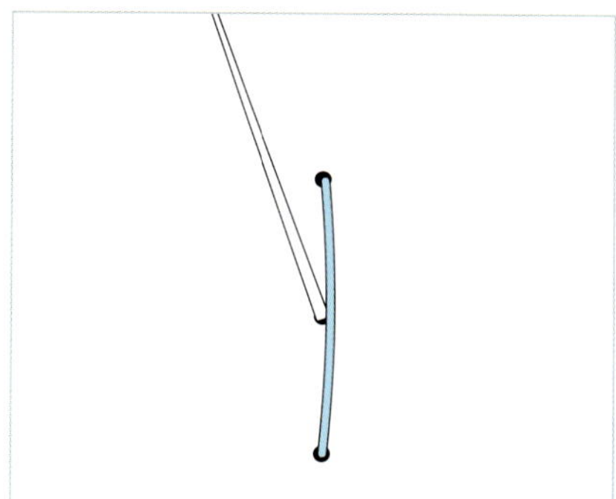

5 Leave the needle in the fabric while you tighten the slack on the loop against your needle.

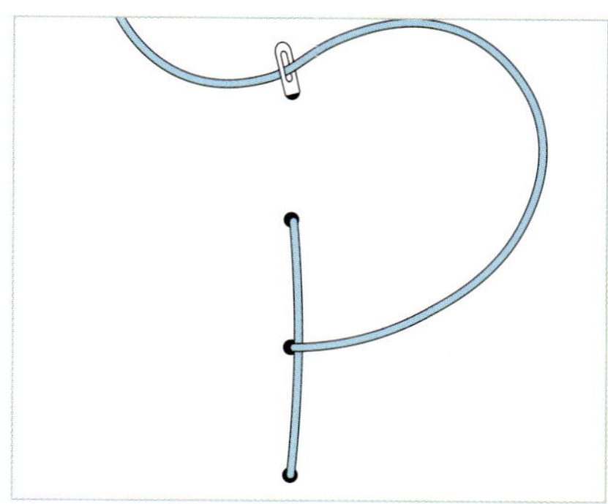

6 Pull the needle up through the fabric and make another looped stitch, equal in length to the first.

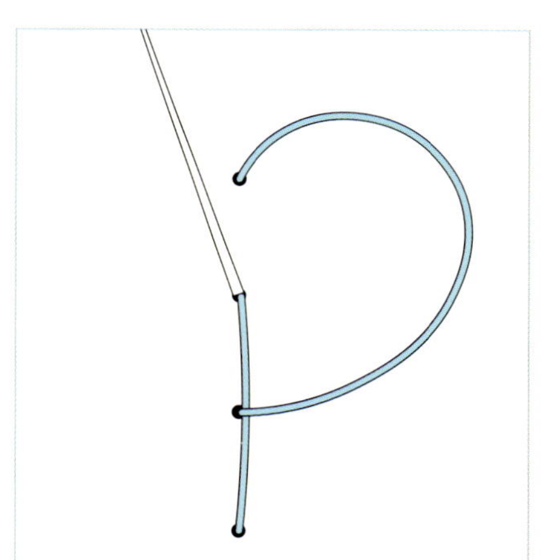

7 Repeat step 4, bringing the needle up halfway again between the stitch length.

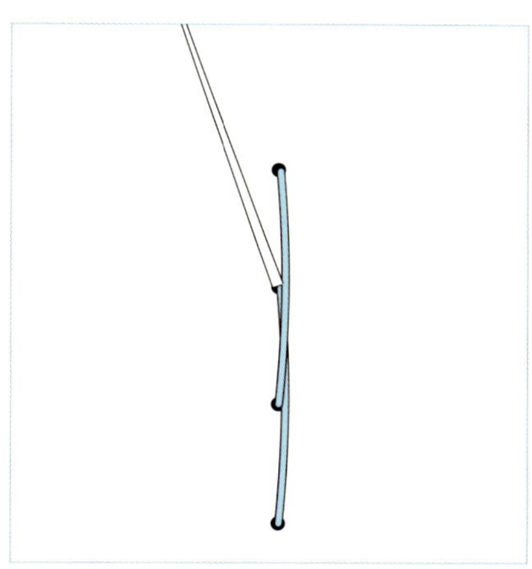

8 Again, leave the needle in the fabric while you tighten the slack on the loop against your needle.

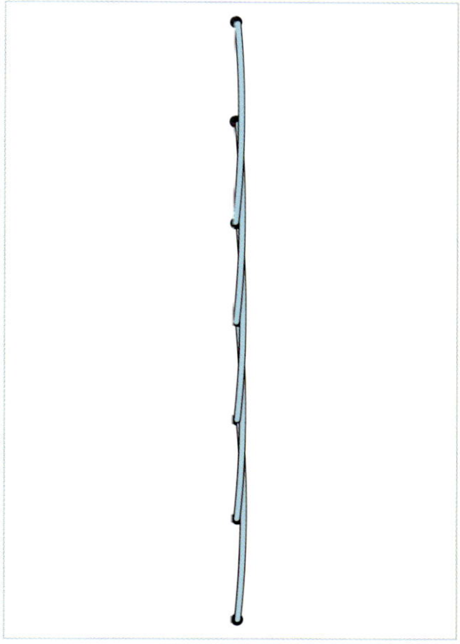

9 Repeat to the end of the line. Each stitch should be equal in length and begin halfway along the previous stitch.

STRAIGHT STITCH

Basic; Crewelwork; Surface; Ribbonwork.

Also known as Single satin stitch, or Stroke stitch.

Straight stitch is literally a stitch which is straight.

It can be worked in any thread and can add areas of interest and texture through small and delicate stitches or larger and heavier ones. Straight stitch is a particularly useful stitch when working with fine silk ribbons. Groups of single straight stitches, worked using thread, ribbon or a combination of both, can be used to create clumps of grasses, legs of insects, leaf veins and so on.

METHOD 1

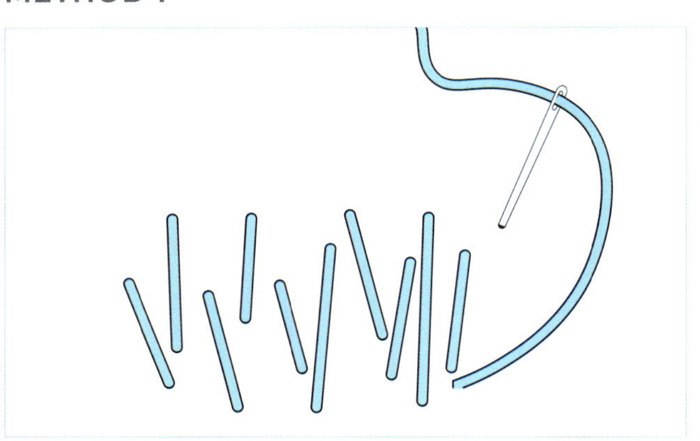

1 Work groups of single straight stitches with a thread to create a clump of grass. Always pull the thread through completely at the start and end of each stitch.

METHOD 2

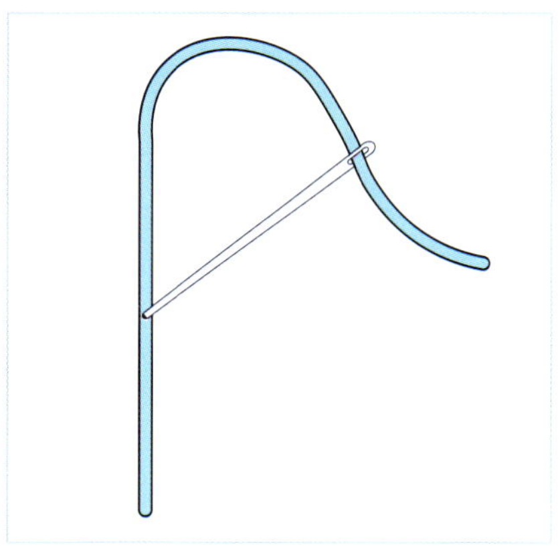

1 To make a straight stitch with ribbon, pass the ribbon through to the front of the fabric. Hold it taut in your left hand and take the needle down through the centre of the ribbon.

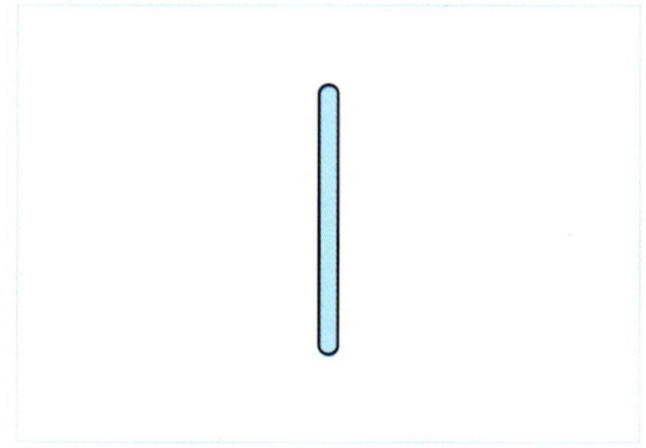

2 Pull the fabric through to the back of the fabric.

3 Use the ribbon to make some more stitches of varying length.

WHIP STITCH

Appliqué; Surface; Bead embroidery.

Also known as Diagonal basting.

Worked from bottom to top, whip stitch is a simple diagonal stitch with a whipping/wrapping motion. It is often used to sew two pieces of fabric together, and it can be used in appliqué to attach a small piece of fabric to the ground fabric (in this regard it is similar to stab stitch on page 200, but the stitches are slightly longer and diagonal). It can also be used as a surface stitch, and is a very simple, effective way to create a rope effect in bead embroidery. You can vary the length of the stitches, or alternate between different beads, or combinations of beads and sequins in order to achieve various interesting effects.

This stitch should not be confused with the action of whipping another stitch: whipping is done by diagonally wrapping a thread around an existing line of stitches, the needle is always inserted from the same side so that the slanted wrappings are parallel and crucially it does not pierce the fabric.

The image shows (from left to right) whip stitch used to apply a piece of fabric, as a beading stitch and as a surface stitch.

METHOD

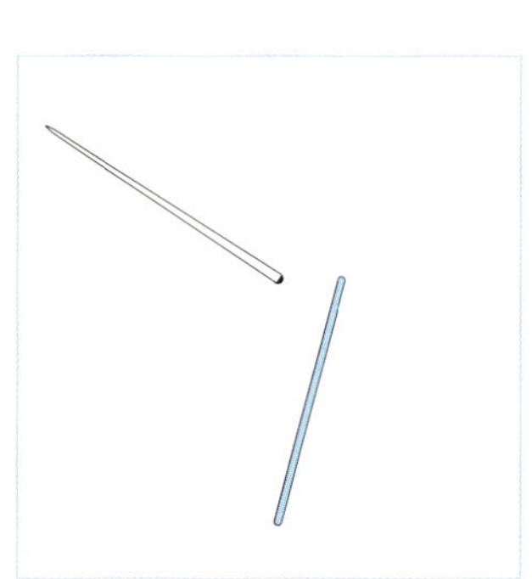

1 Work a diagonal straight stitch; your needle should emerge level with the end of the previous stitch.

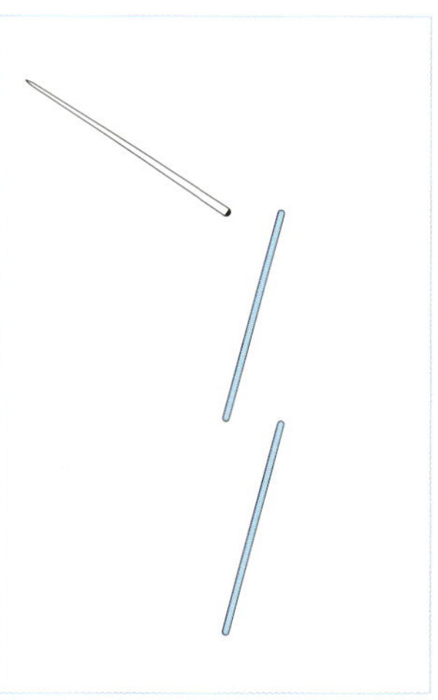

2 Continue working diagonal stitches in the same way.

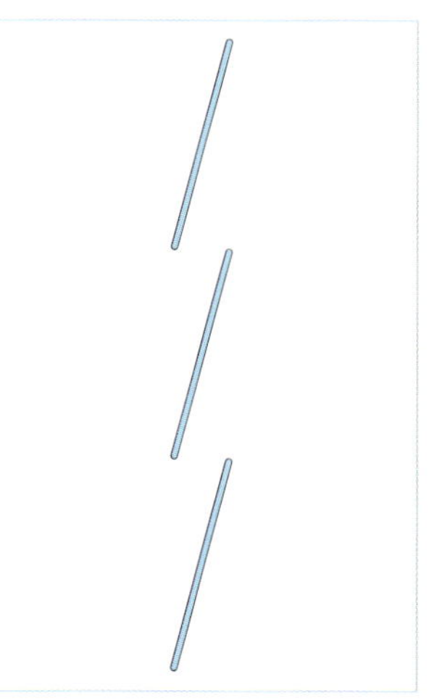

3 Work from bottom to top. It is quite open when worked in embroidery thread only.

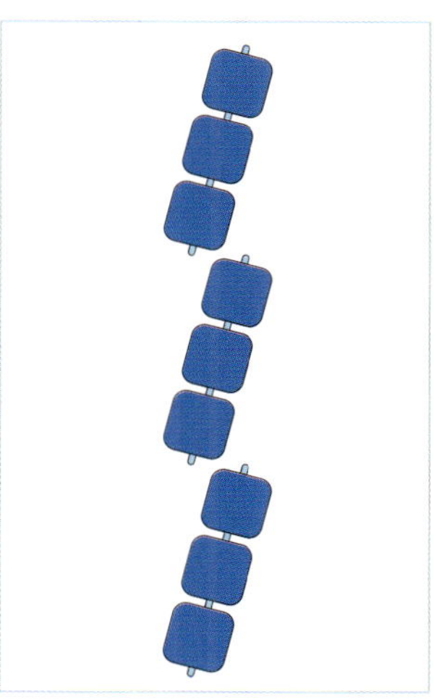

Whip stitch becomes more linear and closed when worked in beads, or a combination of beads and sequins.

OUTLINE AND BORDER STITCHES

These stitches lend themselves to working any type of line: those which edge a motif; those which are freestanding; and those which form wide, straight borders. Within these divisions there are various styles of line stitch which all have different attributes.

Heavy, textured lines – of the type which feature frequently in Elizabethan embroidery where they form curving stylized stems, called 'rinceaux' – can be worked in stitches such as heavy chain stitch, braid stitch or Pekinese stitch. More delicate, branching stems can be worked in stitches such as fern stitch, Mountmellick stitch or one of the versions of feather stitch; while for a more textured but still delicate line, consider Portuguese knotted stem stitch, scroll stitch, or either version of cable chain stitch.

Smooth line stitches, such as couching, pearl purl application and trailing, can be used both to edge motifs and as freestanding lines.

Straight borders, which traditionally adorn the edges of items such as tray cloths and hems, can be worked in one of the many variations of herringbone stitch, raised chain band stitch or double buttonhole stitch. For a canvaswork line stitch which forms a subtly textured straight line, consider using long-armed cross stitch. This stitch is used across the world to create an intricate crossed line which, once the structure has been mastered, is quick to work.

Stitched lettering can be worked in Quaker stitch (indeed, the stitch was invented for the purpose) or any of those listed above which create a smooth line. Finally, don't forget running, stem, split back and chain stitches from the Basic stitches section and their whipped versions, all of which offer further options for outlines and borders.

▲▲ Panel, RSN Collection COL.1

This square zardozi embroidered panel, worked in silk and metal threads on a white silk ground, was stitched in India in the late 19th or early 20th century. At its centre is a peacock with its padded wings outstretched and feathers on display. A design of peacock feathers adorns all four borders.

Couching, an important technique for outlines and borders, is used prominently throughout. The peacock and feathers are worked in silk threads and silver and gold metal threads, namely passing threads, bullion, purl, pearl purl, and bright check. The goldwork stitches used include flat cutwork (goldwork), pearl purl application, and s-ing (see pages 97 and 318–319 for the latter two).

The body of the peacock and the feathers' eyes are three-dimensional, padded and covered in purple satin stitches and red French knots. This object's imagery and techniques are typical of Indian embroidery. The panel is backed with linen.

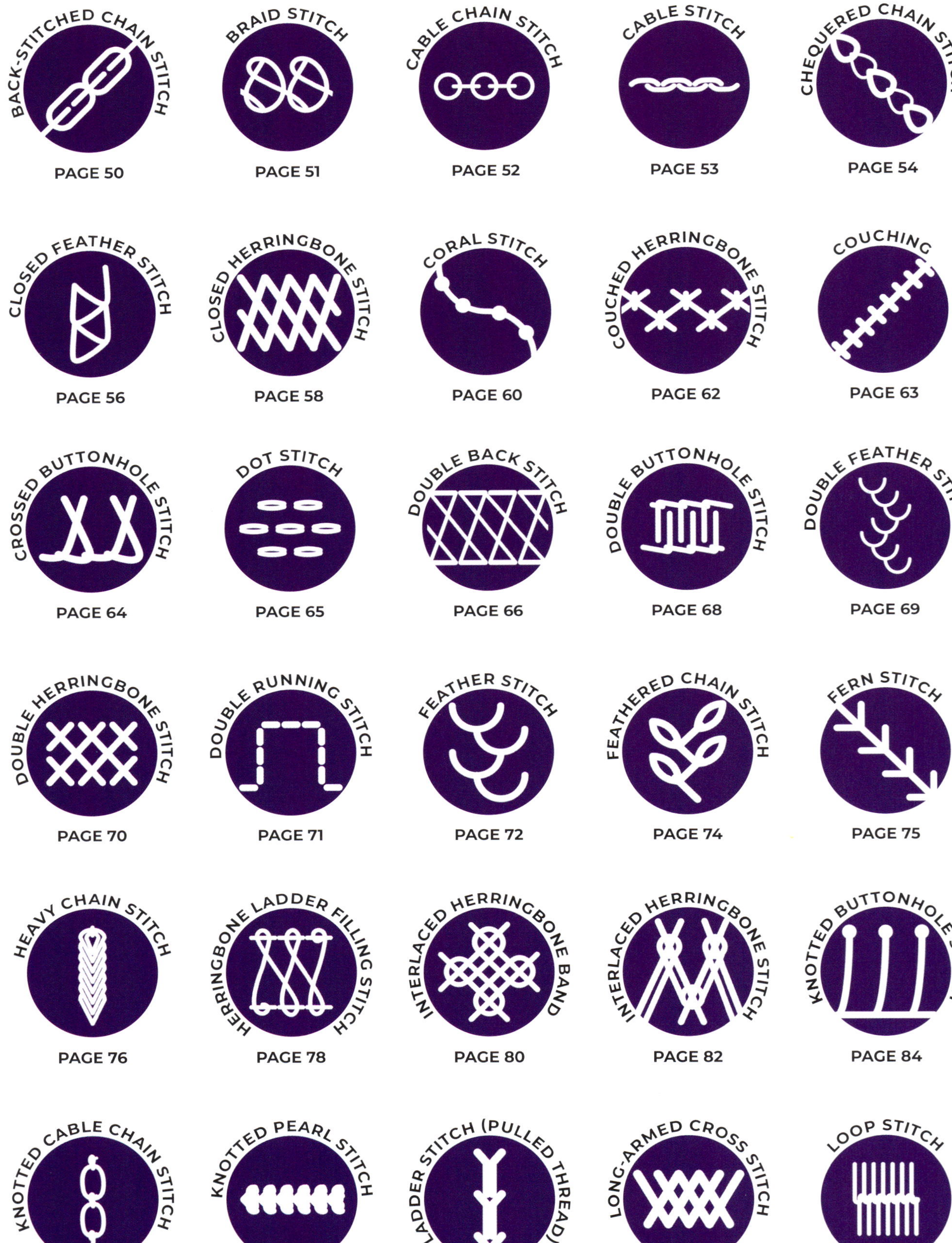
BACK-STITCHED CHAIN STITCH
PAGE 50
BRAID STITCH
PAGE 51
CABLE CHAIN STITCH
PAGE 52
CABLE STITCH
PAGE 53
CHEQUERED CHAIN STITCH
PAGE 54
CLOSED FEATHER STITCH
PAGE 56
CLOSED HERRINGBONE STITCH
PAGE 58
CORAL STITCH
PAGE 60
COUCHED HERRINGBONE STITCH
PAGE 62
COUCHING
PAGE 63
CROSSED BUTTONHOLE STITCH
PAGE 64
DOT STITCH
PAGE 65
DOUBLE BACK STITCH
PAGE 66
DOUBLE BUTTONHOLE STITCH
PAGE 68
DOUBLE FEATHER STITCH
PAGE 69
DOUBLE HERRINGBONE STITCH
PAGE 70
DOUBLE RUNNING STITCH
PAGE 71
FEATHER STITCH
PAGE 72
FEATHERED CHAIN STITCH
PAGE 74
FERN STITCH
PAGE 75
HEAVY CHAIN STITCH
PAGE 76
HERRINGBONE LADDER FILLING STITCH
PAGE 78
INTERLACED HERRINGBONE BAND
PAGE 80
INTERLACED HERRINGBONE STITCH
PAGE 82
KNOTTED BUTTONHOLE STITCH
PAGE 84
KNOTTED CABLE CHAIN STITCH
PAGE 86
KNOTTED PEARL STITCH
PAGE 88
LADDER STITCH (PULLED THREAD)
PAGE 90
LONG-ARMED CROSS STITCH
PAGE 91
LOOP STITCH
PAGE 92

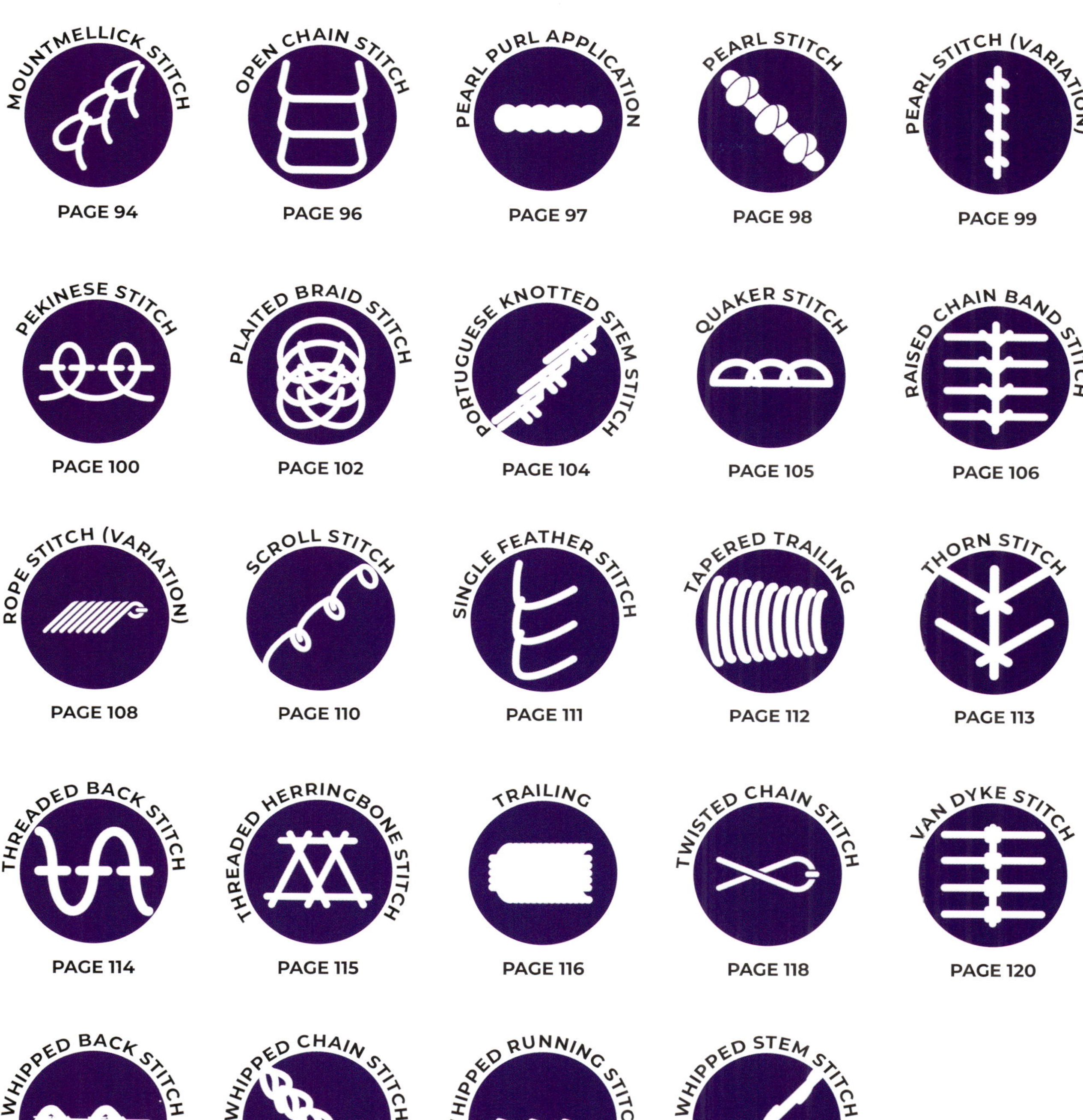

MOUNTMELLICK STITCH
PAGE 94
OPEN CHAIN STITCH
PAGE 96
PEARL PURL APPLICATION
PAGE 97
PEARL STITCH
PAGE 98
PEARL STITCH (VARIATION)
PAGE 99
PEKINESE STITCH
PAGE 100
PLAITED BRAID STITCH
PAGE 102
PORTUGUESE KNOTTED STEM STITCH
PAGE 104
QUAKER STITCH
PAGE 105
RAISED CHAIN BAND STITCH
PAGE 106
ROPE STITCH (VARIATION)
PAGE 108
SCROLL STITCH
PAGE 110
SINGLE FEATHER STITCH
PAGE 111
TAPERED TRAILING
PAGE 112
THORN STITCH
PAGE 113
THREADED BACK STITCH
PAGE 114
THREADED HERRINGBONE STITCH
PAGE 115
TRAILING
PAGE 116
TWISTED CHAIN STITCH
PAGE 118
VAN DYKE STITCH
PAGE 120
WHIPPED BACK STITCH
PAGE 122
WHIPPED CHAIN STITCH
PAGE 123
WHIPPED RUNNING STITCH
PAGE 124
WHIPPED STEM STITCH
PAGE 125

EMBROIDERY TECHNIQUE: SURFACE

Also known as Freestyle.

Surface embroidery is a catch-all term which refers to any technique which is worked independently of the weave of the ground fabric. Stitches can be worked in any direction and can use a multitude of threads, although stranded cotton is probably the most popular. The stitcher uses an embroidery or crewel needle (i.e. a needle with a sharp point) as the needle pierces the threads of the ground fabric, rather than being inserted between them.

It can be worked on any fabric, although if worked on an evenweave fabric, the weave is ignored with regard to the placing of the needle. Designs are normally drawn onto the fabric, or they can be worked by eye.

Techniques such as canvaswork, counted thread, blackwork, drawn thread and pulled thread would not be considered surface embroidery as they rely on counting threads to determine where to insert the needle. Techniques which are very raised from the fabric or which use specialized materials (such as stumpwork or goldwork) would also not normally be described as surface embroidery. Note that some techniques combine surface embroidery with other styles, such as pulled thread.

▸▸ Silk collar, RSN Collection COL.2

This large collar was stitched in China, probably in the late 19th century, towards the end of the Qing dynasty (1644–1911). The detachable collar, which is made of blue silk satin and has a scalloped edge and a symmetrical embroidered design, was likely worn as part of a woman's formal dress. This collar shares similarities with cloud collars, embroidered Chinese collars with a circular centre and four panels in the shape of ruyi clouds.

The entire collar is worked in Pekinese stitch, with selected areas worked in satin stitch. The embroidery is wrought in silk threads, with many of the motifs bordered in gold passing threads.

At the centre front is a lotus flower flanked by other floral blooms and a pair of white cats or dogs. Also present are blue and pink pomegranates, purple, red, and green birds and two pairs of dragons: one pair green, and the others black, blue, and white. At the back of the collar are two women holding flowers. The lotus flower, dragons and women are slightly raised. The motifs are united by scrolling polychrome stems, leaves and curls. Along the edge is a line of embroidered pink flowers and pairs of blue curls, followed by a band of orange ribbon decorated with elongated green circles and red centres and strips of pink, white and purple satin.

▾▾ Detail of Pekinese stitch – pages 100–101

BACK-STITCHED CHAIN STITCH

Whitework; Surface.

This stitch is, as its name suggests, a combination of back stitch and chain stitch. Having stitched a line of chain stitch, a line of back stitch is then stitched over the top: each stitch starts and ends in the centre of each loop of chain.

For more background see the entries for back stitch (see page 16) and chain stitch (see page 22).

METHOD

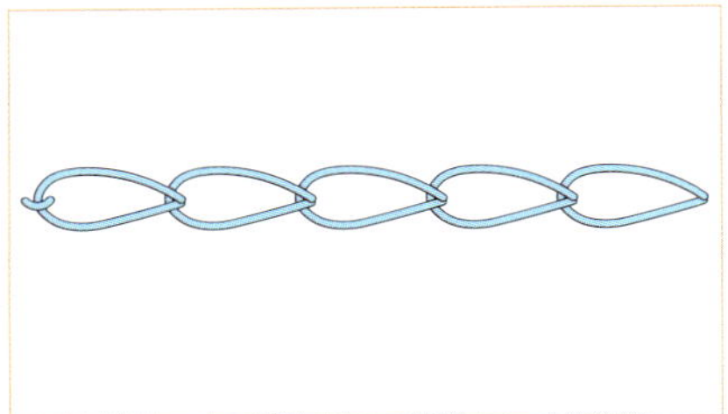

1 Complete a row of chain stitch.

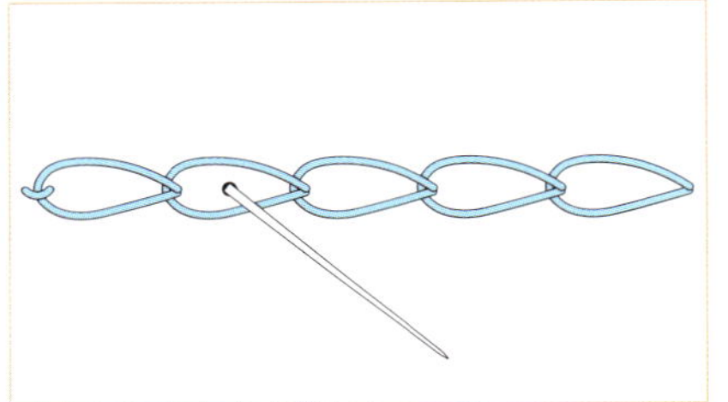

2 After completing a row of chain stitch, work a back stitch over the top by bringing the needle and thread up in the centre of the second loop of chain ...

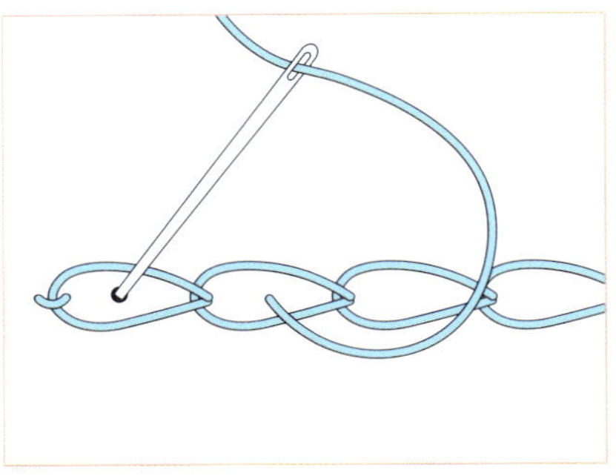

3 ... and taking the needle down in the centre of the first loop of chain. A straight stitch should lie over the intersection of the chain.

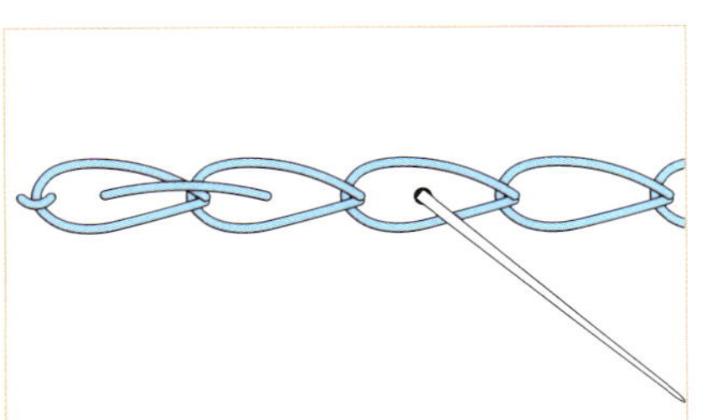

4 Bring the needle up again in the centre of the third loop of chain ...

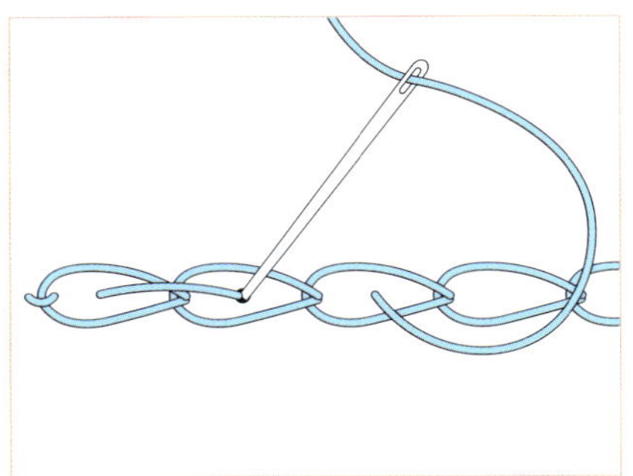

5 ... and back down into the second chain to meet the previous back stitch by sharing the same hole.

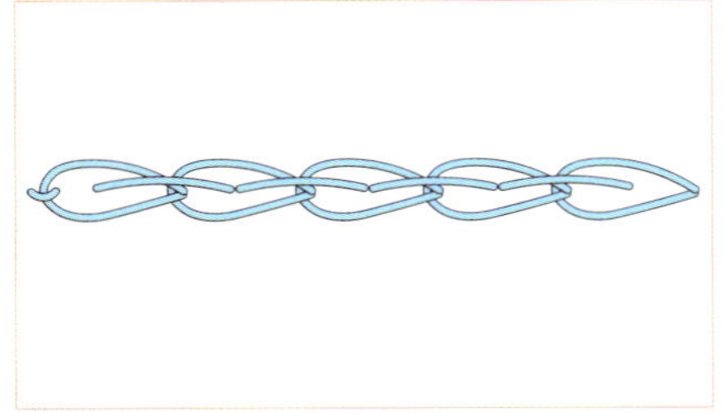

6 Continue to cover each chain intersection with back stitch.

BRAID STITCH

SURFACE; ELIZABETHAN; STUMPWORK.

Also known as Gordian knot stitch.

This stitch is a relatively simple looped braid stitch where each loop is anchored by the needle going either into or out of the fabric.

Elizabethan embroidery is known for a variety of braid stitches besides this one and so historical references to 'braid stitch' may refer to any of the many versions (including heavy chain stitch on page 76), rather than specifically this stitch.

This specific stitch has been first identified on a book cover containing a manuscript written by Queen Elizabeth I in 1544 (it is uncertain whether she stitched the cover). It is also used in another Elizabethan piece from the 17th century, currently held by the Metropolitan Museum in New York.

METHOD

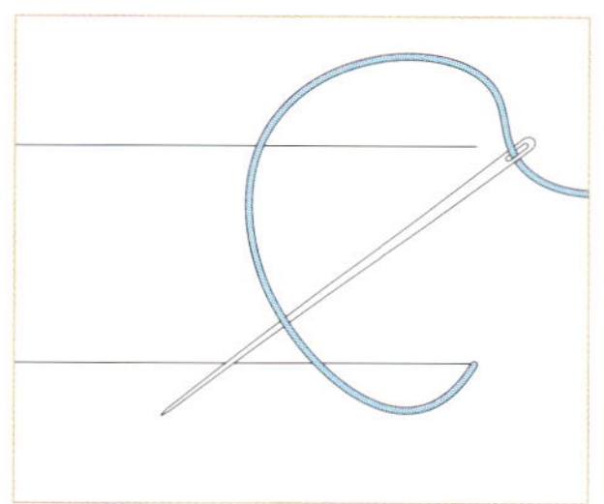

1 Draw a pair of parallel guide lines. Work from right to left. Bring the needle up on the lower line and hold the working thread to the left, passing the needle and thread under it to form a loop.

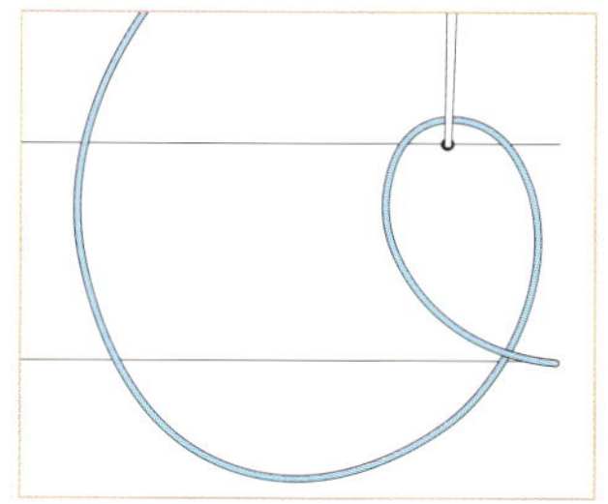

2 Insert the needle on the upper line within the loop you have created, tighten the thread against your needle and draw through, ensuring you leave a secondary loop on the surface.

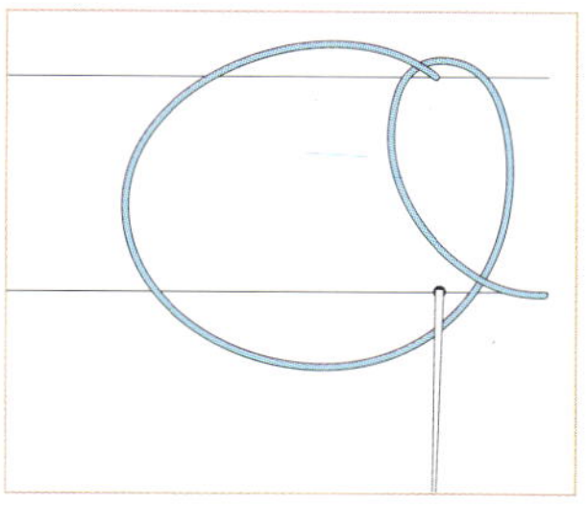

3 Come up in the new loop on the lower line exactly beneath where the needle went down. Pull the loop taut.

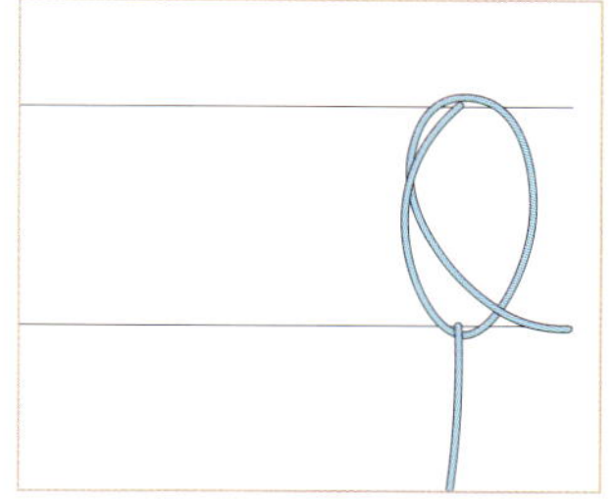

4 Pull the thread through to complete the first braid stitch.

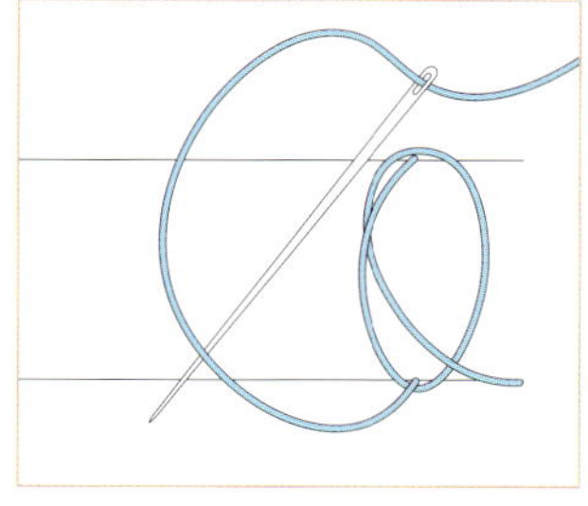

5 Hold the thread to the left again to start the second braid stitch. Pass the needle under the working thread and leave a loop.

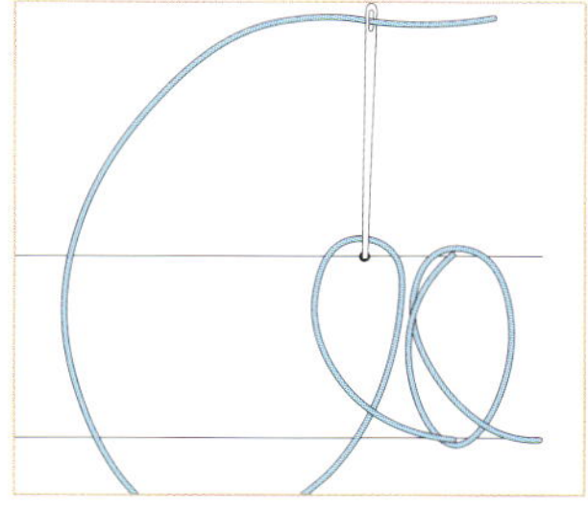

6 Insert the needle on the upper line inside the loop, and tighten the thread against the needle. Pull the thread through, leaving an additional loop on the surface.

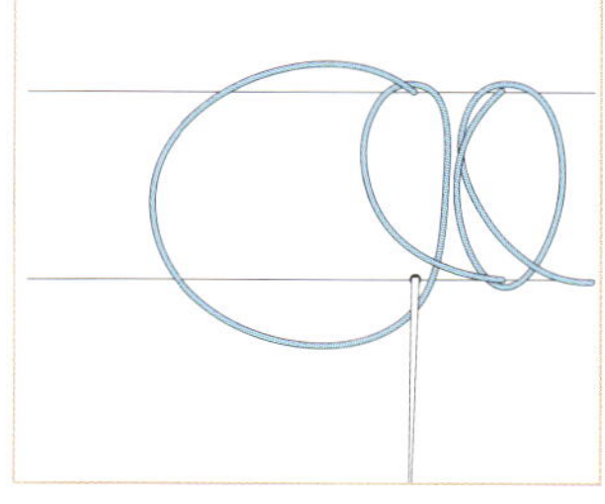

7 Come up on the lower line exactly beneath where the needle went down, and inside the new loop.

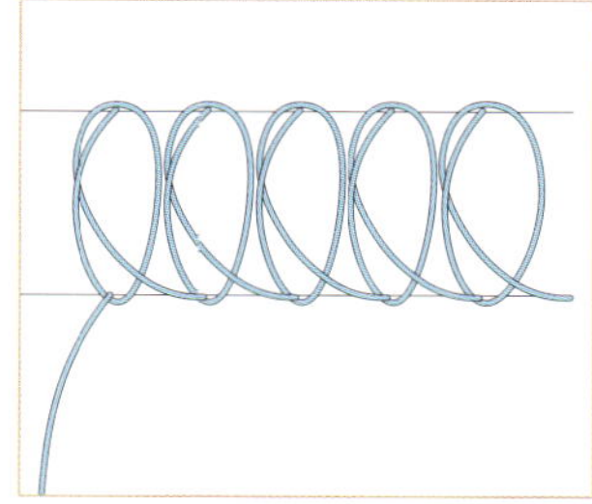

8 Continue to work the braid. The first stage can be awkward so an alternative method is to wrap the needle with the working thread.

CABLE CHAIN STITCH

SURFACE; MOUNTMELLICK.

Also known as Cable stitch.

Cable chain stitch consists of alternate straight stiches and loops so that the finished stitch looks like a length of metal chain.

A variant of chain stitch; for more information see the entry for chain stitch on page 22.

METHOD

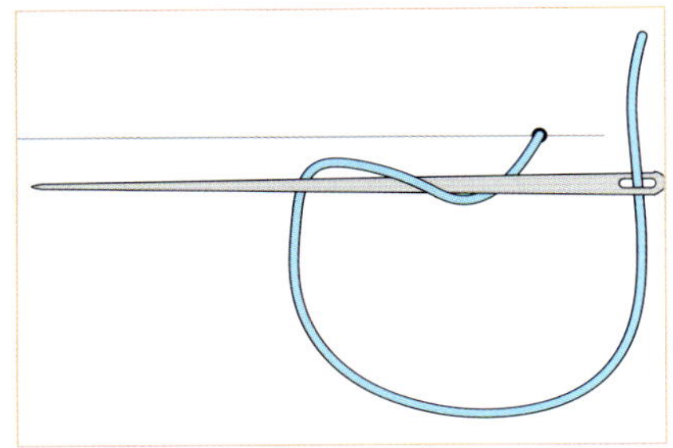

1 Bring the needle and thread to the surface and wrap the needle with the base of the thread.

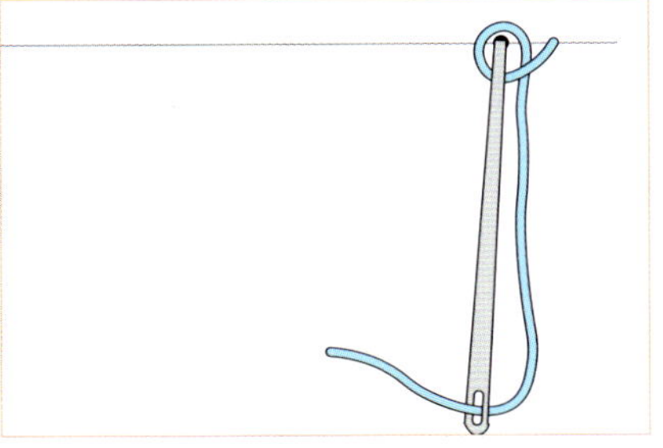

2 Take the needle down through the fabric a few millimetres ahead, leaving a loop on the surface.

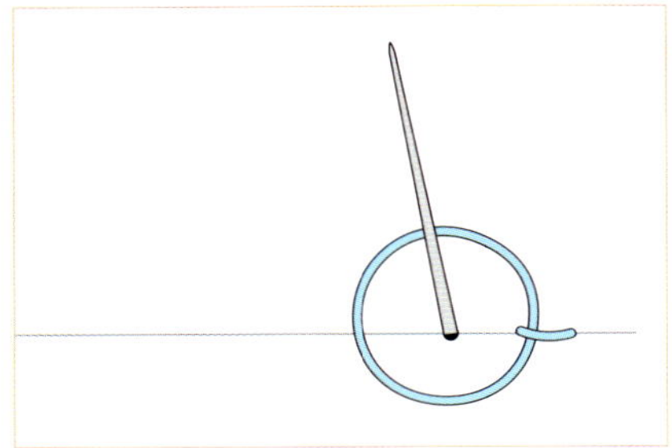

3 Bring the needle up through the fabric within the loop.

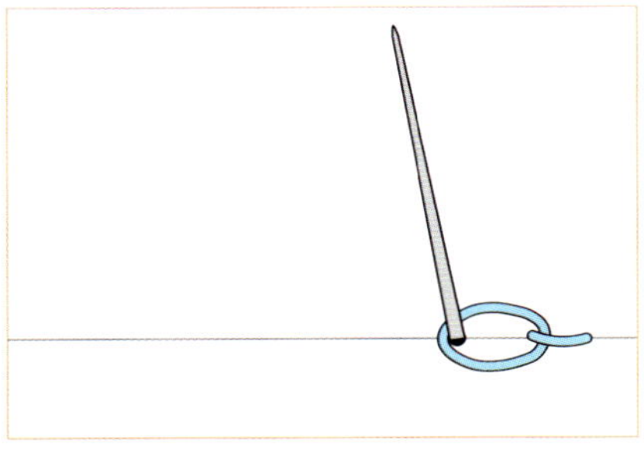

4 Tighten the loop around the needle from the underside before bringing the thread up through the fabric.

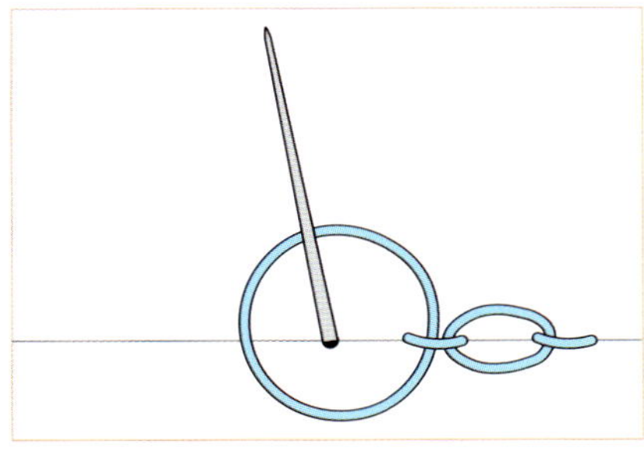

5 Repeat steps 1–4 to complete another link.

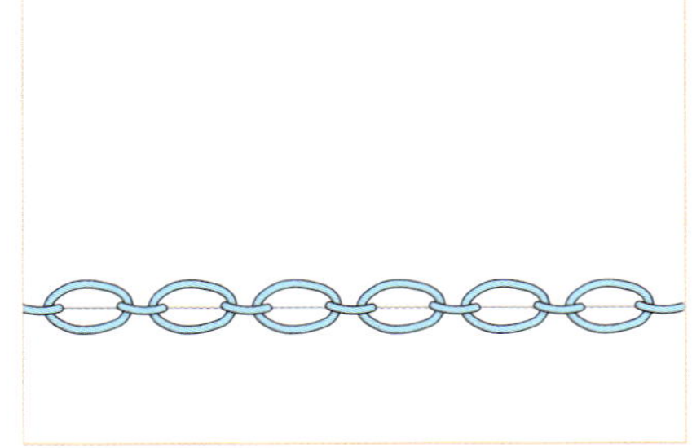

6 Continue to repeat these steps to form more links to produce a cable chain.

CABLE STITCH

SURFACE; HARDANGER.

Also known as Alternate stem stitch, or Side-to-side stem stitch.

This stitch is a combination of stem and outline stitches (see pages 40–41 and 32–33): the two stitches are alternated (so the needle comes up on each side of the previous stitch in turn).

Cable stitch was evidently in use in the 19th century as the V&A South Kensington holds a Turkish towel/napkin from this era featuring the stitch.

METHOD

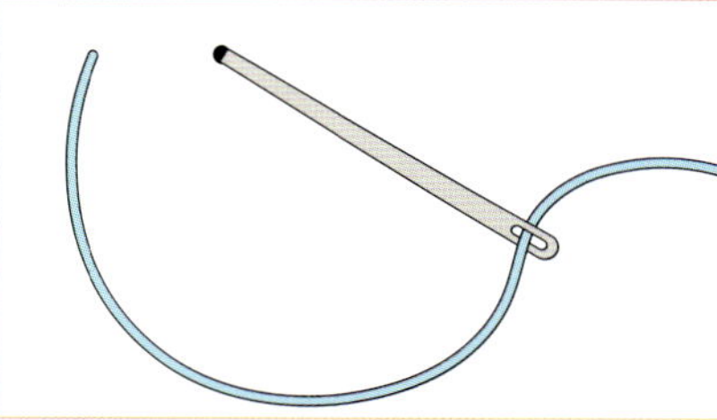

1 Working from left to right, bring the needle up and then back down on the design line, leaving a loop below the design line.

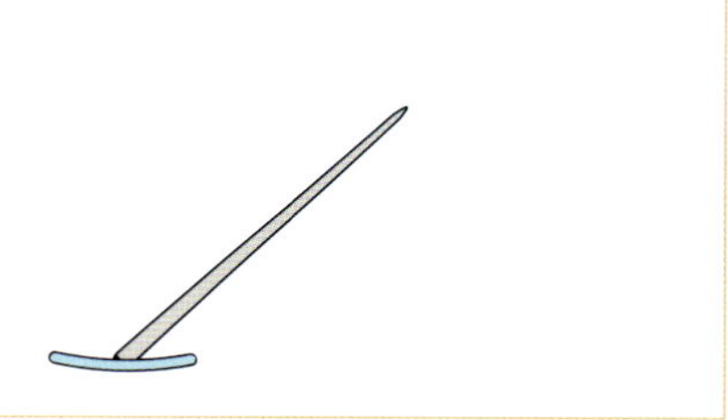

2 Bring the needle back to the surface halfway between the previous start and end points, then tighten the first stitch by pulling the thread through to the back. Your needle should be above the previous stitch.

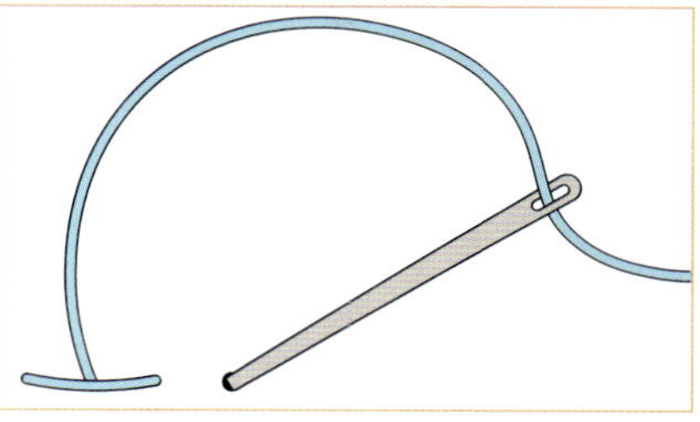

3 Work the second stitch by taking the needle down on the design line, again leaving a loop but this time above the design line. Keep the stitch length consistent.

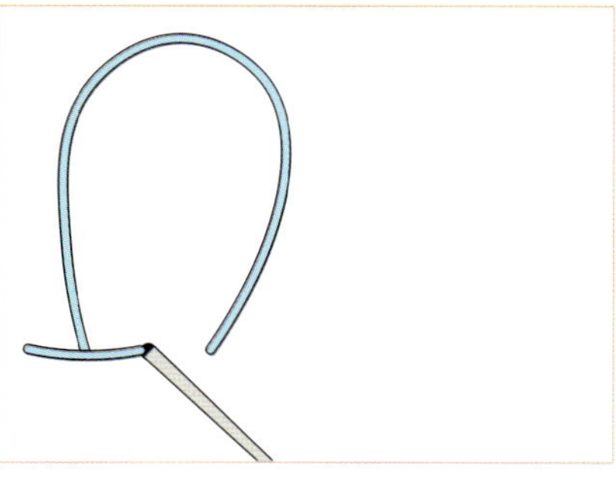

4 Bring the needle up half a stitch length back, this time bringing the thread up below the loop of the second stitch and in line with the first. Pull the thread taut from the back so that the needle is below the previous stitch.

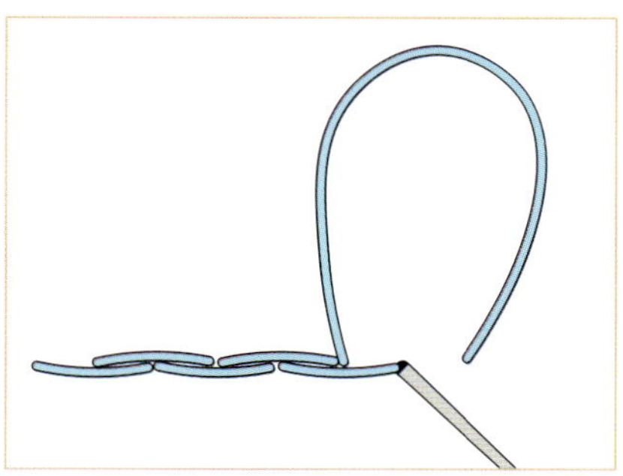

5 Continue to stitch along the line, alternating which side of the previous stitch you bring up your thread.

CHEQUERED CHAIN STITCH

Surface; Crewelwork.

Also known as Two colour chain stitch, Alternating chain stitch, Magic chain stitch, or Magic stitch.

This stitch is a chain stitch where alternate stitches are executed in different colours. It is worked with two different threads in the needle, one of which alternately disappears, hence the alternative name of magic stitch.

For more background see chain stitch on page 22.

METHOD

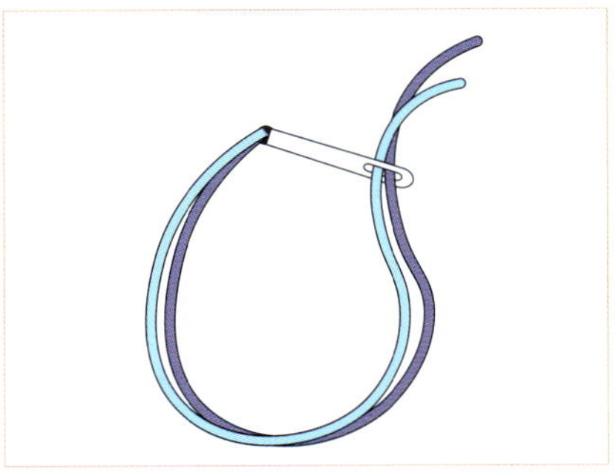

1 Thread the needle with two threads of different shades. Bring the needle up and back down again in the same hole, leaving two loops on the surface. Take care not to catch the thread with the needle and to ensure the same hole is used.

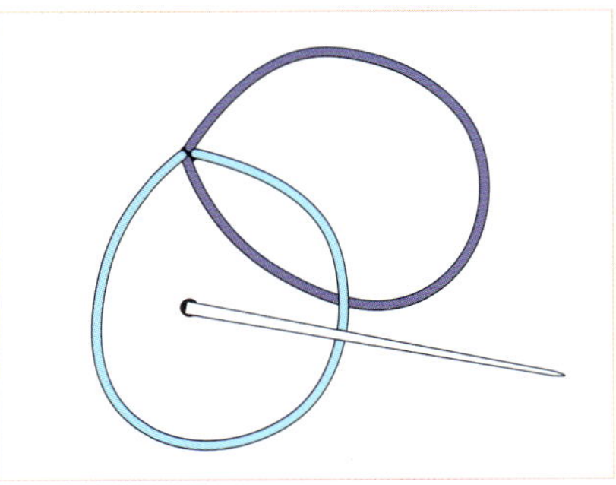

2 Bring the needle up further below and take it through one of the loops.

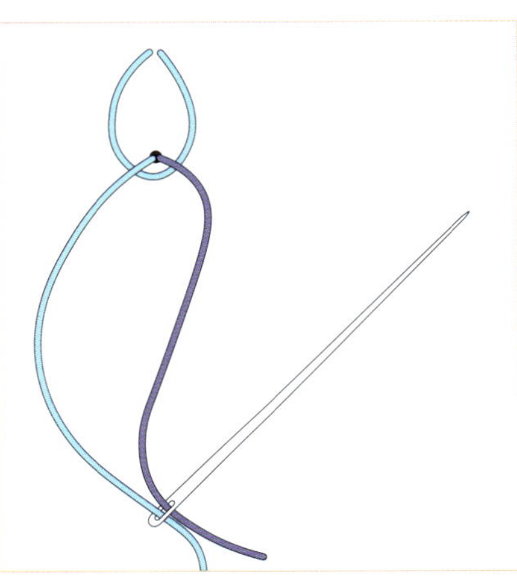

3 Pull both loops tight and one will magically disappear.

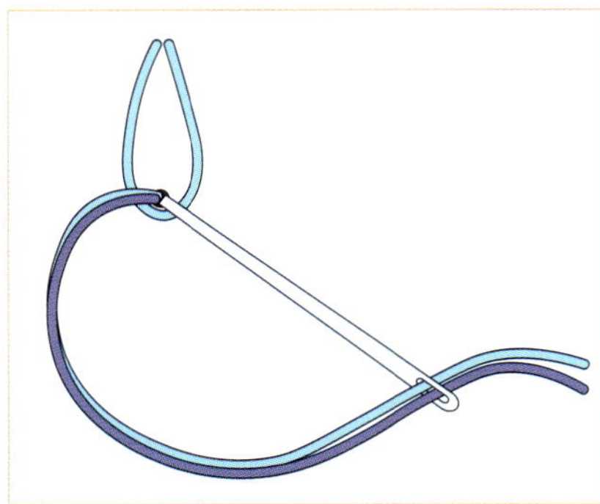

4 Take your needle back down in the same hole again leaving two loops on the surface.

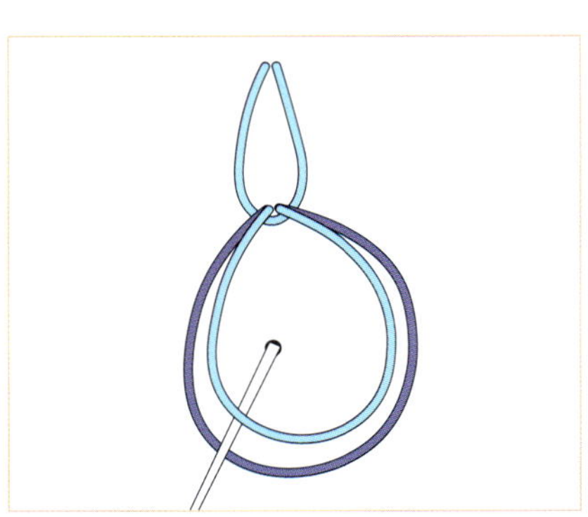

5 Bring the needle back up further down and this time take the needle through the loop of the other colour.

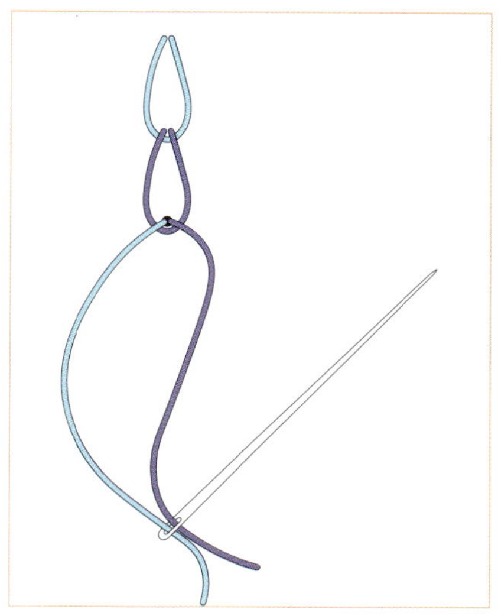

6 Pull both loops tight and you will be left with a chain of each colour.

7 Repeat this process alternating between both colours. To finish, take a holding stitch over the final loop. The holding stitch will be both colours.

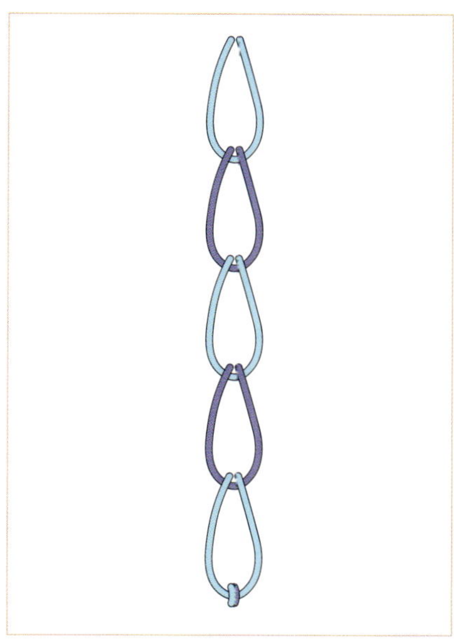

8 The finished magic chain will look like this.

▸▸ Detail from Juno, Venus, Minerva and Proserpine screen, RSN Collection No. 2707

More of this detail can be seen on page 23. It could have been given a very different look in terms of colour if chequered chain stitch had been used for the robes of the figures, but the quality of the line would have remained consistent. This is because both stitches can provide different weights of line through working rows of stitches next to each other, and by varying the number of threads used in the needle, so that there is a play between thicker and thinner sections.

CLOSED FEATHER STITCH

Surface.

This is a variation of feather stitch (see pages 72–73) where each stitch is closed to form a triangle.

This stitch is very similar to double chain stitch: for double chain, the loop of the chain is taken down inside the loop of the previous chain; for closed feather, the needle is taken down just outside the previous loop.

Historic references to closed or close feather stitch may be referring to long and short stitch (see pages 224–225) rather than this stitch, as feather stitch is an alternative name.

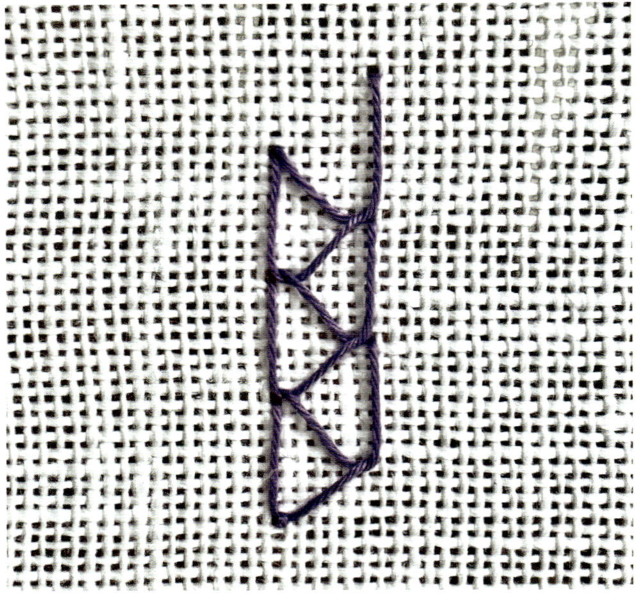

METHOD

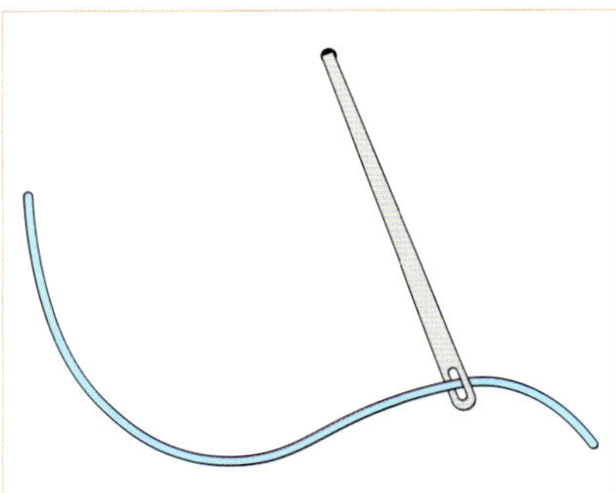

1 Imagine (or draw) two parallel lines and bring your needle up on your left line. Take your needle down on your right line at slightly higher point than where you emerged on your left line.

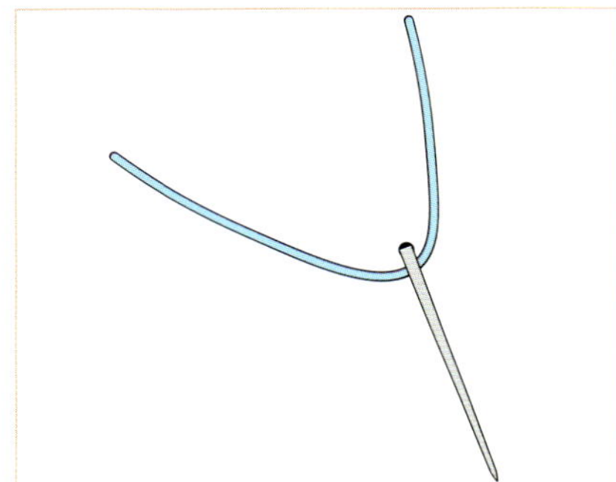

2 Leaving a loop, bring the needle up on your right line, but a little lower than where you first brought the needle up. Pull the thread to create a triangular stitch.

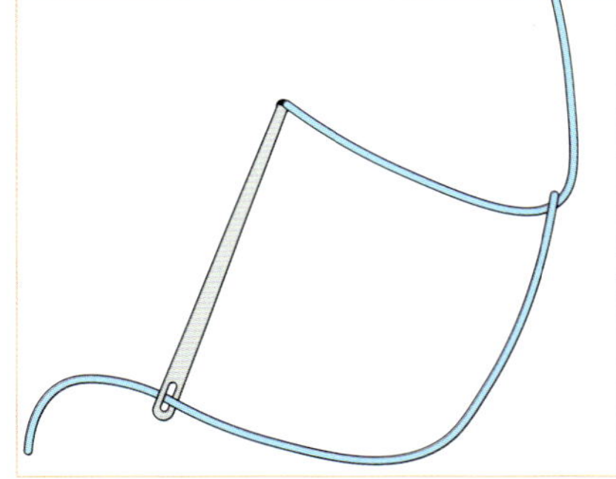

3 Take the needle down on the left line in the same hole that you first brought the needle up.

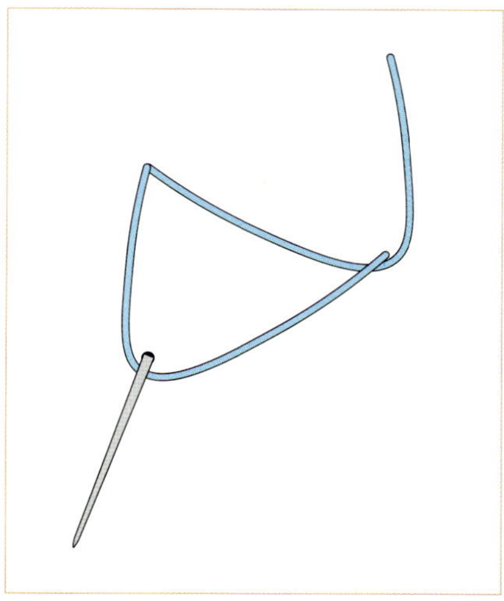

4 Leaving a loop, bring the needle up on your left line, but a little lower than where you brought the needle up for the second stitch.

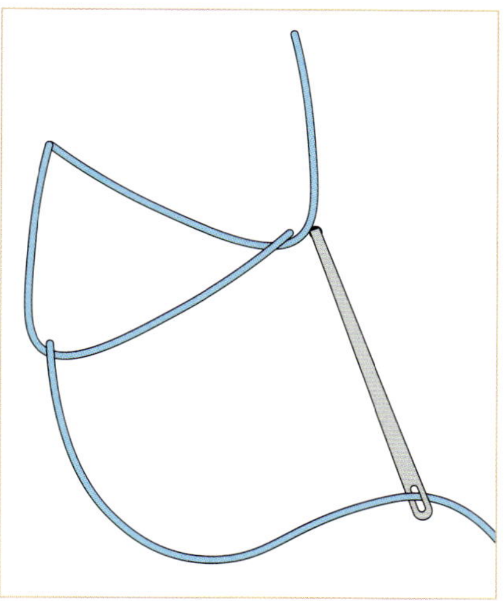

5 Pull the thread to create a second triangle. Then take the needle down on your right line very close to the spot where the second stitch started, but make sure it is outside the loop.

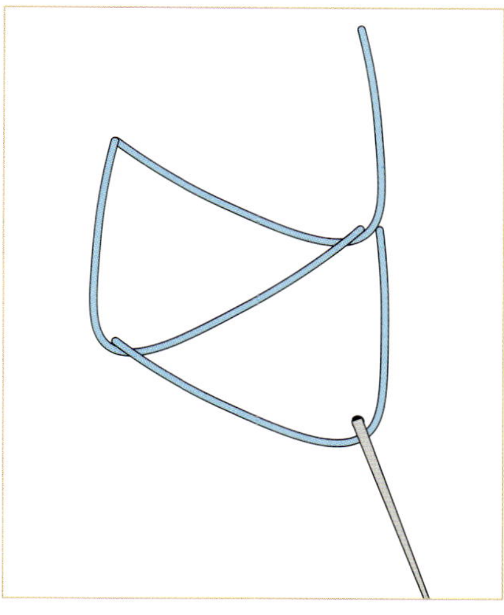

6 Leaving a loop, bring the needle up on your right line, but a little lower than where you started the third stitch. Pull the thread to create another triangle.

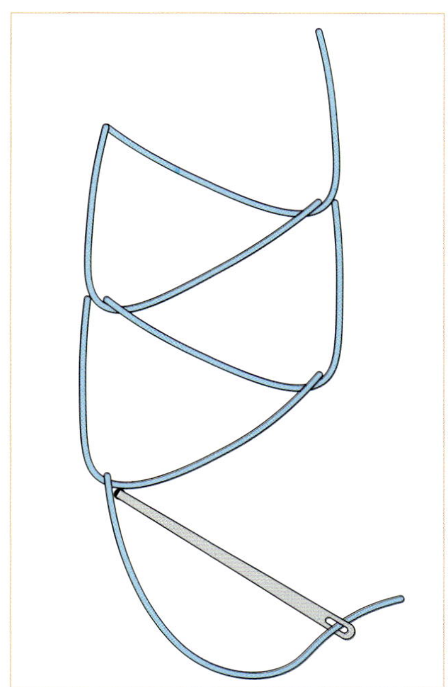

7 Continue working in the same way. When finishing the stitch, take the needle down over the last loop to form a small anchoring stitch.

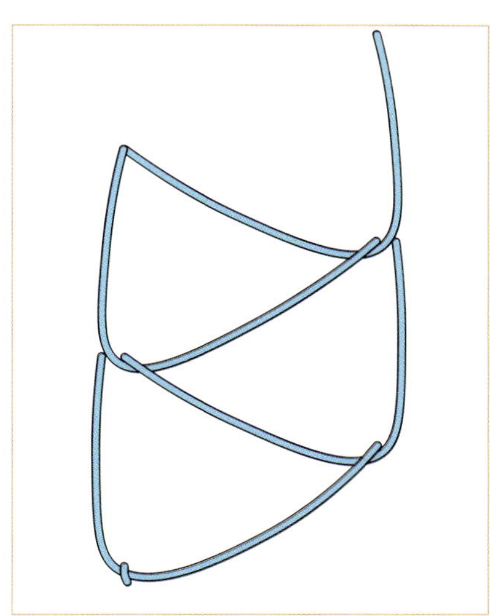

A completed line of closed feather stitch.

CLOSED HERRINGBONE STITCH

Crewelwork; Shadowwork; Surface.

Also known as Persian stitch, Double back stitch, Crossed back stitch, Point croisé stitch, or Close herringbone stitch.

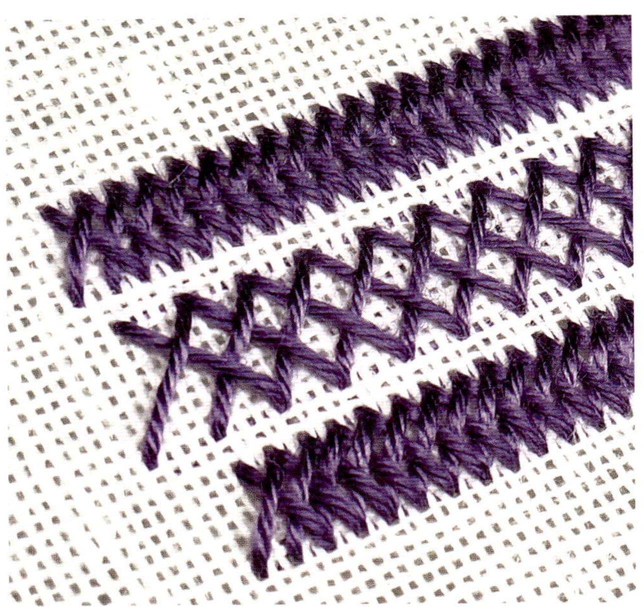

This stitch is a version of herringbone stitch where the stitches are worked closely together to form a solid line.

The reverse of this stitch forms two parallel lines of back stitch (see page 16), which is known as double back stitch (see pages 66–67) although some authors don't clearly distinguish between the two names. The reversible nature of this stitch means it is often used for straight or curved borders.

Closed herringbone stitch certainly dates as far back as the 16th century as it features on a south German/Swiss ecclesiastical panel from that era. The V&A South Kensington holds English items from the 17th century (a crewelwork panel on linen and Margret Mason's sampler) and Turkish pieces from the 18th century.

Contemporary embroiderers in the Hazarajat region of Afghanistan use closed herringbone stitch for bands and borders to embellish garments.

METHOD

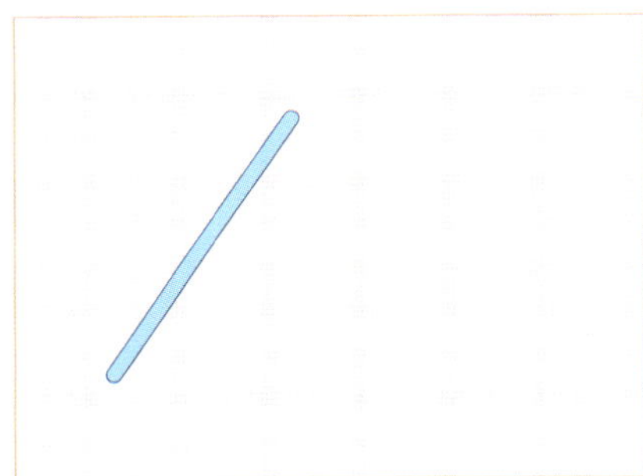

1 Use the grain of the fabric or mark two parallel guide lines to create herringbone stitch. Work a diagonal stitch first.

2 Come up to the left at the same level and go down diagonally at the same level of your starting point. This completes a herringbone stitch.

3 Go back and bring the needle up close to where you inserted your needle. Make another diagonal stitch close to the first herringbone stitch.

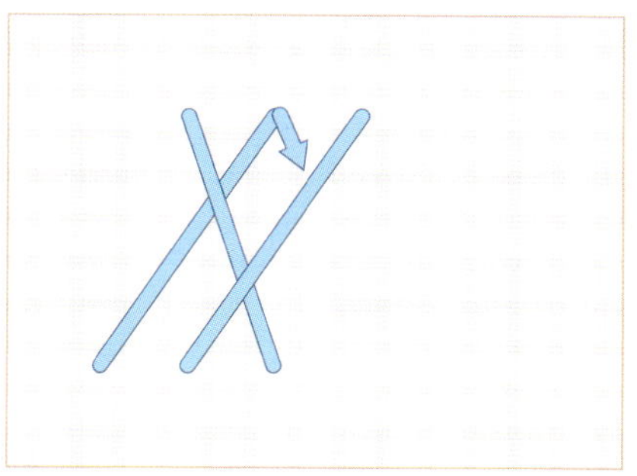

4 Come up where your previous herringbone stitch went in.

5 Go down close to the previous herringbone stitch.

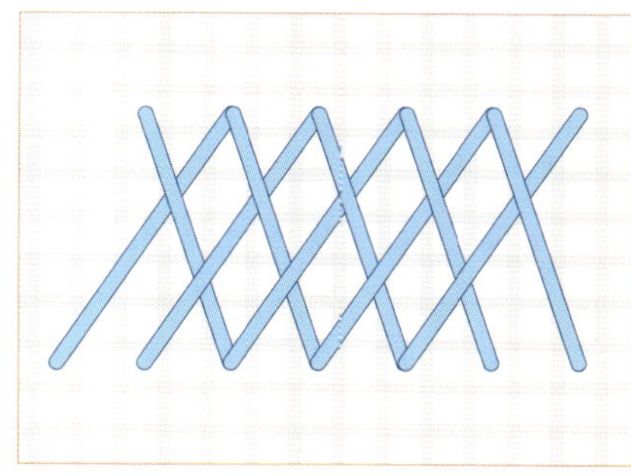

6 Come up where your previous herringbone stitch went in, and then continue in this manner.

The completed closed herringbone stitch.

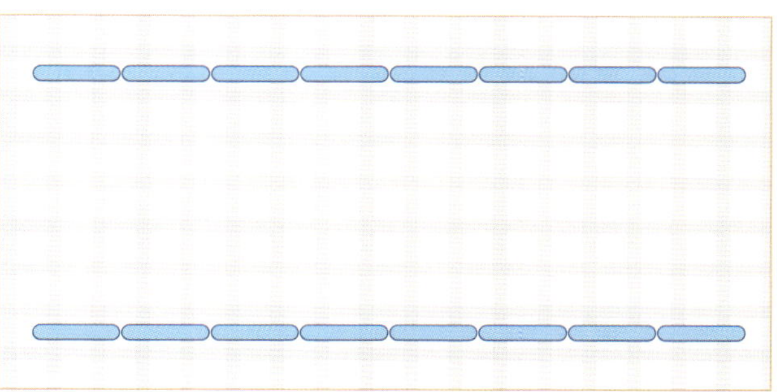

On the reverse side, closed herringbone stitch creates two parallel lines of back stitches.

◂◂ Detail from fragment, RSN Collection COL.1924.20.Grove.2

Fragment of late 17th- or early 18th-century English crewelwork, depicting a stylized flower in blue wool thread. The bottom left of the fabric has a segment of a flower that appears to run to the edge of the embroidery design.

One petal contains cross stitches, while the second appears to contain some form of closed herringbone stitch which is in poor condition, and the final petal has a trellis stitch creating more dense coverage than any other petals in the piece.

The full fragment can be seen overleaf.

CORAL STITCH

Crewelwork; Mountmellick; Surface; Elizabethan; Blackwork.

Also known as Knotted stitch, German knot stitch, Beaded stitch, Snail trail, Scroll stitch, Running knot, or Single coral.

Coral stitch is a line stitch interspersed with evenly spaced knots. It has similarities to scroll stitch (see page 110) although the line between the knots is straight, rather than curved. Coral stitch is commonly used for outlines and tendrils in floral designs.

The stitch has an ancient provenance, as it is credited with being one of the stitches used by ancient Egyptian stitchers. More recently, it features on the earliest known English sampler, dated 1598, and on a late 16th-century English headdress. It was a popular stitch in 17th- and 18th-century English crewelwork.

It became an integral part of German Schwalm whitework (*Schwälmer Weißstickerei*) in the late 18th century and early 19th century. It is also used in Sardinian knotted embroidery (*Punt 'e Nù*), a form of counted thread whitework from Teulada, Sardinia.

METHOD

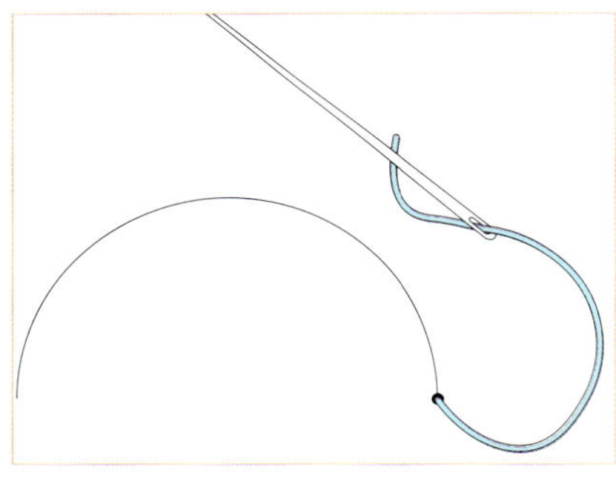

1 Bring your needle to the surface and lay your thread along the design line in the direction of travel.

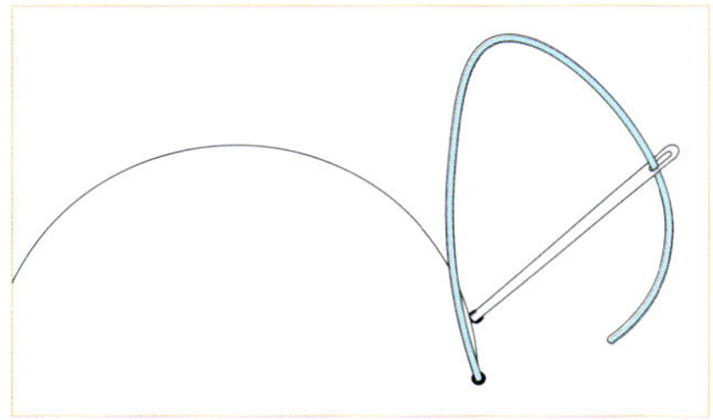

2 Hold on to the thread and take the needle down through the fabric on one side of the laid thread.

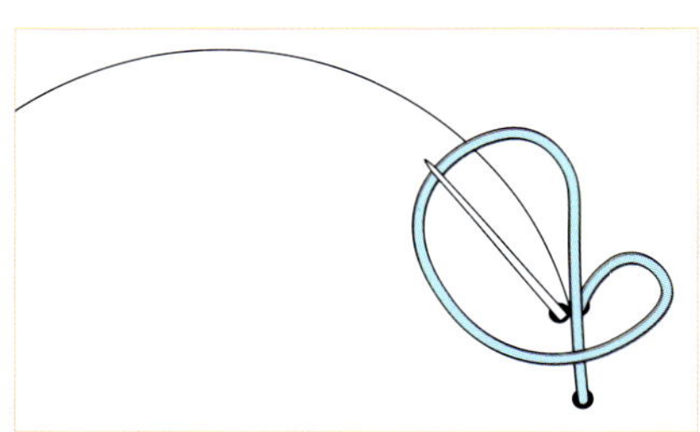

3 Draw the thread through partway to create a loop, then bring the needle back to the surface on the other side of the laid thread and up through the loop.

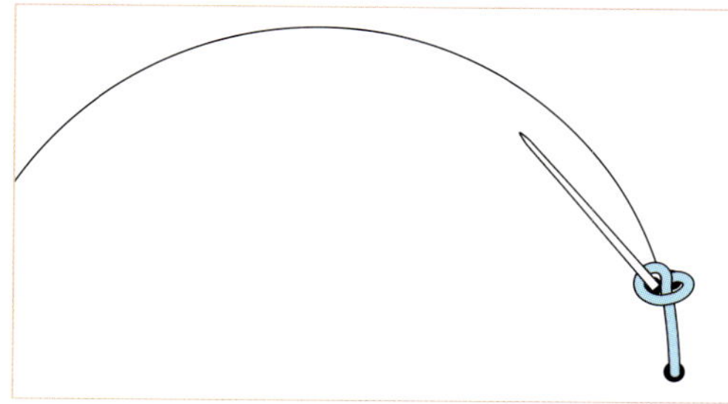

4 Hold on to the needle in the fabric and draw the thread through from the underside, pulling the loop tight against the needle.

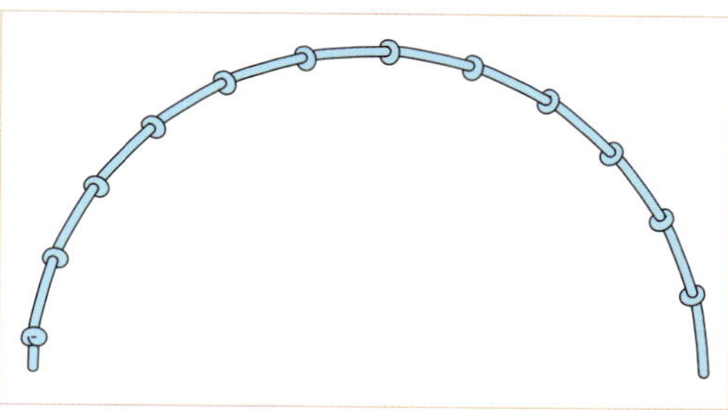

5 Bring the needle up to the surface to repeat. Continue along the line, producing knots at equal intervals.

▴▴ Fragment, RSN Collection COL.1924.20.Grove.2

The design of this English crewelwork fragment, dating from the late 17th or early 18th century, depicts a complete single flower form.

Coral stitch appears on one of the four petals rising up from the centre. From left to right; the first is filled with a combination of detached chain stitches with French knots in the middle and cross stitches. The second has lines made from straight stitches and running stitches, while coral stitch features in the third as part of a vein effect, which is interspersed with French knots. The fourth petal contains a repeated motif which uses French knots and straight stitch arranged in a floral design.

COUCHED HERRINGBONE STITCH

Surface.

Also known as Tied herringbone stitch, or Tacked herringbone stitch.

This version of herringbone stitch has small horizontal couching stitches where the herringbone stitches cross. Its alternative name of tacked herringbone stitch is sometimes used for a version where the couching stitches are vertical rather than horizontal. It is also sometimes known as tied herringbone stitch, although the sources we have used indicate that this name is used for a subtly different version (the second thread in tied herringbone covers more of the original stitching).

Couched herringbone stitch was evidently in use during the 17th century as it features on an English embroidered biblical picture of the creation currently held by the Art Institute of Chicago. The couching stitches on this piece are horizontal, rather than the vertical direction which is currently accepted as standard.

METHOD

1 Work a row of ordinary herringbone stitch.

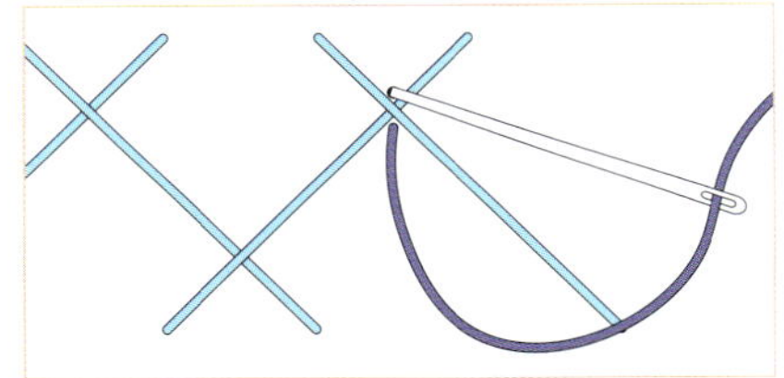

2 Use a different colour for the second thread. Come up just below the intersection of the herringbone stitch, and go down just above the intersection.

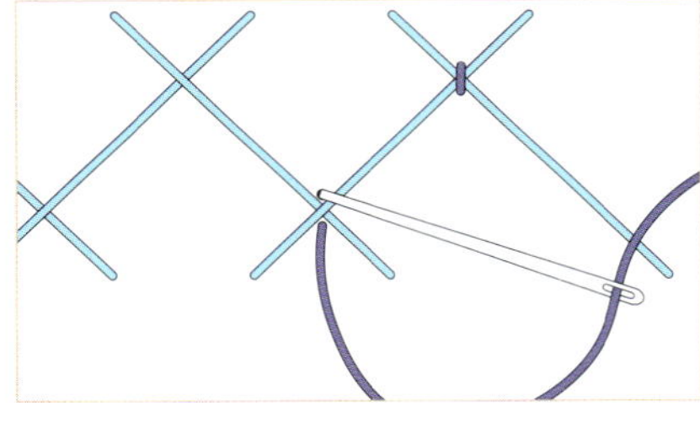

3 Bring the needle up at the next intersection of the herringbone stitch, and take the needle down just above the intersection.

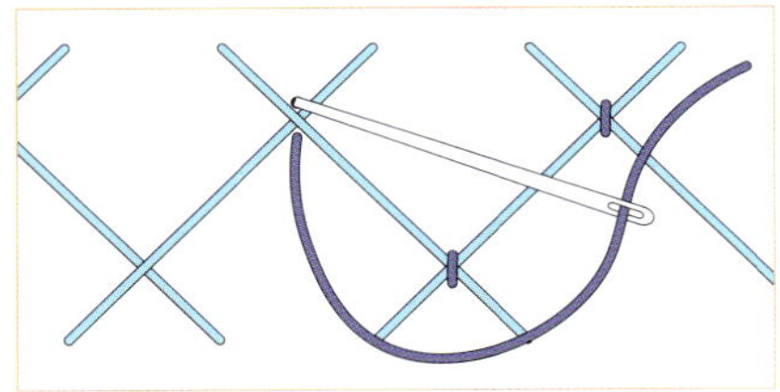

4 Continue couching down the intersections of herringbone stitch.

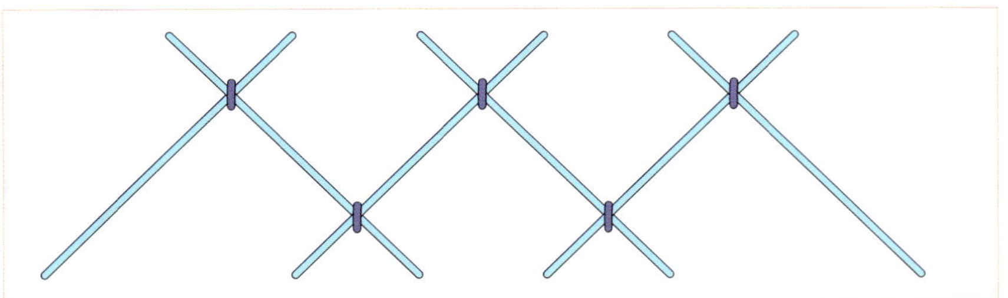

A complete couched herringbone stitch.

COUCHING

Crewelwork; Wessex stitchery; Appliqué; Mountmellick; Ribbonwork; Surface; Stumpwork; Blackwork; Elizabethan.

Also known as Basic couching, Simple couching, Plain couching, Laid embroidery, En couchure stitch, Kloster stitch, or Convent stitch.

Couching is the method used to attach a thread or group of threads to fabric when they are too thick, too highly textured or too fragile to be stitched through the fabric. A second thread, normally finer, is used to stitch over the couched thread, thus anchoring it to the fabric. The name comes from the French word *coucher*, meaning to lay down.

Ideal for covering edges of an applied fabric or embroidery, couching also works well as an outline stitch and is easily scaled up or down by adding more threads. The colour and texture of the couching thread can be chosen to be either invisible or to create a certain effect.

METHOD

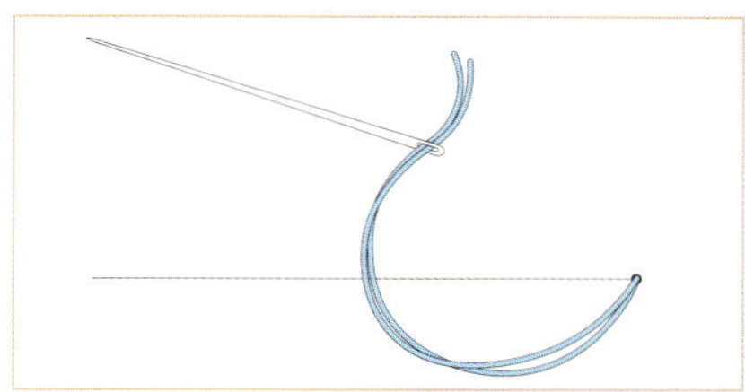

1 Put one or several strands in a chenille needle and bring both ends to the surface separately.

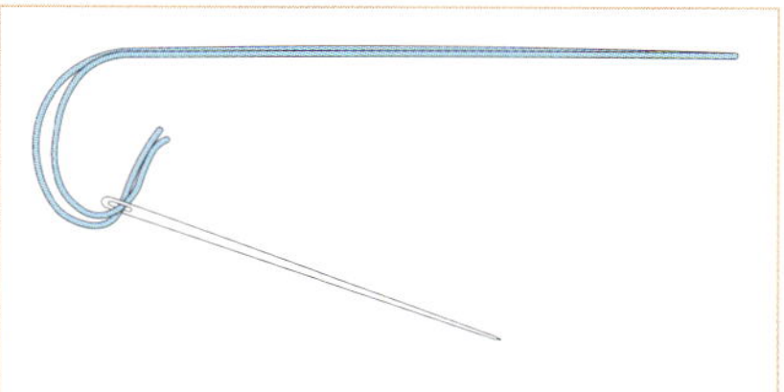

2 Bring all the strands together and lay them along the surface.

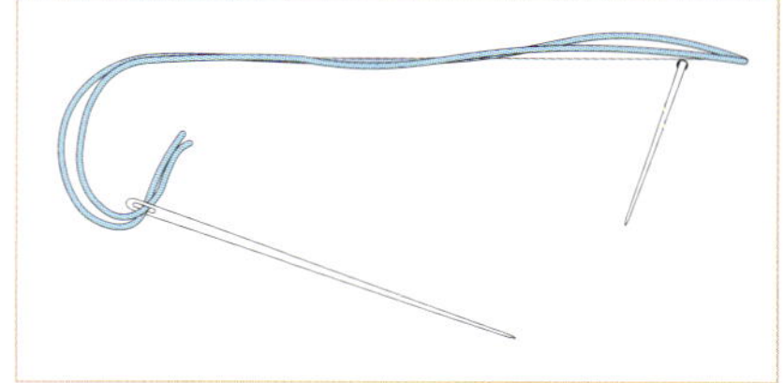

3 Bring another needle and thread up through the fabric on one side of the laid thread.

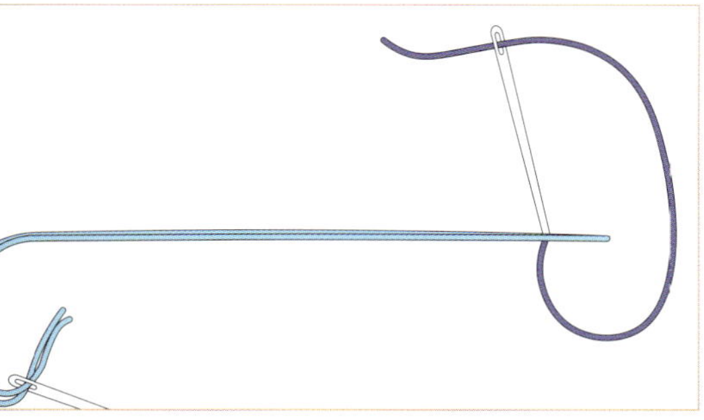

4 Take the needle back down through the fabric on the other side of the laid thread, to secure the surface thread.

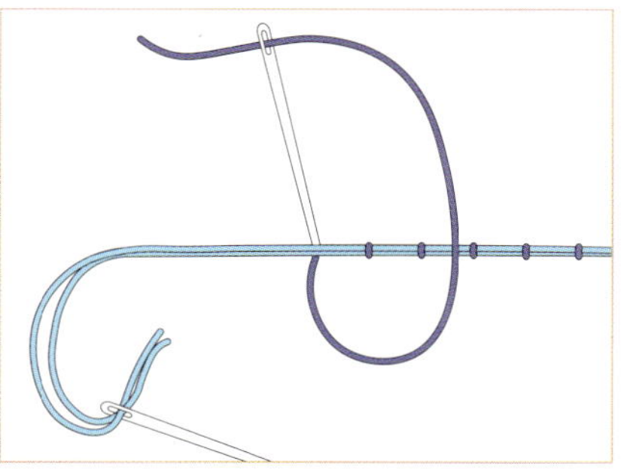

5 Continue couching small stitches over the length of the surface thread at regular intervals.

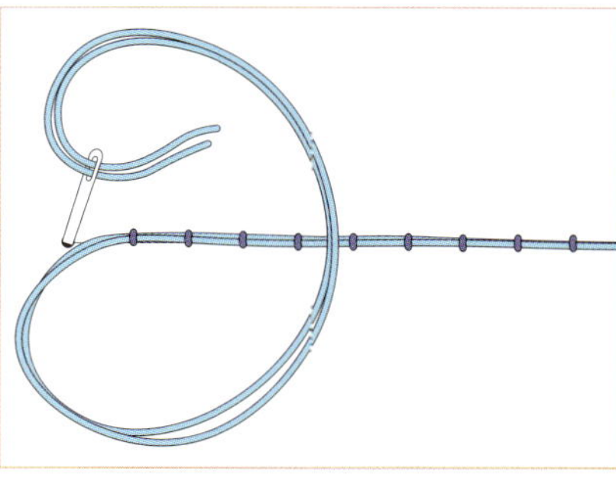

6 To finish, take both the surface thread and the couching thread back to the underside of the fabric and secure in the normal manner.

CROSSED BUTTONHOLE STITCH

Surface.

A variation on buttonhole stitch where the legs of the stitch are crossed. It is an effective border or edging stitch that can also be used for filling.

For more background see the entries for buttonhole stitch (see pages 20–21) and blanket stitch (see page 18).

METHOD

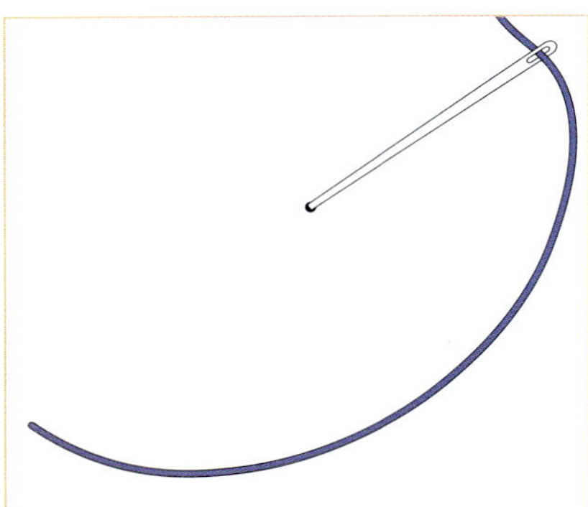

1 Working from left to right, work a diagonal stitch.

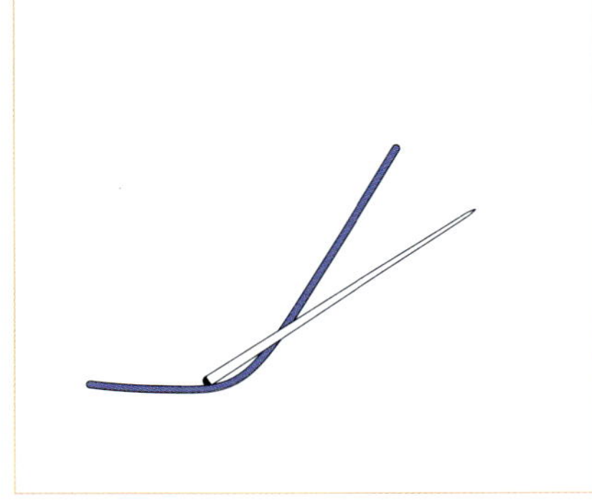

2 Leaving a loop on the surface, bring the needle up in line with the base ensuring the needle comes to the surface left of the loop.

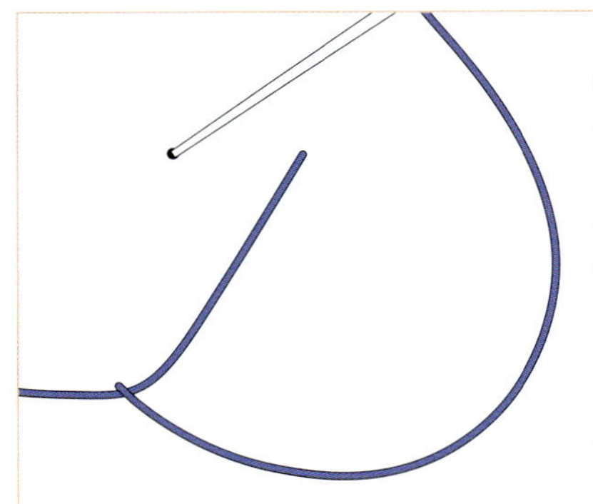

3 Take the needle down by crossing over the last stitch, again leaving a loop on the surface.

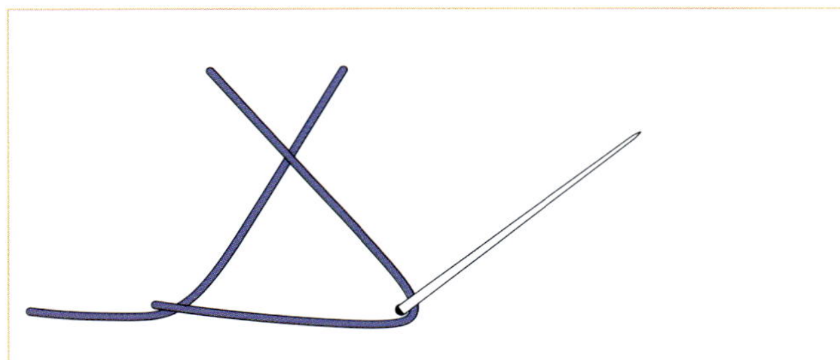

4 Bring the needle up on the base line within the loop.

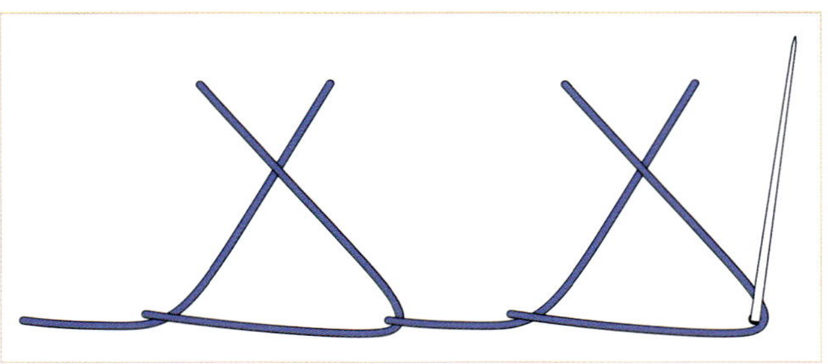

5 Repeat the sequence to create an edge, border or filling.

DOT STITCH

SURFACE; WHITEWORK.

Also known as Simple knot stitch, Point de pois, Point d'or, Point de poste, Dotted stitch, Knot stitch, Spot stitch, Rice stitch, or Rice grain stitch.

This stitch consists of two small parallel back stitches right next to each other so that they form a single dot. They are normally worked in lines and frequently an area is filled with roughly parallel lines of dot stitch; less commonly, they can be scattered randomly like seeding stitch (see page 265). The similarities between the two stitches mean that some authors do not distinguish between them.

Blanche Caulfeild's version in her *Dictionary of Needlework* indicates that more than two stitches can be worked if a more substantial dot is required.

Dot stitch was used as a filling stitch on Victorian whitework garments, including Ayrshire work, although it is hard to ascertain how prevalent it was. Written sources rarely use the name, and it can be difficult to establish on well-worn garments whether a stitch is one single stitch worked with multiple threads, or two parallel ones. The University of Edinburgh archives has a collar from the 1820s which shows dot stitch as a filling for various motifs.

Jacobean crewelwork often features dot stitch as a line of dots, rather than as a filling stitch; but again, written sources rarely identify it. At a casual glance it can look like running stitch in a heavy thread, but it is wider than a running stitch.

METHOD

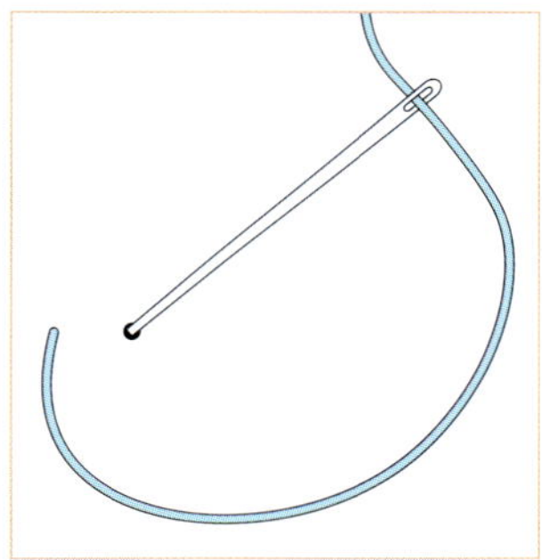

1 Work a back stitch.

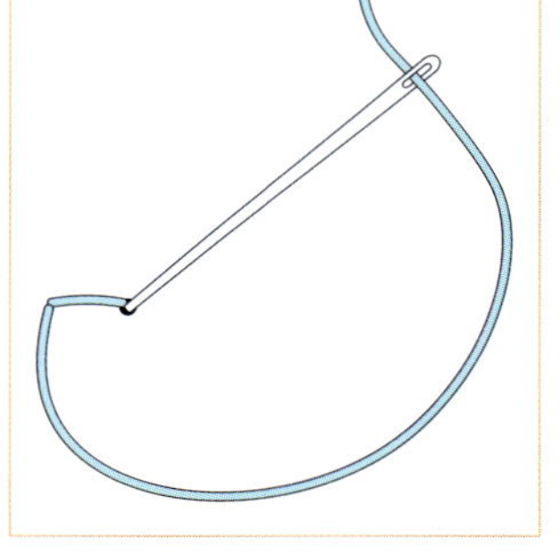

2 Work another back stitch into the same hole.

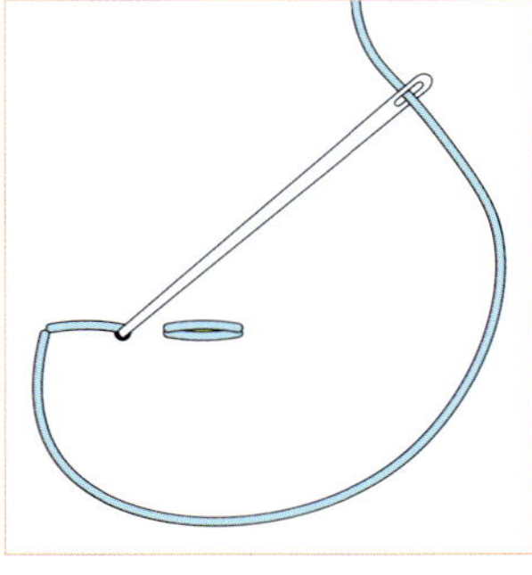

3 Leave a small gap, and work the next pair of back stitches.

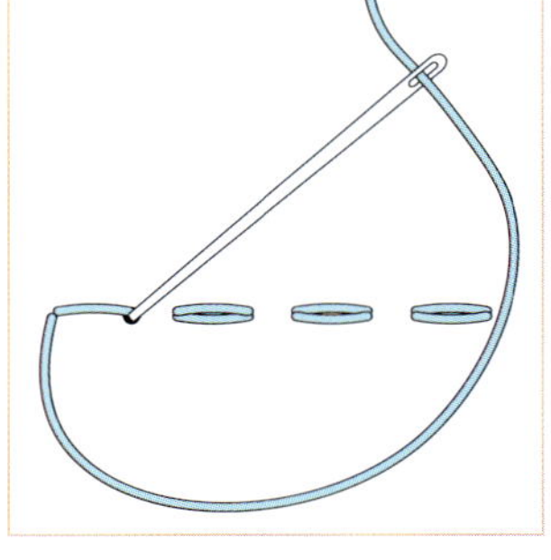

4 Make sure to leave a tiny space between each pair of stitches.

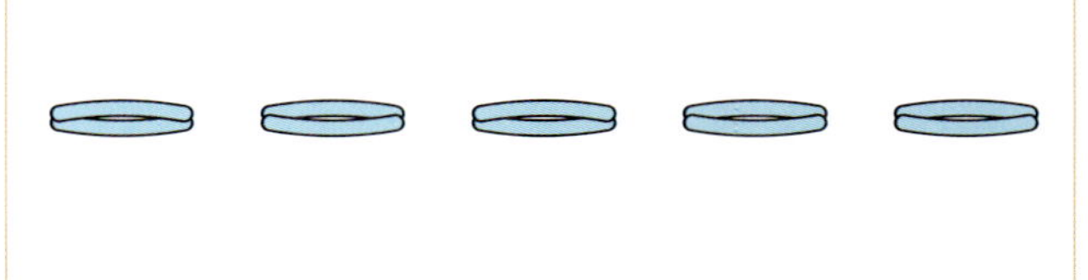

5 Continue working dot stitch as required.

DOUBLE BACK STITCH

Shadow work; Surface; Appliqué.

Also known as Persian stitch, Close herringbone stitch, Crossed back stitch, Point croisé stitch, or Shadow stitch.

Double back stitch is formed by working two parallel rows of back stitch along a narrow shape, crossing from one side to the other to produce an overlapping herringbone stitch on the reverse side. The reverse side of this stitch is known as closed herringbone stitch (see pages 58–59) although some authors don't clearly distinguish between the two names.

This reversible nature of this stitch means it works well in shadow work when using a translucent base fabric, such as cotton organdie, cotton lawn, and so forth.

Indian Chikan work uses double back stitch (*bakhya*) as one of its core stitches. It is thought that this influenced the 18th century development of shadow work.

METHOD

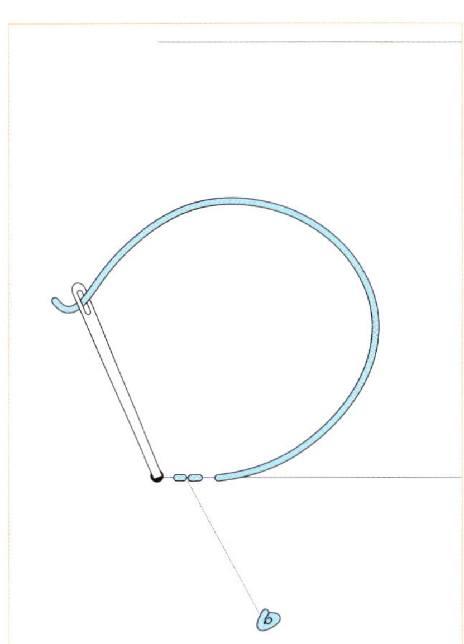

1 Start with a waste knot, a little away from the starting point. Make two tiny holding stitches (see page 31).

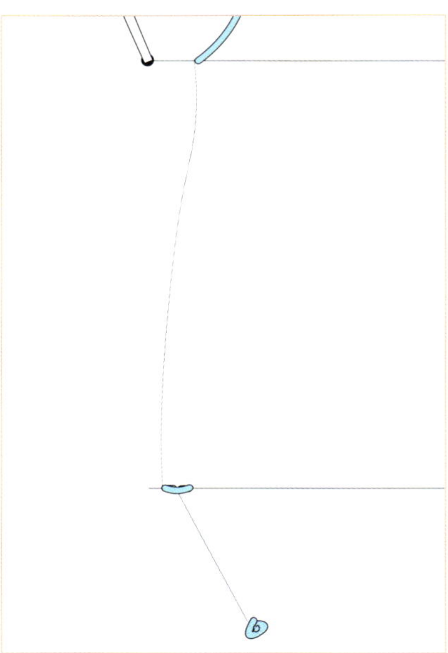

2 Work the first back stitch over the holding stitches so that they are covered. Bring your needle up on the far side of the design area (level with the first back stitch) and work the second back stitch.

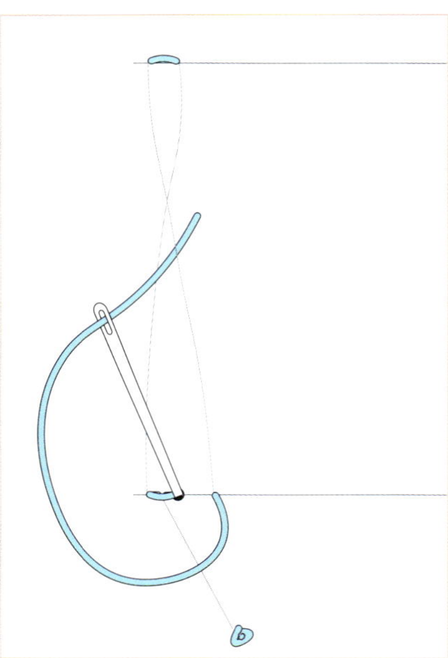

3 Bring your needle up on the opposite side and work the third back stitch.

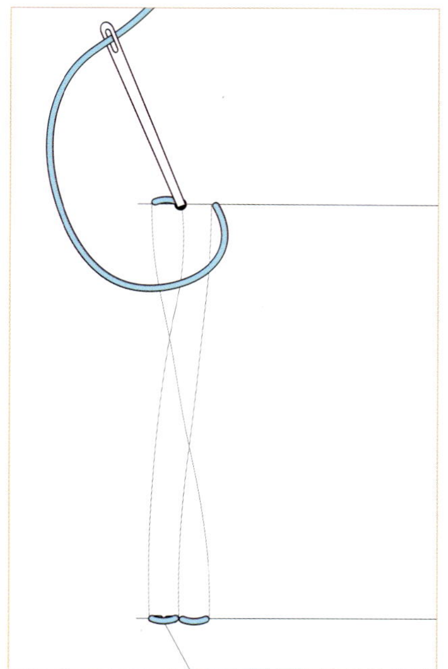

4 Bring your needle up on the opposite side and work another back stitch. The closed herringbone stitch is seen through the fabric as a shadow.

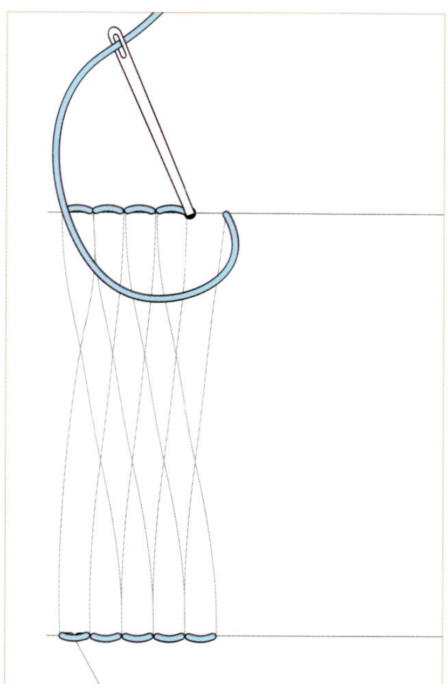

5 Continue working double back stitch. Ensure you take your needle down in the same fabric hole as the previous stich.

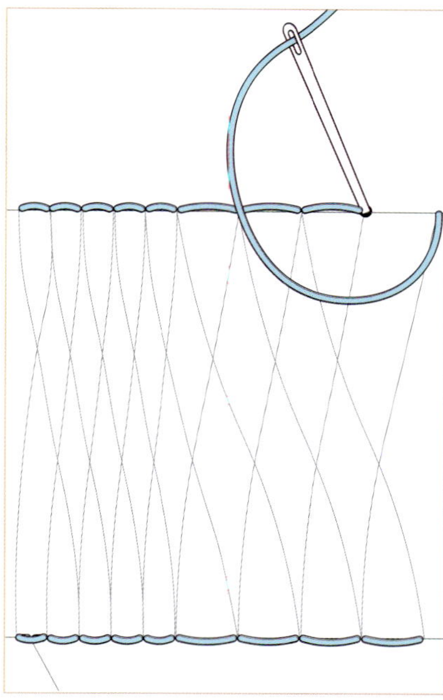

6 Continue along the design shape in the same manner. When your back stitch is small, the shadow of the closed herringbone is darker, and when it is big, the shadow is lighter.

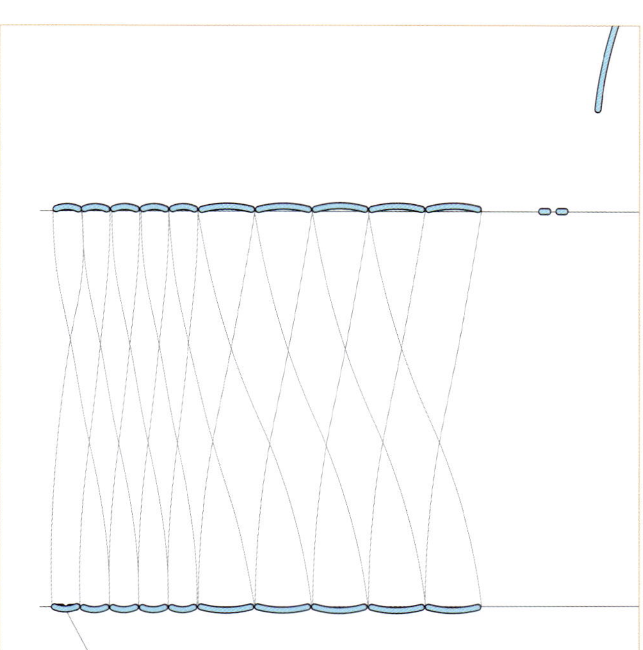

7 To finish your thread, work two tiny finishing stitches (see page 27), which will be covered with a back stitch with the new thread later on. Bring the thread up a little away and leave the tail, which will be cut away later.

DOUBLE BUTTONHOLE STITCH

SURFACE; COUNTED THREAD.

Also known as Double blanket stitch or Dovetail buttonhole.

This stitch consists of two facing rows of buttonhole stitch where the 'legs' of the stitch interlock.

Examples of the use of double buttonhole stitch exist in both historic and contemporary embroidery: the V&A South Kensington holds an early 18th-century whitework *fichu* (neckerchief) which features the stitch; embroidery worked by the nomadic Rabari peoples of north-western India have traditionally used double buttonhole stitch; and Wallachian embroidery, popular towards the end of the 19th century in the USA, features double buttonhole stitch (sometimes known as dovetail buttonholing) as one of its core stitches.

For more background see buttonhole stitch on pages 20–21.

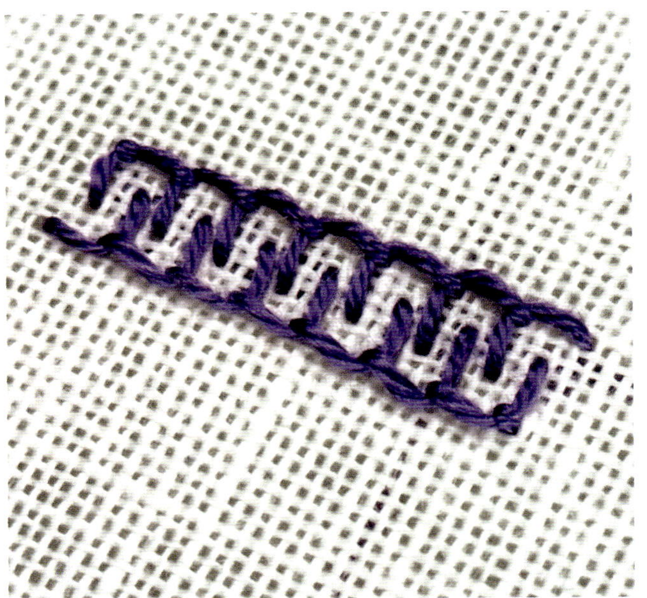

METHOD

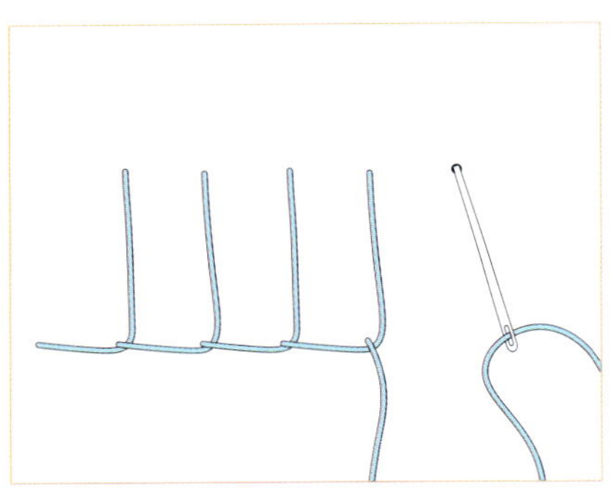

1 Work a row of blanket stitches from left to right.

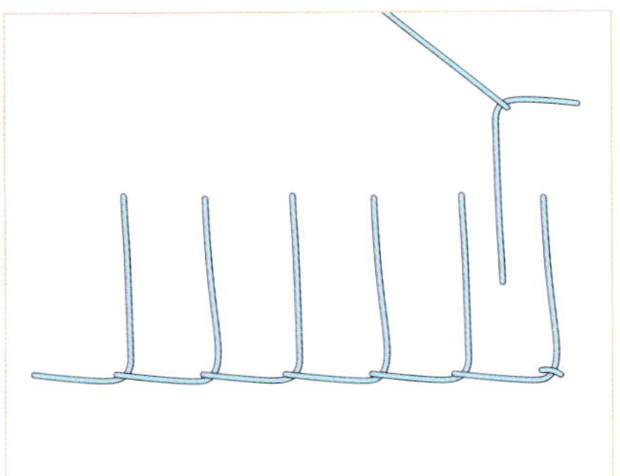

2 Work a second row of blanket stitches from right to left. Make sure that the vertical stitches fit into the spaces between the blanket stitches in the first row.

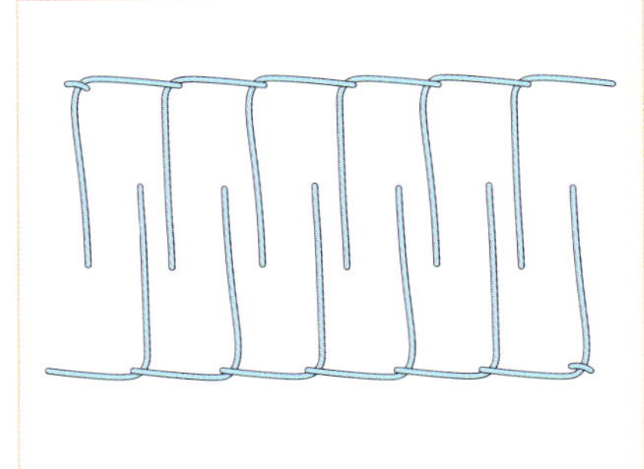

3 Continue as required.

DOUBLE FEATHER STITCH

SURFACE; RIBBON WORK; MOUNTMELLICK.

Also known as Double coral stitch, Point d'epine, Point anglaise, or Briar stitch.

Double feather stitch is a wider, slightly more elaborate stitch than feather stitch: it has three fly stitches in a row before it changes direction, rather than two. If four fly stitches are stitched before the change of direction, the stitch is sometimes known as triple feather stitch.

The descriptive alternative name of briar stitch (a thorny plant) is also used to refer to feather stitch although it seems more apt for the more numerous thorns in this version.

Examples of the use of double feather stitch exist from the 19th century: the V&A South Kensington has a sampler from 1887 which clearly shows a line of double feather stitch. It also features on a crazy quilt from the previous year held by the Art Institute of Chicago where is it used to join quilting blocks. For more information, see feather stitch on pages 72–73.

METHOD

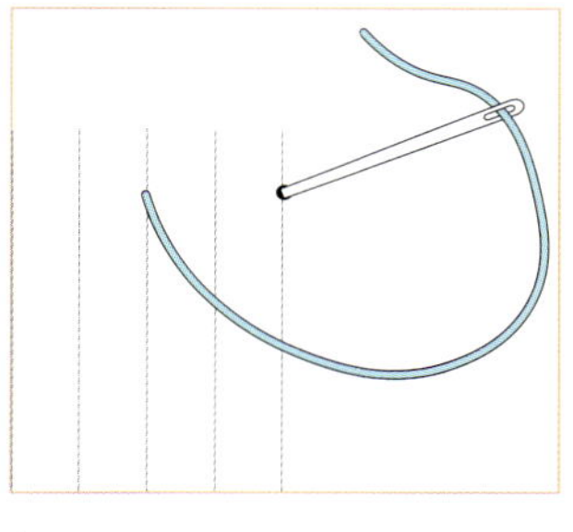

1 Work from top to bottom. Bring the needle up on the middle line, and take the needle down on the far right line.

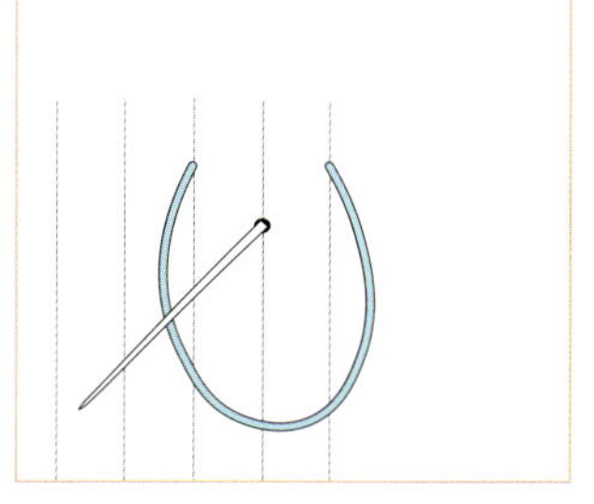

2 Bring the needle up again on the second line from the left, inside the loop.

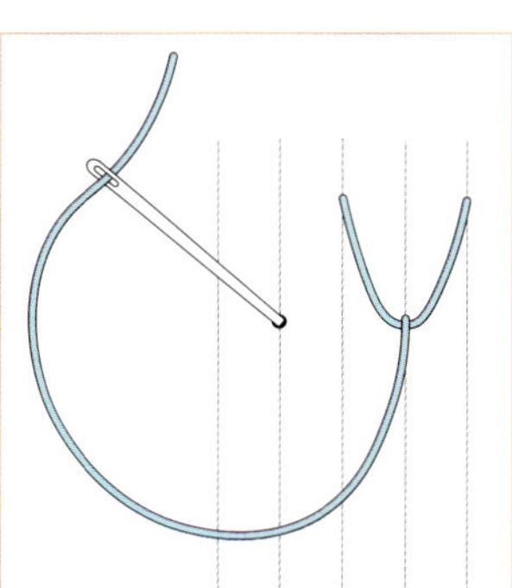

3 Pull the thread gently to make a feather stitch, and then take the needle down on the second line from the left.

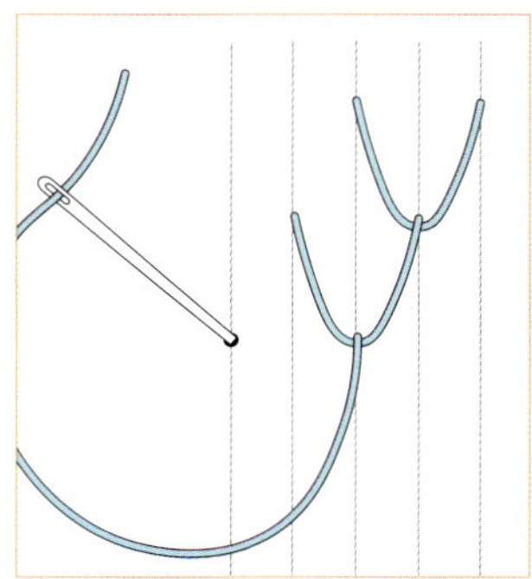

4 Come up on the middle line to make the second stitch, and then take the needle down on the far left line.

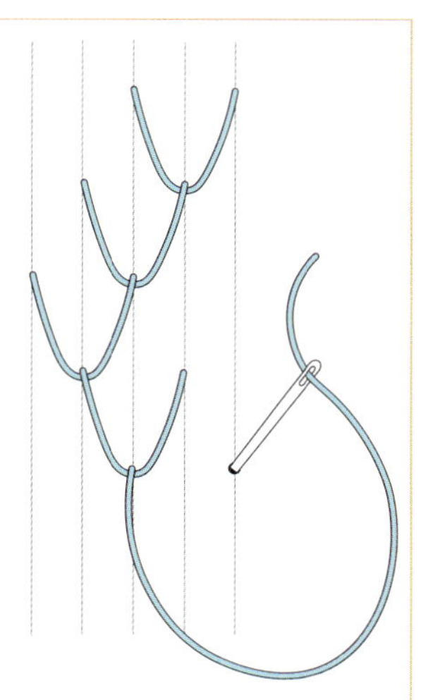

5 After making the third stitch to the left side, continue making two more feather stitches to the right.

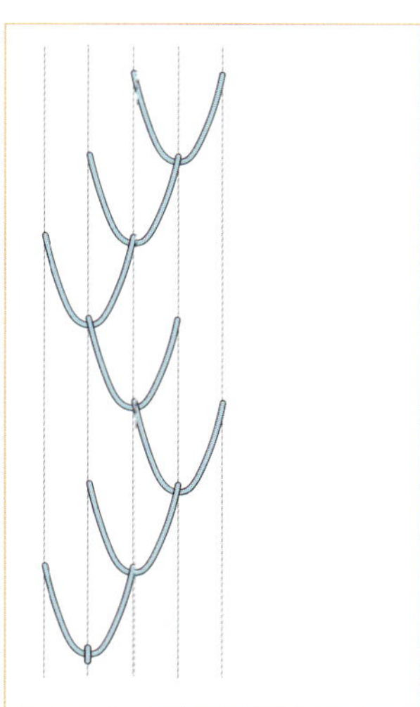

6 Work downwards, making two stitches to the left and two stitches to the right. Make a small straight stitch to secure the last stitch.

DOUBLE HERRINGBONE STITCH

CREWELWORK; SURFACE.

Also known as Indian herringbone stitch, or Double Algerian cross stitch.

Double herringbone consists of two interlocking rows of herringbone stitch.

This stitch can be used as a decorative border.

For more background, see herringbone stitch on page 30.

METHOD

1 Complete a fairly open herringbone stitch (see page 30), leaving enough space to work another herringbone between each stitch.

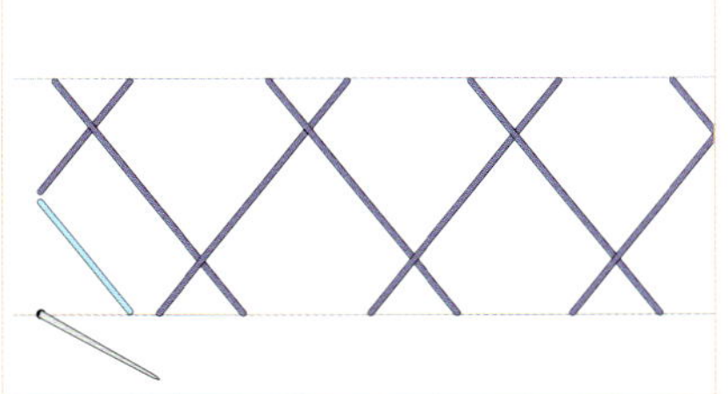

2 Using another colour in the needle, start by bringing the needle up as if working a reflection of the original.

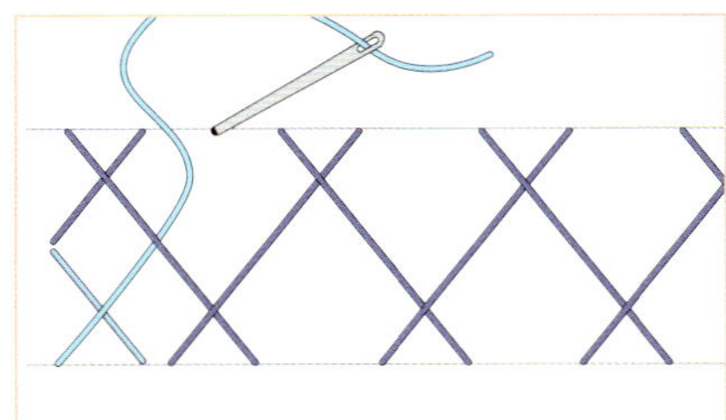

3 Ensure to take the needle under the original diagonal stitches that run top left to bottom right ...

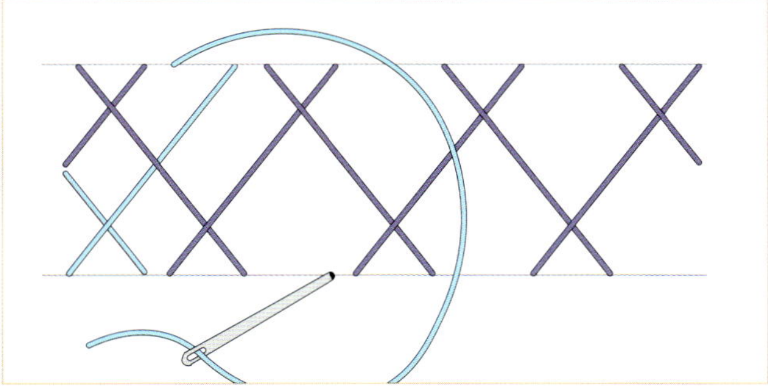

4 ... and over the original stitches that run bottom left to top right.

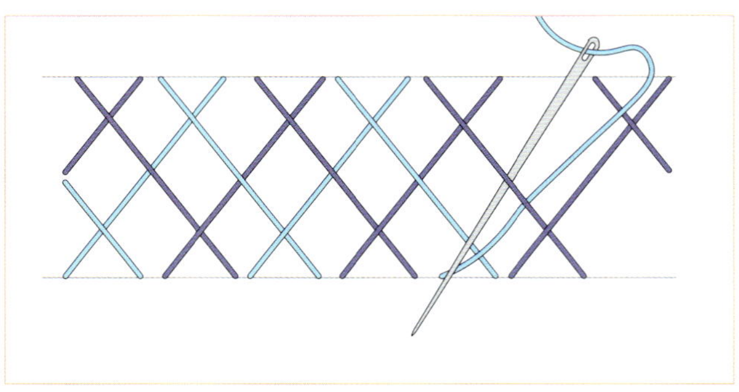

5 Complete to the end of the row.

DOUBLE RUNNING STITCH

Blackwork; Wessex stitchery; Whitework; Surface; Stumpwork.

Also known as Holbein stitch, Line stitch, Spanish stitch, Chiara stitch, Two-sided line stitch, Stroke stitch, or Punto scritto.

Usually worked on an evenweave fabric to ensure equal length stitches, a row of running stitches is worked, then another row of running stitches is worked in between the first row, sharing the same holes in the fabric to create a continuous line.

Double running stitch has been used for centuries: it was found on a medieval fragment which was excavated in Egypt. Ottoman embroideries from the 17th and 18th centuries use rows of double running stitch as a filling stitch. It is also used in Morocco (both Fes style and Meknes) and Syria where it is used on garments in Qalamoun style embroidery.

METHOD

1 Bring your needle up on the design line and, having decided on the length of your stitch, down again. Leave a gap of the same length and bring your needle up.

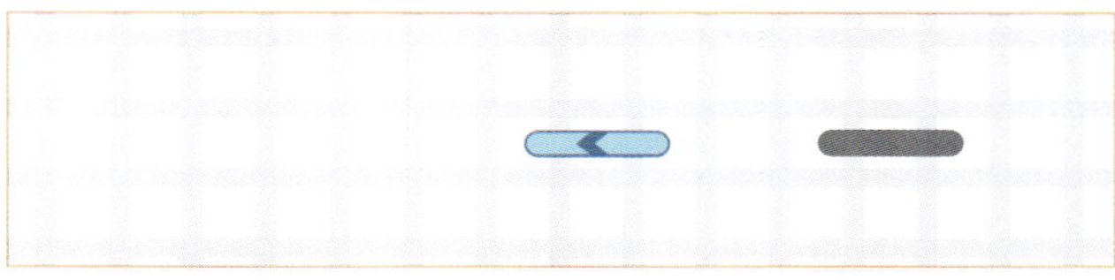

2 Continue along your line producing equal length stitches.

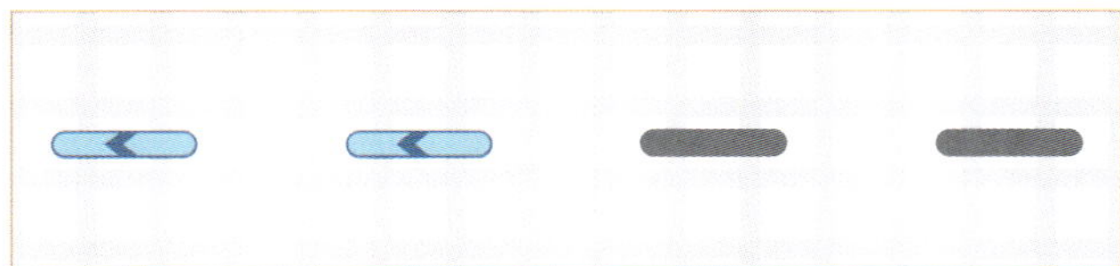

3 Keep the spaces between your stitches the same length as the stitches.

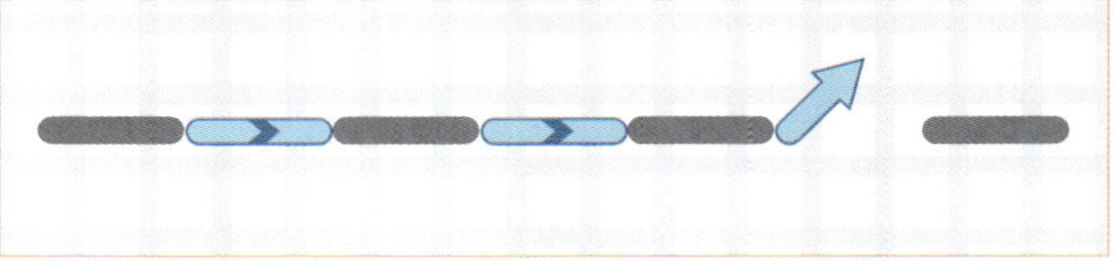

4 Work back along the line filling in the gaps with stitches.

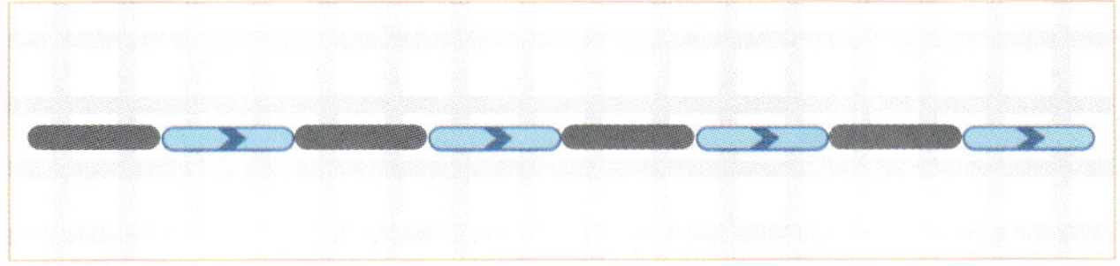

5 Both lines of running stitch should be equal in length to one another to create an even line on both sides of the fabric.

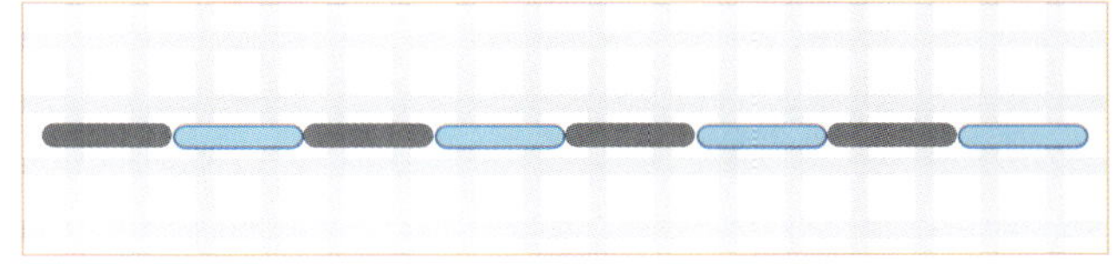

Completed double running stitch.

FEATHER STITCH

Crewelwork; Mountmellick; Ribbonwork; Surface; Stumpwork.

Also known as Single coral stitch, Point anglaise stitch, Point d'epine stitch, Double feather stitch, Briar stitch, or Brier stitch.

This is a series of fly stitches (see page 28) worked under one another and alternately offset to the left and right. The descriptive alternative name of briar stitch (a thorny plant) is also used to refer to double feather stitch. Similarly, the French name *point d'épine* translates as thorn or spine stitch.

Feather stitch has been notably used on English smocks (garments worn by countrymen from the late 18th to mid-19th century). The stitch played both a decorative and practical function as it gathered the cloth to give shape to the clothing. Historically, the terms 'feather stitch' or Opus Plumarium have also been used for long and short stitch (see pages 224–225).

METHOD

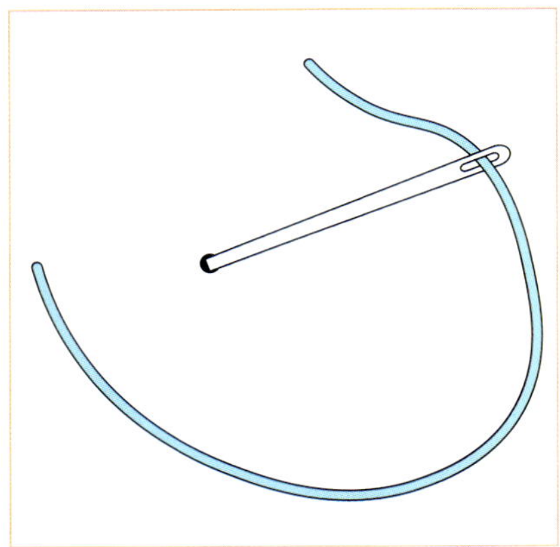

1 Bring the needle up through the fabric, then take it down to the right.

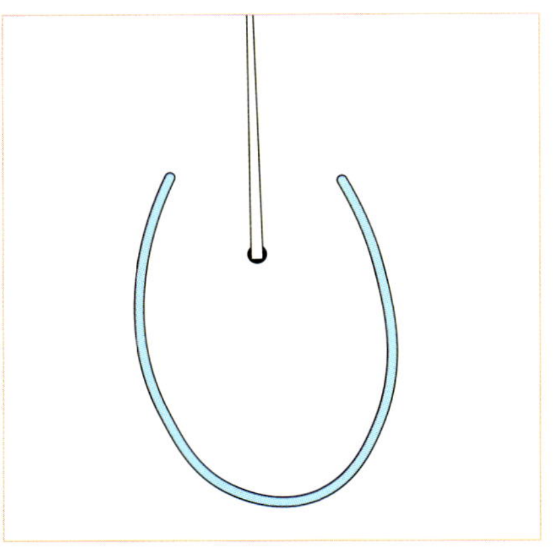

2 Pull the thread through, leaving a loop. Bring the needle up inside the loop, below and between the holes, as shown.

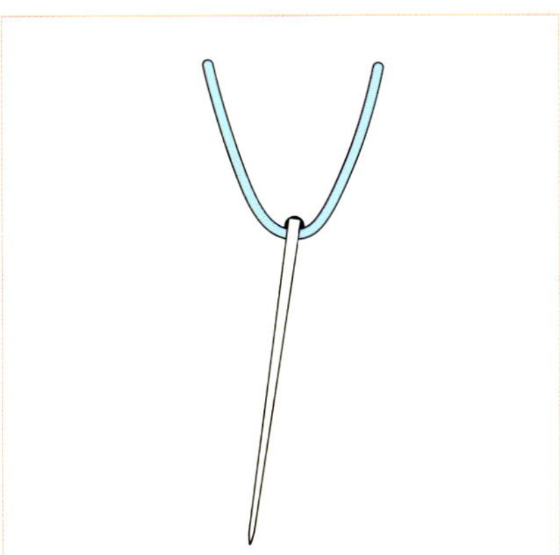

3 Tighten the loop against the needle.

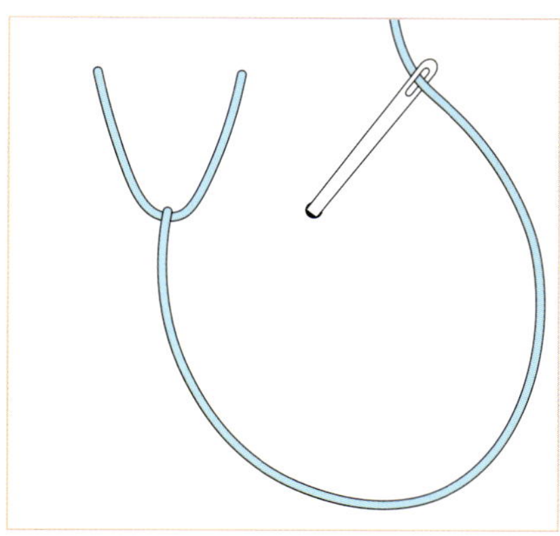

4 Pull the thread through and take the needle down to the right, as shown.

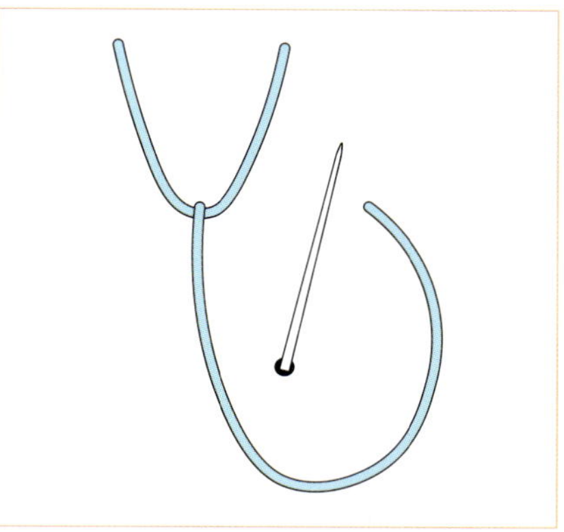

5 Draw the thread through to create a second loop, then bring the needle up below and between the holes.

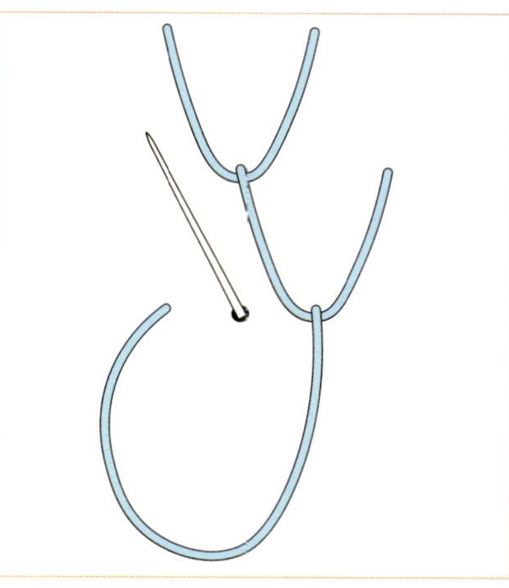

6 Tighten the loop against the needle, then draw the thread through. Repeat the next fly offset to the opposite side.

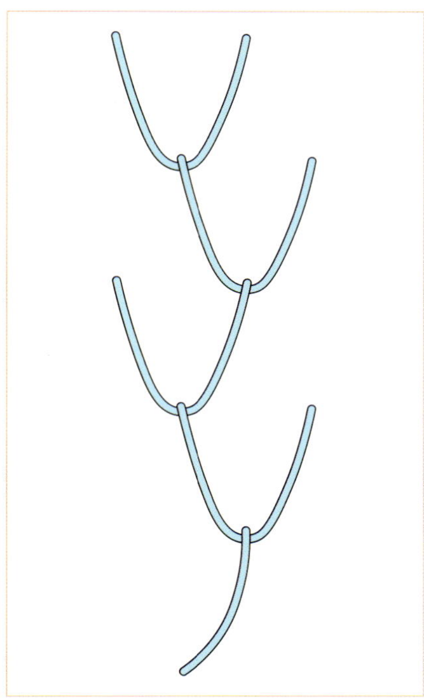

7 Continue, creating stitches to the left and right alternately.

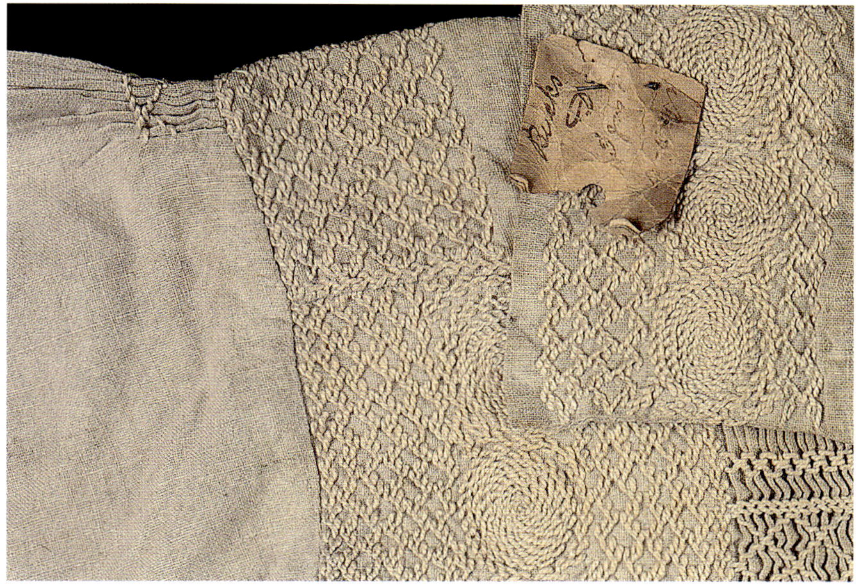

▲▲ Detail from child's buck smock, RSN Collection COL.2023.7

Child's smocked dress in unbleached linen, possibly hand woven. It features extensive smocking and stitching across the chest, back, collar, and cuffs, worked in tan-coloured cotton threads. On the front (shown here) and back are a series of swirling patterns, perhaps reminiscent of hay bales.

The smocking and stitching is worked in back, cable and feather stitches. The smocking on the front and back is nearly identical, as is that on the two cuffs.

FEATHERED CHAIN STITCH

SURFACE.

Also known as Chained feather stitch.

Feathered chain stitch is a wide border stitch comprised of chain stitches linked by diagonal stitches worked in a zigzagging line.

For more background see the entry for chain stitch (see page 22).

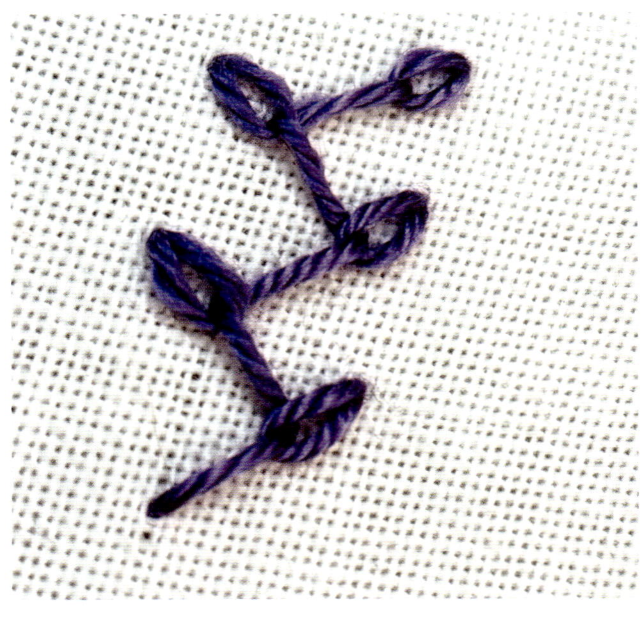

METHOD

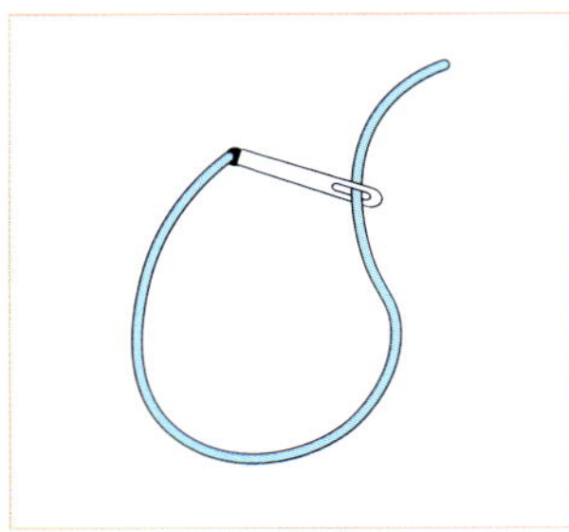

1 Bring the needle up and down in the same hole, leaving a loop of thread.

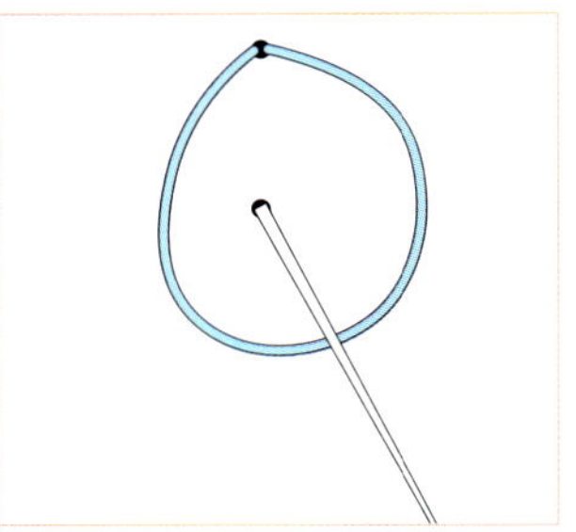

2 Bring the needle up a short distance diagonally down to the left and through the loop.

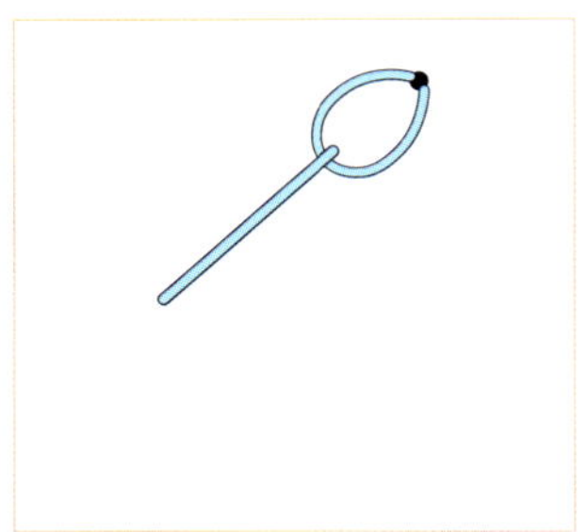

3 Pull the loop tight and take a longer holding stitch continuing the diagonal direction.

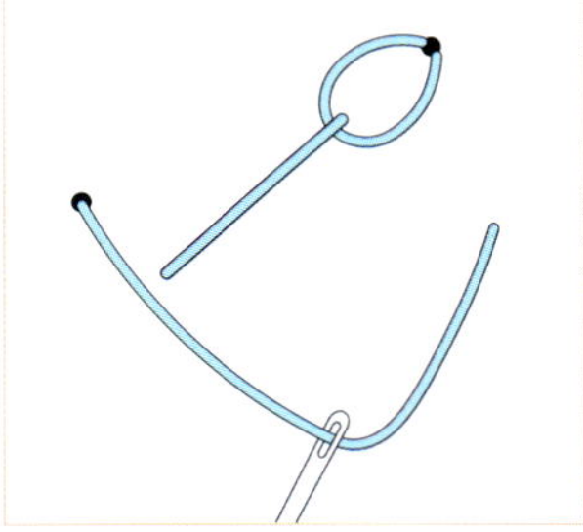

4 Bring the needle up a short distance above and diagonally to the left.

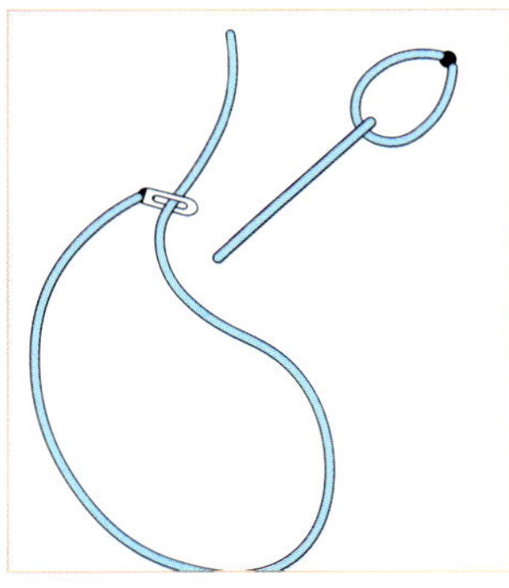

5 Take the needle back down into the same hole again leaving a loop.

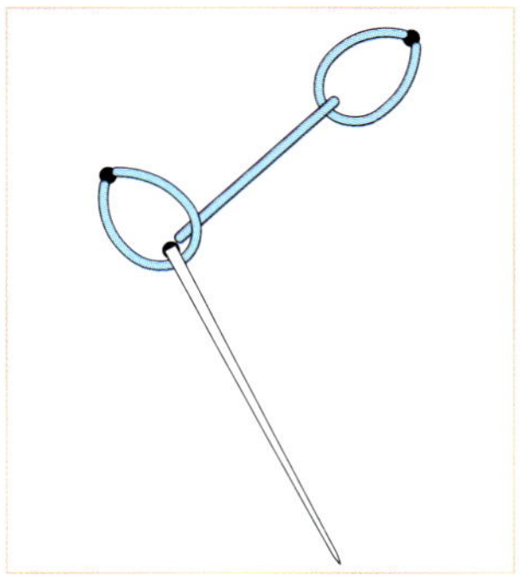

6 Bring the needle up at the end of the long holding stitch and through the loop.

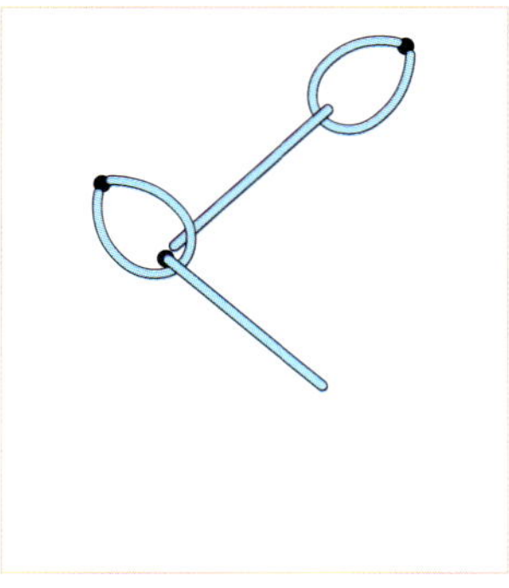

7 Pull the loop taut and take a long holding stitch diagonally down to the right.

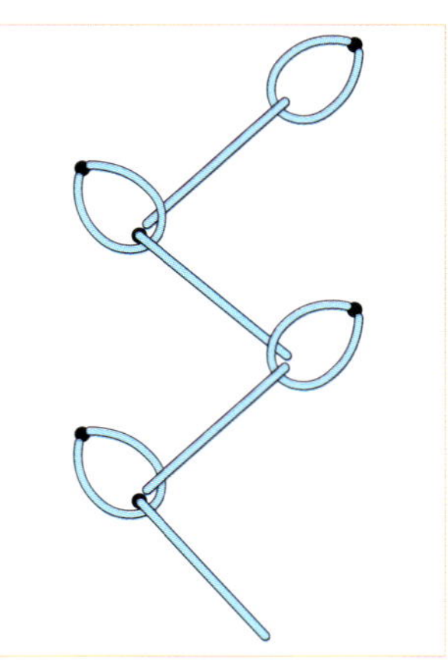

8 Repeat these stitches alternating from right to left.

FERN STITCH

SURFACE; CREWELWORK.

Fern stitch consists of three stitches fanned out from a central point. It can be worked as an isolated stitch or as a line stitch.

It makes a pretty branched line and is often used for decorating leaves and floral shapes.

Fern stitch was used in China from the time of the Ming dynasty as it features as an isolated stitch on Mandarin squares from this time. The V&A South Kensington holds several 18th-century English embroideries which feature the stitch.

METHOD

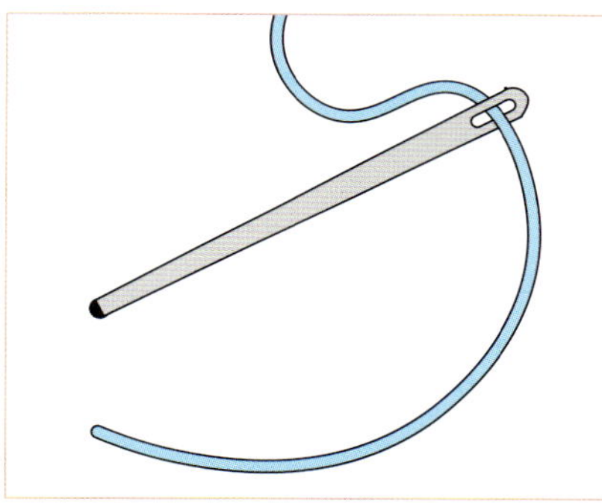

1 Start by making a straight central stitch at the top of the fern.

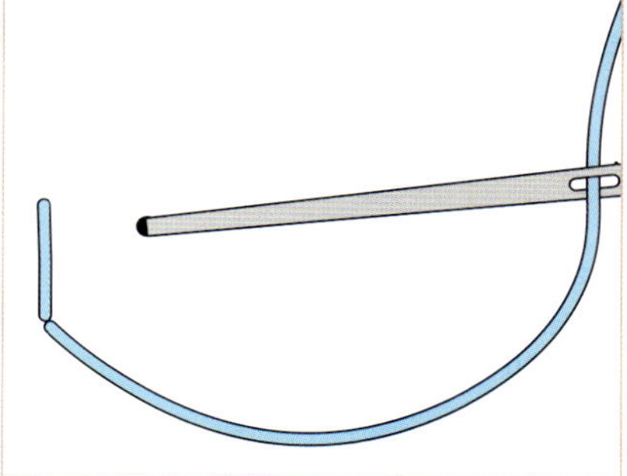

2 Add a two further stitches of equal length worked at angles to one another. All three of these stitches should share the same base hole.

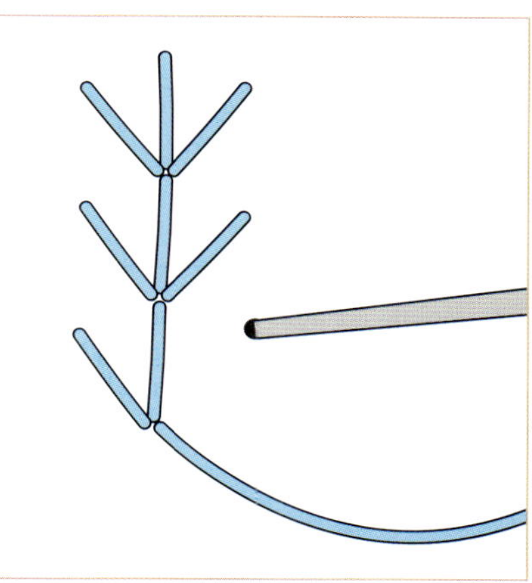

3 Work further groups of stitches downward to form a branched line, as shown.

HEAVY CHAIN STITCH

Crewelwork; Surface.

Also known as Braid stitch.

Heavy chain stitch produces a smooth, bold outline, rather like a braid, and is ideal for heavier outlines. Each chain is produced by threading the needle under the previous loops and worked in the opposite direction from normal chain stitch (see page 22).

Heavy chain stitch evidently dates from at least the 19th century, as it features on a cushion cover from that date currently held by the V&A South Kensington. The cushion is from Kalotaszeg, Romania, and is stitched in wool on a linen fabric.

For more background see the entry for chain stitch.

METHOD

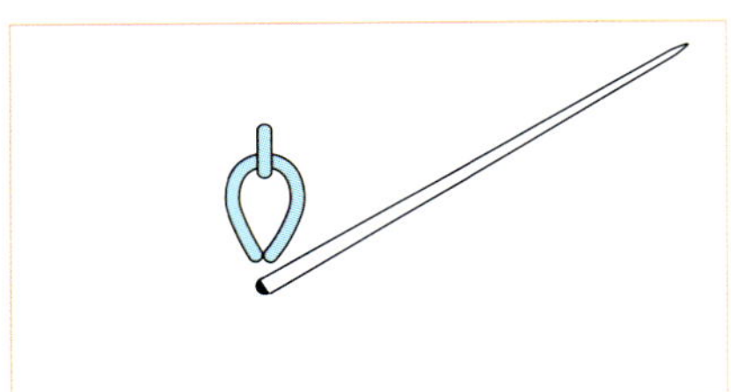

1 Complete a single detached chain stitch (see page 240) then bring the needle back up to the surface just below the point.

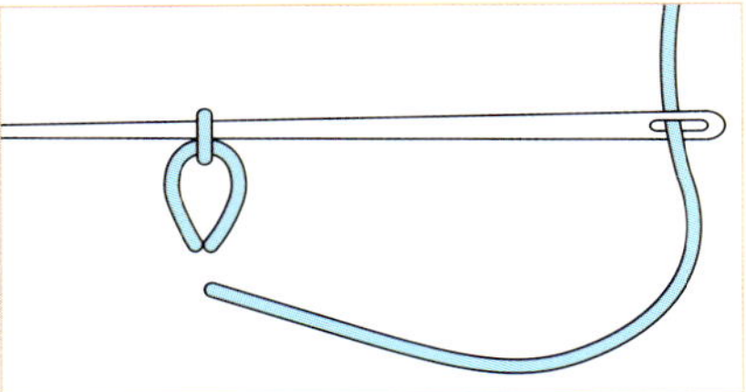

2 Take the needle through the holding stitch of the detached chain stitch.

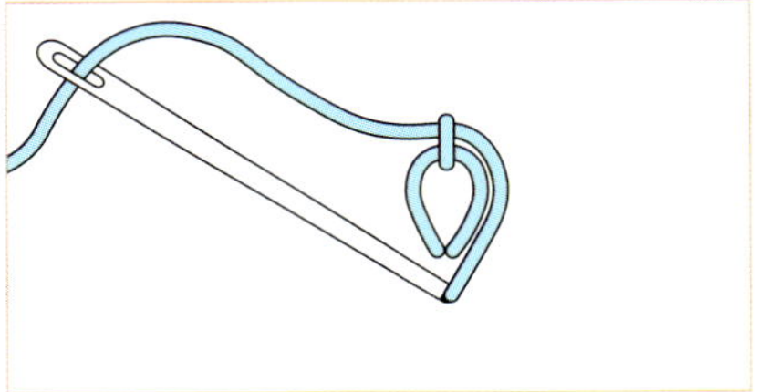

3 Take the needle back down through the same hole and draw the thread through.

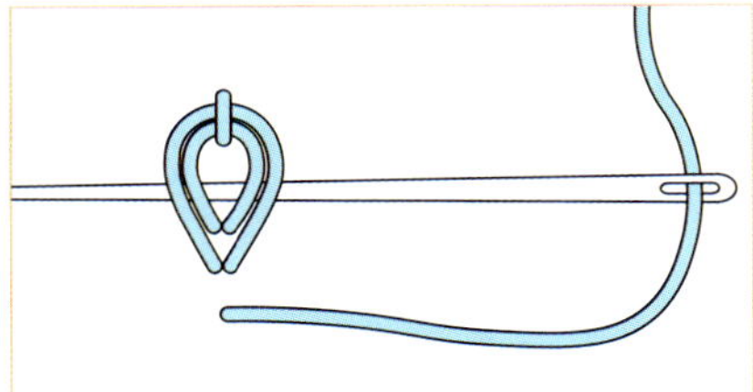

4 Bring the needle back up to the surface just below the point, then pass it under the first chain (two chains back).

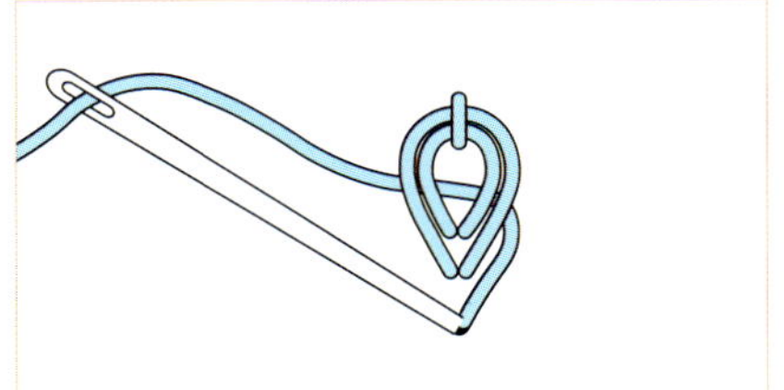

5 Take the needle back down the same hole and draw the thread through.

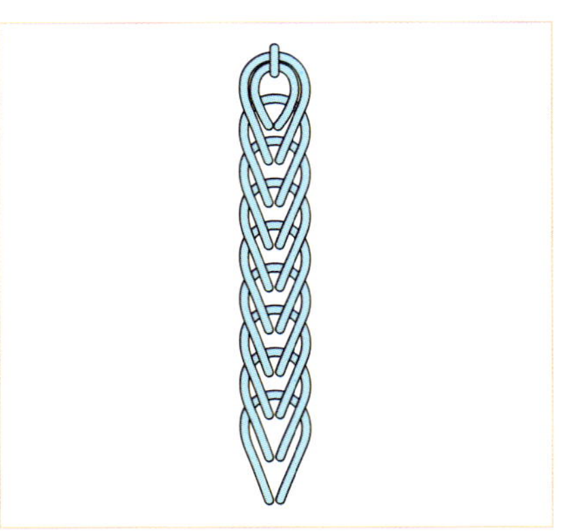

6 Continue along the design and finish in the usual way.

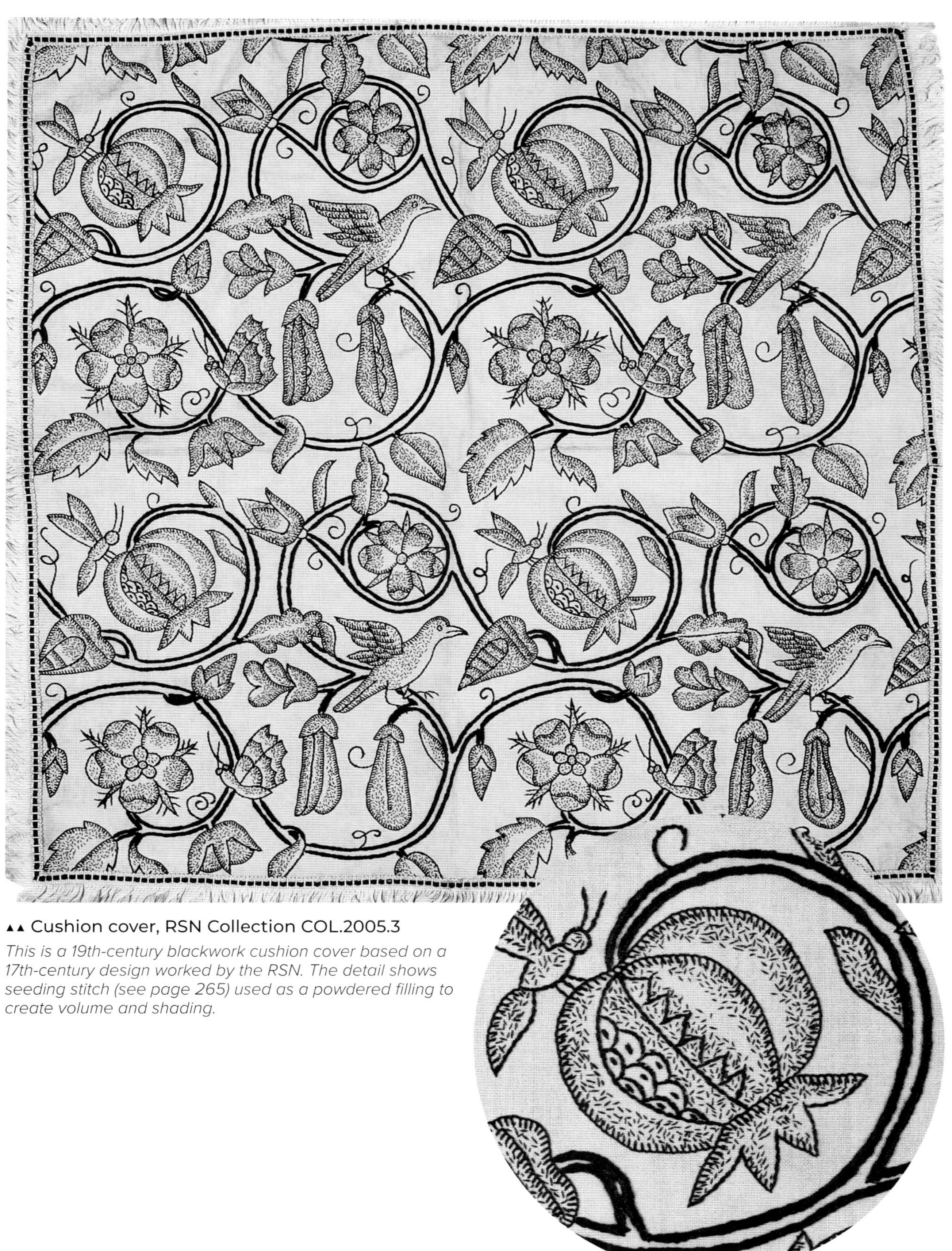

▲▲ Cushion cover, RSN Collection COL.2005.3

This is a 19th-century blackwork cushion cover based on a 17th-century design worked by the RSN. The detail shows seeding stitch (see page 265) used as a powdered filling to create volume and shading.

HERRINGBONE LADDER FILLING STITCH

Surface.

Also known as Interlaced band stitch, Double Pekinese stitch, or Laced Cretan stitch.

This stitch consists of two parallel double running stitch rows, which form the side rails of the ladder, and herringbone stitch, interlaced to form the rungs of the ladder. The herringbone stitch doesn't pierce the fabric.

The method of working back stitch in rows, which are then embellished with loops, has similarities with Pekinese stitch (see pages 100–101), hence the alternative name of double Pekinese stitch. Structurally this stitch is similar to both herringbone and Cretan stitches (see pages 30, 150 and 151 respectively). For more background, see the entry for herringbone stitch.

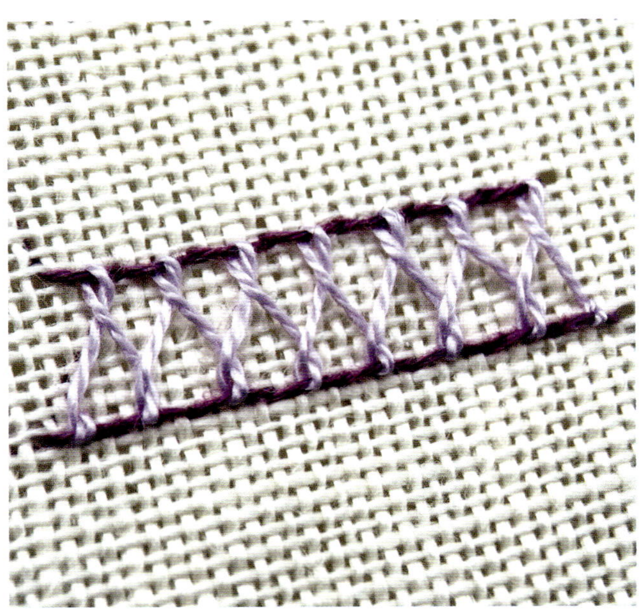

METHOD

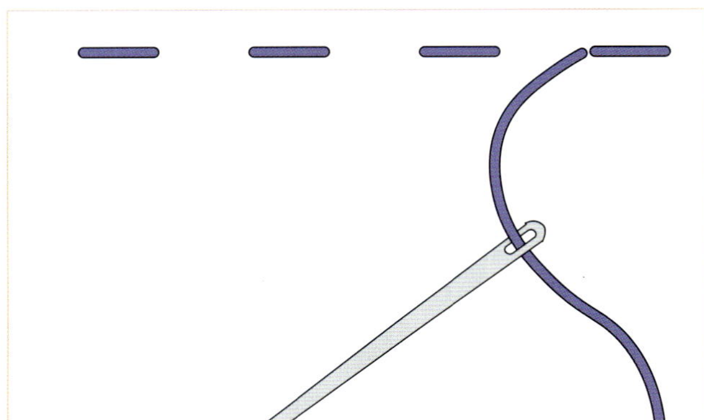

1 Work a line of double running stitch (see page 71), following the grain of the fabric.

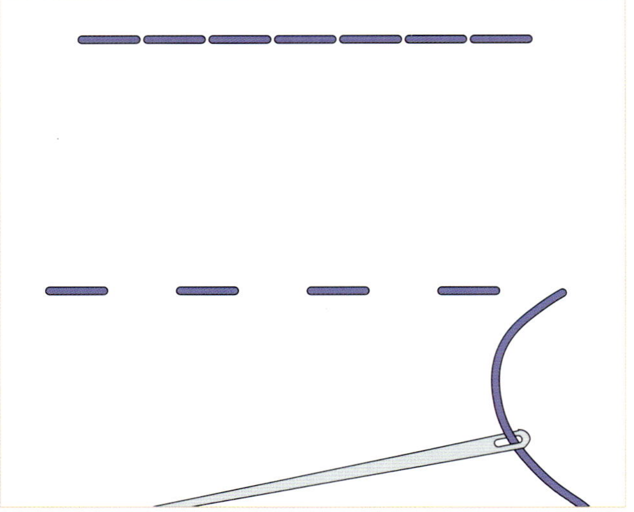

2 Work a parallel row of double running stitch below, ensuring that the two rows of stitches are offset or bricked against one another.

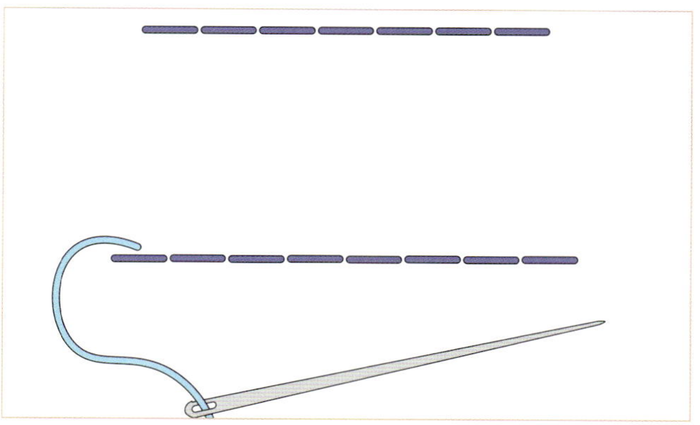

3 Bring the needle up above the first lower double running stitch on the left-hand side.

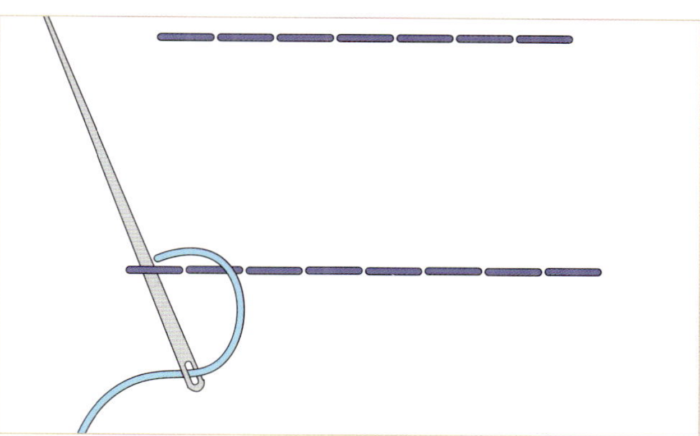

4 It may help to switch to a tapestry needle for the rest of the stitch. Without going through the fabric, take the needle underneath the first stitch from the bottom to the top. Keep the needle pointing to the left with the thread looping to the right.

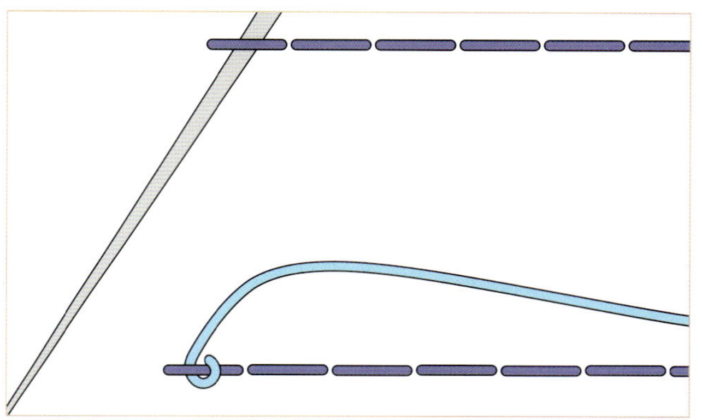

5 Take the needle under the first top double running stitch from top to bottom, bringing it out to the left with the thread looped to the right. Pull the thread tight, ensuring that the double running stitch is not distorted.

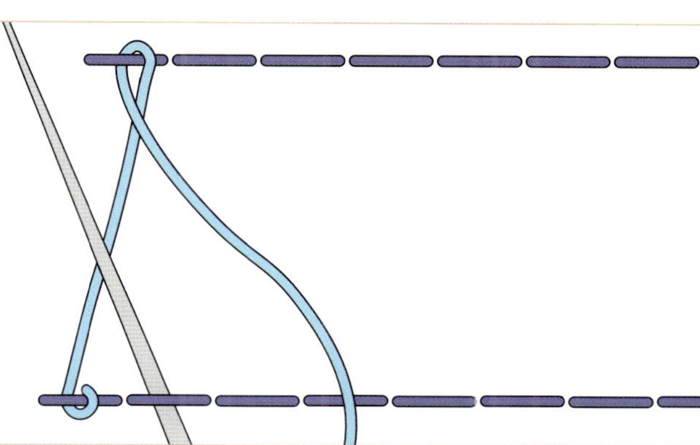

6 Take the needle underneath the second double running stitch on the lower edge. Bring the needle out to the left and keep the thread to the right.

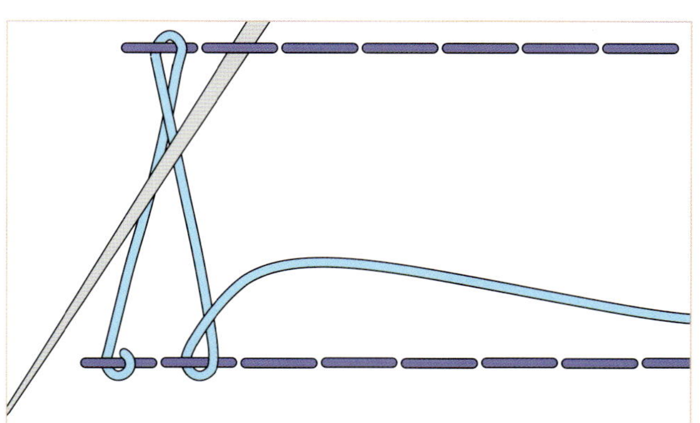

7 Again take the needle underneath the second double running stitch on the top edge. Bring the needle out to the left and keep the thread to the right creating a twist in the herringbone. Ensure each new stitch lays over the top of the previous stitch.

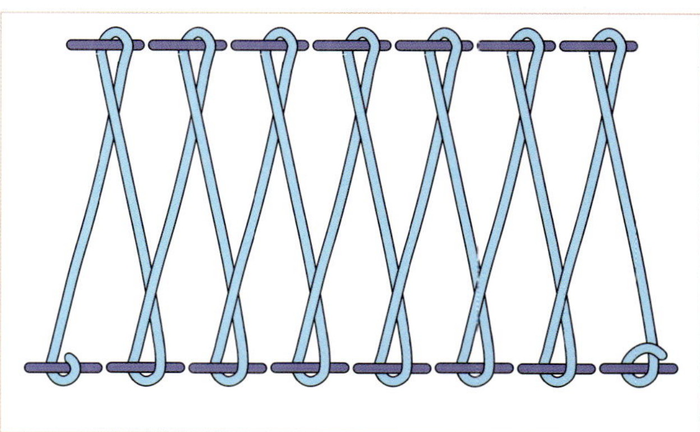

8 Continue alternating between the top and bottom double running stitches to create a continuously laced herringbone stitch.

INTERLACED HERRINGBONE BAND

SURFACE; COUNTED THREAD.

Also known as Double herringbone interlaced, Interlaced herringbone stitch, Interlacing stitch, or Armenian cross stitch.

Interlaced herringbone band is worked over a row of double herringbone stitch (see page 70). It is important to check the sequence of the crossed part of the double herringbone stitch is correct so that this intricate interlacing can be achieved. The two ends of the foundation double herringbone stitch can be made shorter, and the size of the band can be varied, depending on your design.

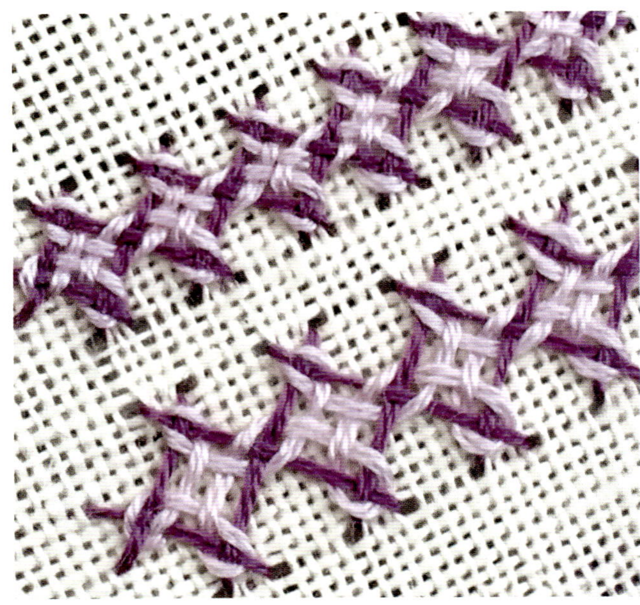

METHOD

1 Work a double herringbone stitch (see page 70) as a foundation. Work the first row of herringbone stitch, making sure to slip the needle under the previous stitch when going downwards.

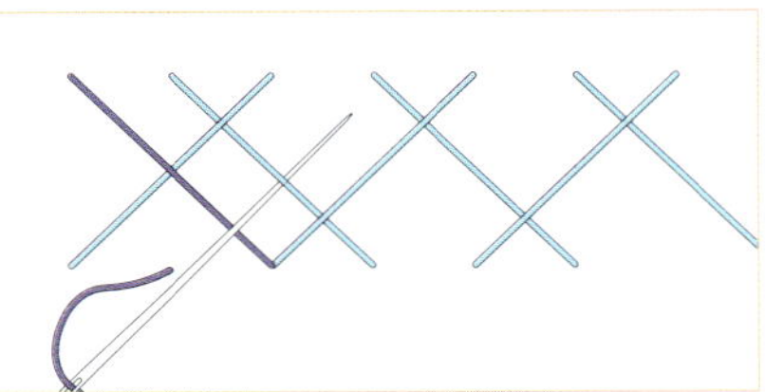

2 For the second row of herringbone stitch, when going upwards pass the needle over the previous stitch and under the first row of herringbone stitch.

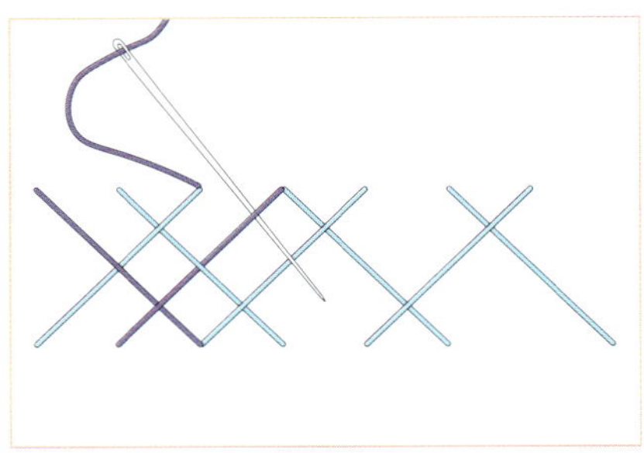

3 When going downwards, pass the needle under the previous stitch and over the first row of herringbone stitch.

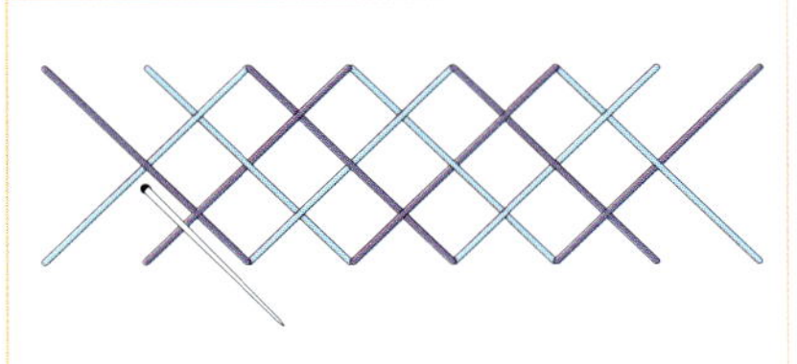

4 After the foundation of herringbone is complete, bring the needle up at the base of the first intersection. Work the interlacing across the top half of the double herringbone stitch from left to right.

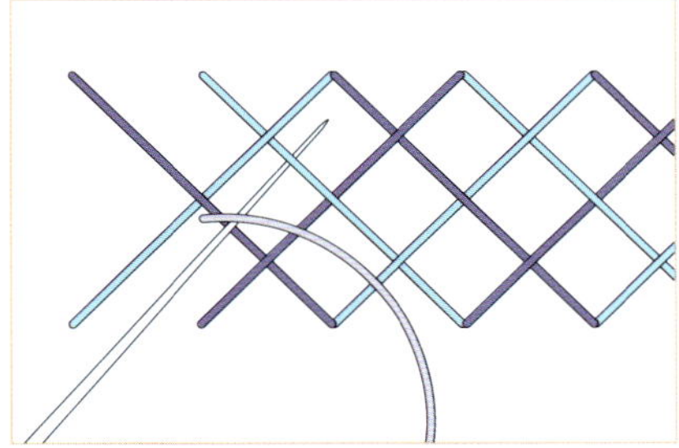

5 Going upwards, pass the needle over and under the foundation double herringbone stitch.

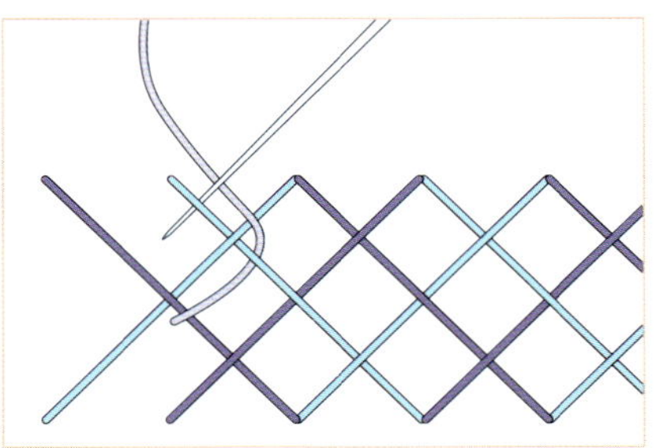

6 Encircle the upper crossed part of the foundation herringbone stitch by passing the needle over and under the crossed area.

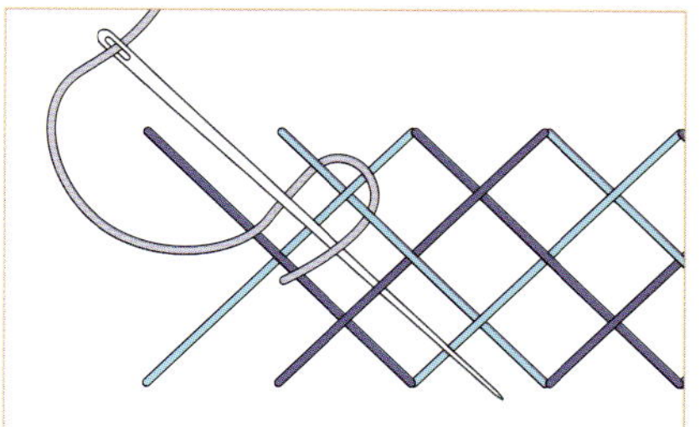

7 Going downwards, pass the needle over the herringbone stitch and under the working thread, and then under the herringbone stitch.

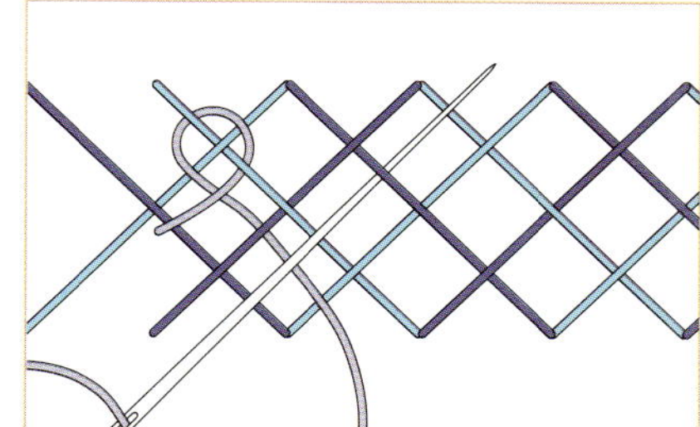

8 Going upwards, pass the needle over and under the herringbone stitch.

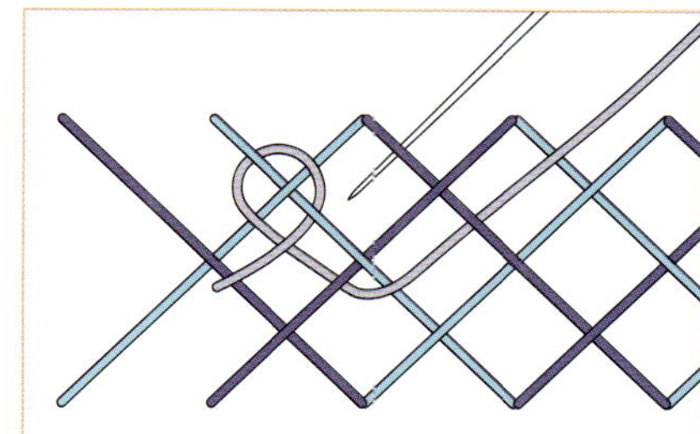

9 Go over and under the upper crossed part.

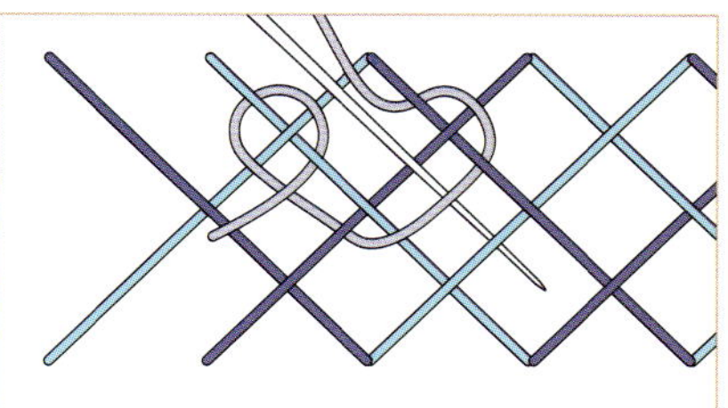

10 Going downwards, pass the needle over the herringbone stitch and under the working thread, and then under the herringbone stitch.

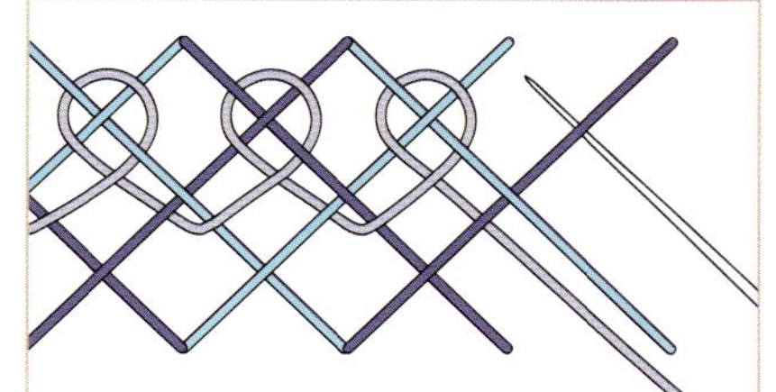

11 Repeat until the end of the foundation herringbone stitch. At the last intersection, pass the needle under, over and under the herringbone stitch.

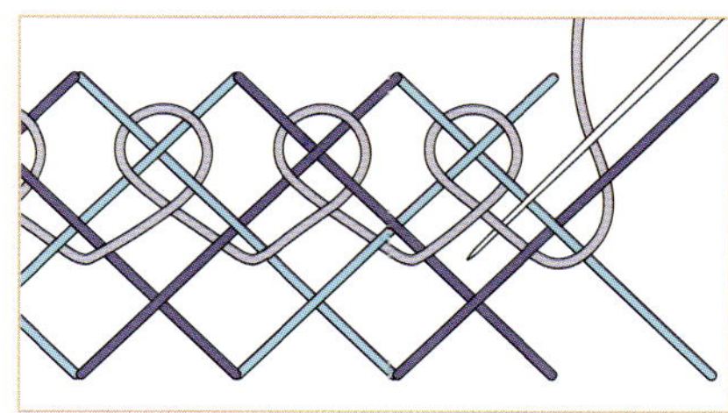

12 Continue working the interlacing across the bottom half of the herringbone stitch, this time from from right to left. Going down, go over the herringbone stitch, under the working thread, and then under the herringbone stitch.

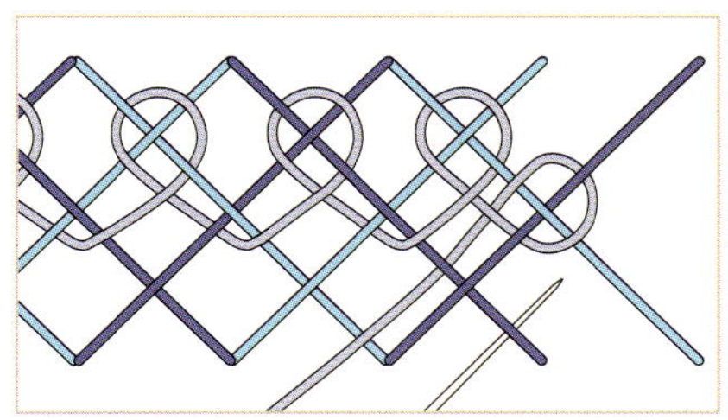

13 Encircle the lower crossed part by going over and under the herringbone stitch.

14 Going upwards, pass the needle over the herringbone stitch, under the working thread, then over the working thread and under the herringbone stitch.

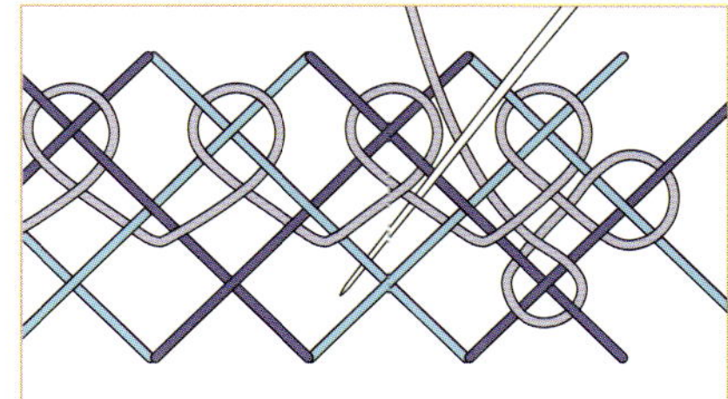

15 Going downwards, pass the needle over the herringbone stitch, under the working thread, and then under the herringbone stitch.

16 Continue until you come back to the beginning of the band. Encircle the intersection by passing the needle over and under the herringbone stitch. Take down the needle through the fabric at the starting point to complete the interlacing.

INTERLACED HERRINGBONE STITCH

SURFACE.

Also known as German interlacing stitch, Laced herringbone stitch, or Woven herringbone stitch.

This version of herringbone stitch (see page 30) is probably the most intricate: the second thread is woven twice around each upper herringbone intersection and one and a half circles around each lower herringbone intersection, always interlacing under and over the foundation stitches and the working thread itself, forming a decorative wreath.

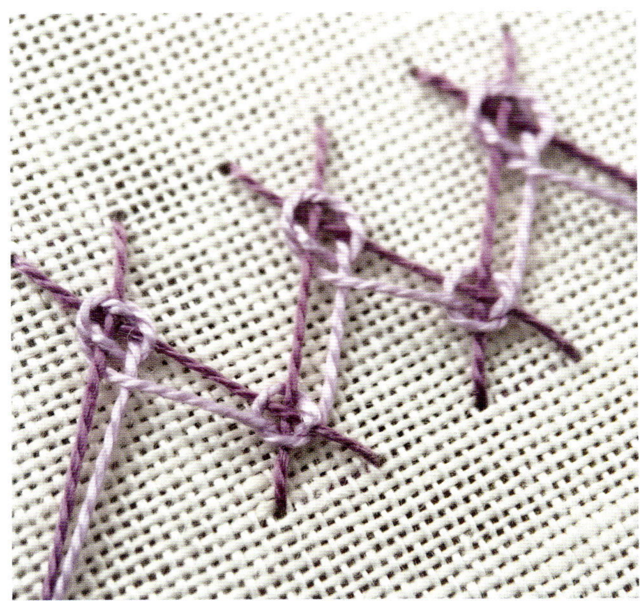

METHOD

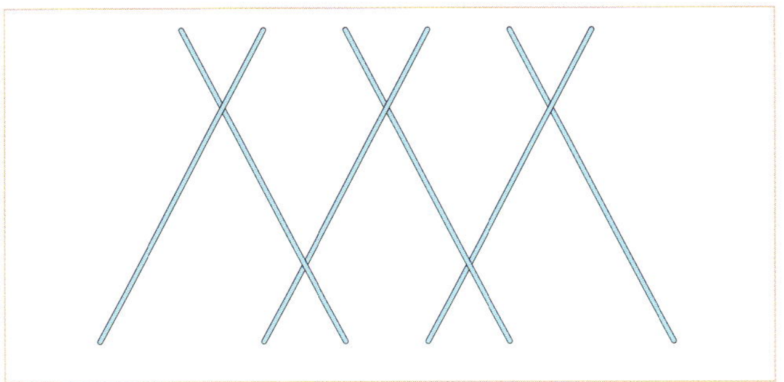

1 Work a foundation row of herringbone stitch from right to left. Alternatively, work from left to right, making sure you slide the needle under the previous stitch where the threads cross so that the working thread is beneath the previous part of the stitch. (This affects how the interlacing will sit.)

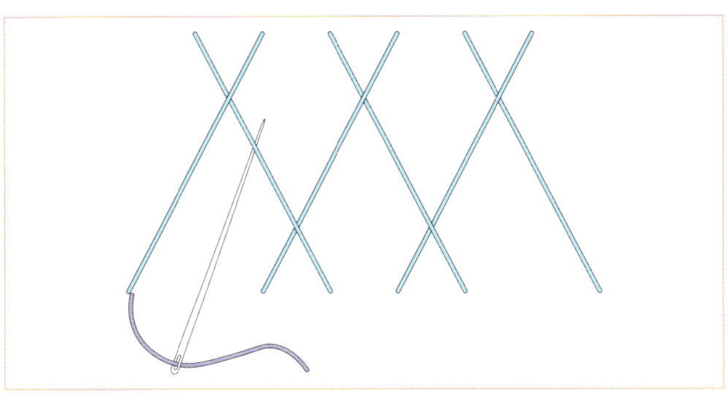

2 Bring up a new thread at the start of the first herringbone stitch.

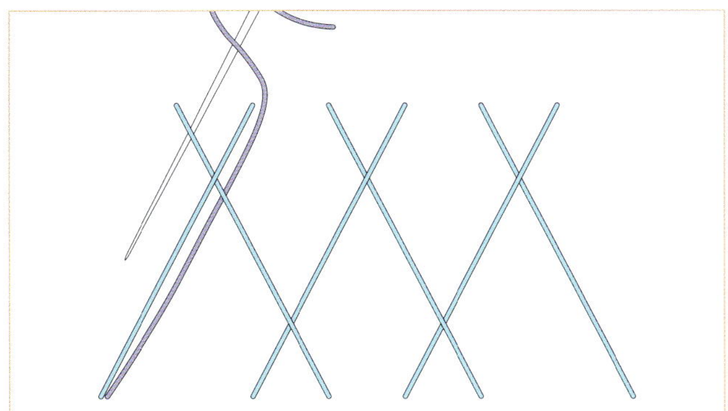

3 Encircle the upper crossed part of the foundation herringbone stitch by passing the needle under, over, and under the crossed area.

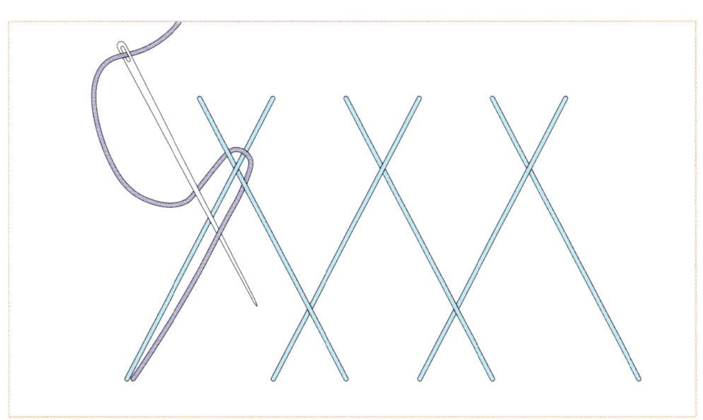

4 Go over the foundation herringbone stitch and under the working thread.

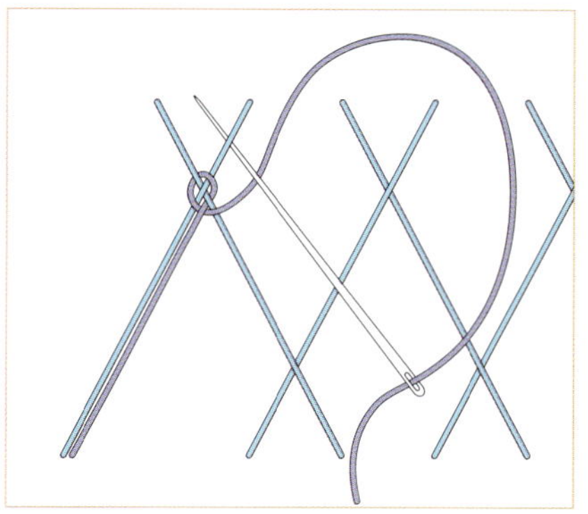

5 Again, encircle the upper crossed area by passing the needle over and under the foundation herringbone stitch.

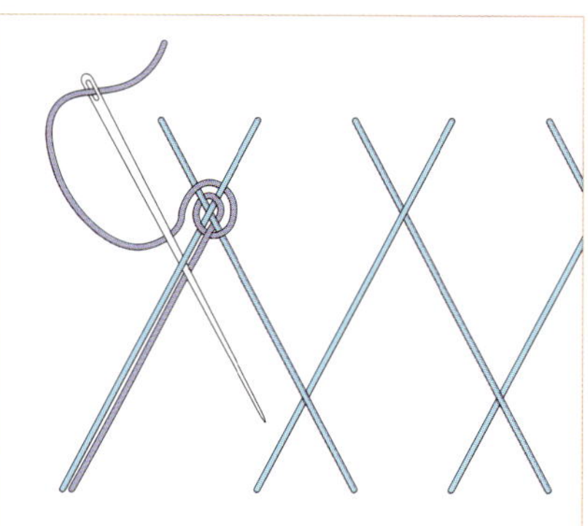

6 Go over and under the foundation stitch and over the working thread. This makes two complete circles round the upper intersection.

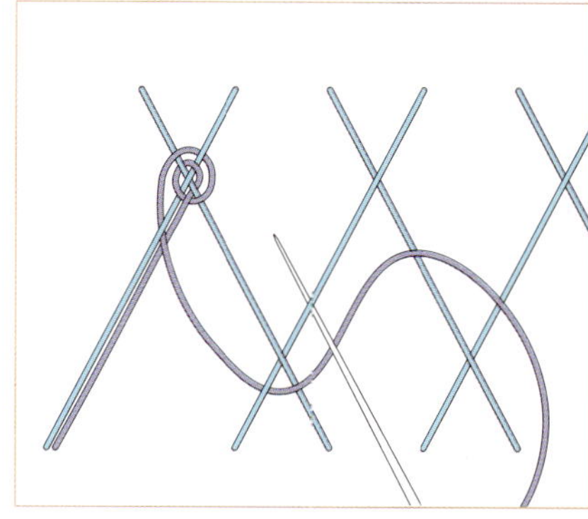

7 Go down to the lower intersection. Pass the needle under, over, and under the foundation stitch.

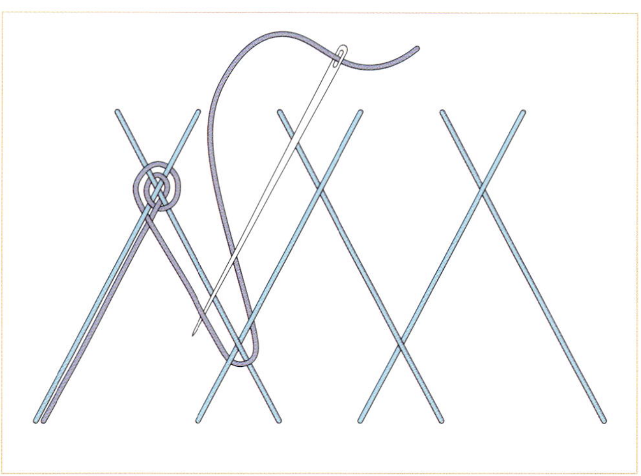

8 Go over the foundation stitch and under the working thread.

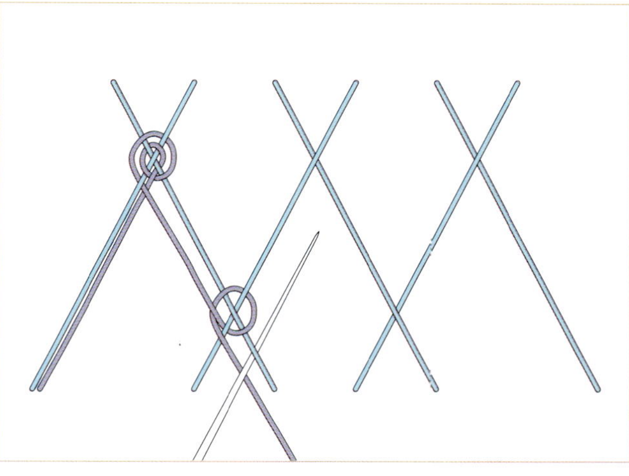

9 Pass the needle over and under the foundation stitch second time. This makes one and a half circles round the lower intersection.

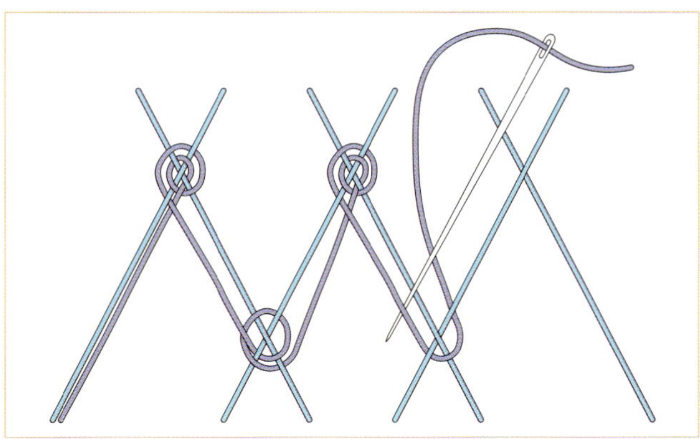

10 Continue interlacing under and over the foundation stitches and the working thread.

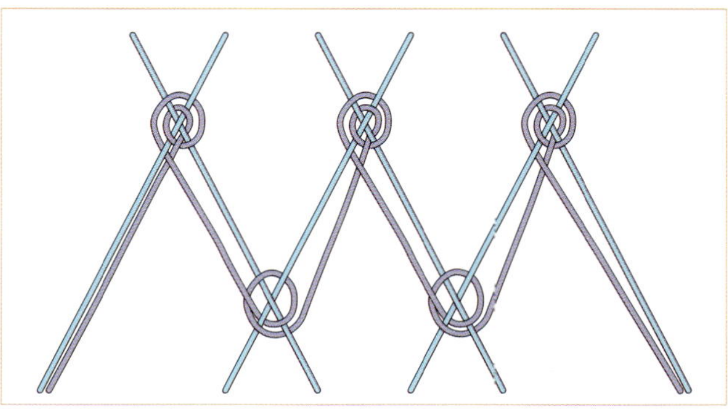

A sample of interlacing herringbone stitch.

KNOTTED BUTTONHOLE STITCH

SURFACE.

A variation of buttonhole stitch (see pages 20–21): this stitch is wider-spaced than a typical buttonhole stitch and has a knot at the end of each of the buttonhole's 'legs'.

It is often confused with knotted blanket stitch – an edging stitch with an additional knot in each buttonhole loop.

A border stitch, knotted buttonhole stitch is sometimes used to simulate fringing. It can also be used an edging stitch.

METHOD

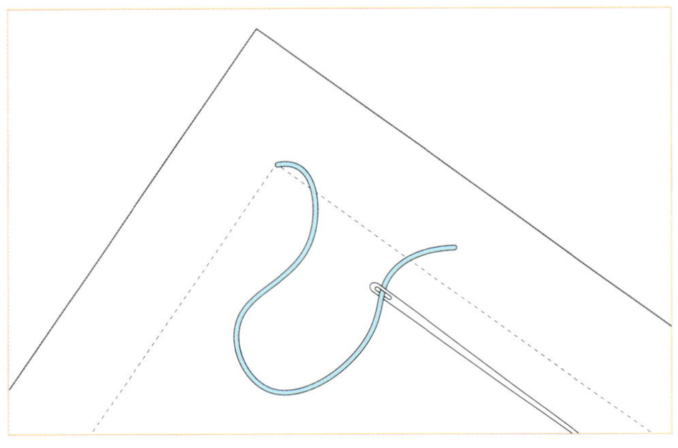

1 Starting from the left-hand side, bring the needle and thread to the surface.

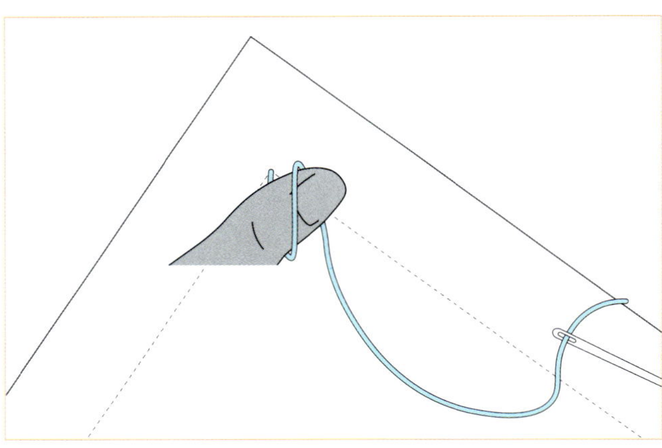

2 Wrap the thread around the left thumb.

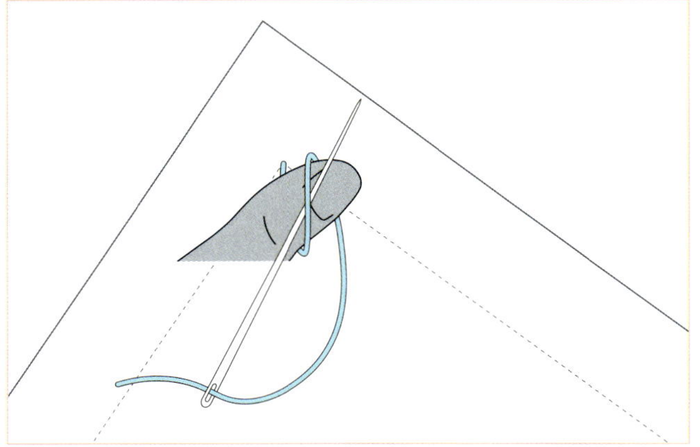

3 Take the needle under the thread towards the tip of the thumb.

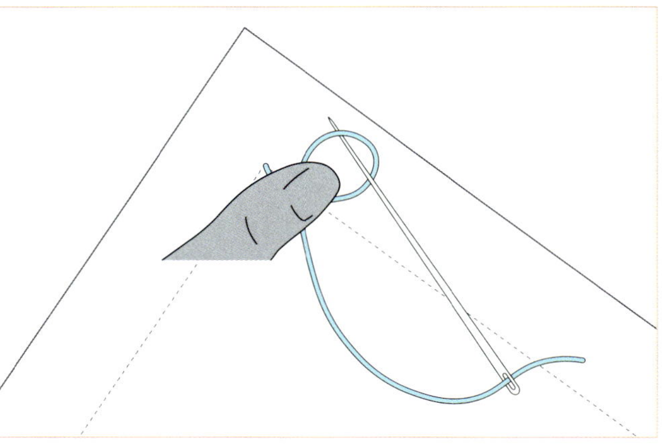

4 Slip the loop off the thumb and take the needle down into the fabric.

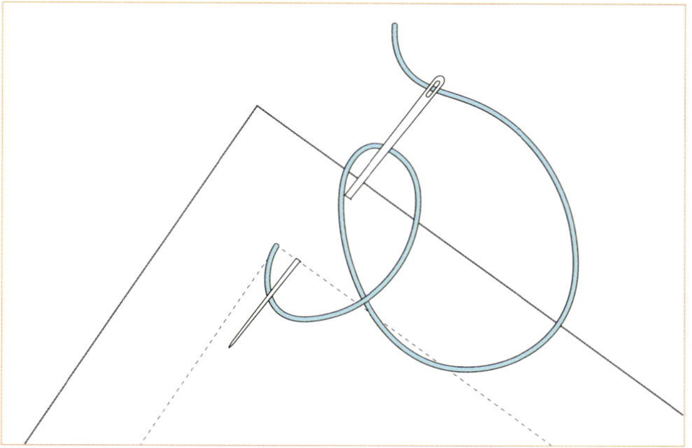

5 Leaving the needle in the fabric, bring the point up again on the base line, ensuring the needle goes over the base of the surface thread to anchor it (as you would for a normal buttonhole stitch).

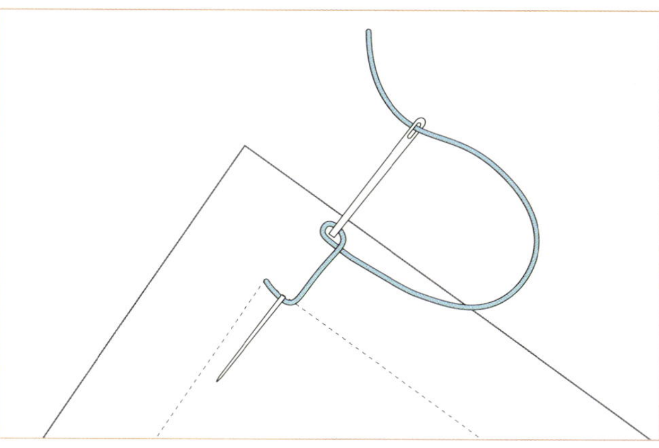

6 Tighten the thread against the needle.

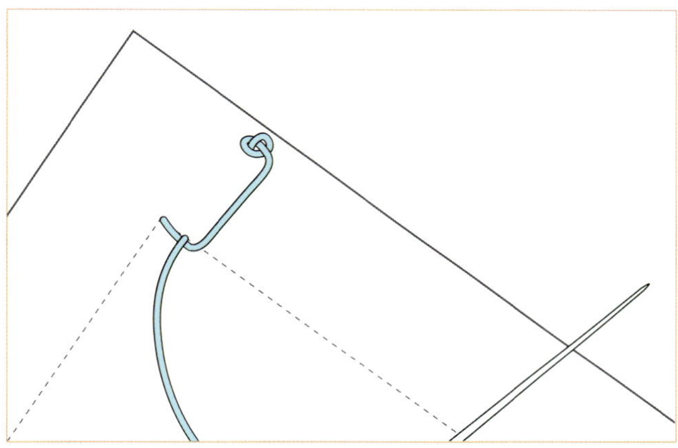

7 Pull through the thread to complete the first knotted buttonhole stitch.

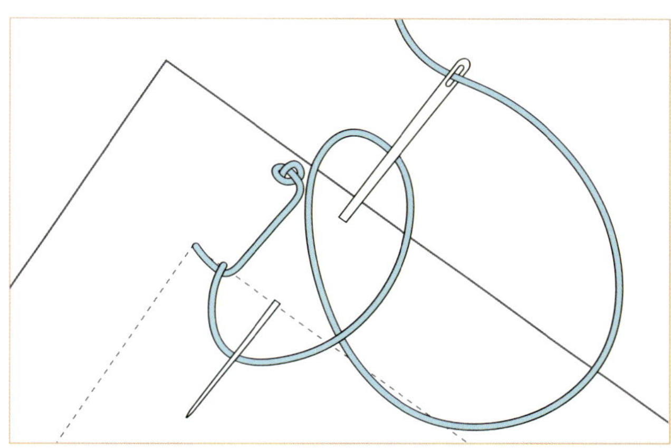

8 Repeat the sequence ...

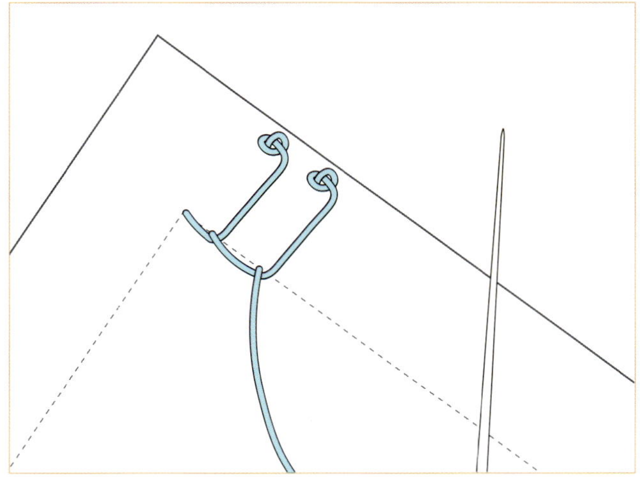

9 ... to complete another knotted buttonhole stitch.

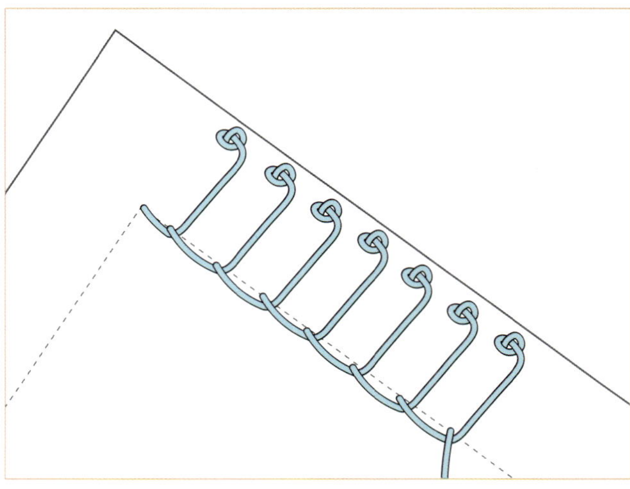

10 Continue along the line to produce a border.

KNOTTED CABLE CHAIN STITCH

SURFACE.

Also known as Knotted cable stitch.

This surface stitch is a more decorative version of cable chain stitch (see page 52). A coral knot (see coral stitch on pages 60–61) is added to the straight stitches, which gives more texture.

The stitch is presumably a development of cable chain stitch; it first appears in early 20th-century publications.

METHOD

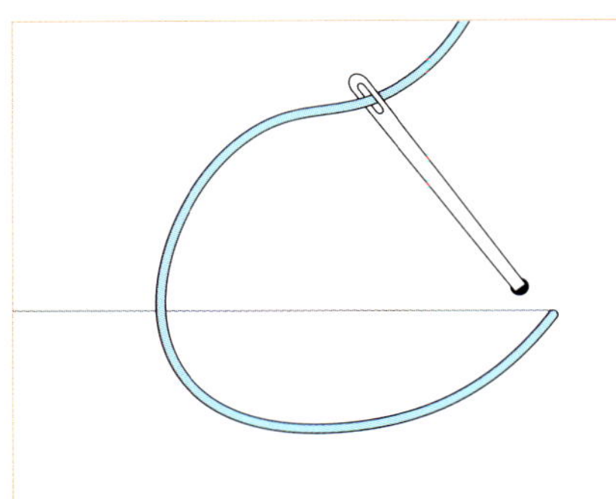

1 Bring your needle up on the right-hand end of your guideline, and take it down through the fabric just above the line and slightly along. Leave a loop on the surface.

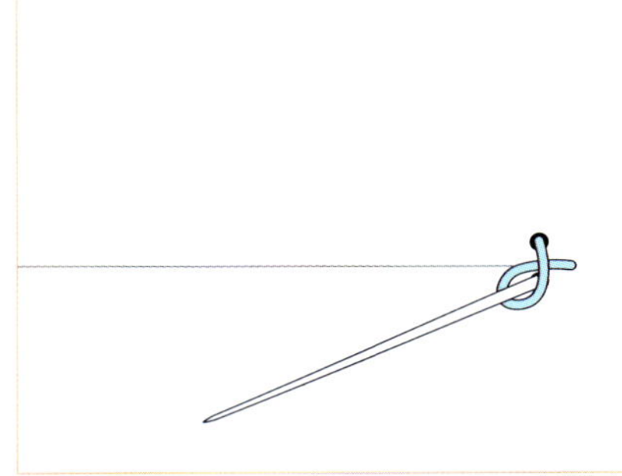

2 Twist the loop so that the second part of the twist is uppermost and bring your needle up inside it, just below the line.

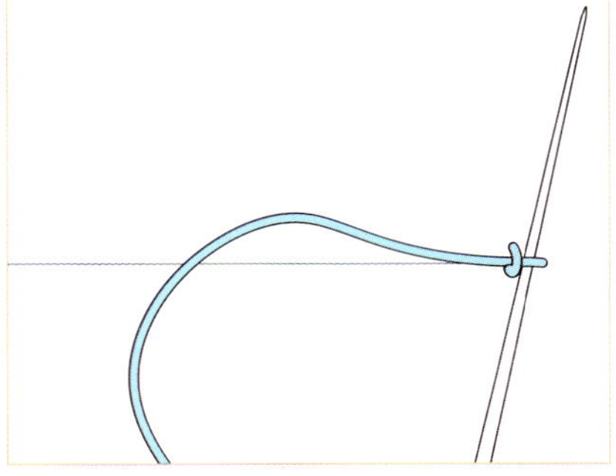

3 Pull your needle through to form a knot, then slide your needle under the straight stitch to the right (do not pierce the fabric).

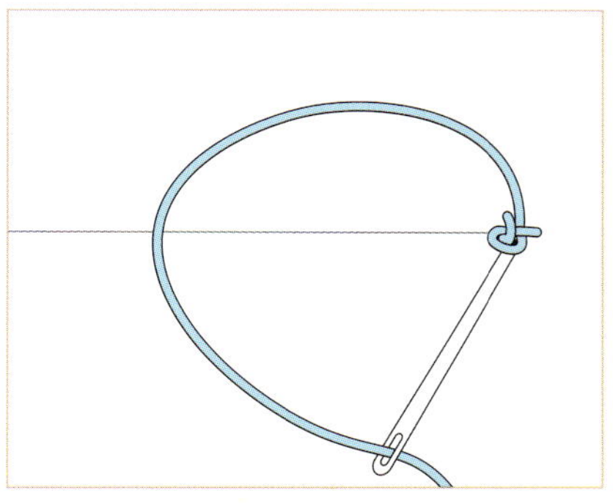

4 Leave a loop on the surface and take your needle down immediately below the coral knot.

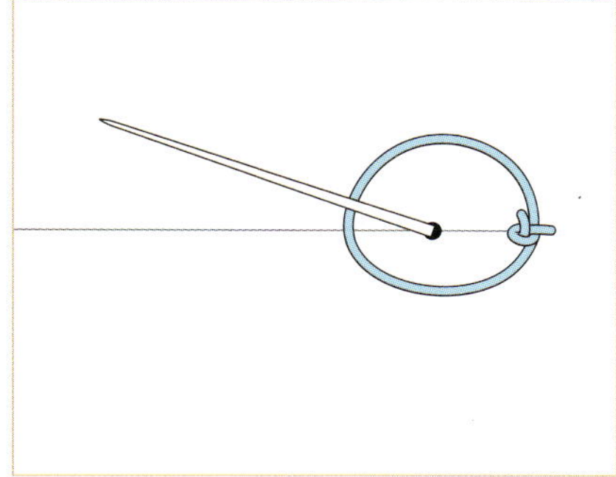

5 Bring your needle up on the line, inside the loop.

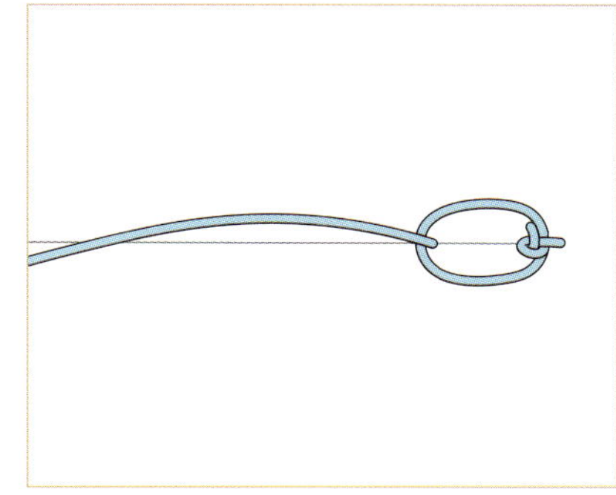

6 Pull through to form a chain stitch. This is your first knotted cable chain stitch.

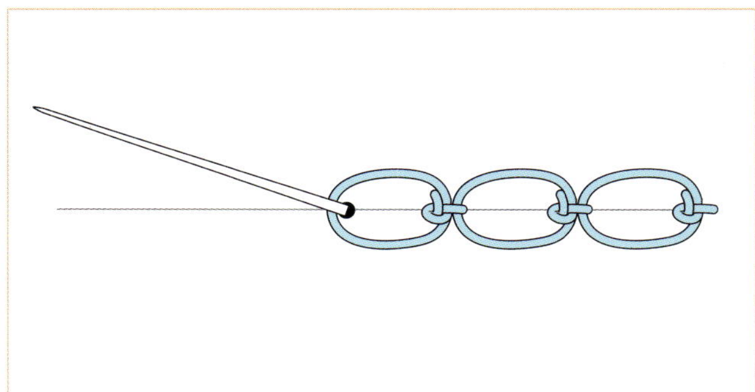

7 Continue working the stitch as before.

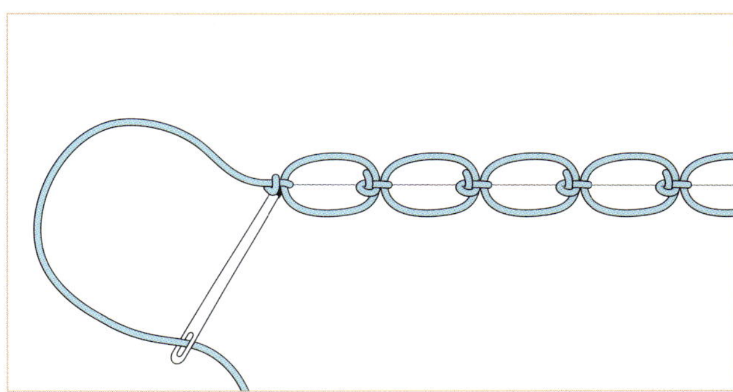

8 To finish, work the coral knot to hold your chain stitch in place and take your thread through the fabric.

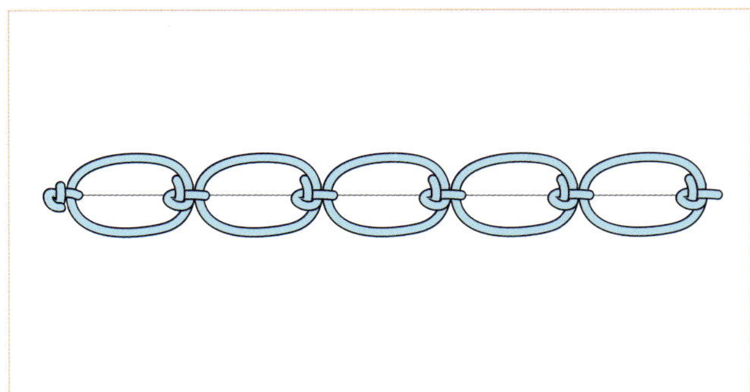

A completed line of knotted cable chain stitch.

KNOTTED PEARL STITCH

CREWELWORK; WHITEWORK; SURFACE.

Also known as Basque knot stitch, or Reverse Palestrina knot.

Knotted pearl stitch is a raised outline stitch. It is best used to give textural detail to your designs, as it emphasizes shapes well when contrasted with flat stitches.

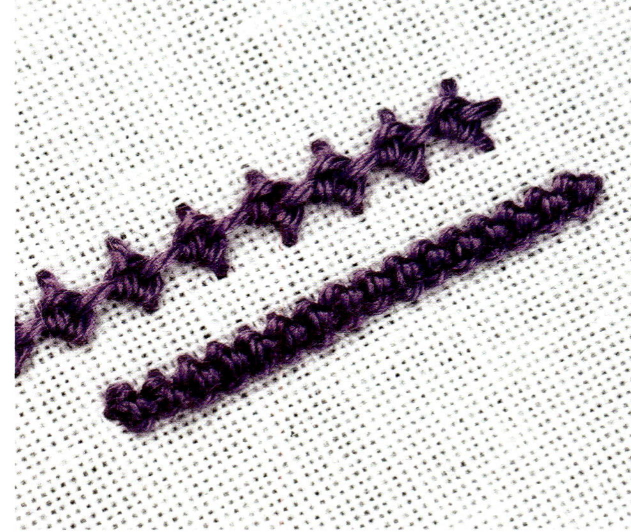

METHOD

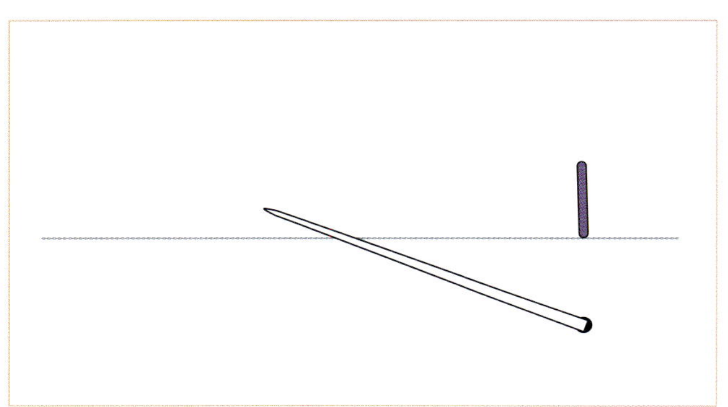

1 Bring your needle and thread up at the start of your line, then down directly above to make a straight stitch. Bring your needle up an equal distance below the line and draw your thread through.

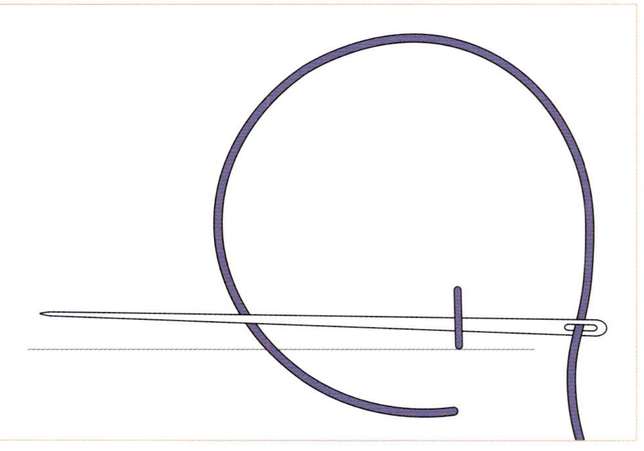

2 Take the needle under the straight stitch and over the end of your thread.

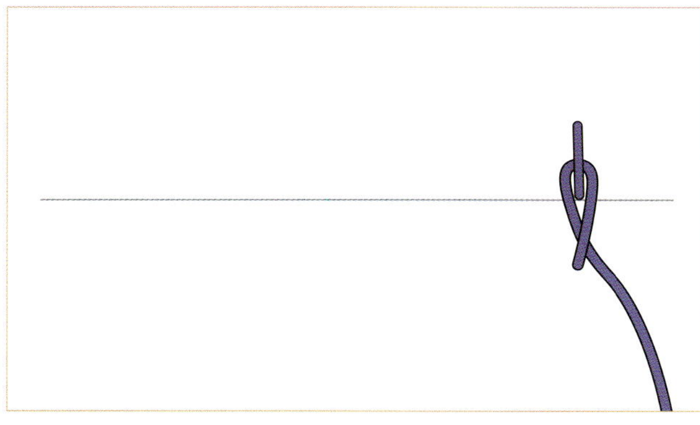

3 Draw the thread through and gently pull taut.

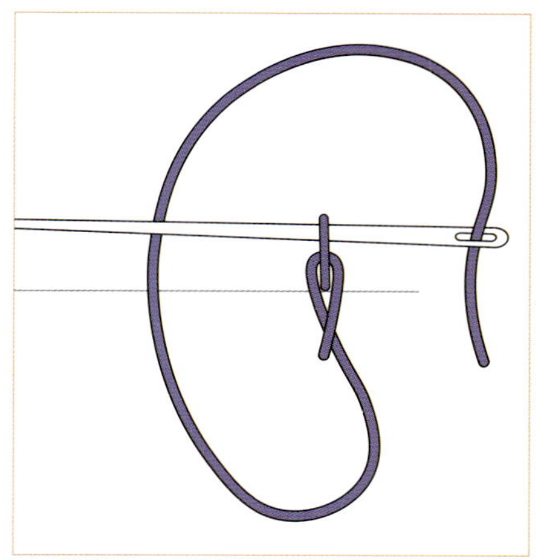

4 Take the needle back under the straight stitch at the top and over the end of the thread again.

5 Draw the thread through, gently pull back on itself to tighten and then lay in the direction of your line. This is your first stitch completed.

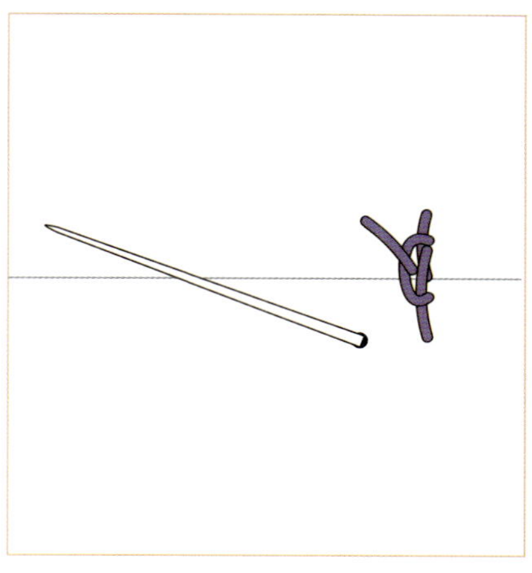

6 Take the needle down above and slightly further along the line (it should be level with the edge of your first stitch). Draw the thread through and bring the needle up and an equal distance directly below the line.

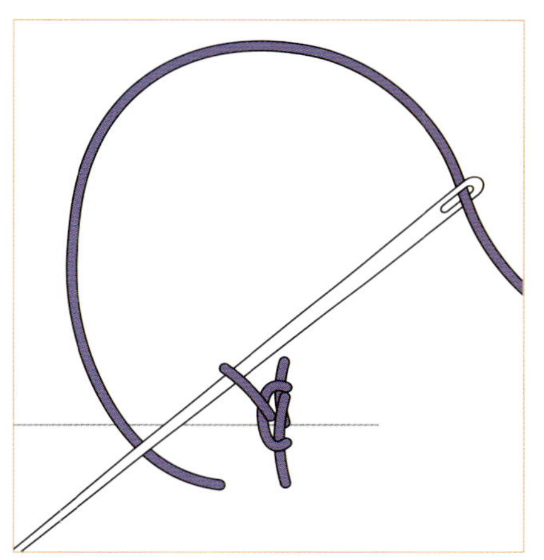

7 Take the needle through the new straight stitch and over the loop of the thread.

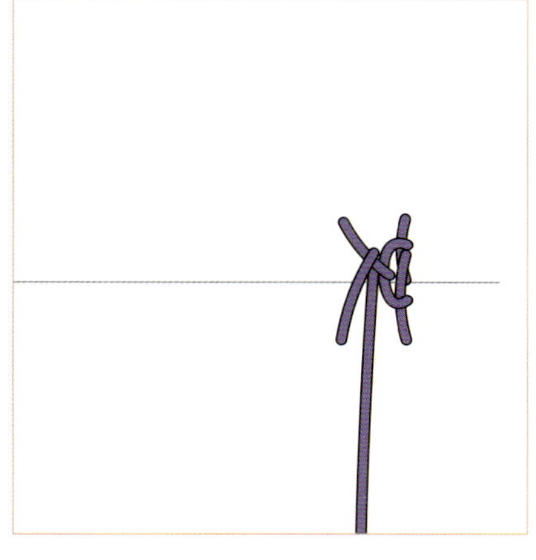

8 Draw the thread through and down.

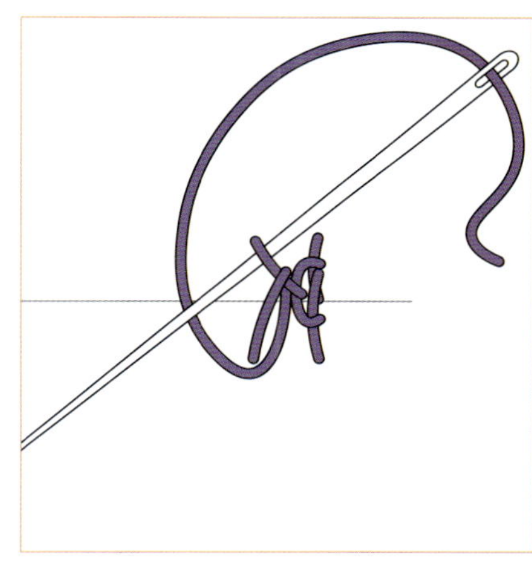

9 Take the needle once more through the new straight stitch and over the loop of the thread.

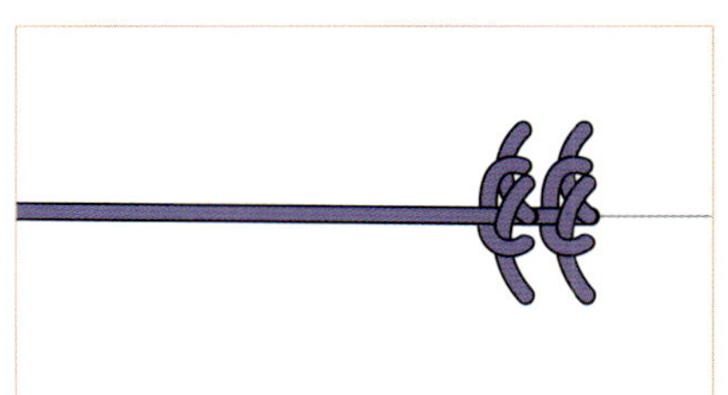

10 Pull the thread through then back on itself to draw it taut, and finally back across in the direction of your line.

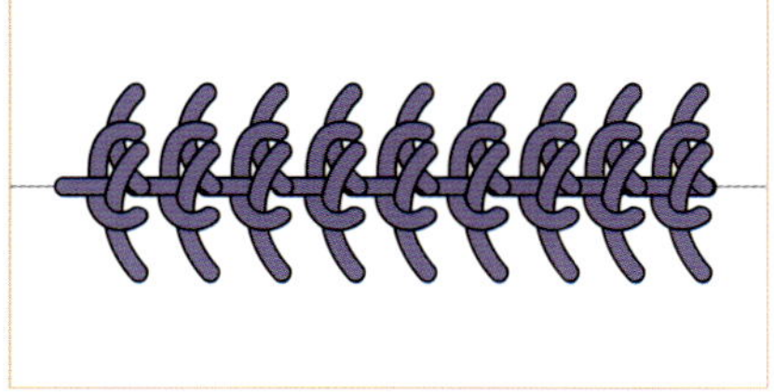

11 Work along your painted line using the same method, and secure the thread in the usual way.

LADDER STITCH (PULLED THREAD)

PULLED THREAD; WHITEWORK.

A pulled thread band used in whitework, resulting in what looks like a series of very small eyelets in a line, ideal for stems and veins. It can be worked either with the grain or across it for a diagonal or curved line.

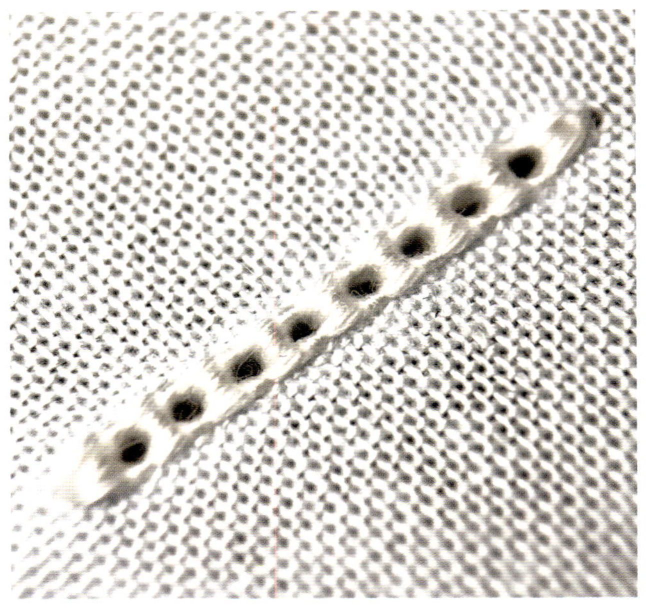

METHOD

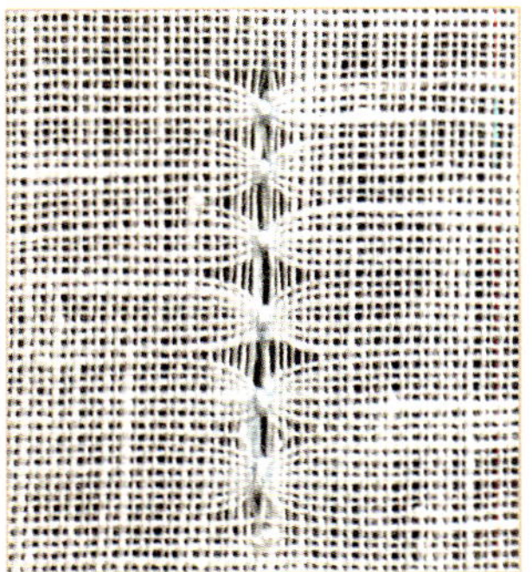

1 Begin with a couple of holding stitches, then work an even back stitch, pulling the thread to create holes between each stitch.

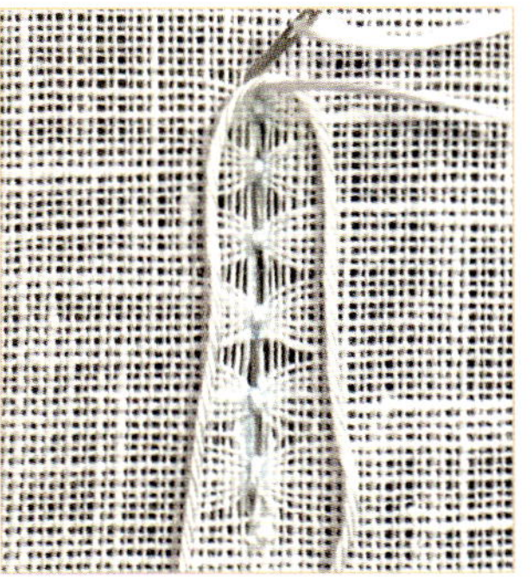

2 Lay a couching thread down each side of the back stitch and attach at the top with a small stitch.

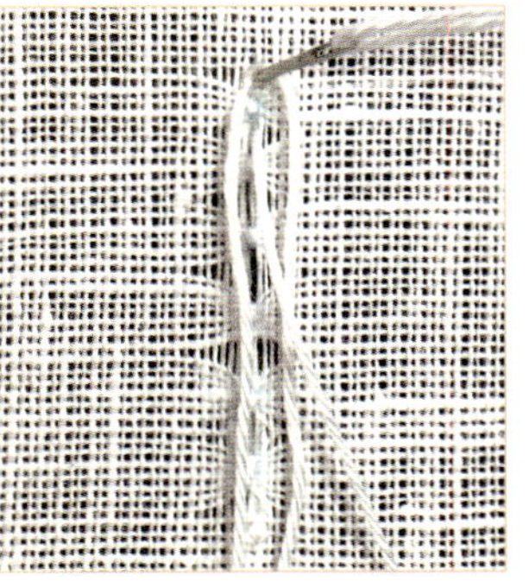

3 Bring the needle up in the first hole and stitch over the first back stitch with good tension.

4 Bring the needle up in the fabric to the right of the first hole and stitch over the laid thread by taking the needle back down into the first hole.

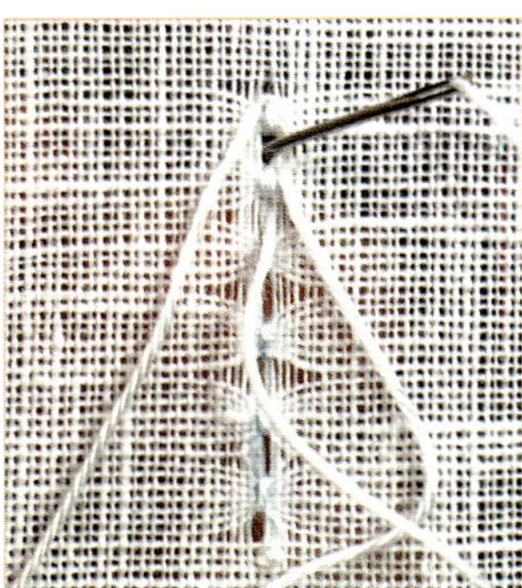

5 Bring the needle up in the second hole and stitch over the back stitch above, again with good tension.

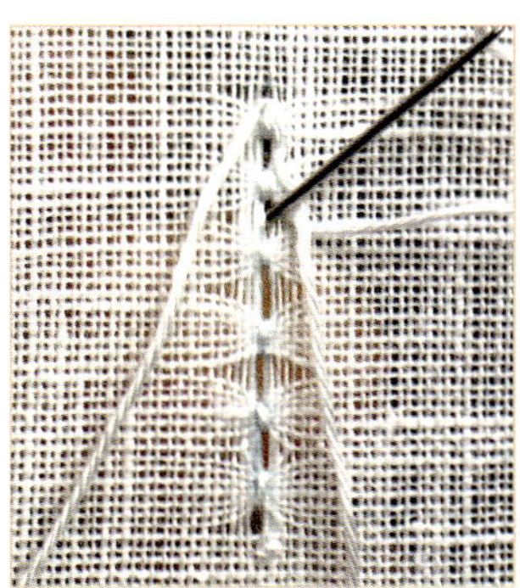

6 Continue securing the laid thread on the right side in the same way to the end of the area.

7 Repeat this pattern down the left-hand side.

8 Plunge the couching thread neatly at the bottom of the back stitch.

LONG-ARMED CROSS STITCH

CANVASWORK; COUNTED THREAD.

Also known as Long-legged cross stitch, Long-arm cross stitch, Plaited Slav stitch, Slav cross stitch, Portuguese stitch, Twist stitch, or Persian cross stitch.

This is an asymmetrical cross stitch where long diagonal stitches are worked over twice the number of vertical threads used for the short diagonal stitches. It can be used as a filling stitch or alternatively as a wide border which accentuates its interwoven appearance.

The earliest evidence of long-armed cross stitch is from 10th–12th century Egypt. Later examples include 16th-century pieces, as demonstrated by the Elizabethan embroideries of Hardwick Hall, and Icelandic embroideries from the 17th century. Elsewhere it featured in embroidery from the Greek islands and Morocco; in Assisi embroidery from Italy and in early 19th-century samplers in the United States.

METHOD

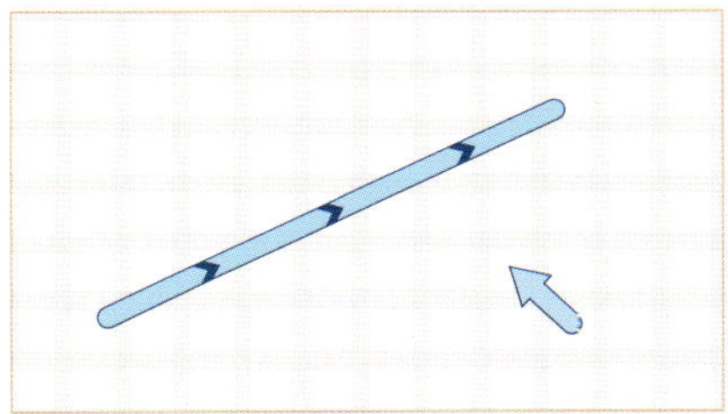

1 Work from left to right. Start with a long diagonal stitch over eight vertical and four horizontal canvas threads, then bring the needle up over four canvas threads below.

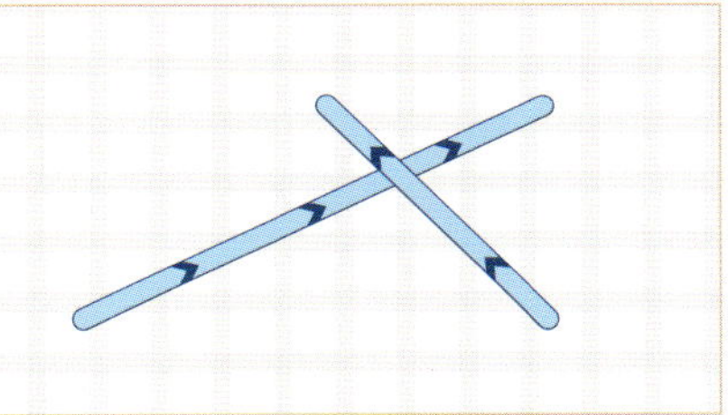

2 Cross the long stitch with a shorter diagonal stitch which spans the square of four threads from bottom right to top left.

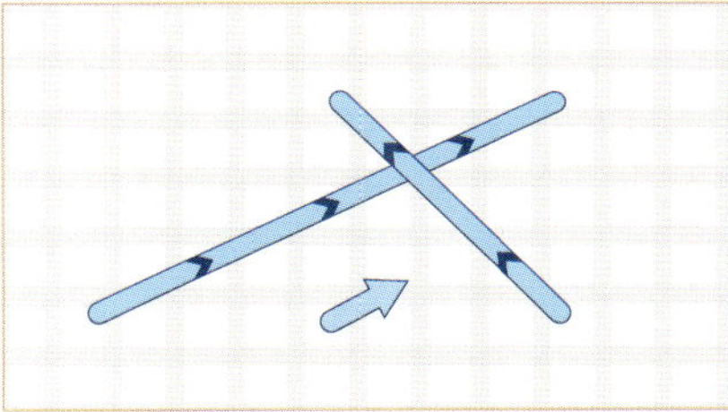

3 Come up four threads below.

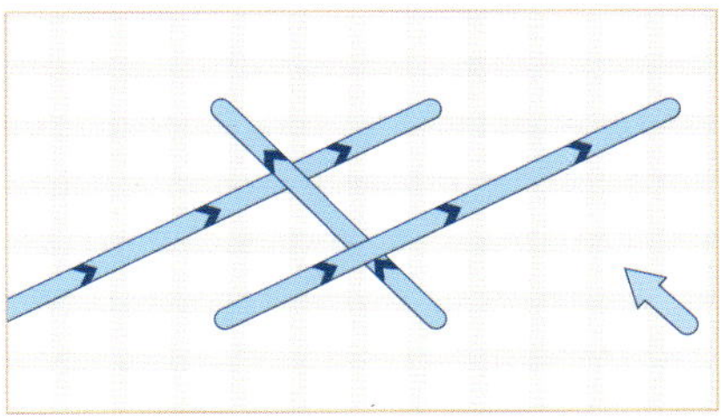

4 Make another long diagonal stitch as shown, then bring up the needle over four threads below.

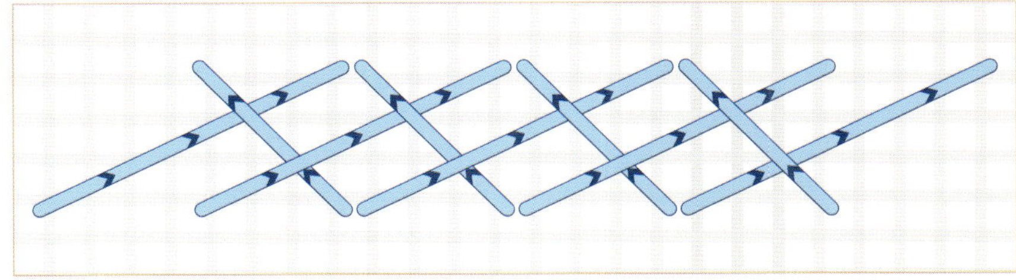

5 Make another short diagonal stitch, then continue until you fill the area or you reach the finishing point.

LOOP STITCH

SURFACE; MOUNTMELLICK.

Also known as Centipede stitch, Knotted loop stitch, or Double buttonhole stitch.

Loop stitch is a line stitch with a raised, plaited centre. It is often worked in straight or gently curved lines, but it can be used for an open filling.

METHOD

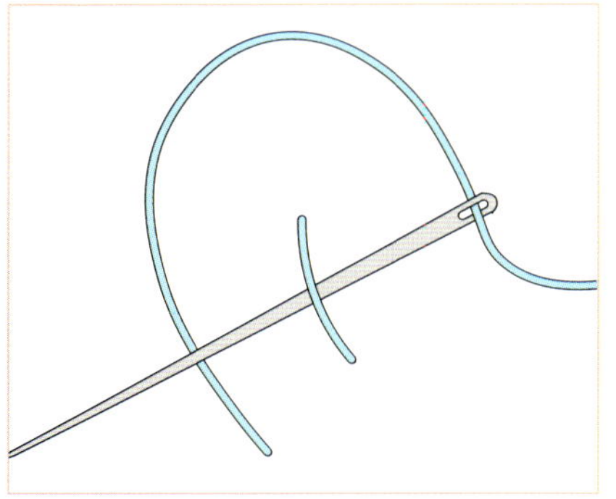

1 Bring the needle up at the centre between the two guidelines, then insert it on the top guideline to make a diagonal stitch. Come up at the lower guideline. Work a buttonhole stitch (see pages 20–21) over the first stitch.

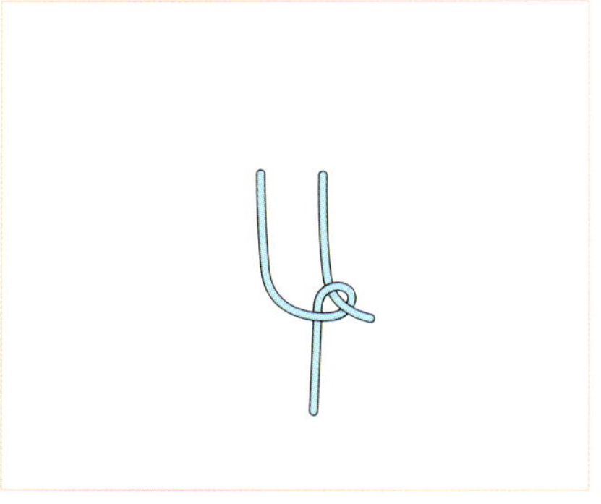

2 Take the needle down on the top line to work the next diagonal stitch.

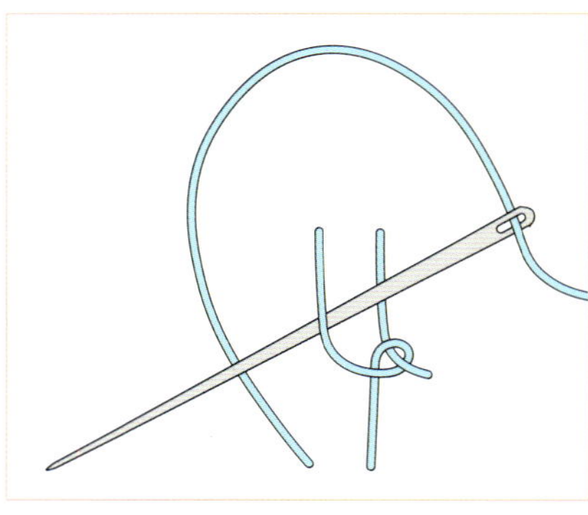

3 Bring the needle up at the lower guideline and work a buttonhole stitch over the previous diagonal stitch.

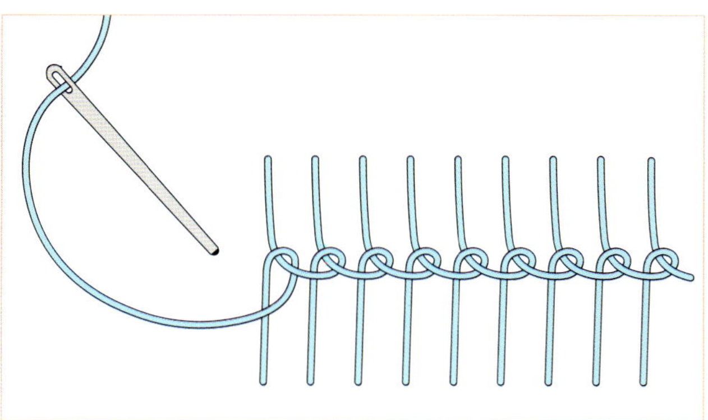

4 Continue in the same manner as required. To finish, take the needle down at the centre between the two guidelines.

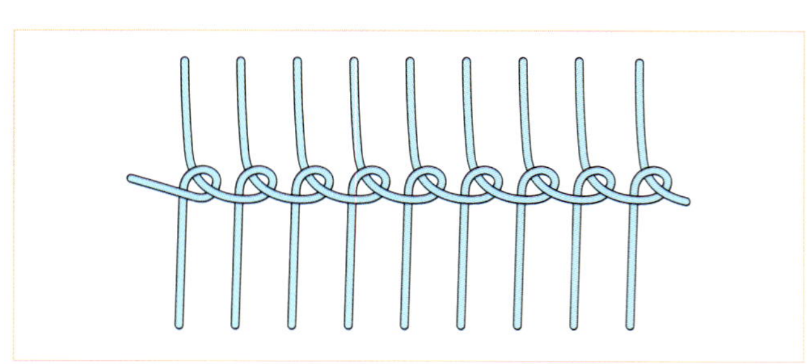

A completed row of loop stitch.

▲▲ Detail from sampler, RSN Collection COL.2018.69

Crewelwork sampler worked by RSN Diploma student Beryl Penson, likely in the late 1930s. In the top right quadrant are a variety of standalone flower and leaf motifs. They are worked in a combination of wool and cotton thread.

The outlines of the flowers are worked in loop stitches. French knots, cloud filling, split, pearl stitch variation and couching stitches (see pages 29, 234, 99 and 63 respectively) are also used for the flower petals and leaf interiors.

More of this sampler can be seen on pages 215 and 227.

MOUNTMELLICK STITCH

Whitework; Mountmellick; Surface.

This stitch looks like a chain stitch with a little leg, and it is often used for thorny stems in foliage. It is one of the outline stitches used in Mountmellick embroidery.

METHOD

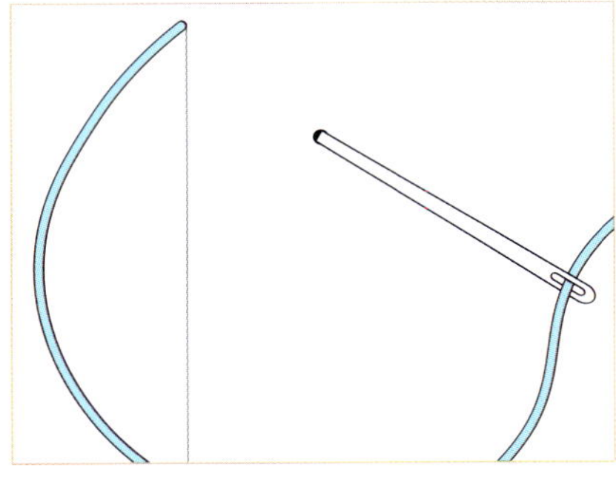

1 Bring the needle up at the top of the line. Go down diagonally to the right and pull through.

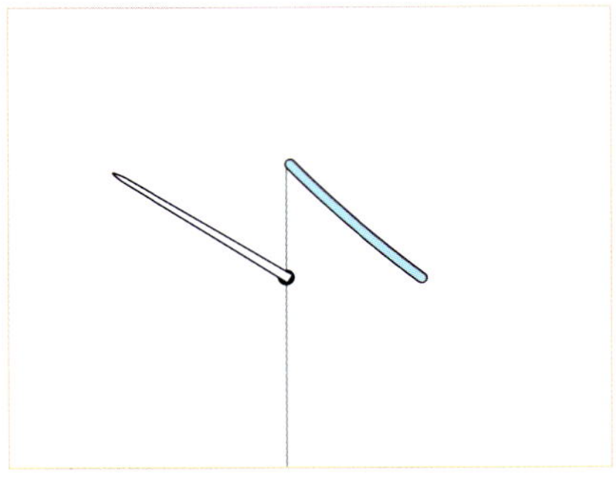

2 Come back up horizontally on the line below the starting point.

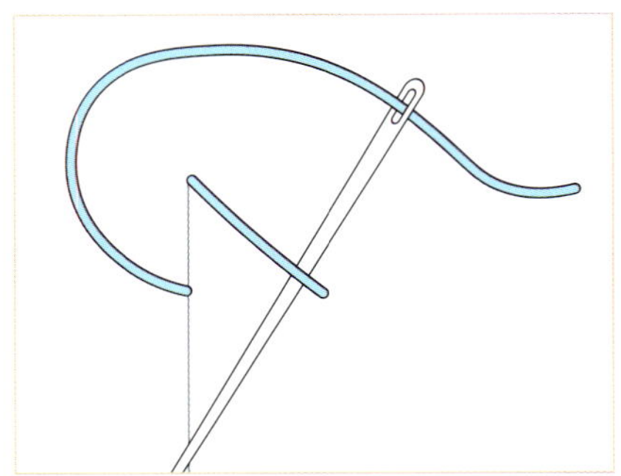

3 Pass the needle under the first diagonal stitch from top right to bottom left.

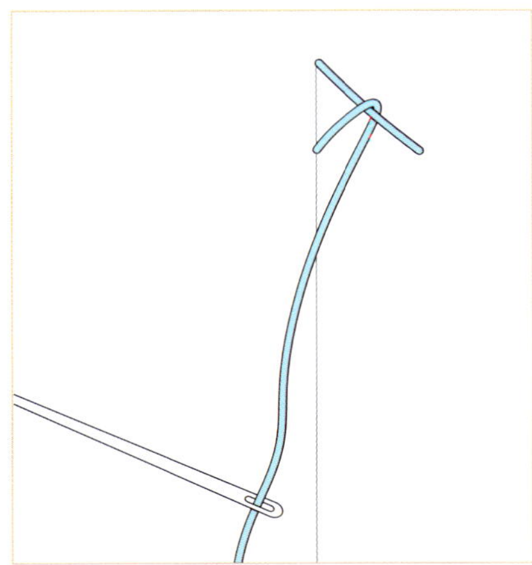

4 Pull through.

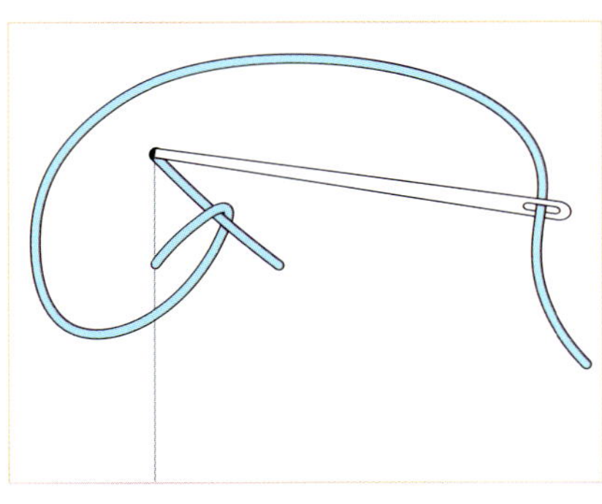

5 Go down the same hole of your starting point. Keep the thread in clockwise direction and leave a loop.

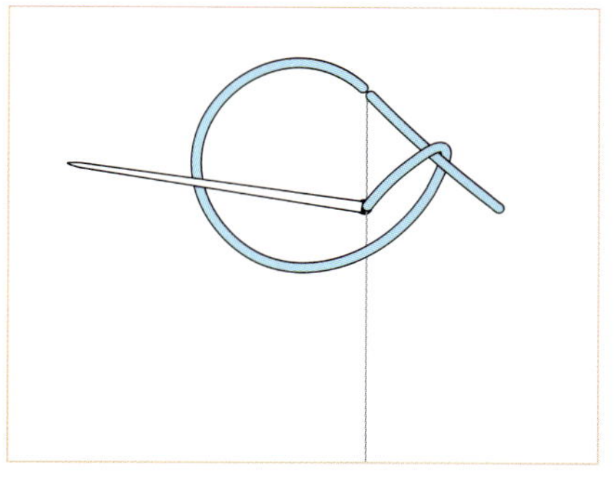

6 Come out at the same hole you came out the second time on the line. Make sure the needle is inside the loop.

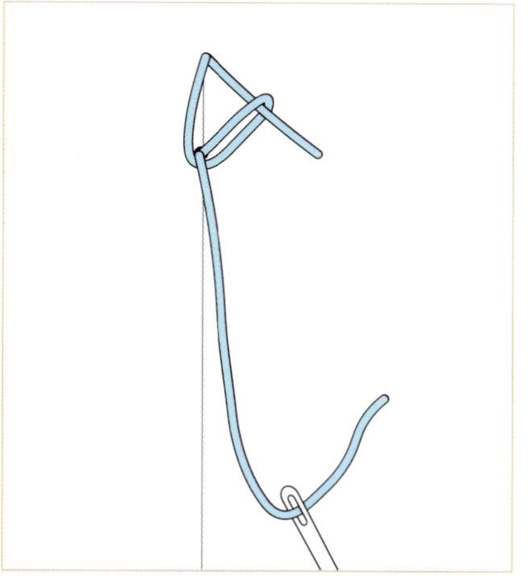

7 Now pull out the needle gently to make a chain. This completes a Mountmellick stitch.

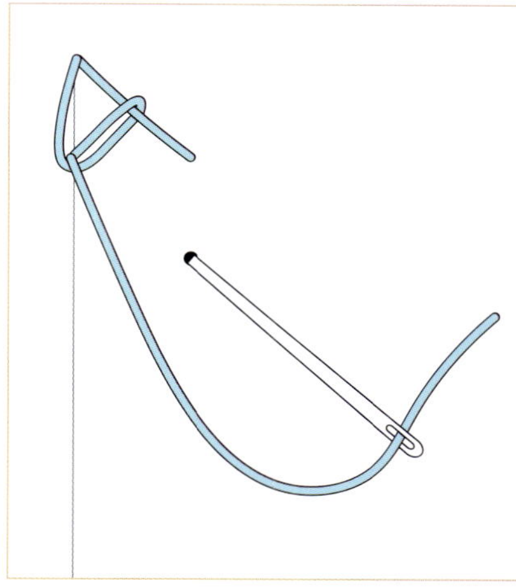

8 Continue with a diagonal stitch to the right.

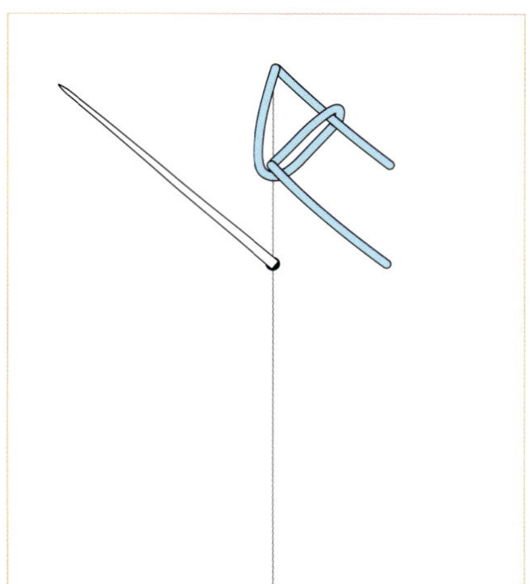

9 Come back out on the line.

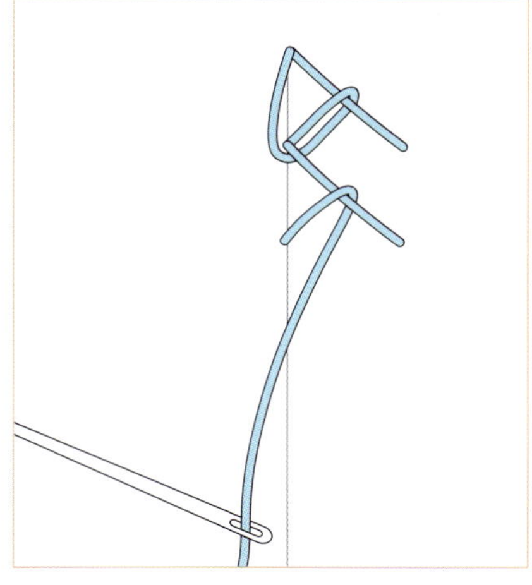

10 Pass the thread under the diagonal stitch.

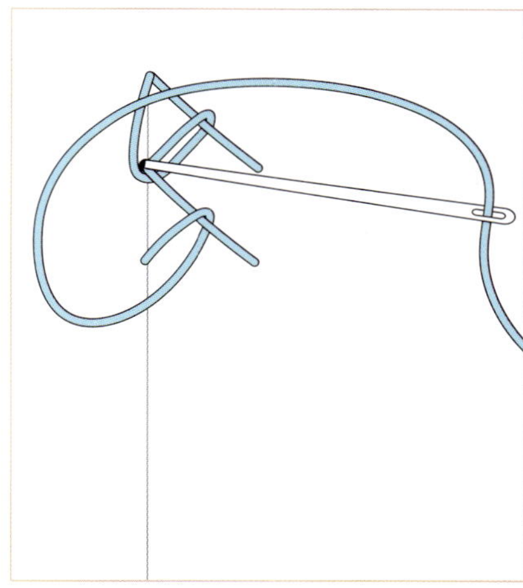

11 Keep the thread in clockwise direction and take the needle down at the same hole you started the second diagonal stitch. Make a chain as before and continue.

OPEN CHAIN STITCH

SURFACE; CREWELWORK.

Also known as Square chain stitch, Roman chain stitch, Small writing, Big writing, or Ladder stitch.

This is a variation on chain stitch (see page 22) where the stitches are wider than the standard variety. The loop of each stitch is pulled wider which can result in a squarer appearance, hence one of its alternative names of square chain stitch and ladder stitch.

METHOD

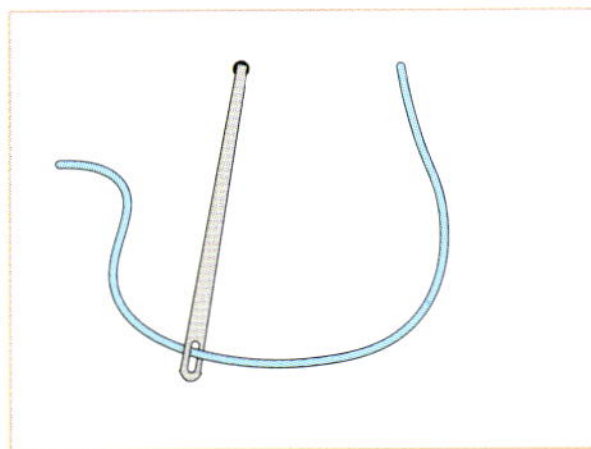

1 Bring the needle up on the right-hand side of the stitch area and down at the same level on the left-hand side, leaving the thread loose.

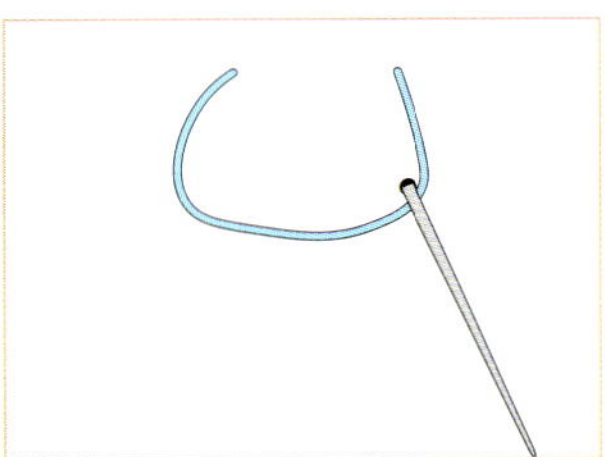

2 Bring the needle back up on the right, below the first stitch and through the loop. Do not tighten the loop yet.

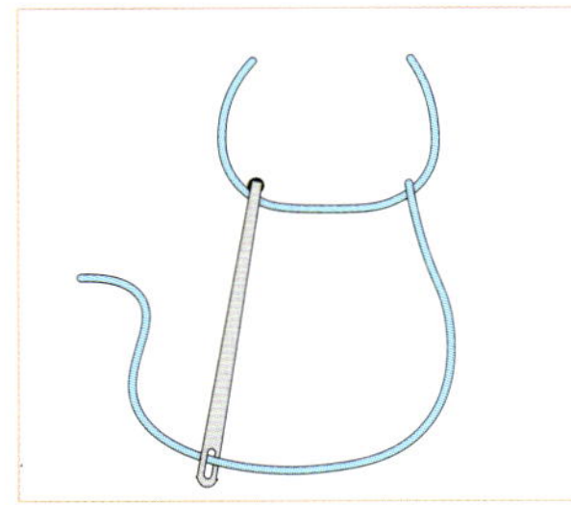

3 Take the needle down through the loop, level with where the needle was brought up, leaving the thread loose. Tighten the first loop to form the first open chain stitch.

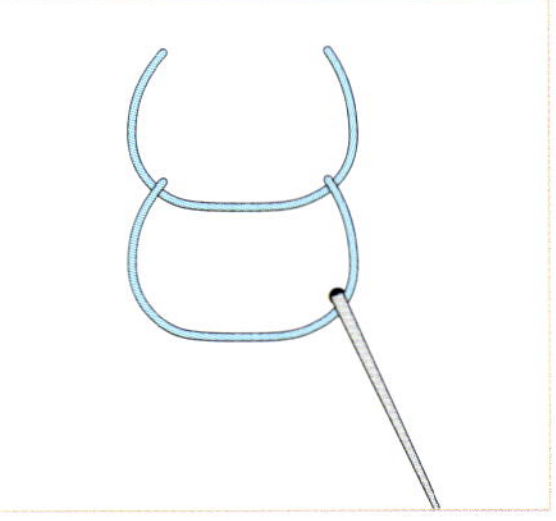

4 Bring the needle up on the right-hand side, through the next loop, keeping it in line with the previous open chain stitch.

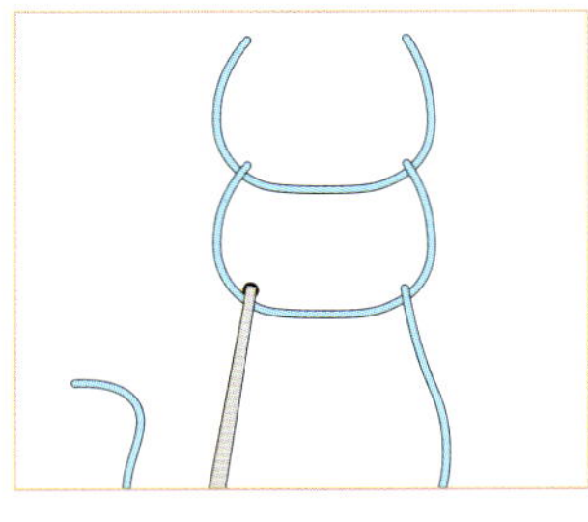

5 Take the needle down on the left-hand side, through the loop to form the second open chain stitch. Continue working from right to left, creating as many stitches as required.

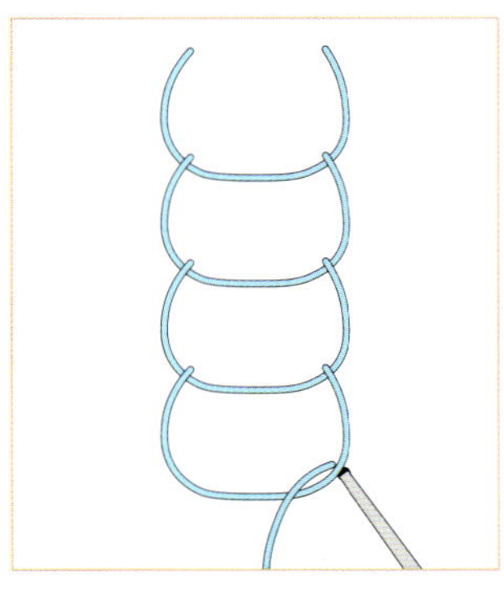

6 Make a small holding stitch over the last open chain at the bottom right-hand corner.

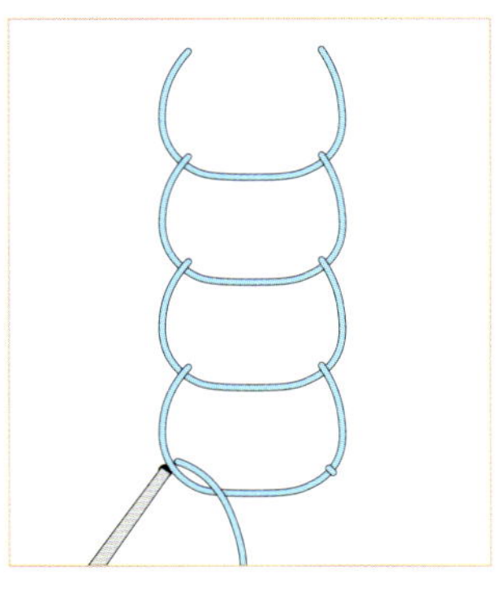

7 Make another small holding stitch at the bottom left-hand corner.

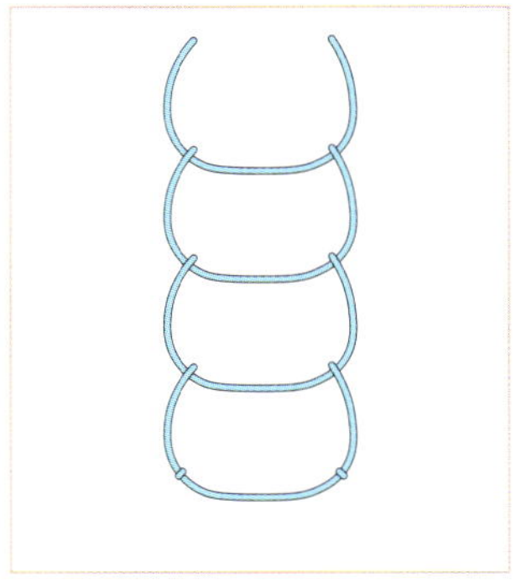

A completed line of open chain stitch.

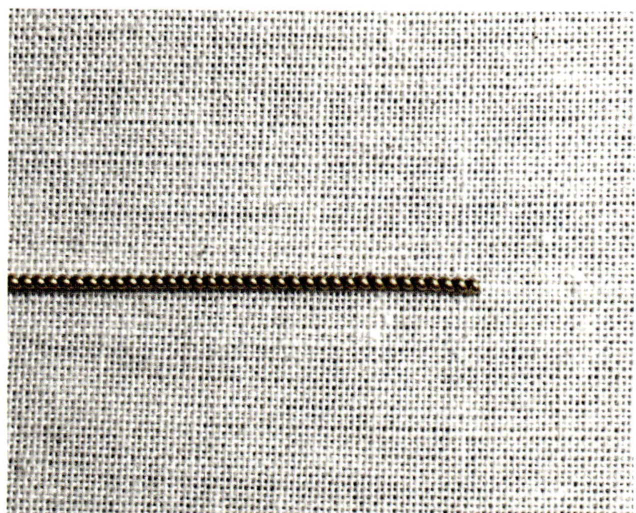

PEARL PURL APPLICATION

GOLDWORK.

Pearl purl is a spiral metal thread ideal for lines or to outline areas. It can be used in lines of couching or overstretched and wrapped with a coloured thread as its core.

Pearl purl was certainly in evidence in the 17th century as the National Museum of Ireland holds a pair of gauntlets originally owned by William of Orange, and the V&A South Kensington museum holds several artefacts from this era featuring various types of purls, including an embroidered book binding probably stitched by a member of the Broderers' Company in London.

A – Unstretched
B – Stretched

PREPARING PEARL PURL

Before using pearl purl, stretch it slightly to loosen the coils. To stretch pearl purl for normal use, hold one end gently but firmly with a pair of embroidery scissors and the other end with tweezers and gently pull the two ends apart with a bouncing movement.

The stretch should be even across the entire length so that the individual twists in the metal appear at regular intervals. This allows the thread with which you attach the pearl purl to sit comfortably between the coils.

Do not confuse this with overstretched pearl purl (see above).

METHOD

1 Using a sewing thread that closely matches the colour of the pearl purl, bring the thread to the front and take it over the pearl purl, about 1cm (½in) from the end.

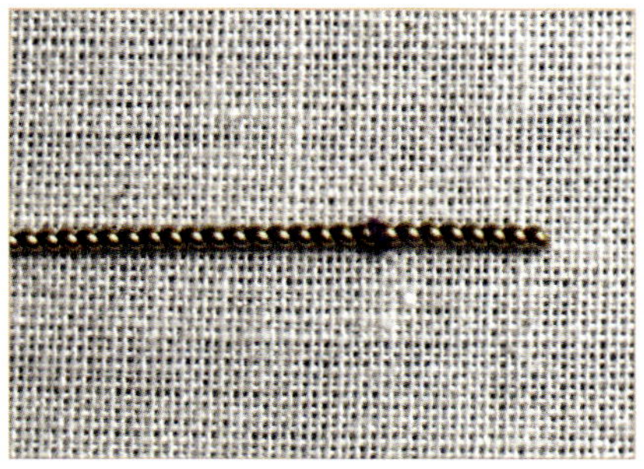

2 Pull the thread tight to form the stitch. Here, the stitch is lying on top on the pearl purl and is clearly visible.

3 Keep pulling until the thread pops between the coils and becomes invisible. Continue attaching the pearl purl in this way.

PEARL STITCH

SURFACE.

Pearl stitch is a looped stitch which, when worked closely together, resembles a string of pearls. It is formed by consecutive loops, each of which are anchored by a short, slanted stitch. The similar pearl stitch variation, shown opposite, is more angular. This rounded version of pearl stitch features in Mrs Christie's 1920 book *Samplers and Stitches*, whereas the variation doesn't appear until later publications which suggests that this was the original stitch.

Pearl stitch is a characteristic stitch in Wallachian embroidery, a technique from Wallachia in what is now Romania. Examples of Wallachian embroidery were displayed in the 1851 Great Exhibition in London.

METHOD

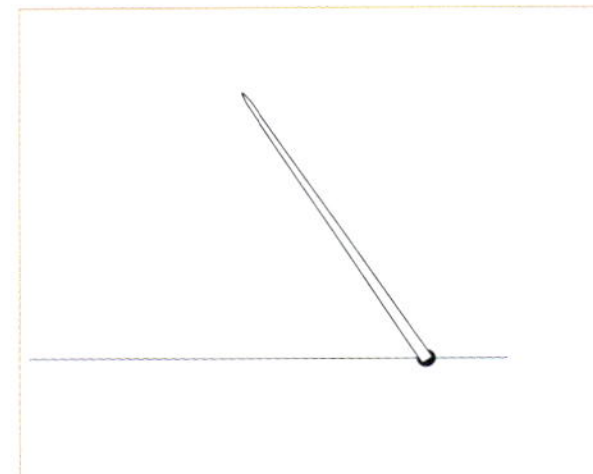

1 Bring the needle up at the right-hand end of the design line.

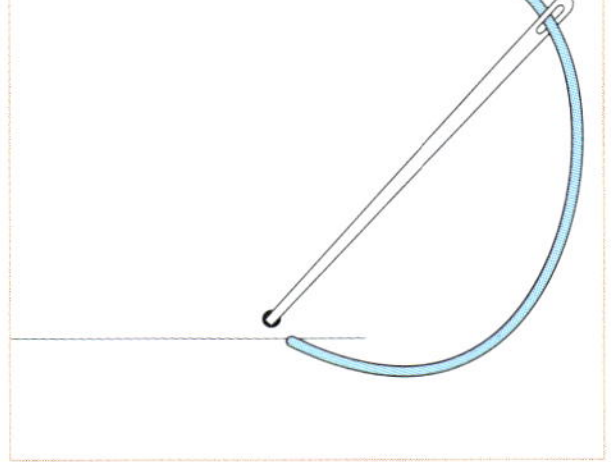

2 Take the needle down a little to the left and just above the design line.

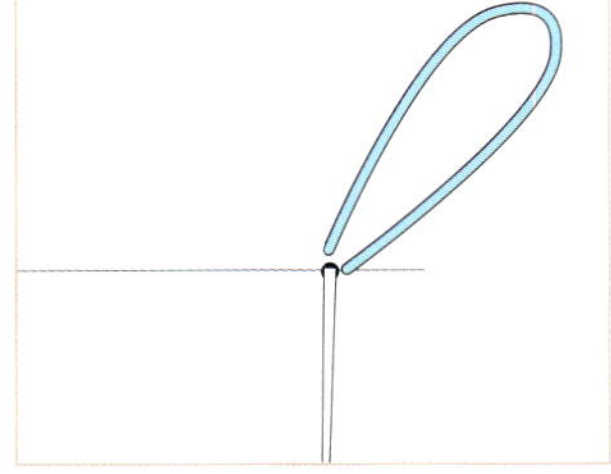

3 Leave a loop and bring the needle up immediately below, on the design line.

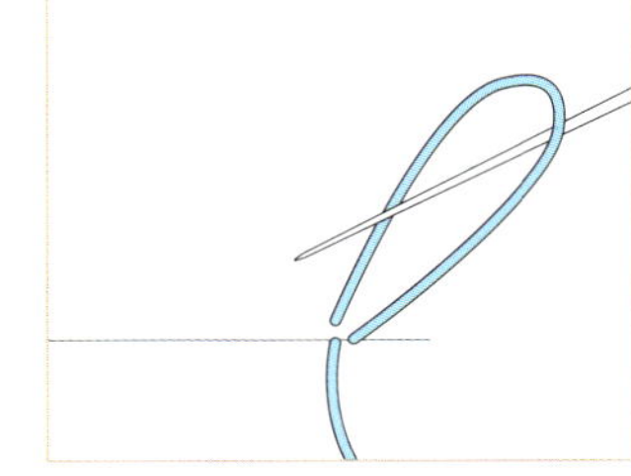

4 Pass the needle through the loop from right to left without piercing the base fabric.

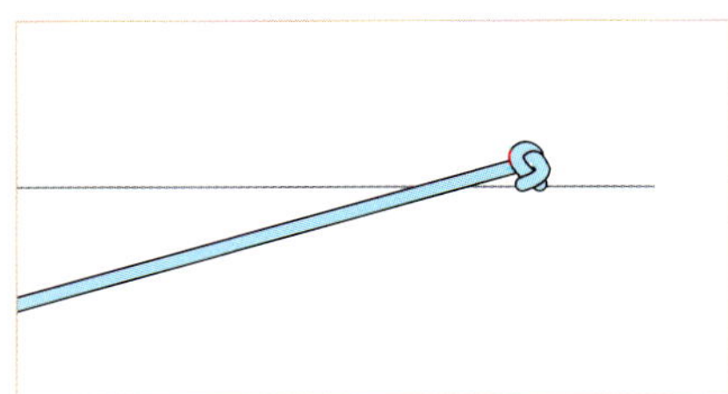

5 Pull the thread through and you will see the first pearl stitch.

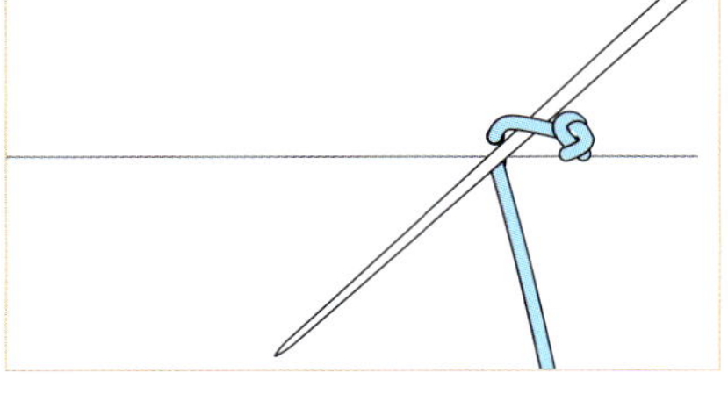

6 Take your needle down a little to the left and just above the design line, and repeat these steps for the next stitch.

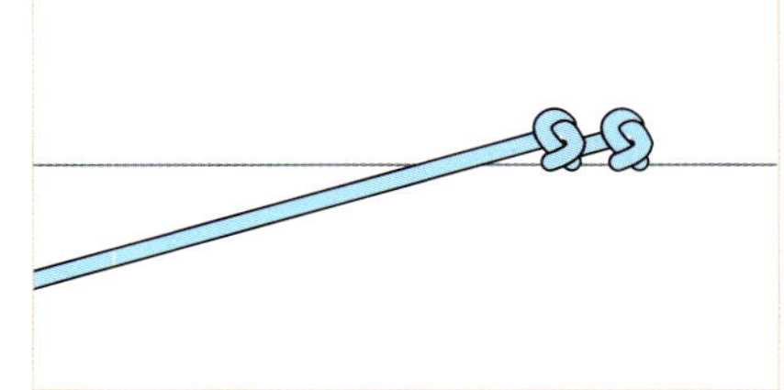

7 Continue working pearl stitch as required.

PEARL STITCH (VARIATION)

CREWELWORK; SURFACE.

This variation of pearl stitch is a line stitch of evenly spaced triangles, created by looping alternate stitches through each other.

It is believed that this stitch is a development of the version of pearl stitch (see opposite) which closely resembles a string of pearls. The circumstances of this divergence is unclear, although it would seem likely that it was after the publication of Mrs Christie's 1920 book, *Samplers and Stitches*, which clearly documents the original version.

METHOD

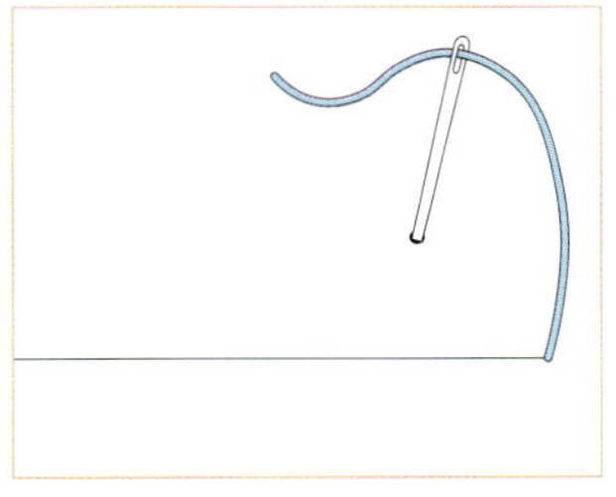

1 Bring your needle and thread up to the surface on the line, create a small diagonal stitch above the line. Pull the thread through.

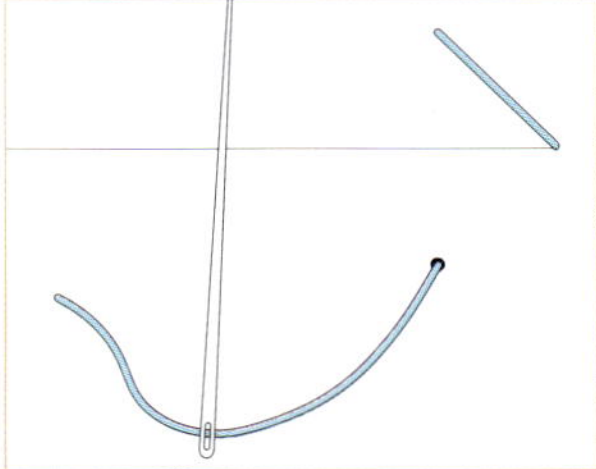

2 Bring the needle up on the opposite side of the line and draw the thread through.

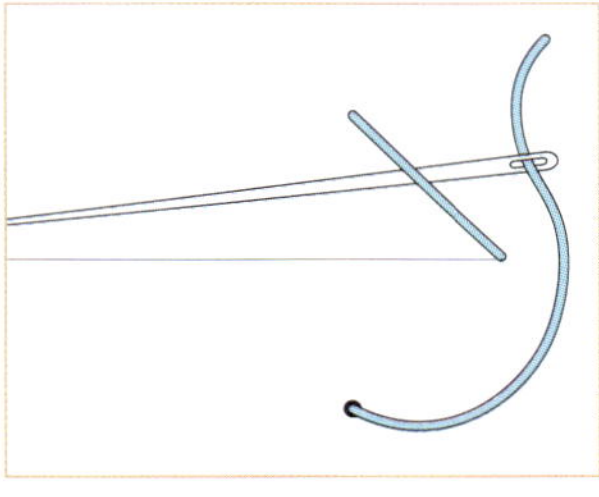

3 Pass the needle under the diagonal stitch created. Pull on the base of the slack loop to tighten the first stitch.

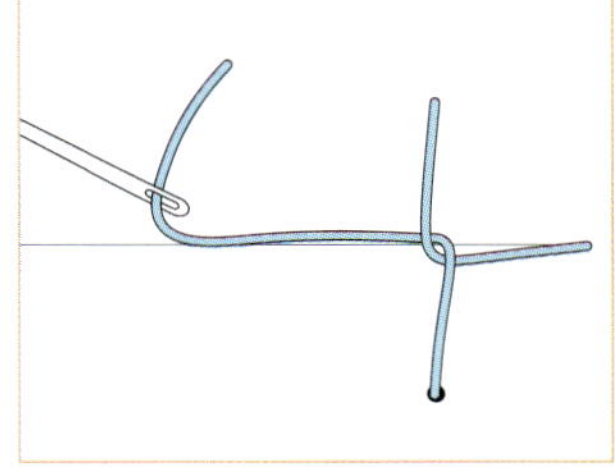

4 Take the needle through and draw the thread taut along the marked line.

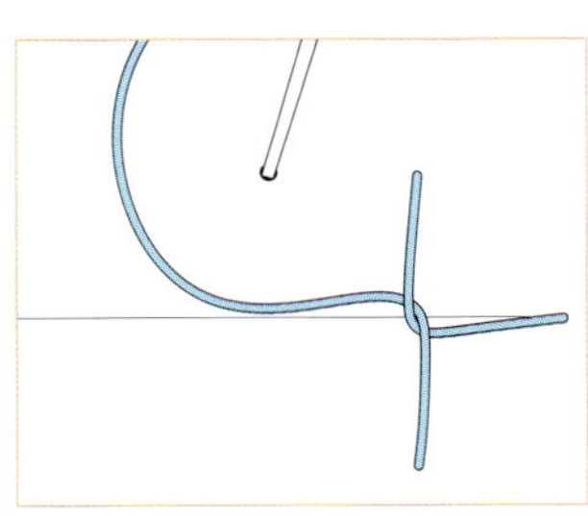

5 Take the needle down through the fabric above and slightly further along the line, parallel with the top of the first stitch to create a second diagonal stitch.

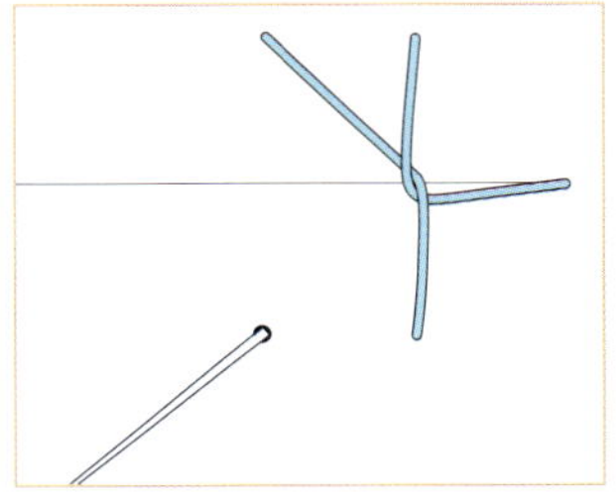

6 Bring the thread back up to the surface on the opposite side of the line.

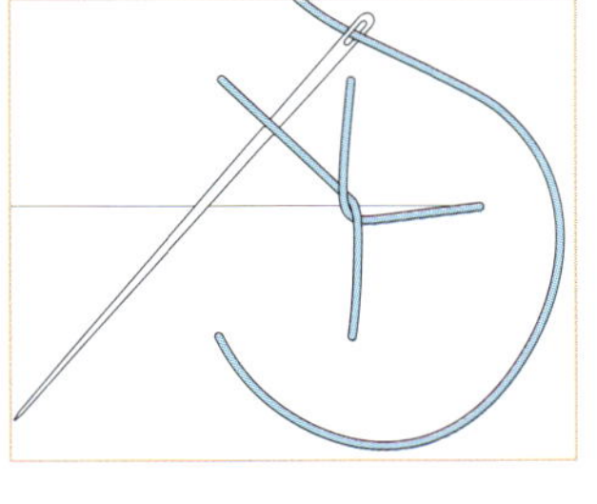

7 Pass the needle through the second diagonal stitch ...

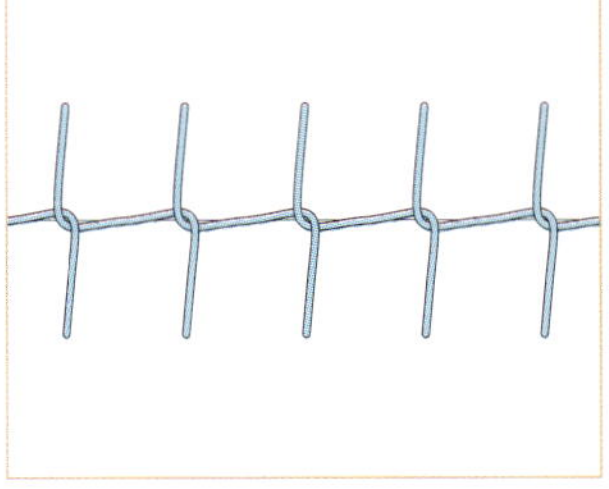

8 ... then repeat the method to the end of the line and secure in the usual way.

PEKINESE STITCH

CREWELWORK; GOLDWORK; SURFACE; STUMPWORK.

Also known as Chinese stitch, Forbidden stitch, Blind stitch, or Peking stitch.

Pekinese stitch consists of a line of back stitch (see page 16) with a second thread looping through it.

Pekinese stitch is credited as originating in and being very common in China, but there is no evidence for it there prior to 1900. The Chinese Mandarin squares which feature it all date from the early 20th century. It is used as a filling stitch, particularly on squares from the late Qing dynasty.

It is traditionally used in Chinese embroidery with silk thread on silk fabric.

METHOD

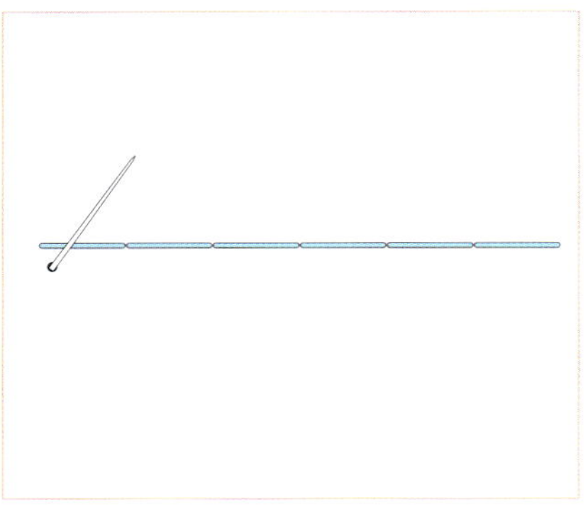

1 Stitch a line of back stitch, then bring your needle up just below the start of your line and swap for a tapestry needle.

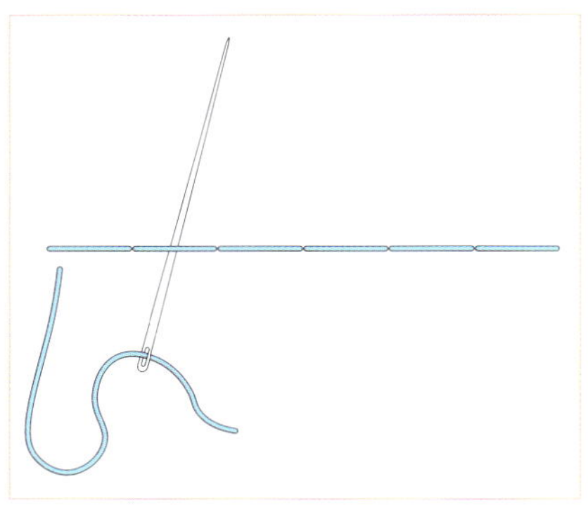

2 Weave the needle upward between the loop of the next back stitch and the surface of the fabric.

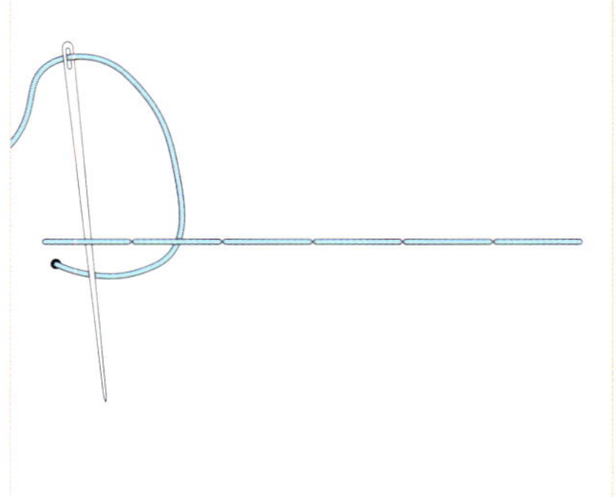

3 Weave the needle downward under the previous loop and over the Pekinese thread.

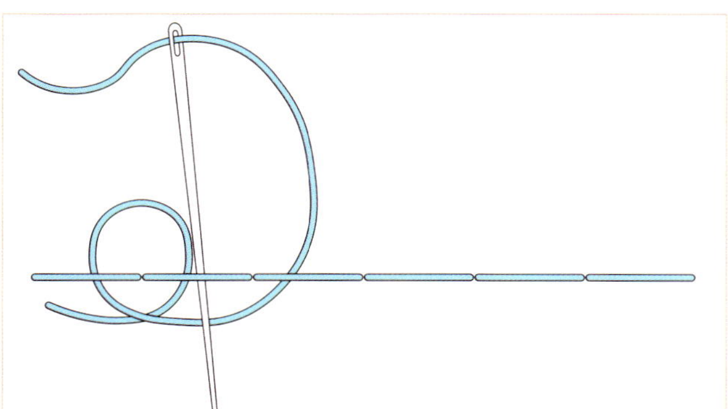

4 Repeat by weaving the needle upward under the back stitch two stitches ahead, then downward under the previous loop and over the Pekinese thread.

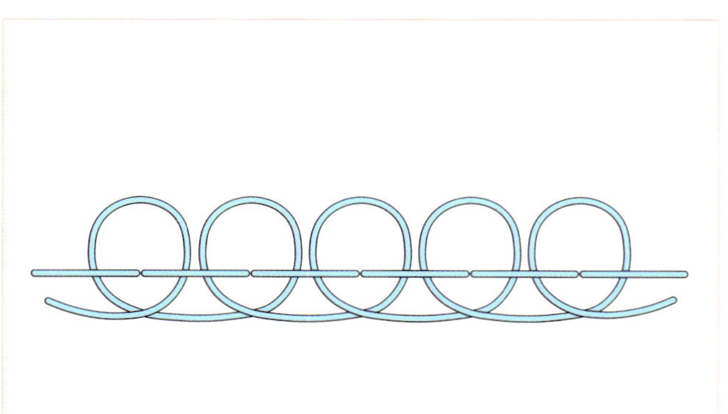

5 Try to keep each loop of the Pekinese stitch equal in size by tightening each loop as it is produced, and continuing along the back stitch.

▲▲ Detail from silk collar, RSN Collection COL.2

This detail shows Pekinese stitch in context. You can see the complete collar on page 49.

PLAITED BRAID STITCH

SURFACE; ELIZABETHAN; STUMPWORK.

This stitch consists of interlocking loops of thread which form a solid raised line of zigzag threads. The majority of the thread remains on the surface of the stitch.

Braid stitches have been popular through history, particularly in the Elizabethan era when many versions were used, but they were not well-documented. This means that historical references to 'braid stitch' may refer to any of the many versions (including heavy chain stitch on page 76), rather than specifically this stitch.

However, research has shown that this plaited braid stitch has its origins in the Bronze Age – a woman buried in South Jutland, Denmark in approximately 1300BC wears a blouse embellished with this stitch. More recently, this stitch was used extensively in Elizabethan embroidery, most commonly using metal threads. The V&A South Kensington holds many examples. These include a coif and forehead cloth which show a quintessentially Elizabethan design of flora, with curvilinear lines executed in plaited braid stitch using metal thread.

METHOD

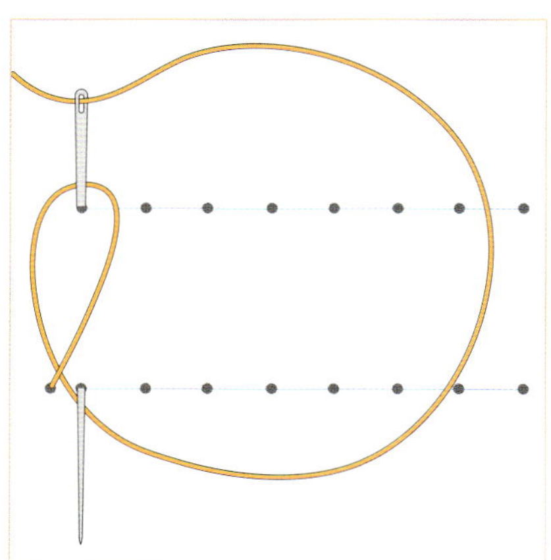

1 Bring your needle up at the end of the bottom guideline and make a loop with your thread. Take your needle down inside the loop on the top guideline (a short distance from the end), and back up on the bottom guideline, over your working thread. Your needle should emerge level with where it went down.

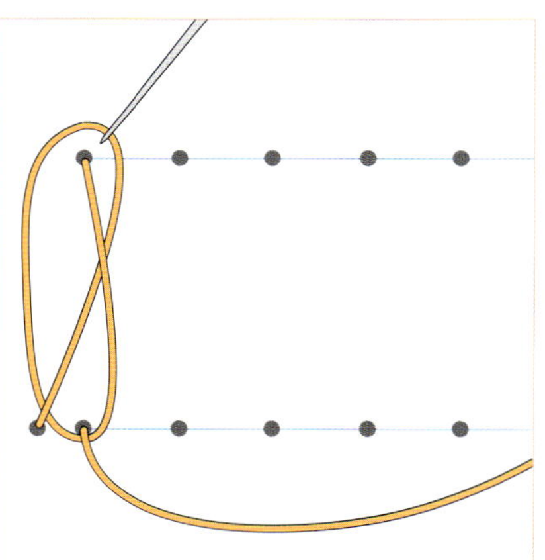

2 Use your needle to manipulate both sides of the braid so it resembles a pretzel.

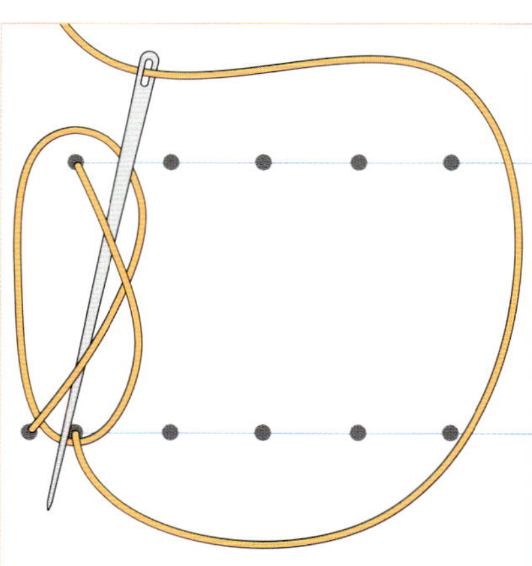

3 Motion 1: Slide your needle under where the threads form a cross, from top to bottom, without piercing the fabric. Your needle should go over the top outer loop of the pretzel, under the cross and over both your working thread and the bottom outer loop of the pretzel. Pull your thread through.

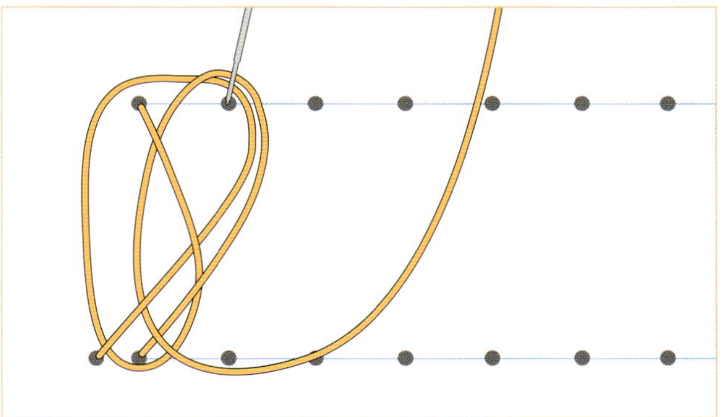

4 Use your needle to manipulate both loops of the braid so it resembles a pretzel. When ready, position the needle to enter the fabric on the top guideline.

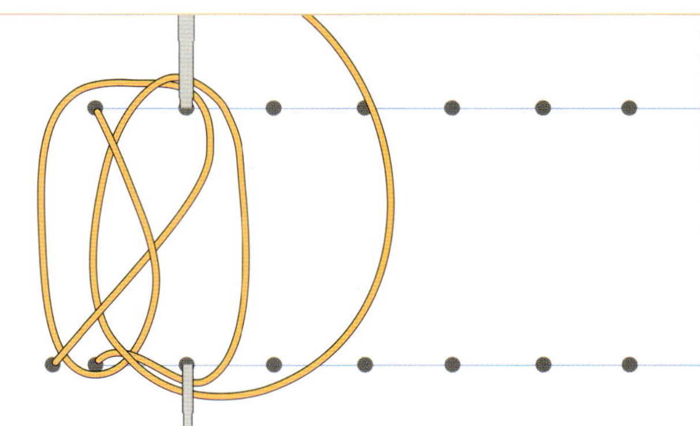

5 Motion 2: Take your needle into the fabric on the top guideline, inside two loops of thread. Bring it back up on the bottom guideline over your working thread and the outer loop. Ensure that the needle emerges outside of the diagonal thread of the pretzel. You may find it helpful to use a tapestry needle or mellor to open up the second loop in order to bring your needle up.

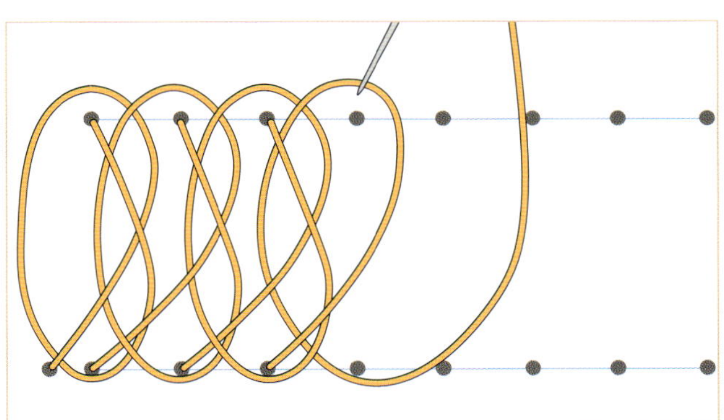

6 Continue working the braid by repeating Motion 1 and Motion 2, alternately. Adjusting the loops of the pretzel after each motion makes it easier.

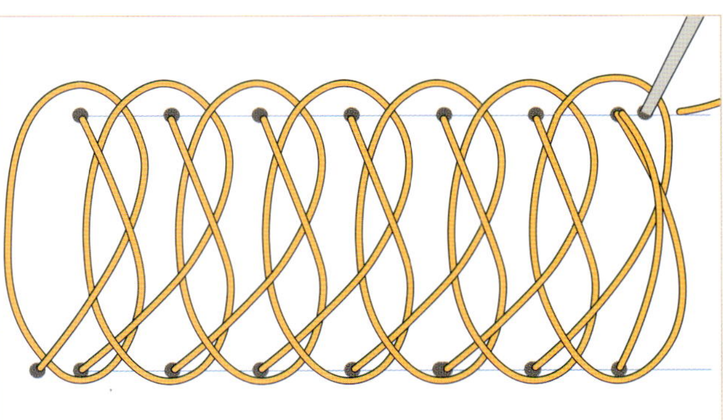

7 When you have reached the desired length, bring your needle out next to one of the loops and anchor it with a small stitch.

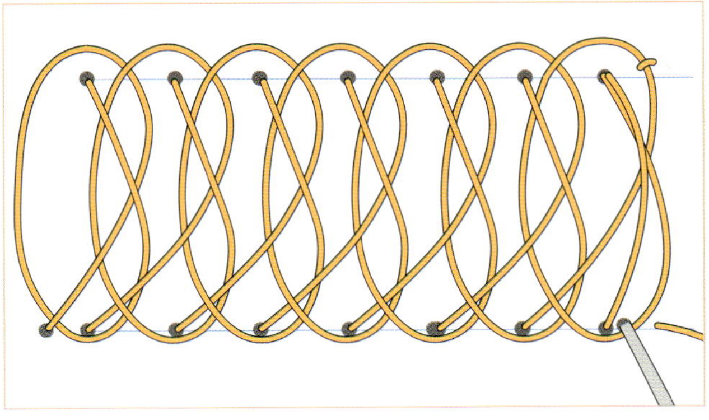

8 Repeat the small anchoring stitch on the other loop.

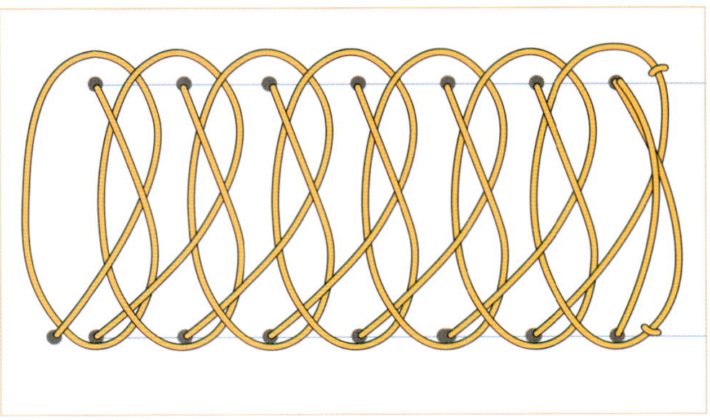

A completed length of plaited braid stitch.

PORTUGUESE KNOTTED STEM STITCH

Crewelwork; Surface; Mountmellick.

This stitch is not actually a knotted stitch. However it visually gives the impression of a knotted version of stem stitch (see pages 40–41) and it creates a textured, rope-like line when stitched with a thick twisted thread.

METHOD

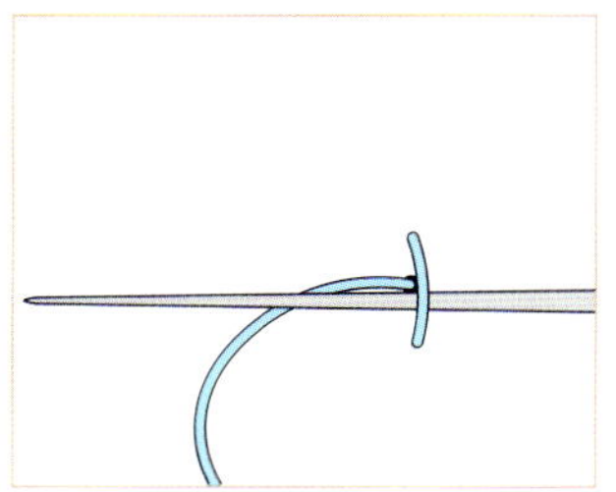

1 Start by working a stem stitch. After bringing up a needle halfway, slide the needle under the first stitch. Do not go through the fabric.

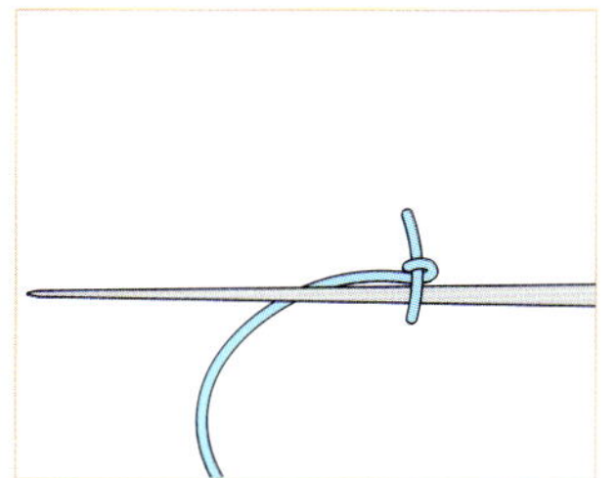

2 Pull the thread tight to wrap the stem stitch, and then slide the needle under the first stitch again. The second wrap sits just below the first wrap.

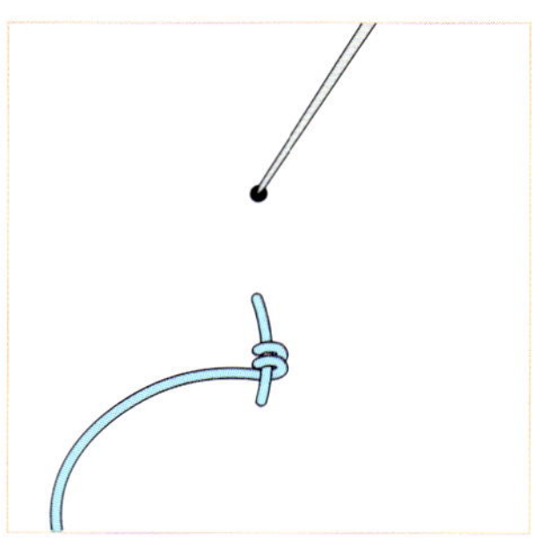

3 Pull the thread to tighten the wraps, and then start another stem stitch.

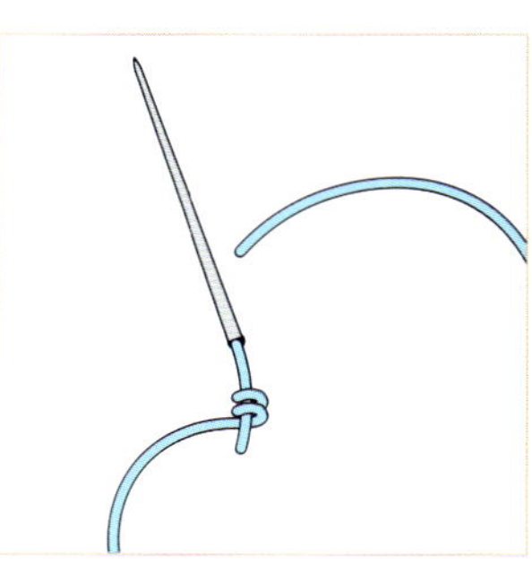

4 Keep the loop to the right of the needle and come up in the same hole at the end of the first stem stitch.

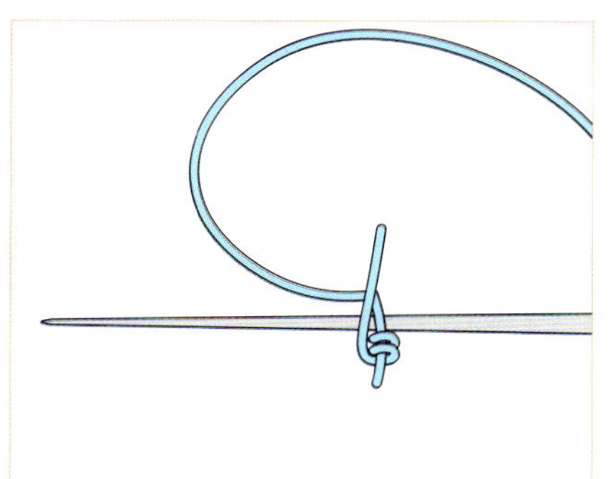

5 Slide the needle under both the first and the second stem stitches.

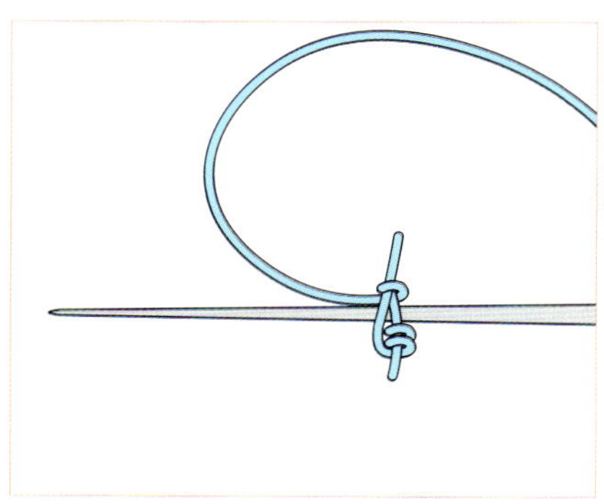

6 Work another wrap so that it lies in place below the first wrap. Make sure not to pick up the fabric when whipping.

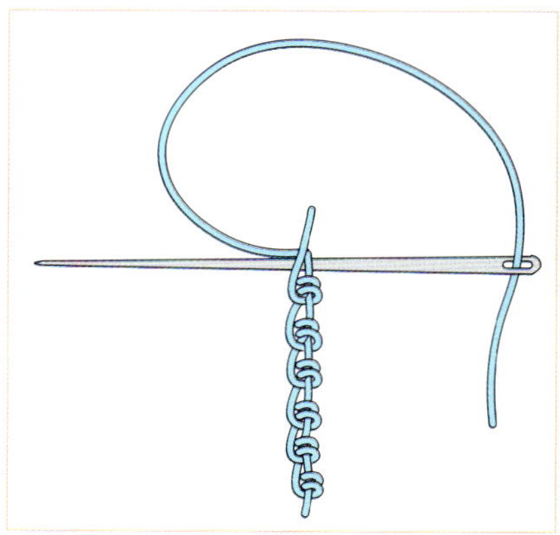

7 Repeat the procedures and continue stitching upwards.

QUAKER STITCH

Crewelwork; Surface.

Quaker stitch is a stem stitch (see pages 40–41) that has been combined with a split stitch (see page 39) to anchor the thread as it turns corners.

It was specifically developed to produce clear and defined lettering on the Quaker Tapestry, a 20th-century crewelwork piece that documents the history of Quakerism.

METHOD

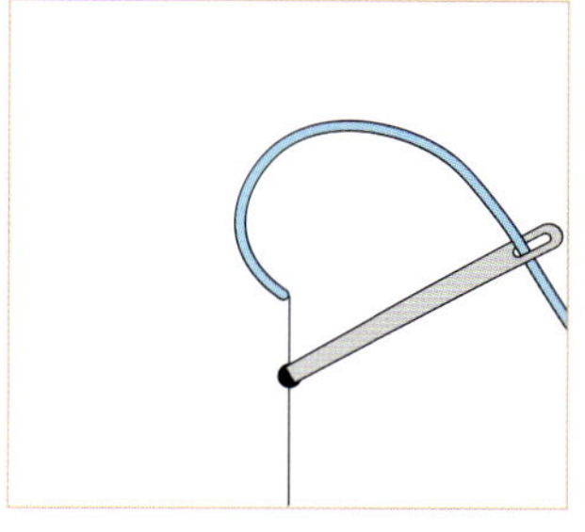

1 Bring your needle to the surface at the top of your marked line, then take the needle down through the fabric further along the marked line to make an initial stitch.

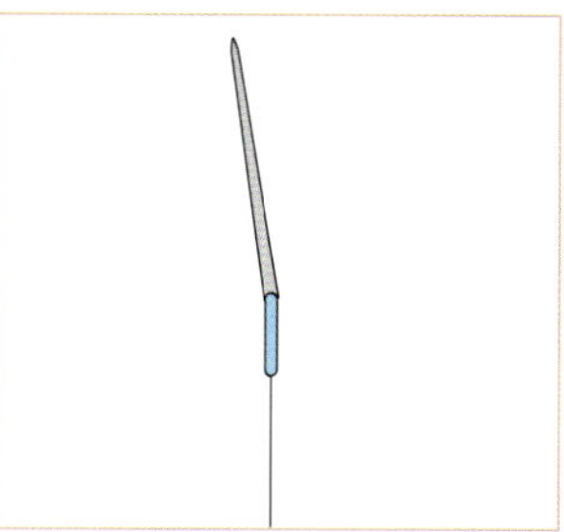

2 Bring the needle up again in the same hole as the initial stitch.

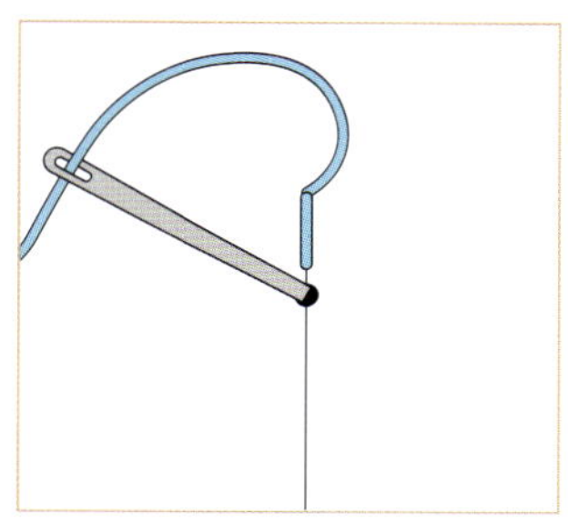

3 Push the needle down through the fabric one third longer than the first stitch. Draw the thread through, leaving a small loop on the left.

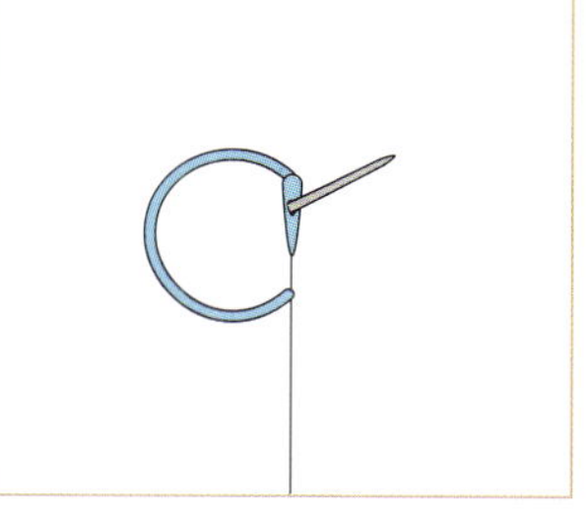

4 Keeping the loop on the left, bring the needle back to the surface, splitting the initial stitch in its centre.

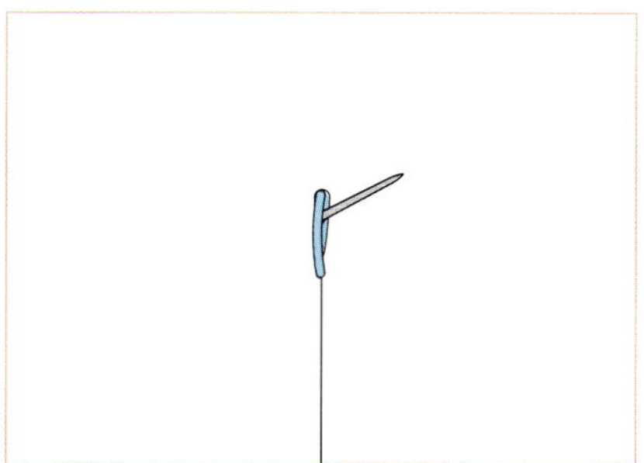

5 Pull through the slack on the loop with your underneath hand and draw the needle and thread to the surface.

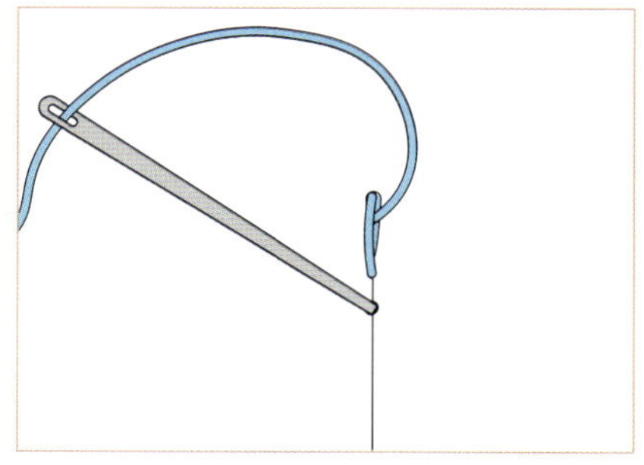

6 Repeat from step 3, bringing the needle up two-thirds of the way through the previous stitch, and then continue along your marked line to the end.

A completed line of Quaker stitch.

RAISED CHAIN BAND STITCH

Crewelwork; Stumpwork; Surface.

Also known as Raised chain band, or Raised chain stitch.

This is a decorative band stitch worked on a foundation ladder of parallel stitches.

METHOD

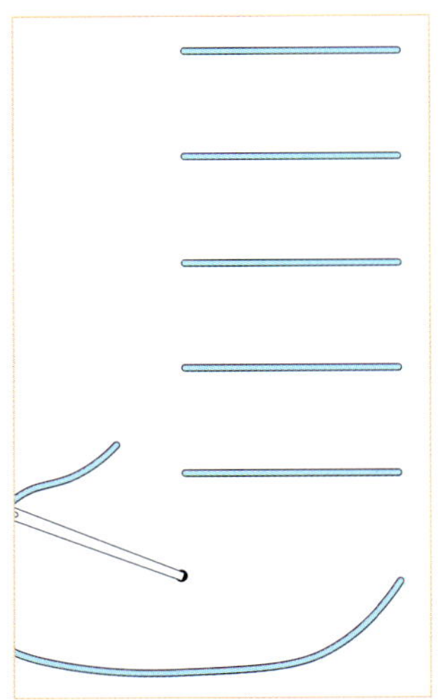

1 Start by stitching a ladder, bringing the needle up on alternate sides in order to make short stitches on the back.

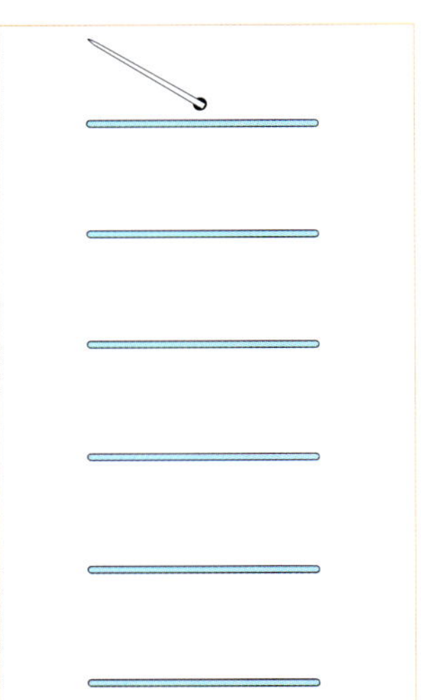

2 Thread a needle with another colour and bring the needle through at the top of the ladder in a central position.

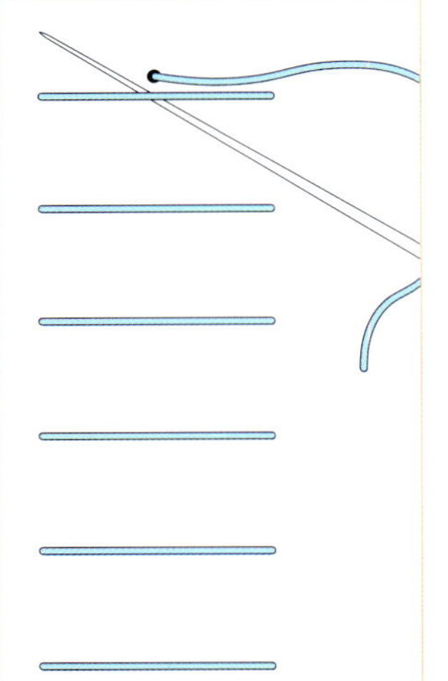

3 Draw the thread through and swap to a tapestry needle. Pass the needle upwards and left under the top stitch of the ladder.

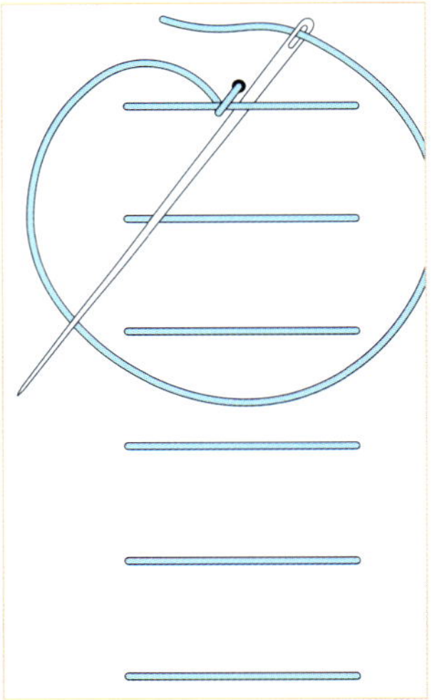

4 Draw the thread through and pass the needle downward on the right-hand side under the same top stitch of the ladder. Ensure the loop of the thread lies under the needle.

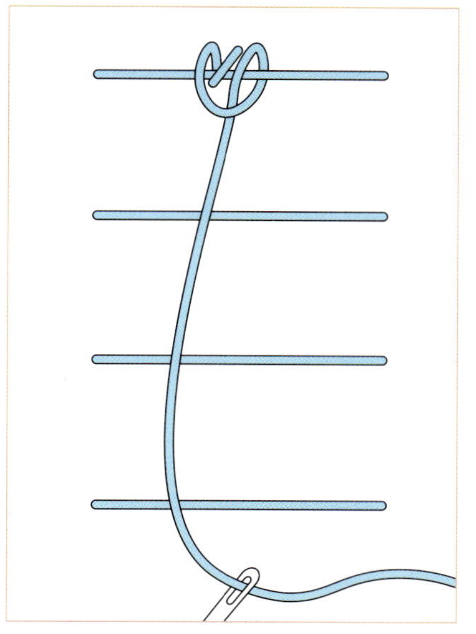

5 Pull the thread through and then down to create a 'Y' shape.

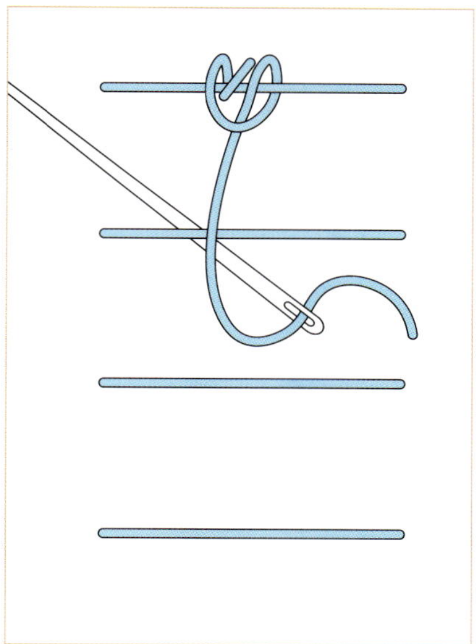

6 Pass the needle upwards and left under the second straight stitch of the ladder.

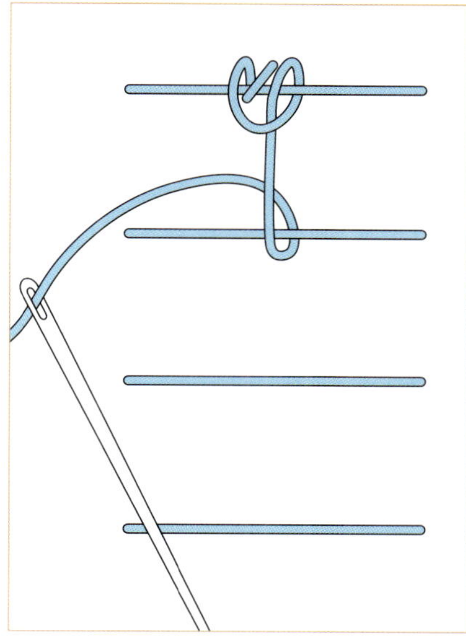

7 Draw the thread through.

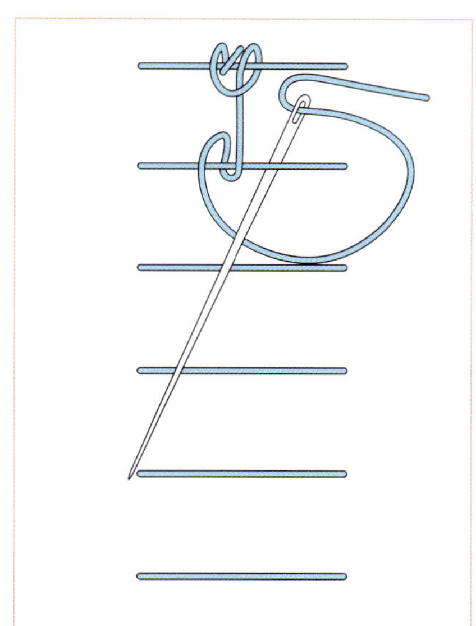

8 Pass the needle downward on the right-hand side under the same straight stitch. Ensure the loop of the thread lies under the needle as before.

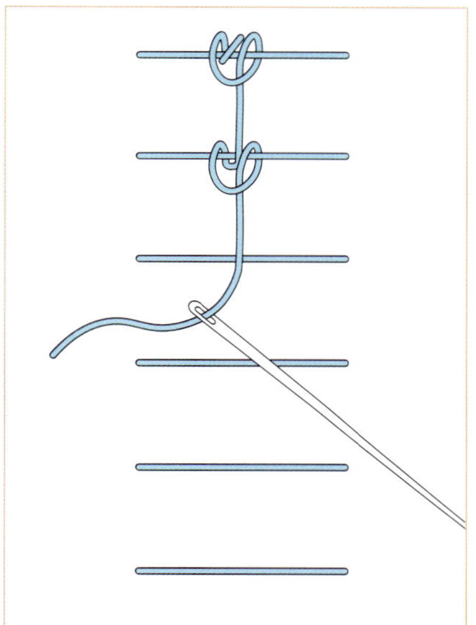

9 Pull the thread through and then down to create a 'Y' shape.

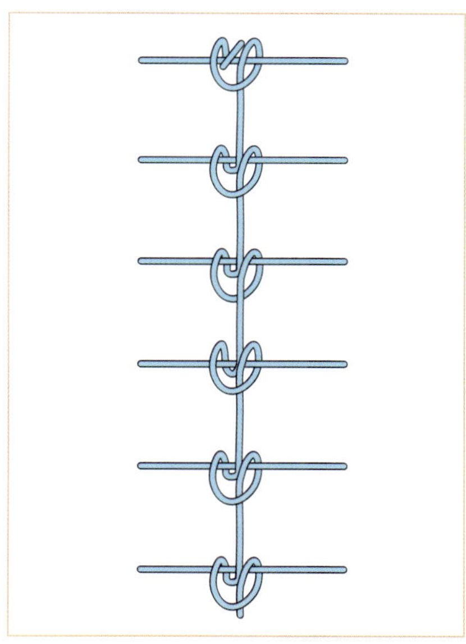

10 Repeat along the line to the bottom of the ladder.

ROPE STITCH (VARIATION)

Surface.

This stitch resembles a slanted satin stitch where one edge of the stitch is raised from the surface of the fabric by forming a small loop.

There is a different stitch, also called rope stitch, which more closely resembles a twisted rope.

The stitch seems to have evolved from twisted chain stitch (see pages 118–119): the RSN's 1880 *Handbook of Embroidery* by Letitia Higgin shows a version listed under both names. This is an elongated version of twisted chain stitch where the needle is taken down halfway along the length of the previous stitch, and slid underneath the loop so the stitches overlap.

METHOD

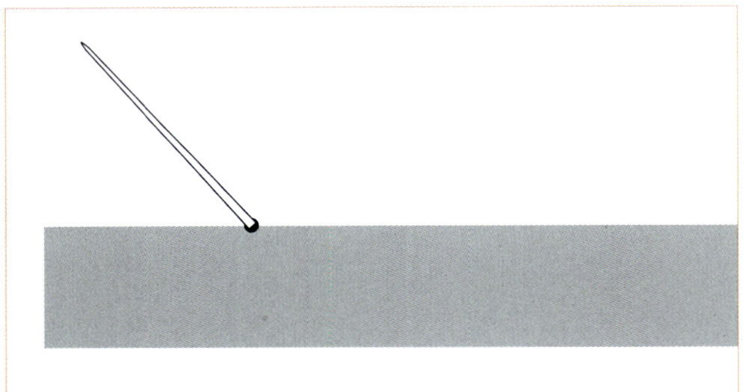

1 Draw a wide guideline. Bring your needle up on the top edge of the guideline, a short distance from the left end.

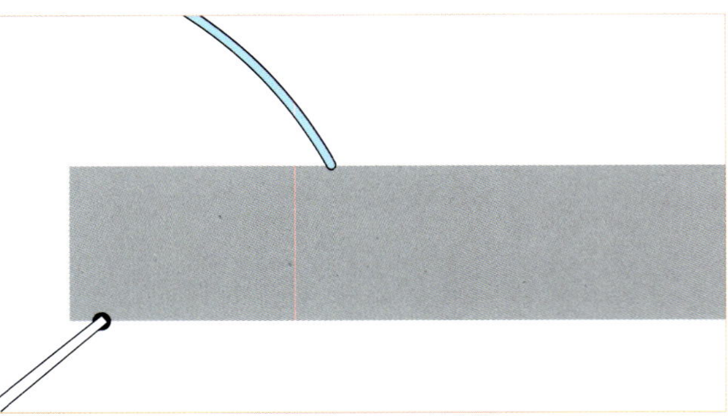

2 Take your needle down on the bottom edge of the guideline, at the left end.

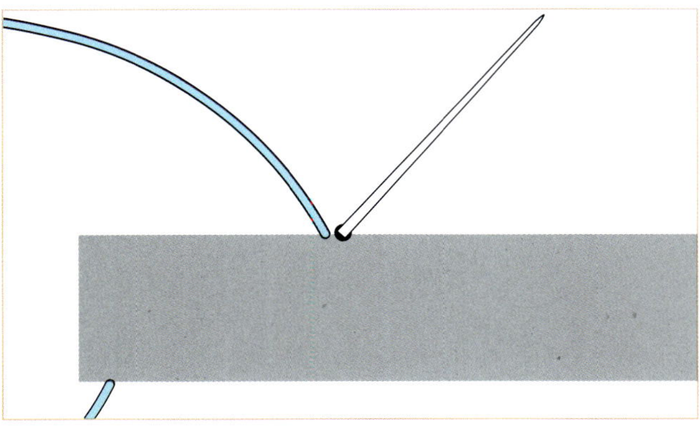

3 Bring your needle back up on the top edge, just to the right of the previous stitch.

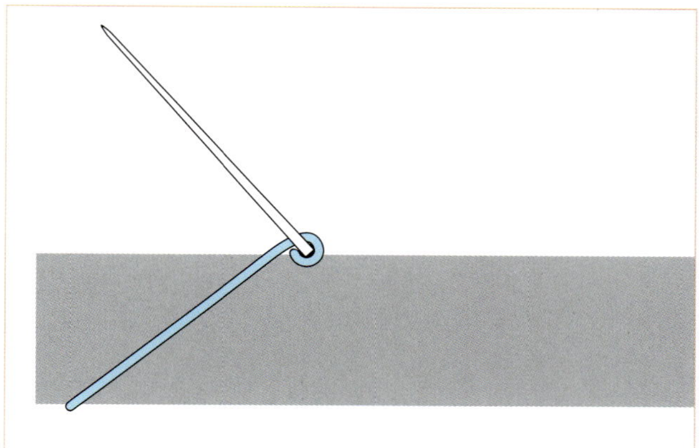

4 Loop the thread around the needle in an anti-clockwise direction and pull your thread taut against the needle.

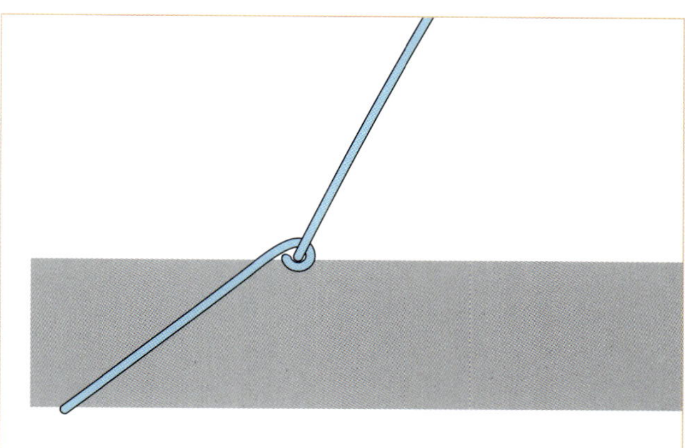

5 Pull the needle through.

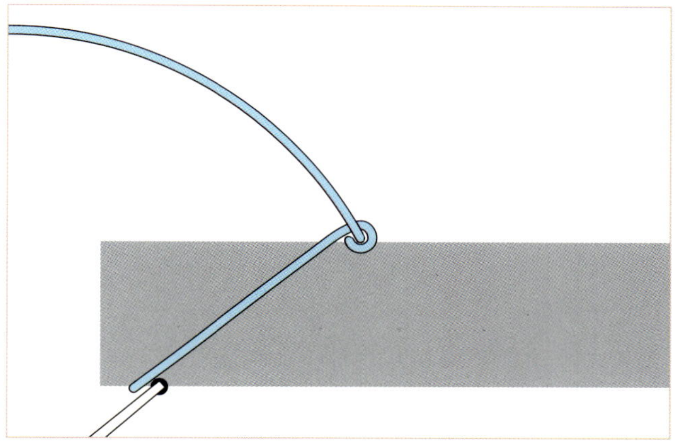

6 Take the needle down on the lower edge, just along from where the previous stitch was taken down.

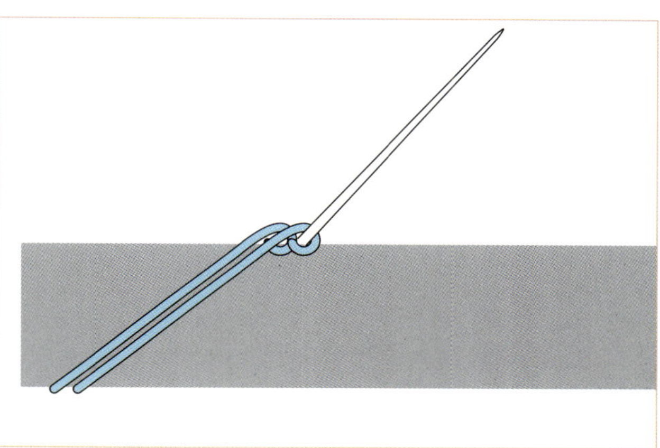

7 Bring the needle up on the top row and wrap the thread in the same way as before.

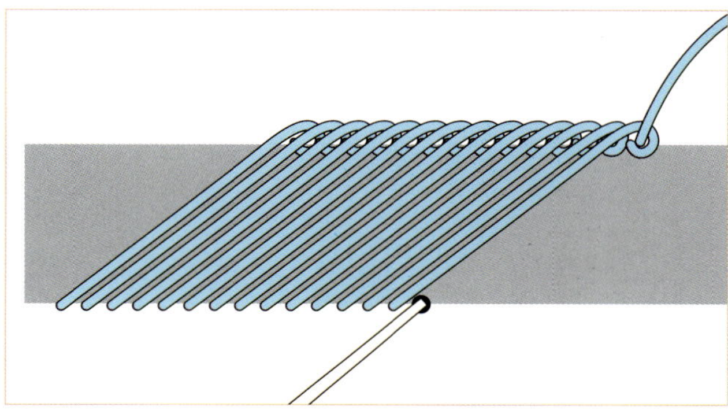

8 Continue working stitches in this way, taking care to keep your stitches parallel.

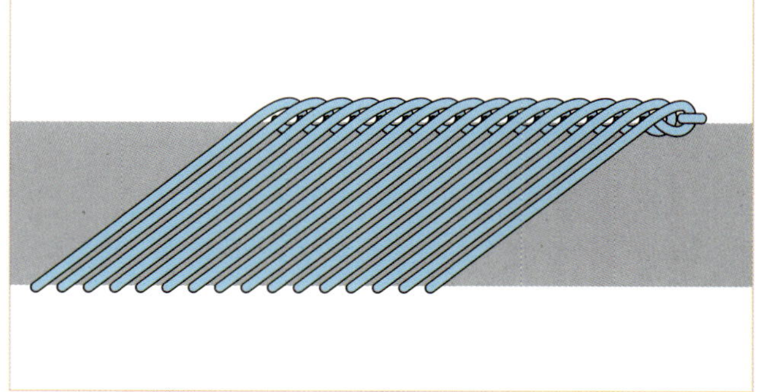

9 Finish the stitch by making a tiny anchoring stitch over the last loop.

SCROLL STITCH

SURFACE.

Also known as Single knotted line stitch.

This surface stitch consists of a line interspersed with small knots. It has similarities with coral stitch (see pages 60–61), but the working method is subtly different which results in a wavy rather than a straight line in between the knots.

Scroll stitch was certainly in existence by the early 20th century, as it features in stitch books from that era.

METHOD

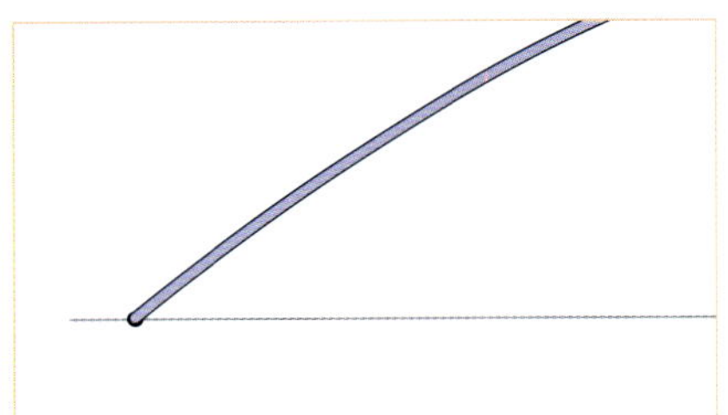

1 Bring your needle up at the left-hand end of your design line, and throw your thread forward.

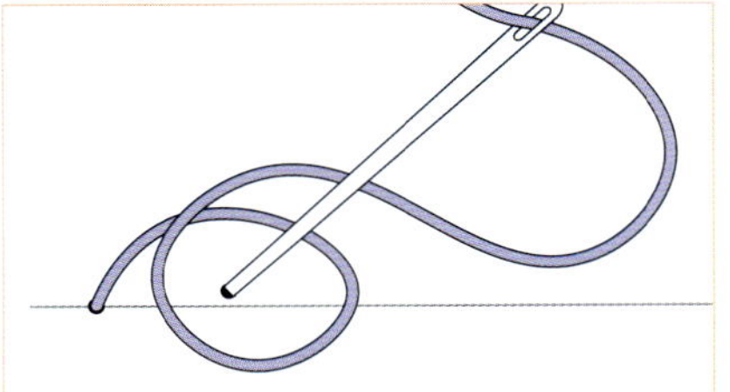

2 Form a loop, keeping your working thread uppermost and take your needle down inside the loop, just above the design line.

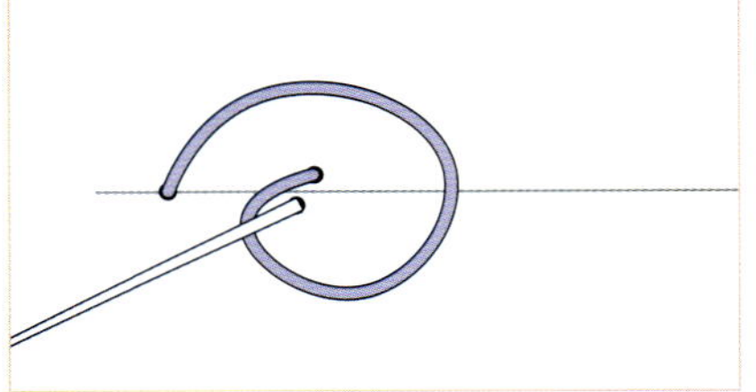

3 Bring your needle up just below the design line and slightly back from where it went down. Pull your thread taut against your needle.

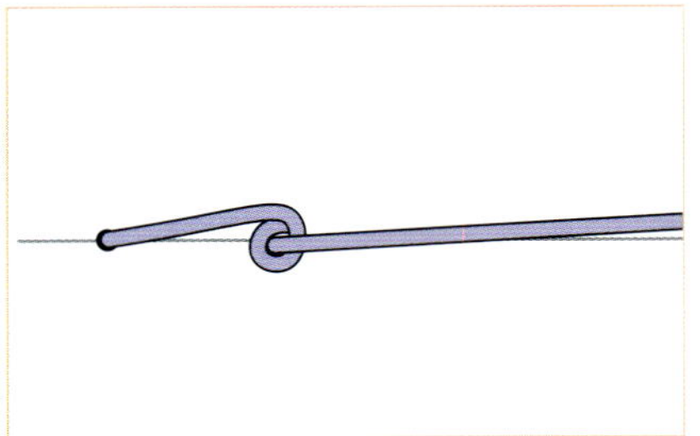

4 Pull your thread through to complete your first scroll stitch.

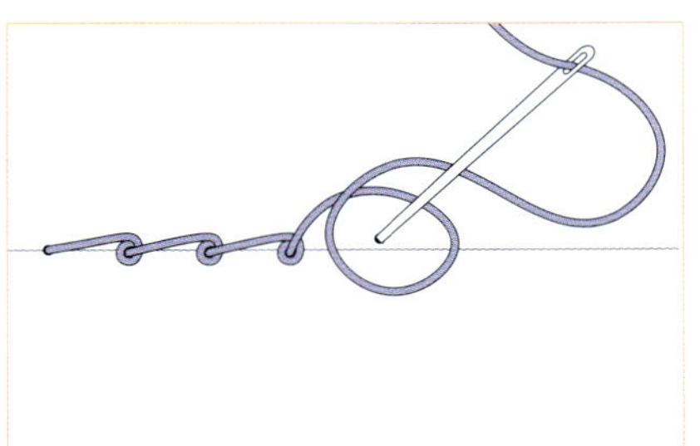

5 Repeat steps 1–3 to continue forming scroll stitches.

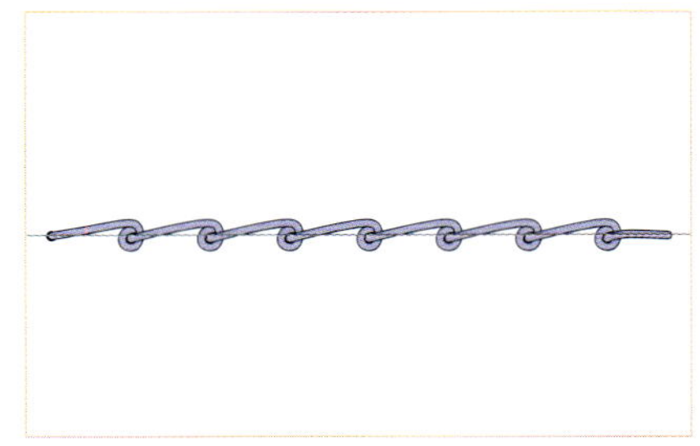

A completed line of scroll stitches.

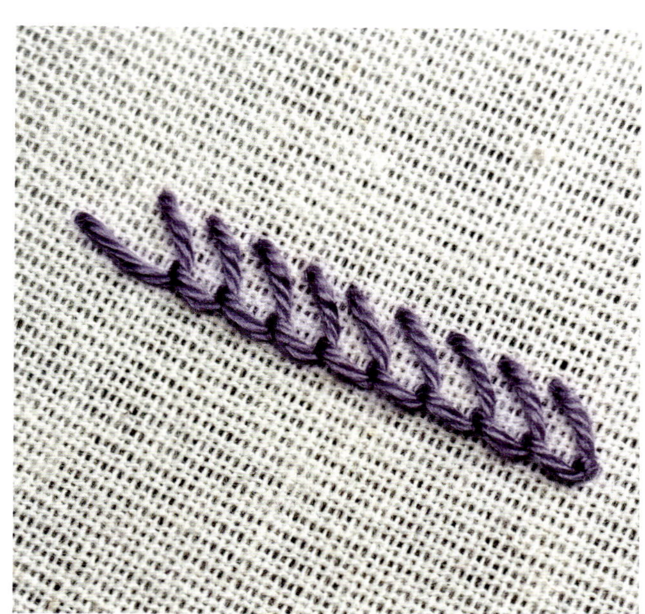

SINGLE FEATHER STITCH

Surface.

Also known as Point d'épine, Point Anglaise, or Slanted buttonhole stitch.

Single feather stitch is a simple variation of ordinary feather stitch (see pages 72–73) which produces a less intricate line. It is also a slanted version of blanket stitch (see page 18).

Unlike feather stitch, the looped stitches are only on one side of the line being followed; they are also all the same length, at the same angle and spaced evenly.

This stitch can either be worked in a straight line or it can be made to follow a gradual curve, with the looped edge facing the inside or the outside of the curve. It can also be worked in multiple rows with the lines of stitches touching along their lengths to make a lacy filling stitch.

METHOD

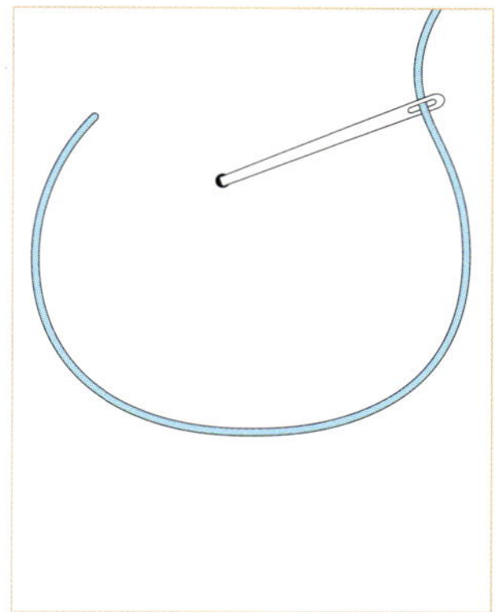

1 Working from the top down, bring the needle up on the line. Take the needle down on the right-hand side of the line.

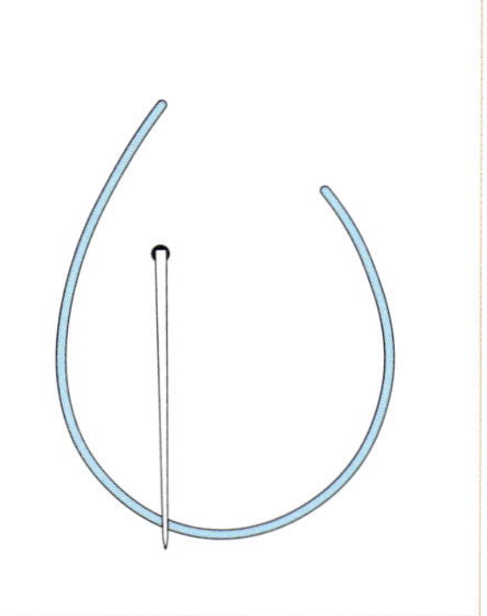

2 Leaving the working thread on the surface, bring the needle up again on the line, making sure the needle is inside the loop.

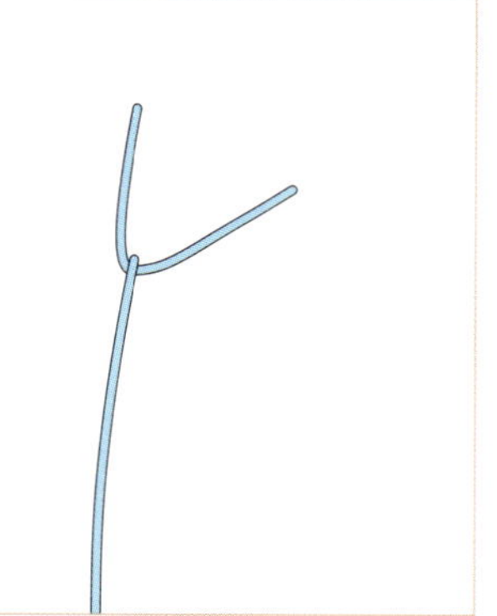

3 Tighten the thread against the needle before bringing the thread up to the surface.

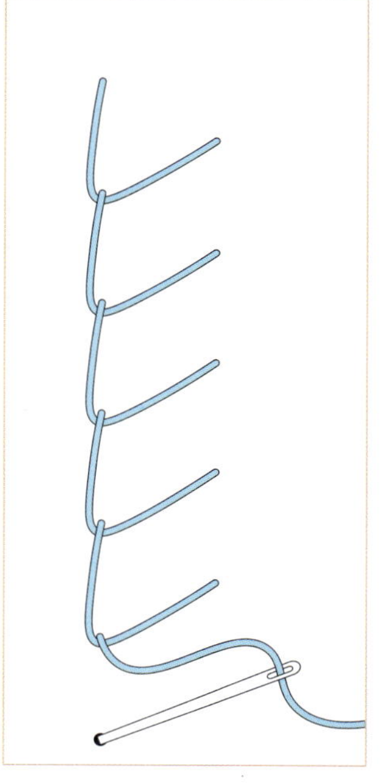

4 Repeat the last three steps and continue along the line.

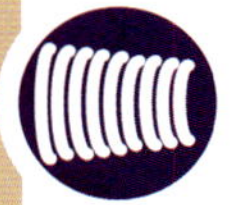

TAPERED TRAILING

Whitework.

Tapered trailing is, as its name suggests, a tapered version of trailing (see pages 116–117). It consists of a core of laid threads which are completely covered with small couching stitches. The number of padding threads varies so that the shape alters in thickness: you can start with any number of core threads and work down to very few or none.

METHOD

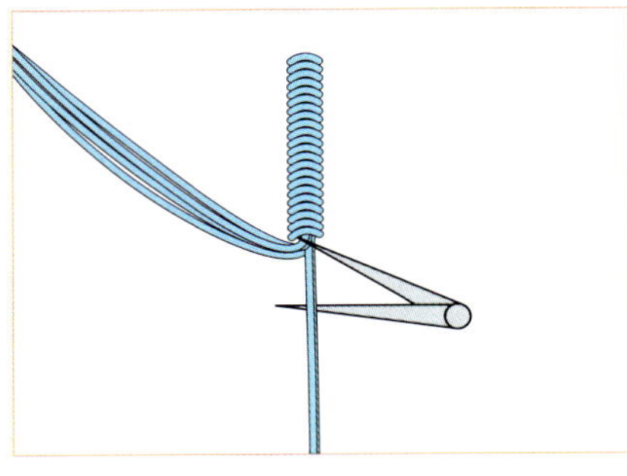

1 Begin working your trailing stitches. Angle your needle out from under the core threads and back underneath them with each stitch. To gradually taper the line, separate the core threads, lift the top threads out of the way and carefully snip a few of the strands closest to the fabric.

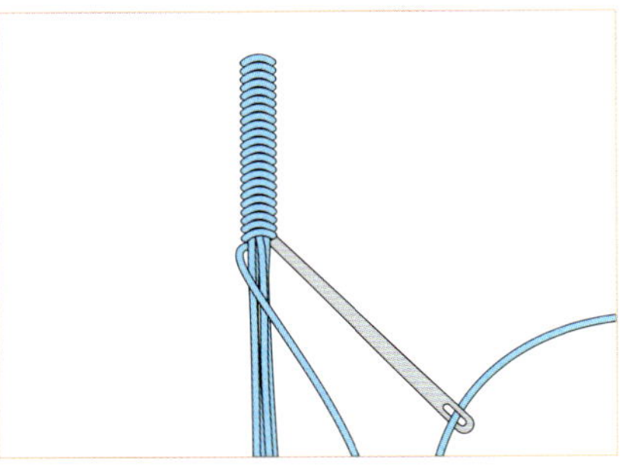

2 Continue to couch over the remaining core threads, holding the core threads in place to keep them taut. Make sure no fluff shows where the threads were cut.

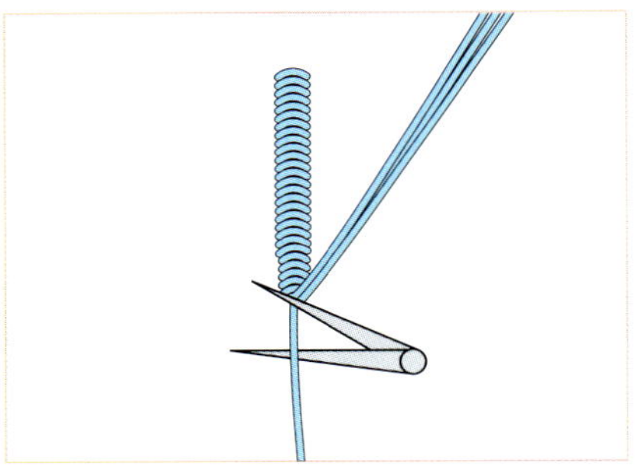

3 Repeat the trimming process as many times as necessary, to gradually taper your line. Make sure you always trim the underneath threads.

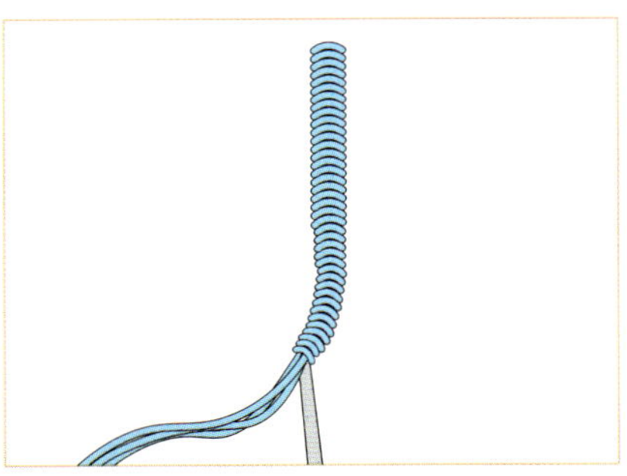

4 When you are near the end of the line, take your last core thread(s) to the back of the fabric, finish stitching to the end and secure your couching thread.

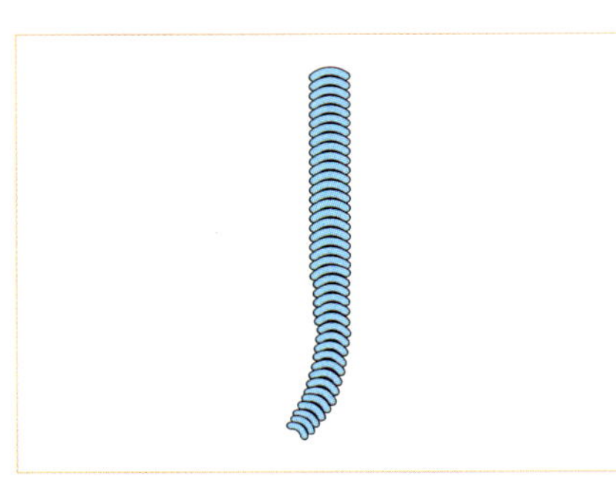

5 On the back, trim your final core thread(s) as close as possible to the fabric so that no shadows will show on the front.

THORN STITCH

Surface.

Thorn stitch is a decorative form of couching where a long thread is held down by an off-centred cross. It is often used to depict thorny stems or ferns, hence its name.

Any type of embroidery thread can be used to work this stitch: both couched and couching elements can be worked with a single thread or you could use a different type or colour of thread for the pairs of crossing stitches.

The example shown has been worked with the thorns crossing the stem; you can instead curve the end of the thorn around the stem to give a more naturalistic appearance.

METHOD

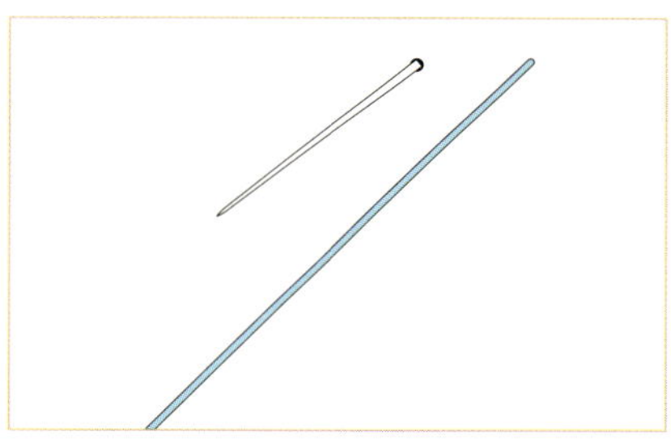

1 Bring the needle up and work a long straight stitch. Then bring the needle up near the end of the first long stitch.

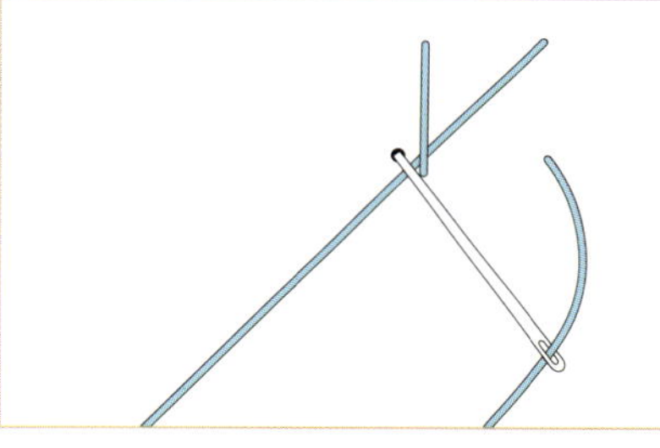

2 Work a pair of diagonal stitches so that they cross over the first long stitch.

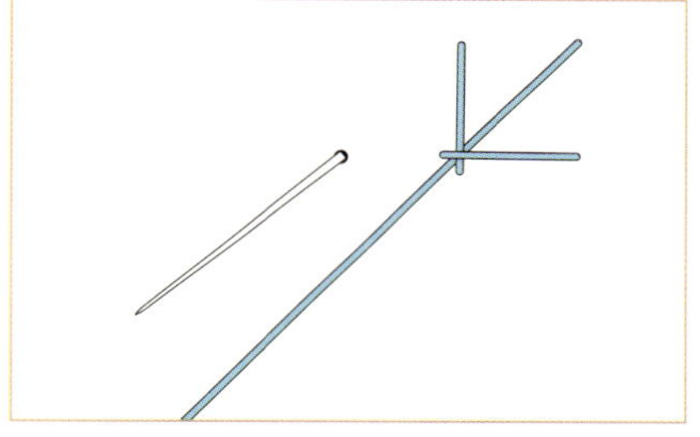

3 Bring the needle up again to begin the next diagonal stitch.

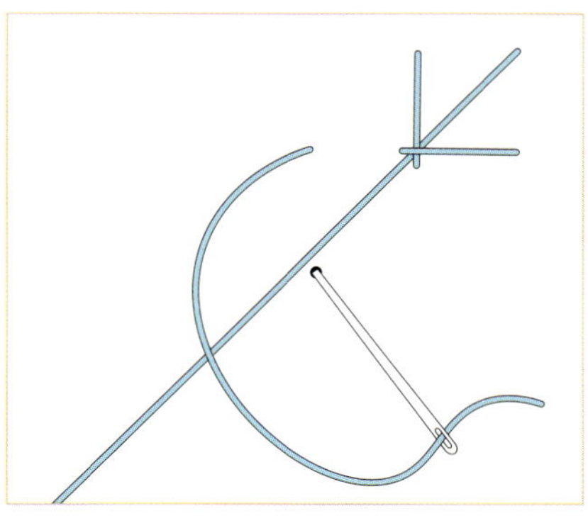

4 Work a diagonal stitch, crossing over the first long stitch.

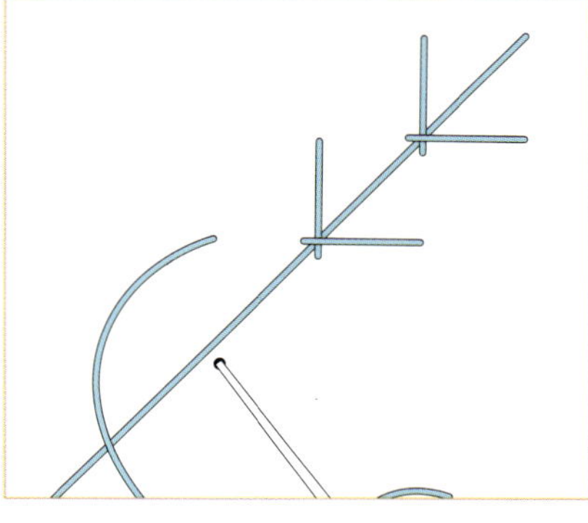

5 Continue working pairs of diagonal stitches as required.

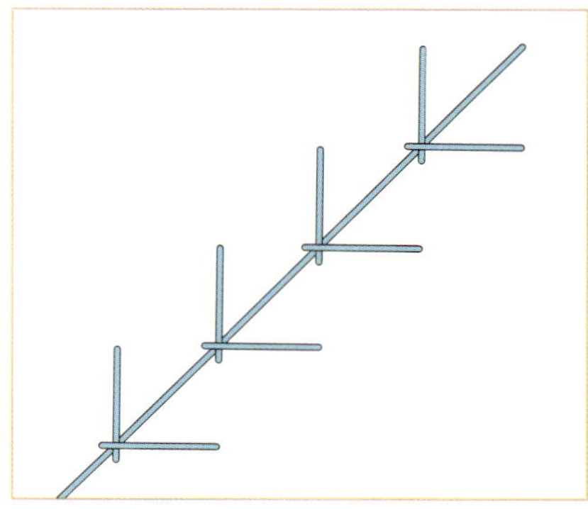

6 The pairs of diagonal stitches create the 'thorns' at each side of the long stitch.

THREADED BACK STITCH

SURFACE.

Also known as Double threaded back stitch.

Threaded back stitch consists of a foundation of ordinary back stitch (see page 16) with either one or two additional threads woven back and forth under the back stitch. If a single thread is threaded, the line has a wave effect; if two threads are used the line of back stitch has a scalloped effect on both sides. Some authors call this latter version double threaded back stitch.

It is often used for outlining shapes or as a border; each component can be worked in a different thread or colour to create different effects.

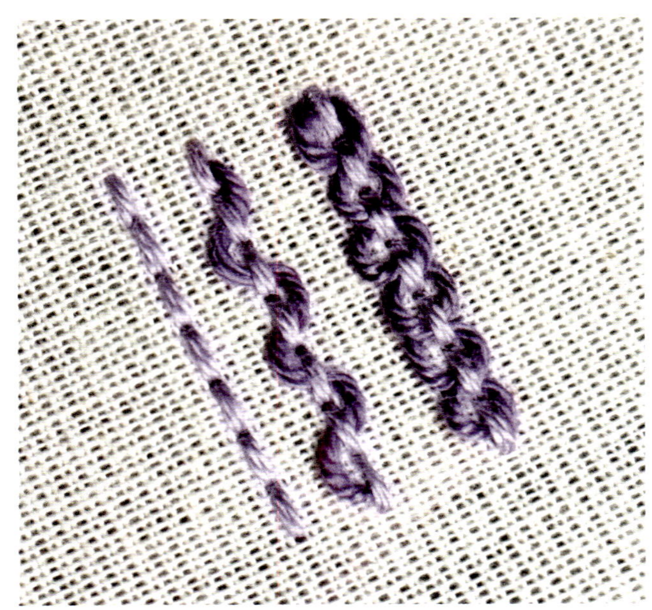

METHOD

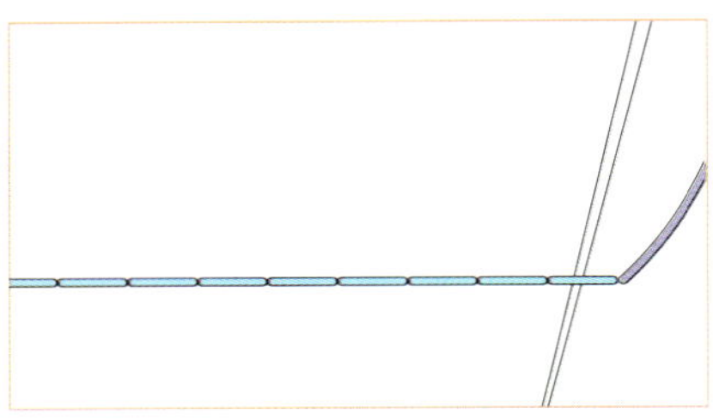

1 Work a foundation row of back stitch. Using a different thread, come up at the end of the back stitch. Slide the needle under the back stitch without piercing the fabric.

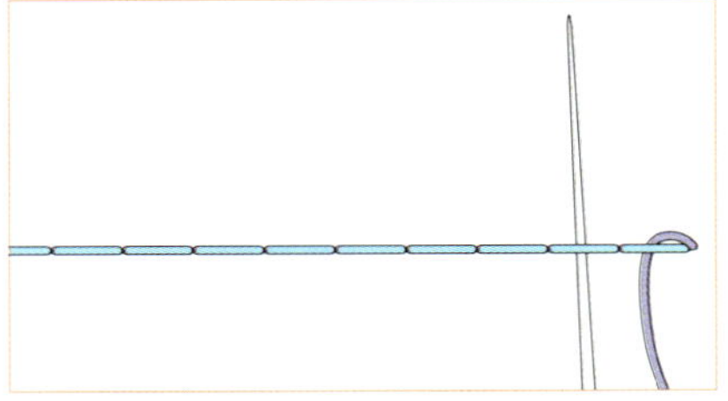

2 Starting from the same side of the back stitch line, slide the needle under the second back stitch.

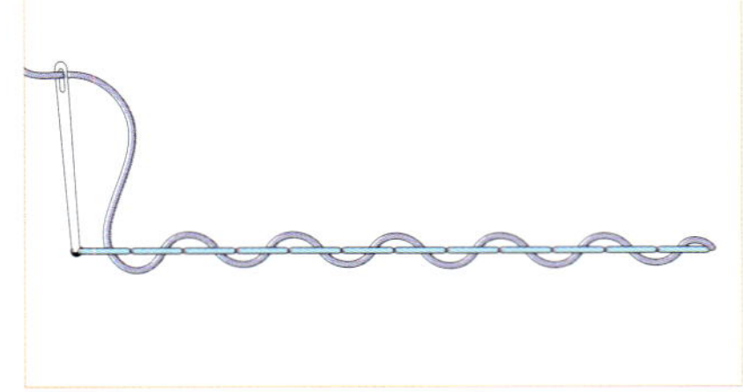

3 Pass the thread back and forth under the back stitches, and take down the needle at the end of the back stitch.

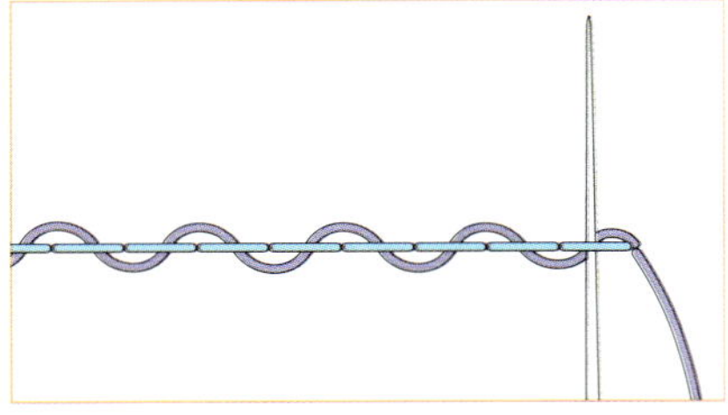

4 A second thread can be worked from the same starting point: slide the needle under the first back stitch in the opposite direction from the previous threaded line.

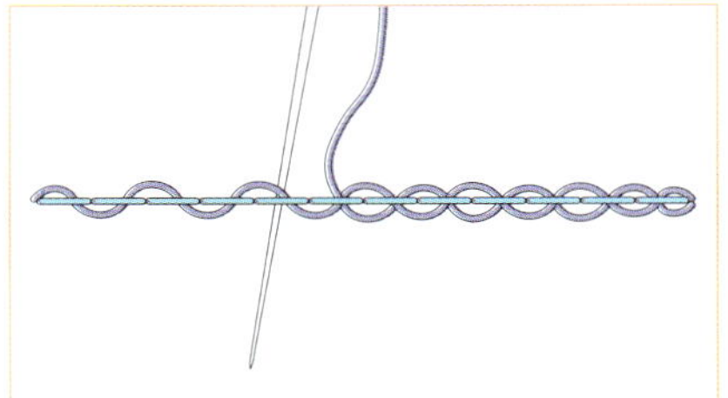

5 Now pass the needle under the second back stitch. The second threading fills in the spaces left on the first threading so that the stitch is symmetrical. Work the second threading alternately back and forth.

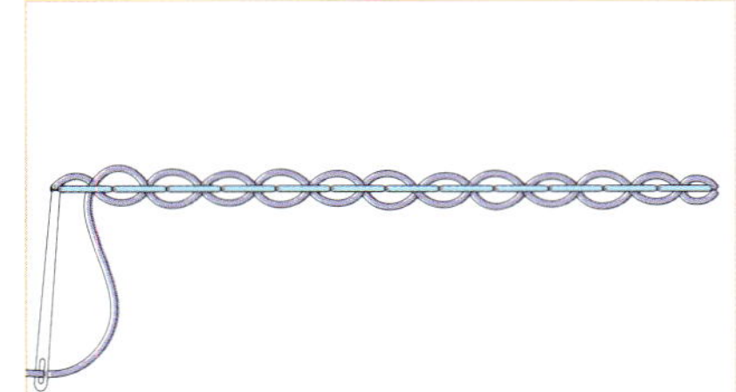

6 Take the needle down at the end of the back stitch.

THREADED HERRINGBONE STITCH

SURFACE.

This stitch is constructed from a line of herringbone stitch, with a thread woven over the crosses and under the length of the stitch. The threading can be done with the same colour as the original thread or a contrasting colour of thread.

For more background, see the entry for herringbone stitch on page 30.

For threading, use a tapestry needle.

METHOD

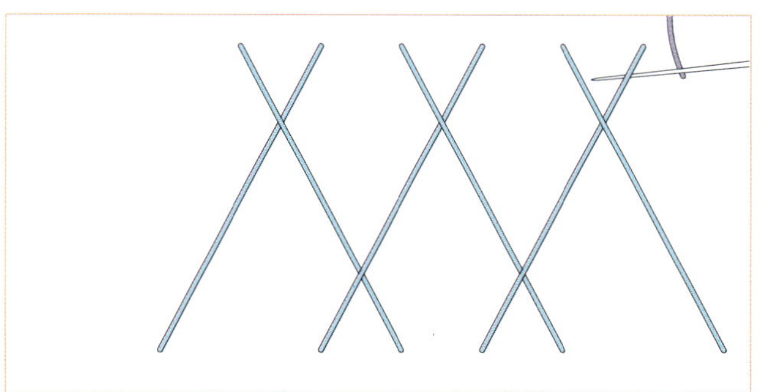

1 Work a row of herringbone stitch. Bring the tapestry needle up to the right of the top intersections, just below the top of the stitching, then slide the needle under the right diagonal stitch and over the left diagonal stitch, above the cross.

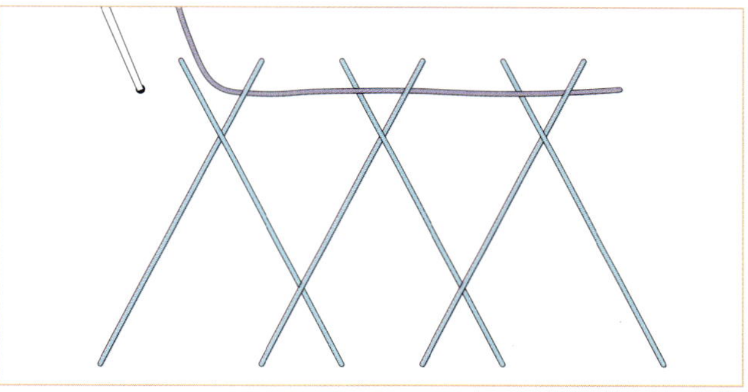

2 Continue sliding the needle under the stitches in the same way. At the end, take the needle through the fabric to the left of the top intersection.

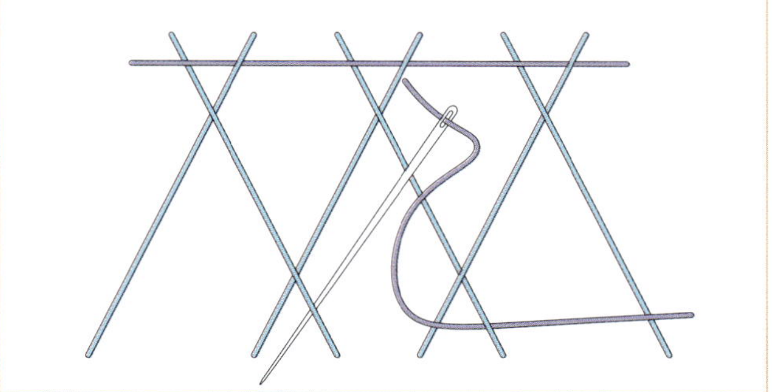

3 For the second threading, bring the new thread up to the right of the bottom part of the herringbone stitch, just above the bottom of the stitching, then work in the same way as the first threading.

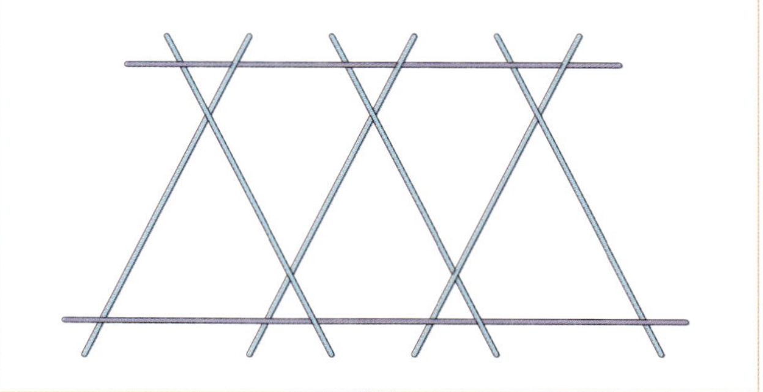

A completed row of threaded herringbone stitch.

TRAILING

WHITEWORK; AYRSHIRE.

Also known as Trailing couching stitch, Overcast stitch, Cording, Satin couching, Cord stitch, or Overcasting.

A precise overcast stitch producing a bold smooth outline over a thread core, suitable for lettering, monogramming and crisp edges.

For a tapered version, see tapered trailing on page 112.

The earliest references to trailing date from the 1970s although it is hard to be sure whether this was the start of the use of multiple core threads, or the first time it was recorded and named.

METHOD

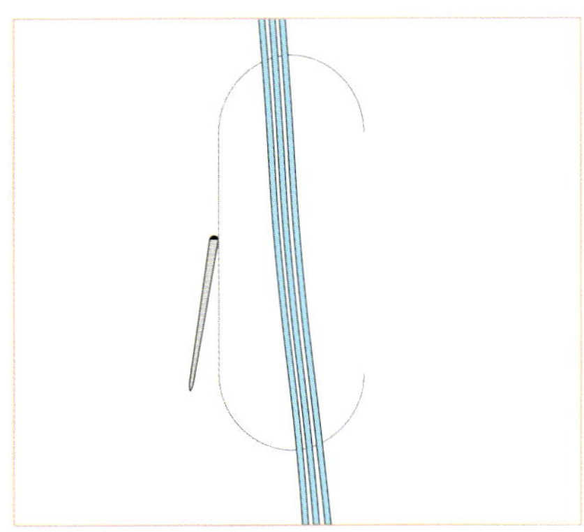

1 Begin part way along the line, preferably on a straight section. Decide how many threads to use as the core. Bring the needle up just one side of the line.

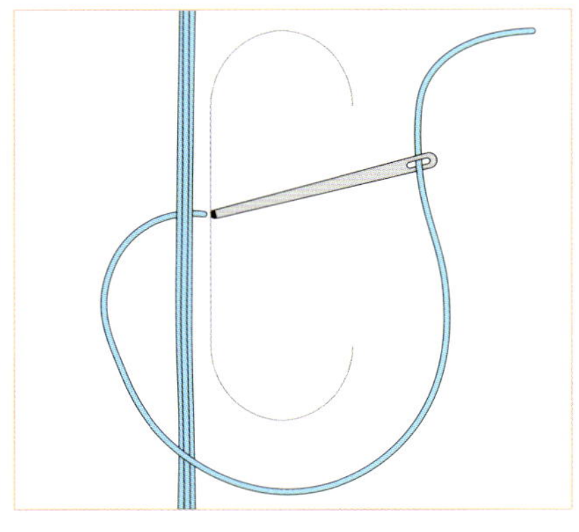

2 Bring the needle over the core threads and take it down just on the other side of the line. The stitch should be at right angles to the line. Pull fairly tight on the first stitch and maintain the tension as you work the next stitch.

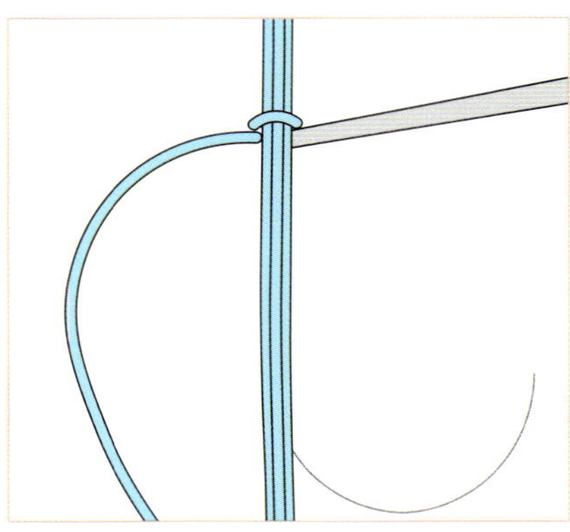

3 For each subsequent stitch, bring the needle up from underneath the core threads and take it down underneath them. The stitches should be as close together as you can manage, so as not to let any of the core threads show through.

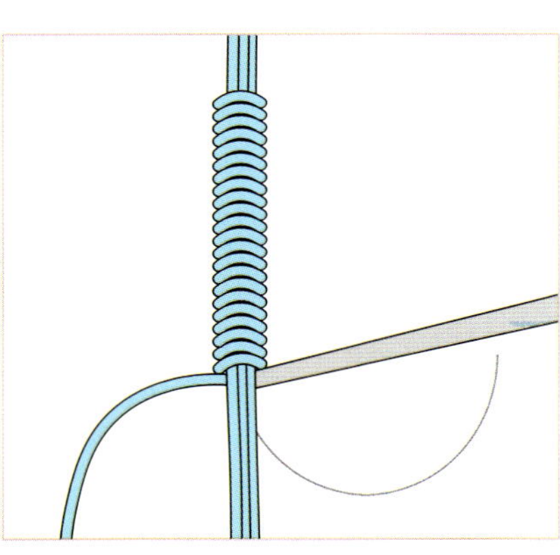

4 As you turn a corner, change the angle of the stitches so that they stay at right angles to the line at all times. They will be spaced a little further apart on the outside curve and even closer together on the inside curve.

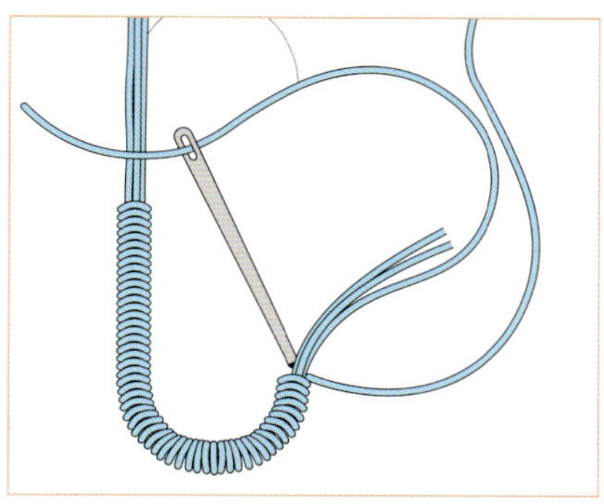

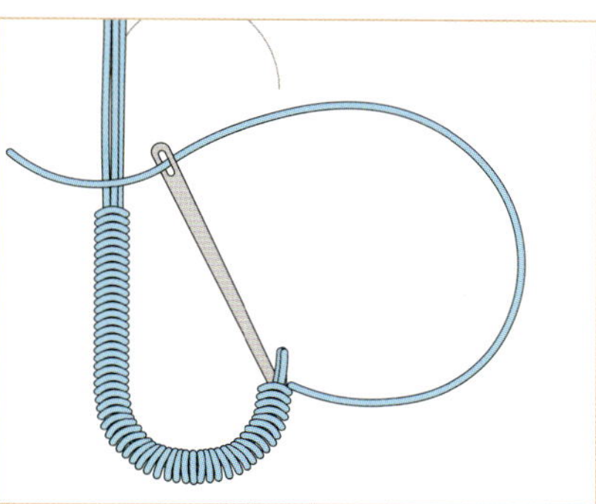

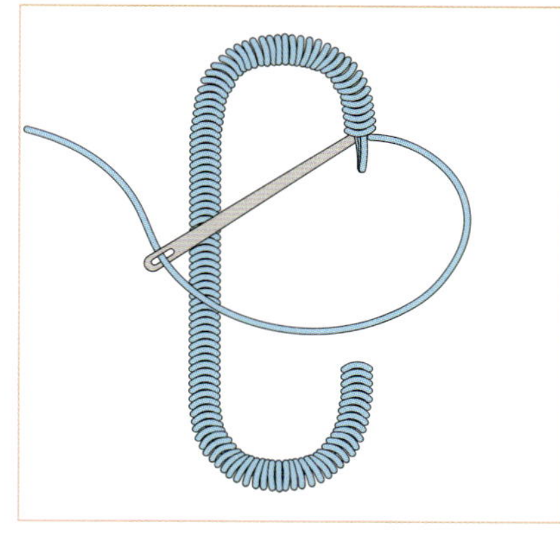

5 To finish a line, stop stitching just before the end of the line. Thread one of the core threads into a large chenille needle and take the needle down at the end of the line to plunge the thread through. Bring it up a short distance away.

6 Repeat for the rest of the core threads and then continue to stitch. Holding the core threads to keep some tension helps.

7 Finish stitching to the end of the line, angling the needle out from under the core threads and back underneath them with each stitch.

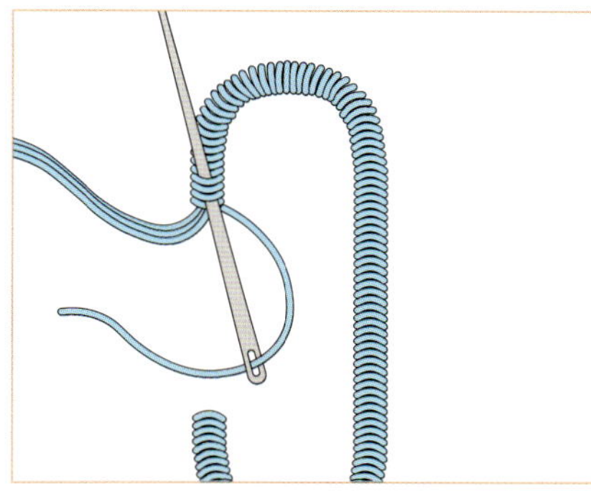

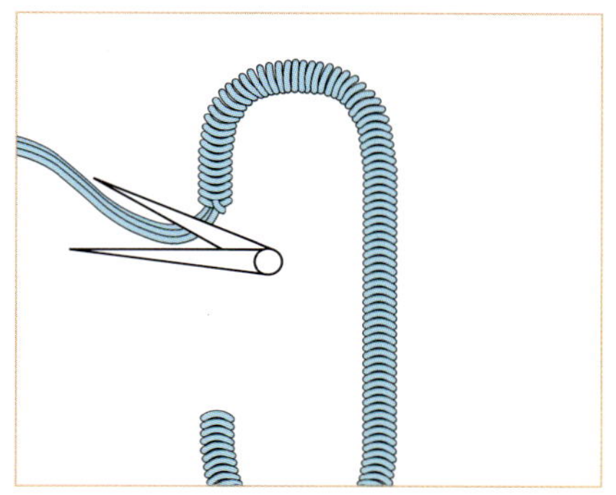

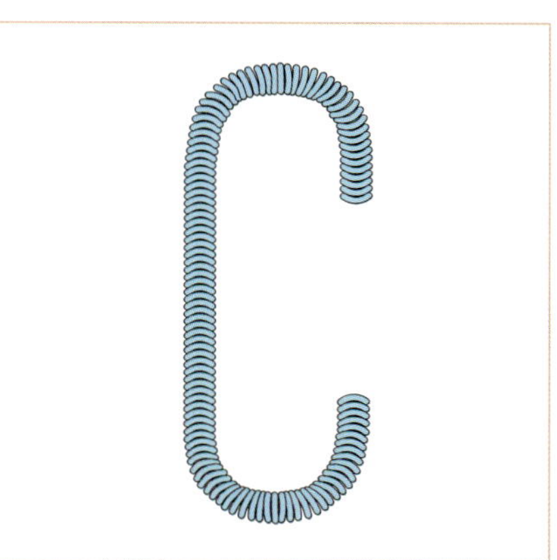

8 If the trailing finishes away from any other stitching, turn to the back to cast off. Run the needle underneath the last few stitches, pull the threads through and trim.

9 On the back, trim the core threads as close as possible to the fabric so that no shadows will show on the front. Trim each thread individually for the neatest result.

A finished example.

◂◂ Detail of bed jacket, RSN Collection COL.42

An example of another overcast stitch; to achieve this highly raised satin stitch (see page 37), the motif would have been worked in a number of layers. Each layer of padding is worked at a different angle, normally 90 degrees, from the layer below. The satin stitch is also worked at a different angle from the top layer of padding.

TWISTED CHAIN STITCH

SURFACE.

Also known as Charles II stitch.

This line stitch has a twisted, rope-like effect as the uppermost threads on each part lie diagonally across it. It is worked in a similar way to chain stitch (see page 22) with two crucial distinctions: each loop of the chain is twisted, and the needle is taken down outside of the previous loop. Some authors take the needle down slightly wide of the design line; others tuck it slightly under the stitch just made for a sleeker look.

The stitch can also be worked as an isolated stitch, either singly or in groups.

The stitch was evidently in use in the 17th century, as it features on a partlet (a garment used to fill in a low-cut gown), currently held by the V&A South Kensington. It is worked in silver-gilt thread to form the narrow tendrils which protrude from the quintessentially Elizabethan plant stems.

Victorian authors indicate that the stitch was also known as Charles II stitch: 'not that he embroidered with it himself; but it is found in work of the time of Charles II', according to *Art-needlework for Decorative Embroidery* from 1879, although we don't know of any examples from this era.

The stitch seems to be the forerunner of rope stitch (variation) on pages 108–109: the RSN's 1880 *Handbook of Embroidery* by Letitia Higgin shows an elongated version listed under both names where the needle is taken down halfway along the length of the previous stitch, and slid underneath the loop so the stitches overlap. By 1885, Higgin shows a more contracted version (again using both names) which is very similar to the modern version of rope stitch, and by the time of 1898's *Corticelli Home Needlework* the stitch is no longer being called twisted chain stitch, and has become the modern version of rope stitch. Twisted chain stitch seems at some point to have contracted so that both sides of the chain are of similar length.

The picture at the top shows (top right to bottom left) the 1880 version of twisted chain stitch, the modern version with the end tucked under, and the modern version with the end protruding.

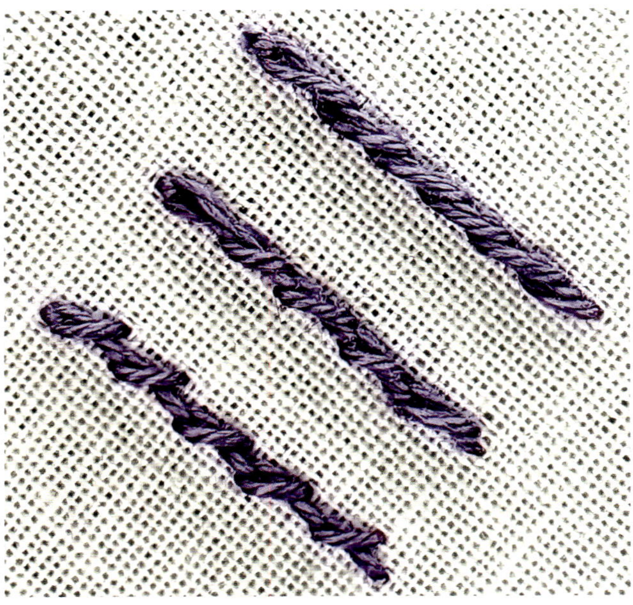

METHOD

1 Bring your needle up slightly above the design line.

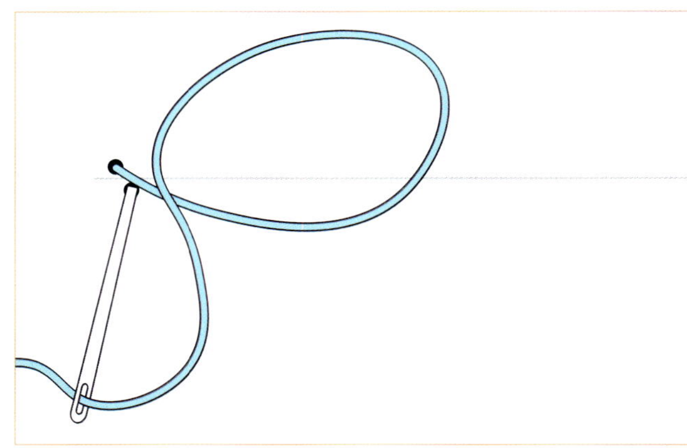

2 Leave a loop on the surface as if you were working a standard chain stitch, and then take your needle down outside the loop, just below the design line and slightly forward of where your needle came up. Your working thread should cross itself.

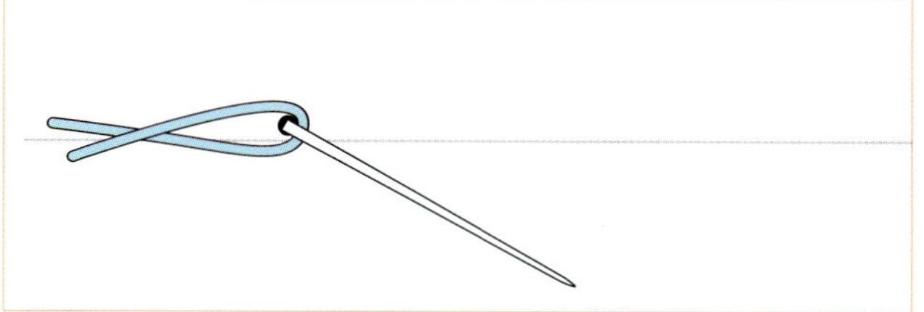

3 Bring your needle up inside the loop, slightly above the design line and a stitch length ahead. Tighten your loop against your needle.

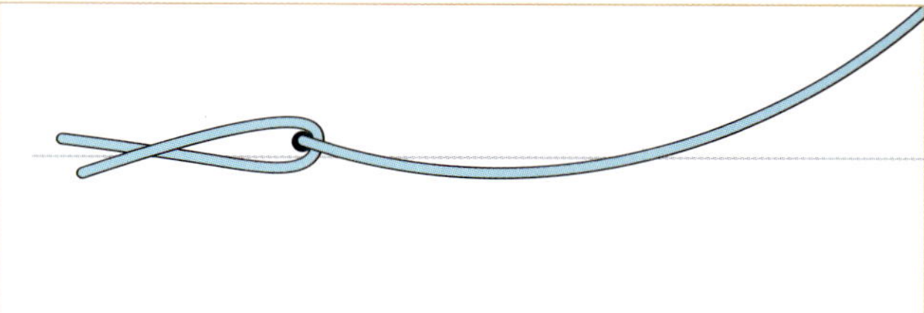

4 Pull through to form your first twisted chain stitch.

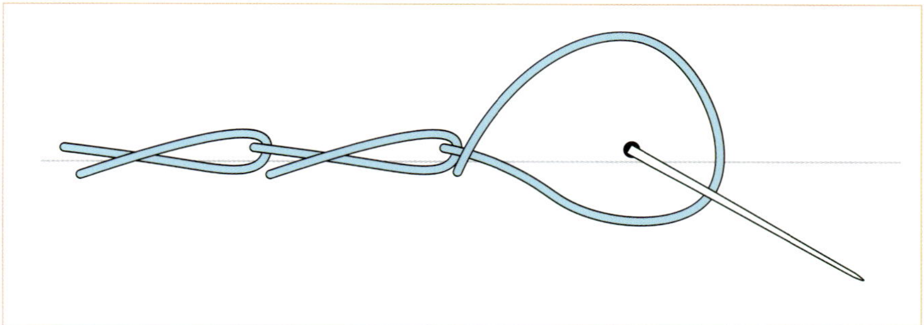

5 Continue working twisted chain stitches in this way.

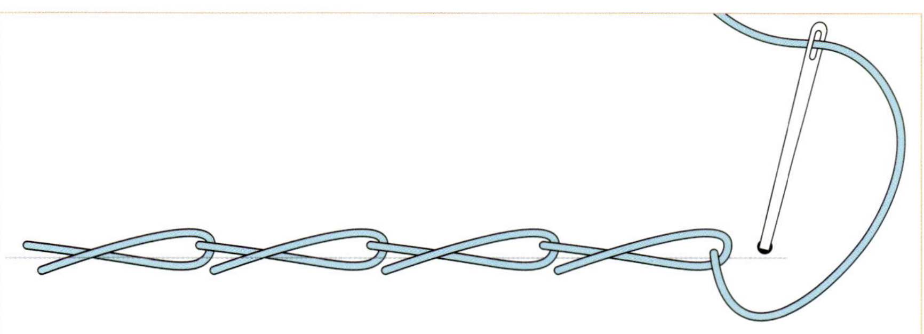

6 To finish, take a small anchoring stitch over your final chain.

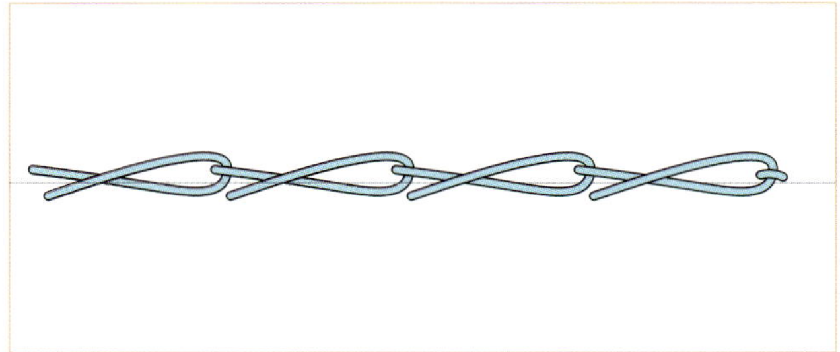

A line of twisted chain stitches.

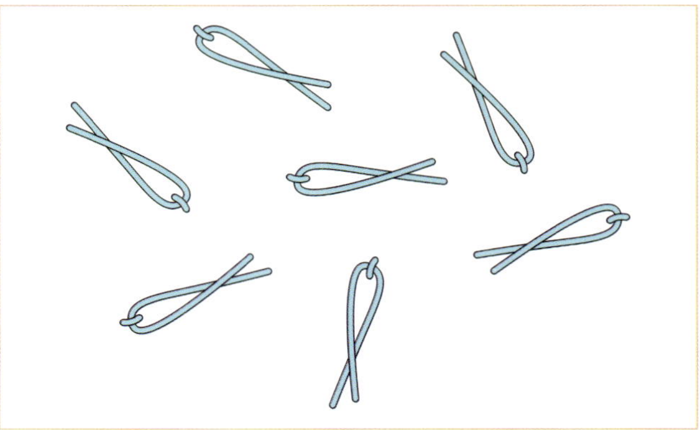

Detached twisted chain stitches in varying styles.

VAN DYKE STITCH

SURFACE; CREWELWORK; MOUNTMELLICK.

A row of equally-spaced cross stitches is worked, with each woven on to the previous stitch. Once pulled taut, this produces a very attractive pattern that looks like a ladder with a central plaited vein. It is ideal for borders or leaf shapes.

METHOD

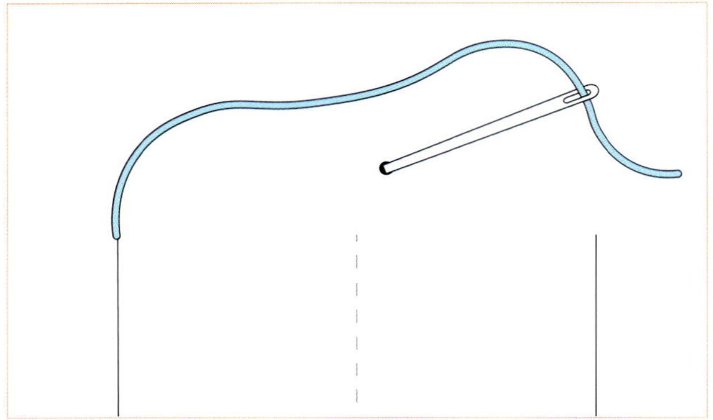

1 Imagine or faintly draw a single central line the length of your shape. Bring the needle up through the left outer edge of the shape on the top of the marked line, then take the needle down just to the right of and above the centre line.

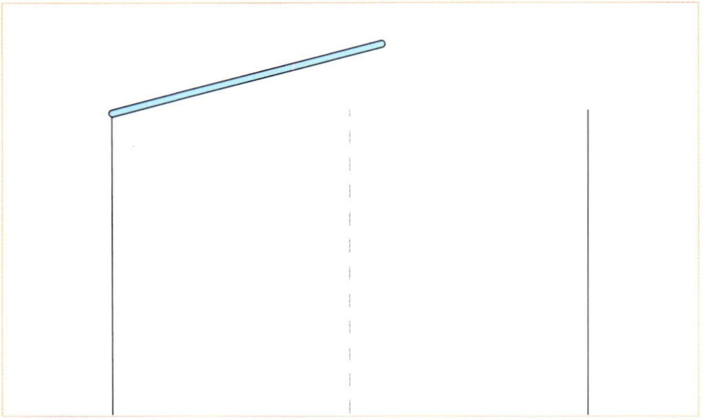

2 Draw the thread through to produce a diagonal stitch just over halfway across the design.

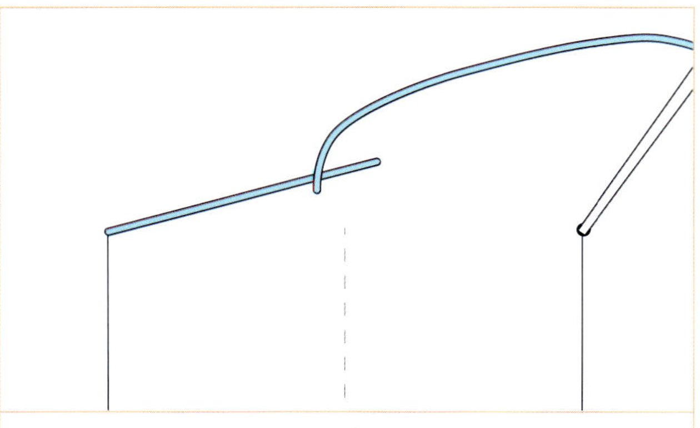

3 Bring the needle up left of the centre line, and take it down on the right edge level with the base of the first stitch. Draw the thread through.

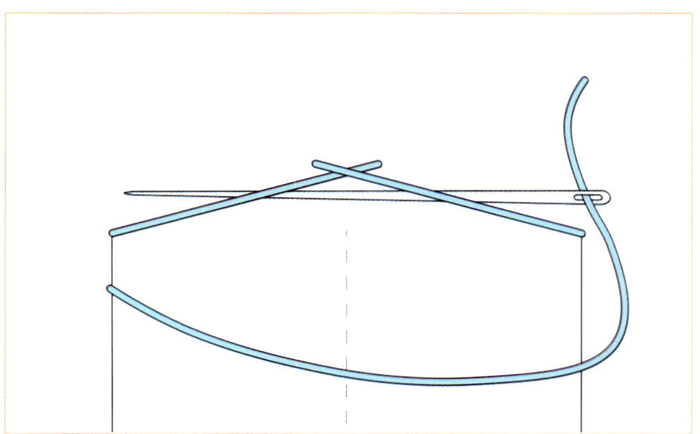

4 Bring the needle up on the left outer edge of the shape a little way along the marked line, then pass the needle under the cross formed by the last stitch.

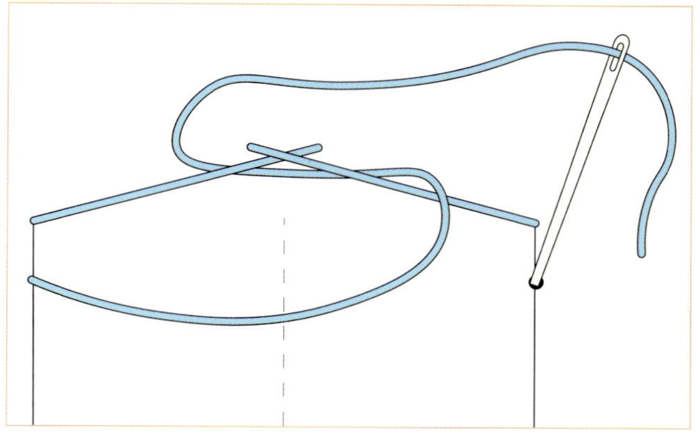

5 Draw through and pull on the thread to create tension before taking the needle down on the right edge level with the base of the left stitch.

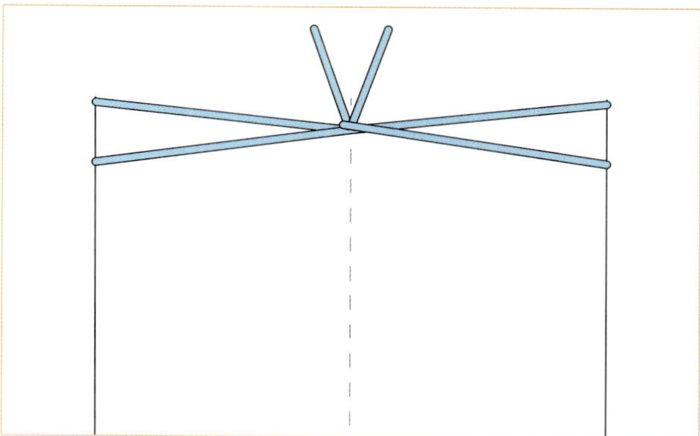

6 Draw the needle through.

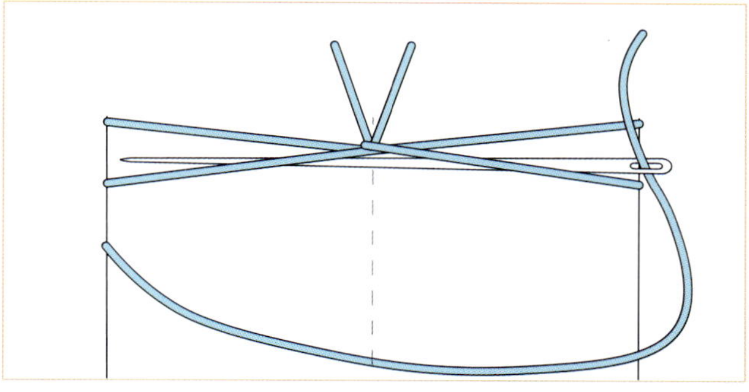

7 As you continue, take the needle only under the cross formed by the stitches made immediately previously, as shown.

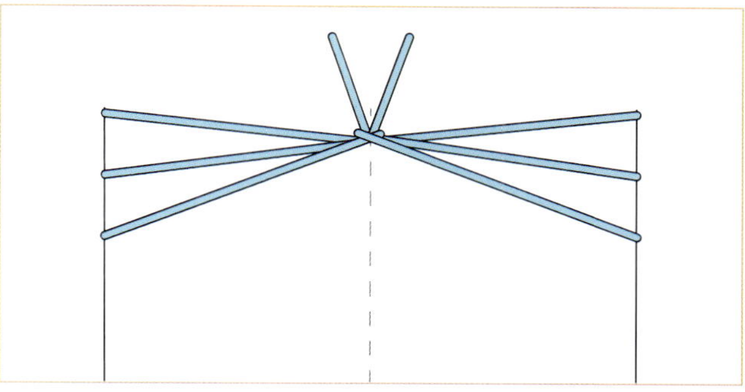

8 Continue working the stitches towards the base of your design.

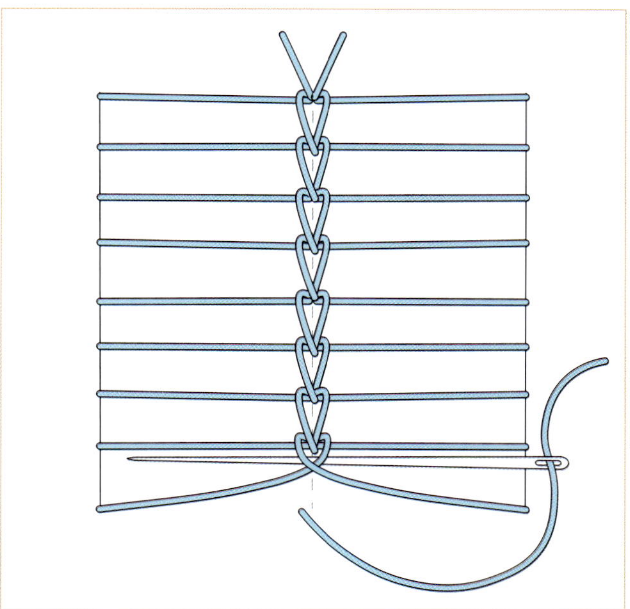

9 At the end, bring the needle up on the left of the central line. Take the needle and thread through the final cross as before.

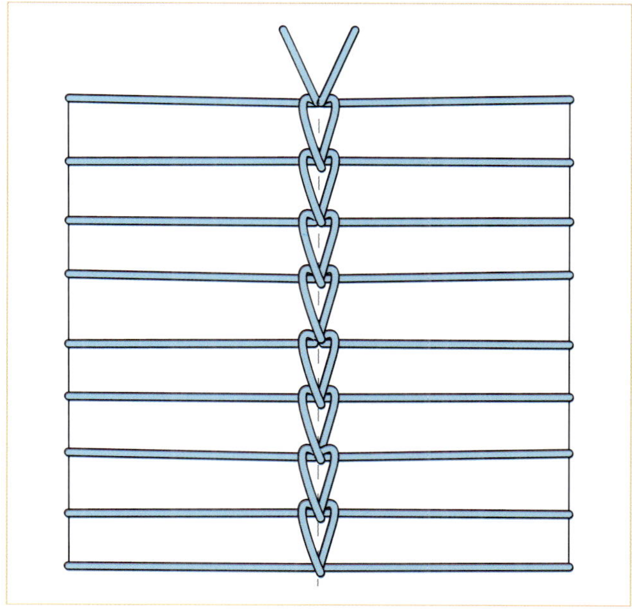

10 Take the needle down on the right of the central line. Fasten off as normal to finish.

WHIPPED BACK STITCH

Crewelwork; Ribbonwork; Surface.

Whipped back stitch makes a heavier line than a back stitch. It gives a similar effect to a stem stitch but a touch finer with the added bonus that it can be stitched in two separate colour threads if required. This technique is useful when a raised line is required on a fabric which is too delicate for a heavy thread to be embroidered directly through the weave.

For more background see the entry for back stitch on page 16.

METHOD

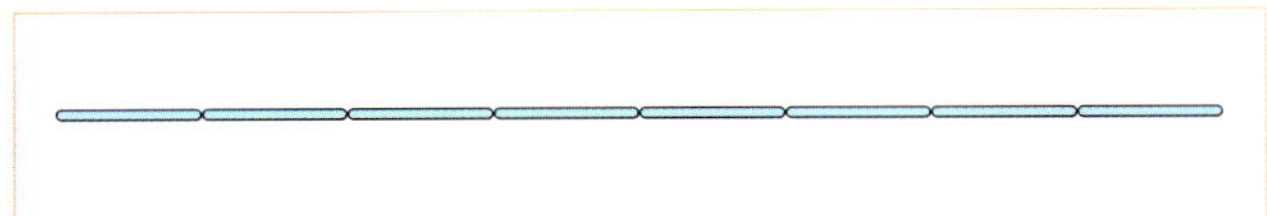

1 Work a foundation row of back stitches, ensuring each stitch is equal in size and not too small.

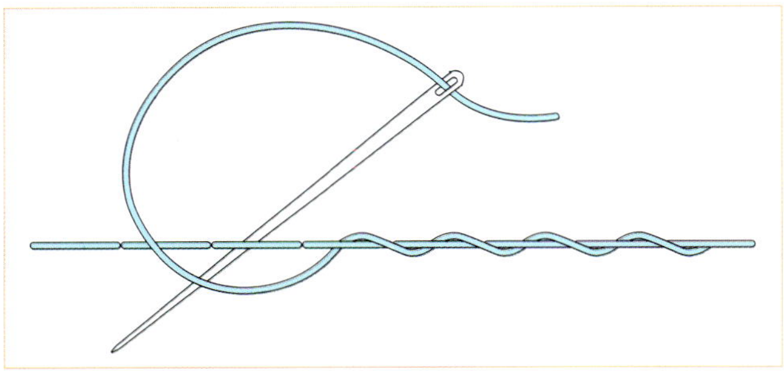

2 Using a second thread, whip over this line from right to left, as shown, without picking up any ground fabric. Use a blunt-ended tapestry needle for the whipping thread to avoid splitting the foundation stitches.

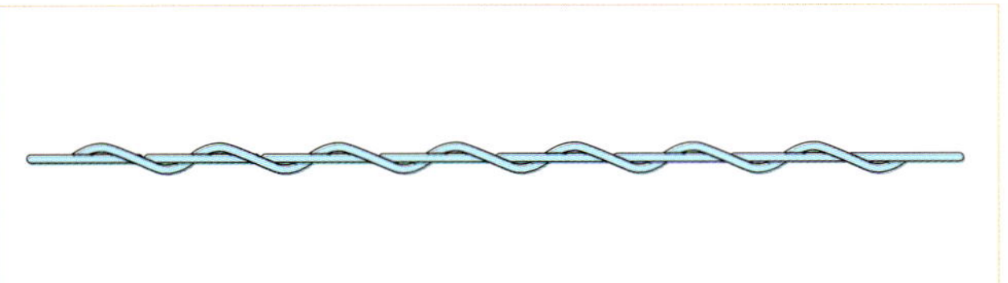

3 Continue whipping along the line. Note the benefit of having slightly larger foundation back stitches, which allows the tapestry needle to pass easily under each stitch.

WHIPPED CHAIN STITCH

SURFACE.

This stitch is formed of a line of chain stitch (see page 22) with a thread whipped around it. The whipped thread can be the same as the chain stitch thread, or a contrasting one.

METHOD

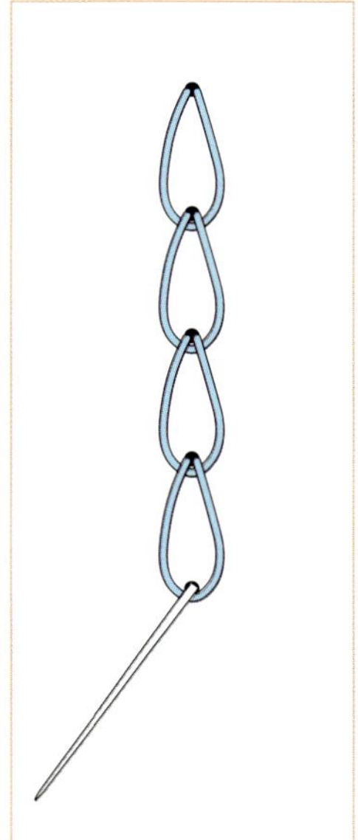

1 Working from top to bottom, make a line of chain stitch first.

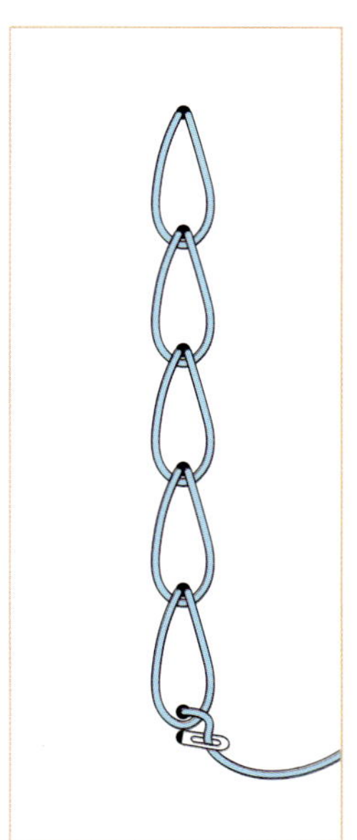

2 At the end of the chain stitch, make a small straight stitch to anchor the last chain.

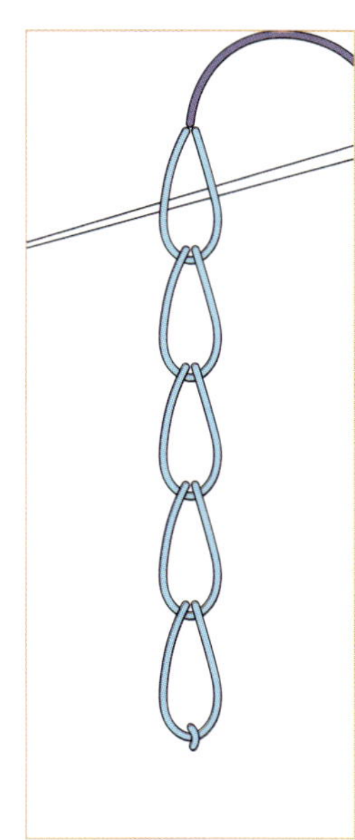

3 Introduce a new thread at the top end of the chain stitch. You could use a contrasting colour for a striking effect.

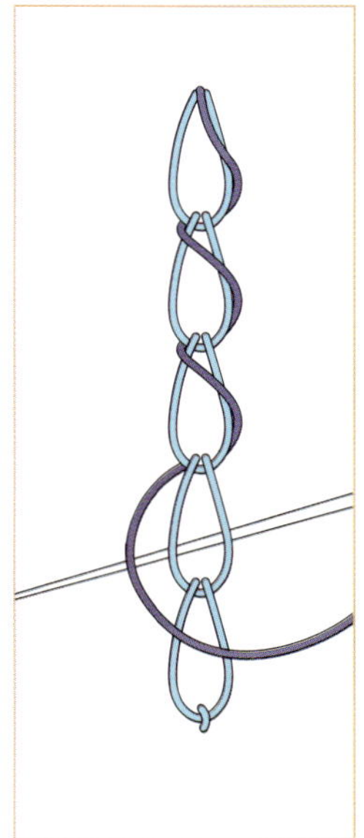

4 Whip the new thread by passing the needle under each chain stitch. Make sure not to pierce the fabric.

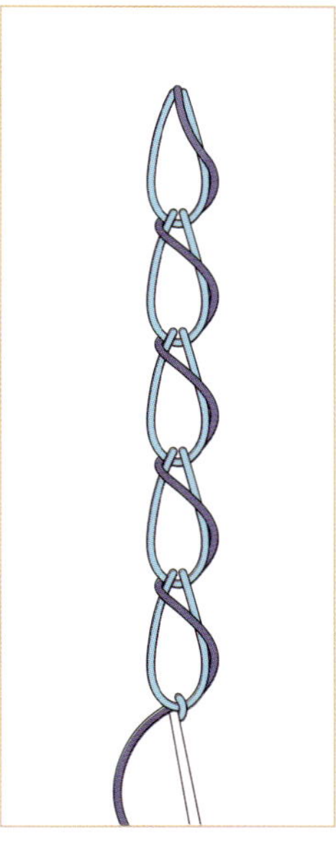

5 At the end of the chain stitch, simply take down the needle and secure the thread with a finishing stitch.

WHIPPED RUNNING STITCH

SURFACE; CREWELWORK; RIBBONWORK.

Also known as Whipping, or Cordonnet stitch.

Whipped running stitch is an embellishment to a normal running stitch (see page 36). By entwining or 'whipping' another length of thread through the original base of running stitch, you can produce some interesting effects, particularly when combining different colour and texture threads.

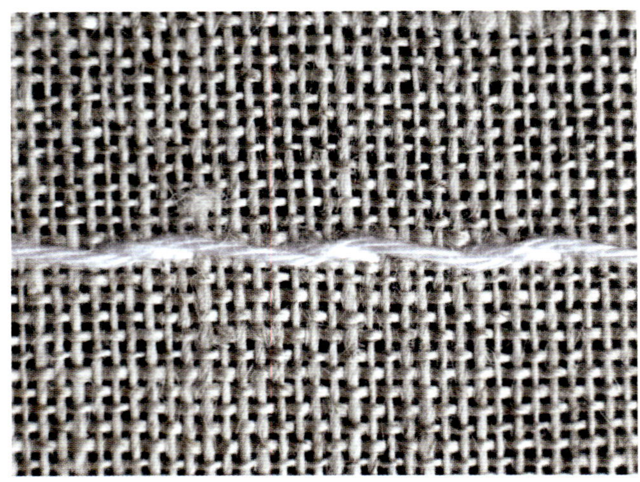

METHOD

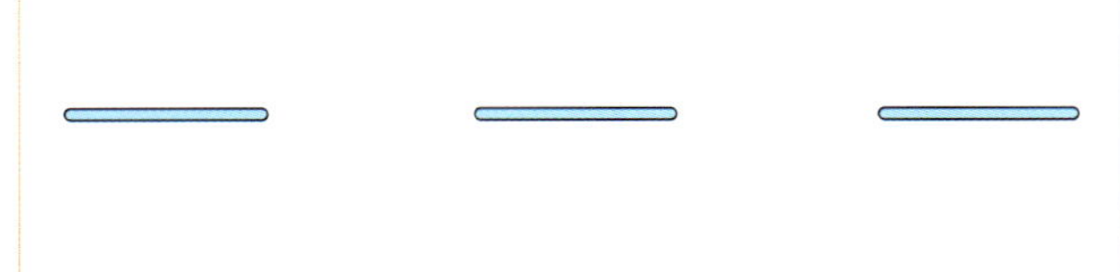

1 Complete a line of equally spaced running stitches.

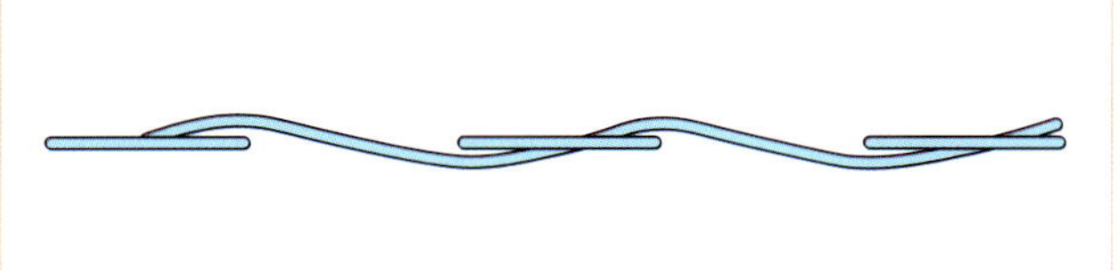

2 Using a tapestry needle, take the needle under each surface stitch. Remember to approach each loop from the same direction.

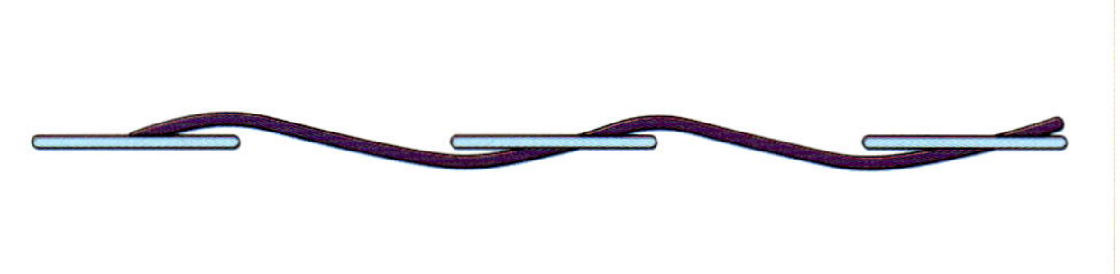

Whipping can be worked in a similar or contrasting thread.

WHIPPED STEM STITCH

SURFACE.

This is a variation on stem stitch: a line of stem stitch is worked, and then a thread is threaded through each stitch, always in the same direction to give a rope-like effect. The whipping thread can be the same as the stem stitch thread or a contrasting one.

Whipped stem stitch was certainly in use by the 16th century: it features on a 16th century border fragment of unknown origin and an ecclesiastical panel from the same era made in Switzerland. It also features on an English band sampler from the following century.

METHOD

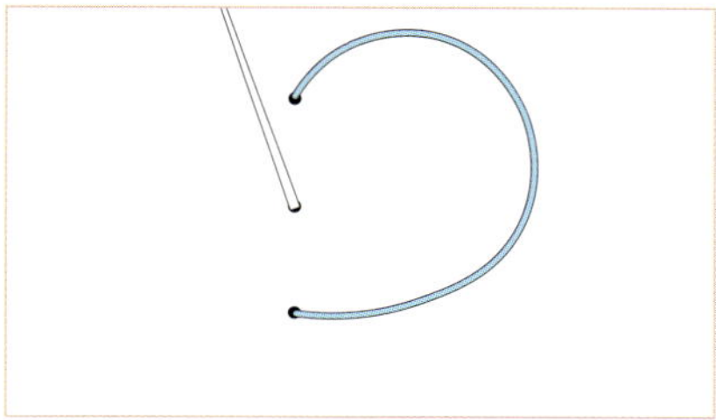

1 Working from bottom to top, make a first straight stitch, leaving a loop. Bring up the needle halfway, keeping the loop on the right-hand side.

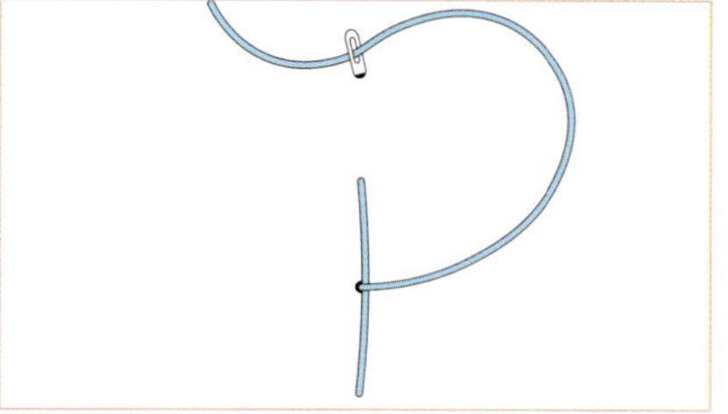

2 Continue the stem stitch as required.

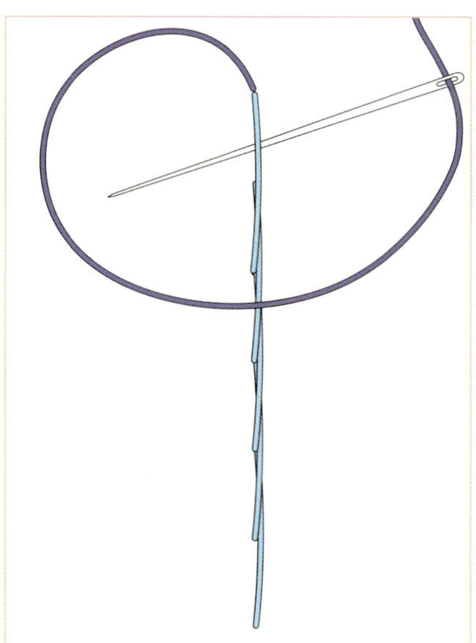

3 Introduce a new thread in a contrasting colour, coming up at the end of the stem stitch.

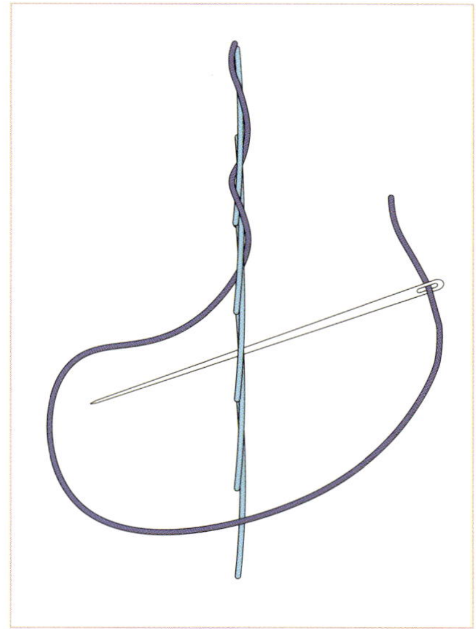

4 Use a tapestry needle to pass the new thread under each stem stitch. Make sure not to pierce the fabric.

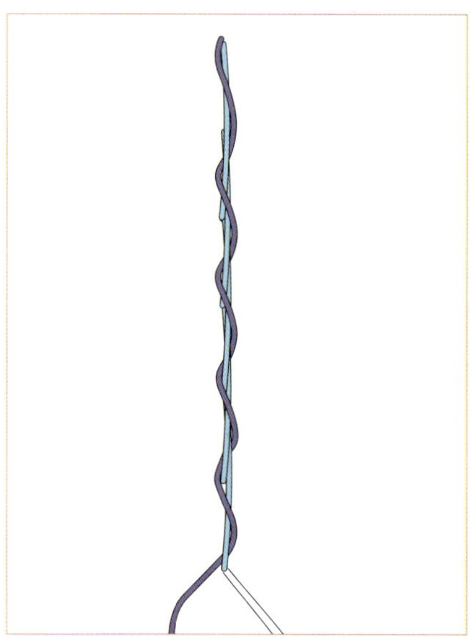

5 When you reach the end of the stem stitch, simply take the needle down through the fabric.

FILLING STITCHES

The attribute common to all of these varied stitches is that they lend themselves to completely filling an area of a design, large or small, so that the ground fabric is obscured.

This section is probably the most varied: it includes blackwork and canvaswork stitches, goldwork and needlelace.

Those filling stitches which are routinely used to shade an area in different tones or colours are grouped within the Shading stitches chapter (see pages 214–225). Those which partially fill an area, either as a spot motif or where the ground fabric is visible are listed under Open and powdered filling stitches (see pages 226–277).

Note that some stitches in Outline and border stitches (see pages 44–125) can also be used as filling stitches by working rows or spirals to fill an area. Even the humble French knot, in the Basic stitches chapter, can be used in this way.

▲▲ **RSN Student laid work, RSN Collection No. 2121**

One of a number of different designs, this was a standard piece to be made by students in the RSN Training School in the 1940s and 1950s. This example, by Lynette de Dene, shows the bird worked in silk shading (see long and short stitch on page 224–225) and the flowers and leaves in laid work (see pages 174–175).

PAGE 132

PAGE 133

PAGE 134

PAGE 136

PAGE 138

PAGE 139

PAGE 140

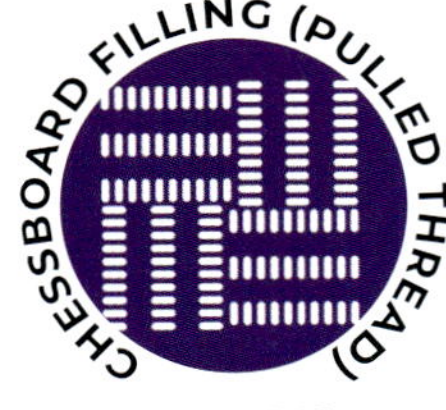

PAGE 142

PAGE 144

PAGE 145

PAGE 146

PAGE 147

PAGE 148

PAGE 149

PAGE 150

PAGE 151

PAGE 152

PAGE 154

PAGE 156

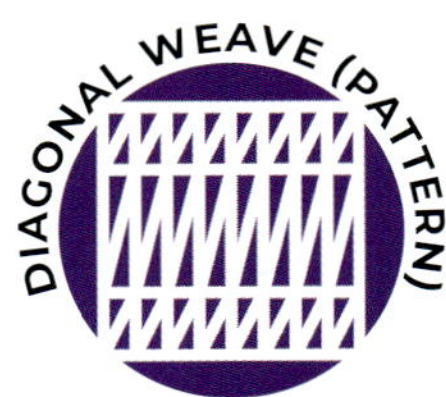

PAGE 157

PAGE 158

PAGE 160

PAGE 162

PAGE 163

PAGE 164

PAGE 165

PAGE 166

PAGE 167

PAGE 168

PAGE 170

EMBROIDERY TECHNIQUE: BLACKWORK

Also known as Spanish blackwork.

Blackwork is a form of monochrome embroidery generally using black thread, although other colours are also used on occasion. It can be worked as a counted thread technique which creates patterns on evenweave fabric or as freeform embroidery. Traditionally, blackwork is stitched in silk thread on white or off-white linen or cotton fabric; sometimes metallic or coloured threads are used for accents. Some pieces are worked in another single colour, most commonly red but also blue or green; very occasionally multiple colours are used in a single piece, although individual motifs tend to be monochrome.

Chaucer, writing in the 14th century, references a blackwork collar, but it is impossible to know if this embroidery was the same as that worked in the 16th century when it was used to embellish linen collars and cuffs. Some authors credit Catherine of Aragon for introducing blackwork into England, but there is no conclusive evidence.

By the end of the 16th century, blackwork was being used to decorate linen coifs (a close-fitting head covering) and other garments, some of which feature gold and silver thread and spangles, as well as black thread. Extant garments, particularly those which feature the flora and fauna and curving stems (known as rinceaux) which epitomize Elizabethan embroidery are often freeform embroidery, rather than counted thread. Motifs are normally outlined in black and either filled with blackwork patterns, or embellished with stitches, especially seeding to give a more naturalistic effect. The counted thread version of the technique was revived in the 20th century when blackwork patterns started to be documented.

▸▸ Sampler, RSN Collection COL.2014.25

Blackwork technique sampler worked by Dorothy Abnett, involving black cotton and gold threads on bleached linen. The sampler comprises outline shapes that are filled in with different blackwork patterns which have been further embellished with the use of fine gold thread. This combination of black and gold was a hallmark of pieces from the 1950s.

The sampler features stylized birds, flowers, and foliage. The outlines have been created using both black and gold threads. The black outlines have been done in stem stitch. For the gold threads, passing threads have been couched down with cotton thread and twist threads have been stitched down through the twist. The design has been filled with a variety of different blackwork patterns (diapers), which have been further embellished with the use of fine gold thread. Blackwork patterns featured in this piece include variations on honeycomb and tulip. The blackwork patterns are worked in double running stitch.

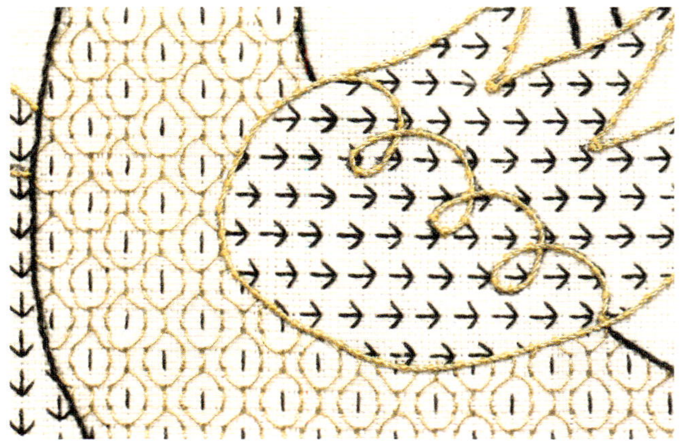

▴▴ Detail of hexagonal lozenge (pattern) – page 167

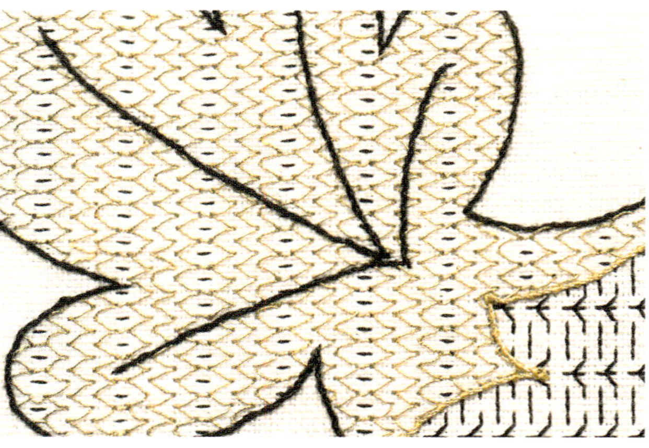

▴▴ Detail of tulip (pattern) – pages 204–205

ARROWHEAD STITCH

COUNTED THREAD; CREWELWORK; SURFACE; BLACKWORK.

Arrowhead stitch can be used as a filling stitch, as shown in the method below, or as a line stitch. It can also be worked individually.

Arrowhead stitch is featured on a 16th-century sampler in the V&A South Kensington. Most of the sampler is worked in cross stitch, but a motif of a dog uses arrowhead stitch.

Several centuries later, arrowhead stitch became one of the stitches used by women in Aleppo, Syria to embellish the wedding outfits of their future husbands.

METHOD

1 Bring the needle up at the top left-hand corner, and then take down the needle a little lower to the right. This example moves two threads to the right and three down, but different spacing will produce a different effect.

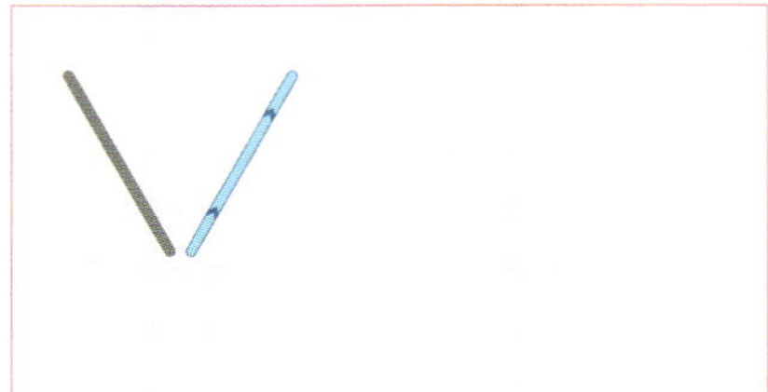

2 Come up to the right on a level with the spot where the thread first emerged. Then insert the needle at the same spot where it last entered to form the arrowhead.

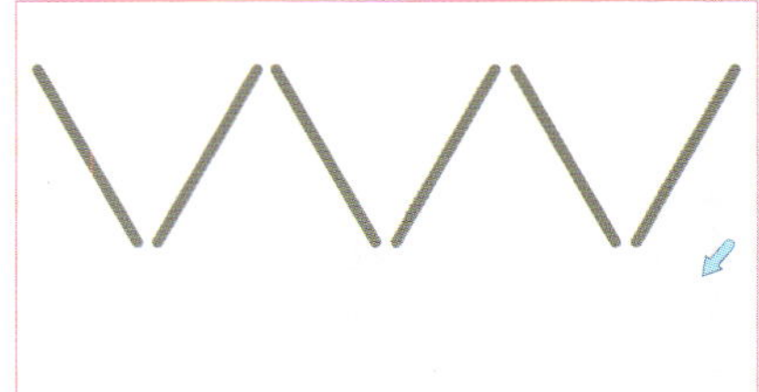

3 Continue the arrowhead stitches from left to right, making sure they are equally spaced. To start the next row, bring up the needle at the top right-hand corner on the same level as the arrowhead tip.

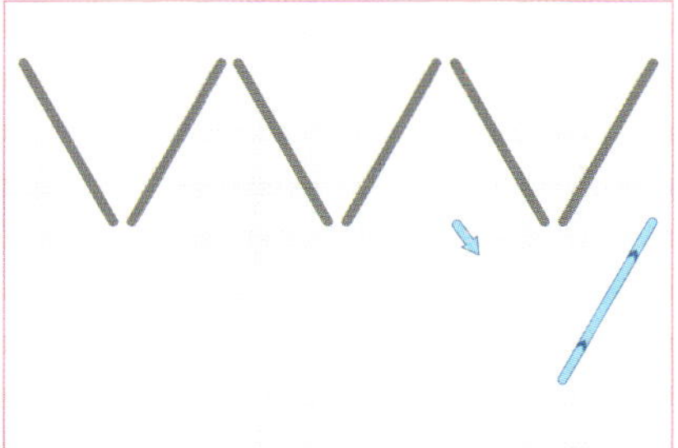

4 Continue the arrowhead stitch from right to left, keeping the spacing even throughout.

Arrowhead stitch can be used as a filling or as a line stitch.

BASKET FILLING STITCH

CREWELWORK; COUNTED THREAD; SURFACE; CANVASWORK; STUMPWORK.

Also known as Basket satin stitch.

Basket filling stitch is made up of squares of satin stitches (see page 37). Each square alternates in direction – either vertical or horizontal – to provide a basketweave pattern.

This version works four stitches over five threads, but this can vary depending on the size of the area to fill or the effect you require. For example, it can be worked with three satin stitches over four fabric threads, or five satin stitches over six fabric threads.

METHOD

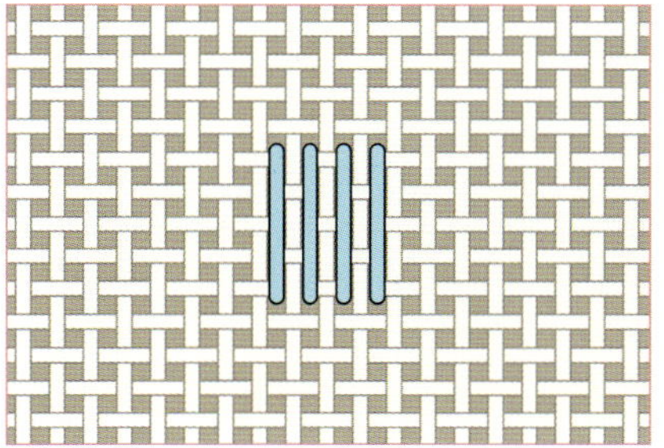

1 Work four vertical satin stitches each over five fabric threads.

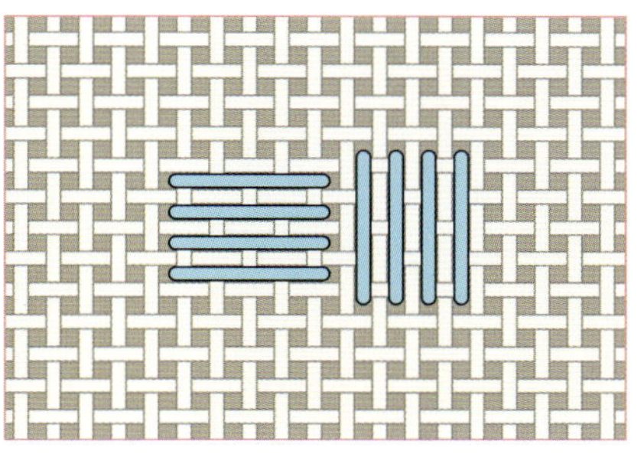

2 Next to this block, work four horizontal satin stitches over five fabric threads.

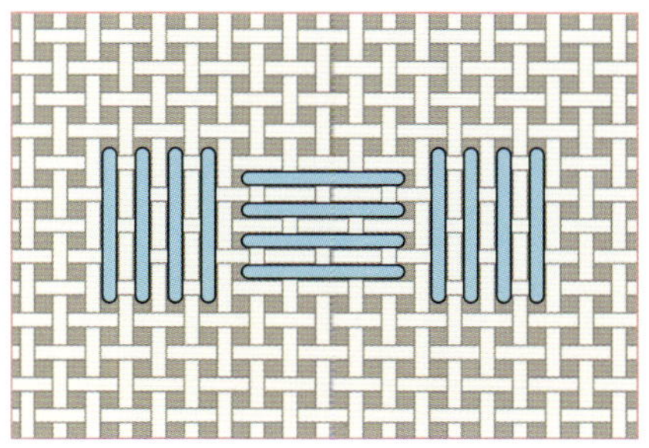

3 Work alternate groups of vertical and horizontal satin stitches in a row.

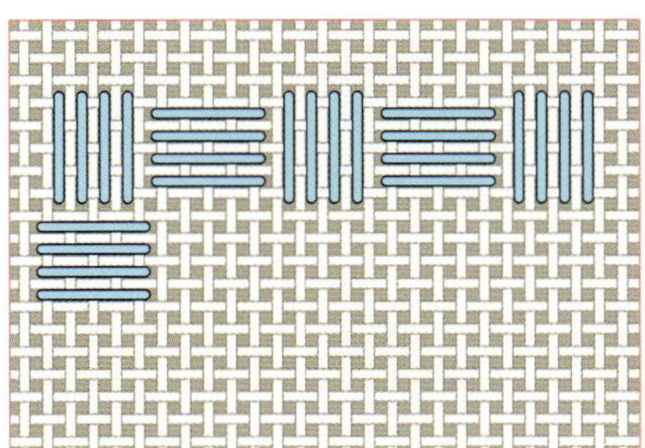

4 Continue onto the second row, alternating the direction of each block of stitches with the row above.

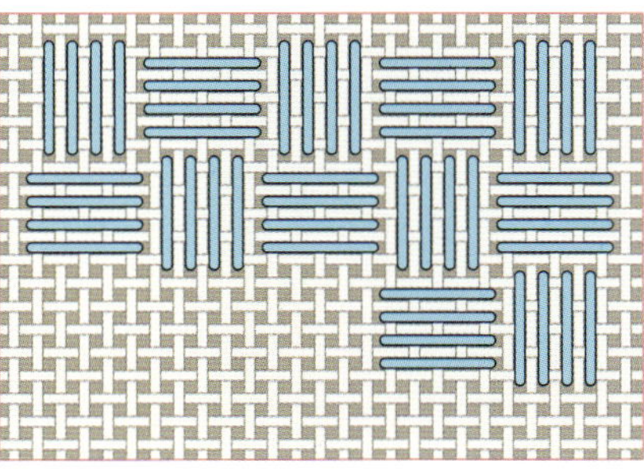

5 Repeat until you fill the area.

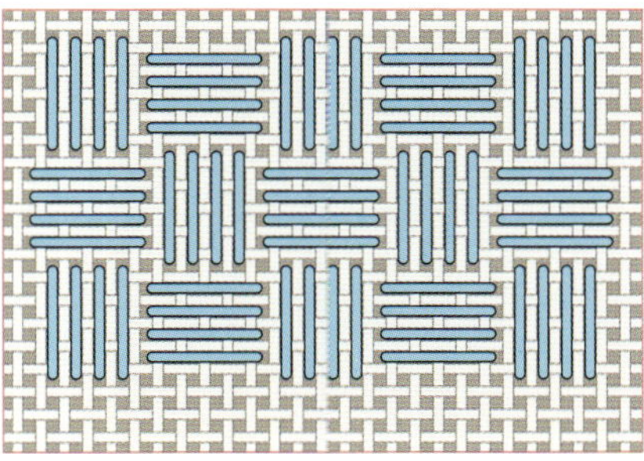

Completed basket filling stitch.

BASKETWEAVE (GOLDWORK)

GOLDWORK.

Also known as Basket stitch.

Basketweave in metal thread embroidery refers to couching gold, silver or copper threads over rows of hard string padding. The couching stitches pull the metal thread down between the padding which creates a woven effect. Many different patterns can be achieved by stitching over different numbers of string padding in different sequences.

Basketweave has long been a feature of ecclesiastical embroidery: Notre Dame church in Montreal has an altar frontal dating to the early 19th century which features this stitch. A 19th-century publication, *Art Amateur*, says that Spanish embroiderers were particularly known for basketweave and they did not confine the technique to churchwork.

METHOD

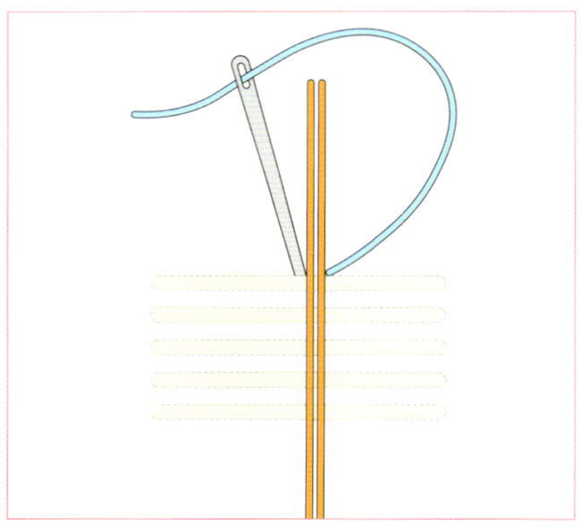

1 Starting in the centre of your shape, lay a pair of gold threads (4cm/1¾in longer at each end than the shape to be covered) across the hard string padding. Secure by couching over the gold using a single waxed sewing thread, above the top length of hard string padding.

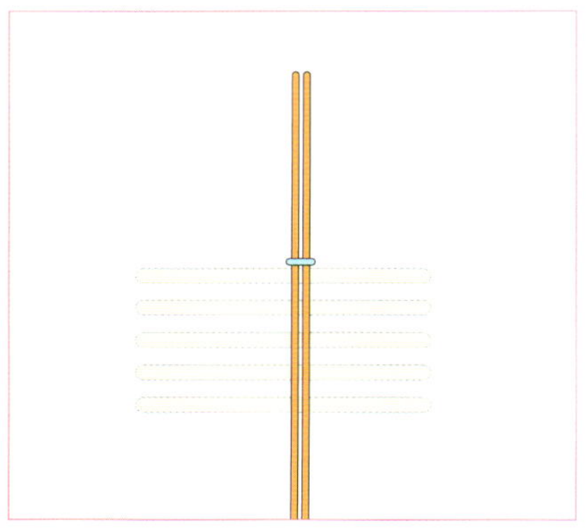

2 Pull the thread firmly to ensure that it holds the gold securely.

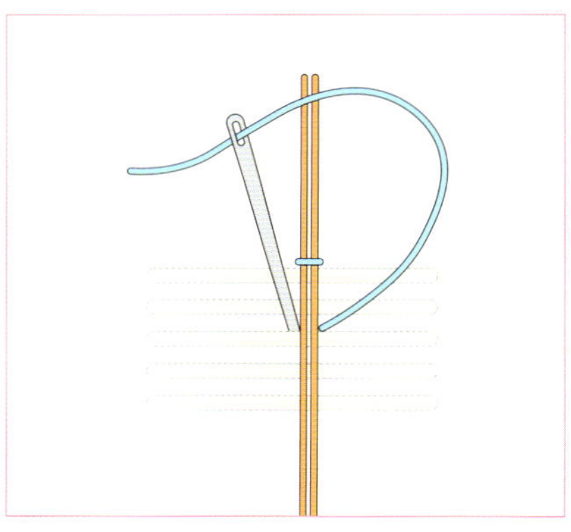

3 Couch another stitch over the gold between the second and third strings and pull firmly so that the gold thread buckles/creases and sits neatly on the fabric surface between the string padding.

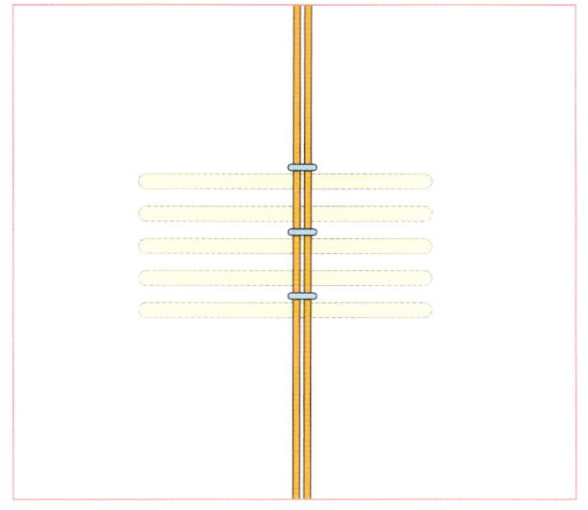

4 Lay the gold threads over each subsequent pair of strings, securing them into position with a stitch. Ensure the gold threads lie as straight as possible, with no twist.

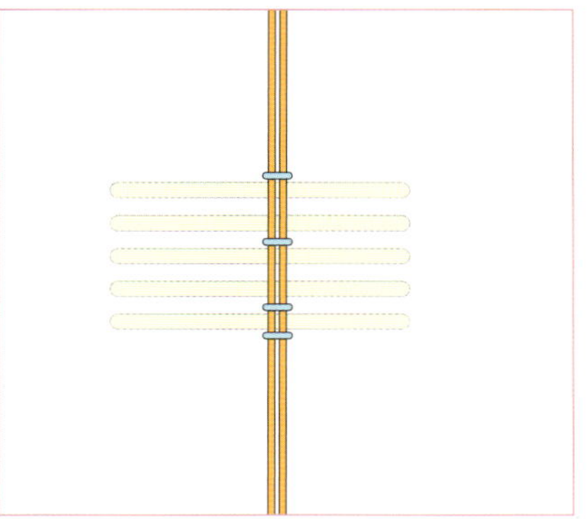

5 Complete the pattern by couching over the gold threads below the bottom piece of string.

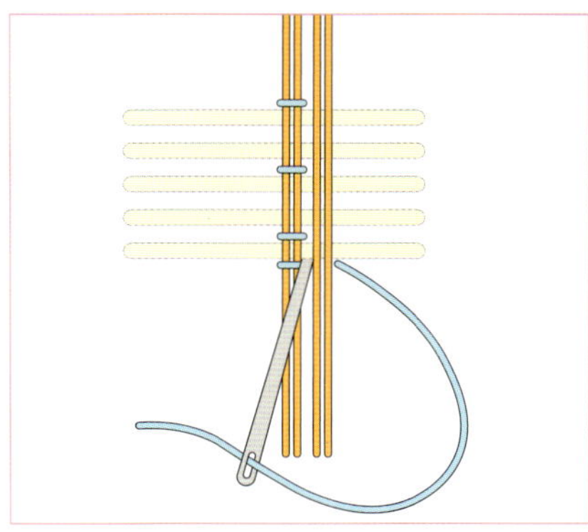

6 Lay another pair of gold threads adjacent to the first. Working up from the bottom, secure by couching into position below the bottom string.

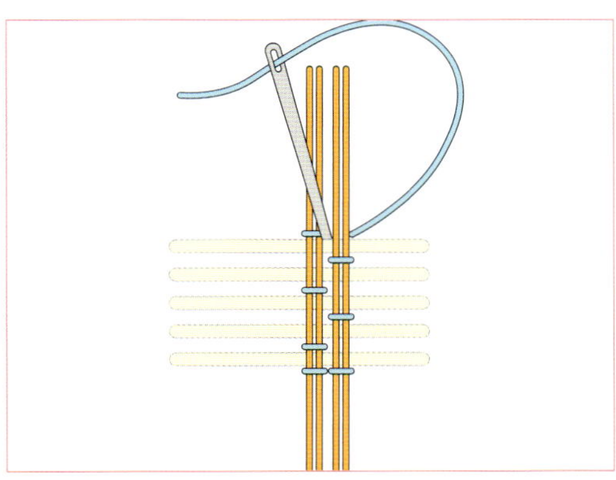

7 Work upwards to the top of the padded shape, securing the gold over pairs of strings alternate to the previous row.

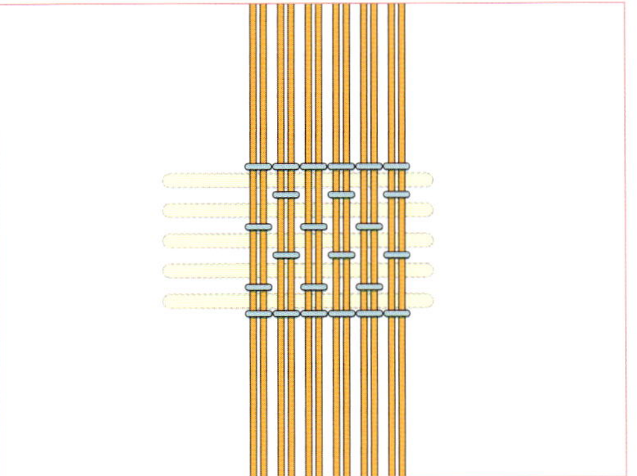

8 Continue working up and down over the string padding to create a basketweave pattern. Complete one side, then return to the centre to complete the other side. Plunge the ends of the gold threads below the fabric surface and secure.

▲▲ Detail from hanging, RSN Collection COL.2013.64.a

Gifted to the RSN Collection by Marion Cantrell, this is a late 19th- or early 20th-century hanging with an angel in purple robes, holding a Tudor rose. Basketweave has been used on the halo, the centre of the Tudor rose, and on the collar and cuffs of the robes in a chevron pattern.

BRICKING

GOLDWORK.

Also known as Couching, or Brick stitch.

Bricking is a method of holding down couched threads: the threads are laid in pairs and couched with small stitches at 90 degrees to the couched thread. The couching stitches for each pair of threads are offset so that they form a pattern like brickwork. This is the most common method for holding down couched threads as it creates a firm, stable embroidery with an even finish.

Bricking was certainly in common usage by the 19th century: articles in contemporary publications frequently refer to it, often mentioning that it is the easiest form of gold couching. Notre Dame parish church in Montreal contains an altar frontal which is documented as dating from this era. Interestingly, the contemporary articles refer to the stitch sometimes being executed in floss crossed with gold (the reverse of the metal crossed with sewing thread which is currently standard).

There is another (canvaswork) stitch called brick stitch (see page 219), also named for the offset pattern of the stitches.

METHOD

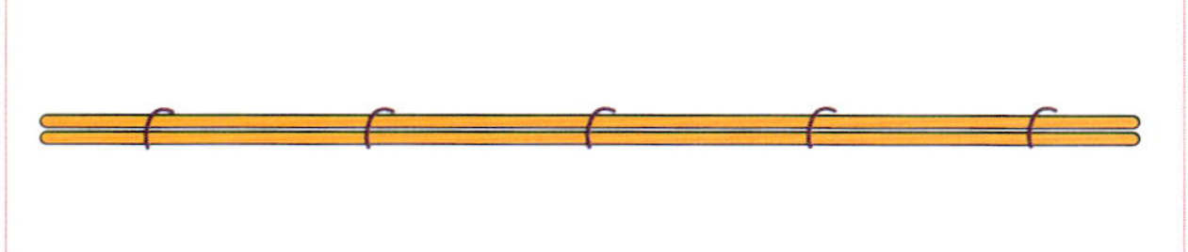

1 Lay down a pair of threads (the image shows Japanese gold threads) and couch into position using a single waxed thread. The couching thread should lay at 90 degrees to the gold threads at intervals of 4mm (¼in) or so, it should be tight enough to hold the gold securely but not so tight that it dents the gold threads. Ensure the gold threads lie flat and parallel without crossing and try not to over-tighten the stitches.

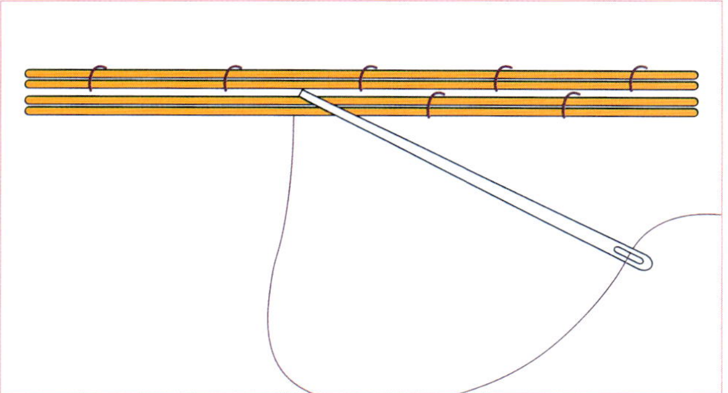

2 Lay another two gold threads parallel to the first. Holding the gold threads firmly in place, secure them in place by couching a stitch between those of the previous row, producing a brickwork pattern. Bringing the needle up on the outer side of the threads and down between the current threads and the previous row will help to avoid puncturing the gold threads.

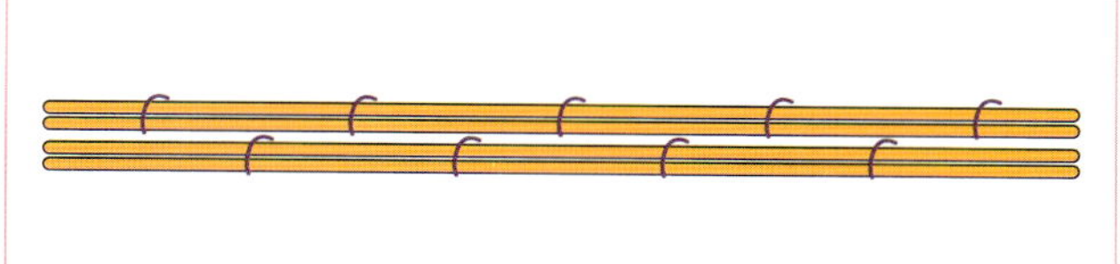

3 Continue to stitch along the gold thread, ensuring the stitches are evenly spaced and all lie at 90 degrees to the threads. Make sure the gold threads do not twist over and do not over-tighten the stitches.

4 Continue to add more rows of gold to fill the space, placing the stitches in between those of the previous row, in a brickwork pattern. When you have completed the area to be filled, plunge the gold threads separately and secure on the reverse with a curved needle.

◂◂ Detail from cherub's face hanging, RSN Collection COL.2016.65.a

A hanging of a cherub's face, halo and feathered wings. The wings, comprised of pink and purple feathers, take the place of the angel's body. The hanging is worked in silk and metal threads and paint on a linen ground.

The halo is in passing thread couched in a brick pattern and outlined with gold twist. The passing threads have been painted over in blue and green tones. Within the halo, the word 'SANCTUS' is rendered in flat cutwork and stem and straight stitches in black silk thread.

BYZANTINE STITCH

Canvaswork.

This pattern is worked in long diagonal bands of satin zigzags. Each stitch is worked from bottom left to top right across four intersections of canvas, or four threads up and across. The repeat of this stitch is quite large, which means that it covers the canvas quickly. It is a flat stitch and very good for backgrounds.

See Jacquard stitch on page 173 for a development of this stitch.

METHOD

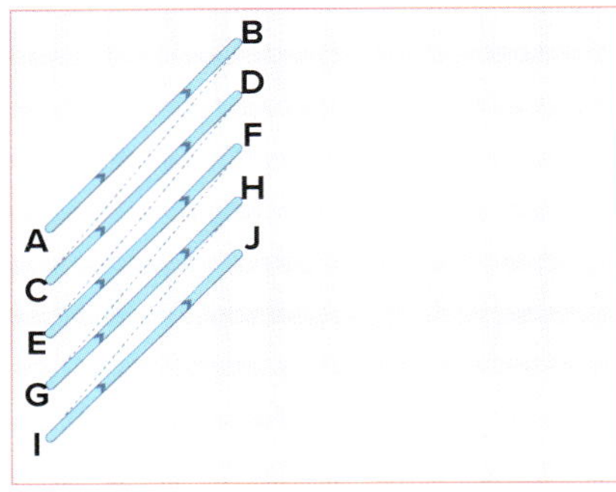

1 Make five diagonal stitches in a vertical band. The stitch at the bottom of these will be the corner.

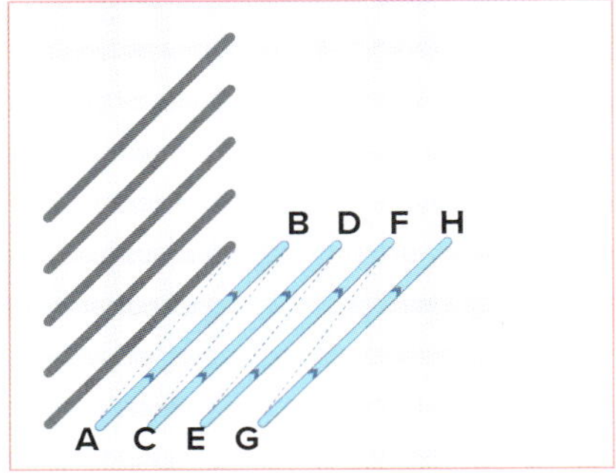

2 Next, make four stitches horizontally across from the corner stitch. This will make five stitches in total for this row, the last stitch being the corner stitch.

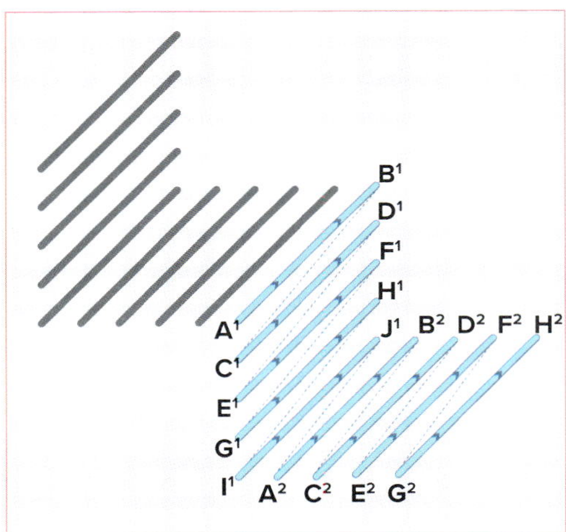

3 Alternate between vertical (marked with 1) and horizontal (marked with 2) bands of stitches to make the stepped pattern.

4 The second row can be worked above or below the first, fitting into the steps. The corner stitches of each row should meet.

CASHMERE STITCH

CANVASWORK.

This stitch consists of diagonally stitched rectangles, two threads wide and three threads high, made up of four diagonal stitches. The rectangular blocks repeat with each block sitting in line with those to the side, above and below to form a grid.

For a condensed version, see page 149; for a staggered version, see page 202.

METHOD

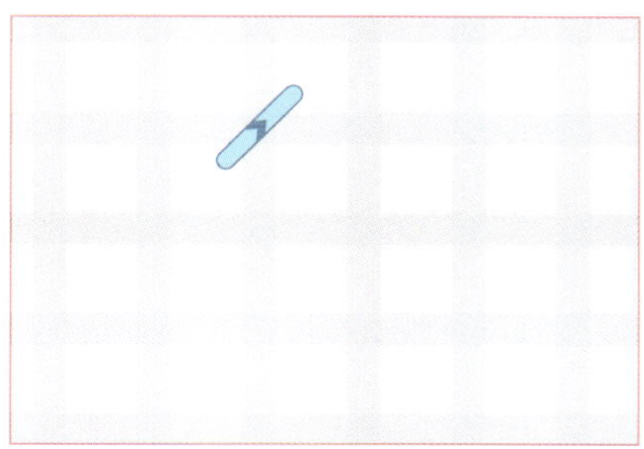

1 Complete one diagonal tent stitch (see basketweave tent stitch on page 218) from bottom left to top right over one intersection.

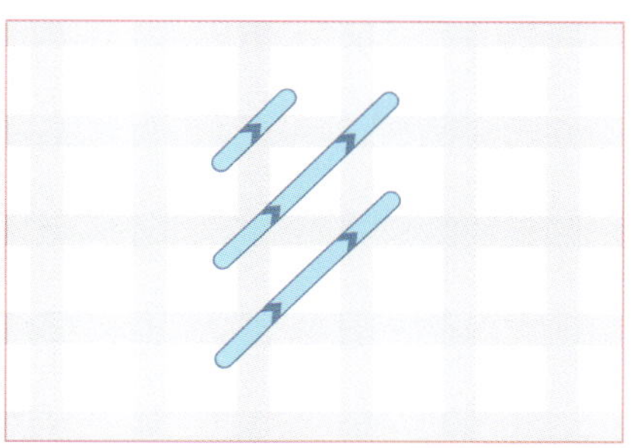

2 Starting directly beneath this stitch make a diagonal stitch across two intersections of canvas. Repeat to make a second stitch across two intersections of canvas.

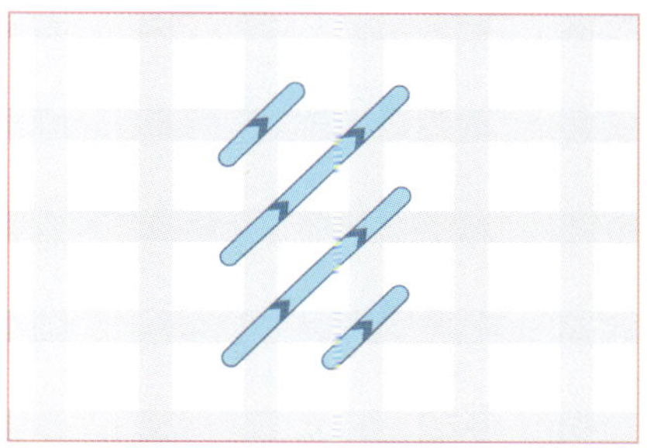

3 And finally make another tent stitch to complete the block.

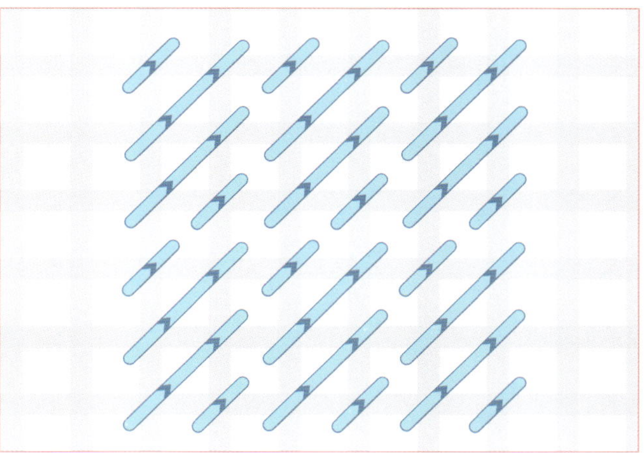

4 Continue the sequence to produce identical blocks that line up vertically and horizontally.

CEYLON STITCH

Stumpwork; Needlelace.

Also known as Cross-knit loop stitch.

This needlelace stitch consists of a series of chained loops, anchored by a foundation line of stitches. It resembles a knitted sweater and is therefore a good stitch to sample in wool, but can be just as effective in any thread. A back stitch outline is used in this example, but Ceylon stitch could be achieved without a foundation outline by anchoring the row of loops with a tiny stitch.

The earliest evidence of Ceylon stitch is from the Iron Age: impressions made on ceramics from Masbate in the Philippines feature the impression of cloth woven using the same structure as the stitch. Slightly more recently, use of the stitch itself has been found on textile artefacts from Peru, dated to the early Nazca period (1st–5th centuries AD). The name 'cross-knit loop stitch' is used by academics for this stitch.

METHOD

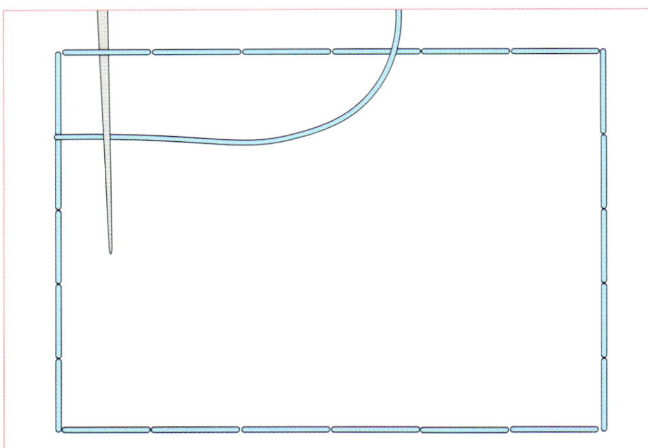

1 Bring the needle up on the left-hand side of the shape, just below the top foundation outline.

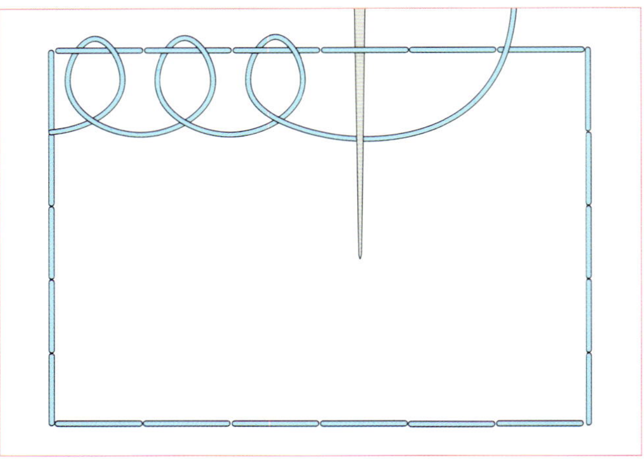

2 Work a row of loops across the shape. Pass the needle under the foundation line as you work each loop.

3 At the end of the first row, take the needle down to the back of the fabric.

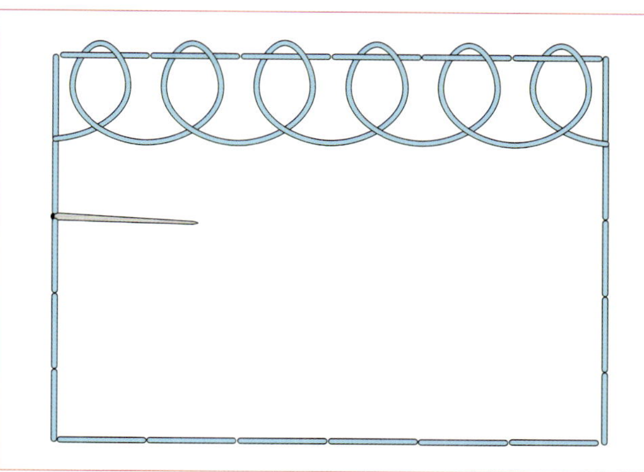

4 Bring the needle back up to the front on the left-hand side, just beneath the previous row.

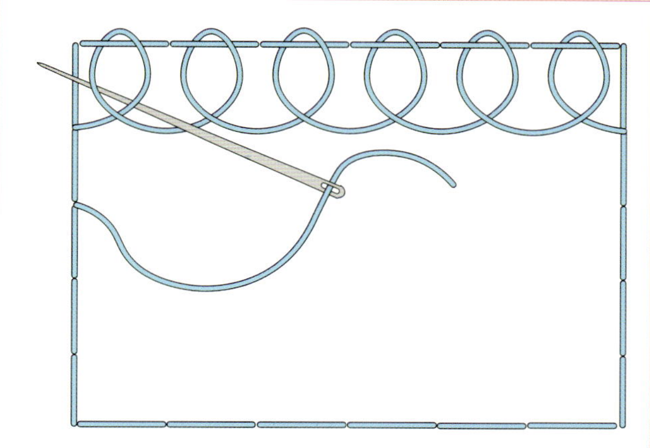

5 Pass the needle behind two threads of the loop above without piercing the fabric. Pull the thread through to form the stitch.

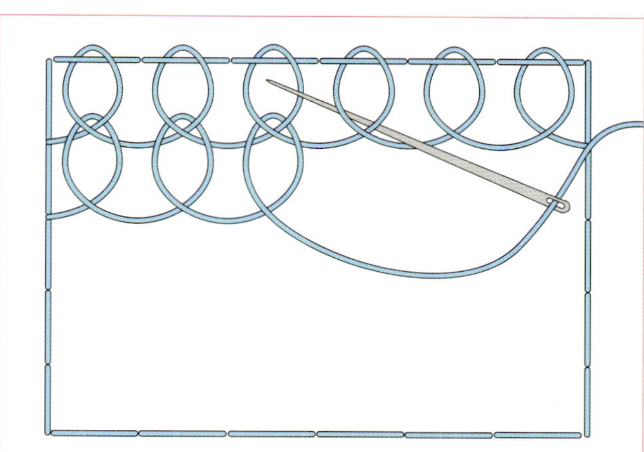

6 Continue working the second row by passing the thread through the loops of previous row.

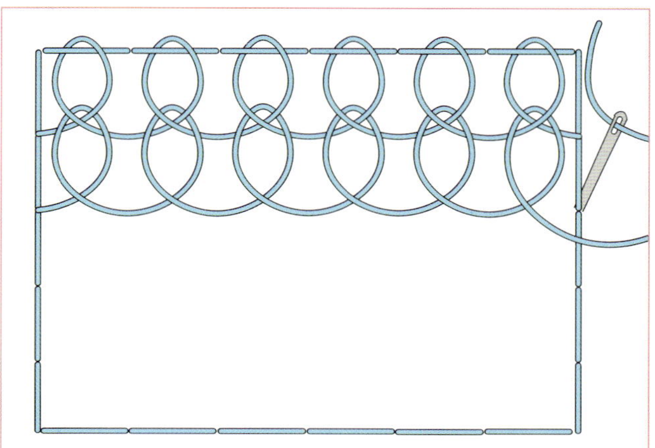

7 At the end of the row, take the thread through to the back of the fabric.

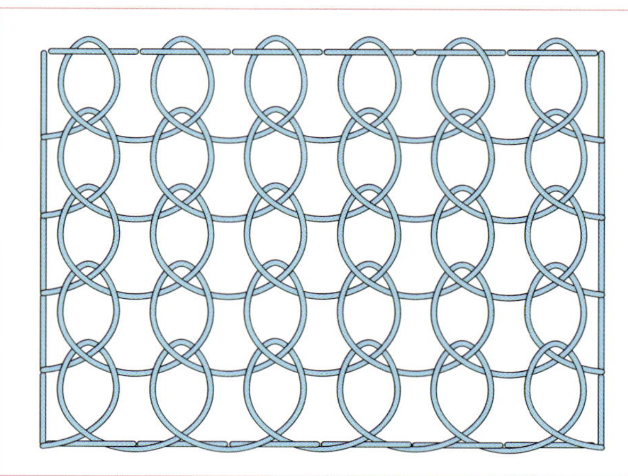

8 Continue working in this way until the shape is filled. On the last row, take the needle through the foundation outline as you work each stitch.

CHESSBOARD FILLING (PULLED THREAD)

Counted thread; Pulled thread; Whitework.

This pulled thread stitch consists of regular blocks of satin stitches, worked in alternating directions to form a chequerboard effect.

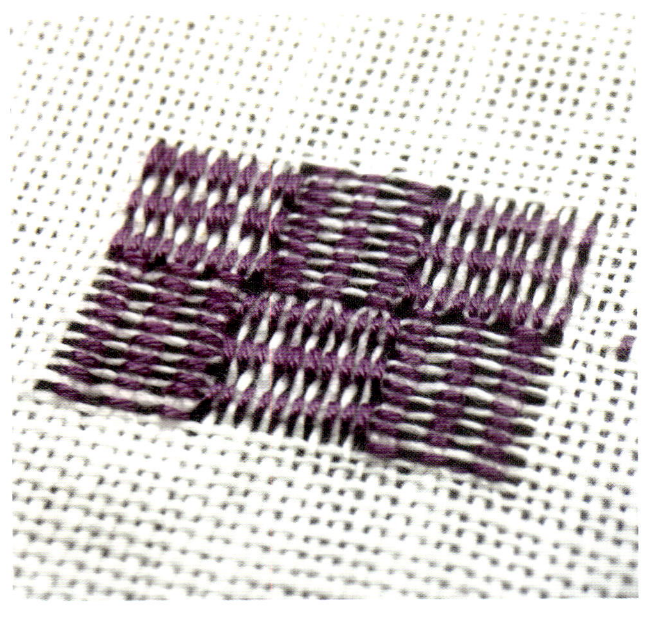

METHOD

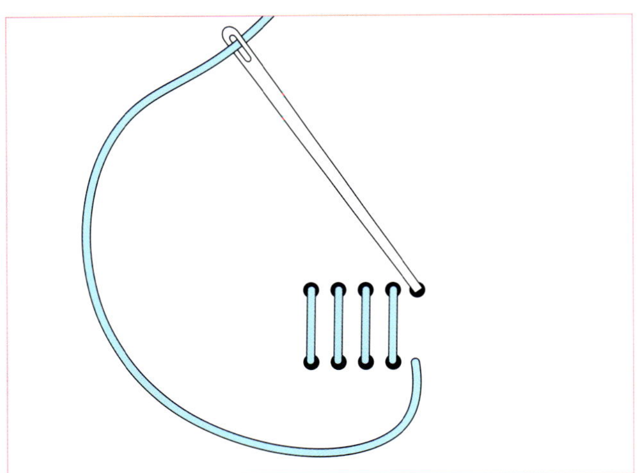

1 Work a row of ten vertical satin stitches over three fabric threads.

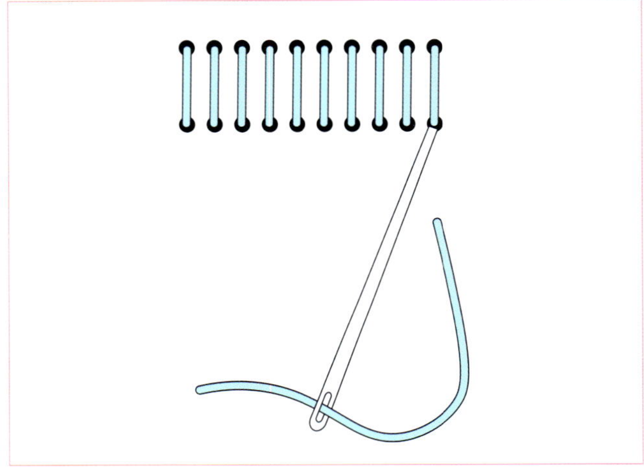

2 Start the second row by bringing the needle up three holes below the bottom of the last stitch. Take the needle down in the same hole as the bottom of the last stitch to make a vertical satin stitch in line with the previous one. Continue the row.

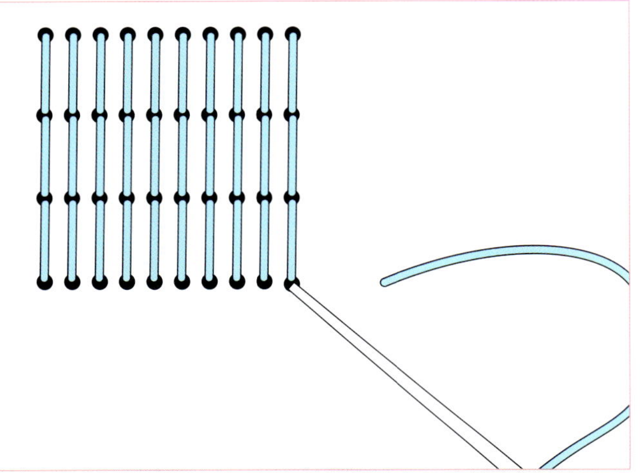

3 Complete the first block with a third row of satin stitches, and move onto the second block. This time, make three columns of ten horizontal satin stitches across three threads.

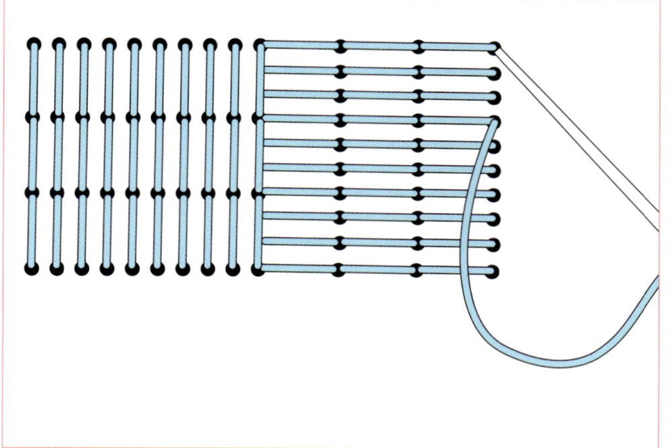

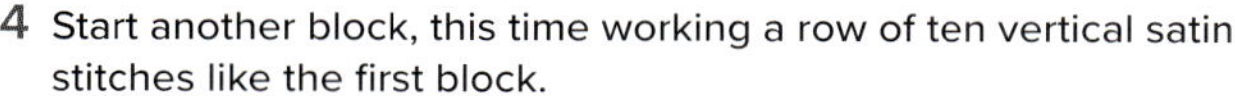

4 Start another block, this time working a row of ten vertical satin stitches like the first block.

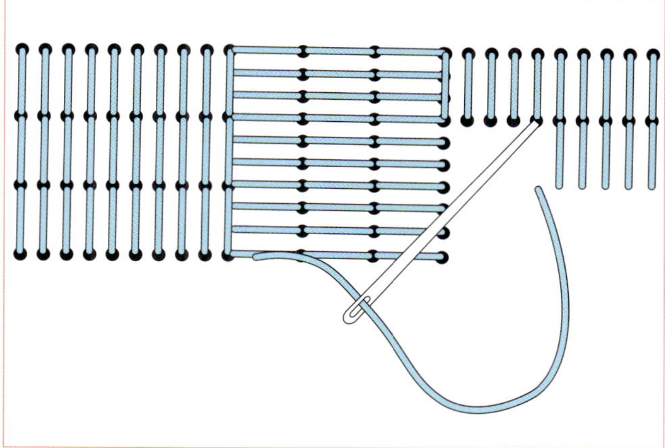

5 Continue with two more rows of ten vertical satin stitches to complete the block.

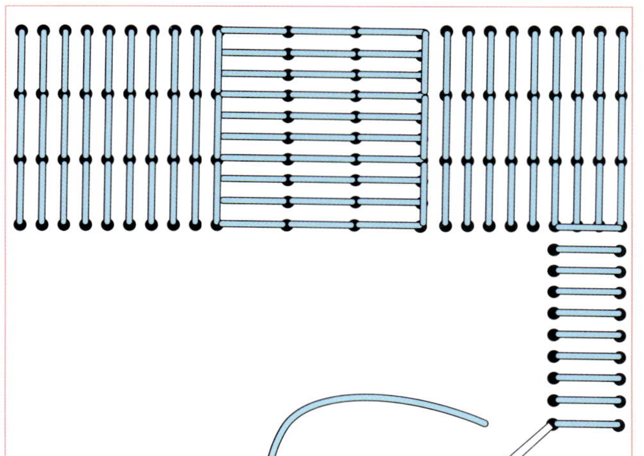

6 Alternate the direction of stitches for each block in order to make a chessboard pattern.

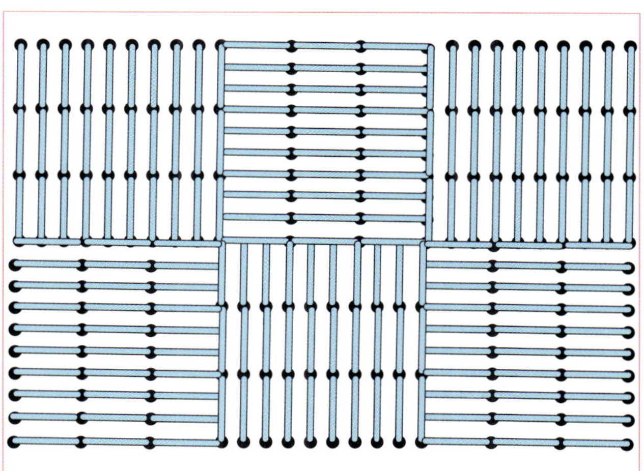

7 Continue until the design area is filled.

CHEVRON (PATTERN)

Blackwork.

A pattern made up of diagonal 'V' stitches with vertical stitches in between. It is a small, dense pattern which is suitable for more linear designs.

METHOD

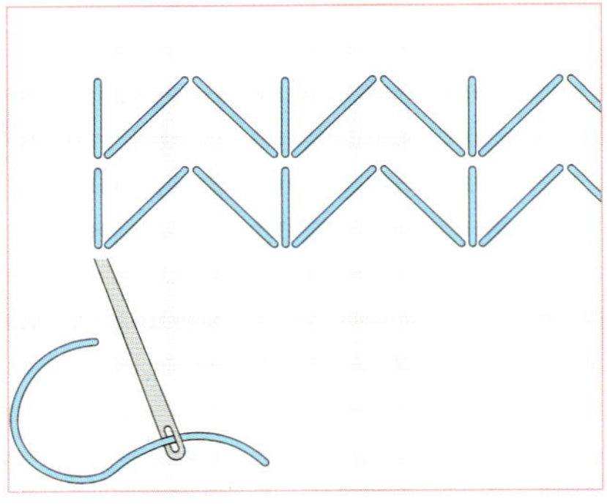

1 All stitches are worked across the fabric in a band covering two threads. Complete a vertical stitch over two fabric threads.

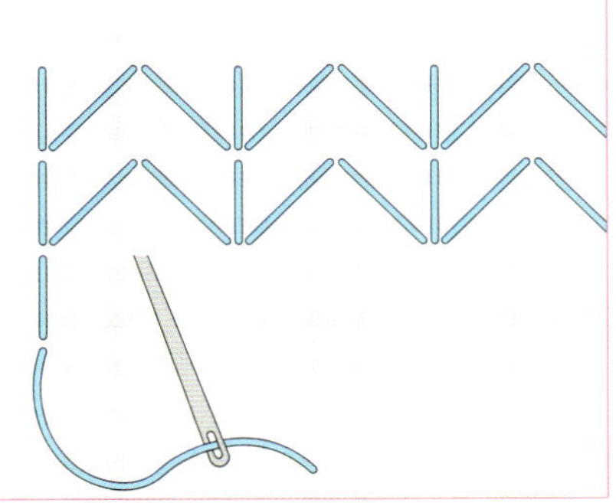

2 Bring the needle up at the base of the first stitch. Count two threads to the right and two threads up and take the needle down.

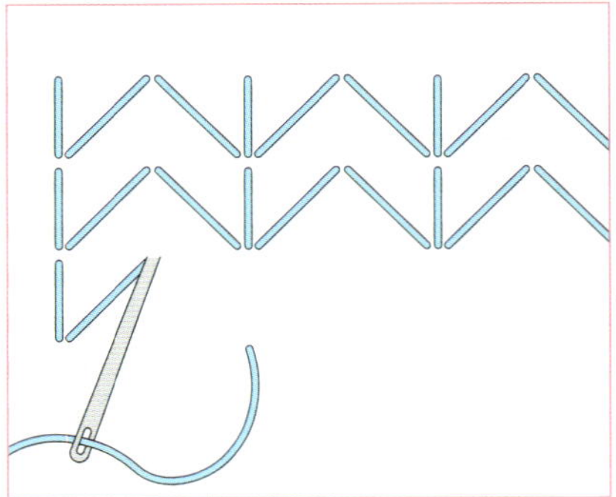

3 Count two threads to the right and two threads down and bring the needle up. Take it down at the top of the previous stitch.

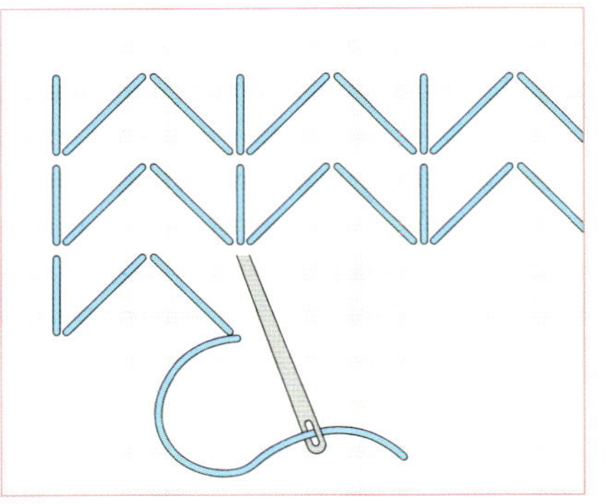

4 Repeat the previous three stitches in the same direction.

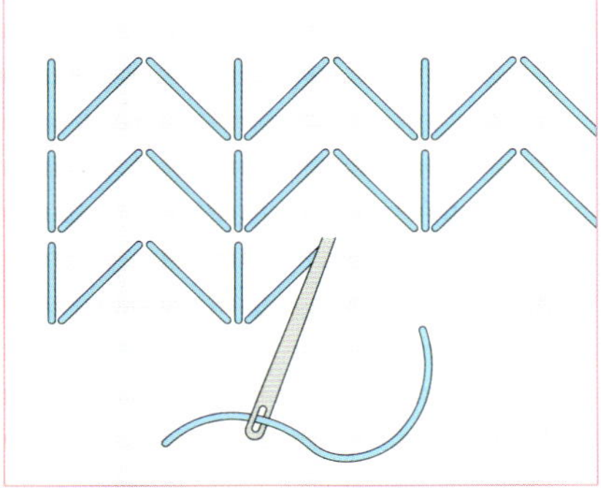

5 Continue along the row in the same sequence.

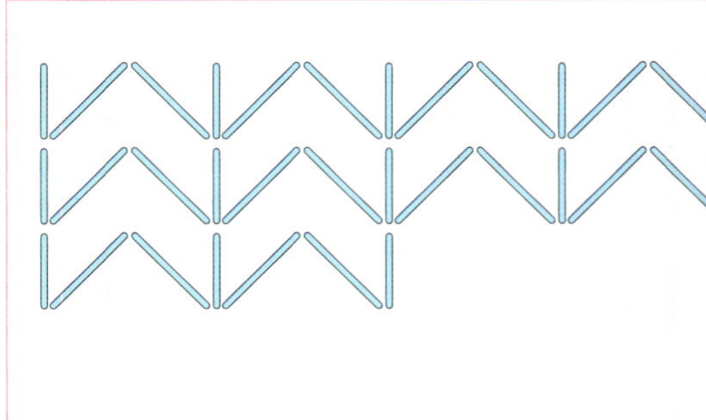

6 To start your next row, bring the needle up two threads below the bottom of the last stitch. Continue with the same pattern in the opposite direction.

CHIPPING

GOLDWORK.

Also known as Bright check, or Goldwork chips.

Chipping is the use of short lengths of hollow metal thread which are stitched down like beads. The placement of the chips at different angles makes them reflect the light and gives a glittery appearance.

METHOD

1 Cut a good number of small chips from a length of metal thread, they should be as long as they are wide. This example shows bright check.

2 Use a length of machine sewing thread, waxed and folded double. Bring the needle through to the front of the fabric from underneath, thread a chip onto the needle and gently manoeuvre it to the base of the thread.

3 Take your needle through the fabric, and stitch the purl in place. Your stitch length should be long enough to allow the chip to lie flat without arching up but not too long so that the thread is visible at the end of the chip.

4 Use the tip of a mellor or laying tool to help direct the sewing thread into position and avoid catching the sharp end of surrounding chips.

5 Continue to fill the shape with chips by varying the angle and stitching them close to one another so that no padding is visible.

CLOSED DIAGONAL DARNING (PATTERN)

Blackwork.

This stitch consists of long straight stitches, each offset by one thread, to form subtle diagonal stripes. It provides dense, flat coverage.

METHOD

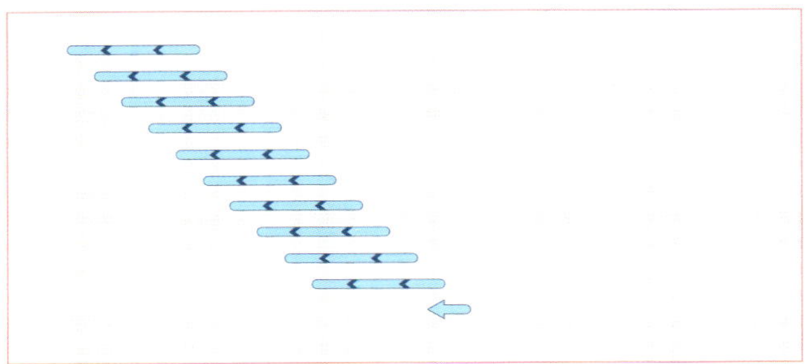

1 Work a series of straight horizontal parallel stitches over five fabric threads. Each stitch should be offset horizontally by one fabric thread from the stitch above.

2 Work back up the shape repeating the same stitch over five threads, ensuring each stitch shares a hole with the previous stitch on that line.

3 Continue to fill the space by working back and forth across the area to be filled.

CLOSED FLY STITCH

SURFACE.

Also known as Close-stacked fly stitch, Attached fly stitch, Fly stitch, or Antique embroidery.

This stitch is formed of a line of fly stitches (see page 28) worked so that the anchoring stitches touch each other. It has similarities with a line of closely-worked fern stitches and is often used to portray leaves or feathers.

The origins of this stitch are unclear: the name does not feature in any prominent 19th century sources, nor Mary Thomas' 1934 *Dictionary of Stitches*. However, an 1891 publication shows the stitch under the name 'Antique embroidery'; and another from 1888 doesn't name it specifically, but indicates that is used in Berlin wool work.

METHOD

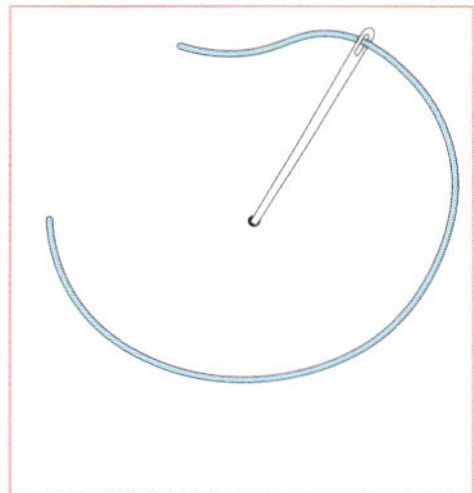

1 Bring the needle up through the fabric and back down short distance apart – this will be the width of your stitch.

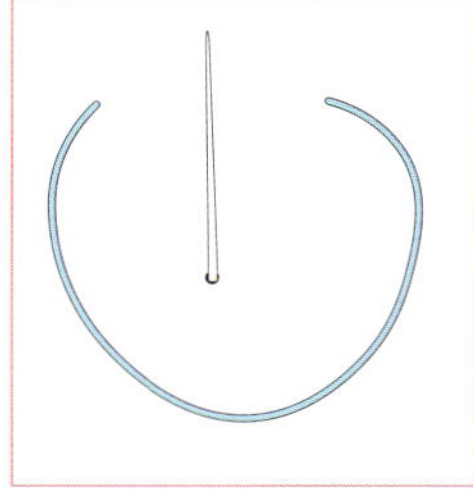

2 Leaving a loop on the surface, bring the needle up inside the loop, equidistant between the start and end points.

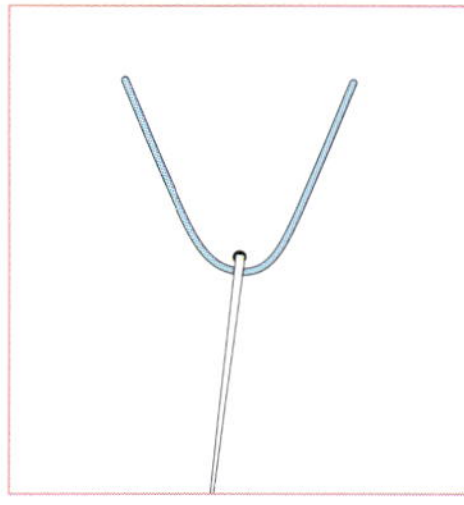

3 Tighten the loop against the needle by pulling the thread underneath your fabric.

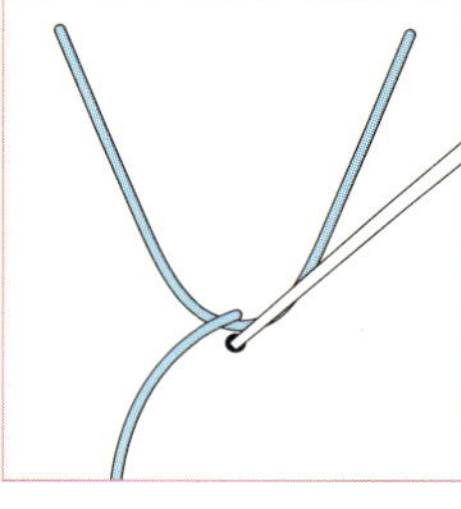

4 Pull the thread through to the surface and take the needle down the other side of the loop to secure.

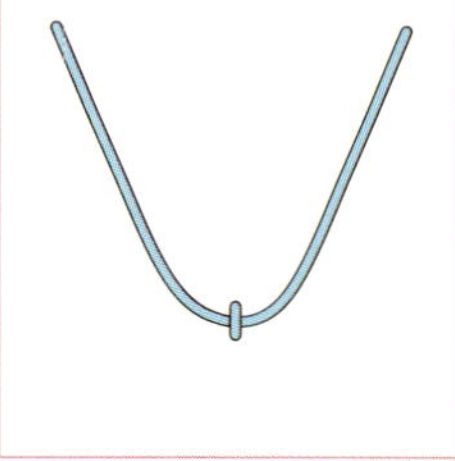

5 Pull through to complete a fly stitch.

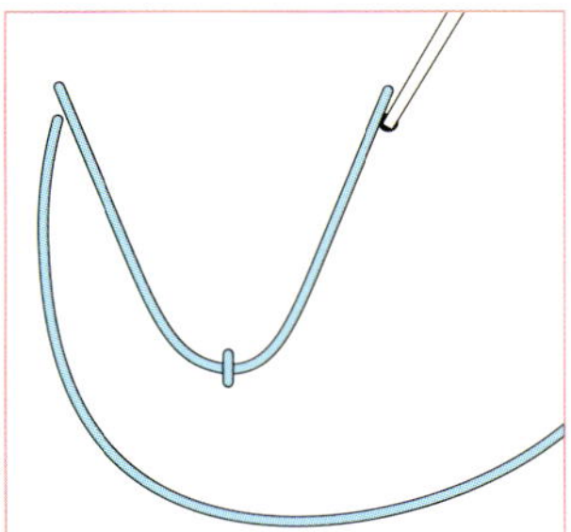

6 Come up and go down for the second loop just below the first fly stitch.

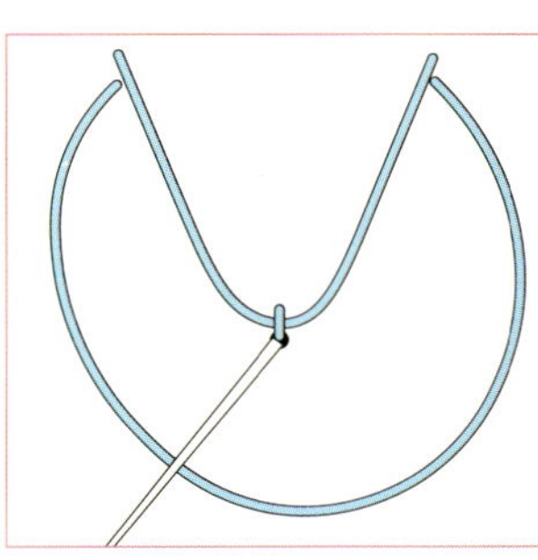

7 Bring the needle up inside the loop, where the first fly stitch ended.

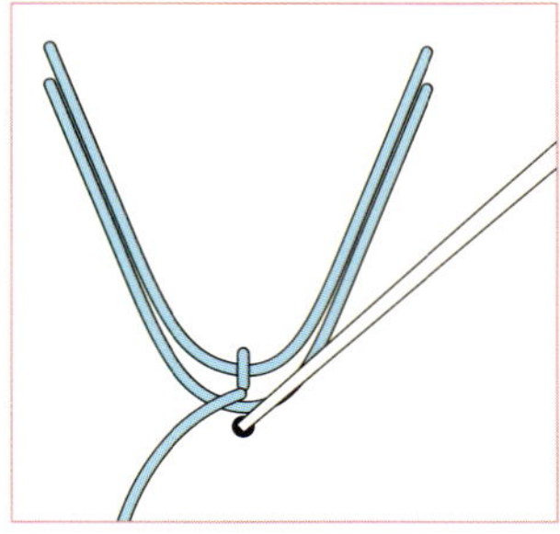

8 Take the needle down the other side of the second loop to secure.

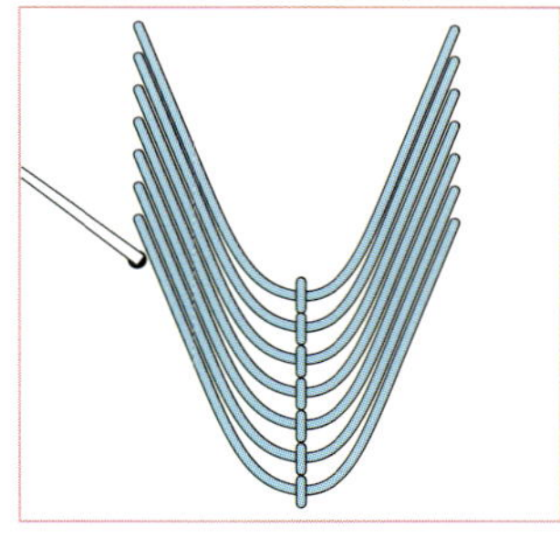

9 Continue and work a series of fly stitches closely together.

COLONIAL KNOT

SURFACE; SILK SHADING.

Also known as Candlewicking knot, or Figure of eight stitch.

The colonial knot creates a larger, rounder and more raised knot than the French knot (see page 29).

Colonial knots are part of the Candlewick embroidery tradition, developed in the USA during the early 18th century. The tradition started by using cotton from the wicks of candles (hence the name) to embellish empty flour bags and then developed into using more conventional materials. Items such as bedspreads are embellished with traditional patterns, some of which use colonial knots as the only stitch on the item.

METHOD

1 Bring the needle and thread to the surface. With both hands on the surface, hold the needle with one hand and the tension of the working thread in the other.

2 Bring the needle to the inside of the working thread and take it under the thread away from you.

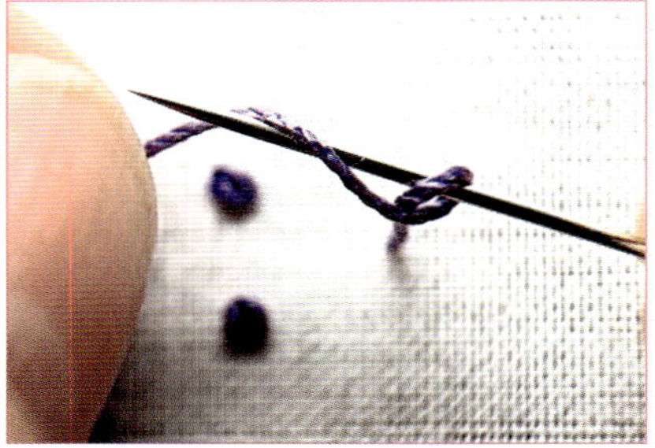

3 Use the working thread to wrap the pointed end of the needle.

4 Take the needle back down through the fabric, at the place it surfaced or very close to that point.

5 Draw the knot down the shaft of the needle so that it sits firmly on the fabric.

6 Take the needle through the fabric and draw through the excess thread to the back of the fabric.

CONDENSED CASHMERE STITCH

Canvaswork.

Also known as Diagonal cashmere stitch.

This is a diagonal stitch with a small pattern repeat of offset rectangles. The rectangles are condensed which means that the end of one rectangle overlaps the start of the next. Each rectangular cashmere block of this pattern is worked across two canvas threads by three.

Mary Thomas calls this version of the stitch 'Cashmere stitch' in her *Dictionary of Embroidery Stitches*, but she is alone in this and so we use the more common name. See cashmere stitch on page 139 for the original version of this stitch.

METHOD

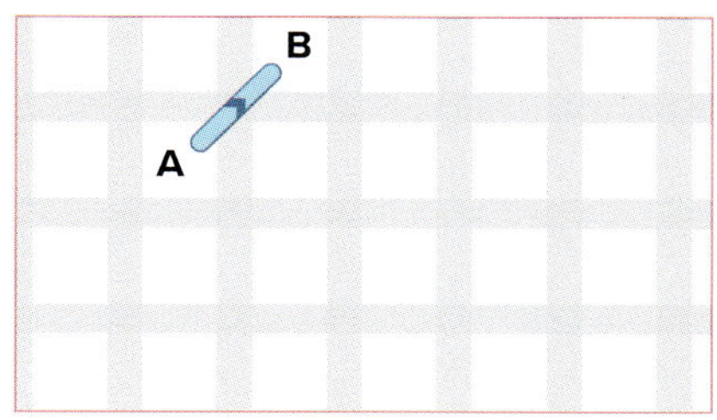

1 Make a tent stitch (see basketweave tent stitch on page 218) across one intersection of canvas.

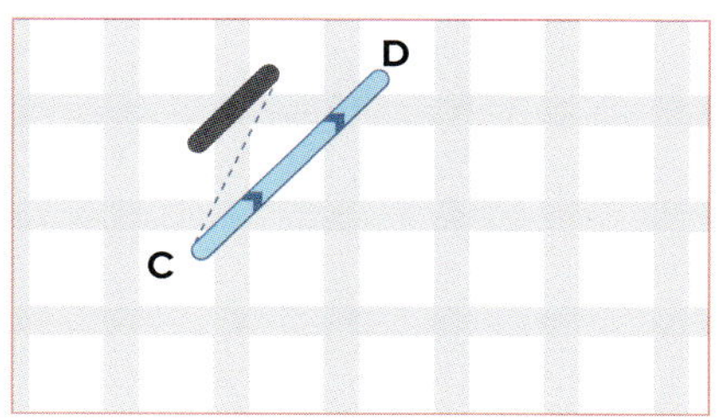

2 Starting directly beneath this stitch, make a diagonal stitch across two intersections of canvas.

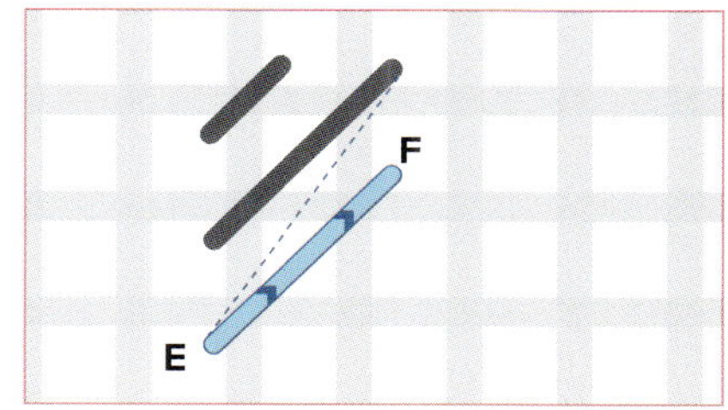

3 Repeat to make a second stitch across two intersections of canvas.

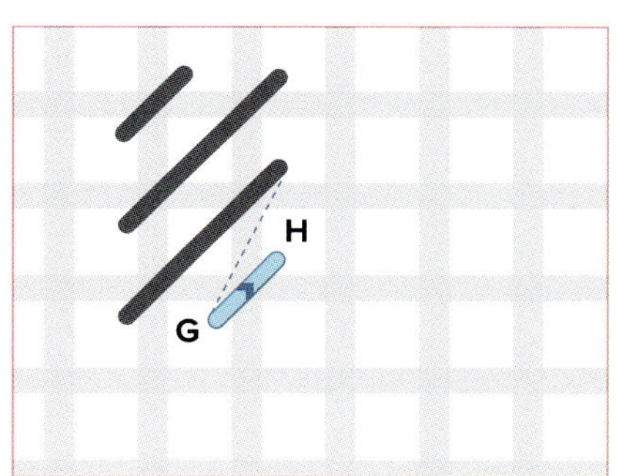

4 Finish off the rectangle with a second tent stitch at the bottom right corner of the block.

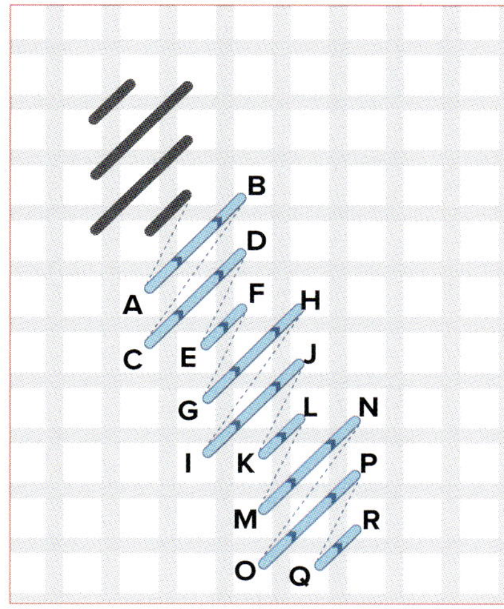

5 To work a diagonal row, continue the pattern with two longer stitches, then a tent stitch.

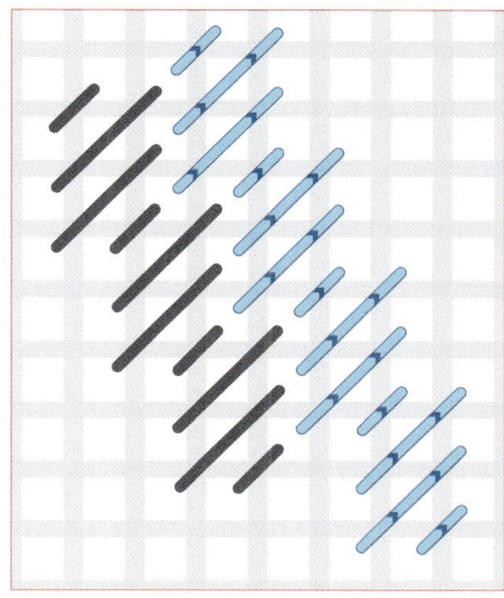

6 When working the next row to the right, the first tent stitch of each cashmere block should meet the top right-hand corner of the previous row's cashmere blocks.

CRETAN STITCH (CLOSED)

CREWELWORK; SURFACE.

Also known as Closed cretan stitch, Persian stitch, Long-armed feather stitch, or Cretan feather stitch.

This surface stitch consists of long, almost parallel stitches which anchor the previous stitch from alternate sides. This results in a filling stitch where the central area is more closely worked than the edges.

While it was certainly used in Cretan embroidery, there is no evidence to indicate that it originated on the island. The first evidence of its use is on a piece of 16th century Swiss/south German ecclesiastical embroidery currently held by the Cleveland Museum of Art, Ohio.

METHOD

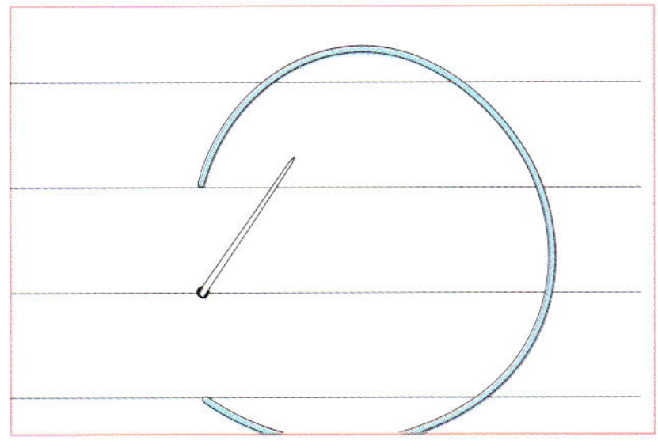

1 Draw four lines to divide the area to be filled into three equal columns. Bring the needle up on one of the central lines and take it down on the farthest outline. Leaving a loop on the surface, bring the needle up in the centre of that stitch.

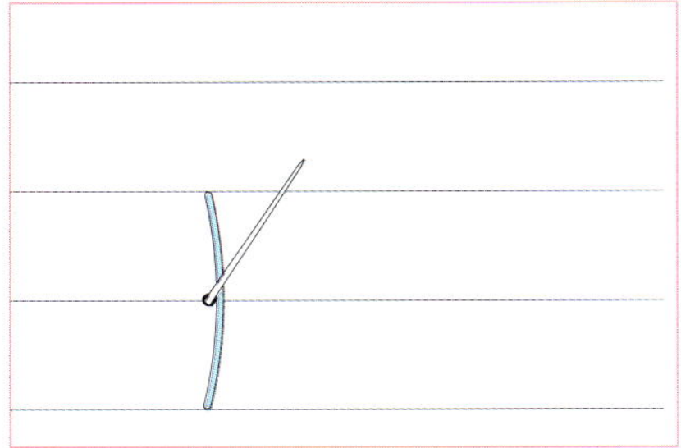

2 Take the slack on the thread to the underside and pull against the needle then draw the thread through to the surface.

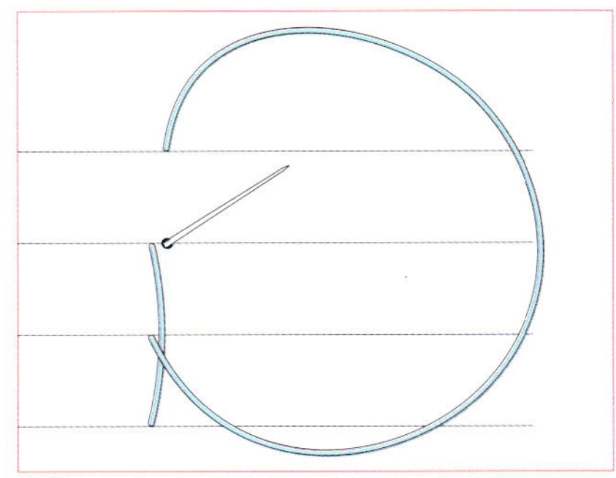

3 Take the needle down on the opposite outer line (fractionally below the previous stitch) and back up again in the centre of that stitch.

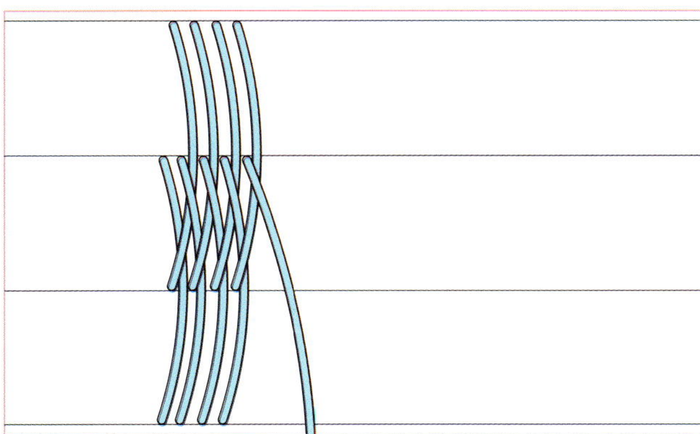

4 Continue working from side to side keeping the stitches close so as not to reveal too much background fabric.

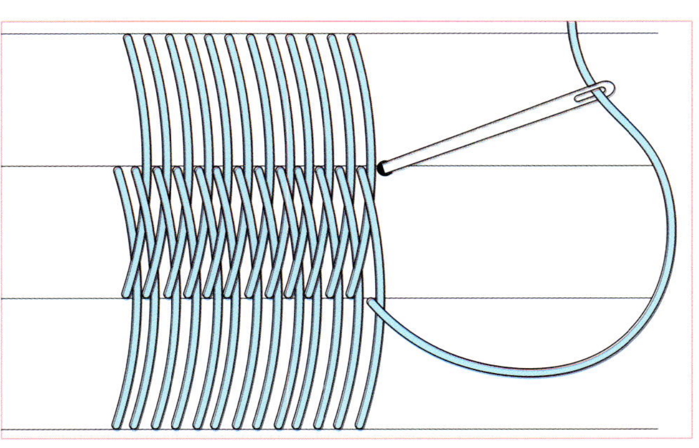

5 Secure the last stitch by couching over it at an angle and taking the needle down into the other central stitch.

CRETAN STITCH (OPEN)

CREWELWORK; MOUNTMELLICK; SURFACE.

Also known as Long-armed feather stitch, Quill stitch, Persian stitch, or Cretan stitch.

This stitch is a series of widely offset fly stitches.

As its alternative name of long-armed feather stitch suggests, Cretan stitch has structural similarities with feather stitch. It has a broad history: it features on a piece of 16th-century southern German/Swiss ecclesiastical embroidery currently held by the Cleveland Museum of Art, Ohio; it is used on an embroidered skirt from mid 18th-century Crete, now held by the V&A South Kensington; and it is used to decorate garments in Oman.

METHOD

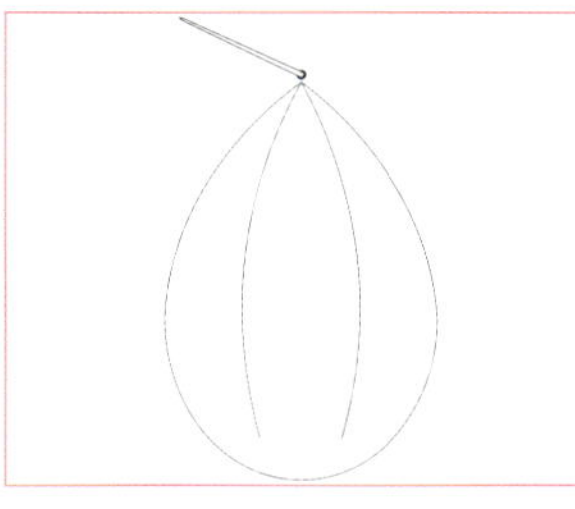

1 Draw a double stem line. Starting at the tip of your leaf shape, bring the needle up just outside the marked line.

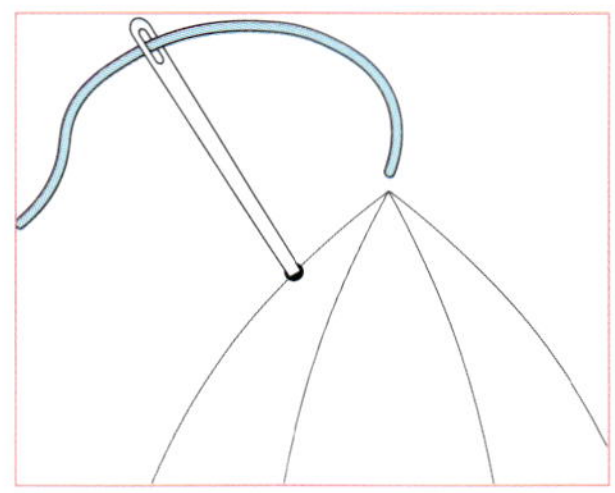

2 Take the needle down through the fabric on the line left of the protruding thread.

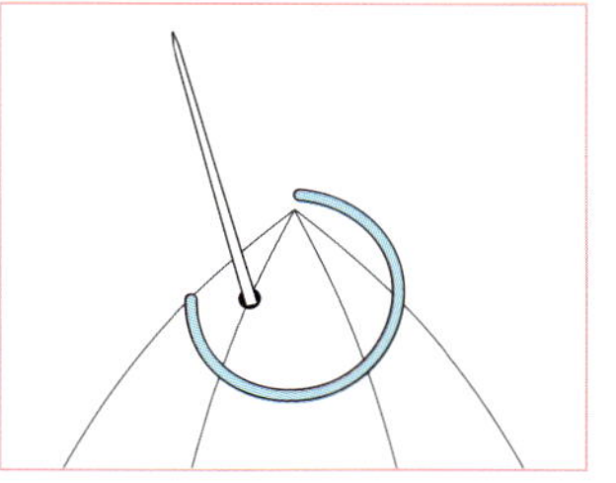

3 Draw the needle through to create a loop. Hold the loop and bring the thread up inside it from the back, on the left-hand stem line.

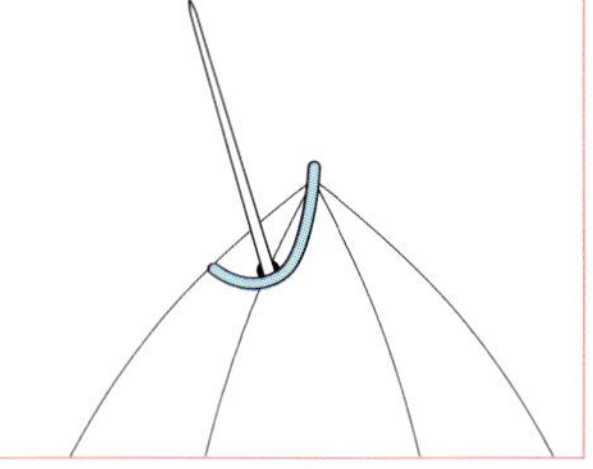

4 Draw the thread through to tighten the loop against the needle.

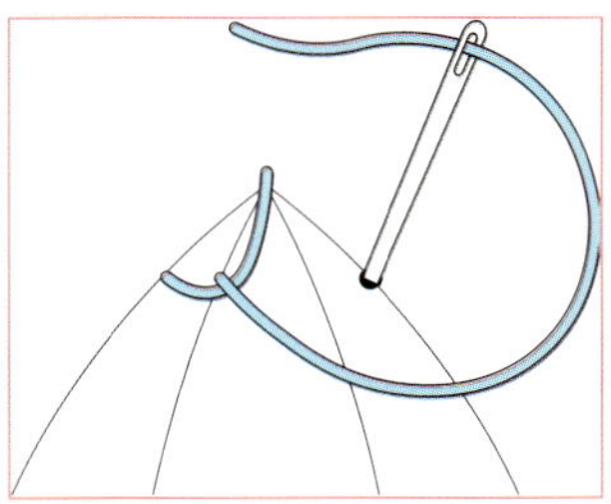

5 Draw the needle and thread through, then take the needle down through the fabric on the outer marked line to the right of the first stitch.

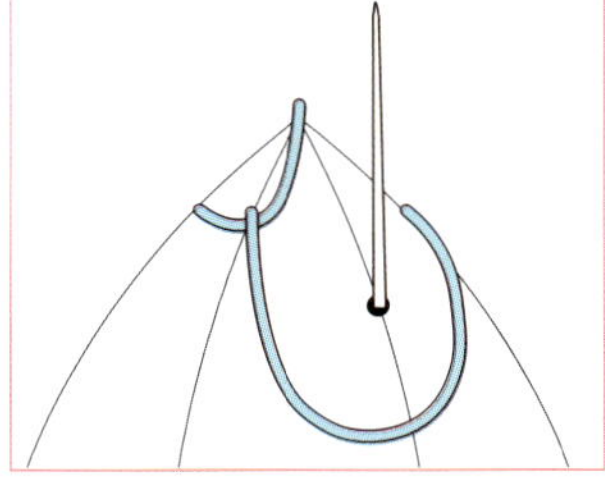

6 Pull the thread through to create a loop. Hold the loop on the surface, and bring the needle up on the stem line on the right-hand side.

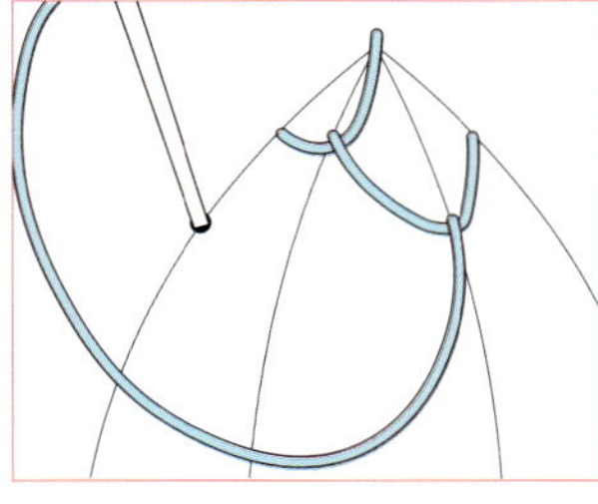

7 Tighten the loop on the needle, draw the thread through and take it down on the outer line on the left-hand side.

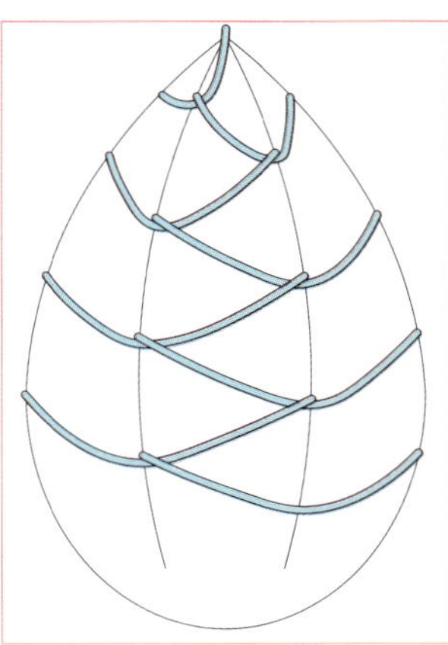

8 Continue to work down towards the base by filling in alternate sides.

CUSHION STITCH

Canvaswork.

Also known as Scotch stitch, or Diagonal satin blocks.

This canvaswork stitch consists of five diagonal stitches combined to form a square block. Multiple blocks form a grid pattern.

The stitch is also widely known as Scotch stitch; hence the naming of some of its variations: condensed Scotch stitch and Scottish squares (see page 195). Confusingly, both reversed cushion stitch and Scottish squares are sometimes also known as cushion stitch.

METHOD

1 Begin with a tent stitch in the top left-hand corner.

2 Move one canvas thread along and make a stitch across two intersections; repeat across three intersections ...

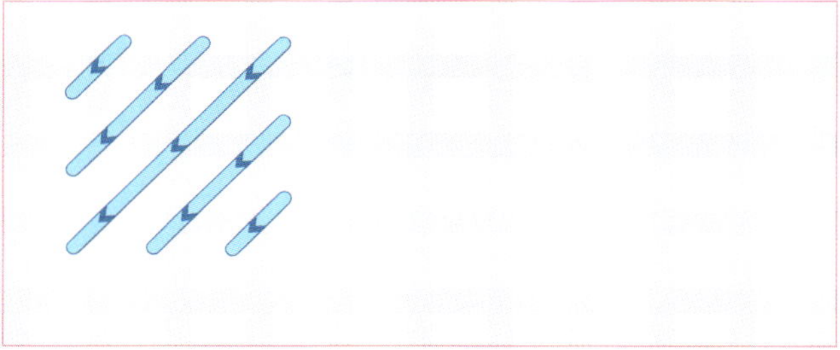

3 ... then two, and finally make another tent stitch.

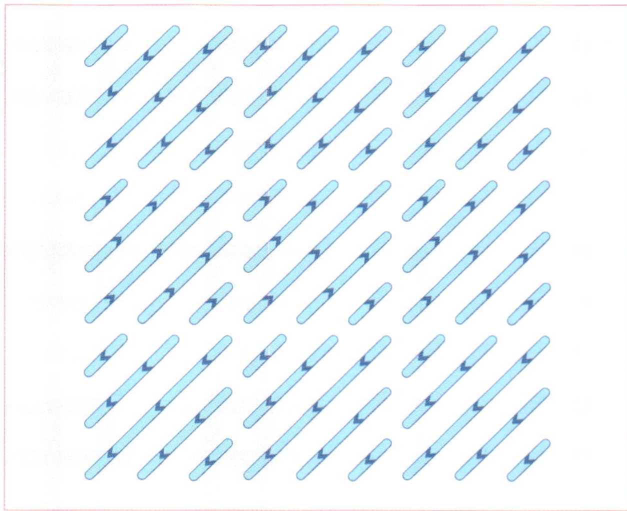

4 Continue the sequence to produce identical blocks that line up vertically and horizontally.

▲▲ Sampler, RSN Collection COL.61

Worked by Kathleen Barnard while a student at the Royal School of Needlework's Training School in 1932, this sampler, with its four different border patterns and floral arrangement, is typical of the whitework samplers made at the school during this period.

It uses a number of drawn and pulled thread whitework techniques and surface stitches to depict several flowers and a butterfly. These are surrounded by a drawn and pulled border with four corners, which is completed with a hemmed edge. Each side of the border is unique.

A small butterfly (see detail) features on the right of the motif. Its head is rendered in French knots (see page 29) and its wings feature a burden stitch (see page 220) filling and cushion stitches with eyelets, as well as drawn work in the form of woven bars. The back end of its body is worked in satin stitch (see page 37).

CUTWORK PURLS OVER SOFT STRING

Goldwork.

Cutwork purls is the stitching of lengths of metal purl at a 45 degree angle over a padded shape. Metal purl is fine wire tightly wound into a delicate coil; it is available in a variety of colours.

For more background about purls generally, see pearl purl application on page 97.

METHOD

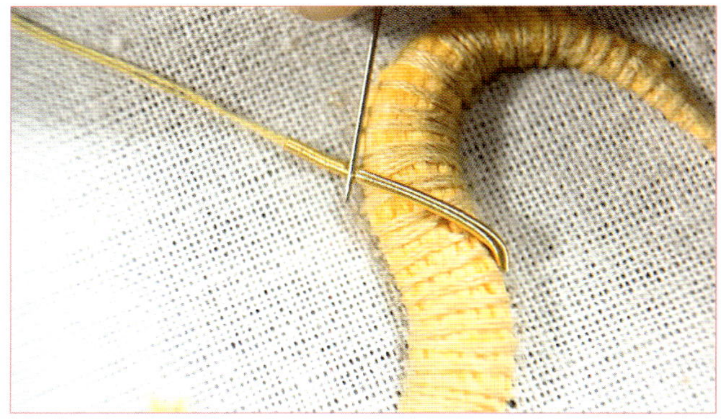

1 Using a double waxed thread, bring the needle to the surface at one side of the padded shape, halfway down the length of the padding. Cut a piece of purl to the estimated length required, thread the purl and hold it in position across the padding at 45 degrees. Use the needle to dent it at the point where it touches the fabric on the other side – this marks where it needs to be cut.

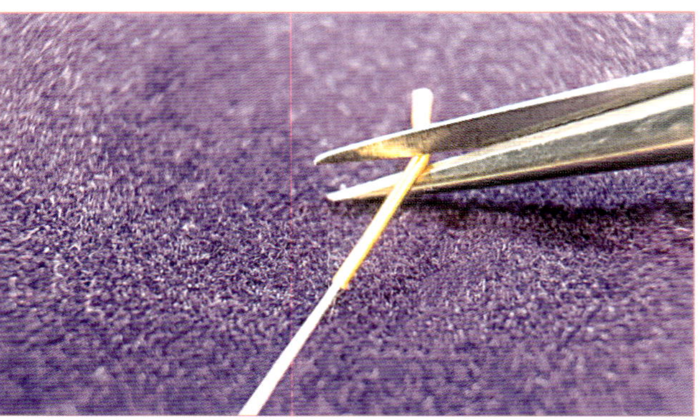

2 Remove the purl from the thread and 'cut' to the required length. You can use this piece as a guide to measure and cut more purls to the desired length.

3 Re-thread the cut purl and gently manoeuvre it to the base of the thread. Avoid touching it with your fingers, as this can encourage tarnishing.

4 Stitch the purl over the padding at 45 degrees. Place the tip of a mellor under the gold to ease it around the padding and prevent it from cracking.

5 Gently pull the purl in place so that it hugs the padding.

TIP

If you thread a cut purl and find that it is too long or short, repeat the unthreading process and re-cut the piece. If it is too short, keep it as you should be able to use it for a narrower section.

6 Continue to secure more purls in the same way and cut purls to the length that suits the shape to be filled. When bringing the needle down into the fabric, an acute angle will help you get the purl close to the previous purl and maintain the 45 degree angle.

7 Pay attention to the spacing between each purl to achieve a sweeping angle: tighter on the inside of the curve and more spaced on the outside. Complete one half of the shape before returning to the centre to start the other half.

DIAGONAL WAVE (PATTERN)

Blackwork.

This blackwork stitch, as its name suggests, is formed of asymmetrical diagonal waves. They form slanted jagged lines from top left to bottom right.

The pattern works best in larger areas.

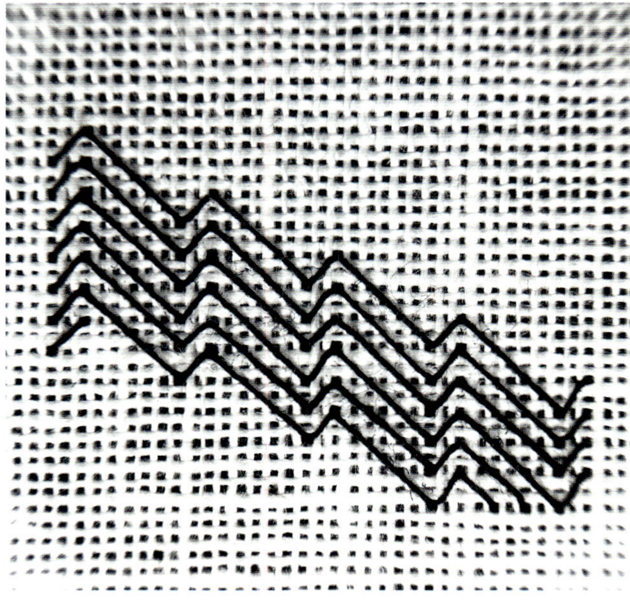

METHOD

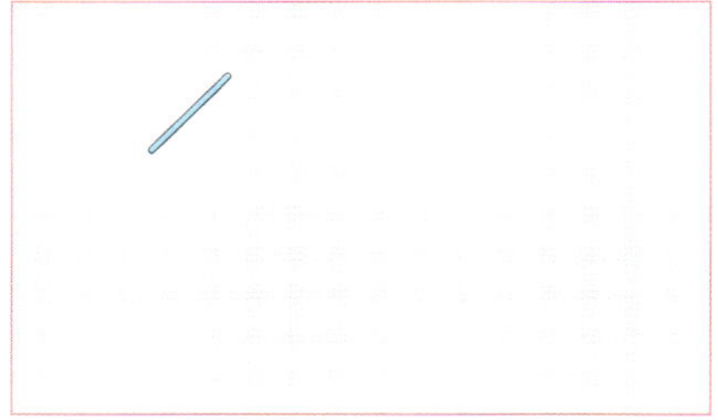

1 Make a diagonal stitch from top right to bottom left over two intersections.

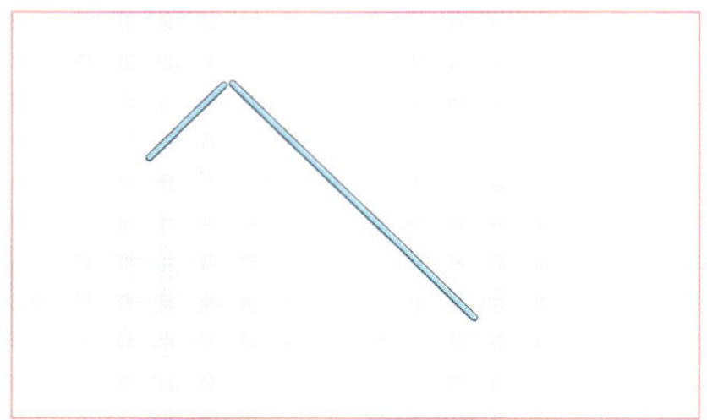

2 Bring the needle up again where you started and make a diagonal stitch from top left to bottom right over six intersections.

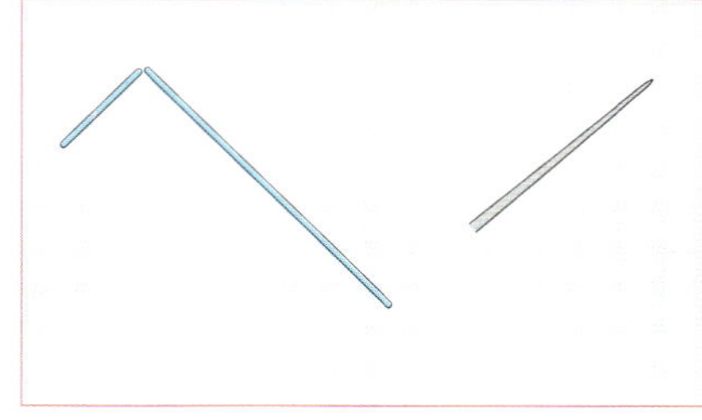

3 Bring the needle up again two intersections up to the right and repeat the last two steps.

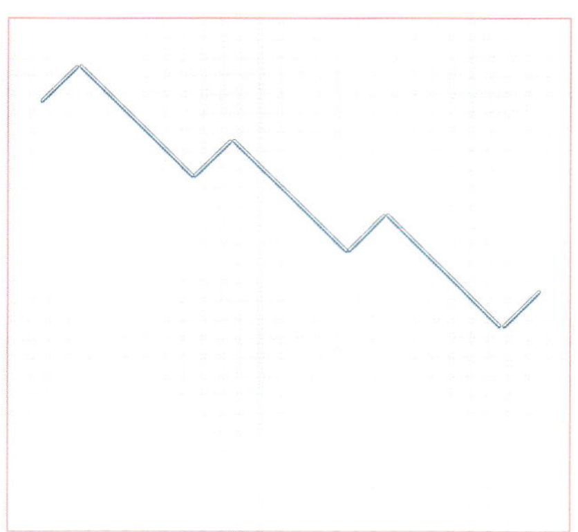

4 Continue to the other side of the shape.

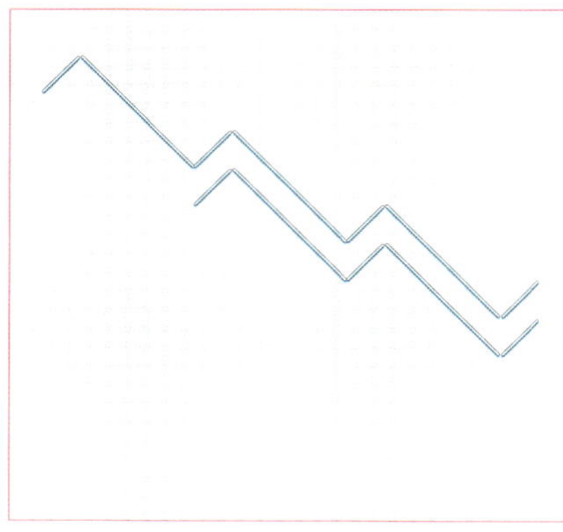

5 Complete a parallel line two threads below. This time work diagonally upwards; each stitch should be directly below the one above.

6 Continue to fill the shape.

DIAGONAL WEAVE (PATTERN)

Blackwork.

This complex pattern is made up of alternate rows of tall and short rectangles, each crossed with a diagonal stitch. It is a fairly dense pattern and works well in architectural shapes.

METHOD

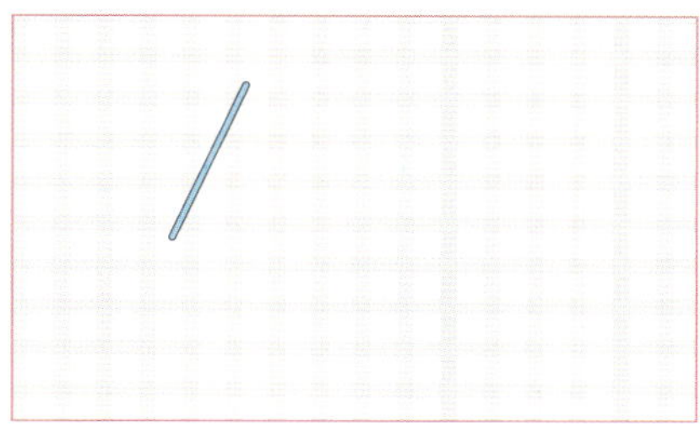

1 Work a diagonal stitch over two vertical and four horizonal threads, top right to bottom left.

2 Bring your needle up in the original hole, and work three sides of a box around the diagonal stitch in a combination of straight and back stitches.

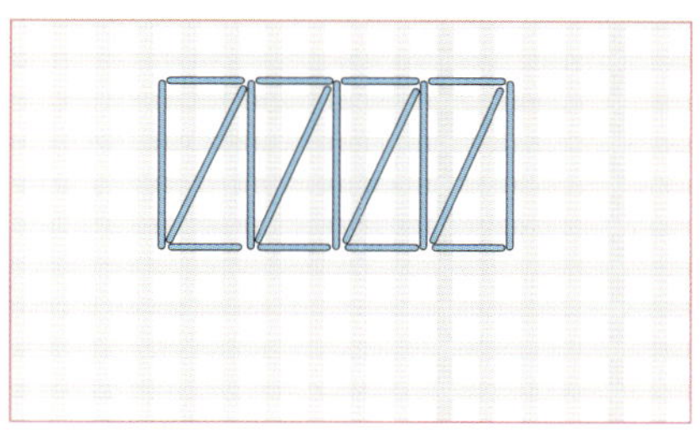

3 Repeat working from left to right to complete the row.

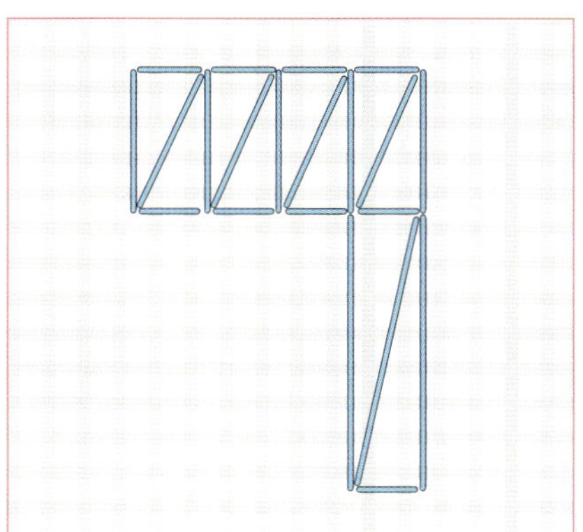

4 Work the next row from right to left: this time the diagonal and vertical stitches should be twice the height, so over eight threads.

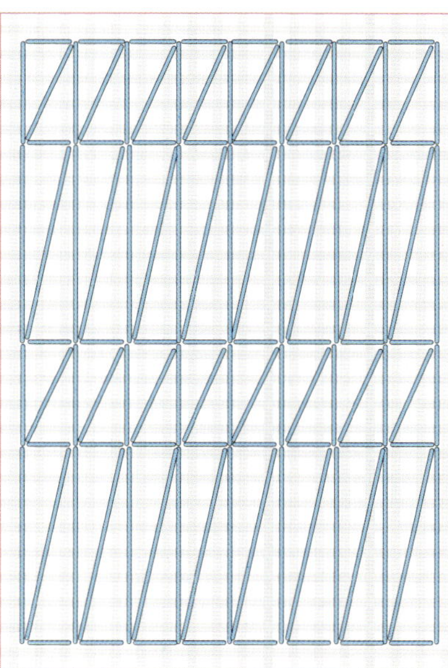

5 Continue to work alternate rows over four and eight threads.

DIAPER COUCHING (GOLDWORK)

GOLDWORK.

Also known as Diapering, or Pattern couching.

Diaper couching is the method of stitching coloured thread over laid metal threads to create a patterned effect.

Originally a diamond motif, today 'diapering' or 'diaper patterns' can describe any textured background with a small repeating pattern. Diaper patterns were first woven into fabric rather than embroidered – many Egyptian examples survive from the 5th century AD and some fabrics are still produced in this way. This explains the origin of the term 'diaper' in North America for babies' nappies – it describes the pattern in the weave of the original fabric.

Threads couched in diaper patterns feature in many Opus Anglicanum pieces from the 12th to 14th centuries, although most of these are worked in underside couching so, unlike our examples, there is no visible couching thread. It is not until the late 1800s that the modern version of diaper couching is documented, when it is described as 'worked so as to form zigzag lines, diamonds, and crosses'.

METHOD

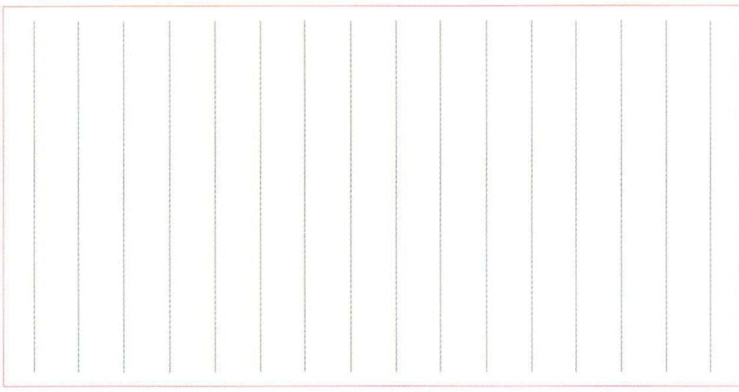

1 Begin by drawing evenly spaced lines on to the background fabric. The lines represent where the couching stitches are to be placed.

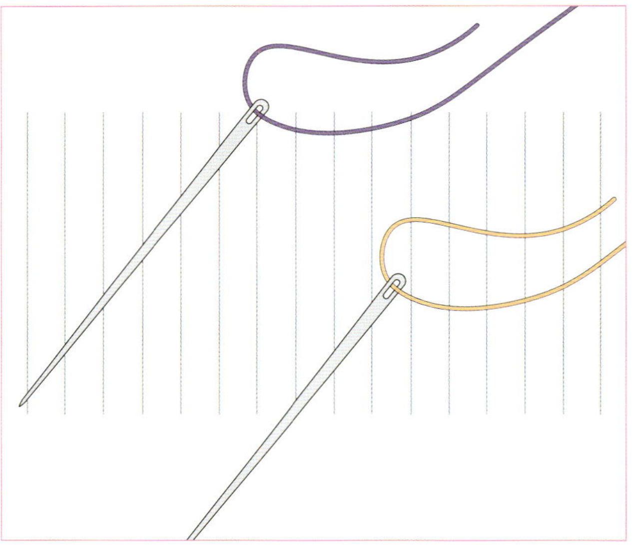

2 Thread two needles: one with a single strand of self-coloured thread (matching the metal thread) and the other with a single strand of a coloured thread of your choice.

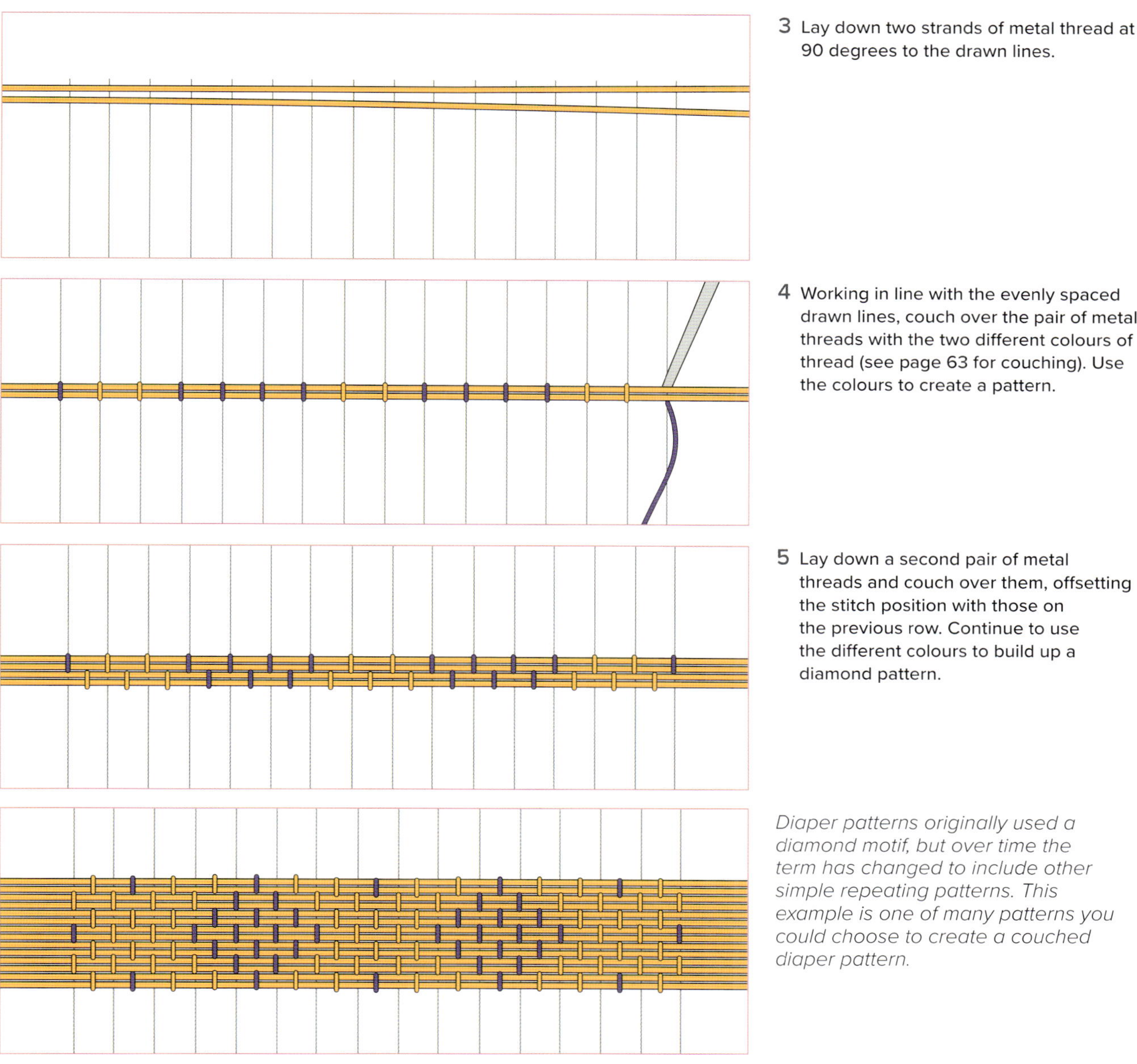

3 Lay down two strands of metal thread at 90 degrees to the drawn lines.

4 Working in line with the evenly spaced drawn lines, couch over the pair of metal threads with the two different colours of thread (see page 63 for couching). Use the colours to create a pattern.

5 Lay down a second pair of metal threads and couch over them, offsetting the stitch position with those on the previous row. Continue to use the different colours to build up a diamond pattern.

Diaper patterns originally used a diamond motif, but over time the term has changed to include other simple repeating patterns. This example is one of many patterns you could choose to create a couched diaper pattern.

DOUBLE CROSS STITCH

Canvaswork; Berlin wool Work; Counted thread; Hardanger.

Also known as Star stitch, Devil stitch, Leviathan stitch, Smyrna cross stitch, or Railway stitch.

This stitch consists of a diagonal cross stitch, with an upright cross stitch of the same size placed directly on top.

Double cross stitch has multiple names, one of which is 'railway stitch', which apparently comes from the fact it covers the ground so quickly. This presumably dates from the 19th century, but double cross stitch certainly dates from before this time, as there are early 18th-century pieces showing it used as a surface embroidery stitch, rather than a canvaswork/counted thread one.

METHOD

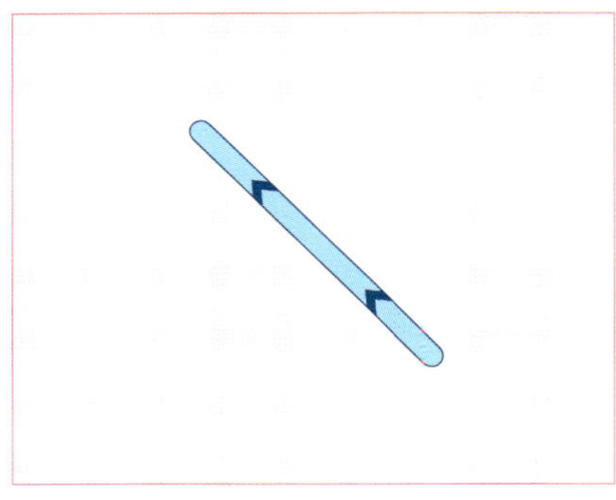

1 Bring the needle up at the bottom right corner to work a half cross stitch over four vertical and four horizontal canvas threads.

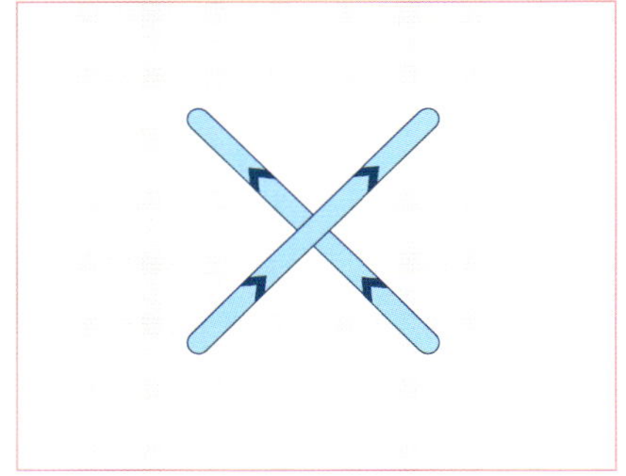

2 Bring up the needle at the bottom left corner to complete a cross stitch over four vertical and four horizontal canvas threads.

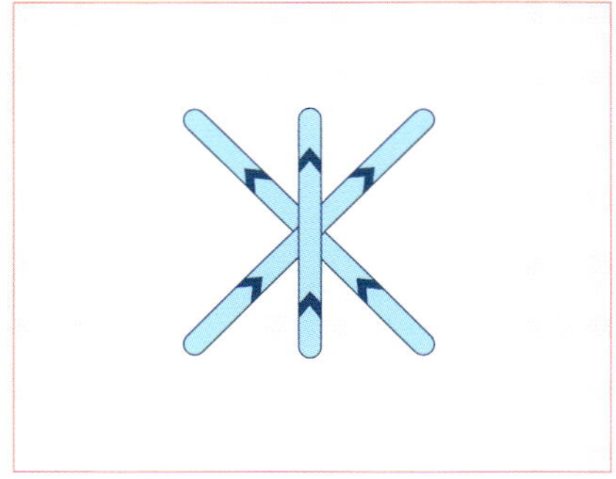

3 Then work an upright cross stitch by starting from the bottom centre to the top centre.

4 Finish the upright cross stitch by going from left centre to right centre. This completes a double cross stitch.

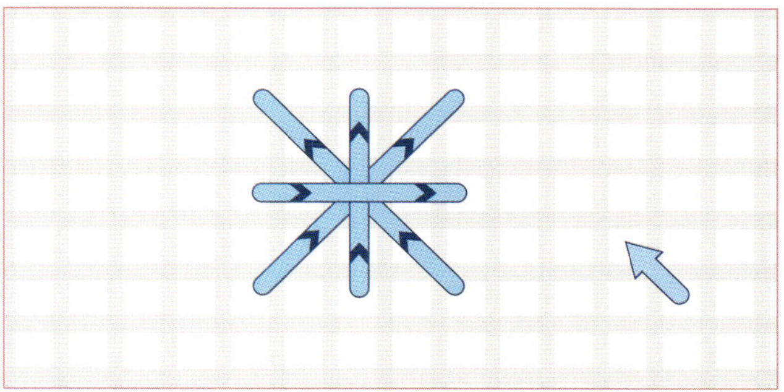

5 To continue, bring up the needle to the right (four canvas threads from the bottom right corner of the first double cross stitch).

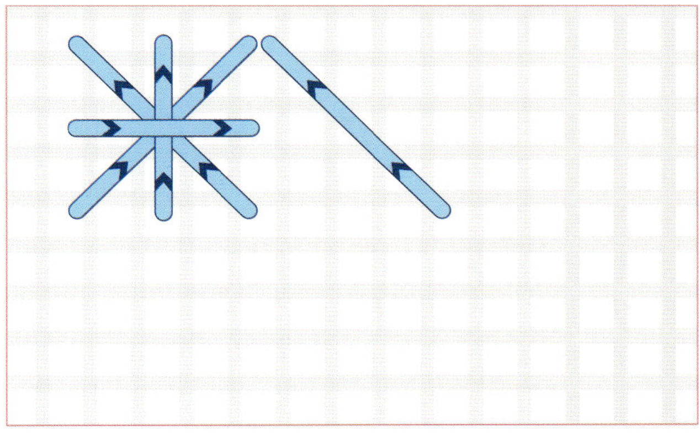

6 Starting from step 1, repeat working an ordinary cross stitch and then an upright cross stitch.

7 When the first row is finished, bring the needle up at four canvas threads below the bottom right corner of the last double cross stitch.

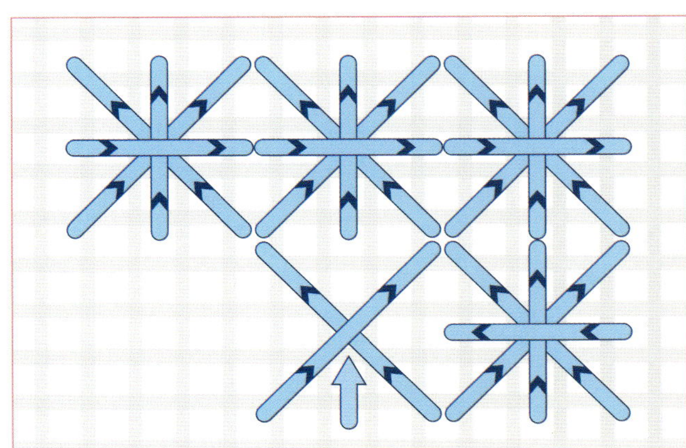

8 Continue working double cross stitch on the second row from right to left, making sure the stitches of each double cross stitch are worked in the same order and direction.

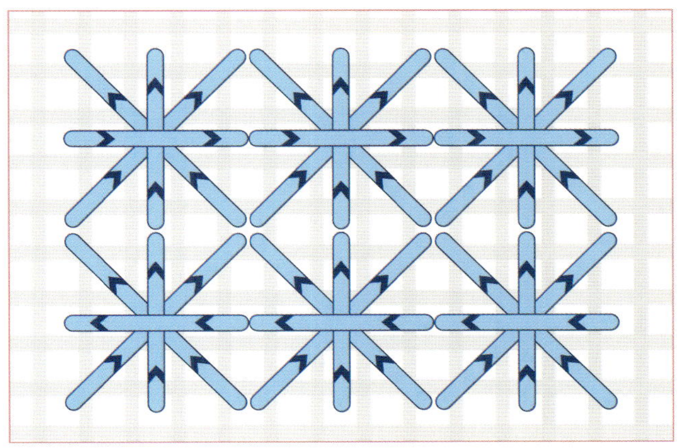

Completed double cross stitch as filling.

DUTCH STITCH

CANVASWORK.

Also known as Dutch cross stitch.

This canvaswork stitch consists of three crossing stitches which form a six pointed star. When worked in rows the stars are offset so that they fit together.

It is a raised, medium-sized stitch that is good for adding texture.

METHOD

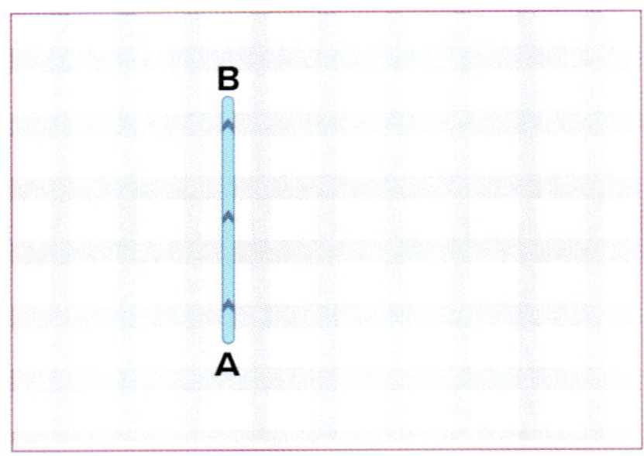

1 Make a vertical stitch from bottom to top across four threads of the canvas. Bring the needle up one thread down and two threads to the left (this corresponds to 10 on a clockface).

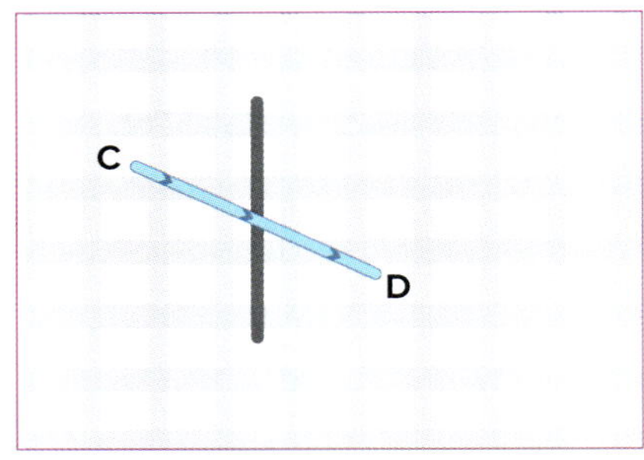

2 Make a diagonal stitch across four threads and down two threads of the canvas (corresponding to 4 on a clockface).

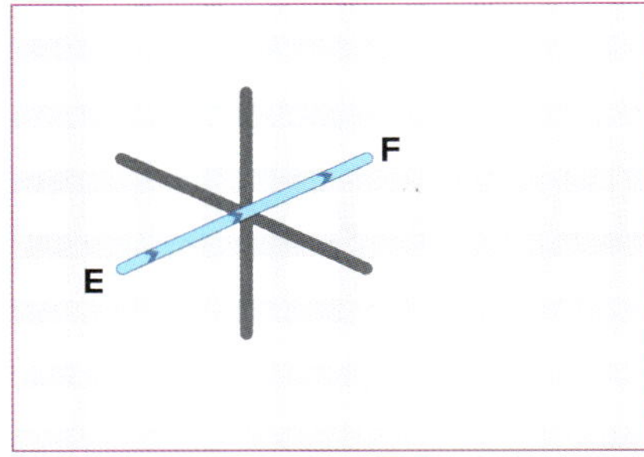

3 Bring your needle up across four canvas threads to the left (8 on a clockface) and make a diagonal stitch across four threads and up two (2 on a clockface).

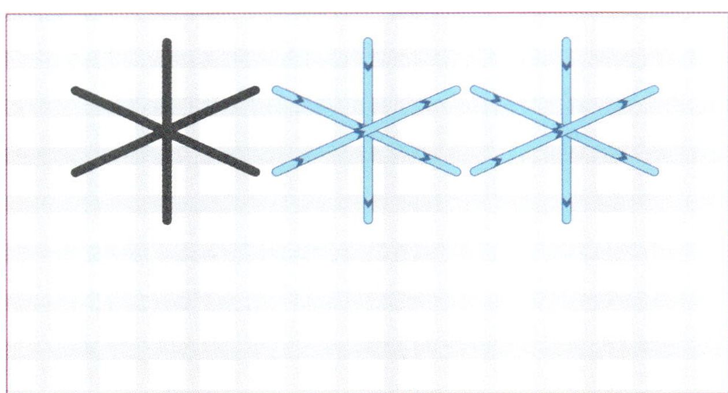

4 Work the pattern in horizontal rows so that the edges of the crosses touch.

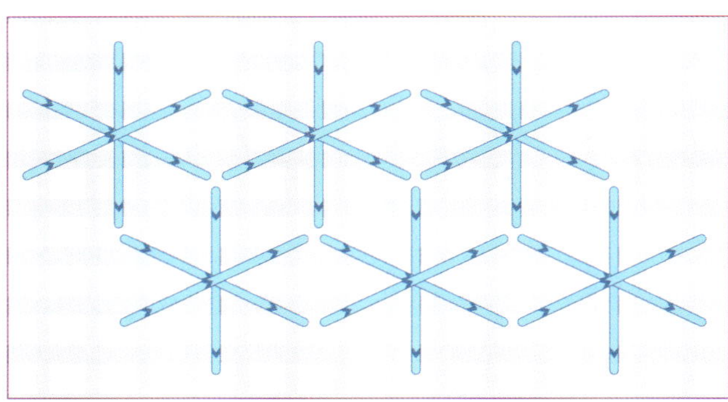

5 The row below should fit into the gaps of the first, touching at the corners of the crosses.

ENCROACHING STRAIGHT GOBELIN STITCH

CANVASWORK.

This stitch features parallel bands of satin stitch that interlock slightly into the stitches of the bands above and below. This gives a smooth appearance ideal for flat or shaded backgrounds.

For more information see straight Gobelin stitch on page 203.

METHOD

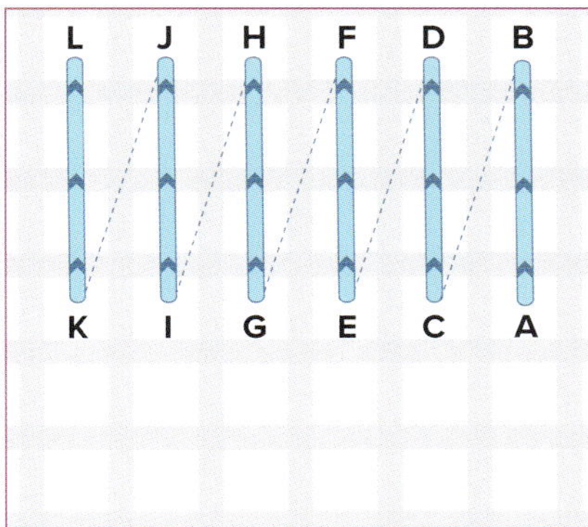

1 Start by making a row of vertical stitches over three threads of the canvas.

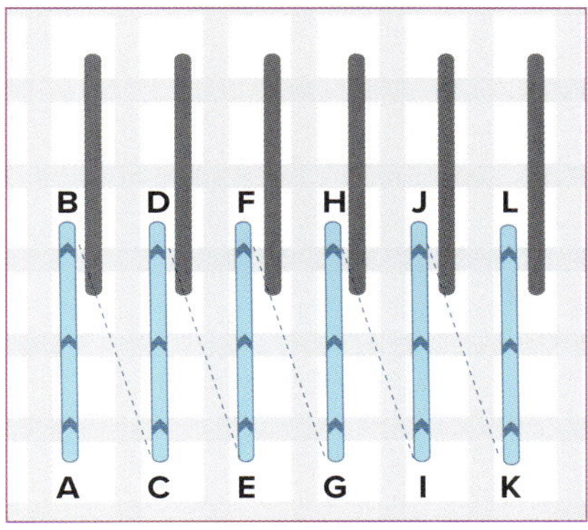

2 Begin the second row two threads below the first, and again make a row of vertical stitches over three threads, allowing for the encroachment of one thread between rows.

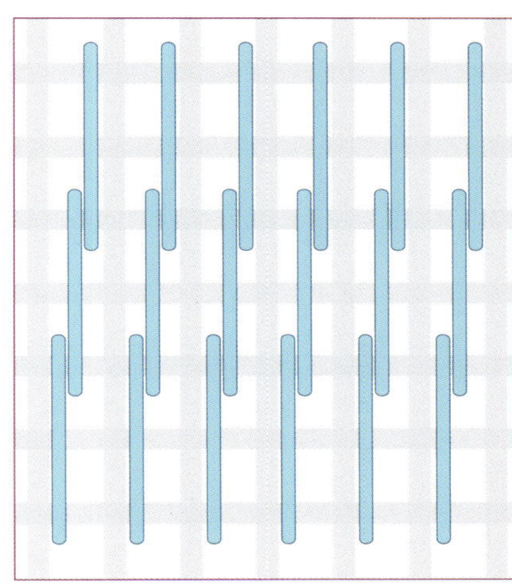

3 Always take the needle down into the previous row between stitches. Do not bring the needle out of the previous row, as this can disturb the lay of the stitches.

FELT PADDING

Goldwork; Stumpwork; Appliqué.

Felt padding is a method of raising up metal threads. It can consist of one or more layers of felt in a colour that complements the chosen metal: yellow for gold, white or light grey for silver, and brown for copper or bronze.

METHOD

1 Thread a needle with a multipurpose thread in a colour that complements the metal thread you will use (see the text at the top of the page). Use a waste knot or holding stitch to start your thread.

2 Bring your needle up in the fabric and take it down into the edge of your first piece of felt at a slight angle (about 45 degrees to your base fabric), making a small stitch on the top surface of the felt.

3 Stitch around the piece to prevent it from moving while you work. The number of stitches will depend greatly on the size of your felt: as a rough guide, if it is large, leave gaps of about 1.5–2cm (½–¾in); if it is small, reduce the gaps to less than 1cm (½in) or even smaller.

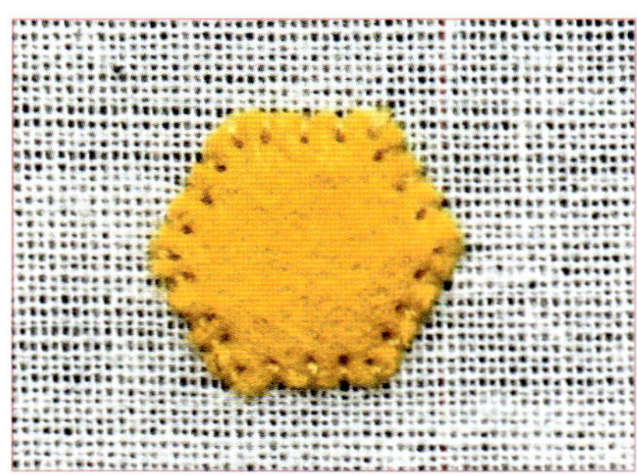

4 Go back around your shape, filling in the gaps with more stitches so that they are 2mm (⅛in) or so apart.

5 Once the whole shape is held down, either add the next layer of felt in the same way on top of your first piece, or finish off the thread using two tiny stab stitches on or next to each other, in an area to be covered or slightly under the felt.

6 Add a third layer of felt, following the same method, if required.

FLYING CROSS STITCH

CANVASWORK.

Also known as Long cross stitch.

Flying cross stitch is a slightly elongated cross stitch that is worked in diagonal rows. Each cross stitch is made across two by three threads of the canvas.

METHOD

1 Work an elongated cross stitch, across two by three threads (making sure that the top stitch is worked from bottom left to top right).

2 Bring your needle up one canvas thread below the top right-hand corner of this stitch. Start your second cross from here.

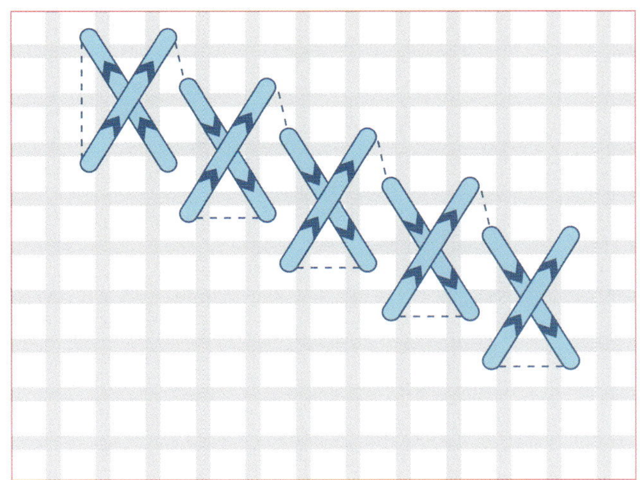

3 This and every following cross should start one canvas thread below the previous cross.

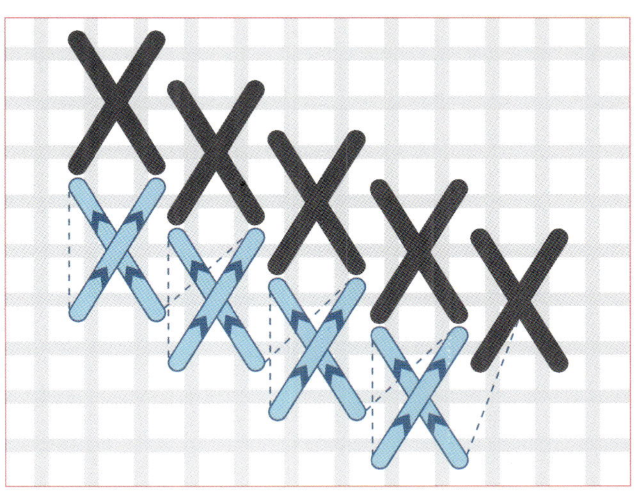

4 Work the second row directly beneath the first.

HARLEQUIN (PATTERN)

Blackwork.

This blackwork stitch consists of horizontal diamonds, hence the name 'Harlequin' after the costume of the pantomime character.

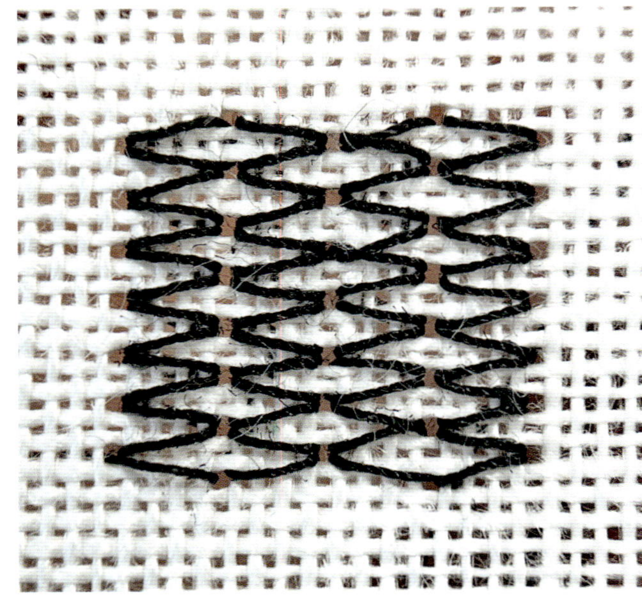

METHOD

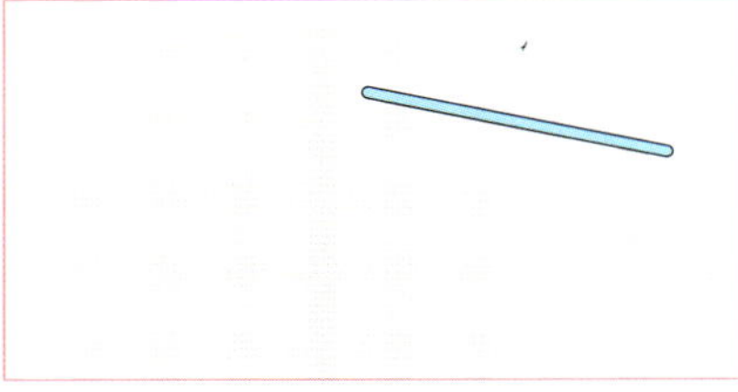

1 Make a diagonal stitch across four threads and down one thread from top left to bottom right.

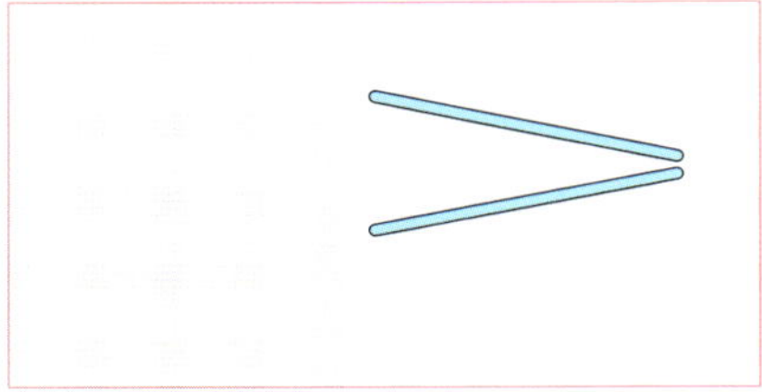

2 Bring the needle up two threads below where you started and make a diagonal stitch across four threads and up one thread; take your needle down in the same hole as the end of previous stitch.

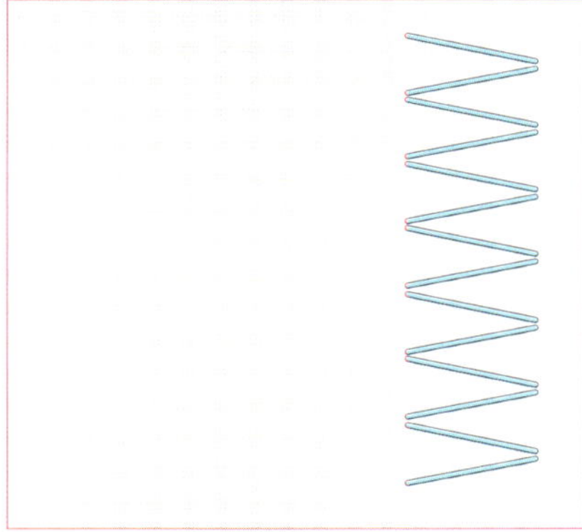

3 Repeat steps 1 and 2 to complete a vertical row of zigzags.

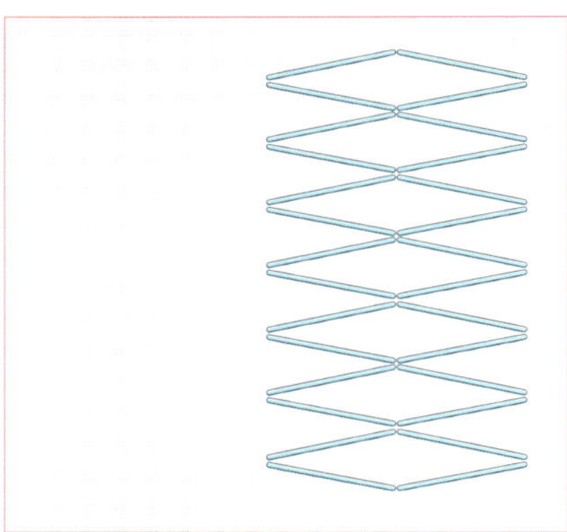

4 Work the next vertical row by completing the diamond shapes: stitch a mirror image zigzag which shares the holes of the first row.

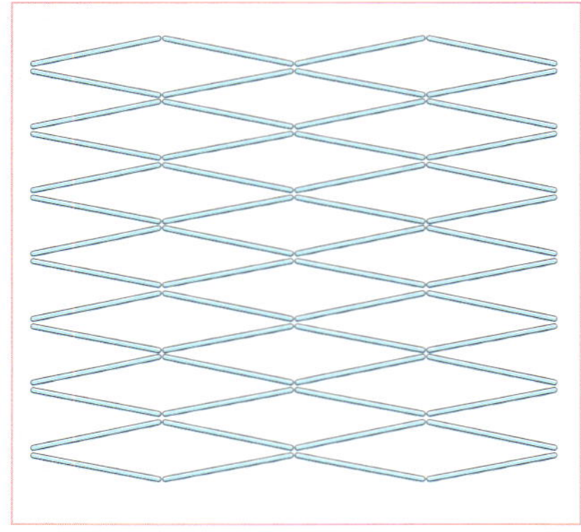

5 Continue working up and down across the shape to complete the pattern.

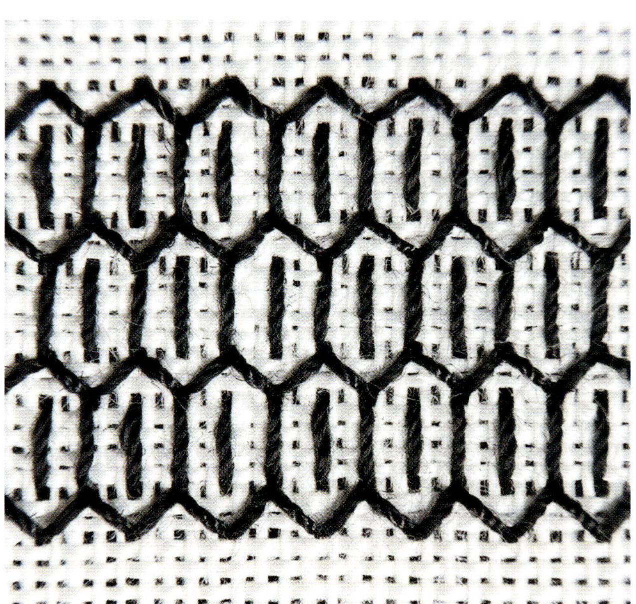

HEXAGONAL LOZENGE (PATTERN)

Blackwork.

This pattern is made up of adjoining elongated hexagons with a long stitch through the centre. It is a fairly open pattern and works well horizontally or vertically.

METHOD

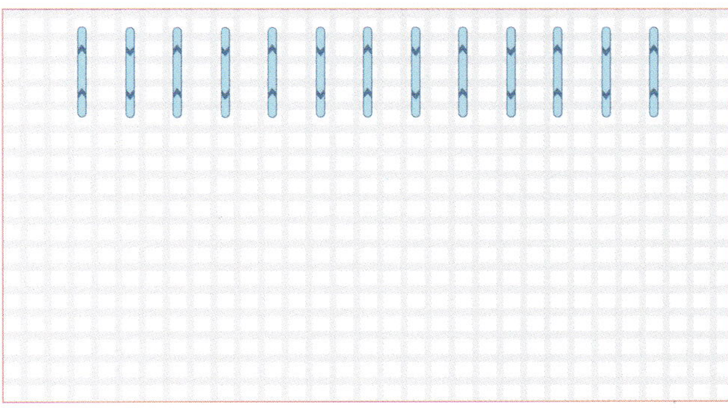

1 Complete a row of vertical stitches over four threads of the fabric, each two fabric threads apart.

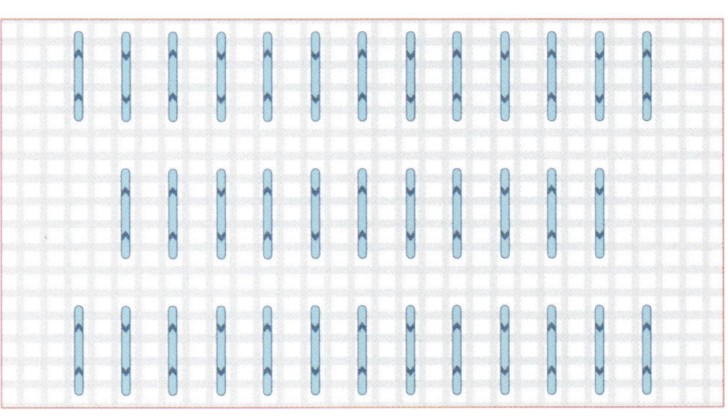

2 Continue with any subsequent rows needed to fill the area; each row should also be two fabric threads apart. Add each stitch in line with the previous row.

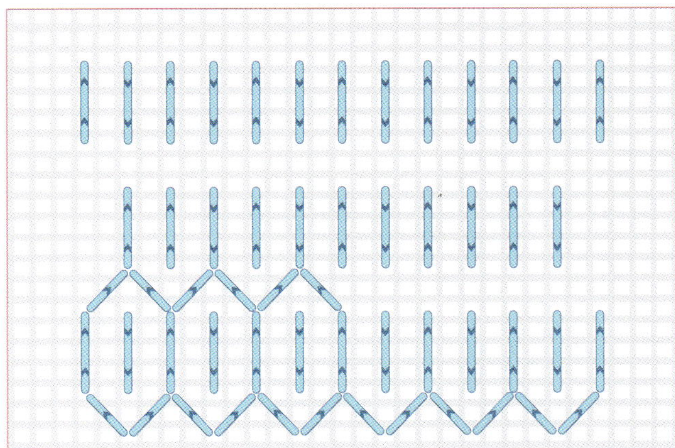

3 Next, stitch a zigzag pattern between each row with the apex of the zigzag meeting alternate vertical stitches.

4 Continue to complete the area.

HOLLIE STITCH

NEEDLELACE; AYRSHIRE; WHITEWORK; STUMPWORK.

Also known as Holy stitch, Holy point, Hollie point, Point d'Espagne, Spanish point, or English stitch.

Hollie stitch is a corded needlelace stitch which is similar to corded Brussels stitch, but each buttonhole stitch has an extra twist. It is worked from left to right, but some authors whip the thread back along the previous row of stitching rather than laying a cord.

It is historically used to create patterns or lettering by missing stitches to leave holes. When used in the round, it is also a feature of Ayrshire work.

The origins of hollie stitch are hard to ascertain: some writers claim it was originally used to adorn medieval ecclesiastical pieces, and it wasn't used for secular items until the Jacobean era. However, others suggest that early references to it refer to other forms of whitework stitched by nuns (the confusion arising from the term 'holy work'). There is also a school of thought which suggests the name comes from the holes created by the patterns in needlelace.

The Cooper Hewitt Museum in New York holds amongst the earliest extant pieces. They have several 18th-century samplers (including examples which show the use of the stitch to form letters) and a baby's cap. The stitch was frequently used at this time to embellish caps and small garments, especially Christening gowns.

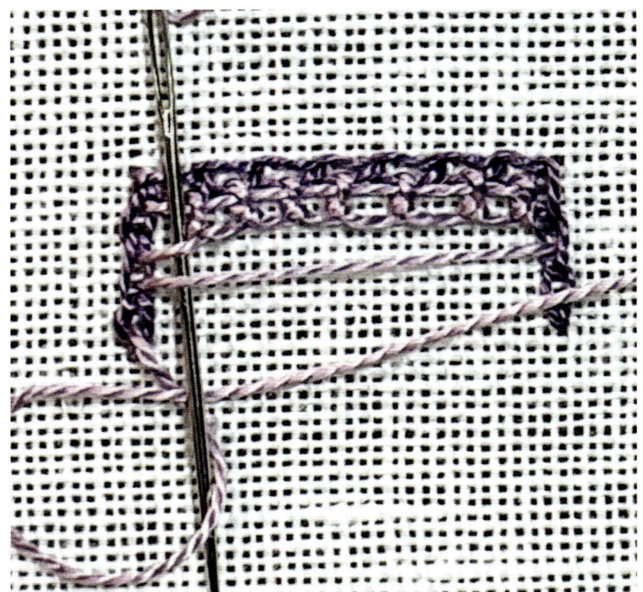

METHOD

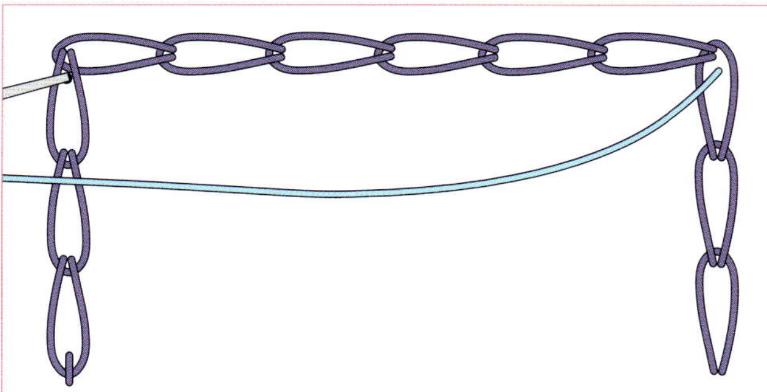

1 Outline the shape to be filled with a row of chain stitches. Bring the needle up at the top right corner, carry the thread across the shape and take the needle down on the left side to make a long cording stitch. Bring your needle back up just underneath where it went down.

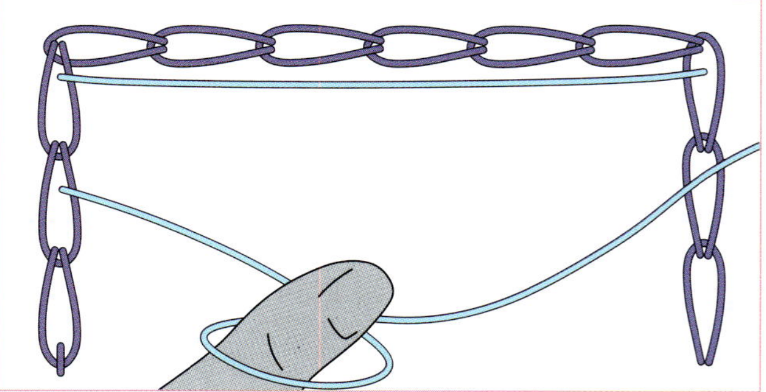

2 Loop the thread around your thumb: take the thread under your thumb, over the top of it and back under it.

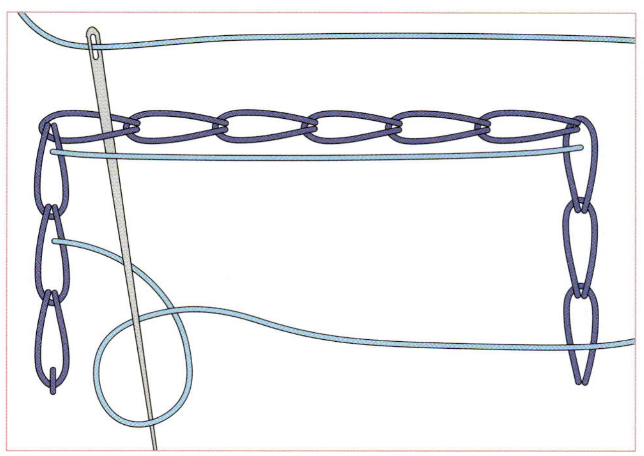

3 Pass the needle under both the outlining stitch and the long cording stitch, then go over the cross and into the loop in order to make a knotted stitch.

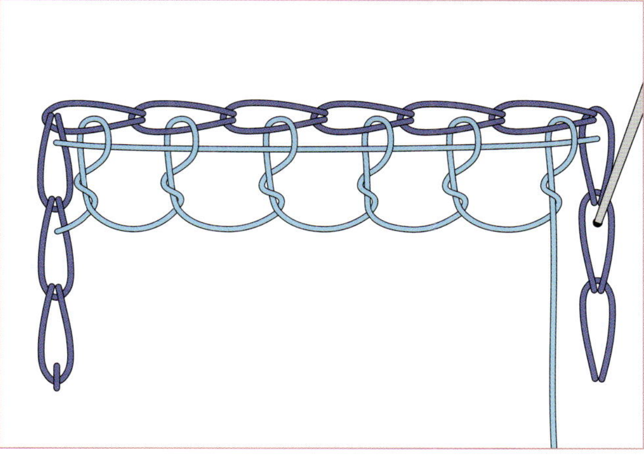

4 Continue in the same manner. When you reach the end of the line, take the needle down on the right side.

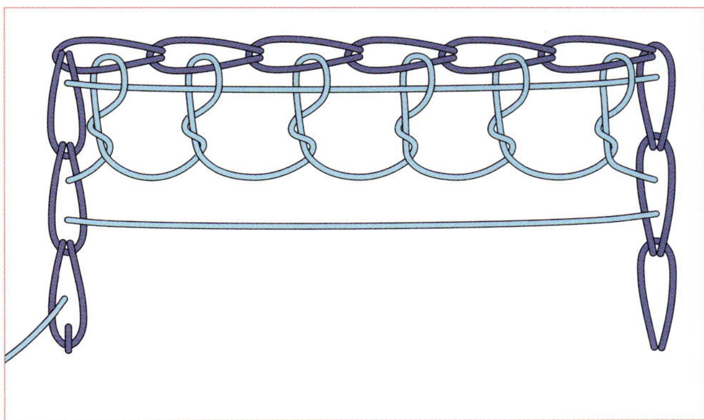

5 Bring the needle up just below on the right side, and throw the thread across the shape. Take the needle down on the left side and come up just below.

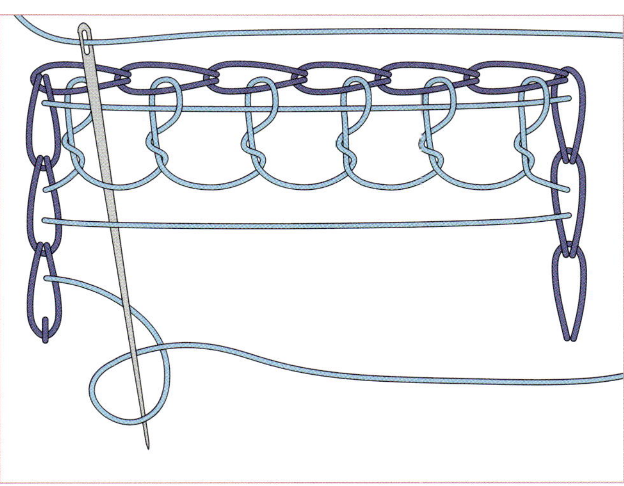

6 The following row will be worked in a similar way. Twist the thread using your thumb. Pass the needle through the previous row and the second long cording stitch, then go over the cross and under the loop.

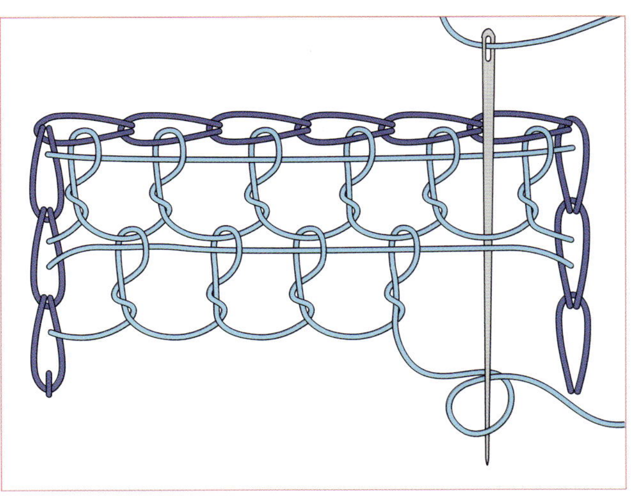

7 Continue as required to fill the shape.

HUNGARIAN STITCH

Canvaswork.

This stitch produces a pattern of small diamond-shaped blocks. It consists of three vertical stitches, worked over two, four, then two canvas threads. It can be worked in one colour or in rows of different colours.

Hungarian stitch is very similar to mosaic stitch (see pages 178–179) but it is worked vertically, rather than on the diagonal.

Hungarian stitch certainly dates to the late medieval period as there is evidence it was used in German ecclesiastical embroidery from this time. It was still being used in the 17th century as the Metropolitan Museum of Art in New York has a stitched portrait of King Charles II which, unusually, includes Hungarian stitch alongside petit point.

METHOD

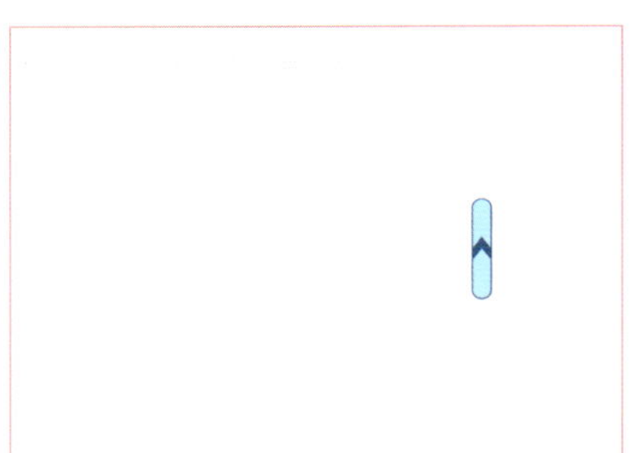

1 Work from right to left. Bring up the needle at a starting point, over two horizontal canvas threads, then down.

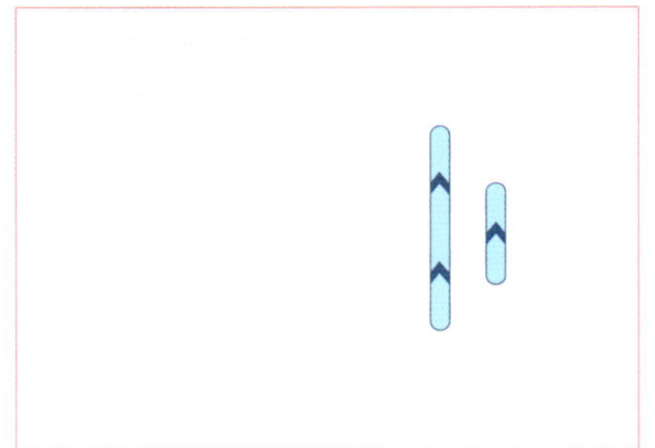

2 Work the next stitch to the left over four horizontal canvas threads as shown in the picture.

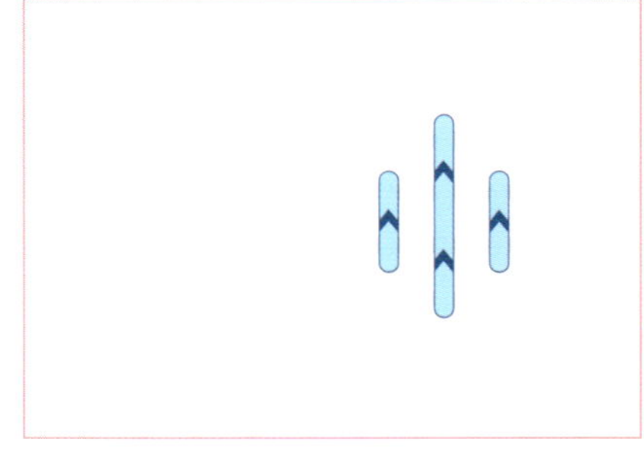

3 The third stitch is again over two horizontal canvas threads. This makes a small diamond shape.

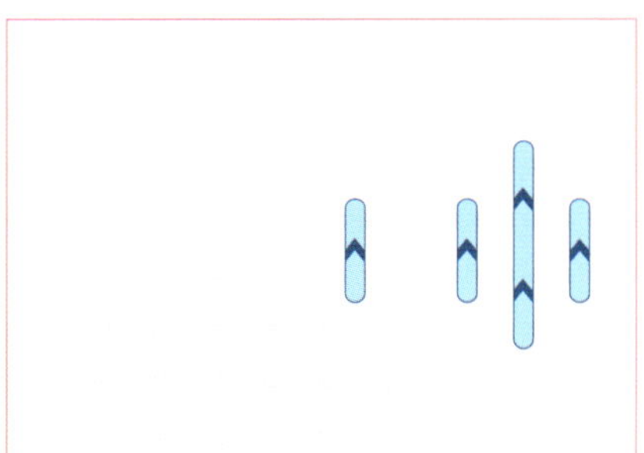

4 Leave two vertical canvas threads and start the next stitch.

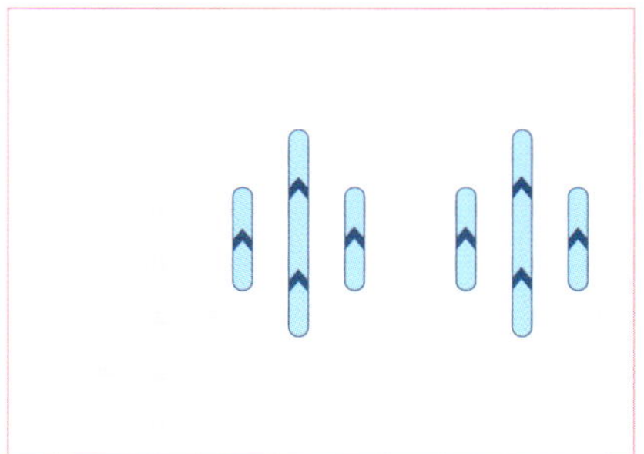

5 Continue working another small diamond-shaped block.

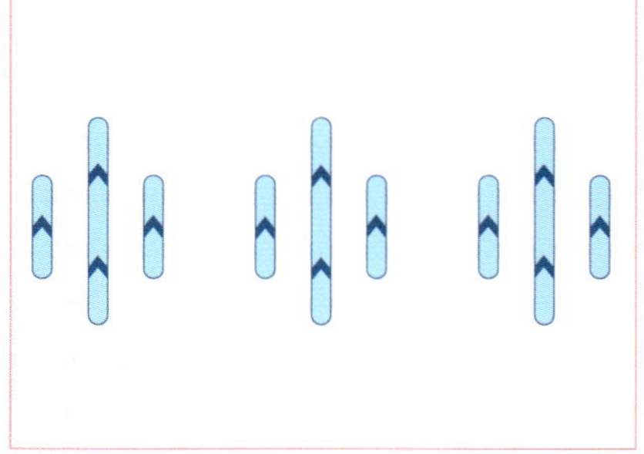

6 Repeat until the end of the row.

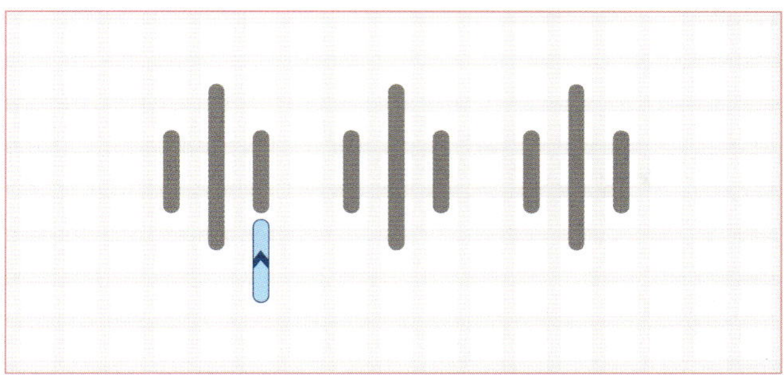

7 The second row is worked from left to right. Work the first stitch over two horizontal canvas threads just under the first row as shown in the picture.

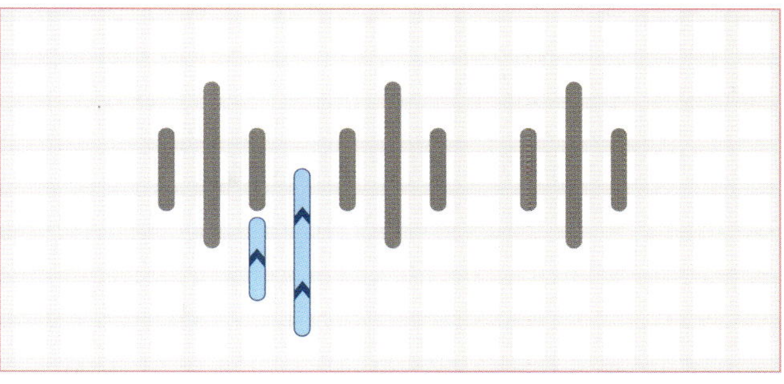

8 The second stitch over four horizontal canvas threads is worked to fit into the spaces left in the first row.

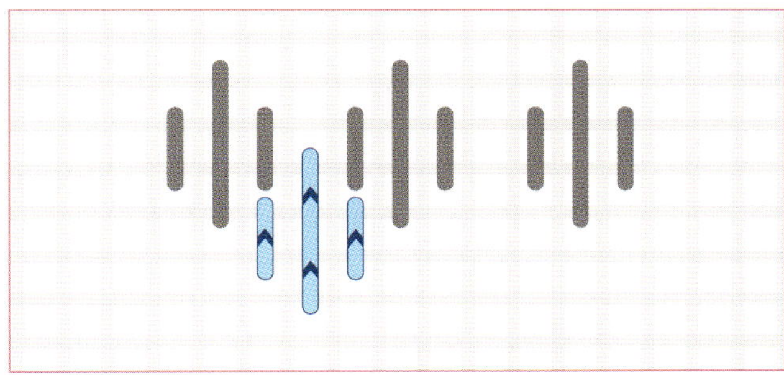

9 The third stitch over two horizontal canvas threads is worked to complete the small diamond-shaped block.

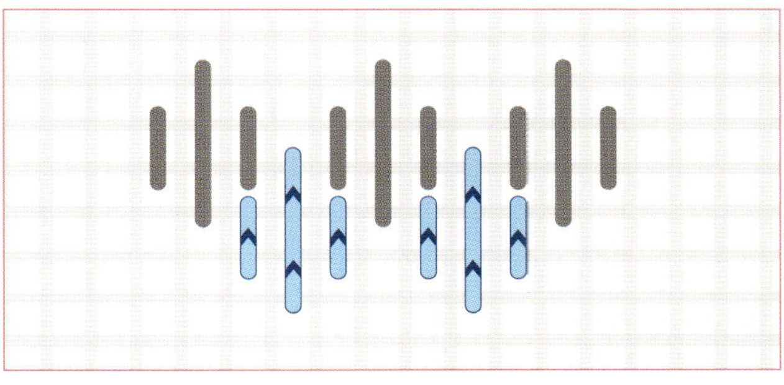

10 Continue working the blocks to fit into the spaces left in the previous row.

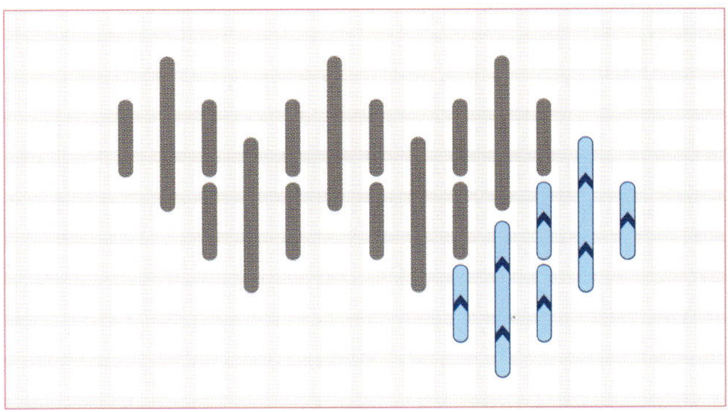

11 The third row is worked from right to left. Work the small diamond-shaped blocks and make sure that the long stitches are worked into spaces between the two blocks in the previous row.

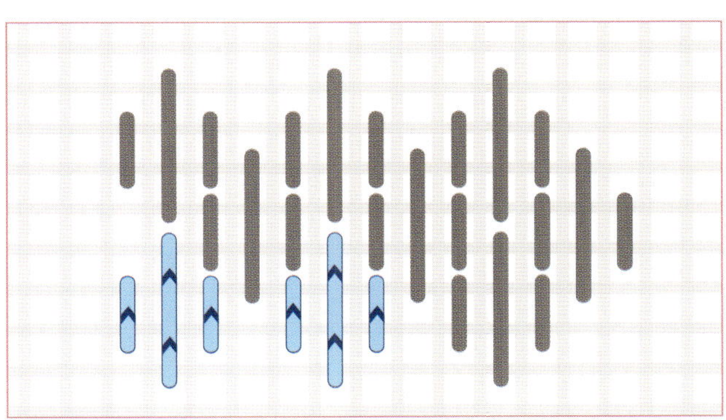

12 Continue until the area is filled.

INTERLOCKING 'I'S (PATTERN)

Blackwork.

This blackwork pattern is made up of rows of long straight stitches with a bar at either end. It is fairly large in scale and is good for creating a linear texture.

The pattern can be worked across the shape horizontally or vertically, depending on the design.

METHOD

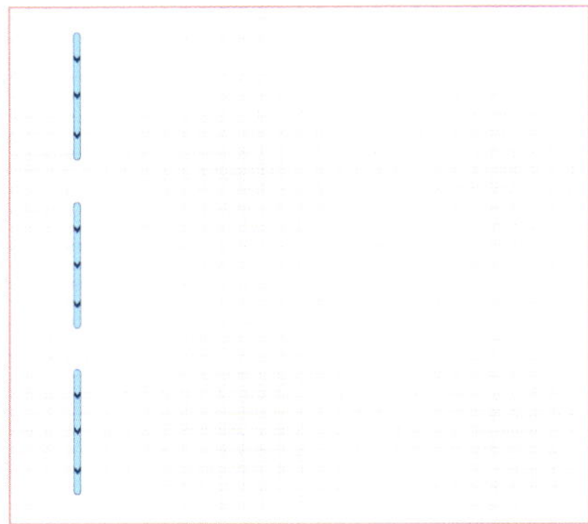

1 Start by completing a running stitch over seven threads and under one thread of openweave fabric.

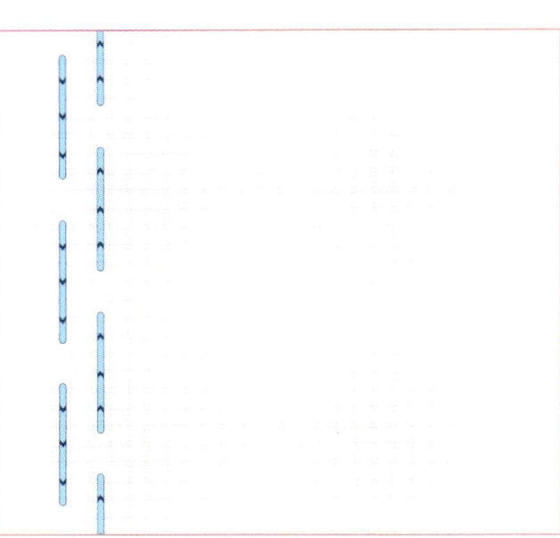

2 The second row should be placed two fabric threads away, each running stitch should be offset from the previous line.

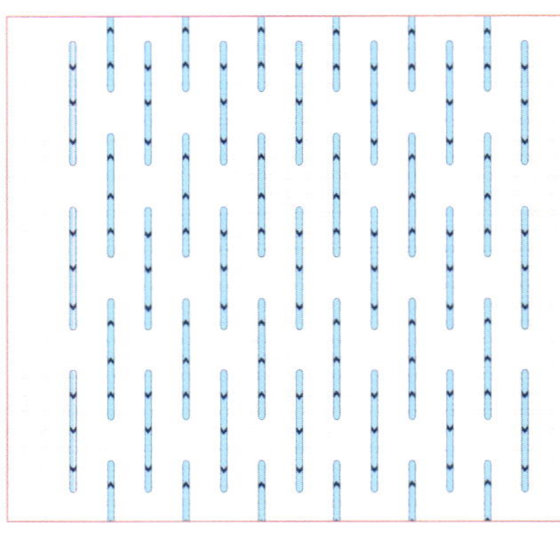

3 Continue to fill the area.

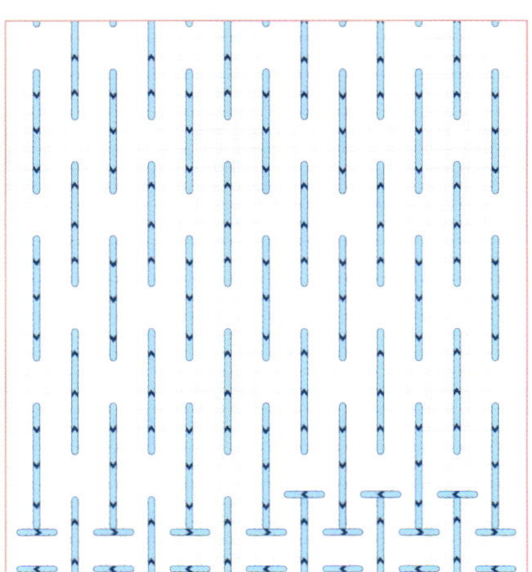

4 The next step is to work a small running stitch over two threads across the shape in the opposite direction. Each stitch should be placed at each end of the large straight stitches previously worked.

5 Continue to fill the area.

JACQUARD STITCH

CANVASWORK; BEAD EMBROIDERY.

This canvaswork stitch consist of alternate diagonal rows of Byzantine stitch (see page 138) and tent stitch (see basketweave tent stitch on page 218). It is useful for filling large areas: the two stitches create diagonal zigzag stripes, alternately wide and narrow, producing the effect of a woven fabric.

The name 'Jacquard' presumably refers to the Jacquard machine, a device fitted to a loom which enables the weaving of complex designs. The machine was patented in 1804, which suggests the stitch must date from the 19th century. Thérèse de Dillmont's 1890 *Encyclopedia of Needlework* supports this theory as she says it can be used to 'produce the effect of brocaded stuff'.

METHOD

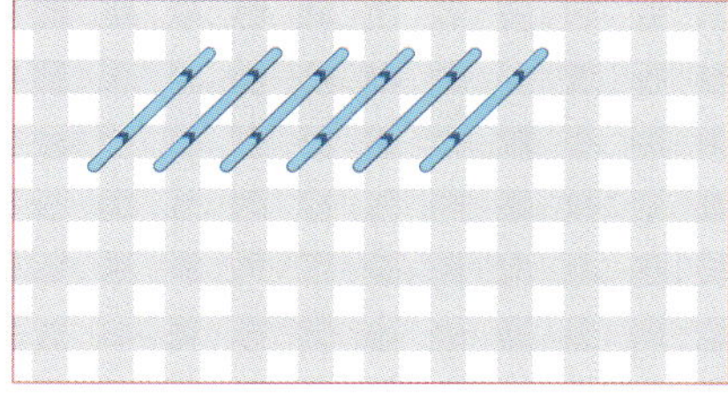

1 Start with a horizontal row of six diagonal stitches, each over two intersections of the canvas, laying bottom left to top right.

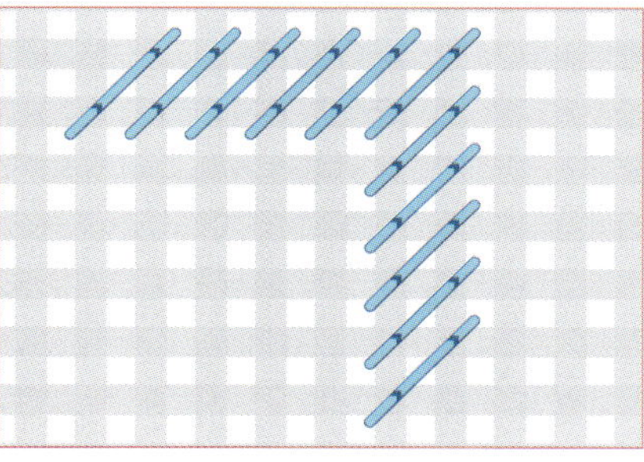

2 To achieve the stepped appearance, complete a further five diagonal stitches in a vertical column.

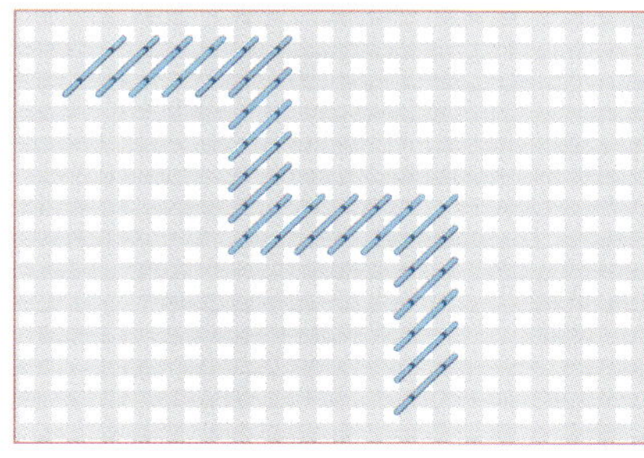

3 Continue across the shape with five stitches across and five stitches down.

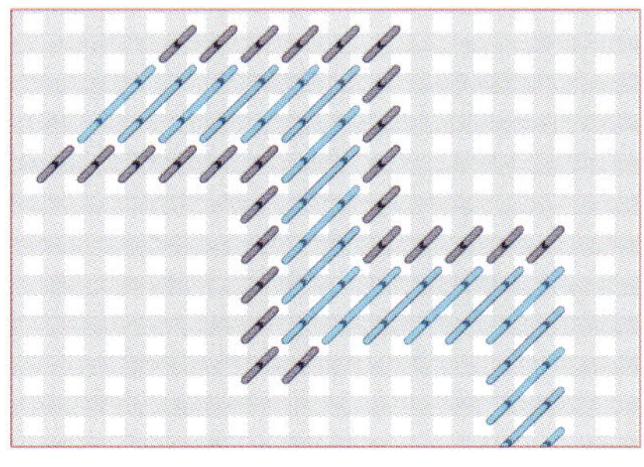

4 The adjacent rows are again worked in a stepped appearance but with a shorter stitch over one intersection of the canvas, like a tent stitch.

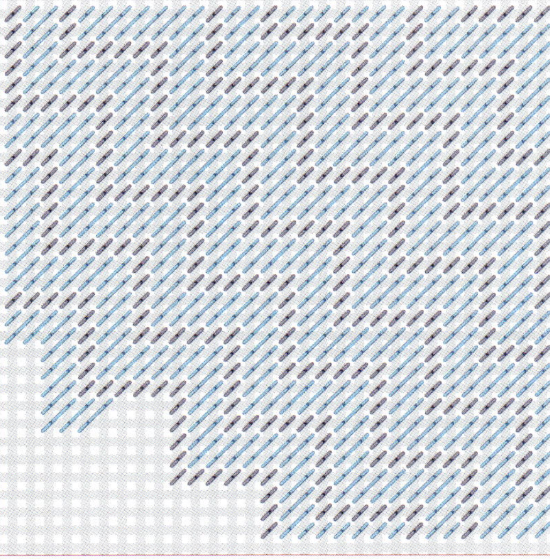

5 Continue to fill the shape with alternate rows of longer and shorter stitches. The pictures shows the stitches in two shades in order to illustrate the pattern clearly.

LAID WORK

CREWELWORK; SURFACE; ELIZABETHAN.

Also known as Surface satin stitch, Bayeux stitch, False satin stitch, Up and down shading, or Thread saver stitch.

Laid work covers the front of the fabric with long stitches which are stitched in alternate directions, resulting in short stitches on the reverse of the fabric.

One of the main stitches used to fill the Bayeux Tapestry, laid stitch fills areas quickly without using up too much thread.

METHOD

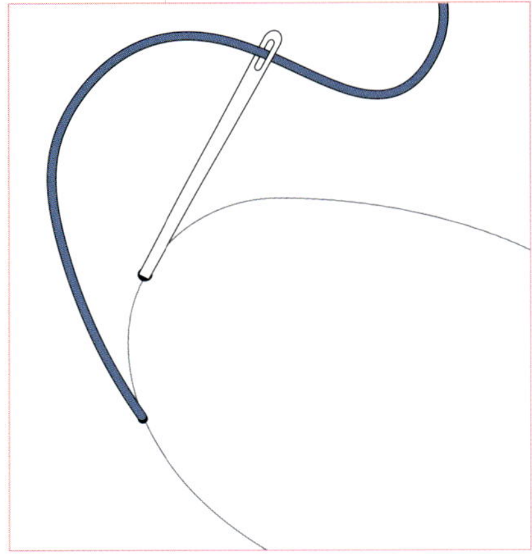

1 Bring the needle up on the painted line and take it down directly opposite. Pull the thread down through the hole and bring the needle up directly adjacent. If you think you may struggle to ensure threads lay parallel, start in the centre of the shape.

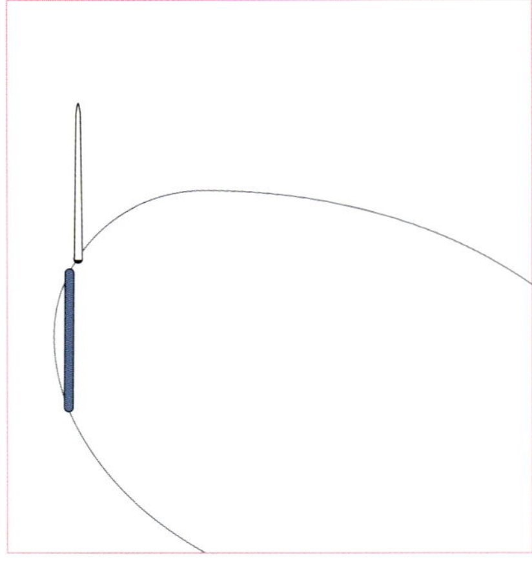

2 Take the thread back down directly opposite, adjacent to where you first brought the needle up.

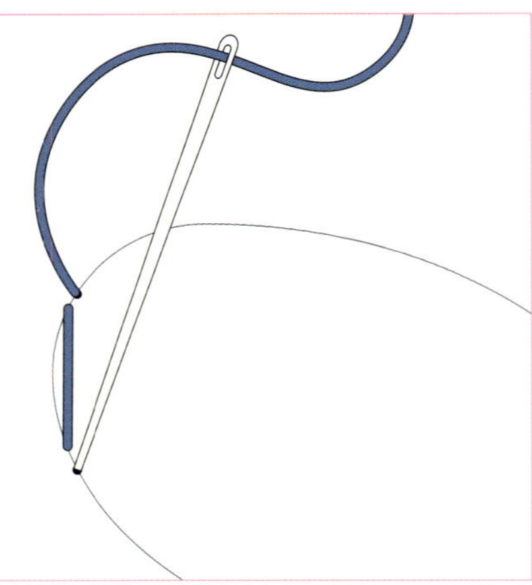

3 Draw the thread through to create a parallel stitch, then start to work parallel stitches up and down across the shape.

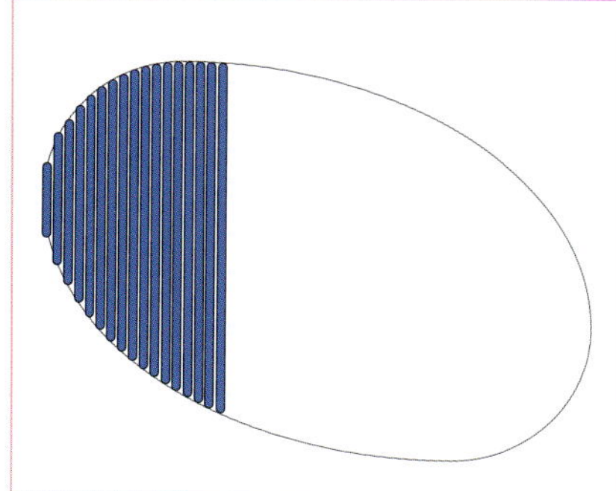

4 If you wish to shade the area, gently introduce a second colour by laying in a single stitch then returning to the original colour for two stitches. Reverse the sequence (two of the new colour then one of the old), then continue with the new colour.

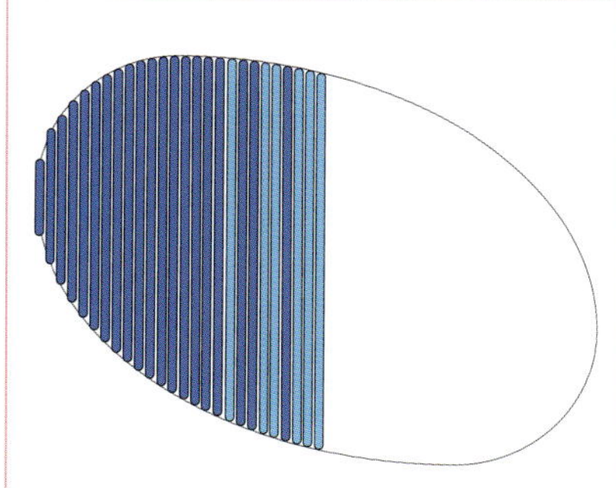

5 Complete the laid filling to the edge of the area to be filled before returning to the centre of the shape to work the other side.

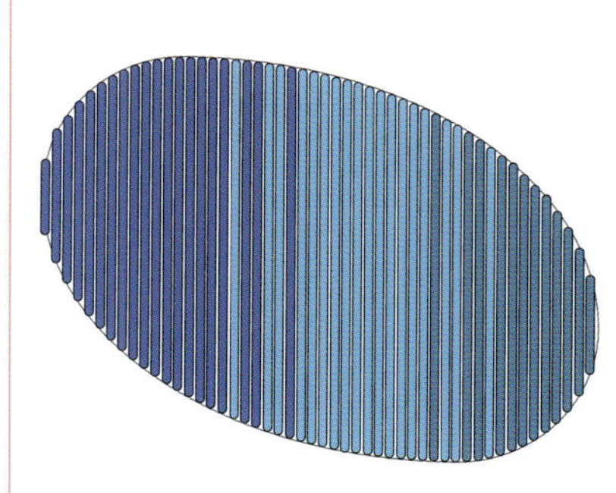

6 Continue in the same direction, adding new colours as you wish and following the sequence in step 4 to blend them in. Once the shape is filled, secure the thread to finish.

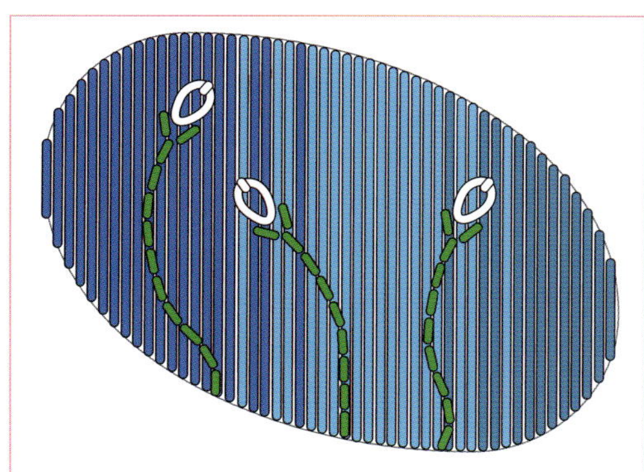

On traditional examples you will find that these long stitches are held down with several couched threads to prevent them from gaping.

However you can use any surface stitches to hold the threads in place. The illustration and photograph shows fly stitch, back stitch and detached chain stitch (see pages 28, 16 and 240, respectively).

▲▲ Detail of Peranakan slippers, RSN Collection COL.31.a-b

Each slipper top is bordered in royal blue silk and the embroidery itself is worked on red, yellow, green, and blue velvet. The intricate and densely worked embroidery, which includes laid work alongside other filling stitches including basketweave (goldwork), and bricking (see pages 134–135 and 136–137, respectively), would have taken great skill.

LEAF STITCH (SURFACE)

CREWELWORK; SURFACE.

Leaf stitch is a series of overlapping open diagonal stitches. It is easily adapted to forms of varying width, such as petals and leaves.

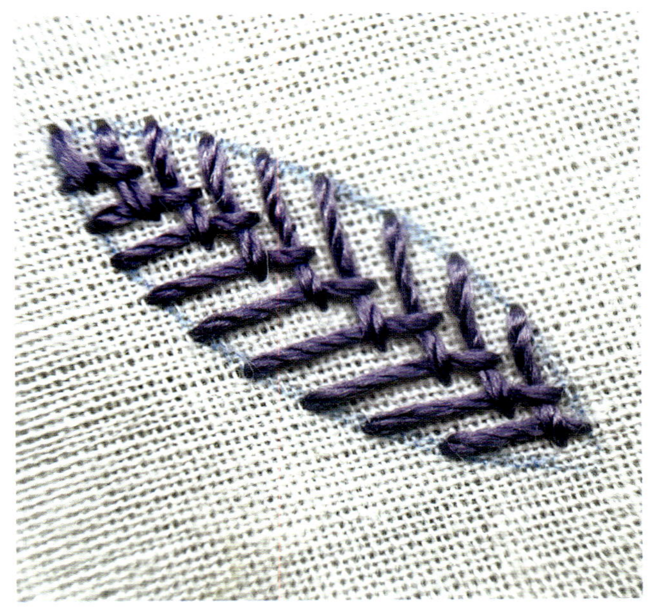

METHOD

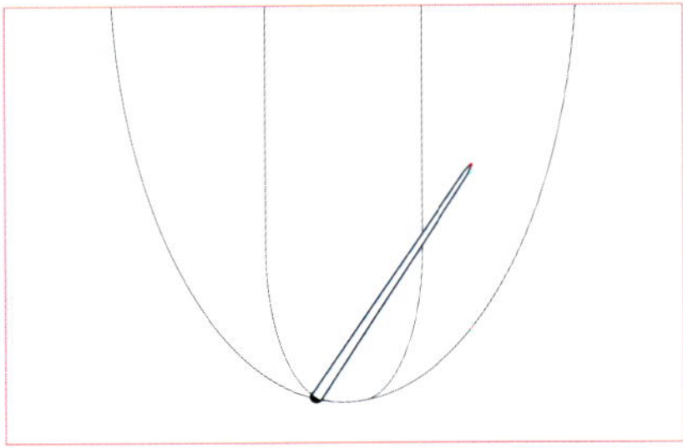

1 Imagine or faintly draw a double stem line. Starting at the base of your shape, bring your needle up through the fabric on one of the stem lines.

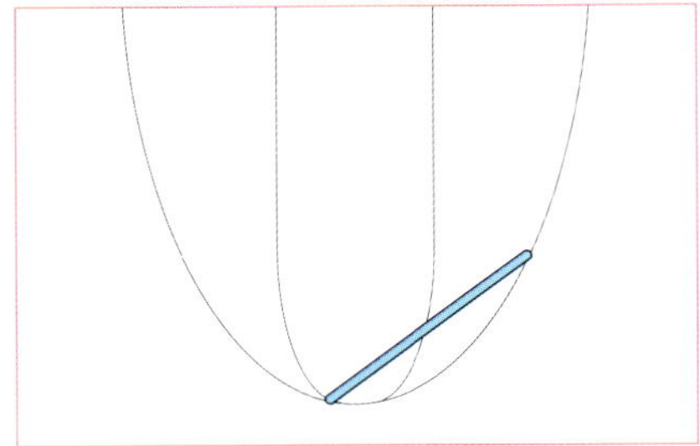

2 Take the needle to the opposite side of the shape and take it down through the fabric on the line, creating a straight slanted stitch.

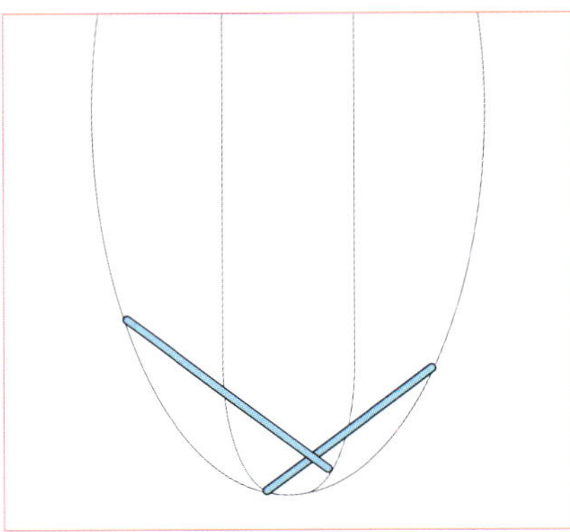

3 Do the same on the opposite side by bringing the needle up through the fabric on the other stem line, just under the previous stitch, and taking it down on the opposite side of the leaf.

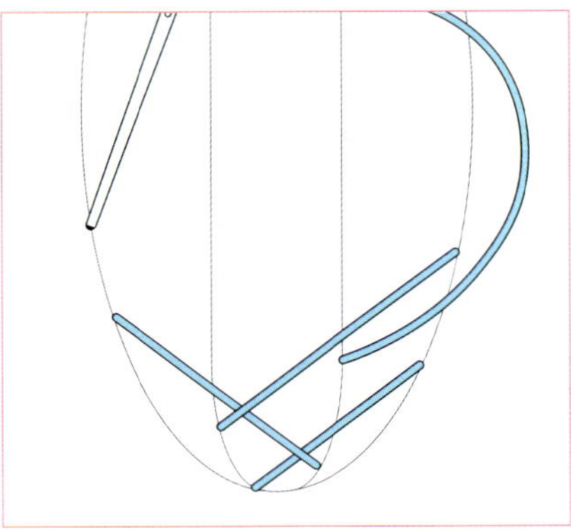

4 Repeat the process, bringing the needle up just under the previous stitch and above the rest.

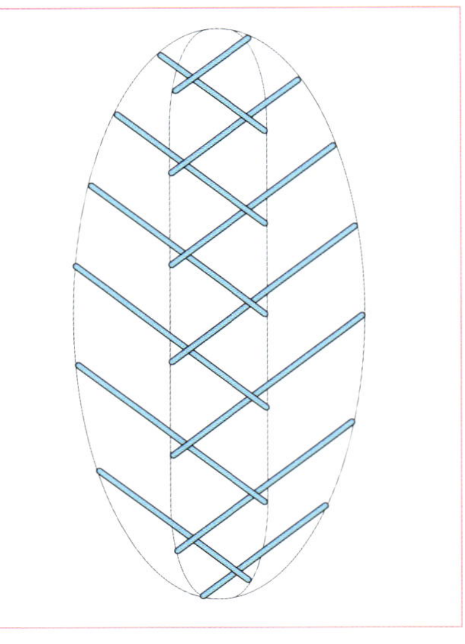

5 Continue by working up towards the tip of the shape until it is filled.

MILANESE STITCH

Canvaswork.

This is a canvaswork filling stitch consisting of diagonally offset triangles.

For information on the tent stitch used in step 1, see basketweave tent stitch on page 218.

METHOD

1 For the first unit, make a tent stitch across one canvas intersection.

2 Below it make a stitch across two intersections, then three, then four.

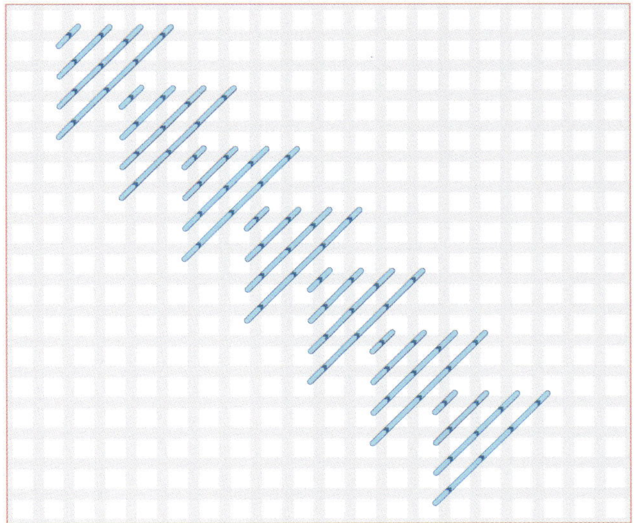

3 Repeat this sequence of stitches over one, two, three and four canvas intersections in a diagonal row from top left to bottom right.

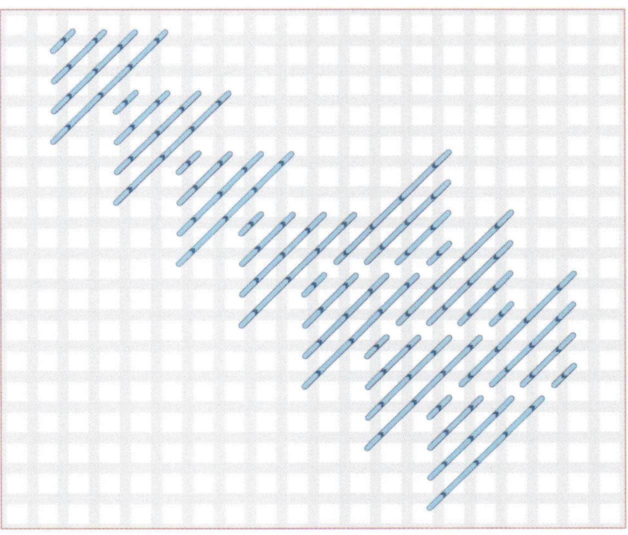

4 Work the next row of triangles in reverse, so that they fit into the gaps of the first row. The smallest stitch of one row should always be next to the largest stitch of the following row.

MOSAIC STITCH

Canvaswork; Berlin wool work.

Also known as Double stitch.

Mosaic stitch is a small square stitch, and it is useful for backgrounds. Each square block consists of a group of three diagonal stitches worked over two horizontal and two vertical canvas threads.

There are two methods for working this stitch; both give a visually similar result from the front.

METHOD A

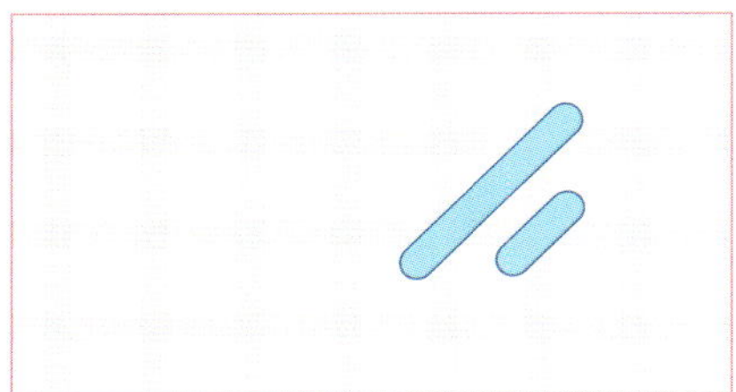

1 Work in horizontal rows. The first diagonal stitch is worked from bottom left to top right over one intersection of the canvas, and the second diagonal stitch is worked over two intersections.

2 The third diagonal stitch is worked over one intersection, and this completes a square block.

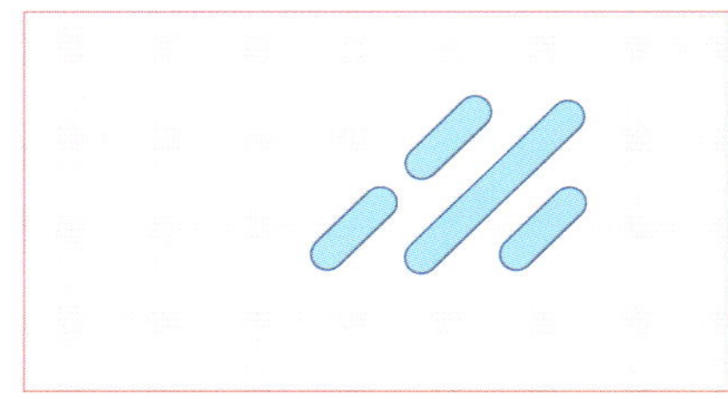

3 Work from right to left in the first row. Bring up the needle right next to the bottom left corner of the first block.

4 Work from left to right in the second row. This time, work diagonal stitches from top right to bottom left.

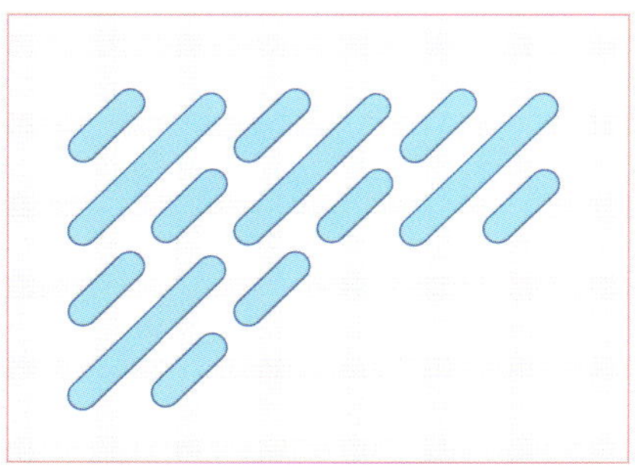

5 Repeat blocks to the right.

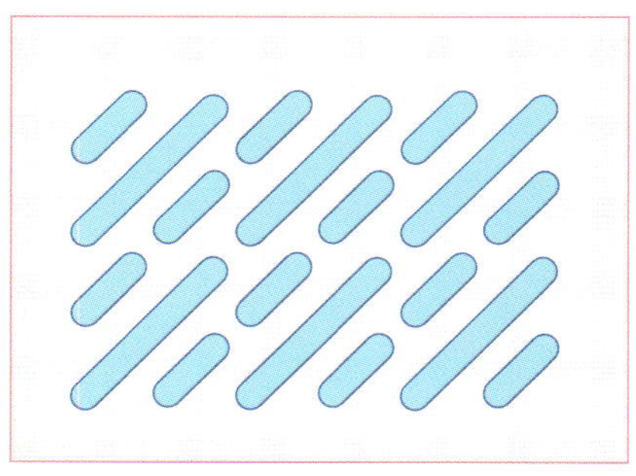

6 Continue until the area is filled.

METHOD B

This method is very similar to Hungarian stitch (see pages 170–171), but worked diagonally.

1 Work in diagonal rows. The first diagonal stitch is worked from bottom left to top right over one intersection of the canvas, and the second over two intersections.

2 When one square block is completed, leave one canvas hole and work the next block.

3 Continue working the blocks until the required area is filled. Work the next diagonal row in the same manner.

A complete area of mosaic stitch.

OBLIQUE GOBELIN STITCH

CANVASWORK; BERLIN WOOL WORK; ELIZABETHAN.

Also known as Gobelin stitch, Oblique Slav stitch, Diagonal Gobelin stitch, or Slanted Gobelin stitch.

Oblique Gobelin stitch is a slightly elongated diagonal stitch; it is traditionally worked over two horizontal and one vertical thread. It produces smooth bands, useful to simulate architectural detail such as shiplap or panelling. It also works well used as a single band to produce a border stitch.

This is the slanted version of Gobelin stitch (see straight Gobelin stitch on page 203 for the upright version). Historically, the name Gobelin stitch has been used for both this version and the straight version.

METHOD

1 Working left to right, start with a diagonal stitch running top right to bottom left, down over two horizontal threads and across one vertical thread.

2 Bring the needle up one thread to the right of the top of the completed stitch and repeat. There should be a long diagonal stitch on the reverse of the canvas.

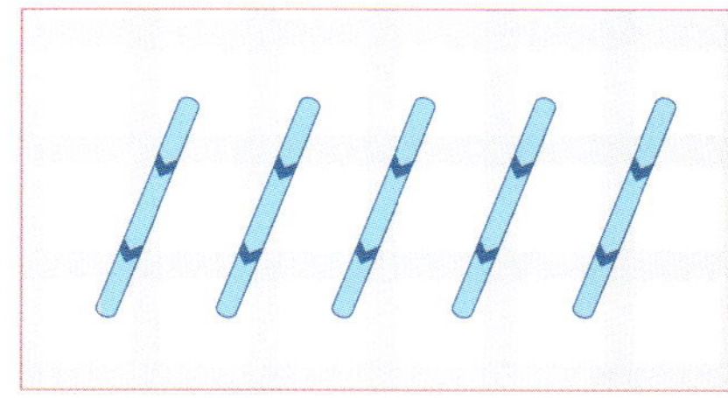

3 Continue to complete the row.

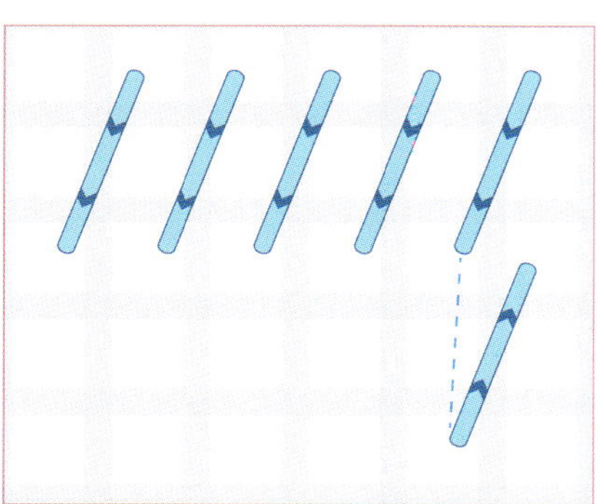

4 Return in the opposite direction by bringing the needle up two threads below the bottom of the last stitch and taking it down one thread to the right of the base of the stitch above.

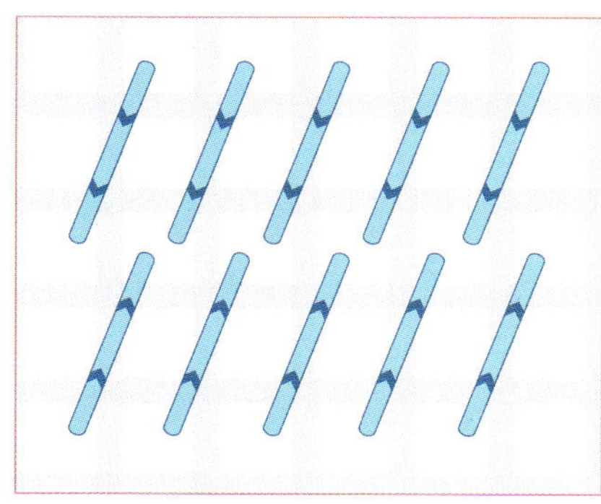

5 Continue to complete the row.

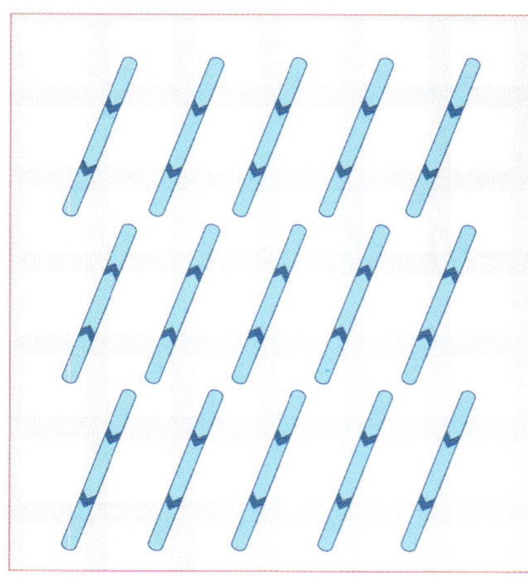

6 Repeat steps 1 and 2 when working from left to right.

OPEN ZIGZAG (PATTERN)

BLACKWORK.

A blackwork pattern made up of columns of zigzag lines, with an added horizontal stitch at each point. It is a mid-scale pattern and is suitable for creating a geometric effect within more linear shapes.

METHOD

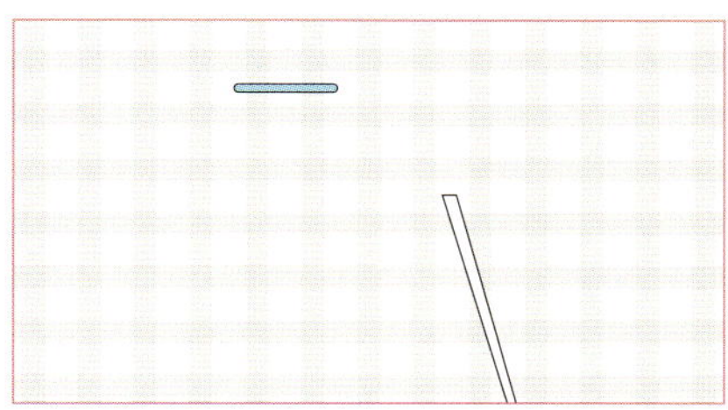

1 Make a horizontal stitch over two threads then bring the needle up diagonally under two intersections below and right.

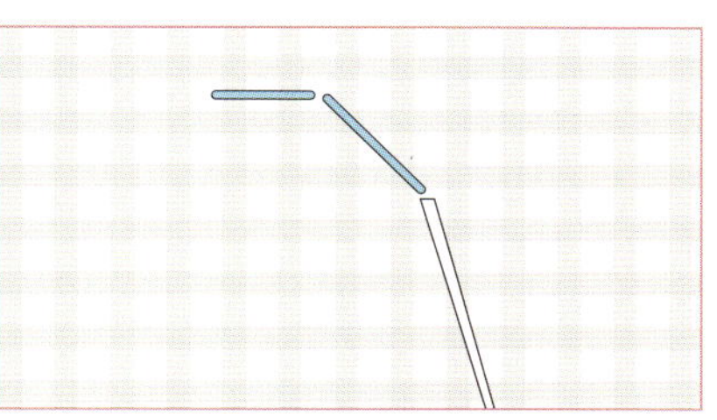

2 Complete a back stitch into the same hole the previous stitch ends and then bring the needle up at the end of that stitch so that the thread on the back is obscured by the last surface stitch.

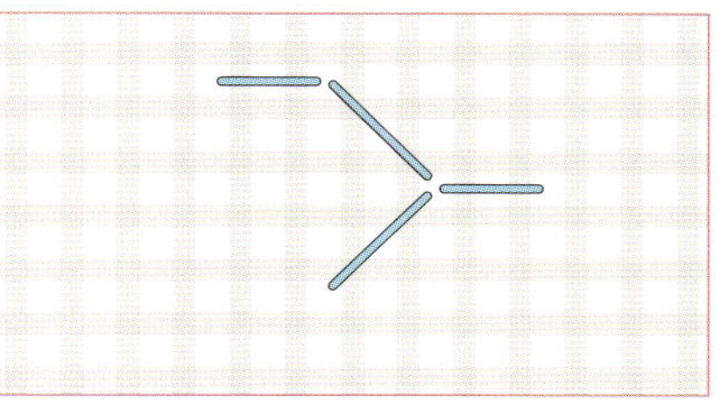

3 Repeat the last two stitches in the opposite direction.

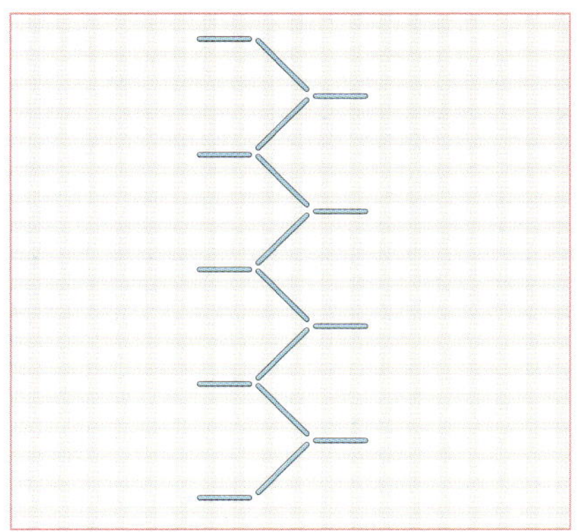

4 Continue alternating from side to side to complete the column.

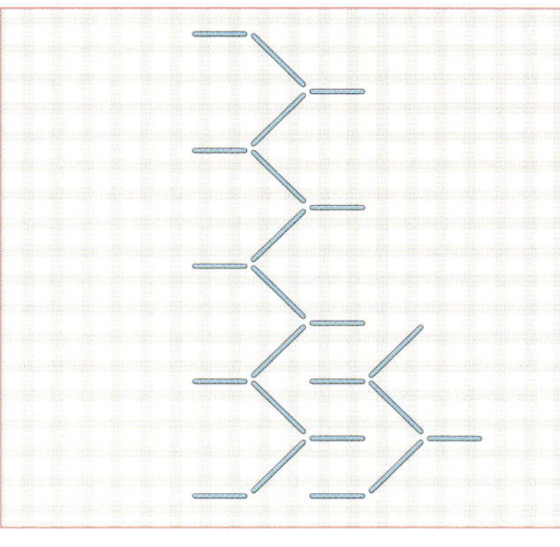

5 Each zigzag should be in line with previous columns.

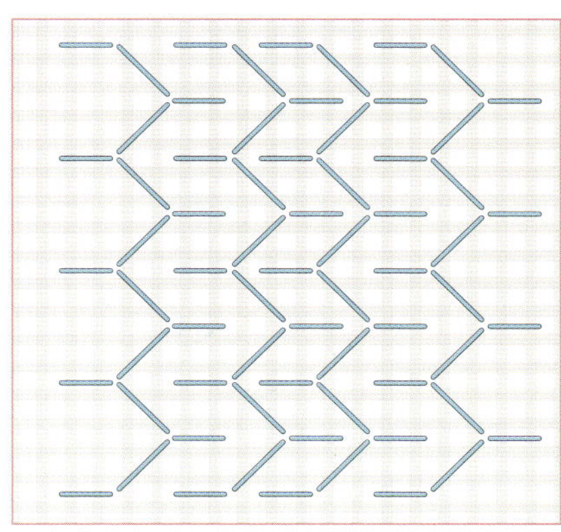

6 Add more columns to cover the area.

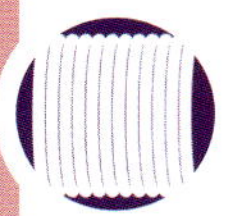

PADDED SATIN STITCH (LAID WORK PADDING)

Crewelwork; Stumpwork; Whitework; Surface; Mountmellick.

Padded satin stitch is a satin stitch with padding underneath the stitching to create a raised motif. This technique catches the light, particularly in monochrome embroidery.

This method of padding is the use of laid work (long stitches); for an alternative method see the entry for padded satin stitch (split stitch padding) overleaf.

Padded satin stitch was used in Ming-era China using either a coarser thread than the silk which was used for the satin stitch itself or sometimes even cloth or paper (it is unclear whether the padding was laid work or split stitch). The stitch was also used as part of the Kyoto tradition in Japan (which dates from the 8th century, although the stitch itself may not be as early). Different European Whitework traditions used padded satin stitch: Mountmellick embroidery from Eire; *Omvendt Udklipshedebo* in Denmark; Venetian embroidery; French embroidery; and later Broderie Anglaise.

TIP

Laid work (see page 174–175) is used for this padding in order to minimize the amount of thread on the back of the fabric.

METHOD

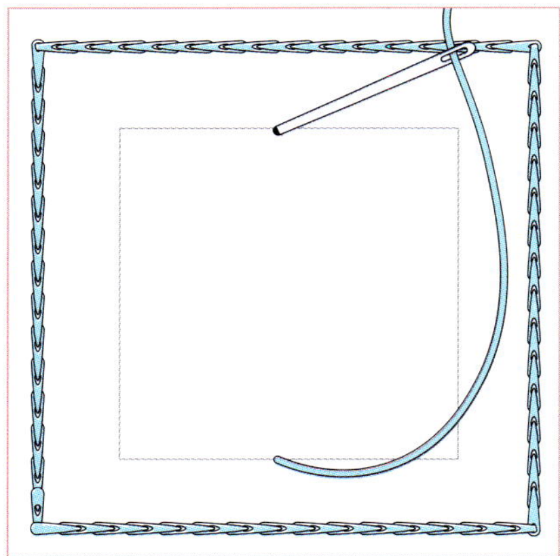

1 To begin, outline the shape with split stitch (see page 39). Next, use a thicker thread to make the first stitch for padding in the middle of the shape, across the longest part of the shape.

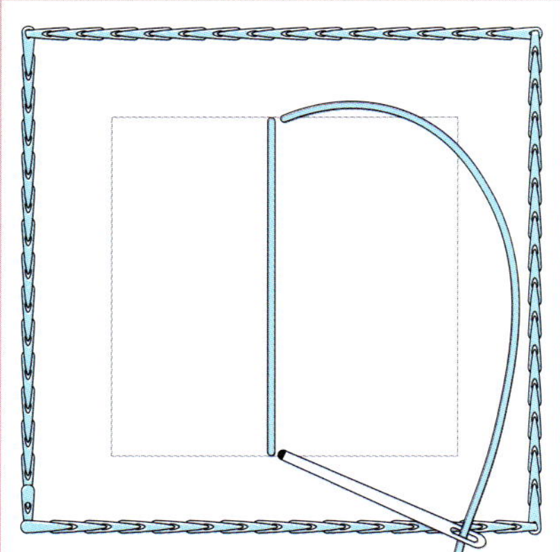

2 Bring the needle up next to where the first stitch ended, and make another stitch parallel to the first. Continue stitching back and forth across the area.

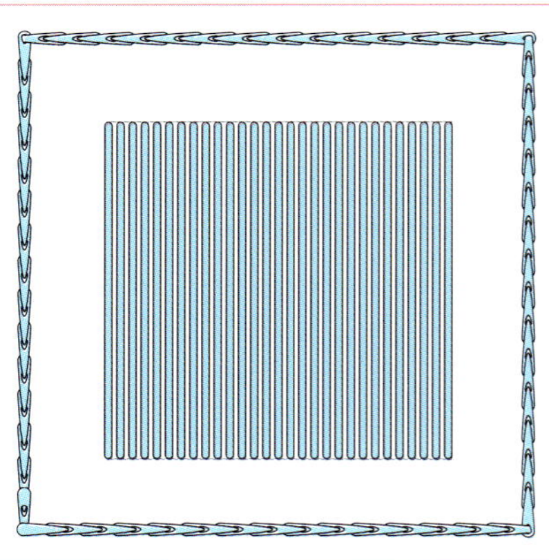

3 When you have filled the first half, return to the middle and fill the second half.

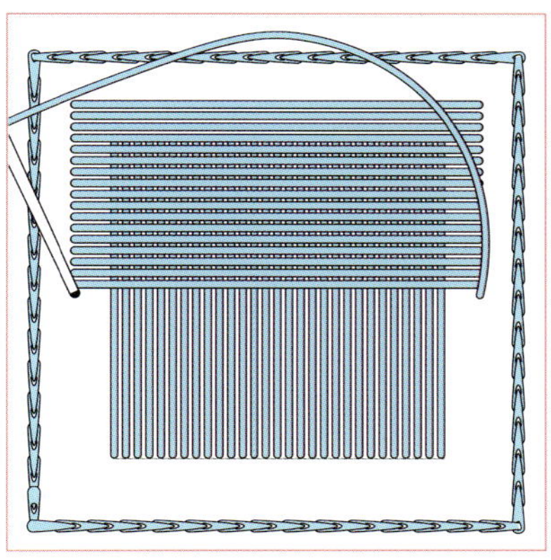

4 Work the next layer of padding at a different angle from the first, starting in the middle and working outwards. Start again in the middle and work to the other end to complete the second layer.

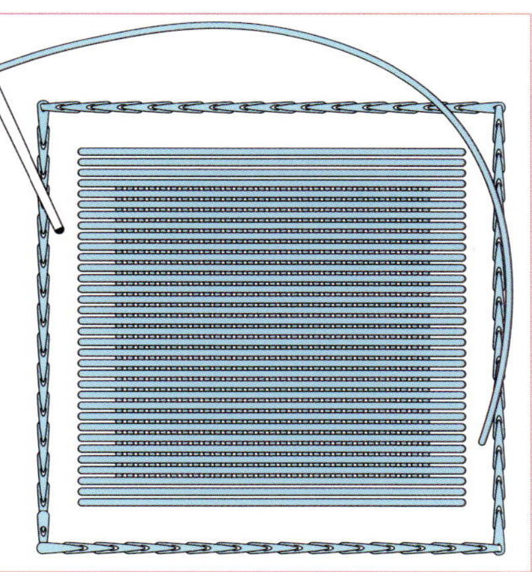

5 Stitch the third layer in the same way at another angle. Ideally, the last layer should be perpendicular to the final satin stitch.

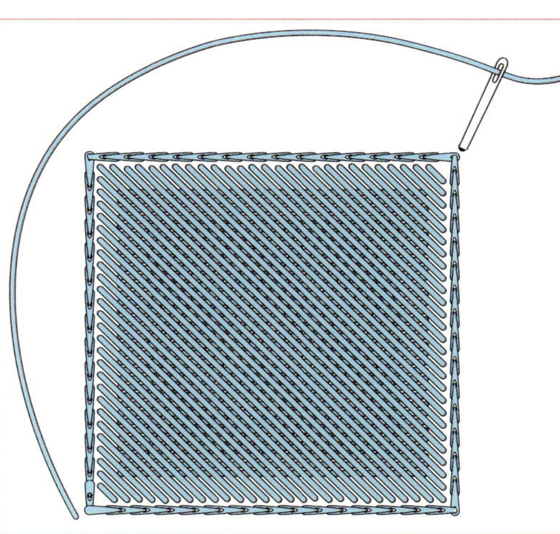

6 Work satin stitch with your chosen thread over the padding. See satin stitch on page 37 for further information.

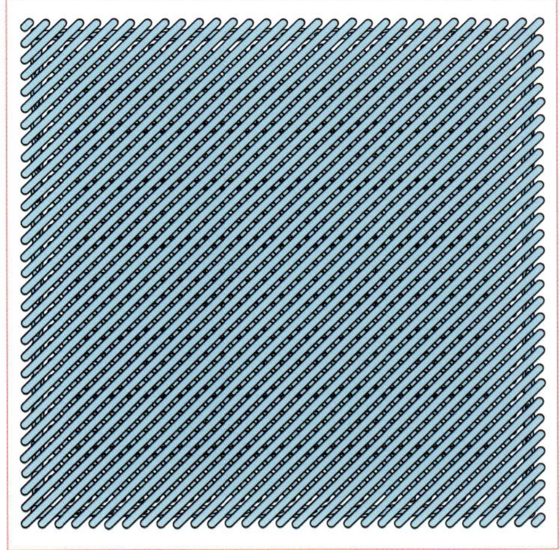

Completed padded satin stitch.

▲▲ Detail from Kyoto panel, RSN Collection No. 1580

In this Japanese piece, padded satin stitch has been used extensively to give height to the leaves.

PADDED SATIN STITCH (SPLIT STITCH PADDING)

Crewelwork; Stumpwork; Whitework; Surface; Mountmellick.

Also known as Raised satin stitch, or French plumetis stitch.

Similar to the technique on the previous pages, this method uses satin stitch (see page 37) over split stitch (see page 39) to create a raised motif, and it is usually best used for long, narrow, curved shapes.

This method can also be worked using running stitch instead of the split stitch.

METHOD

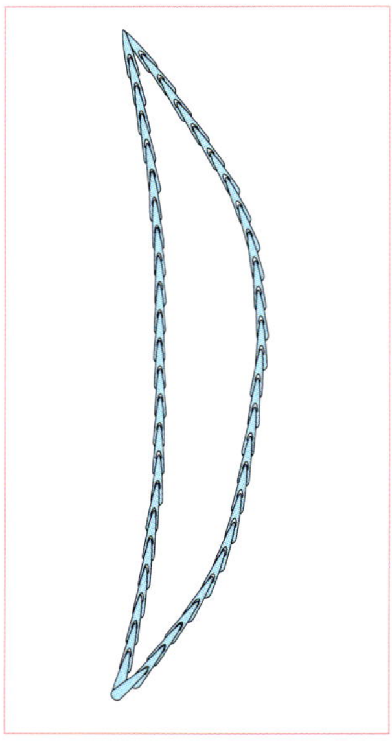

1 Outline your shape with split stitch. Keep your stitches small (approximately 3–4mm) and the line as neat as possible as this will dictate the shape of your satin stitch shape.

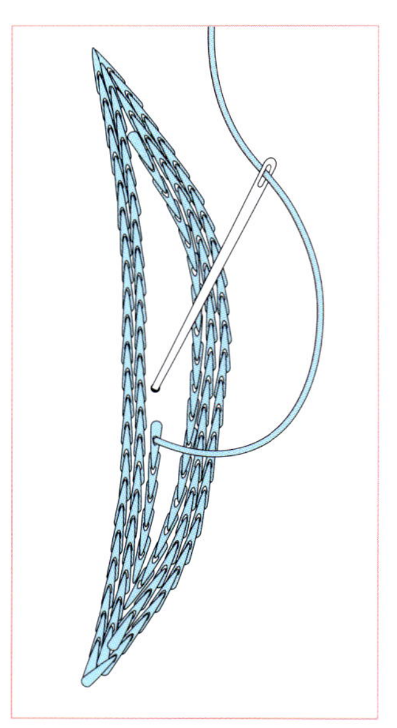

2 Starting within the outlined shape work back and forth with rows of split stitch. Use stitches that are longer than those used for the outline. A thicker thread may be used.

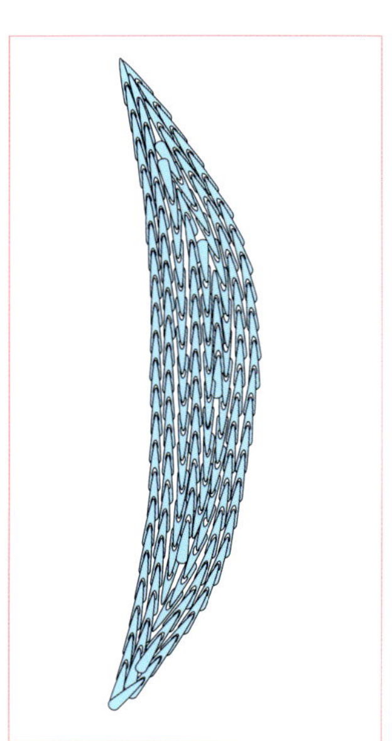

3 Fill the shape with rows of split stitch.

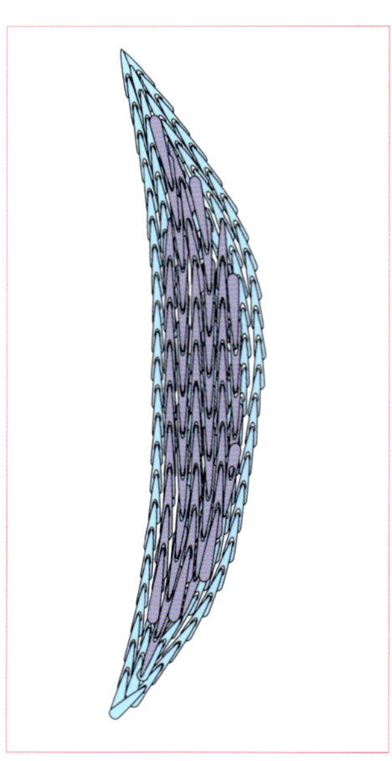

4 Add further layers of split stitch over the first layer until you have as much padding as you require.

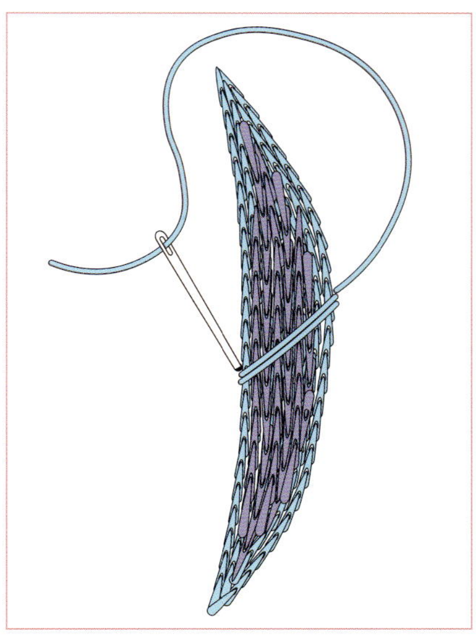

5 Beginning halfway along one side, bring the needle up just outside the split stitch outline. Hold the thread to set the angle of the first stitch and take the needle down accordingly, just outside the split stitch. Bring the needle up on the first side, very close to the first stitch. Make a second stitch, angling the needle towards the previous stitch and towards the split stitch.

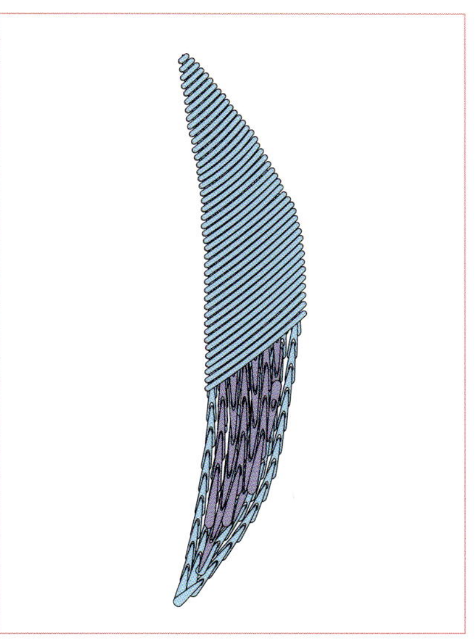

6 Work outwards towards the end of the shape.

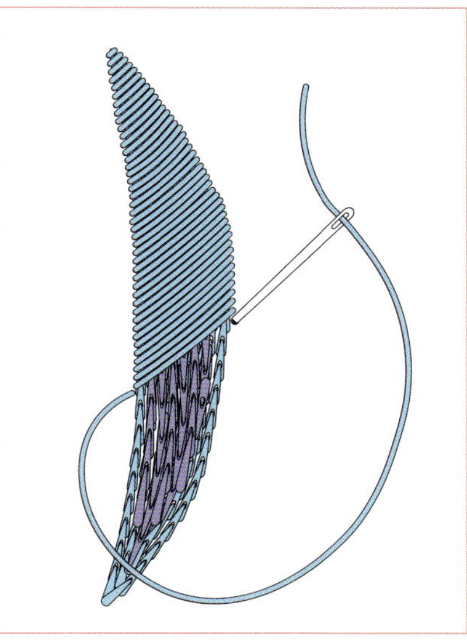

7 Begin again in the middle. This time bring the needle up on the other side of the shape, and angle the needle towards the previous stitch as before.

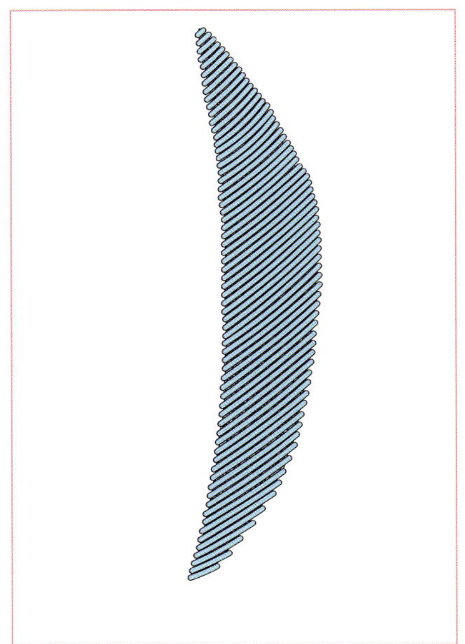

8 Continue working the satin stitch towards the opposite corner until the shape is complete.

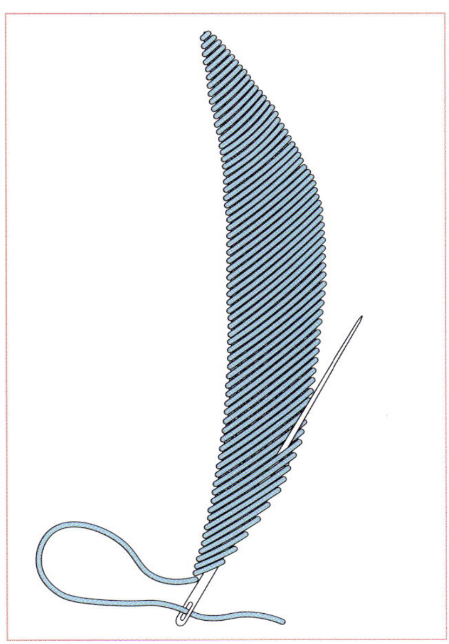

9 Padded satin stitch may be finished from the front by threading the needle under the satin stitch from the finishing point of the stitch.

PLAITED GOBELIN STITCH

CANVASWORK.

This canvaswork stitch is made up of rows of oblique stitches which slant in alternate directions to create a herringbone effect. It is similar to fern stitch (see page 75), but for this stitch the rows encroach on each other.

METHOD

1 Starting at the top right-hand side of your shape, stitch a diagonal stitch from bottom right to top left, up four and across two canvas threads.

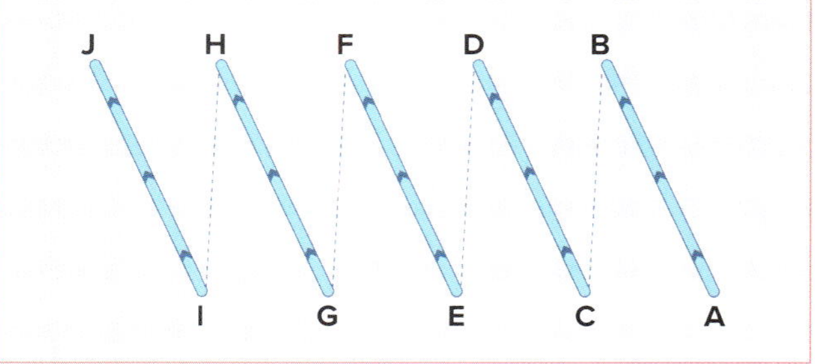

2 Complete a row of diagonal stitches each spaced by two threads of the canvas.

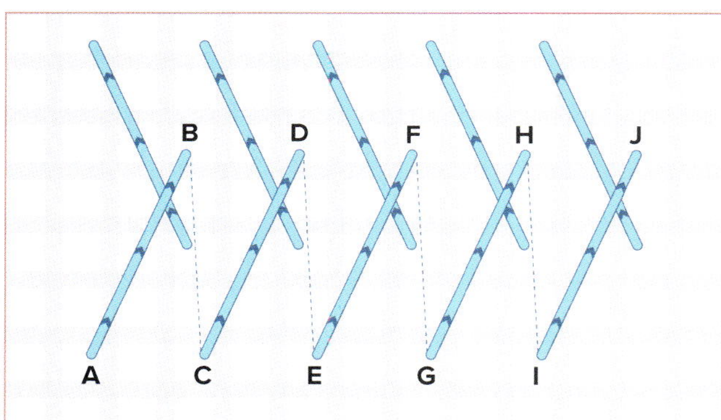

3 Work the next row from left to right , working diagonal stitches from bottom left to top right. Each stitch should lie directly below those on the previous line and encroach by two threads of the canvas so that the new row crosses the previous one.

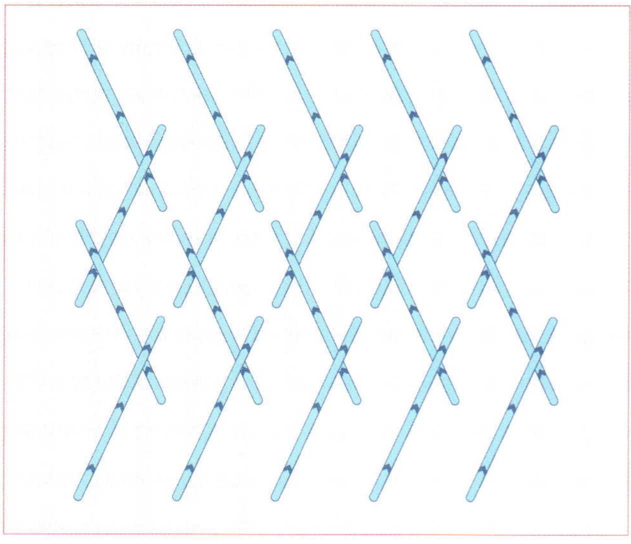

4 Continue working each row back and forth across the shape, each row encroaches on the previous one by two threads of the canvas.

RAISED FISHBONE STITCH

SURFACE; STUMPWORK.

Also known as Overlapping herringbone stitch.

This stitch consists of alternate diagonal stitches which overlap to fill an area, typically a leaf shape. Its alternative name of overlapping herringbone stitch gives an indication of its structure, although due to the amount the stitches overlap this is not readily visible from the finished stitch.

It is well-suited for leaf shapes.

METHOD

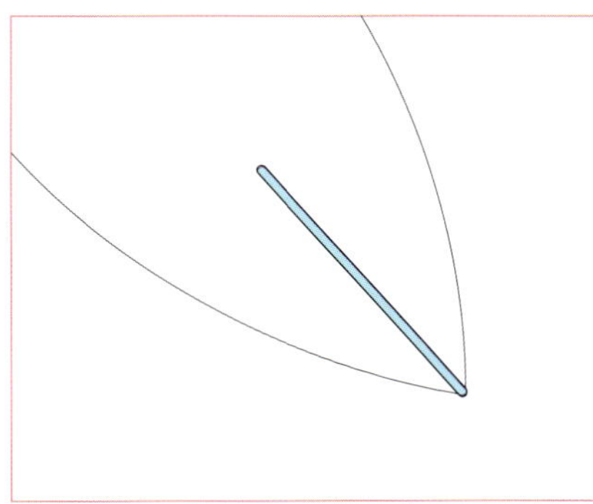

1 Starting at the tip make a straight central stitch into the shape.

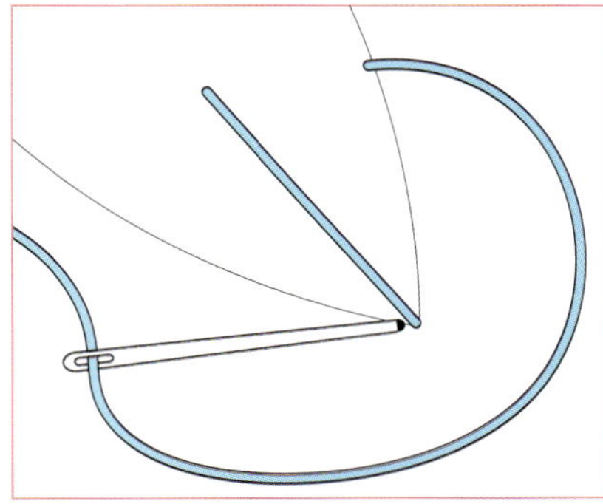

2 Bring the needle up just inside one side of the shape, cross over the central stitch and take the needle down on the edge close to the point.

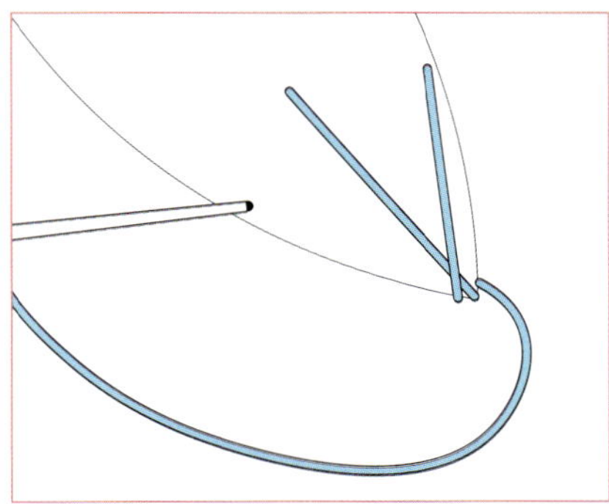

3 Bring the needle up close to the point on the other side of the central line and take it down just inside the outline mirroring the other side.

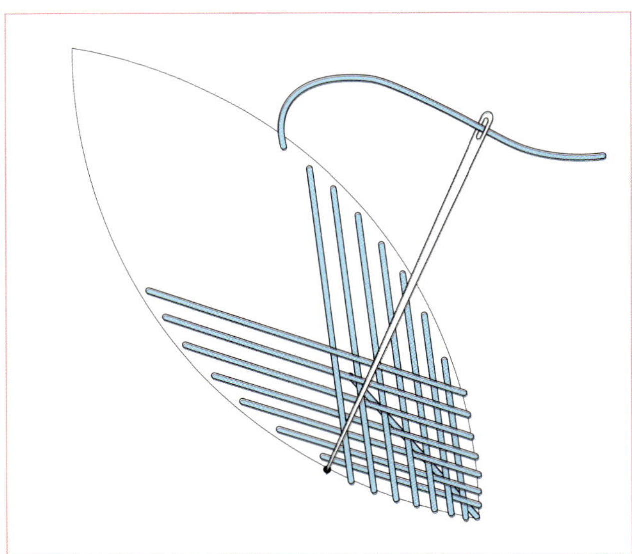

4 Repeat the last two steps over and over to gradually fill the interior, padding and covering the shape at the same time.

RAISED SPOT STITCH

Canvaswork.

This canvaswork stitch is like a very padded version of brick stitch (see page 219): a straight vertical stitch worked as a zigzag in horizontal bands.

Raised spot stitch is useful for creating texture.

METHOD

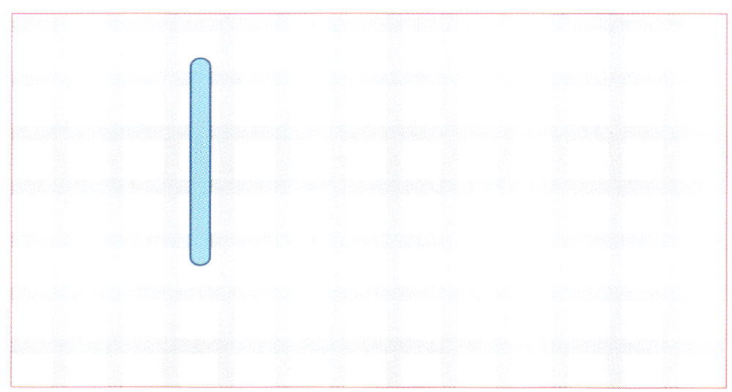

1 Make a vertical stitch across four threads of the canvas, then repeat the stitch through the same holes several times, until no more threads will fit through.

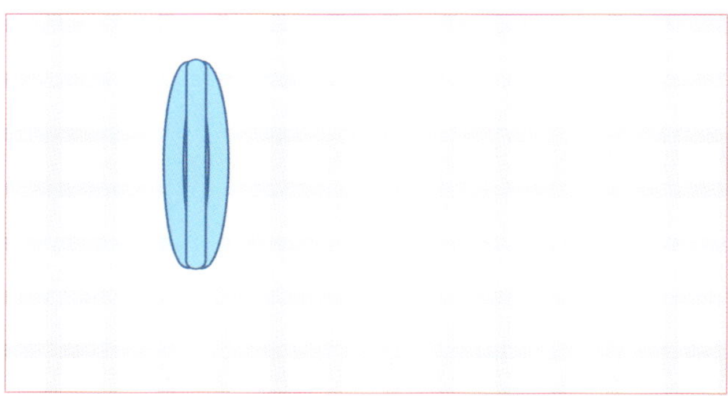

2 Make a note of how many times you are wrapping around each stitch and keep this consistent throughout.

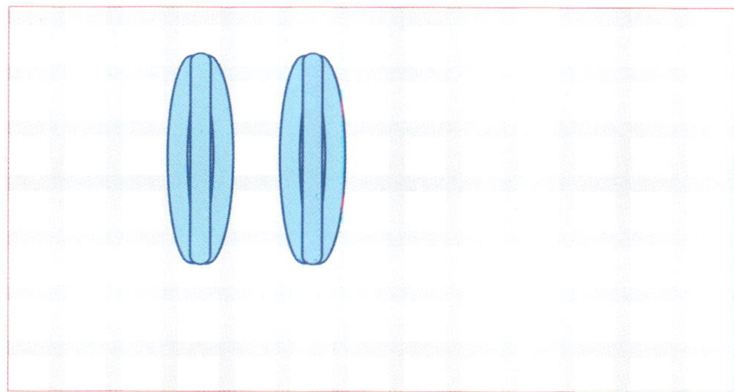

3 Move two canvas threads to the right and repeat to make the next stitch, making sure to match the number of times you wrap around each stitch.

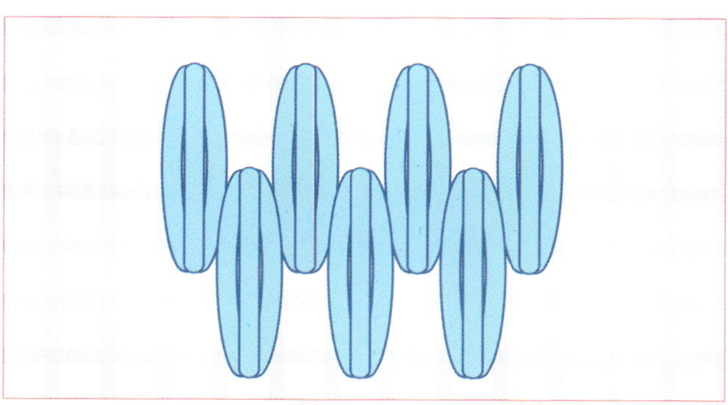

4 The second row fits into the gaps of the first, encroaching by two canvas threads.

RHODES STITCH

CANVASWORK.

This large stitch is made up of square blocks of slightly raised straight stitches. The straight stitches fan out around the grid, crossing in the centre, to fill all 360 degrees.

METHOD

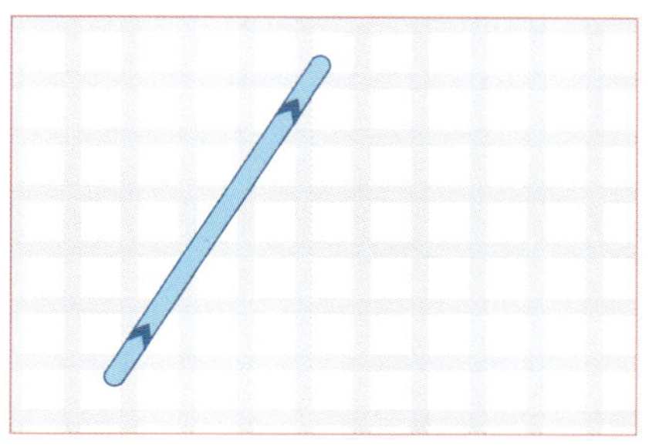

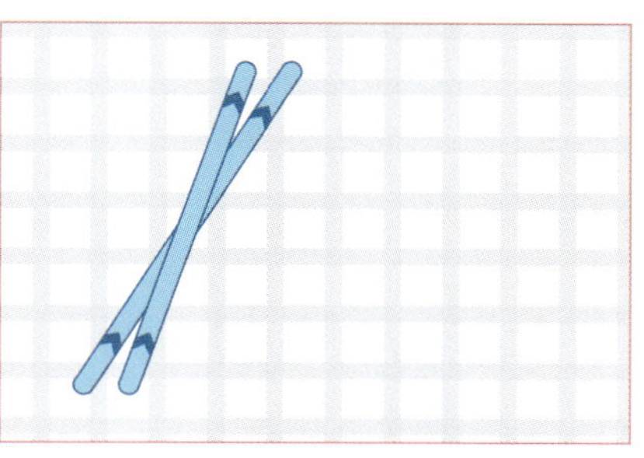

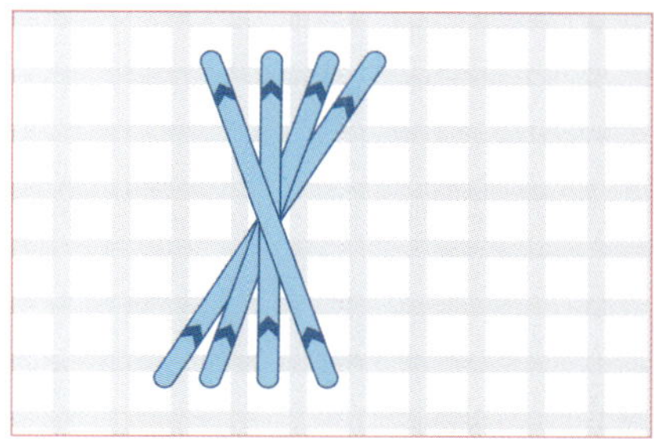

1 Begin one canvas thread in from the bottom left-hand corner and take this over to one thread in from the top right-hand corner of the completed square (i.e. across four threads and up six threads of the canvas).

2 Return to the bottom edge and make a stitch one thread to the right of the first and one thread to the left of the top edge of the first stitch.

3 Continue in an anti-clockwise direction around the square, fanning the stitches.

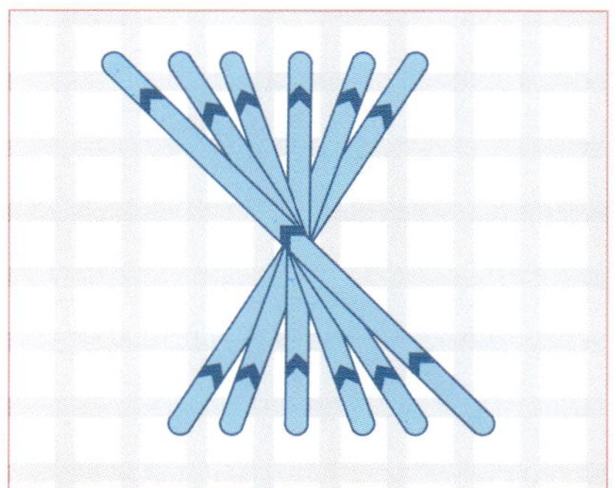

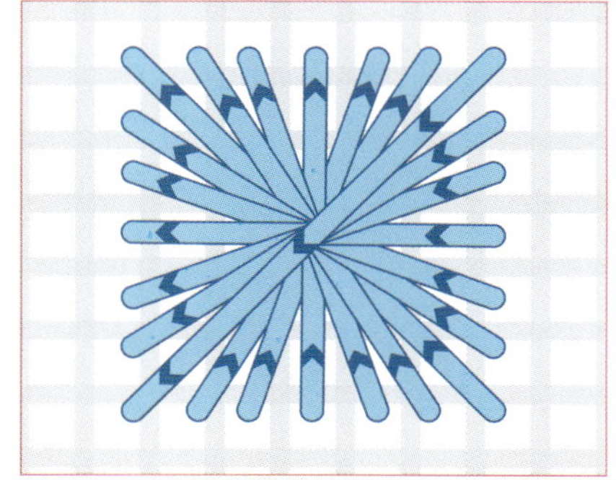

4 The sixth stitch should be from the bottom right-hand corner to the top left-hand corner.

5 Continue around the square until twelve stitches have been made. The last of these should be from the top right-hand corner to the bottom left-hand corner.

6 Move to the next square, either below or across. Always work the stitches in the same order and direction, so that the last stitch is always the same.

RICE STITCH (CANVASWORK)

CANVASWORK.

Also known as Crossed corners, or William and Mary stitch.

This is a large cross stitch with a diagonal stitch over each of its corners to form four small crosses.

Rice stitch is a good basic medium-sized stitch. It is a little raised and has an even textured appearance. It can be used as a single motif or as part of a pattern.

Rice stitch was used as one of the core stitches of Java canvas embroidery (named for the origin of the fabric, rather than the technique). The technique was popular during the late 19th century.

METHOD

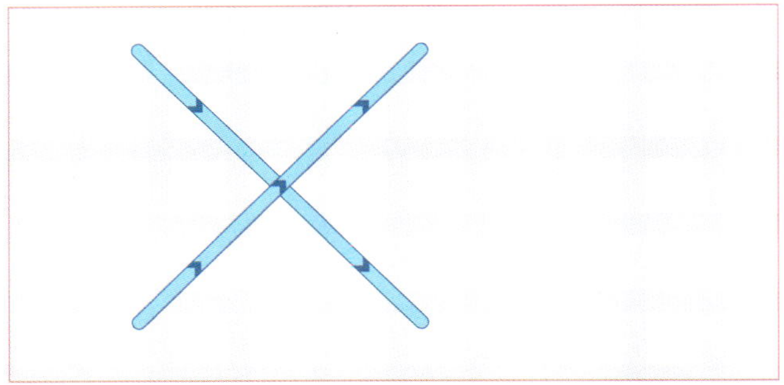

1 Begin by making a cross stitch across four by four threads of canvas. Make sure that the top stitch is always bottom left to top right.

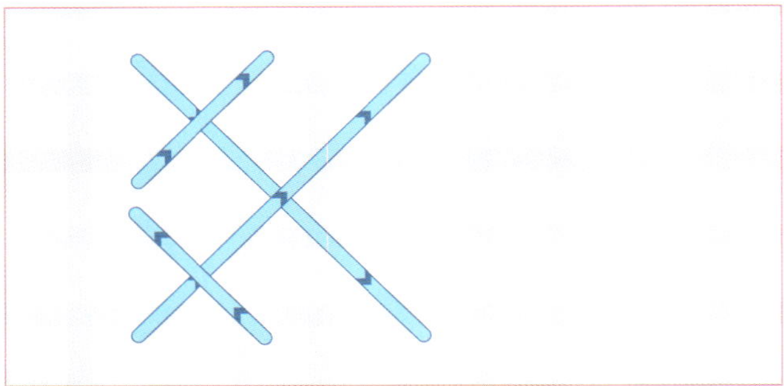

2 Now beginning at the top left-hand corner make a diagonal stitch across two intersections of canvas, crossing the corner of the first cross.

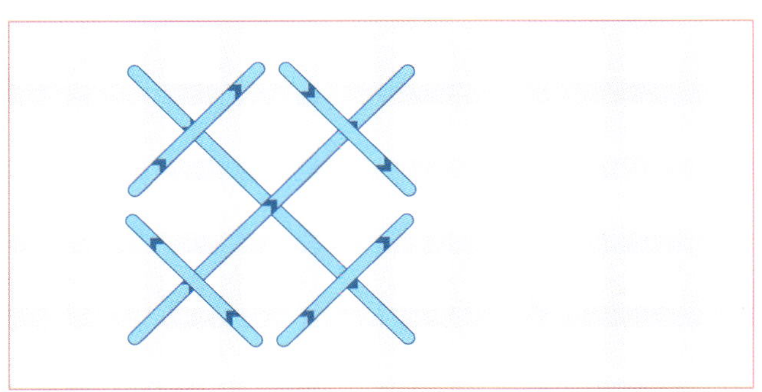

3 Repeat at each corner, so that these stitches meet at the centre points of the sides of the cross.

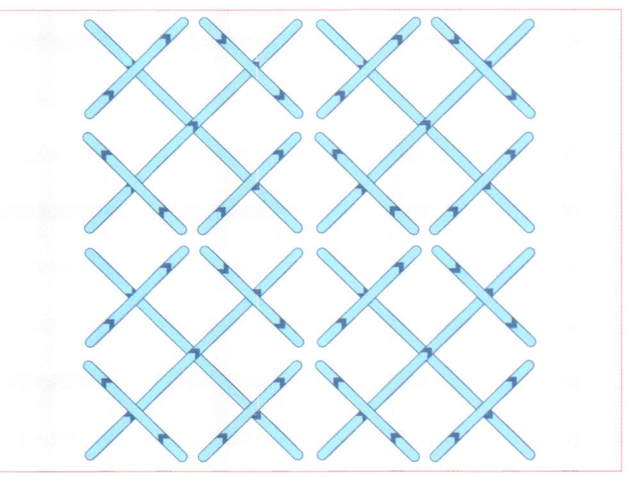

4 Repeat the rice stitch block in horizontal rows.

▲▲ Sweete bag, RSN Collection No. 758

This is an Elizabethan 'sweete bag', stitched using the technique of canvaswork. It was used to contain sweet-smelling herbs to dispel and hide the less nice smells. The designs embroidered on these bags often came from the early pattern books allowing them to be worked by both amateur and professional embroiderers. The example shown here is worked in silk thread using cross stitch. The background is worked in silver gilt thread using encroaching straight Gobelin stitch (see page 163). The bag is finished off with a metallic and silk braid and metallic tassels.

ROCOCO STITCH

Canvaswork; Stumpwork.

Also known as Double square stitch, or Queen stitch.

Rococo stitch is used in canvaswork as a textured filling stitch. Four vertical stitches are couched down with small horizontal stitches to form a diamond shape.

Rococo stitch dates from at least the 17th century, when it was normally known as Queen's stitch: it features on a panel exhibited by the Metropolitan Museum in New York and a casket now held by the V&A Museum in London. Both examples are worked in silk to showcase the intricacy of the stitch. It continued to be popular in the 18th century for chair seats and stools, as well as smaller items such as pocketbooks and pincushions. Historic examples normally have a slightly open appearance, as the canvas pulls apart slightly where the points of the stitch meet.

METHOD

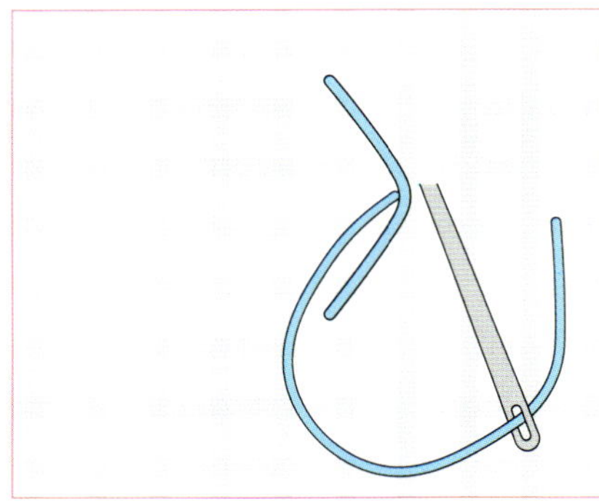

1 Come up to the front of the canvas and go down over four threads above. Pull the stitch out of alignment and make a horizontal stitch across it as shown in the diagram. The couching stitch should be two stitches up and two stitches across from the starting point – make sure that you stitch over the vertical canvas thread.

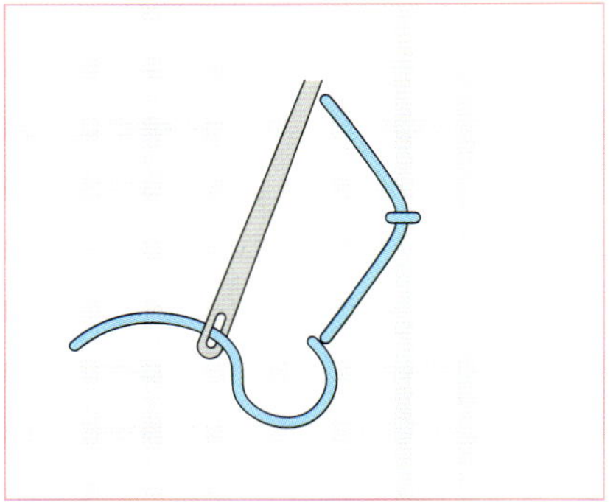

2 Bring the needle up at the same hole as the starting point, and go down in the same hole over four threads above.

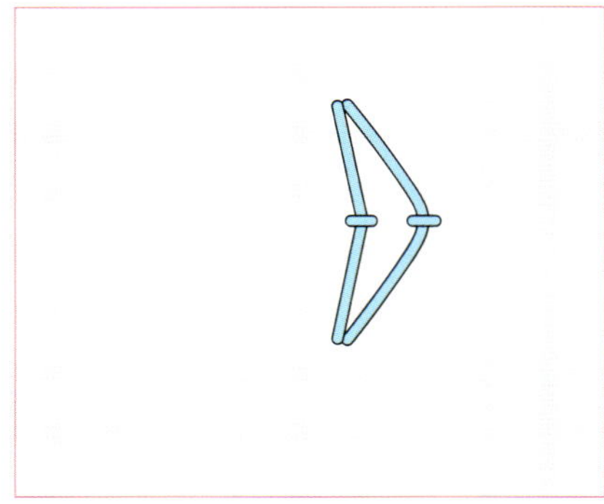

3 Make a small horizontal stitch in the middle one thread over as shown. The couching stitch should be two stitches up and one stitch across from the starting point.

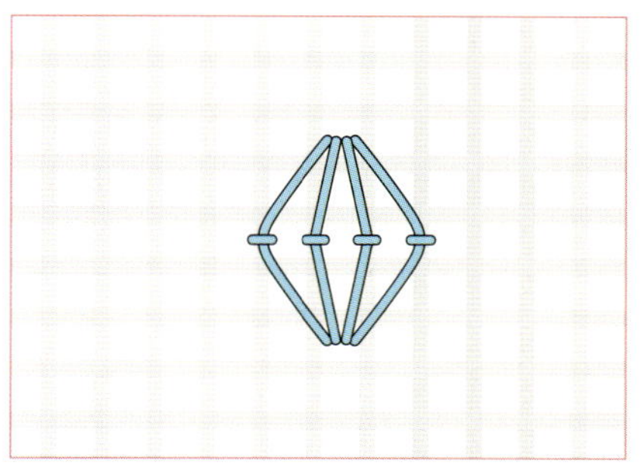

4 Repeat and work two more vertical stitches with a small horizontal stitch across. Make sure these four vertical stitches share the same holes at the top and the bottom.

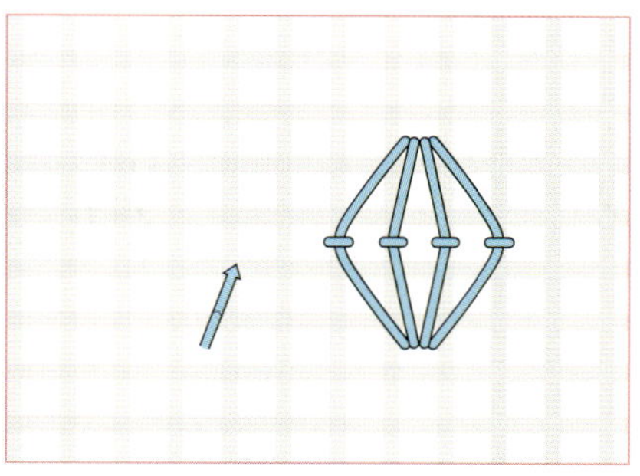

5 To continue, come up at the bottom, four threads over to the left.

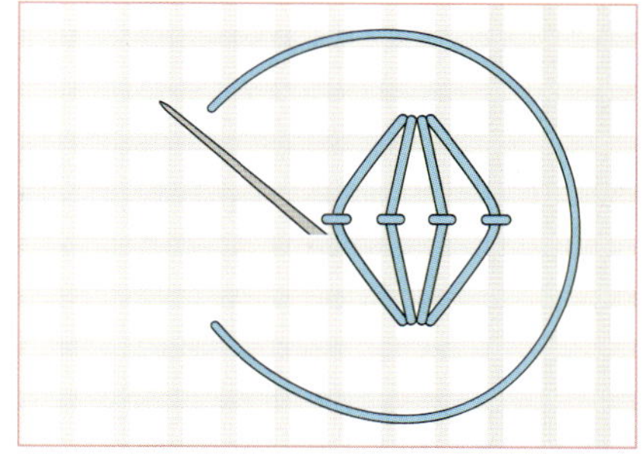

6 Continue the rococo stitch as before.

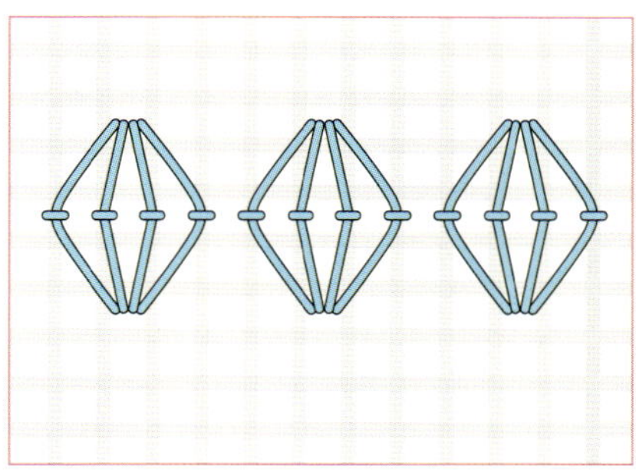

7 The first row of rococo stitch; worked from right to left.

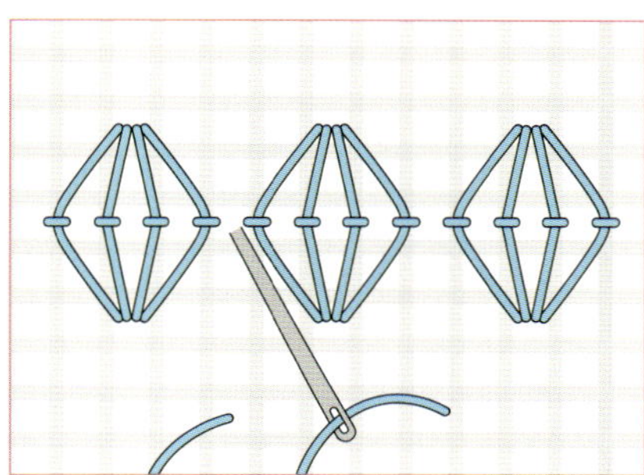

8 To begin the second row, bring the needle up at four threads down from the hole between the two rococo stitches in the first row.

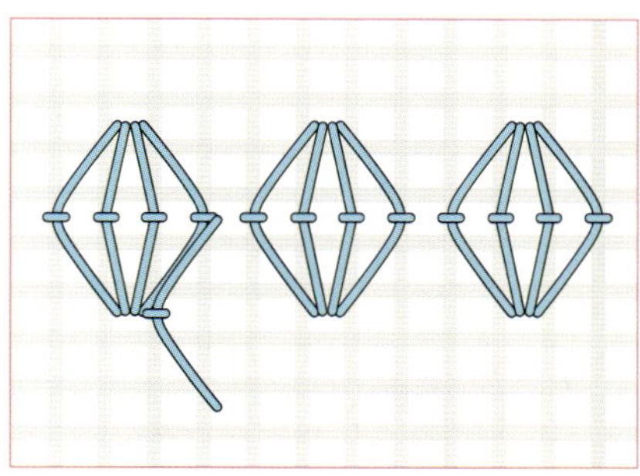

9 The first vertical stitch is couched with a small horizontal stitch as shown (this uses the same hole as the previous row).

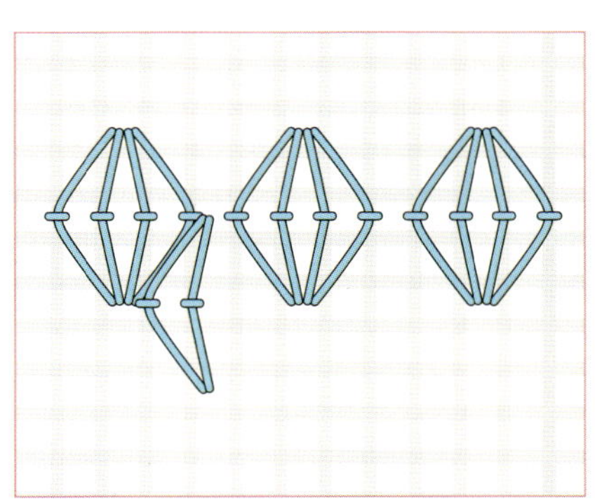

10 Work from left to right.

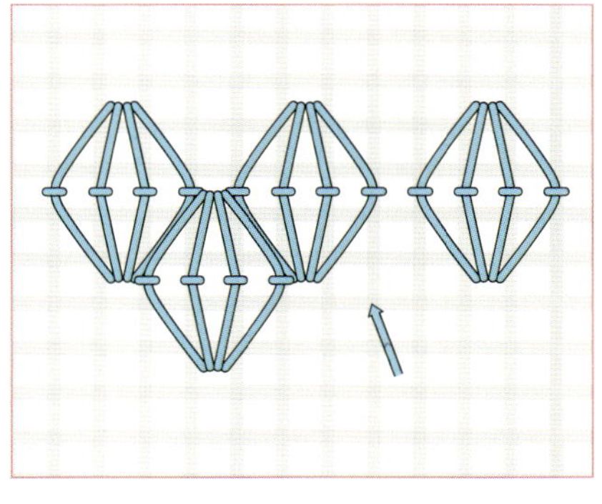

11 Continue to the end of the row.

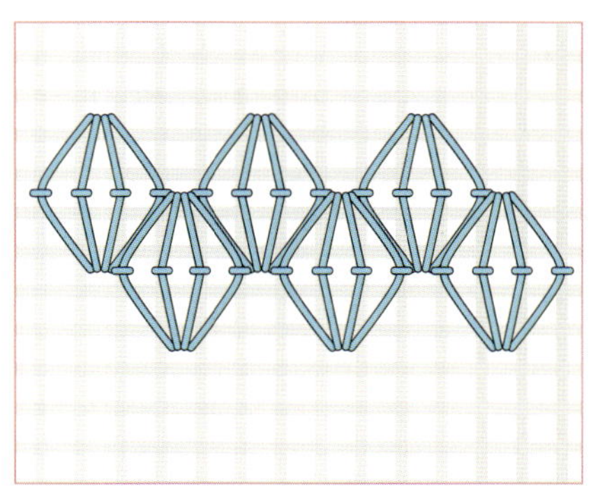

Two rows of Rococo stitch.

ROUNDED EYELET (PATTERN)

BLACKWORK.

This looks like a fairly complex pattern made up of larger, filled octagons joined together by smaller straight squares. In actual fact the pattern is easy to follow by completing a number of offset eyelets and then outlining each eyelet with an octagonal frame.

This works well for an even density and for darker areas.

METHOD

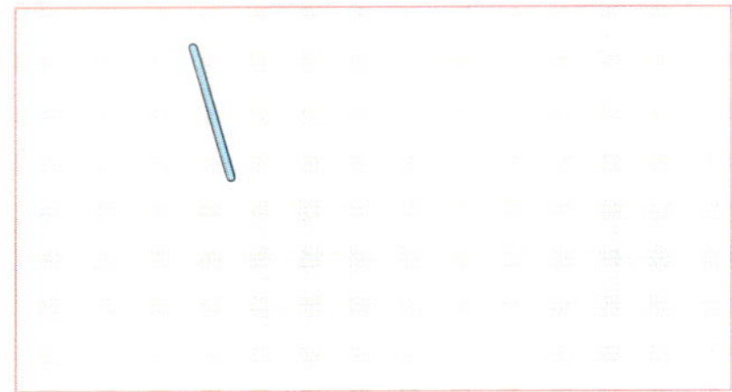

1 Start by completing a single diagonal stitch across one thread and down over three threads.

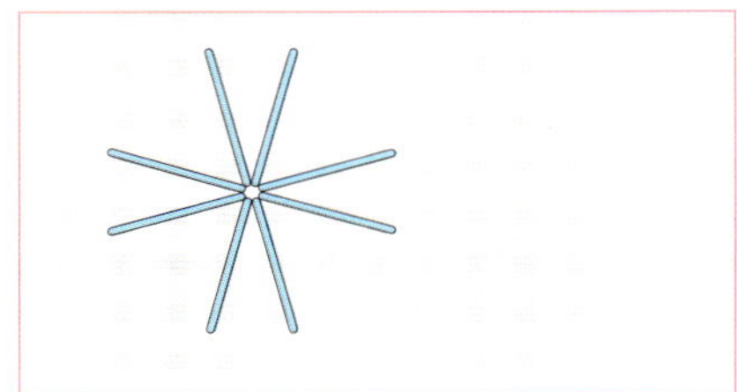

2 Add another seven diagonal stitches of the same length all going down into the same hole to complete an eyelet.

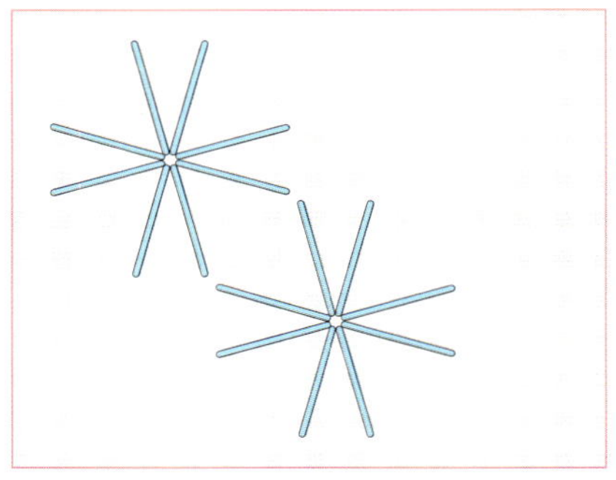

3 The next eyelet should be offset from the last, but touch at the corners.

4 Fill the area with a pattern of offset touching eyelets.

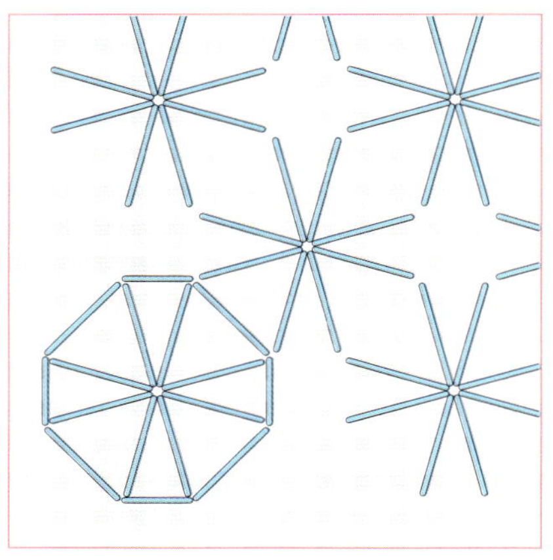

5 Each eyelet should then be framed with an octagonal outline.

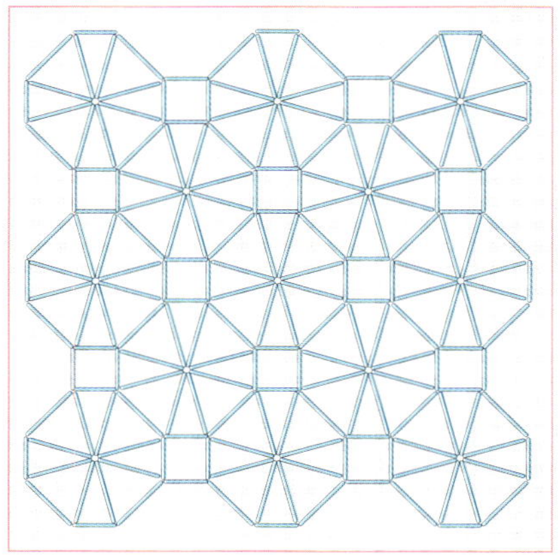

6 Continue to outline the eyelet pattern with the octagons.

SCOTTISH SQUARES

CANVASWORK.

Also known as Scottish stitch, Scotch stitch, Framed scotch stitch, or Cushion stitch.

This stitch is a version of cushion stitch (see page 152), where five diagonal stitches form a square framed by a grid of tent stitch (see basketweave tent stitch on page 218).

In common with the other versions of this stitch, it is known by various names, some of which are used interchangeably for the different versions.

METHOD

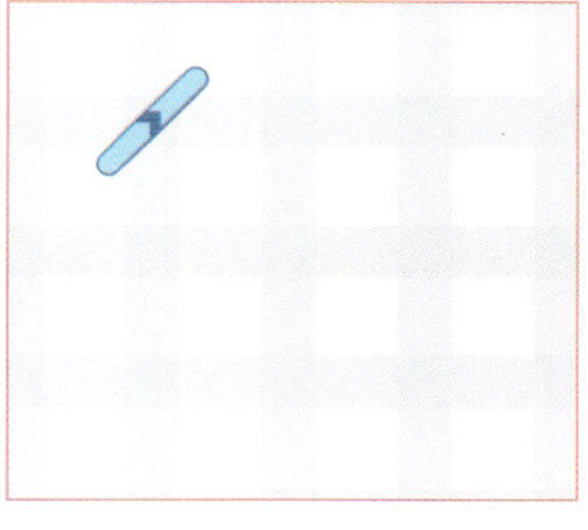

1 Work a diagonal stitch from bottom left to top right, over one intersection ...

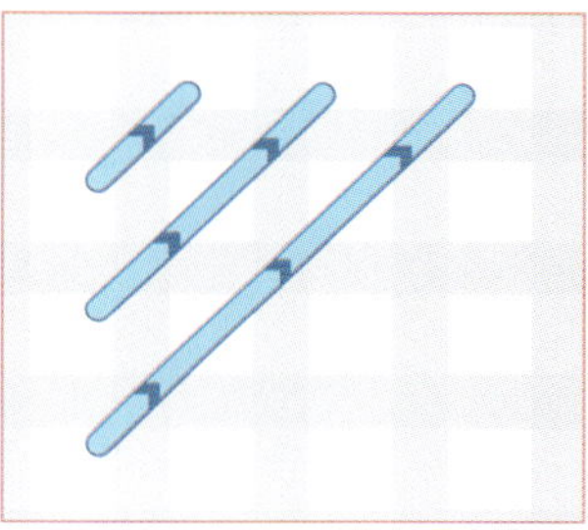

2 ... then over two and three intersections ...

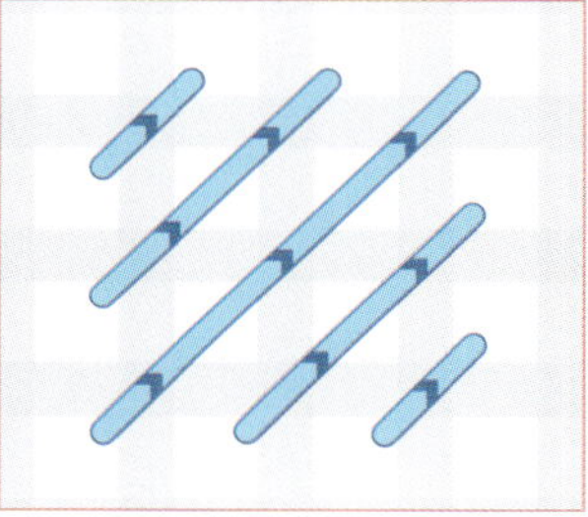

3 ... and finally over two and one intersections to complete a square cushion.

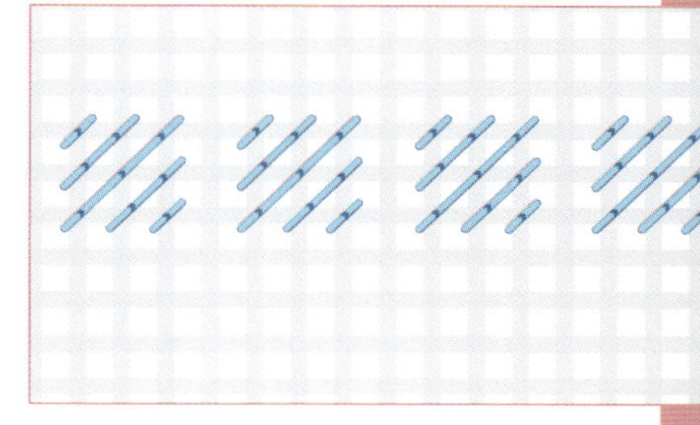

4 Leaving a gap of a single thread, repeat the square cushions across the shape to complete a row.

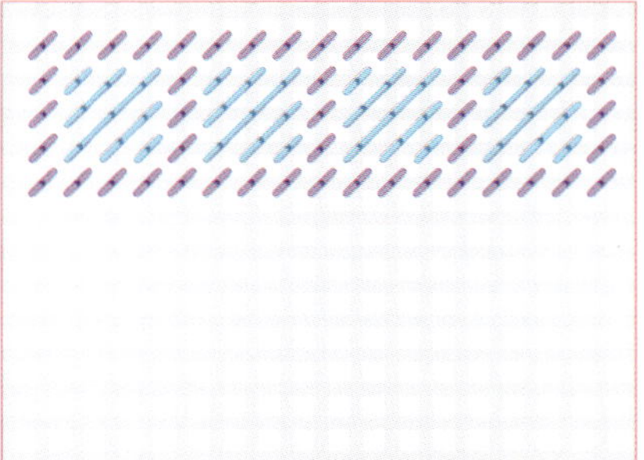

5 Surround the cushions with a single line of tent stitch, either in the same or a contrasting colour.

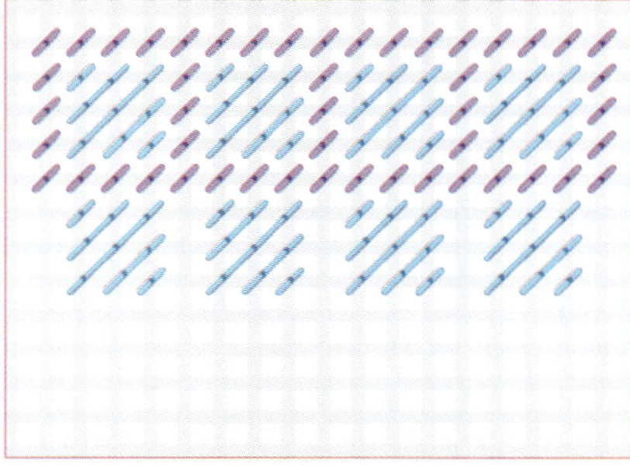

6 Continue to add more square cushions to fill the area.

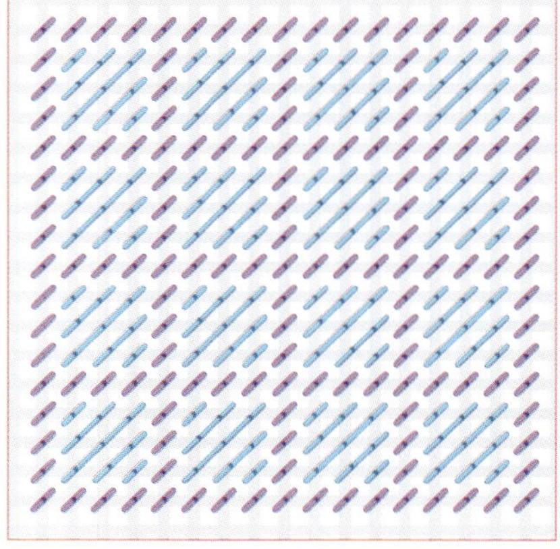

7 Complete by framing the whole area with a single line of tent stitch.

SINGLE BRUSSELS STITCH

NEEDLELACE; STUMPWORK; ELIZABETHAN.

Also known as Detached buttonhole, Buttonhole filling, Open buttonhole filling, Point de Bruxelles, Foundation stitch, Brussels lace stitch, Point de feston, Plain net stitch, Italian lace stitch, Buttonhole net stitch, or Point noné.

Often used in stumpwork embroidery, this is a needlelace stitch, consisting of detached butthonhole stitches worked over a pre-existing outline. After the first row of buttonhole stitches has been completed, the stitch direction is reversed and the next row is worked into the previous row. The stitch can be worked densely by working the first row of detached buttonhole stitches closely together, or as a more open stitch by spacing them apart, as shown below.

Single Brussels stitch is attached to the background fabric only at the edges. A simple back stitch (see page 16) outline is used here, but it could be a cordonnet when making a needlelace slip.

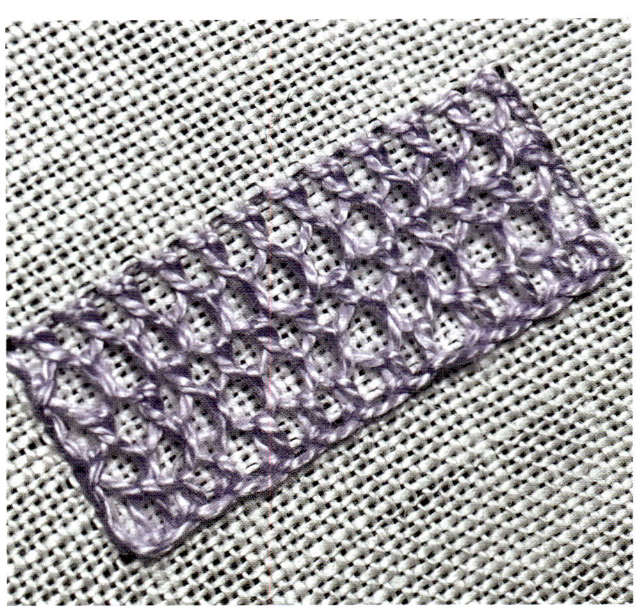

METHOD

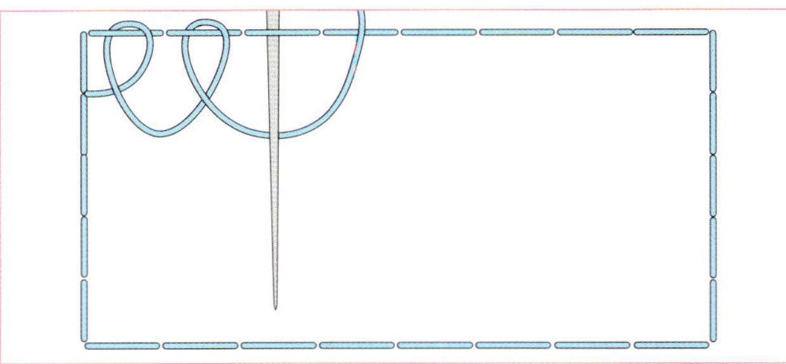

1 Outline the edge of the area which you want to fill with double running stitch. Start just under the top left-hand corner and work a detached buttonhole stitch. The stitch is attached to the fabric by passing through the top outer edge only.

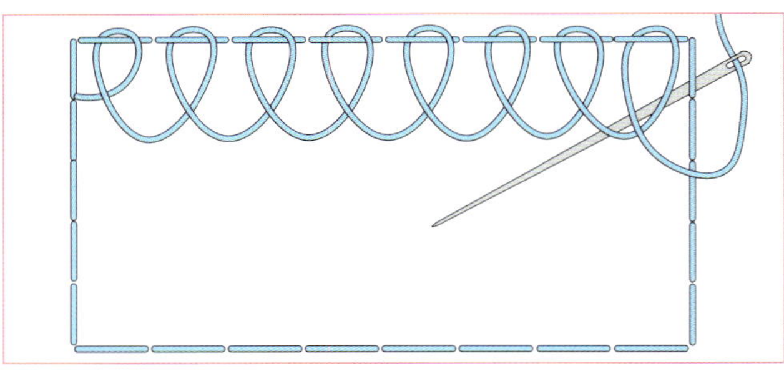

2 Repeat along the row to the right-hand edge of the shape. Attach the stitch to the right-hand side of the shape by whipping the edge.

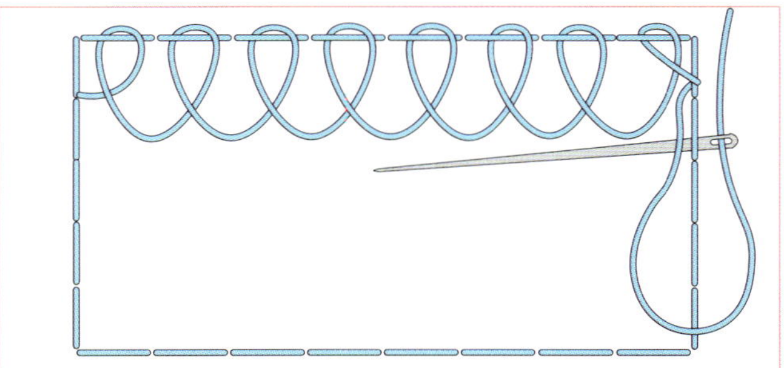

3 Whip the side outer edge again to bring the needle just below the first row.

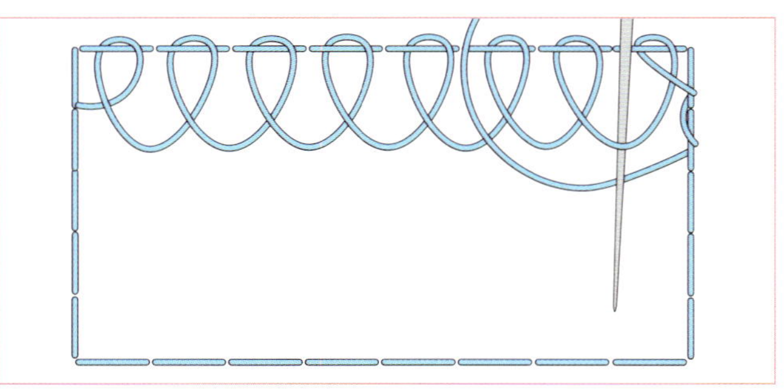

4 Work another row of detached buttonhole stitches from right to left, passing the needle through the loops of the previous row.

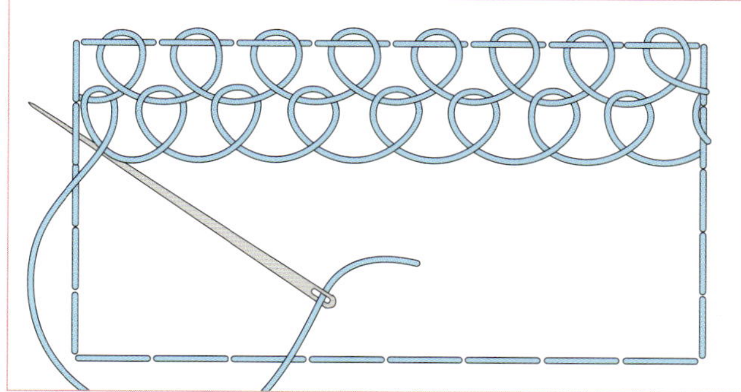

5 Continue to the left-hand edge of the shape, and whip down the left side edge to bring the needle just below the last row.

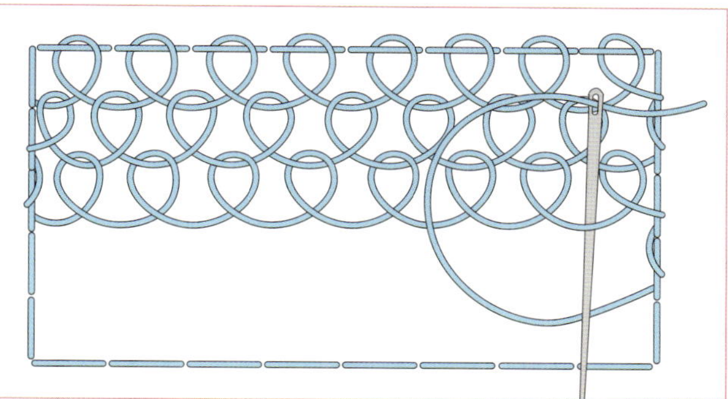

6 Continue to work rows of detached buttonhole stitch back and forth across the shape, forming each stitch by passing the needle through the loop just above it.

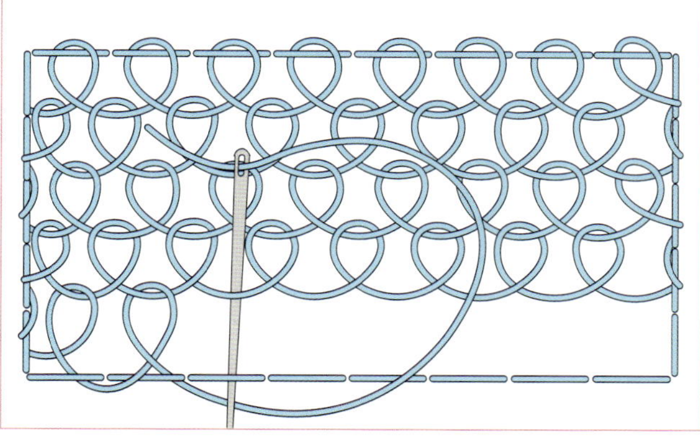

7 On the final row, pass the thread through the loop of the previous row and the bottom outer edge as you form each stitch.

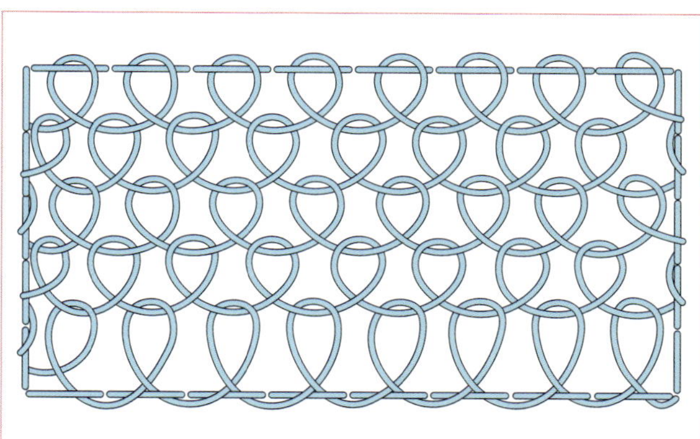

A completed area of single Brussels stitch.

◂◂ Detail from Stumpwork (raised work) casket panel, RSN Collection COL.2006.44

This panel is worked in silk and metal threads on a cream silk ground with a variety of needlelace stitches. It is from an embroidered casket or cabinet that dates from circa 1650–1675, and which possibly depicts Pyramus and Thisbe from the Metamorphoses *by Ovid.*

On the right-hand side of the picture, a man looks out from behind a tree. He wears a knee length, brown, striped tunic over tights and boots, all worked in needlelace techniques. He has a chain stitch (see page 22) belt, a single corded Brussels tunic, and single corded Brussels white collar and cuffs.

SLANTED SATIN STITCH

Crewelwork; Surface; Whitework.

A series of straight parallel stitches worked at an angle across a shape to produce a smooth solid filling.

It is typically used in monogramming, leaves and petals.

For more background see satin stitch (on page 37).

METHOD

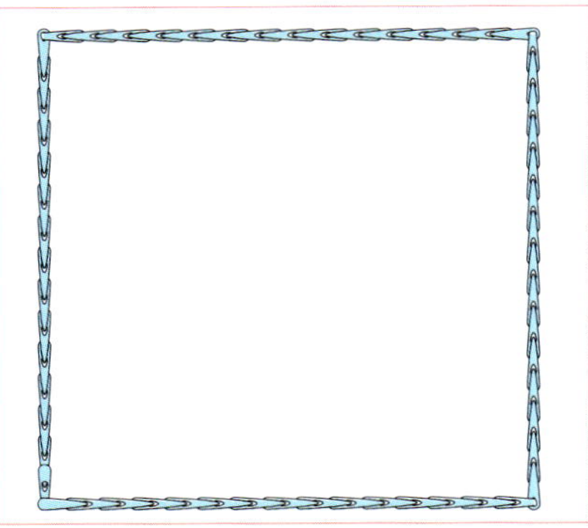

1 Complete a split stitch outline around the shape to be filled.

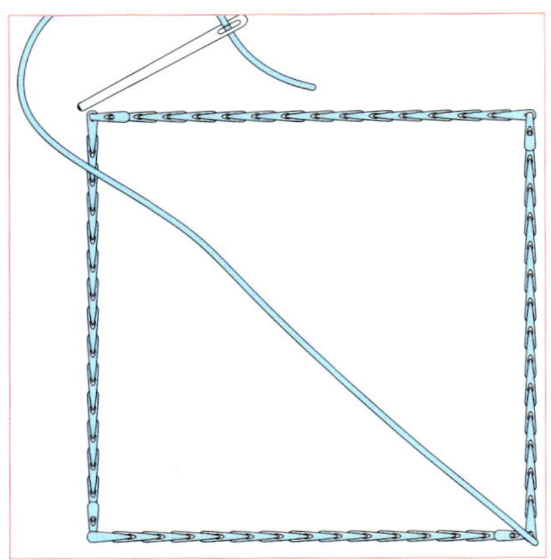

2 Beginning halfway along one side, bring the needle up just outside the split stitch outline. Hold the thread to set the angle of the first stitch and take the needle down accordingly, just outside the split stitch.

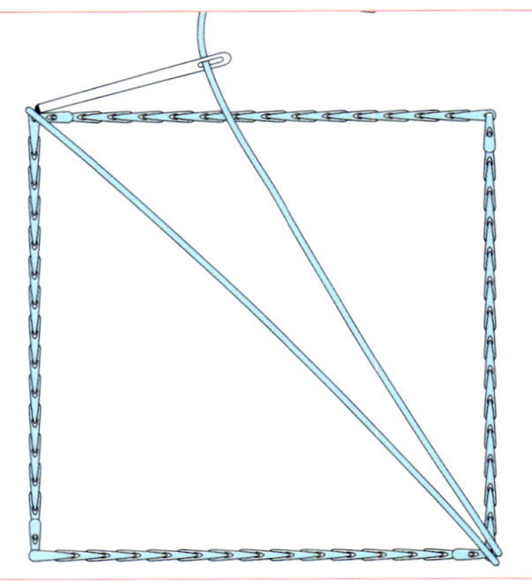

3 Bring the needle up on the first side, very close to the first stitch. Make a second stitch, angling the needle towards the previous stitch and towards the split stitch.

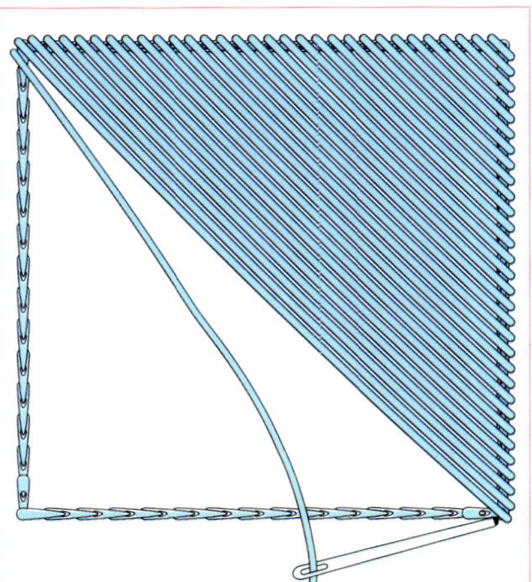

4 Work outwards towards the end of the shape, and then begin again in the middle. This time bring the needle up on the other side of the shape, and angle the needle towards the previous stitch as before.

5 Continue working the satin stitch towards the opposite corner until the shape is complete.

SMALL DIAMOND (PATTERN)

Blackwork.

A blackwork pattern made up of diagonal squares with a vertical straight stitch inside. It is a small-scale pattern suitable for darker tones.

METHOD

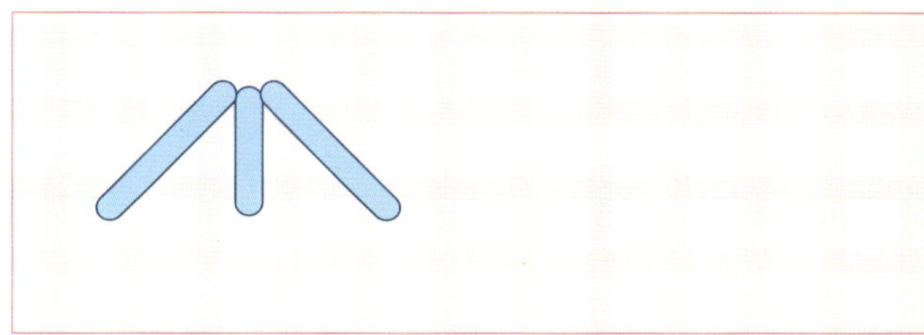

1 Stitch an arrow of three stitches each over two threads (one vertical and two diagonal) each going into the same hole at the top. Each arrow should be symmetrical.

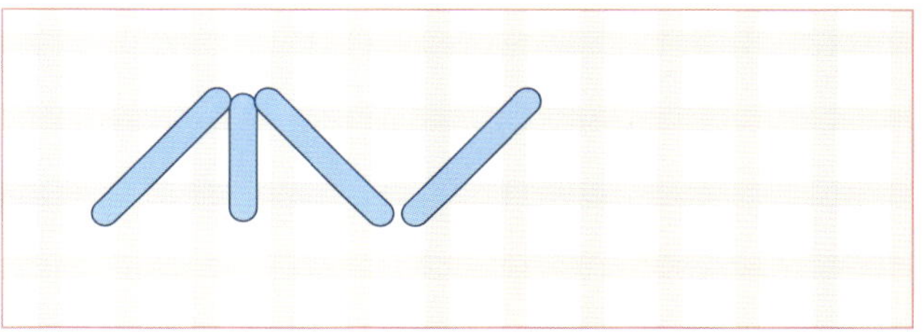

2 The diagonals of each stitch should touch that of the neighbouring stitch.

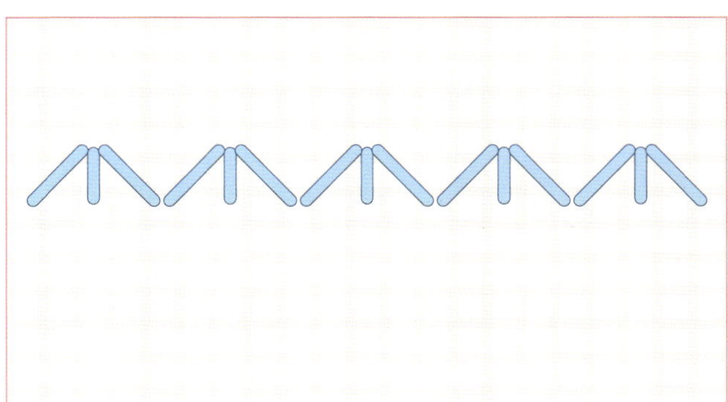

3 Continue the sequence horizontally.

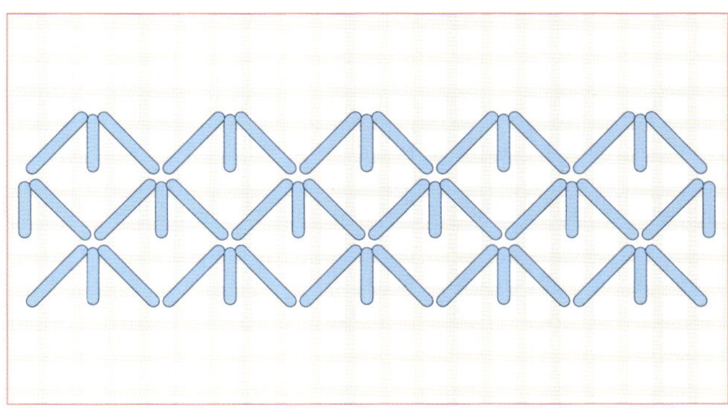

4 Each subsequent row is offset with the previous row to complete the diamond in the pattern.

STAB STITCH

Bead embroidery; Appliqué; Stumpwork; Surface.

Also known as Appliqué stab stitch.

This tiny, simple stitch is really useful for applying one piece of fabric to another by sewing small discrete stitches around the edges, for consolidating layers of fabric or for attaching beads. Using stab stitch to secure a single bead works well as the centre of a circular motif.

For using it to start and finish a thread, see the entries for holding stitch on page 31 and finishing stitch on page 27.

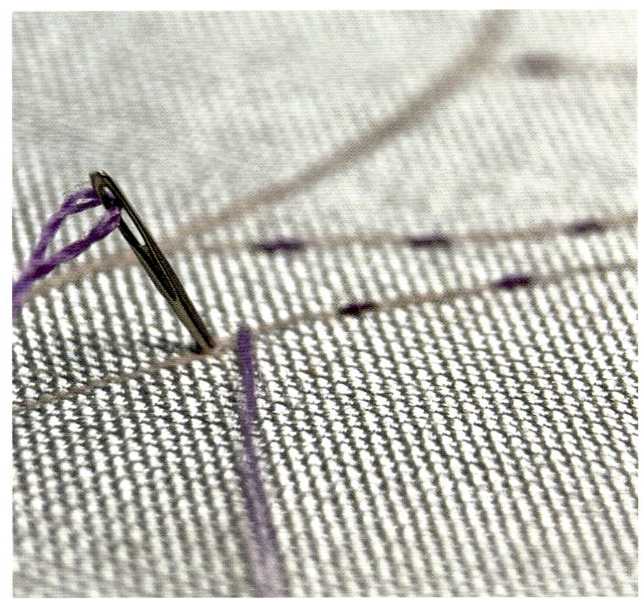

METHOD

Applying fabrics
This image of stab stitch shows how small straight stitches can be used to apply another fabric. The needle is brought up through the base fabric at the edge of the fabric to be applied. The needle is then taken down through both fabrics just inside the applied shape.

For more information about applying felt, see felt padding on page 164.

Securing beads
Bring the needle up through the fabric and thread your chosen base bead onto the needle. Now thread on a smaller bead to act as a stopper and take the needle back through the base bead (but not the stopper bead).

Draw the thread through to secure the beads: the stopper bead will nestle in the top of the base bead.

For more information about using this stitch, see spangles held on with purls on page 268.

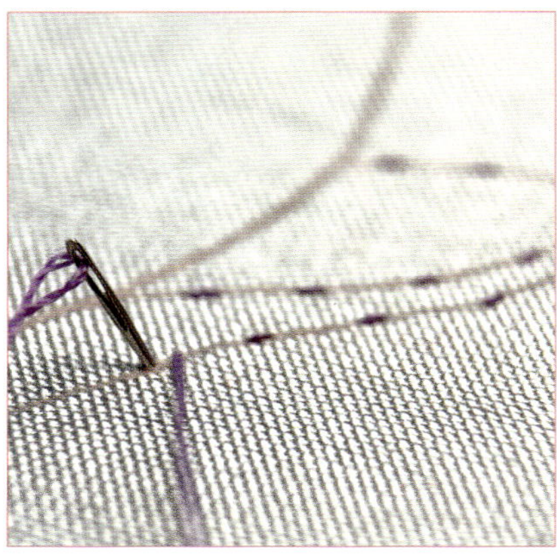

Consolidating fabrics
Small stab stitches are used here to consolidate two different fabrics. The fine silk layer is a background to the embroidery design which has been stabilized with stab stitches to a more durable layer of calico beneath.

▲▲ Detail from cape, RSN Collection COL.86

1890s black silk cape with beads, bows, frills and cut outs. The collar and front of the cape feature ruffles. The back is shown here, focussing upon a pattern of beadwork roses and leaves worked onto net. Down the centre of the cape's back, this beadwork pattern morphs into a geometric series of lines and wheel shapes. The beads appear to be jet.

STAGGERED CASHMERE STITCH

CANVASWORK.

Also known as Diagonal cashmere stitch.

Each rectangular cashmere block of this pattern is worked across two canvas threads by three.

This stitch is very similar to condensed cashmere stitch (see page 139), evidenced by the fact that this version is sometimes also known as diagonal cashmere stitch. Both feature offset cashmere blocks: the difference is that in this version each block is complete, whereas the blocks in diagonal cashmere stitch are condensed.

METHOD

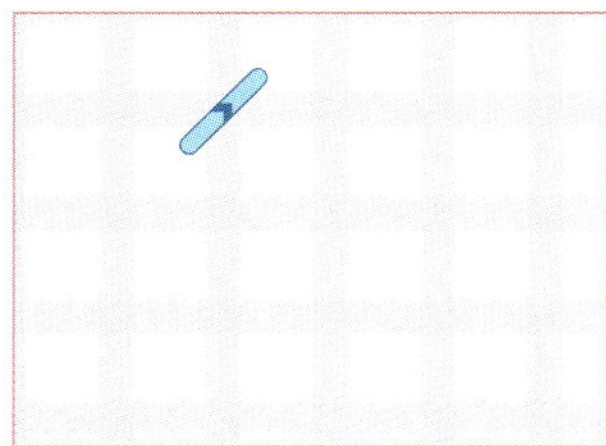

1 Make a single tent stitch across one intersection of the canvas.

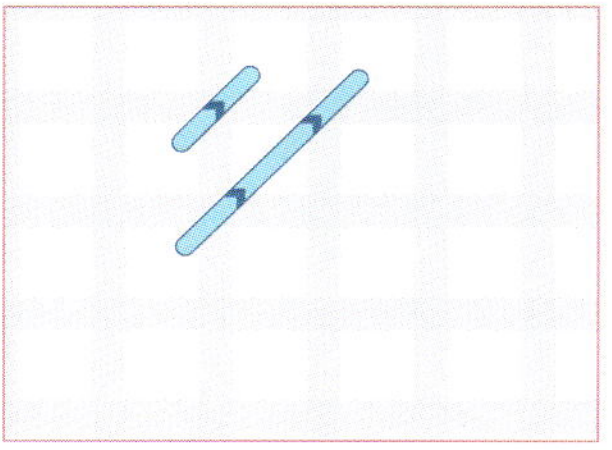

2 Starting directly beneath this stitch make a diagonal stitch across two intersections of canvas.

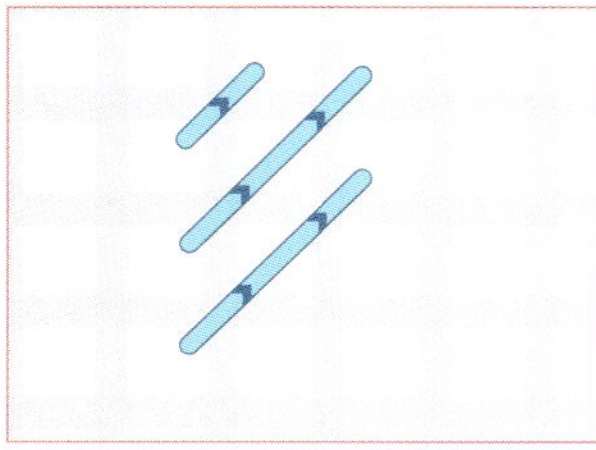

3 Repeat to make a second stitch across two intersections of canvas.

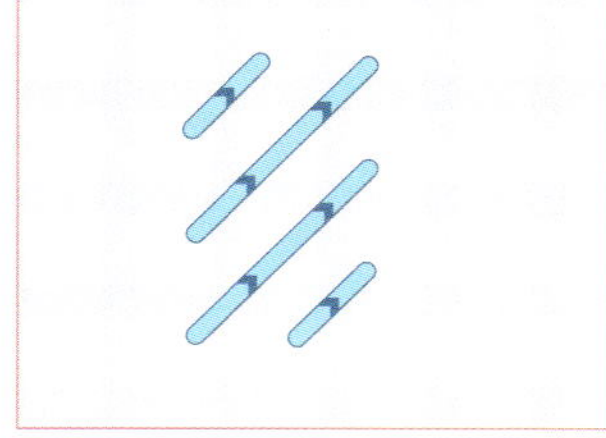

4 Finish off the rectangle with a second tent stitch at the bottom right corner of the block.

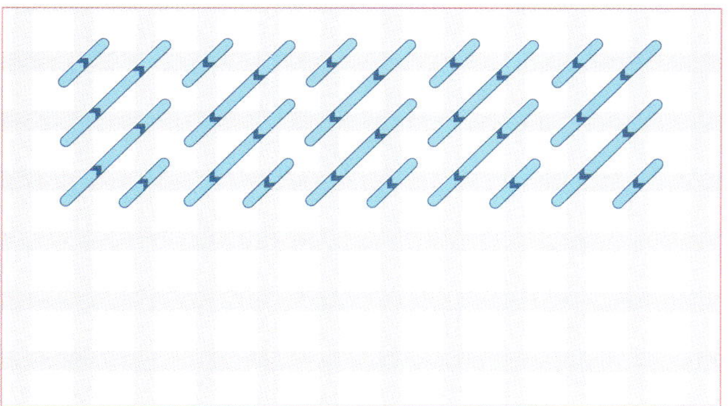

5 Continue the sequence to complete a horizontal row of identical blocks.

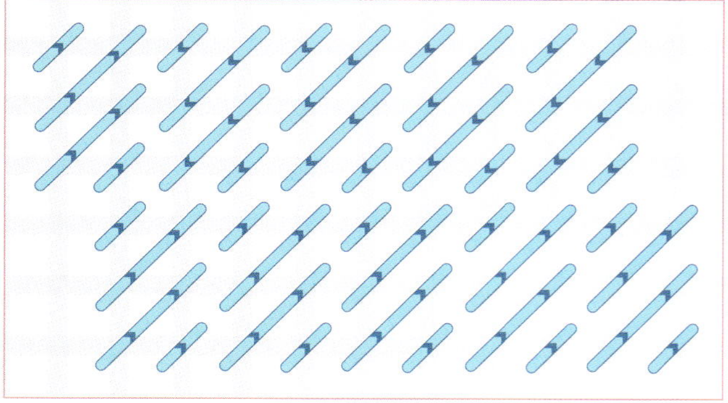

6 Offset the following rows to complete staggered cashmere.

STRAIGHT GOBELIN STITCH

CANVASWORK; BERLIN WOOL WORK.

Also known as Upright Gobelin stitch, Gobelin stitch, or Tapestry stitch.

This canvaswork stitch is a small, neat vertical stitch with a slightly raised appearance. It is good for small striped areas. If desired, it can be trammed (stitched over a long laid stitch to provide a raised effect).

This is the vertical version of Gobelin stitch (see oblique Gobelin stitch on page 180 for the slanted version). Historically, the name Gobelin stitch has been used for both this version and the oblique version.

The name Gobelin is credited with originating from the 17th century Gobelins Manufactory in Paris, but whether the name is connected with the factory or purely a reference to the stitch's tapestry-like appearance is unclear.

METHOD

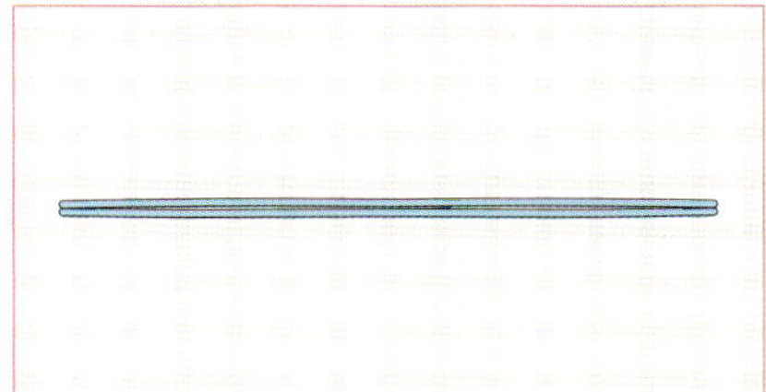

1 Start by making a padding stitch across the width of the area to be covered.

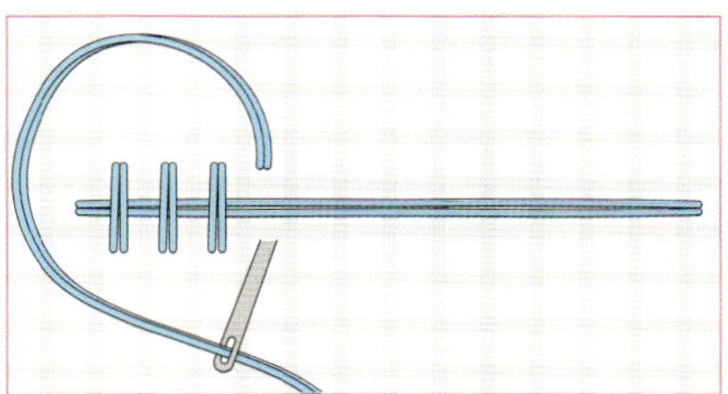

2 Work back over this, adding vertical stitches across two threads of the canvas.

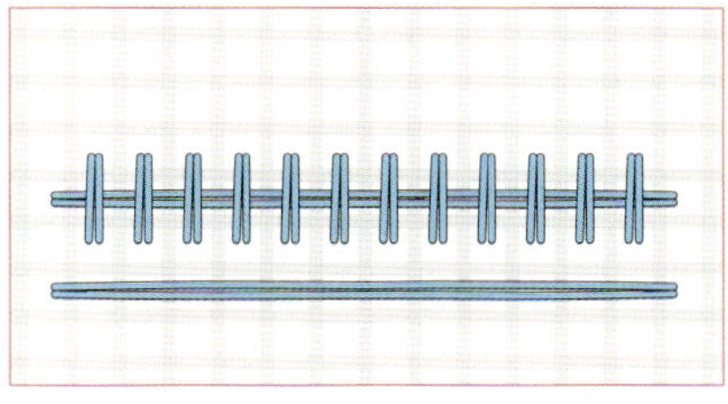

3 Start the padding of the second row two canvas threads below the first padding stitch.

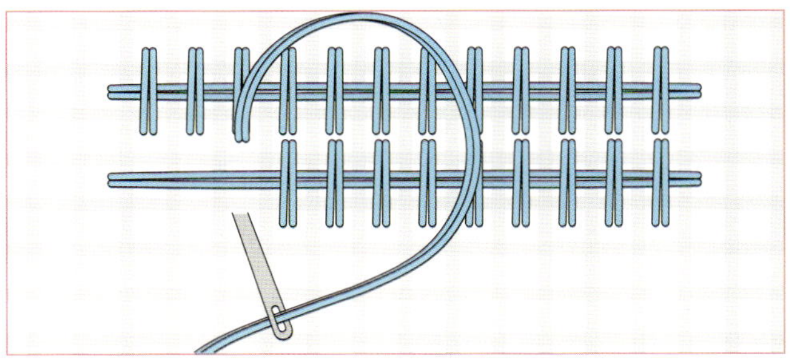

4 Work back across this, working each vertical stitch into the same hole of the previous row of stitches. Always take the needle down into the occupied canvas hole, not out of it.

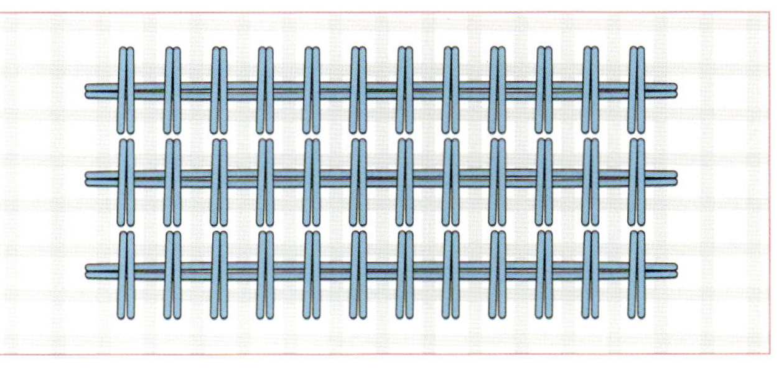

Straight Gobelin does not always have to be worked with the straight padding stitch under the couching stitches.

TULIP (PATTERN)

Blackwork.

This pattern is made up of a series of interlocking hexagons, joined in columns by a straight stitch; the pattern resembles a line of tulips with their stamens. The lozenge pattern can be successfully blended with diamond or hexagon patterns.

It is a mid-scale pattern and works well in more organic designs. Use different weight thread to produce shading within the pattern.

METHOD

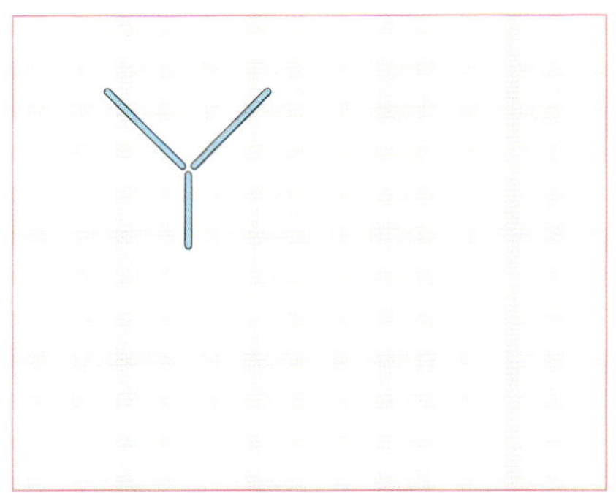

1 Starting from the centre, stitch the first three stitches. Each stitch is over two intersections or two threads of the fabric.

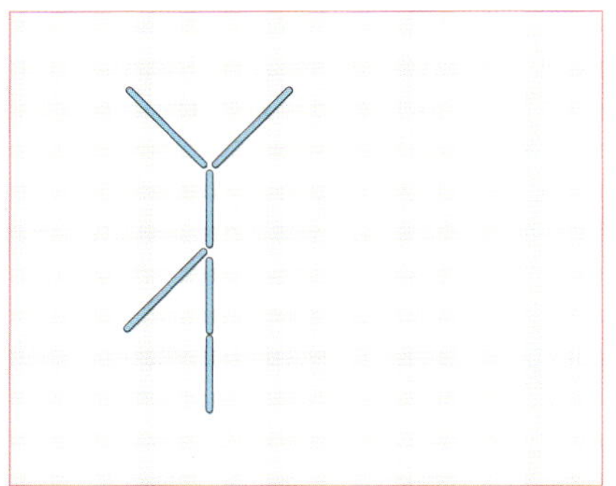

2 Work the vertical stamen using double running stitch, then work a diagonal back stitch to start the outline.

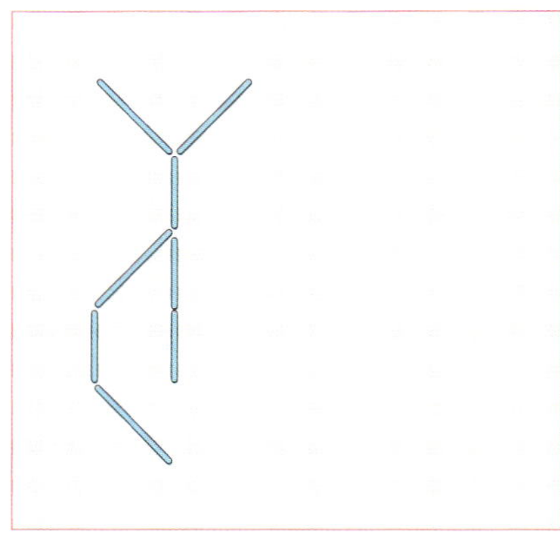

3 Work the left edge of the tulip using running stitch and back stitch, changing to double running stitch for the right edge.

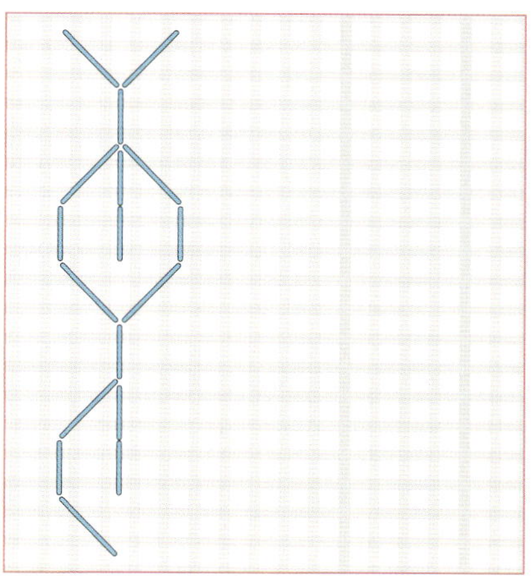

4 Stitch the vertical line in the centre of the flower in double running stitch, before stitching the outside.

5 Complete a vertical row in the pattern.

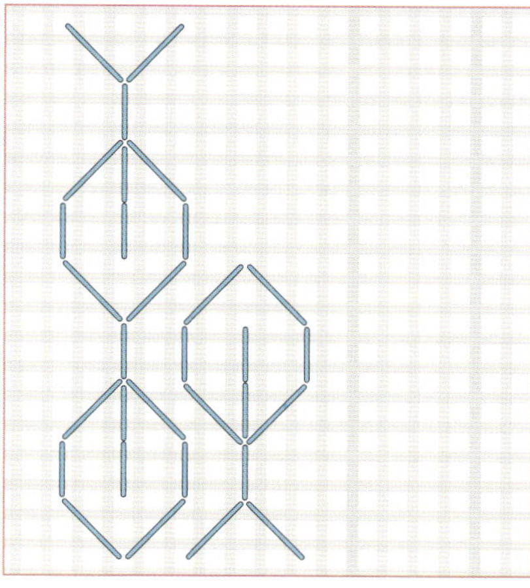

6 Bring your needle up two threads to the right of the tip of the last tulip and work a second row from the bottom up. The pattern should face in the opposite direction.

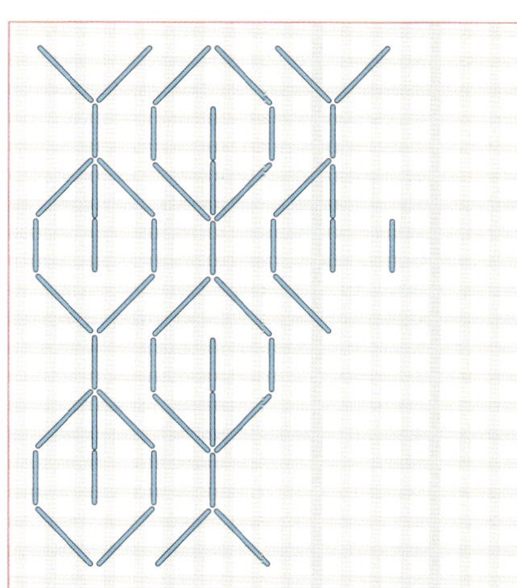

7 Continue with more vertical rows, each with the pattern facing the opposite direction.

8 Continue to fill the shape.

▲▲ Detail from sampler, RSN Collection COL.2014.25

This detail of the bird shows the filling of tulip has been worked in a second colour, with black thread reserved for the central part of the pattern. This principle can be applied to many other patterns, too.

You can see the full piece on page 131.

TURKEY RUG KNOT

CANVASWORK.

Also known as Ghiordes knot, Quilt knot stitch, Single knotted Smyrna rug stitch, Tufted knot stitch, Turkey rug stitch, Turkey stitch, Rya stitch, or Turkey work.

This stitch can be worked on canvas (as shown here) or on fabric, in which case It is known as Turkey rug stitch. It consists of loops of thread which are either left as even length loops, or, more commonly, cut into a pile. This stitch gives a very fluffy texture to an area and can give real height to the work. However, it is also very slow to work.

Turkey rug knot is probably the best known of various canvaswork piled stitches (those made from raised loops, cut into a pile to resemble a rug). They are often referred to as Turkey work (the name originating from their similarity to carpets which were originally imported from Turkey). It is often difficult to be certain which stitch has been used on an artefact as they are all visually similar from the front: they differ purely in the working method. This also means dating the origin of each stitch individually is very hard.

There is evidence of some form of piled stitches on canvaswork chairs from the mid-17th century, and by the 19th century Turkey work was being used on smaller, decorative items.

METHOD

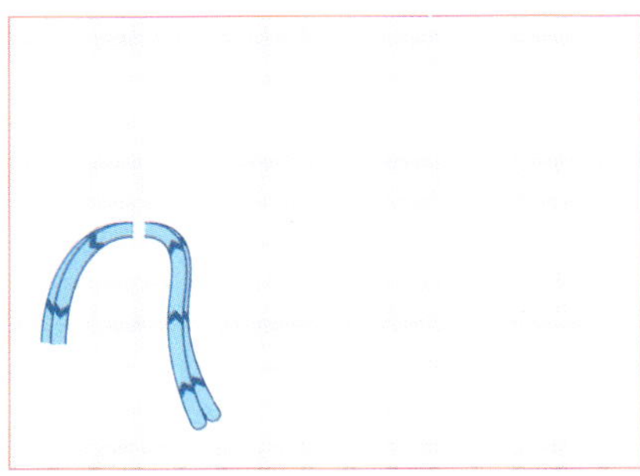

1 Take the needle down through the canvas leaving a tail on the surface. Bring the needle up one thread to the left of this.

2 Take the needle down two threads across from where it came up, leaving a loop on the surface, (keep the loop above the stitch).

3 Bring the needle back up where you initially started and pull the surface loop tight. This will form a horizontal holding stitch to secure the tail ends of the thread.

4 Repeat the stitch to the right by taking the needle down in the next hole. Instead of leaving a tail, leave a loop on the surface, (keep the loop below the stitch).

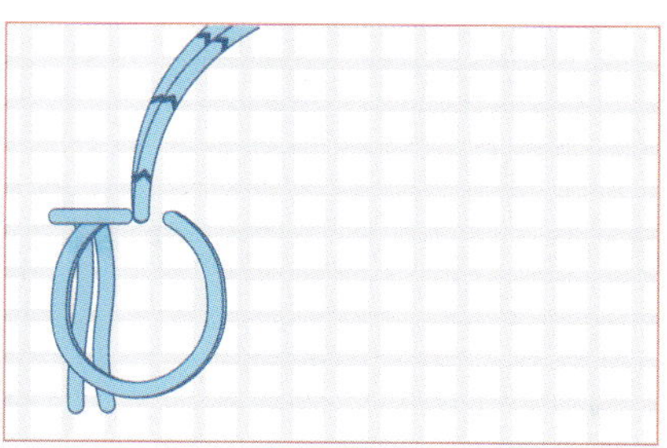

5 Bring the needle up one thread to the left of this, sharing the same hole as the previous stitch.

6 Holding the working loop of the thread above the work, take the needle back down, two threads across to the right but do not pull tight yet.

7 Bring the needle back up where it first began and pull the loop tight.

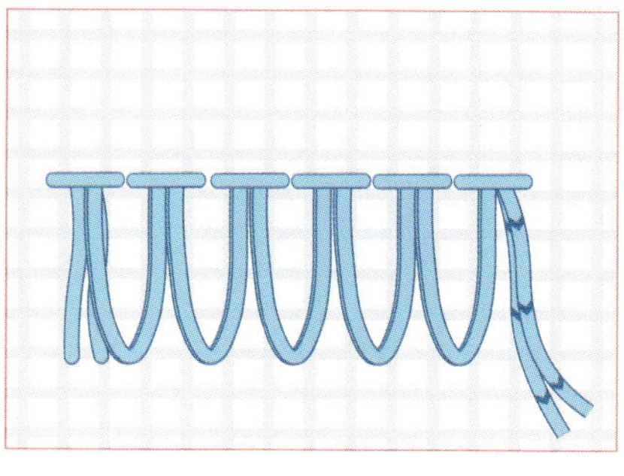

8 Continue looping stitches across the row.

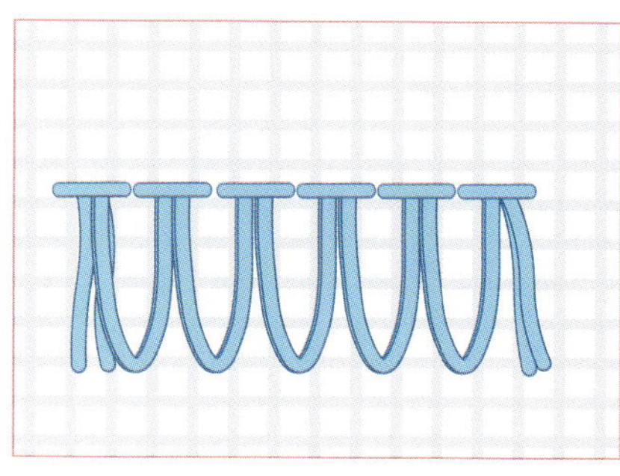

9 Cut the thread at the end of the row and return to the left-hand side of the work.

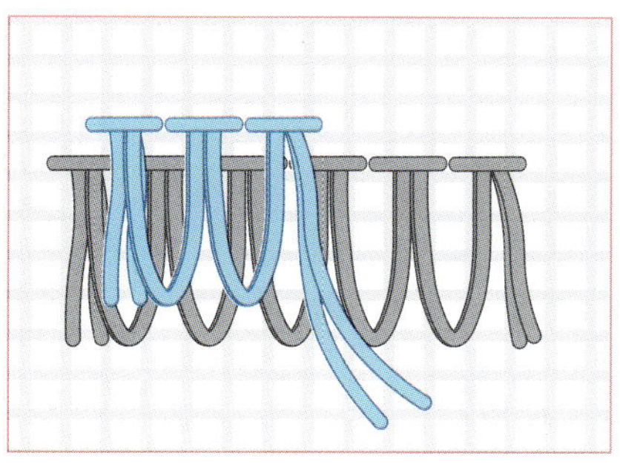

10 Make a second row above the first, beginning one thread to the right, so that the stitches are offset.

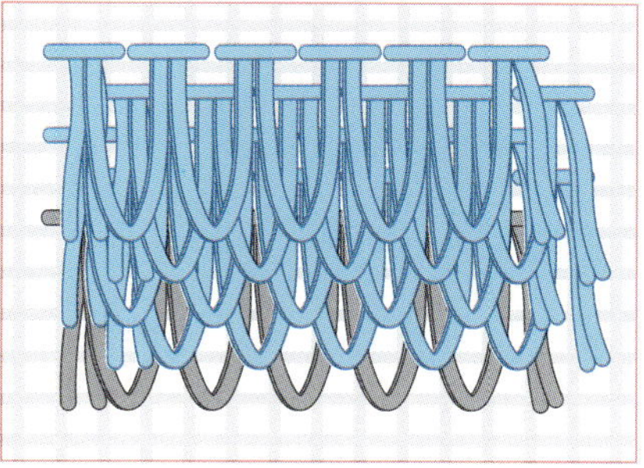

11 Continue with more rows to fill the area.

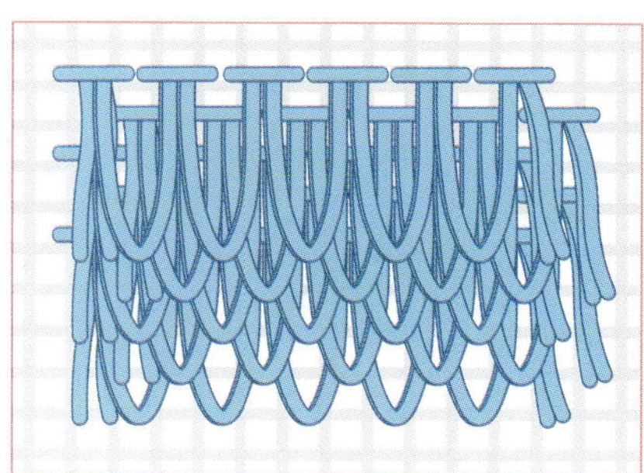

12 When the area is complete, you can either leave the loops as they are ...

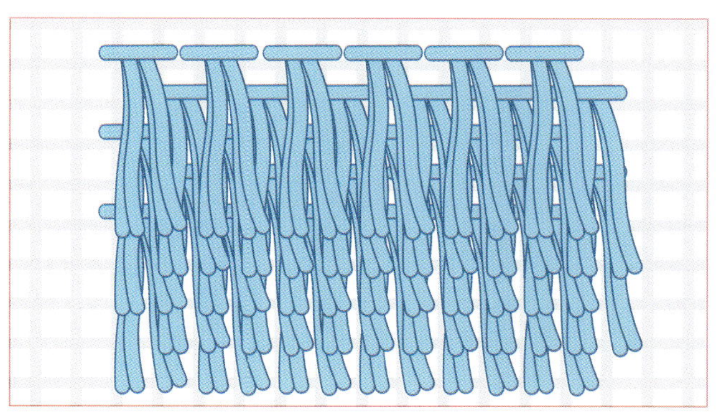

13 ... cut the loops ...

14 ... or trim the loop for a fluffy appearance.

TURNED SATIN STITCH

Whitework; Crewelwork; Mountmellick; Surface.

This is a variation of satin stitch: rather than the stitches remaining parallel across the design area, they are angled so that the stitch direction follows the shape of the design.

For more information see the entry for satin stitch (see page 37).

METHOD

1 Complete a split stitch (see page 39) outline around the shape and fill with padded satin stitch (split stitch padding) (see page 184). Bring the needle up on the inner curve of the shape just outside the split stitch outline where you can easily achieve the required angle for the first slanted satin stitch (see page 198). Then take the needle down on the outer curve, just outside the split stitch.

2 Bring the needle up on the first side again, very close to the first stitch, just outside the split stitch. Take the needle down on the outside of the curve, angling the needle towards both the previous stitch and the split stitch.

3 Work towards the end of the shape. To change the angle gradually, bring the needle up a little closer to the previous stitch on the inner curve and take it down a little further away on the outer curve.

4 The last stitch should cover the split stitch outline. It can be finished by threading the needle under the satin stitch.

5 Using a new thread, resume stitching where you started. This time the direction of the stitch should be reversed, so bring your needle up on the outer curve of the shape.

6 To change the angle, bring the needle up a little further away from the previous stitch on the outer curve and tuck it closer to the previous stitch on the inner curve.

◂◂ Detail from kimono, RSN Collection No. 1359

This chrysanthemum illustrates the use of turned satin stitch, which helps to bring the individual petals of the flower to life.

The kimono on which this motif appears was purchased by the RSN around 1900.

TURNING METAL THREAD COUCHING

Goldwork.

Metal thread couching is the technique of laying down metal threads and using a finer thread to secure them; this entry demonstrates how to turn the couching thread at the end of a line.

Metal thread couching certainly predates the end of the first millennium as it was being skilfully employed in both the UK and China at this point. It was used in the Maaseik Embroideries (credited with being made in England at the turn of the 8th century and considered a precursor to Opus Anglicanum) where it was made from cattle tail hair wrapped with gold foil.

From a century later, artefacts from St Cuthbert's tomb and Chinese Tang embroideries both also feature couched metal threads, the latter referred to as 'flat gold'. Underside couching subsequently took precedence in England for quite some time but by the 1430s the use of metal thread couching had regained popularity. Across the world, it has been used for religious, military, ceremonial and other garments: countries including Turkey, Iran, Yemen, China and Sumatra have long traditions of its use.

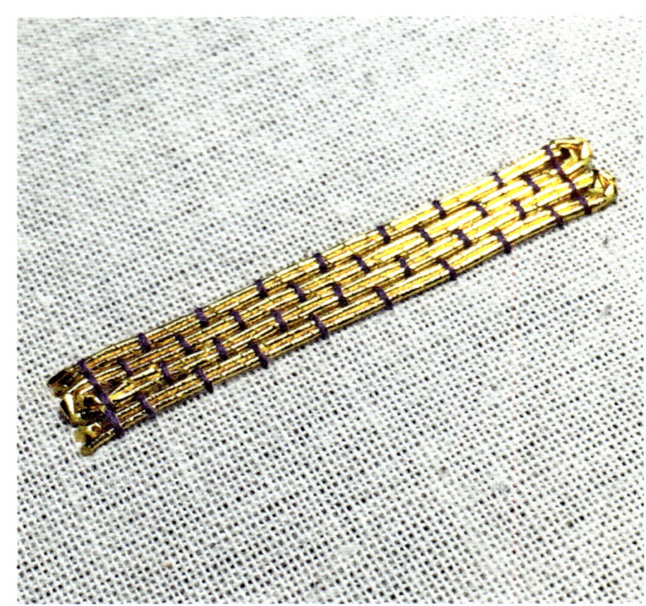

METHOD

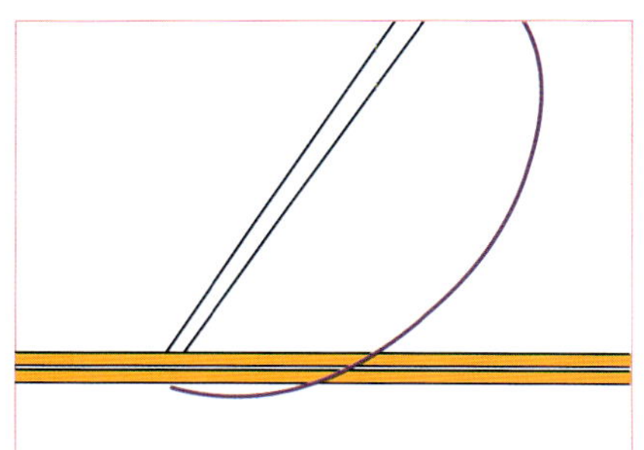

1 Lay down a pair of metal threads and couch into position using a single waxed thread. The couching thread should lay at 90 degrees to the metal threads; it should be tight enough to hold the metal threads securely but not so tight that it dents the metal.

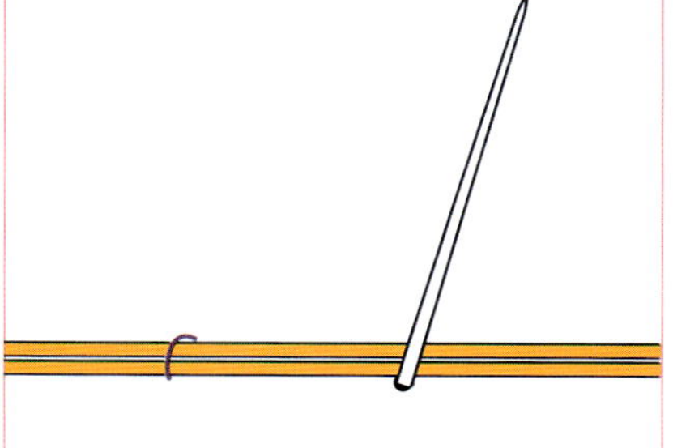

2 Bring the needle to the surface approximately 3–4mm (⅛–¼in) from the last stitch and repeat.

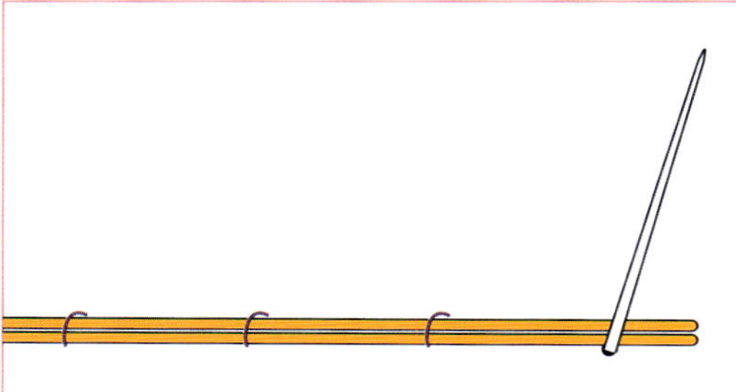

3 Continue to stitch along the metal thread, ensuring the stitches are evenly spaced and all lie at 90 degrees to the threads. The metal threads should lie flat and parallel without crossing, and try not to over-tighten the stitches.

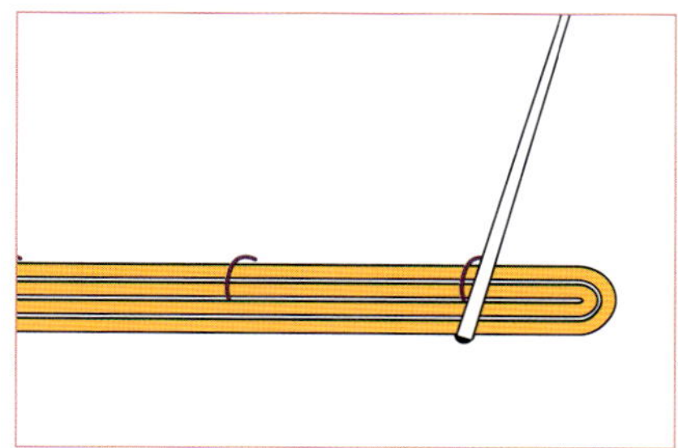

4 Turn the metal thread back on itself and secure in place by couching directly below the last stitch. Bringing the needle up on the outer side of the threads will help to avoid puncturing the metal threads.

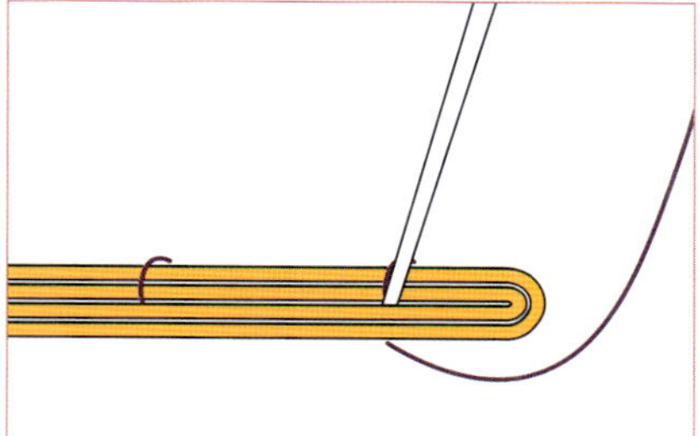

5 Take the needle down through the hole at the end of the last stitch.

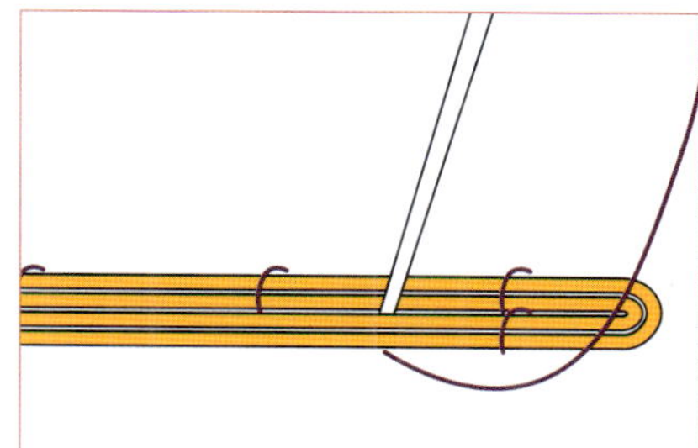

6 Tighten the stitch, making sure the two pairs of metal threads are still lying parallel, and make the next stitch halfway between the last two stitches of the previous row.

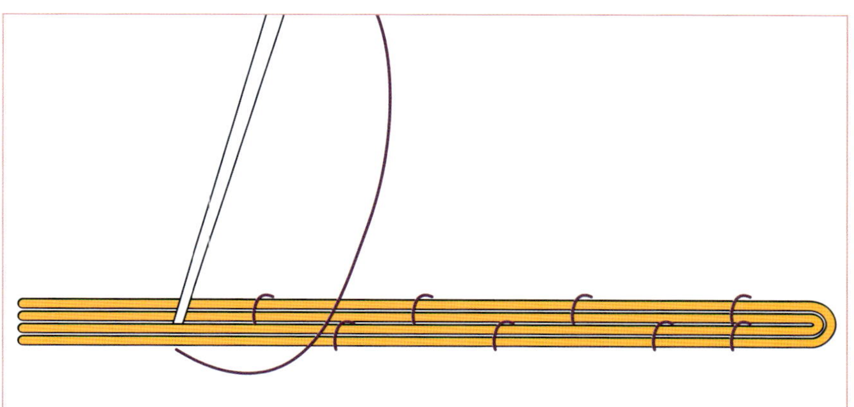

7 Continue working along the metal threads, placing the stitches in between those of the previous row, in a brickwork pattern. When you have completed the area to be filled, plunge the metal threads separately and secure on the reverse with a curved needle.

◂◂ Detail from crest, RSN Collection COL.30

Part of an embroidered crest worked by Royal School of Art Needlework, this is a detail of the coat of arms of King Edward VII.

The panel's background is embroidered in split stitch using red and blue silk thread. The motifs are rendered in goldwork, large stretches of which are completed using bricking (see pages 136–137) and turning metal thread couching.

Another detail of the crest can be seen on page 336.

UPRIGHT CROSS STITCH

CANVASWORK.

Also known as St George cross stitch, or Straight cross stitch.

This stitch consists of small interlocking vertical cross stitches.

METHOD

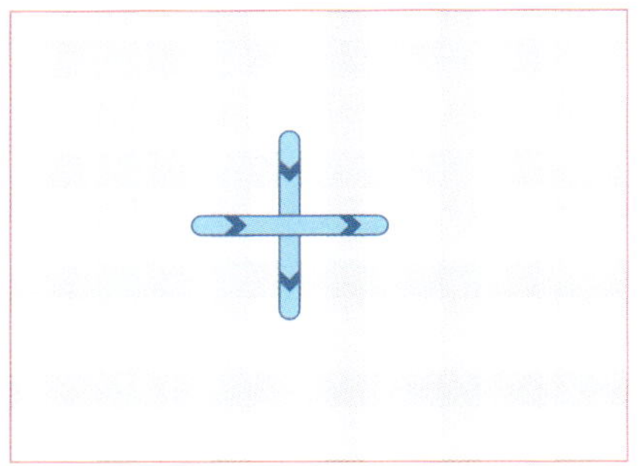

1 First make a vertical stitch across two canvas threads, then cross it with a horizontal stitch across two canvas threads.

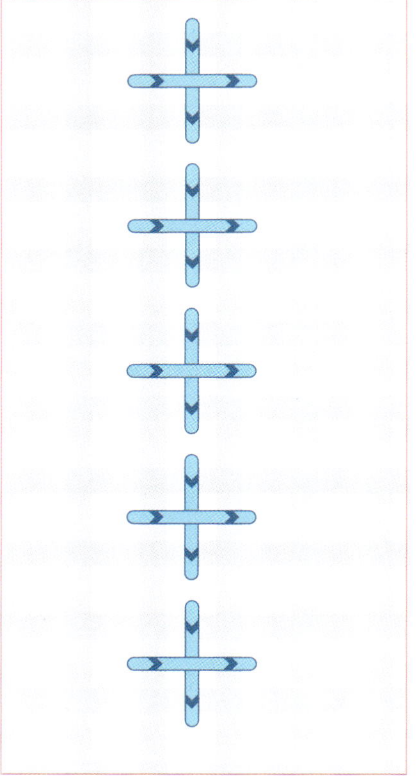

2 Make sure the top stitch is always horizontal.

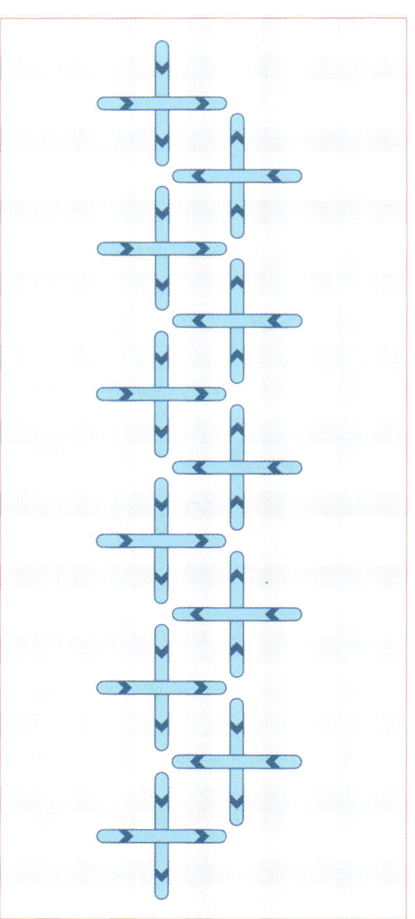

3 Work the crosses in rows. The second row should fit into the spaces of the first.

WAFFLE (PATTERN)

Blackwork.

A detailed blackwork pattern which forms an abstract geometric design. It is made up of rows of eight-spoke eyelets, although each row is offset so the eyelets are not readily apparent. It is fairly small in scale, making for a denser pattern, and is suitable for rounded, natural shapes.

METHOD

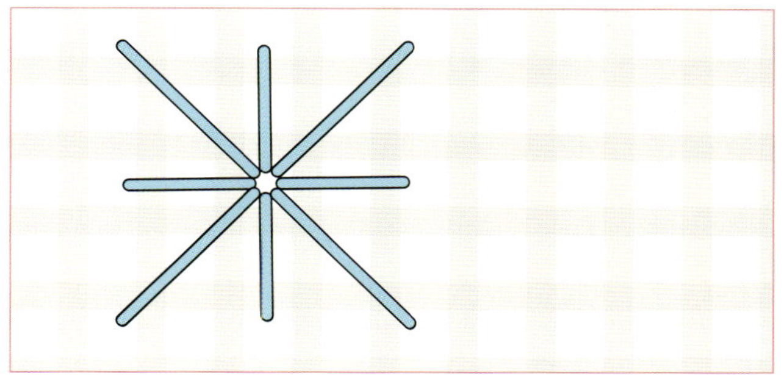

1 Start by working eight spokes into the same hole to produce an eyelet. Each stitch should be over two threads or intersections of the evenweave fabric.

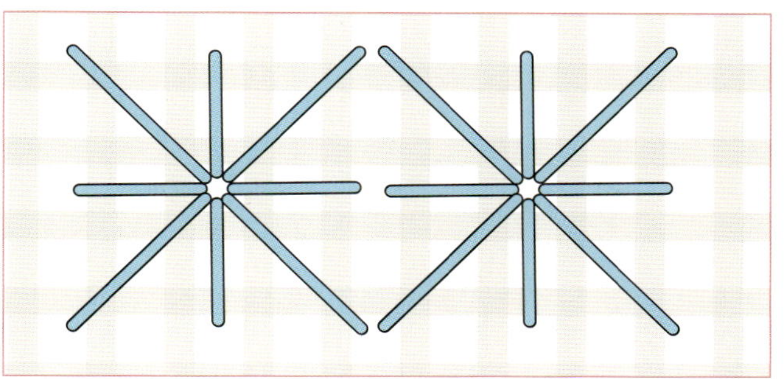

2 Copy step 1 by working horizontally to complete the row.

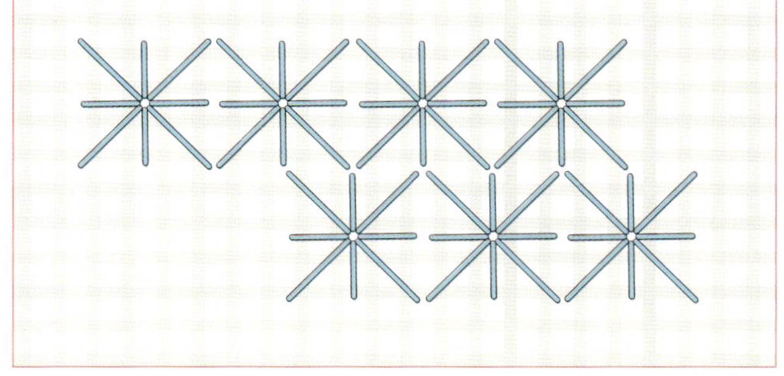

3 Work the next row by continuing to work more eight-spoked eyelets; this time the eyelets are offset from the previous row.

4 Continue to fill the shape.

SHADING STITCHES

These stitches are used to fill an area and, while they can be worked in a single colour, they are either traditionally used to shade an area or lend themselves to doing so.

Probably the most recognizable shaded stitch is the canvaswork Florentine stitch: through history it has been used to work patterns that rise and fall to form geometric waves of shaded colours – it is instantly familiar. By contrast, long and short stitch offers a much more subtle way of shading: this surface stitch is used to portray everything from photorealistic flora and fauna through to stylized Jacobean crewelwork motifs. Burden stitch is also used in crewelwork where it shades hillocks, tree trunks and other motifs in a more geometrical way.

Finally, one of the most widely used shading stitches is tent stitch (explained as part of basketweave tent stitch on page 218) which historically has been used to work both designs and figurative works. The small size of the stitch means that it lends itself to subtle shading, and during the 19th century it became a popular way of working photorealistic pieces as part of Berlin wool work.

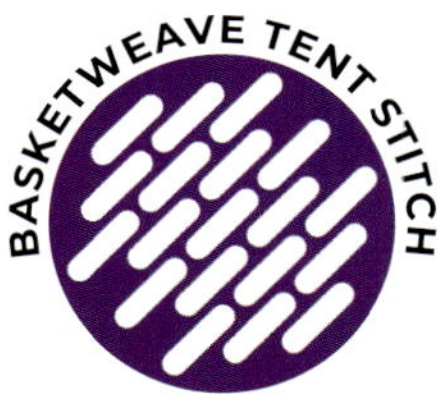

PAGE 218

PAGE 219

PAGE 220

PAGE 221

PAGE 222

PAGE 223

PAGE 224

▸▸ Detail from sampler, RSN Collection COL.2018.69

Beryl Penson, RSN Diploma student, worked this sampler – see also page 93 and 227.

This quadrant features a stylized leaf, flower, stem and pomegranate fruit, all worked in wool threads in long and short stitch. The centre of the flower is embroidered in French knots (see page 29). The leaves are worked in feather stitch (see pages 72–73) and the tendrils are worked in chain stitch (see page 22). These motifs, too, are reminiscent of early modern crewelwork.

EMBROIDERY TECHNIQUE: SILK SHADING

Also known as needle painting, long-and-short stitch embroidery, thread painting, painting with a needle, or Opus Plumarium.

Silk shading is predominantly stitched with just one stitch: long and short stitch. The stitch changes direction, angle and colour to portray flora and fauna, people and landscapes. The techniques are typified by subtle gradations of colour and at its best a photorealistic portrayal.

There are two styles of silk shading: natural silk shading, where both the angle of the stitches and the colour of the thread change to render the shape being depicted, much as strokes of a brush change angle; and tapestry shading, where the stitches are all vertical and the design is rendered purely by changing the colour of the thread. Traditionally, animals and birds are worked in natural silk shading; clothes and people are worked in tapestry shading.

In England, silk shading was first used in the Medieval period where it was used within Opus Anglicanum primarily to portray robes, but also angels and animals. Early Opus Anglicanum is noted for its use of split stitch to depict faces, but later pieces use tapestry shading.

Practically, when working silk shading the stitcher has several needles 'in play' at the same time, all threaded with a different shade. Those needles not in use are rested on top of the fabric, ready to be employed when a stitch or two of that colour is required. Long and short stitch is always the predominant stitch, but it is often edged with a hidden split stitch, and can be embellished with other stitches such as back or stem stitch, French or bullion knots to create certain effects.

Silk shading was originally worked exclusively in silk, but is now frequently worked in stranded cotton or synthetic threads.

▸▸ Silk shaded magnolias, RSN Collection

This piece was embroidered by Miss Bartlett who was the Head of the RSN's Paint Room. The RSN also has Miss Bartlett's watercolour which she used as the starting point for this piece.

While many pieces of silk shading technique are actually worked with cotton thread, this uses silk throughout which gives it the extra lustre.

◂◂ Detail of long and short stitch – pages 224–225

BASKETWEAVE TENT STITCH

Canvaswork.

Also known as Diagonal tent stitch.

This is a form of tent stitch, the simplest and most common stitch in canvaswork and the foundation for many other stitches. Tent stitch is a diagonal stitch, usually worked across a single intersection of canvas from bottom left to top right.

Basketweave tent stitch is the most hard-wearing of the three variants and uses the most thread. The name comes from the appearance of the stitch on the reverse of the canvas, which crosses in a pattern reminiscent of a woven basket. This structure means that basketweave tent stitch is most likely to keep the canvas square while it is being worked, hence it is recommended for large areas of tent stitch. It is worked in diagonal rows, either from the top right-hand corner down, or from the bottom left-hand corner up.

METHOD

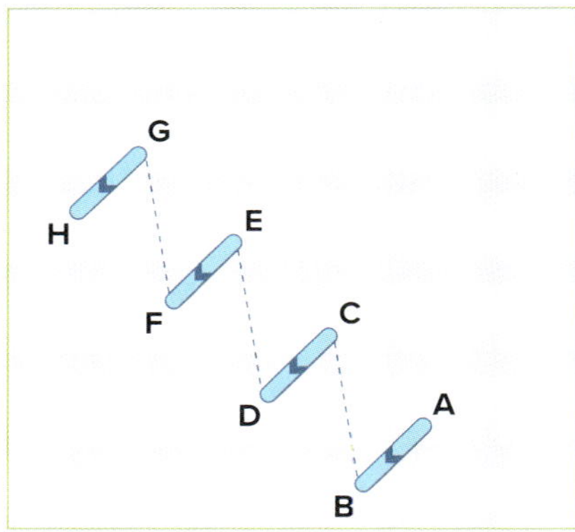

1 Starting from the bottom left-hand corner of the area you want to fill, make a diagonal row of tent stitches, each from top right to bottom left, and with a vertical stitch across two threads on the reverse.

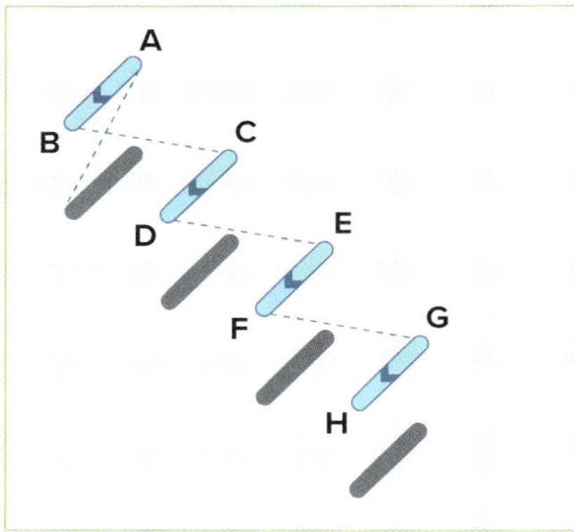

2 On the return row, fit the tent stitches between those of the first row, this time making a horizontal stitch across two canvas threads on the reverse.

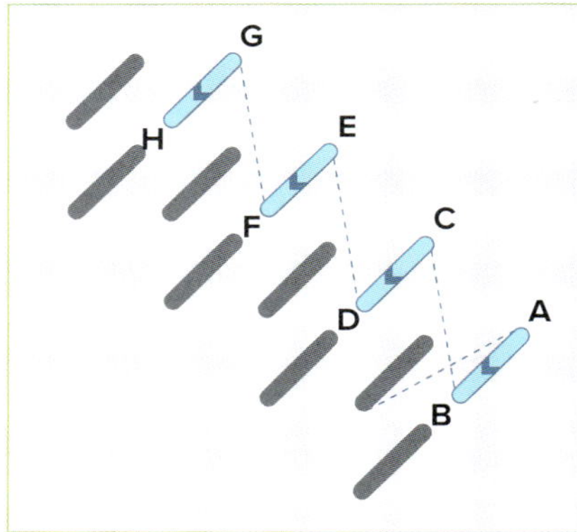

3 When working down a basketweave row, there will be a horizontal stitch on the reverse, and when working up a row there will be a vertical stitch on the reverse.

This image shows the basketweave tent stitch from the underside.

BRICK STITCH

CANVASWORK; CREWELWORK; MOUNTMELLICK; SURFACE.

A simple straight vertical stitch worked as a zigzag in horizontal bands. Each stitch is offset from its neighbour, hence the name brick stitch.

The term brick stitch has been used historically to refer to various offset stitches, including the method of couching called bricking, and so doesn't necessarily refer to this counted thread stitch.

Brick stitch is one of the core stitches in Chinese embroidery, normally executed in silk on gauze fabric. It is also used in Kohistan to embroider patterns of diamonds and zigzags.

METHOD

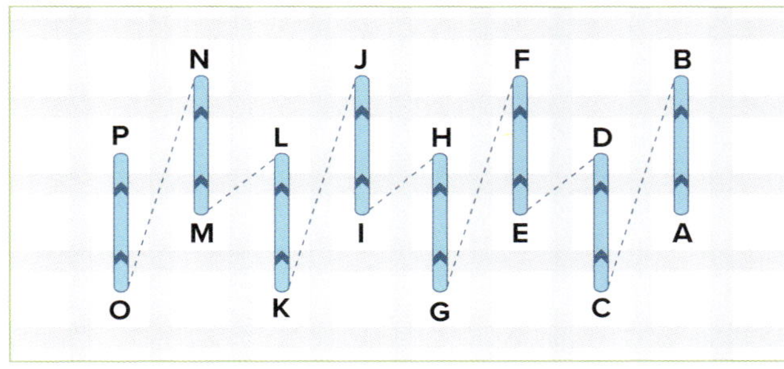

1 This simple stitch is worked as a zigzag in horizontal bands. Make a vertical stitch over two threads of the canvas. Next to it work an identical size stitch one thread down to offset it with the first and continue.

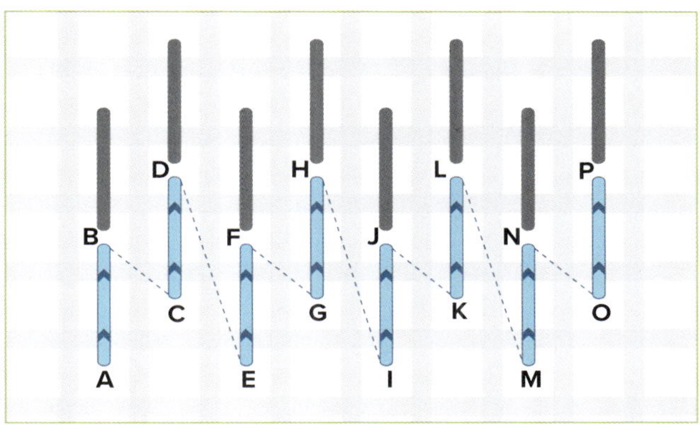

2 Work back along the band ensuring that each stitch touches the stitches in the previous band by interlocking the stitches with the band above.

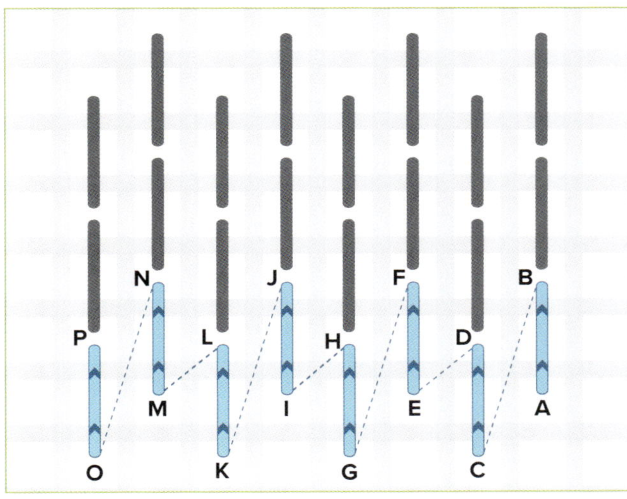

3 Repeat bands to fill your shape.

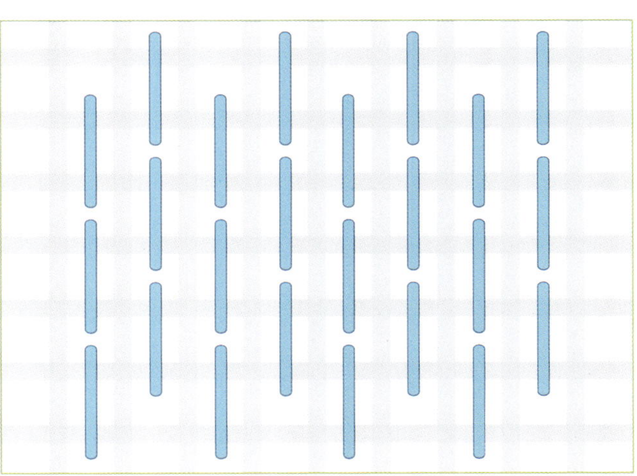

A completed area of brick stitch.

BURDEN STITCH

CREWELWORK; SURFACE; STUMPWORK.

Also known as Cushion stitch.

Burden stitch uses rows of parallel straight stitches to fill an area. Each row is stitched over a single laid thread, and is offset by half of the stitch length. Different coloured threads can be used to shade an area; it is frequently used to portray hummocks in Crewelwork. It can be used quite densely by packing the stitches closely or less densely by spacing the stitches. This latter approach reveals more of the backing fabric.

Burden stitch was named after Elizabeth Burden, who taught the stitch at the Royal School of Needlework (then the Royal School of Art Needlework) during the 1870s. Burden also worked for the embroidery department of Morris, Marshall, Faulkner & Co. and was the sister of Jane Morris and sister-in-law of William Morris.

METHOD

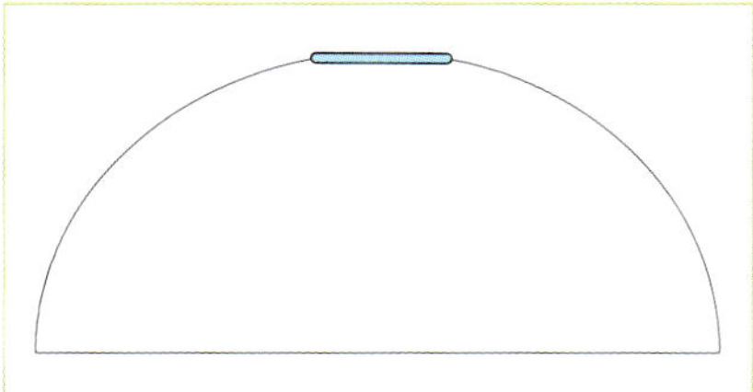

1 Bring your needle up on the edge of the shape, then take it down through the fabric on the opposite side.

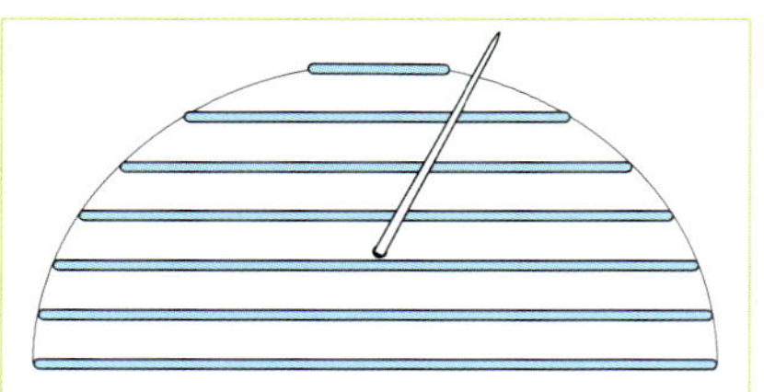

2 Leaving equal gaps, produce parallel stitches, alternating between working from right-to-left and left-to-right. Next, starting in the centre, bring your needle up through the fabric just above one of the horizontal lines.

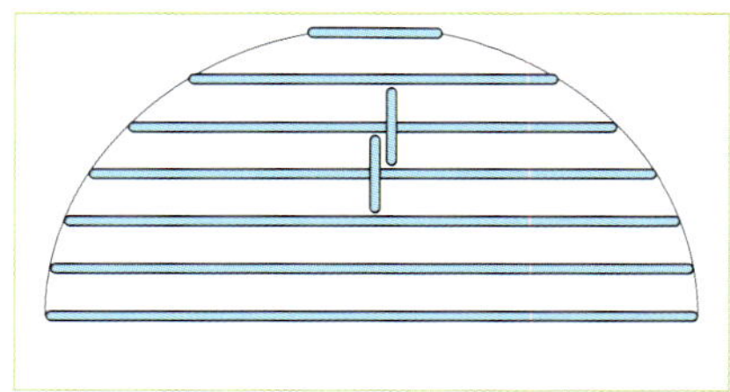

3 Take the needle back down just below the horizontal stitch two rows above. Draw the thread through and trap the middle horizontal stitch. Bring your needle up just above and adjacent to the vertical stitch, then down just below the horizontal stitch two rows above.

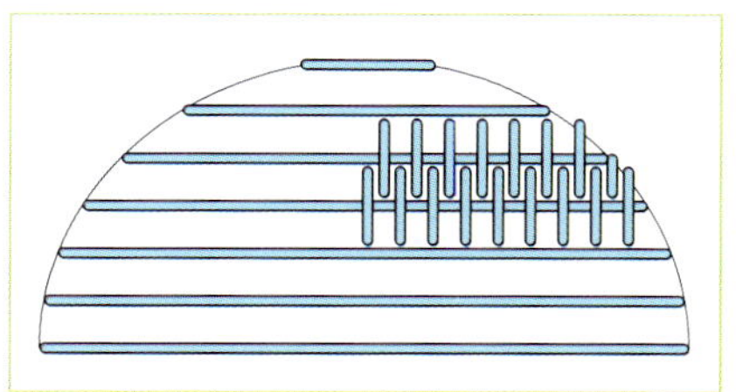

4 Work these two lines of vertical stitches alternately to one side.

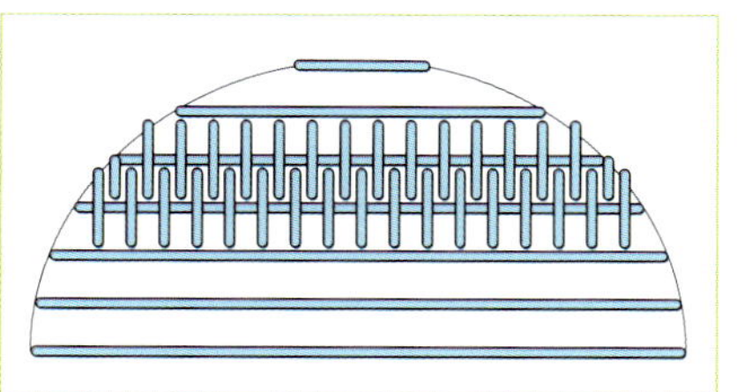

5 Work the two lines to the other side.

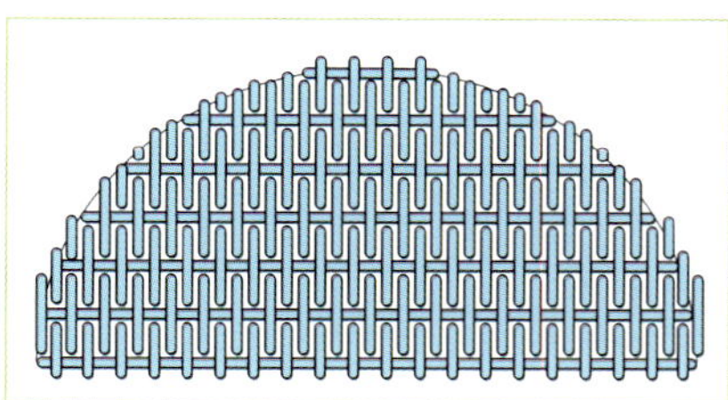

6 Work interlocking rows of vertical stitches over the other horizontal lines.

CONTINENTAL TENT STITCH

CANVASWORK.

Also known as Tent stitch.

This is a form of tent stitch, the simplest and most common stitch in canvaswork and the foundation for many other stitches. Tent stitch is a diagonal stitch, usually worked across a single intersection of canvas from bottom left to top right.

Continental tent stitch is worked in horizontal or vertical rows and makes a diagonal stitch on the back, longer than that on the front. This is a fairly hard-wearing stitch. It uses less thread than basketweave tent stitch (see page 218), but more than half cross tent stitch (see page 223).

METHOD

1 Working from right to left, make a tent stitch from bottom left to top right and bring the needle up one thread to the left of the bottom corner of the first canvas stitch.

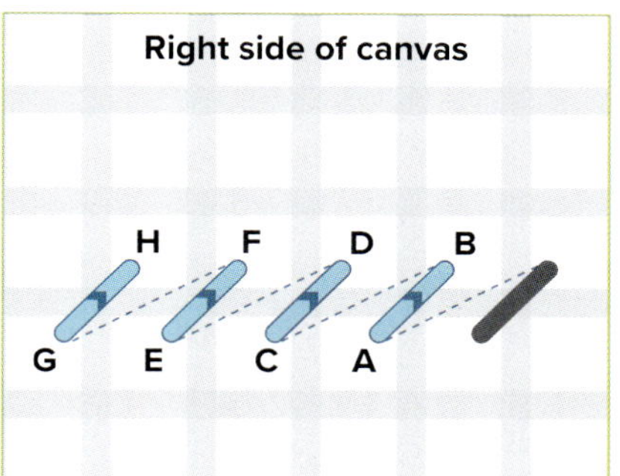

2 Continue across the row in the same way, making the stitches from bottom left to top right. On the reverse of the canvas make a diagonal stitch across two threads of the canvas.

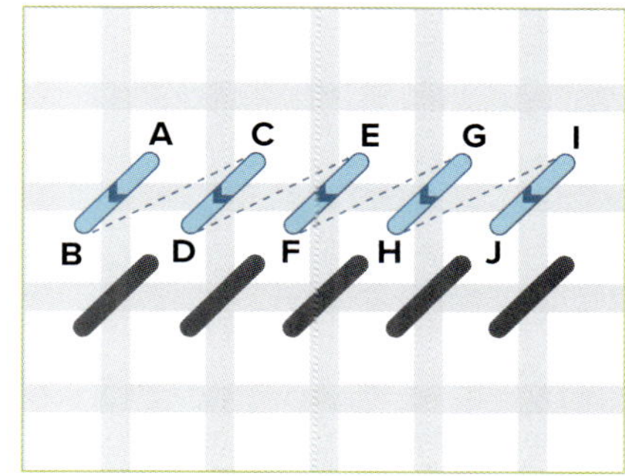

3 To work a row from left to right, the order is reversed: i.e. top right to bottom left.

FLORENTINE STITCH

CANVASWORK; BERLIN WOOL WORK.

Also known as Flame stitch, Bargello work, Irish stitch, Cushion stitch, Hungary stitch, Hungarian stitch, Bargello stitch, or Berlin stitch.

Florentine is a vertical straight stitch (normally across four threads) which is used in different colours to form one of a small number of geometric patterns. The most common is the flame or wave pattern (illustrated here) where the colours rise and fall; others are the oval and stepped patterns. Collectively, these patterns are known as Florentine work or Bargello work. This stitch needs a large area to display its pattern.

The name Bargello work originates from the Bargello Palace in Florence (Italy), where there are a series of 17th-century chairs upholstered with canvas embroidery in this technique. However, the origins of the technique are obscure – it has been suggested that it came from 15th-century Florentine migrants to Hungary, but there is no hard evidence for this.

The technique certainly spread to many different cultures: it features on 17th-century ecclesiastical Icelandic pieces; in England it was popular on samplers from the early to mid 17th century when it went out of fashion, only to regain popularity at the start of the 18th century. It featured on 18th-century Chinese Mandarin squares. In the 20th century, the technique is used by the Banjara people of central Italy and it was embraced in Western Europe and North America in the 1960s.

METHOD

- Each stitch is made across four threads of the canvas, and each step across the pattern is two threads of canvas above or below the previous stitch.
- By varying the number of stitches at each step of the design a pattern of waves is produced.
- The pattern is set by the first complete wave of stitches. Each row above or below this then repeats the same design.

HALF CROSS TENT STITCH

CANVASWORK.

Also known as Half stitch, Tent stitch, Trammed tent stitch, or Half-cross tent stitch.

This is a form of tent stitch (see basketweave tent stitch on page 218), the simplest and most common stitch in canvaswork and the foundation for many other stitches. Tent stitch is a diagonal stitch, usually worked across a single intersection of canvas from bottom left to top right.

Half cross tent stitch is worked in rows and makes a vertical stitch on the back. It uses the minimum amount of thread on the reverse of the canvas.

METHOD

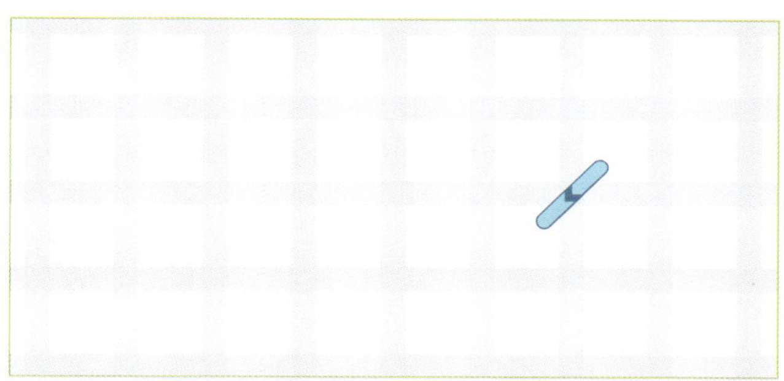

1 Working from right to left, make a tent stitch from top right to bottom left. On the reverse of the canvas, make a vertical stitch up across one thread of canvas.

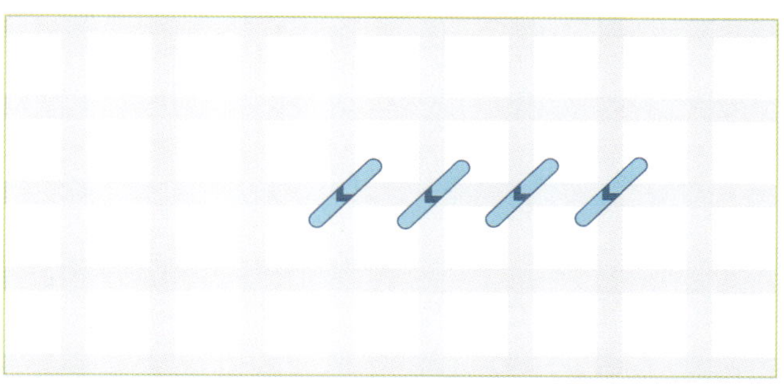

2 Begin the next tent stitch, again working from top right to bottom left. The back of an area worked in half cross will be quite open and will all be vertical stitches.

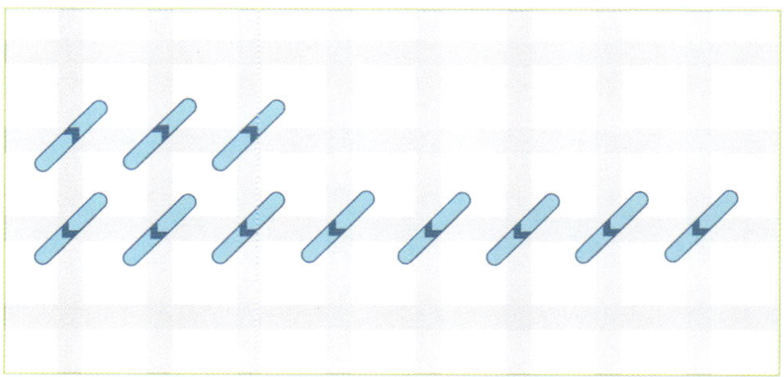

3 To work a row from left to right, the order of the stitch is reversed: in this example, bottom left to top right.

LONG AND SHORT STITCH

CREWELWORK; SILK SHADING; STUMPWORK; WHITEWORK; SURFACE; ELIZABETHAN.

Also known as Long and short satin stitch, Shading stitch, Silk shading, Natural shading, Tapestry shading, Embroidery stitch, Plumage stitch, Feather stitch, Opus Plumarium, or cushion stitch.

A series of long, medium and shorter straight stitches are densely combined to fill and smoothly cover an area of fabric. By using different coloured threads, this enables blending, shading and realism.

The variety of names by which long and short stitch is known gives an indication of how widely-used the stitch has been: some names refer to the resemblance to feathers the stitch bears; others highlight the fact that it's commonly used for shading.

Long and short stitch has been part of both Asian and western European traditions for centuries: it is part of the *sashi-nui* style of Japanese embroidery from Kyoto; it was frequently used in Opus Teutonicum, a German whitework technique; and in China it was an integral stitch in *Gu* embroidery (based on ink brush paintings). Individual surviving embroideries suggest that its use was probably even more widespread: the Museum für Angewandte Kunst in Vienna holds a 13th century chasuble and the V&A South Kensington holds a 14th century cope from Germany.

METHOD

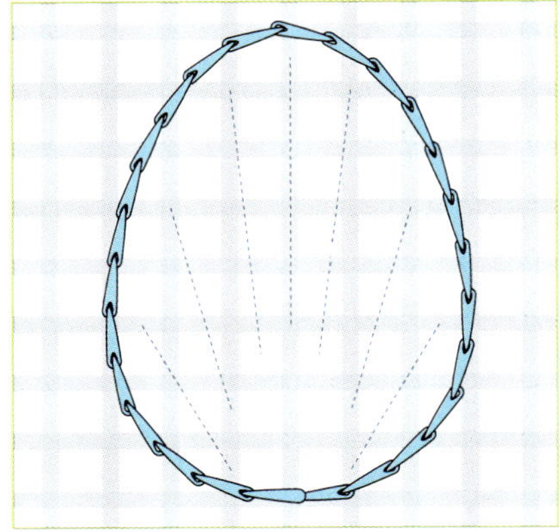

1 Work an outline in split stitch (see page 39) then draw on guide lines to show the angles of your stitches.

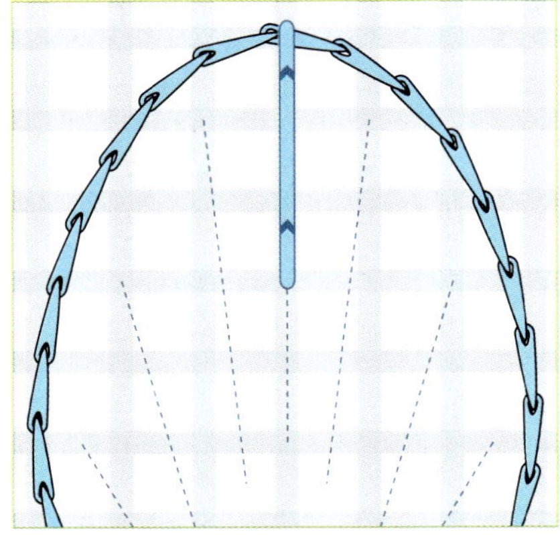

2 Bring the needle up in the centre of the design about 1cm (½in) from the edge, then take the needle down over the split stitch edge to complete the first stitch.

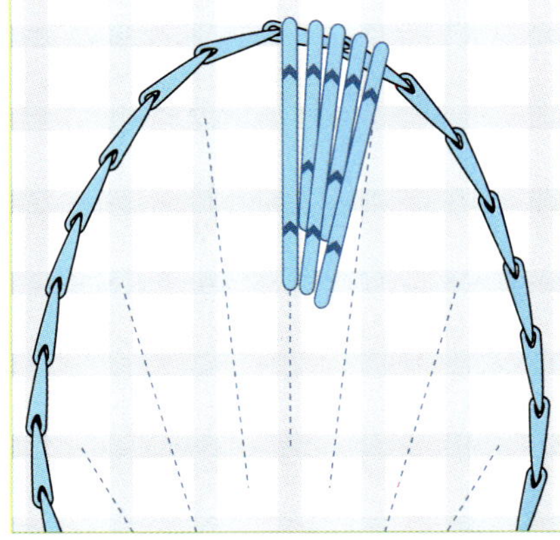

3 Work a few stitches to one side of the first stitch, taking each down over the outline. Vary the length of each stitch: this ensures a smoother surface – and is what gives the stitch its name.

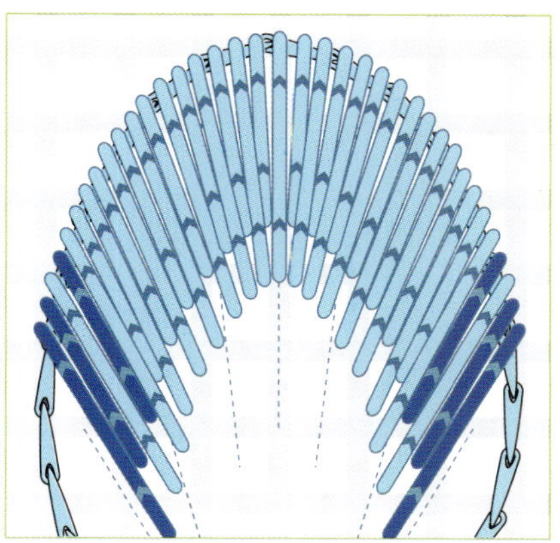

4 Work the other side of your design in the same way, then thread another needle with a second colour. Continue working a few stitches each side by alternating the two colours. Gradually drop out the first colour and work exclusively in the second colour.

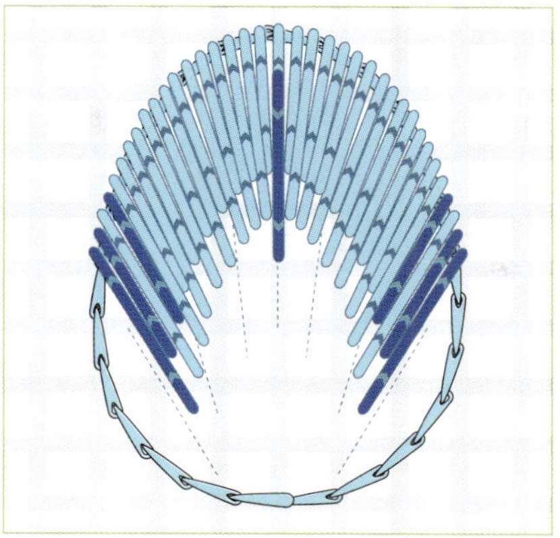

5 To work the inside of the shape, work new stitches in the opposite direction. Bring the needle up to the surface by splitting the original stitch high in its length. Envisage lengthening the first stitch a little and take the needle down at that point. If the shape curves, change the angle of your stitch slightly.

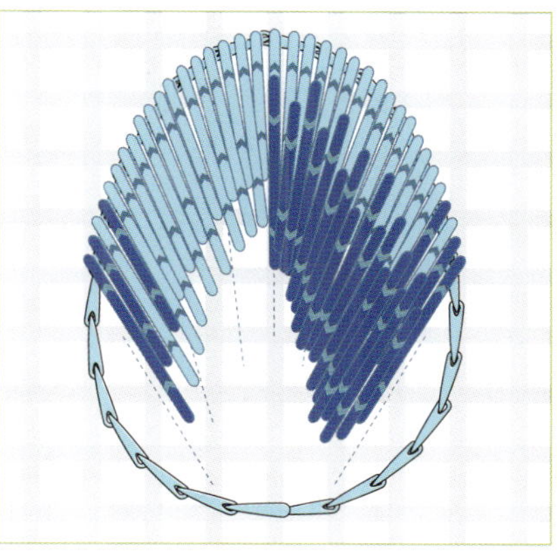

6 To build up the second row, split the stitches in the first row in random distances along their length. Each stitch in the second row should be of a similar length but staggered at different depths across the area to be filled.

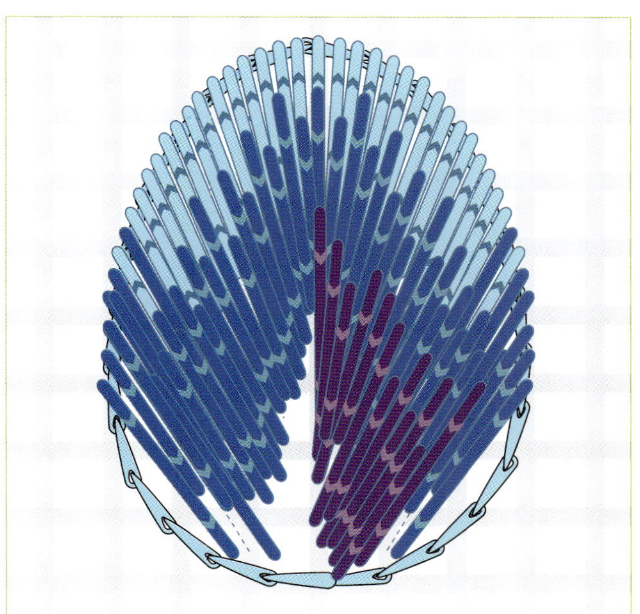

7 Introduce a third colour as you reach the ends of the first row, and gradually drop out the second colour by the time you start the third row. Remember to change the direction of the stitch when covering the split stitch edges.

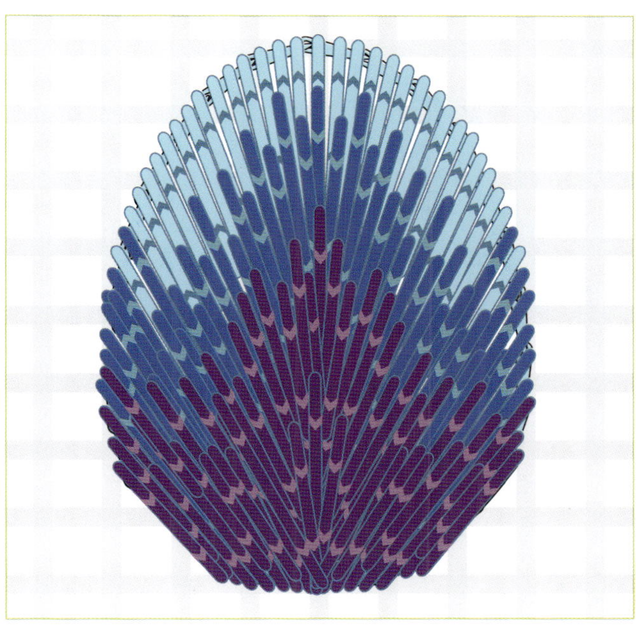

8 Complete the third row and introduce a new colour on each subsequent row, and work only up to the edge of your shape and not into any others.

OPEN AND POWDERED FILLING STITCHES

The common thread between these stitches is that they are used to fill an area while still showing some of the ground fabric. Some by their nature have spaces within them (such as trellis stitches or pulled work stitches); others are isolated stitches (such as detached chain stitch) which are worked to form a powdered filling (like a spot motif on a printed fabric).

The stitches in this chapter come from various stitch traditions: blackwork, pulled work and crewelwork; one notable exception is canvaswork as the canvas is traditionally completely covered by the stitching.

Any isolated stitch can be used as a powdered filling. The stitches are worked individual motifs but can be worked either densely (with small spaces between the stitches) or sparsely or with a density which graduates. The stitches can all be oriented in the same direction, in a varying pattern or randomly.

Blackwork patterns have been included as open filling stitches as their density means that the ground fabric is often visible. The density often varies within a single design area to provide a shaded effect.

Pulled work stitches have also been included in this category as the pulling of the thread means that the ground fabric remains visible (indeed the pattern into which the ground fabric is pulled is an intrinsic part of pulled work).

Trellis stitches fall into this category as the trellis by definition shows the ground fabric between the bars of the trellis and any adornment used.

▲▲ Sampler, RSN Collection COL.2018.69

A crewelwork sampler worked by Beryl Penson while a diploma student at the Royal School of Needlework. This four-part design, likely worked in the late 1930s, was used until the last few years of the RSN's Training School Diploma. The piece is embroidered on linen and is divided into four groups of motifs – you can see some quadrants in more detail on pages 93 and 215. The flower in the top right is a good example of the use of stitches that leave the ground fabric showing, but they are also used elsewhere. For example, cloud filling stitch (see page 234) is used at the top right for one of the flower petals, and again for the acorn cup in the lower left quadrant.

Crewelwork embroidery experienced a revival in the late 19th century and first decades of the 20th century, when it became a popular way to embellish home furnishings. Penson's sampler blends traditional crewelwork imagery with more creative, unusual motifs.

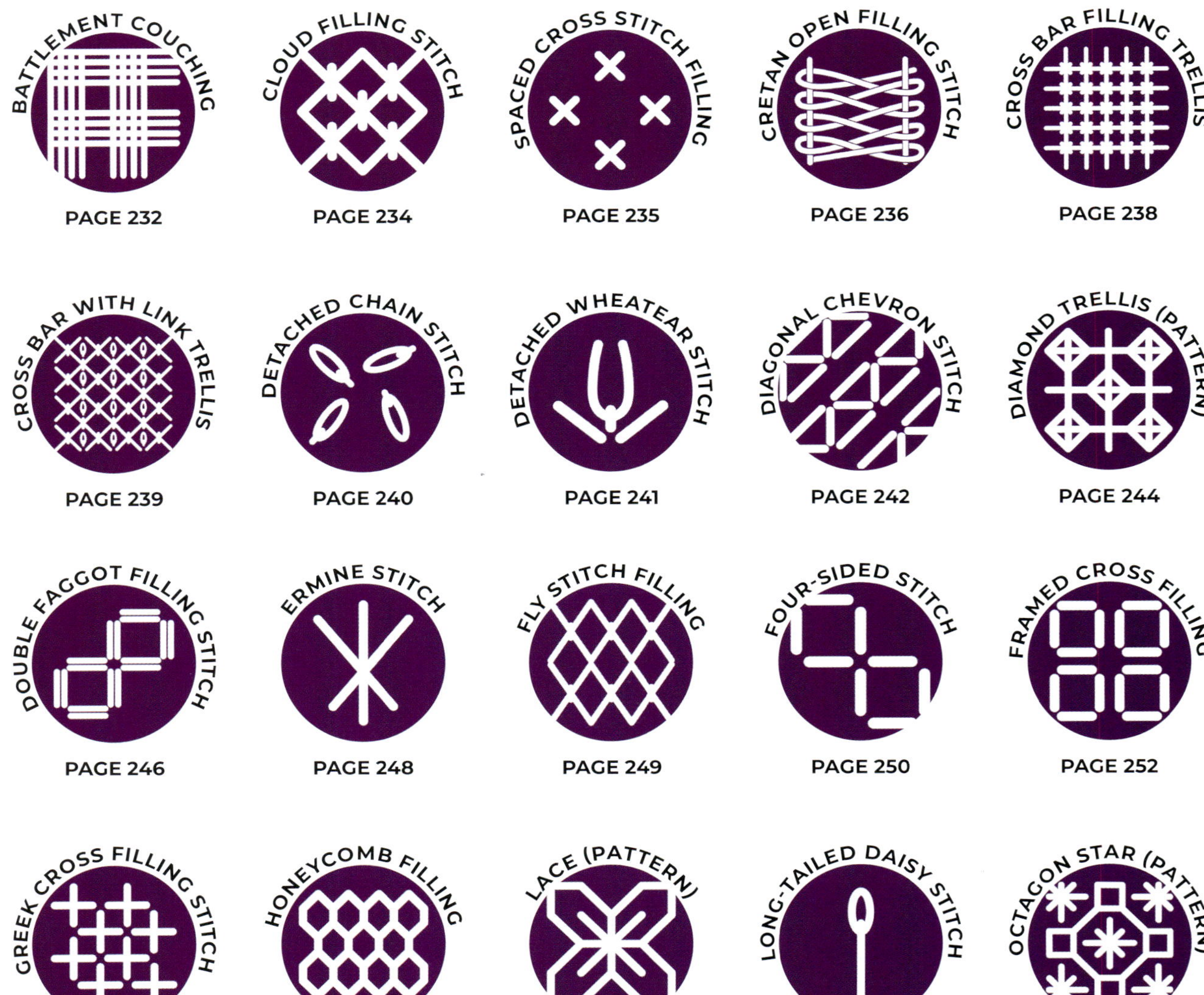
BATTLEMENT COUCHING
PAGE 232
CLOUD FILLING STITCH
PAGE 234
SPACED CROSS STITCH FILLING
PAGE 235
CRETAN OPEN FILLING STITCH
PAGE 236
CROSS BAR FILLING TRELLIS
PAGE 238
CROSS BAR WITH LINK TRELLIS
PAGE 239
DETACHED CHAIN STITCH
PAGE 240
DETACHED WHEATEAR STITCH
PAGE 241
DIAGONAL CHEVRON STITCH
PAGE 242
DIAMOND TRELLIS (PATTERN)
PAGE 244
DOUBLE FAGGOT FILLING STITCH
PAGE 246
ERMINE STITCH
PAGE 248
FLY STITCH FILLING
PAGE 249
FOUR-SIDED STITCH
PAGE 250
FRAMED CROSS FILLING
PAGE 252
GREEK CROSS FILLING STITCH
PAGE 254
HONEYCOMB FILLING
PAGE 256
LACE (PATTERN)
PAGE 258
LONG-TAILED DAISY STITCH
PAGE 259
OCTAGON STAR (PATTERN)
PAGE 260

PAGE 262

PAGE 263

PAGE 265

PAGE 266

PAGE 268

PAGE 270

PAGE 271

PAGE 272

PAGE 274

PAGE 276

PAGE 277

▸▸ Mirror frame, RSN Collection COL.2018.45

This embroidered mirror frame with double doors was gifted to the RSN by Susan Howard in memory of her mother, Alison Mary Taylor née Mills. Dated 1653, during the Interregnum, the depiction of the king on this mirror would have been a political statement of the creator's royalist sympathies.

The acorn caps at the bottom centre are chipping overlaid with trellis stitch, which has come unravelled in some places.

EMBROIDERY TECHNIQUE: APPLIQUÉ

Appliqué is the technique of cutting out small pieces of fabric ('slips') and attaching them to a larger piece of fabric. The term comes from the French verb meaning 'to apply'.

The slips are stitched around the edges with either slip stitch (where the edges have been folded under to form a hem) or stab stitch (where the edges have been cut). This stitching holds the slips in place and can be covered by other more decorative stitches.

Appliqué works from the medieval period still exist, although the technique is almost certainly considerably older. Appliqué is also used in stumpwork and some whitework techniques: needlelace slips are worked and then applied to a ground fabric.

▸▸ Peacock, RSN Collection No. 2076

This stylized peacock, made of layers of fabric, lace and thread, is one of a pair of artworks produced by Thomasina Beck in 1970. Though the peacocks are of a similar shape and involve some similar materials, they differ in their colours, stitches and embellishment.

▴▴ Detail of blanket stitch – page 18

▴▴ Detail of feather stitch – pages 72–73

BATTLEMENT COUCHING

Crewelwork; Surface.

Also known as Battlement trellis, or Shaded cross bar.

A fairly solid and quick filling stitch, battlement couching consists of couched laid threads which form layers of trellis, slightly offset from the previous layer to let all of the layers show.

The earliest evidence we have of this stitch are two 17th-century English embroidered bookbindings held by the British Library. Both books are religious texts; one is dated 1619 and the other 1627. Rather than couching the corners of the trellis, the stitcher has interwoven some of the threads to hold them in place, but the perspective element of the stitch is clearly used.

METHOD

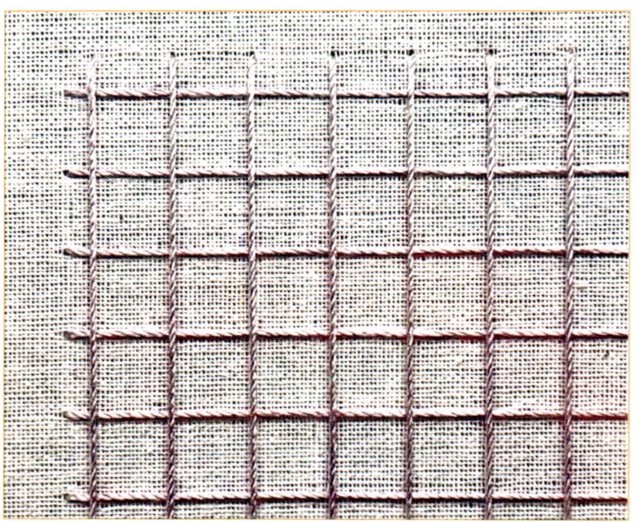

1 Start by laying a basic square trellis (see pages 274–275) without securing the threads at the intersections.

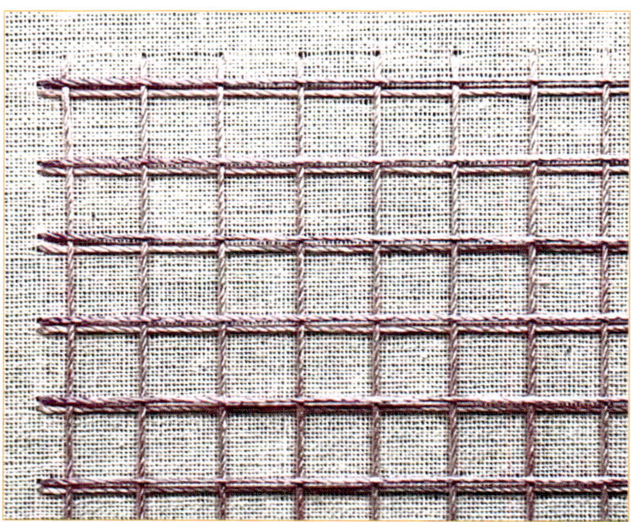

2 Choose another shade or colour and lay another trellis slightly offset from to the first trellis.

3 Ensure you lay the vertical and horizontal threads in the same order as the first layer of trellis.

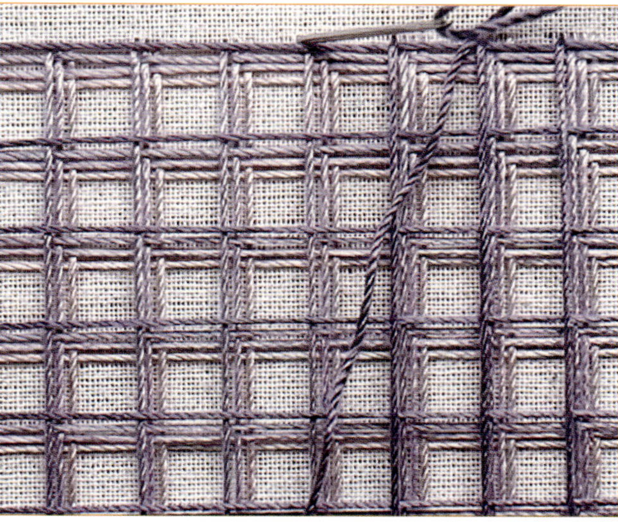

4 You also need to lay both the vertical and horizontal threads to the inside or outside of an intersection, and keep this consistent to achieve the pattern.

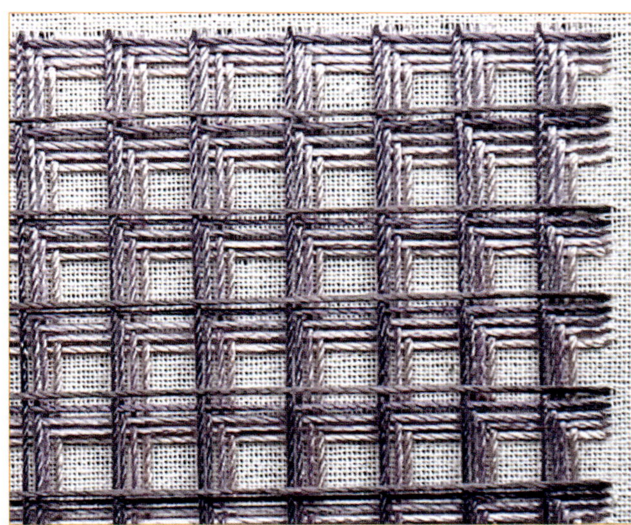

5 Continue to layer extra colours or shades in the same way. Take care not to overcrowd the threads.

6 Once you are satisfied with the number of layers, the top layer should be held down to the fabric with a stitch over each intersection. Start from the centre and work out.

TIP

You can neaten the threads by repositioning any that don't quite line up.

CLOUD FILLING STITCH

Crewelwork; Surface; Stumpwork.

Also known as Mexican stitch, Cloud stitch, or Ukranian interlaced running stitch.

This stitch consists of evenly spaced small vertical anchoring stitches, interwoven with a diagonal trellis. Most trellis stitches are worked with the long threads laid first and then anchored with small crossing stitches; this version is worked with the small anchoring stitches first which softens the lines of the trellis, making it slightly curved.

For a more angular version, see fly stitch filling on page 249.

METHOD

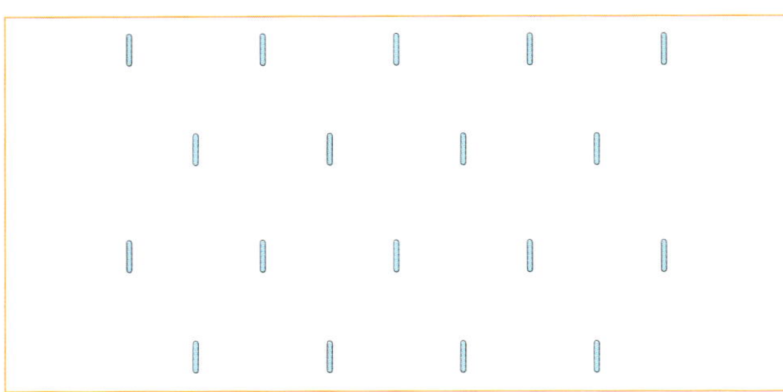

1 Work a row of evenly spaced small vertical stitches. Beneath this, work a second row of alternately spaced vertical stitches. Repeat these two rows as required.

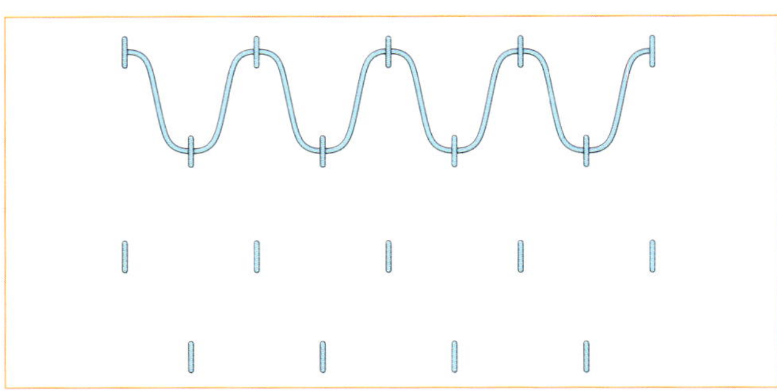

2 To start the weaving, bring the needle up through the fabric so it protrudes to the right of the top left vertical stitch. Working from left to right, weave the needle through the stitches alternating between first and second rows – this will form a zigzag line. While weaving, do not pierce the fabric. Take the needle down underneath the last vertical stitch of the row.

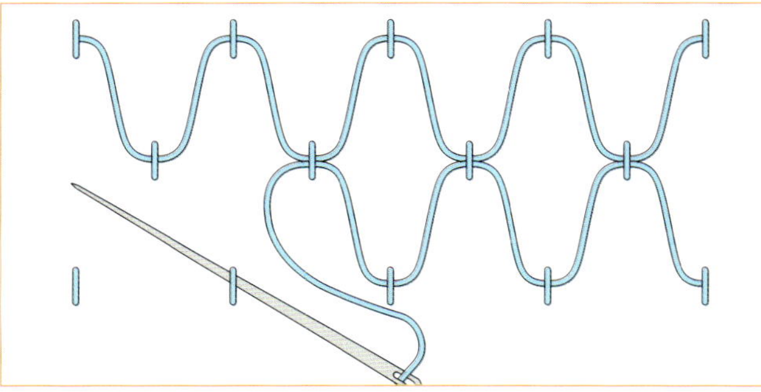

3 The next row is worked right to left. Bring the needle up from underneath the first stitch of the third row and again weave the needle through the vertical stitches alternating between the second and third rows.

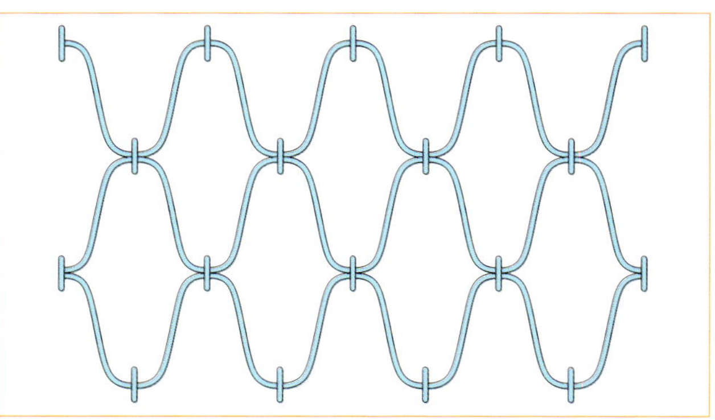

4 Repeat these steps to complete the cloud filling.

SPACED CROSS STITCH FILLING

SURFACE; COUNTED THREAD.

This filling stitch consists of diagonally offset cross stitches (see page 24) spaced across an area. The stitches can be widely spaced, or stitched so that the corners touch. It can be worked on either evenweave or plain weave fabric.

METHOD

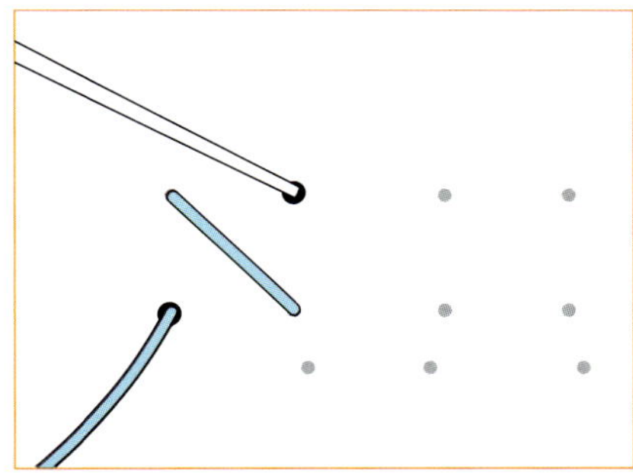

1 Make a diagonal stitch lying bottom right to top left. Bring the needle up at the bottom left and take it down at the top right.

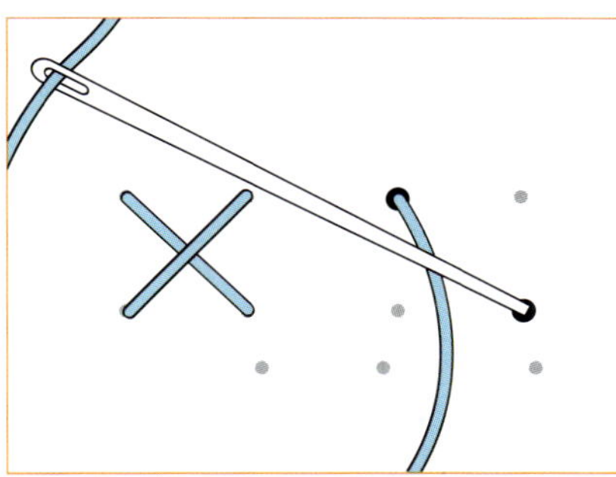

2 Draw the needle through to complete your first cross. Leaving your desired space, continue working cross stitches.

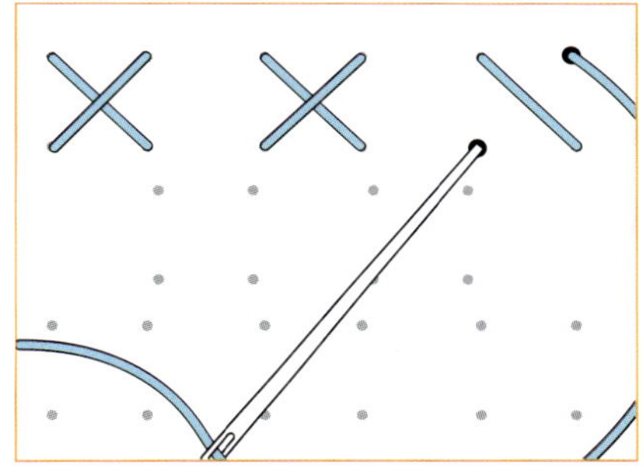

3 Continue to the end of the row.

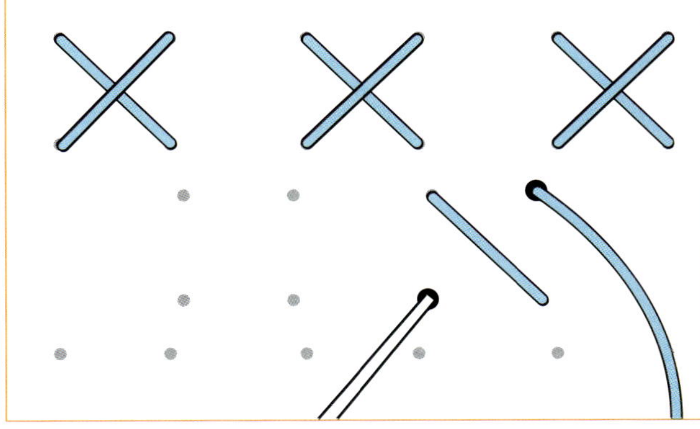

4 To work the next row, offset your cross stitches. Make sure that the orientation of the top stitch is consistent with the previous stitches.

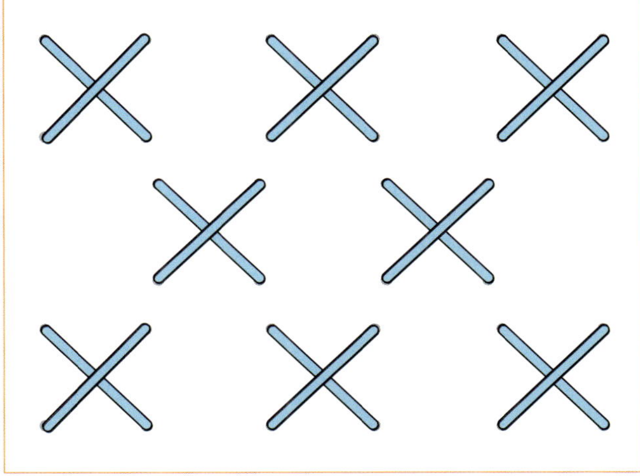

An area of spaced cross stitch filling.

CRETAN OPEN FILLING STITCH

Surface; Crewelwork.

This surface stitch consists of a foundation of long vertical stitches which are woven with Cretan stitch (see pages 150–151) into offset square blocks. The woven element of the stitch is completely detached from the fabric – similar to Russian stitch, although Russian stitch is often used across just a pair of foundation stitches or bars rather than to fill an area.

The action of the weaving is variously described as using a detached buttonhole stitch or a herringbone motion.

It is also visually similar to a closed version of threaded herringbone stitch, although the working method is different.

METHOD

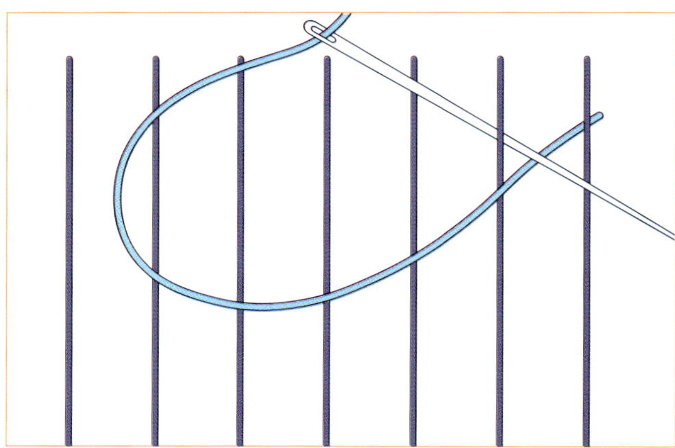

1 Work a group of vertical stitches, evenly spaced, using a strong thread and ensuring they are taut. Introduce the second thread by bringing the needle up just to the right of the rightmost thread. Work blocks of Cretan stitches diagonally from top right to bottom left. Weave the needle horizontally under the vertical foundation thread and over the second foundation thread. Bring the needle back under the second foundation thread, keeping your working thread above the weaving. Cross over the first horizontal stitch and also the first vertical stitch.

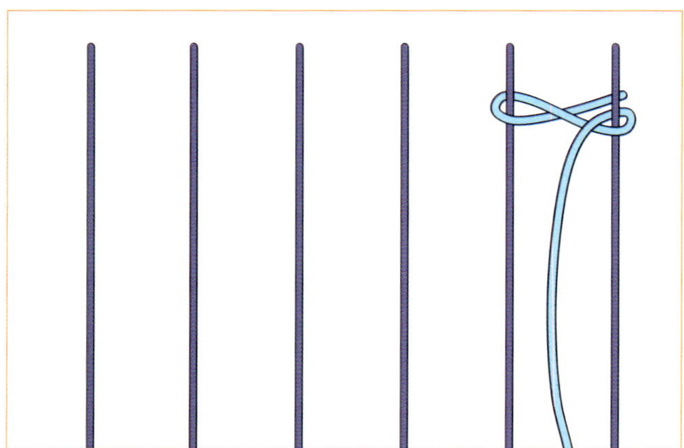

2 Take the working thread under the first vertical thread and over the previous horizontal stitch. The motion is similar to a herringbone stitch: it should form a figure of eight.

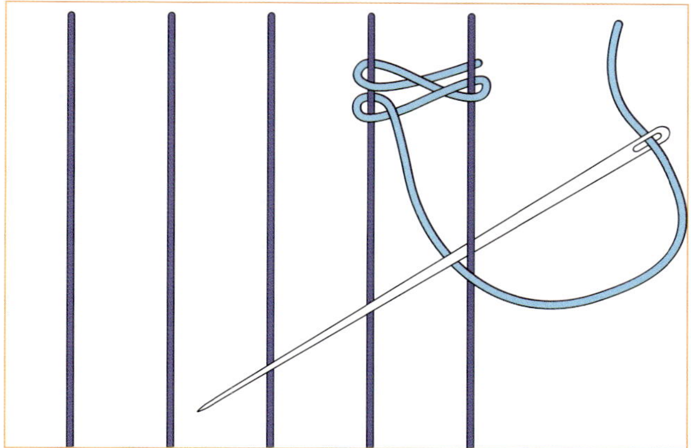

3 Repeat the figure of eight movement.

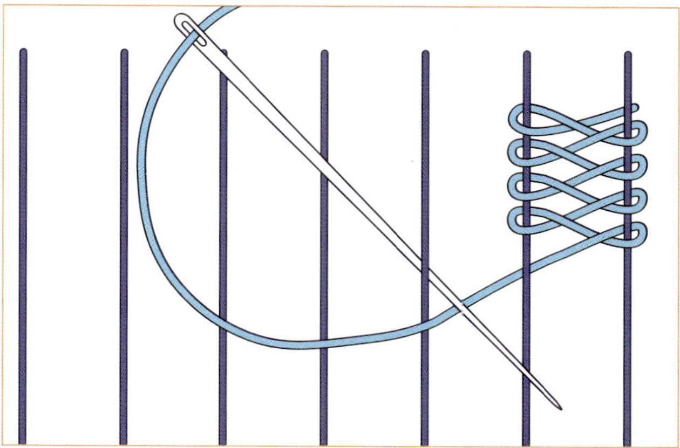

4 Continue in this way until you have completed four Cretan stitches. You will need to use your needle or a mellor to push the stitches together and keep them even. Start a new block by taking the thread under the second vertical thread, and over the third one. Reversing the direction, bring the needle under the third thread and diagonally over the horizontal stitch to form a figure of eight, as before.

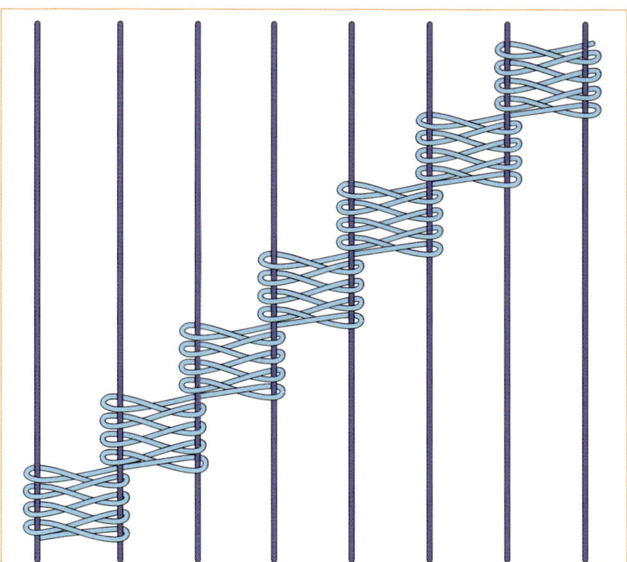

5 Continue working the Cretan stitches in diagonal blocks of four, using your needle or mellor to keep the positioning even. Finish your thread at the leftmost vertical thread.

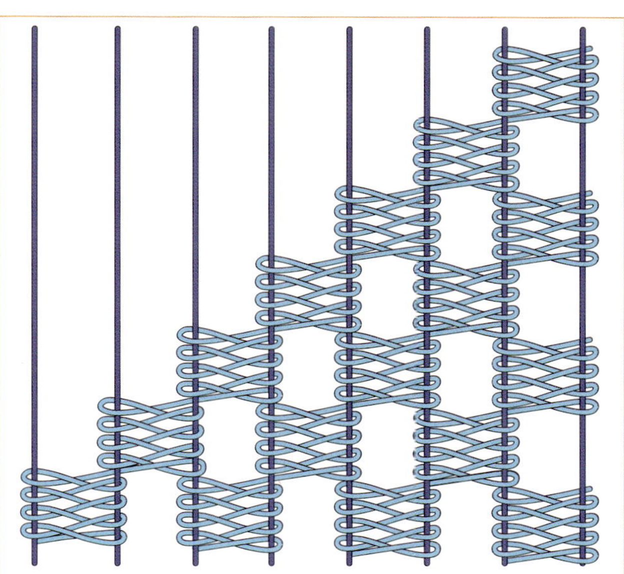

6 Start a new diagonal row on the right side, working it as before. Continue working diagonal rows until the area is complete.

CROSS BAR FILLING TRELLIS

CREWELWORK; SURFACE.

Also known as Trellis filling, Couched filling stitch, or Jacobean couching.

This stitch is a trellis with a cross over each intersection which is used to hold the trellis in position.

This decoration can be done with a larger cross over the trellis intersections for greater visual impact.

For more background see the entry for trellis stitch on pages 274–275.

METHOD

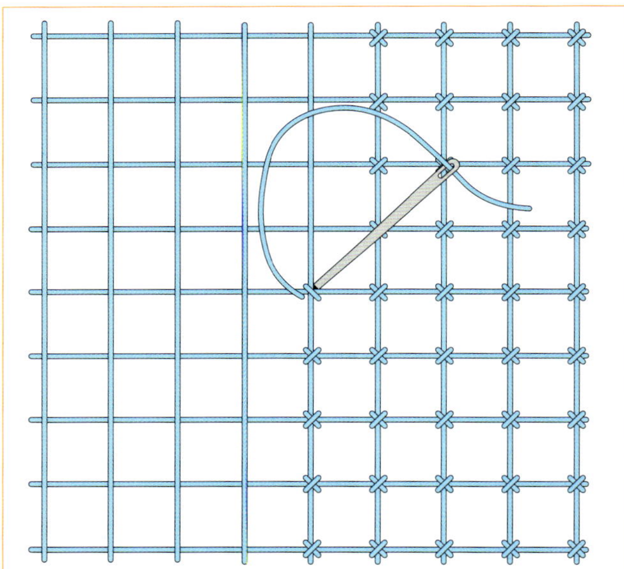

1 Start by filling your shape with a grid framework of basic trellis, either square like this image or on the diagonal as shown opposite. Anchor each intersection with a small cross stitch; ensure the uppermost stitch lies bottom left to top right.

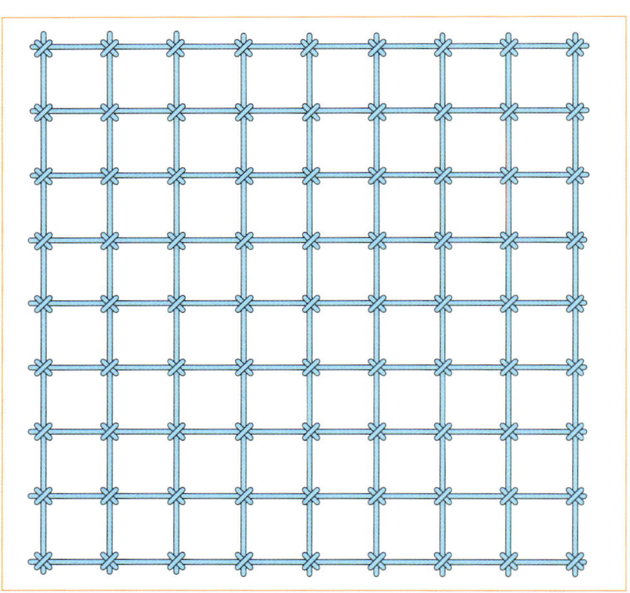

2 Complete every intersection within the shape.

CROSS BAR WITH LINK TRELLIS

Crewelwork; Surface.

A diagonal trellis decorated using detached chain stitch (see page 240) and straight stitches.

The term link in the name comes from the alternative name for detached chain stitch: 'link powdering stitch'.

For more background see the entry for trellis stitch on pages 274–275.

METHOD

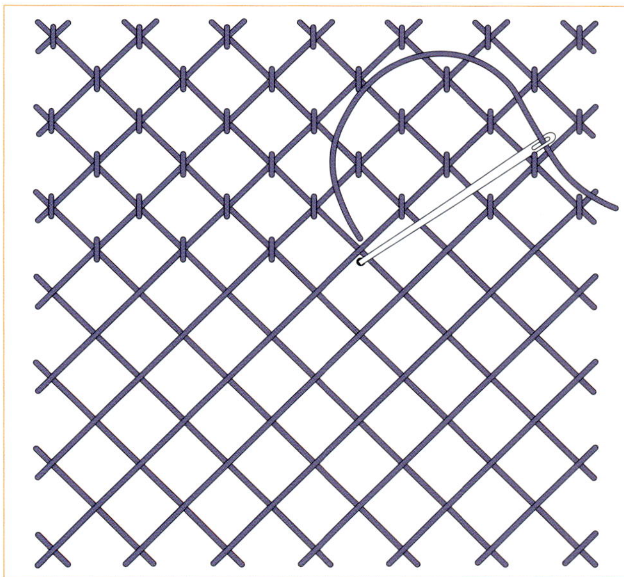

1 Start by filling your shape with a grid framework of basic trellis, either diagonal like this image or square, as in the example opposite. Complete a straight stitch over each intersection.

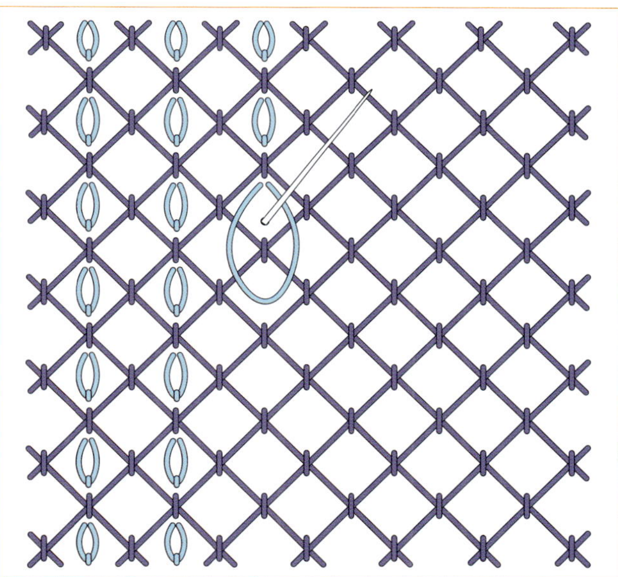

2 Fill some of the squares with a detached chain.

DETACHED CHAIN STITCH

CREWELWORK; WESSEX STITCHERY; MOUNTMELLICK; SURFACE; STUMPWORK.

Also known as Lazy daisy stitch, Single chain stitch, Daisy stitch, Link powdering stitch, Picot stitch, Loop stitch, or Washable knot stitch.

A detached chain stitch is a single chain secured using a holding stitch over the loop instead of another chain. For a slightly different version, see long-tailed daisy stitch on page 259.

For more background see chain stitch on page 22.

METHOD

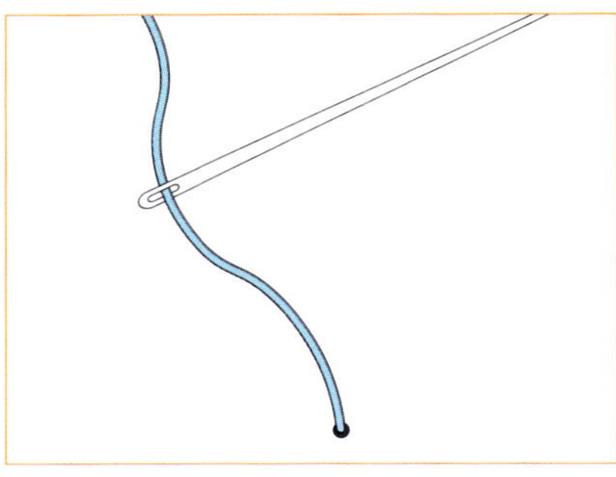

1 Take the needle up through the fabric where you wish the pointed tip of the shape to be.

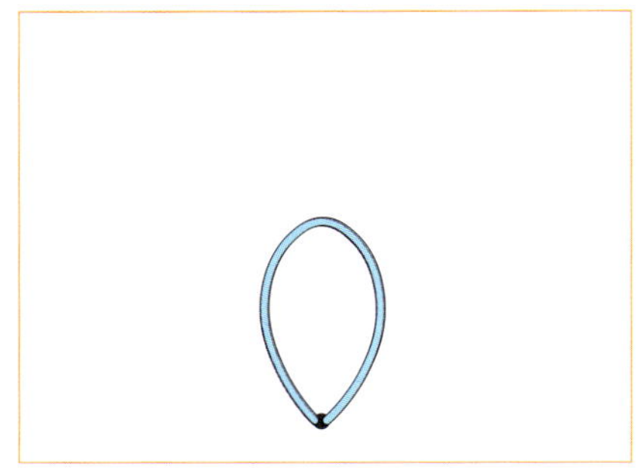

2 Take the needle back down through the fabric, through the same hole, creating a loop on the surface. Hold onto the loop to avoid pulling it through.

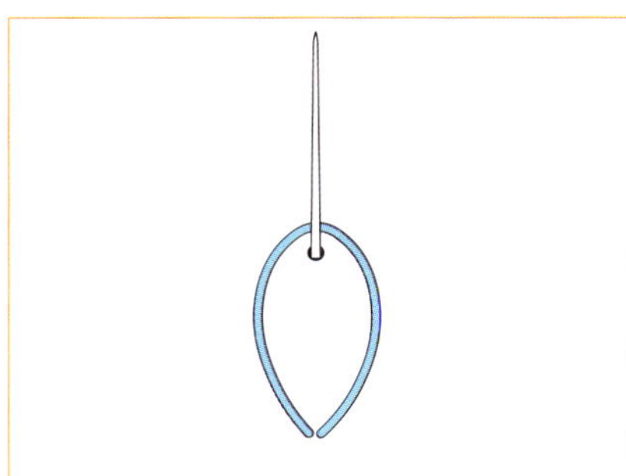

3 Decide on the length you would like the stitch to be and bring the needle up in the inside of the loop at this point.

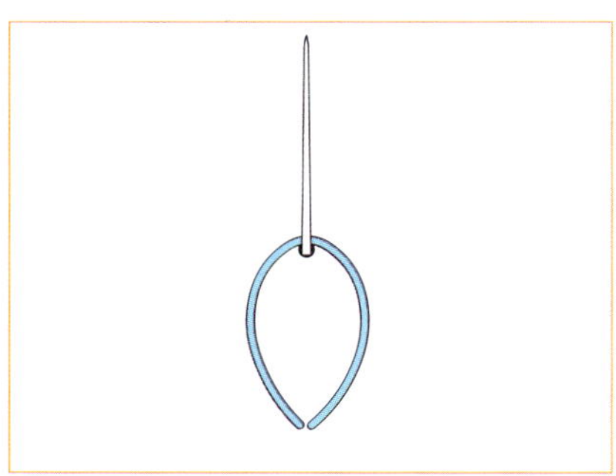

4 Leave the needle in the fabric and draw the thread through to tighten the loop against the needle.

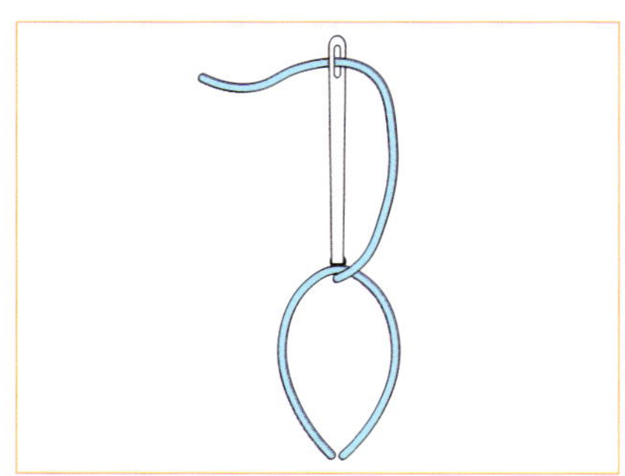

5 Take the needle over the loop then down through the fabric to make a small holding stitch to secure it.

DETACHED WHEATEAR STITCH

SURFACE; CREWELWORK.

Detached wheatear stitch consists of a detached open chain stitch with the addition of two slanting stitches underneath the chain stitch. As the name suggests, the resulting stitch resembles an ear of wheat. It can be used in isolation or scattered as a filling stitch.

Detached wheatear stitch bears a strong resemblance to tête de boeuf stitch (see page 271) as both stitches consist of a detached chain stitch plus two extra small stitches. Over time some embroidery sources have swapped the names of the stitches in error. However, the strong resemblance of this stitch to an ear of wheat (and that of tête de boeuf to a bull's head) suggests that this version is the correct way to stitch it.

METHOD

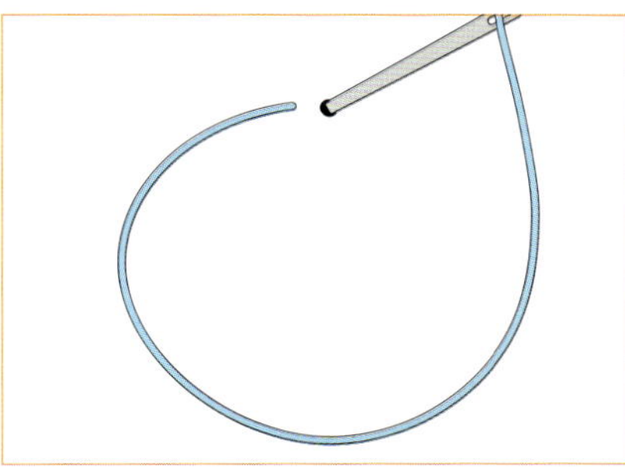

1 Bring the needle and thread to the surface, take the needle back down close by, leaving a loop on the surface.

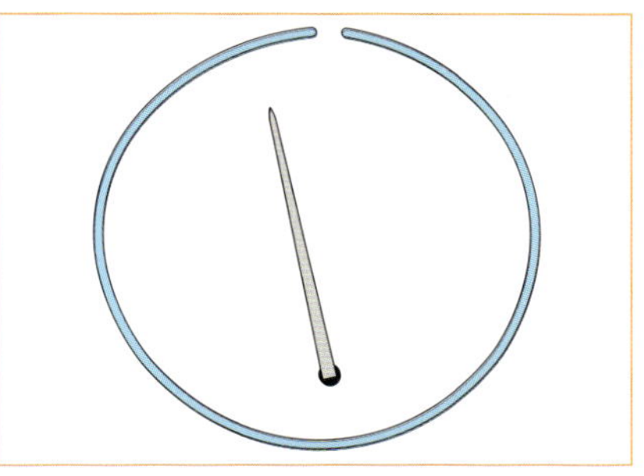

2 Bring the needle up through the loop and tighten the loop against the needle.

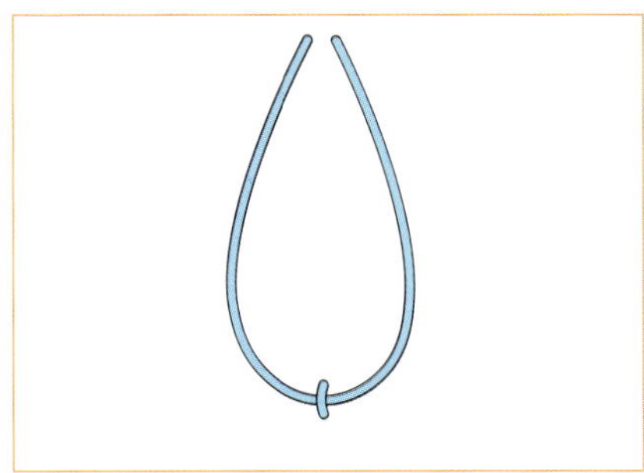

3 Secure the loop with a straight vertical stitch of your preferred length.

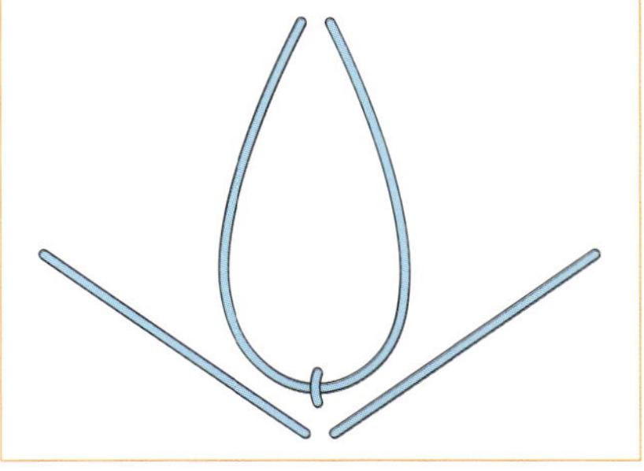

4 Add a straight stitch either side at a 45 degree angle.

DIAGONAL CHEVRON STITCH

WHITEWORK; PULLED THREAD.

This pulled thread stitch consists of diagonal lines of single faggot stitch (see page 266), each followed by a diagonal row of parallel oblique lines or chevrons.

Despite the stitch being worked in diagonal rows, it has a gridded appearance.

METHOD

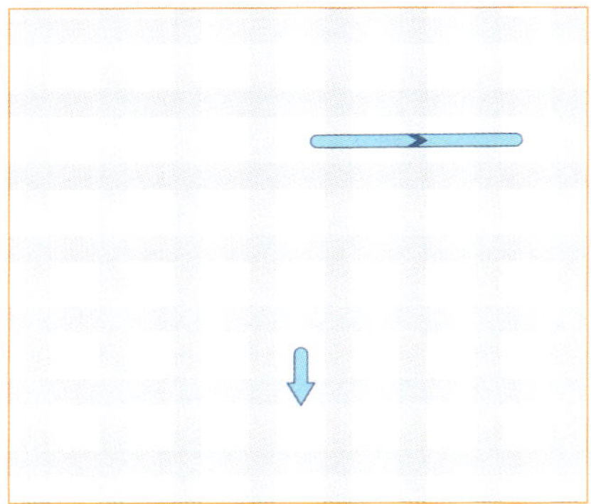

1 Complete a horizontal stitch from left to right over three fabric threads, then count three diagonal intersections down to the left, bring the needle up to the surface and pull firmly on the thread so as to distort the weave of the fabric.

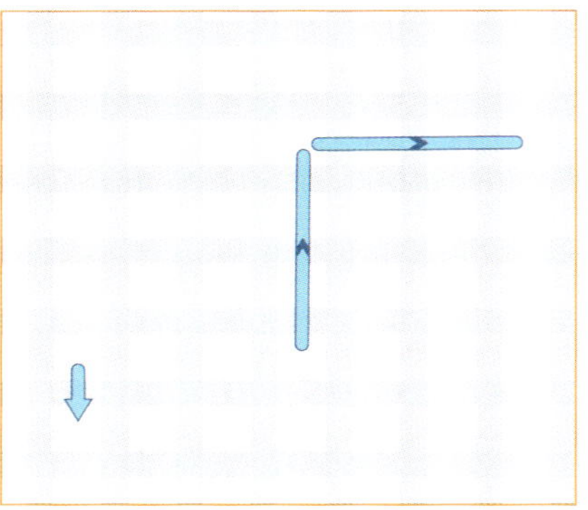

2 Create a vertical stitch taking the needle up over three threads to meet the beginning of the horizontal stitch, then count three diagonal intersections down to the left, bring the needle up to the surface and pull firmly on the thread.

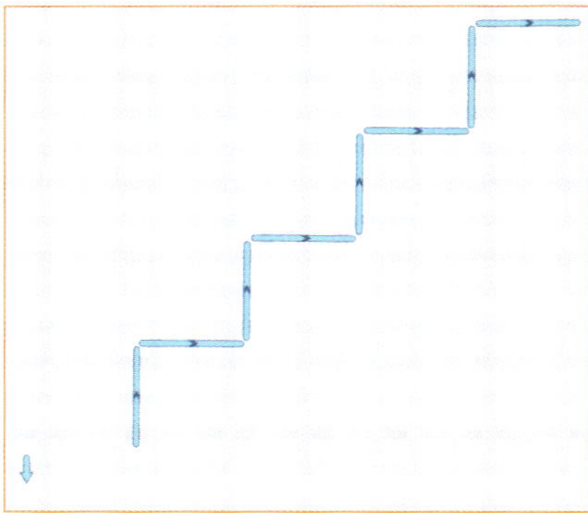

3 Repeat the last two stitches across the fabric in a line running down to the left. This is single faggot stitch.

4 Complete a diagonal stitch from bottom left to top right over three intersections, then count three fabric threads to the left, bring the needle up to the surface and pull firmly on the thread.

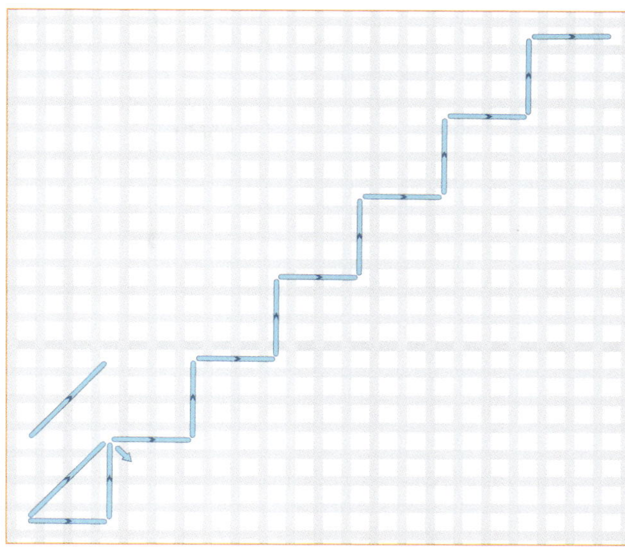

5 Complete another diagonal stitch from bottom left to top right over three intersections, then count down over three horizontal fabric threads and bring the needle up to the surface and pull firmly on the thread.

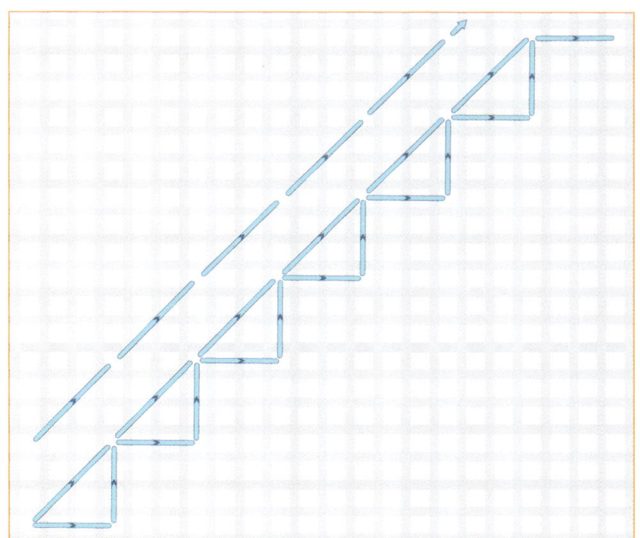

6 Repeat the last two stitches across the fabric in a line running diagonally up to the right.

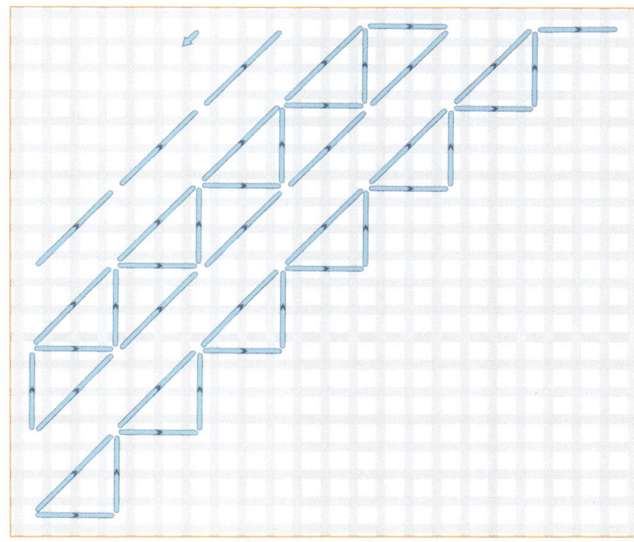

7 Continue to fill the shape.

DIAMOND TRELLIS (PATTERN)

Blackwork.

This blackwork pattern consists of small diamonds inside a vertical trellis.

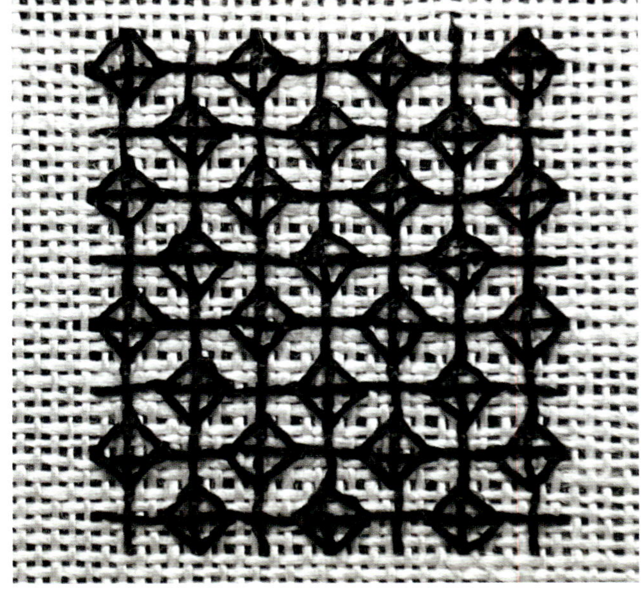

METHOD

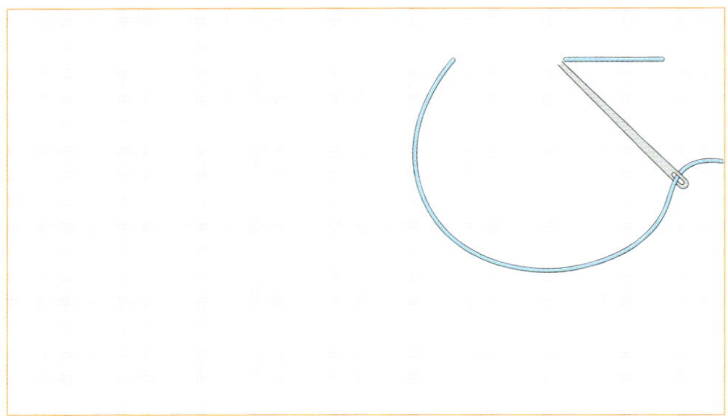

1 Work a line of horizontal back stitches across the design area: each stitch should be over four threads.

2 Leave a gap of four fabric threads and work additional horizontal lines.

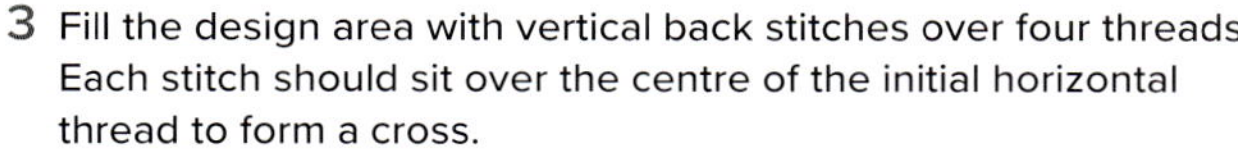

3 Fill the design area with vertical back stitches over four threads. Each stitch should sit over the centre of the initial horizontal thread to form a cross.

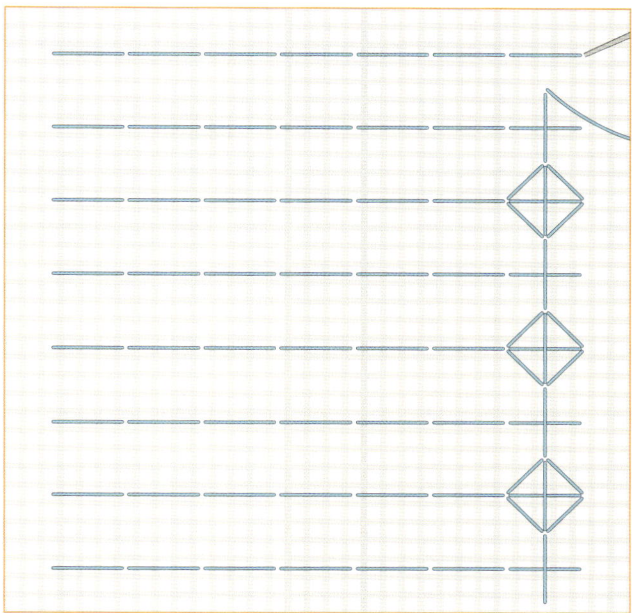

4 Alternate crosses should be surrounded by a diamond: work alternate straight and back stitches over two intersections.

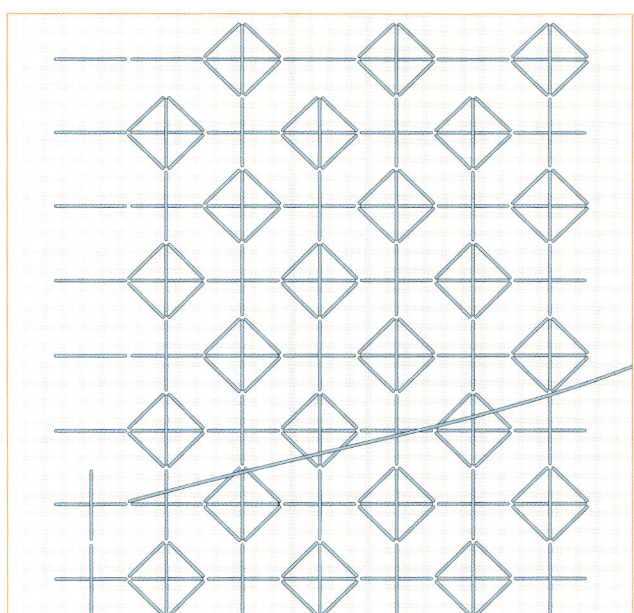

5 Continue working vertically up and down to complete the pattern.

DOUBLE FAGGOT FILLING STITCH

Whitework; Pulled thread.

This stitch is a heavier version of single faggot stitch (see page 266): each stitch is worked a second time over the original one which gives a heavier line and pulls the fabric slightly tighter.

METHOD

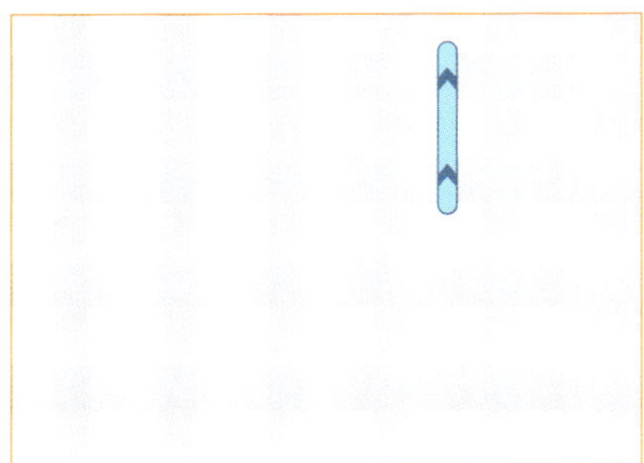

1 Working from the right-hand side of the shape to be filled, work a vertical stitch up over two fabric threads.

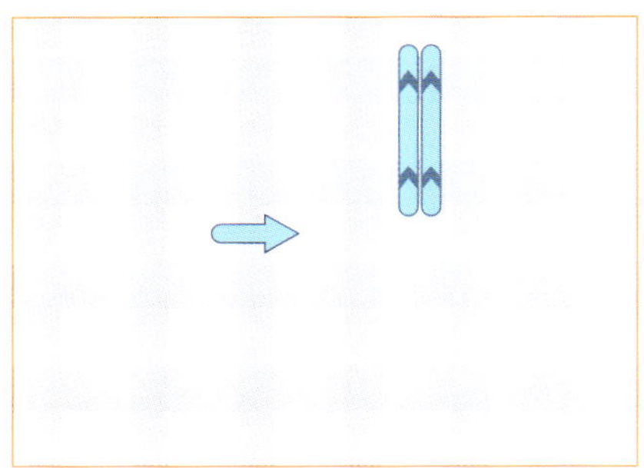

2 Repeat the stitch over the same two threads then count left and down under two intersections, bring the needle to the surface and pull.

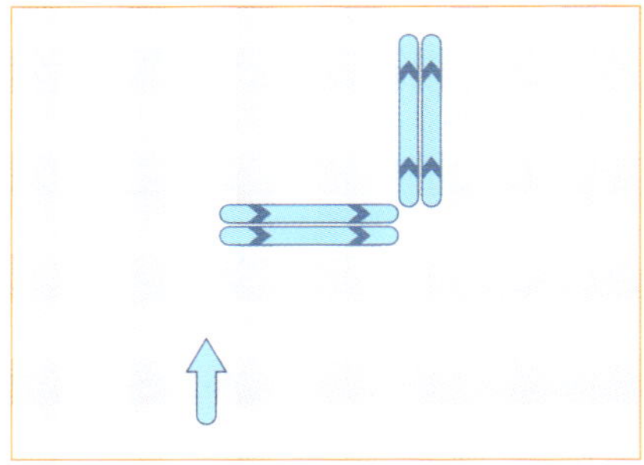

3 Work two horizontal stitches over two fabric threads (into the original hole), one over the other. Count left and down under two intersections, bring the needle to the surface and pull.

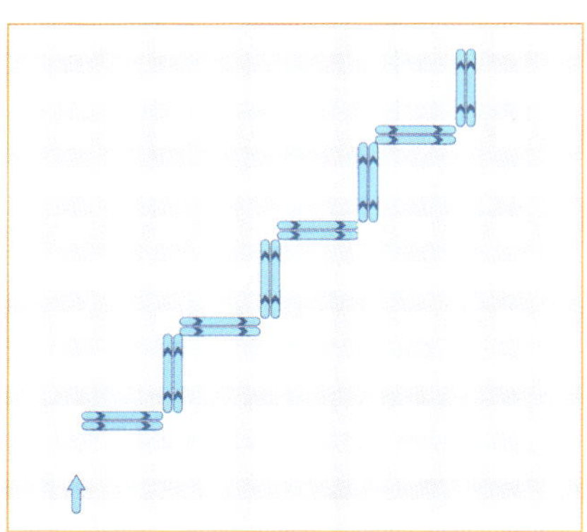

4 Repeat the last three steps until you reach the other side of the shape to be filled.

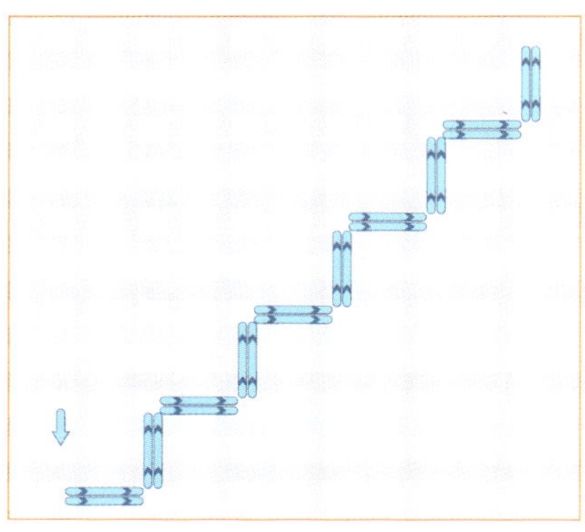

5 Working from the left-hand side, count left and up under two intersections, bring the needle to the surface and pull.

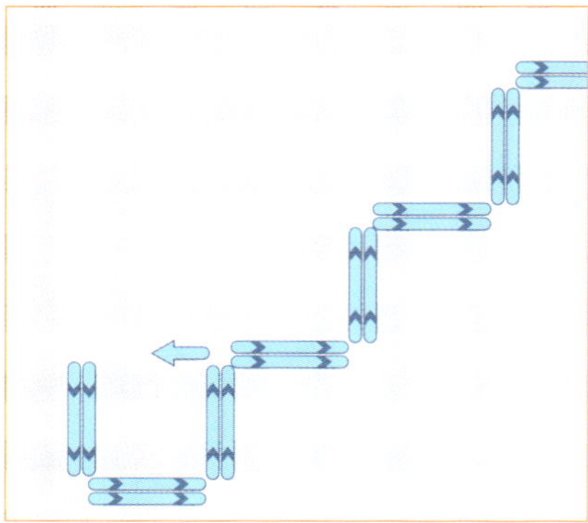

6 Work two vertical stitches down over two fabric threads, one over the other. Count right and up under two intersections and bring the needle to the surface and pull. You will share holes with the previous row of stitching.

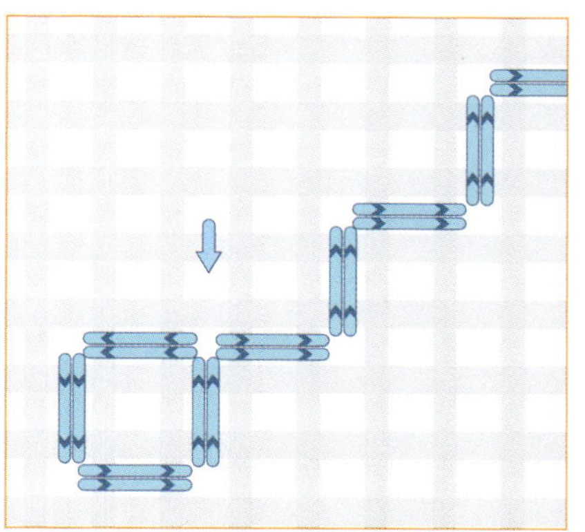

7 Work two horizontal stitches over two fabric threads, one over the other. Count right and up under two intersections and bring the needle to the surface and pull.

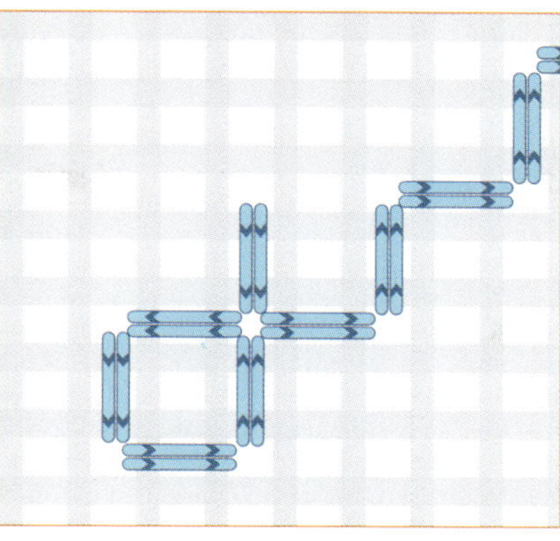

8 Continue in this way until you reach the top of the space.

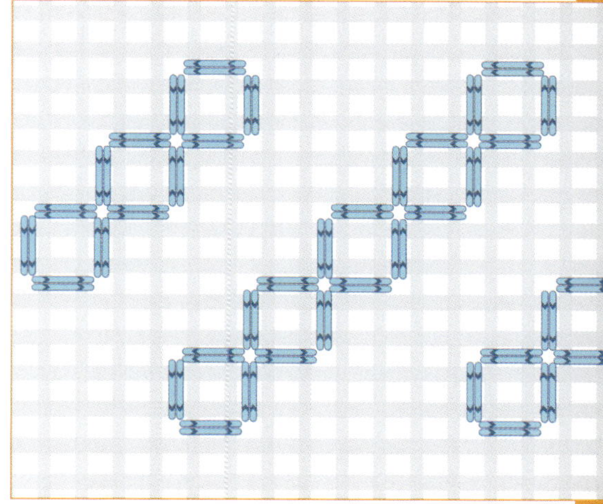

9 Continue to fill the space with more diagonal bands of double faggot stitch, spacing the bands six fabric threads apart.

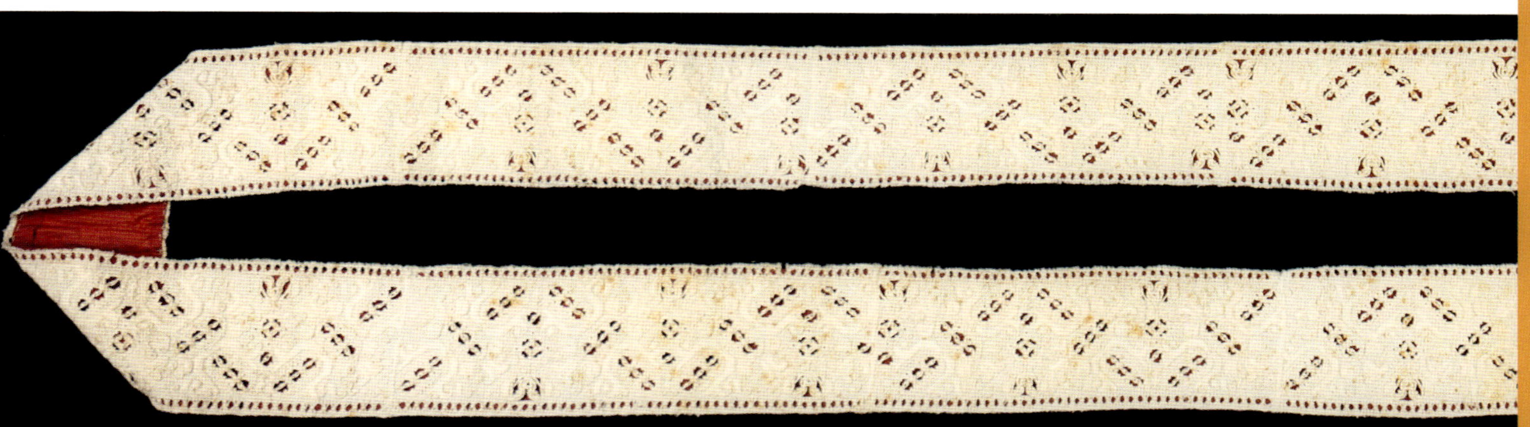

▲▲ Border, RSN Collection COL.37

Late 16th-century linen cutwork border or band with couching, satin stitches, eyelet stitches and wrapped bars (see pages 63, 37, and 312–313 for these stitches), most likely produced in Italy.

Quadratic counted stitch cutwork motifs are interspersed with couched and satin stitch leaves. Double faggot filling stitches have been used throughout, as shown in the detail to the right.

The red backing is likely 20th century and has been applied to several other early modern cutwork borders in the Royal School of Needlework collection.

ERMINE STITCH

Crewelwork; Surface.

Ermine stitch consists of a vertical stitch crossed towards the bottom with two diagonal stitches.

The shape formed is similar to the heraldic pattern called ermine, itself based on the winter coat of the stoat.

METHOD

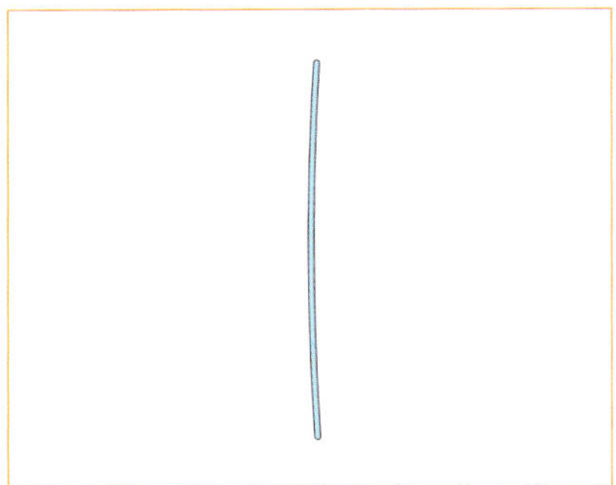

1 Begin by making a vertical, straight stitch.

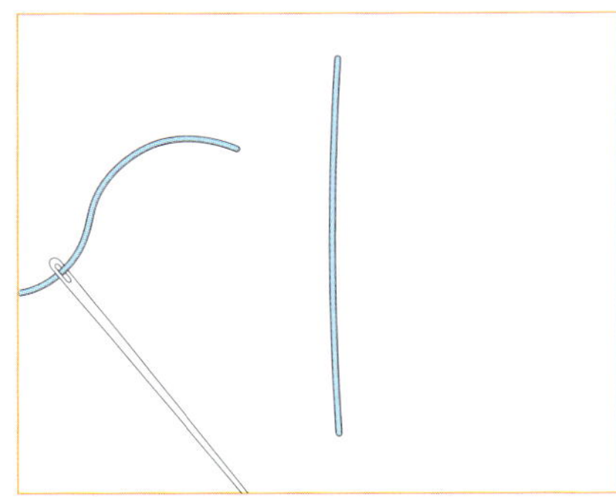

2 Bring the needle out to the left, slightly lower down from the top of the first stitch.

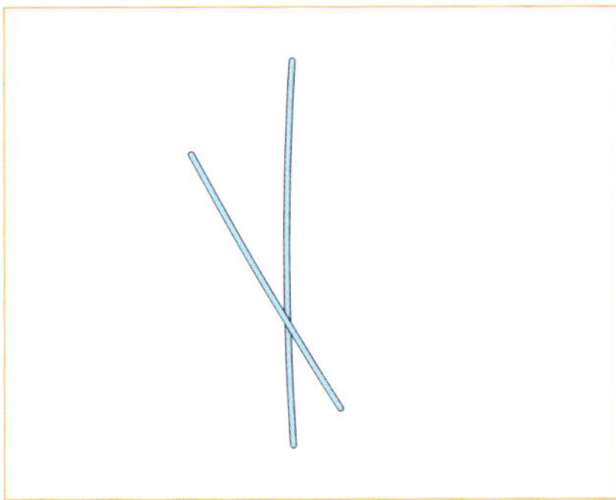

3 Take the needle down diagonally to the right, ensuring it finishes slightly above the bottom of the first stitch.

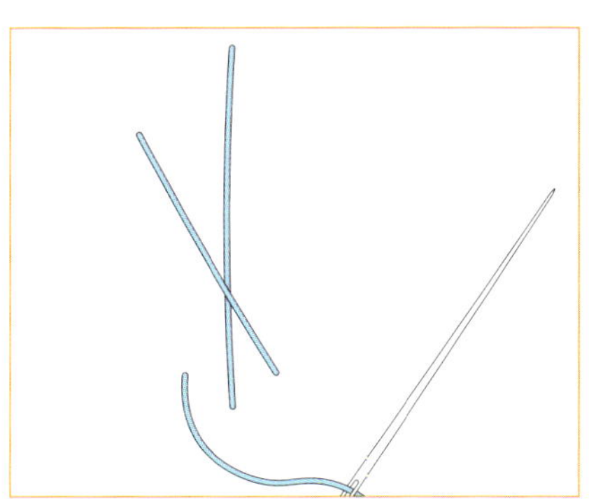

4 Bring the needle up on the left-hand side, parallel with where the needle was just taken down and close to the very first stitch.

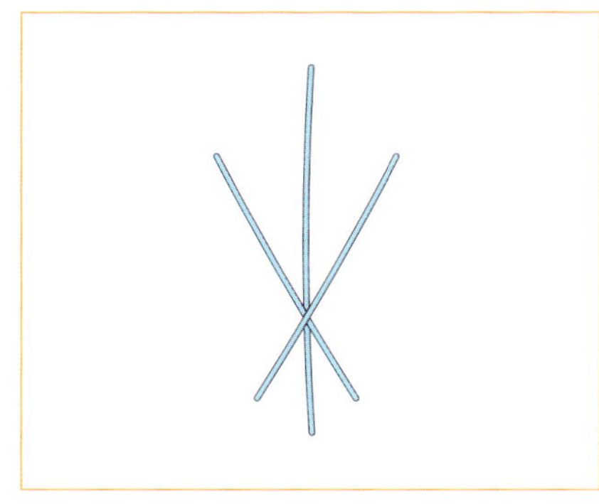

5 Take the needle down diagonally to the right-hand side of the first stitch.

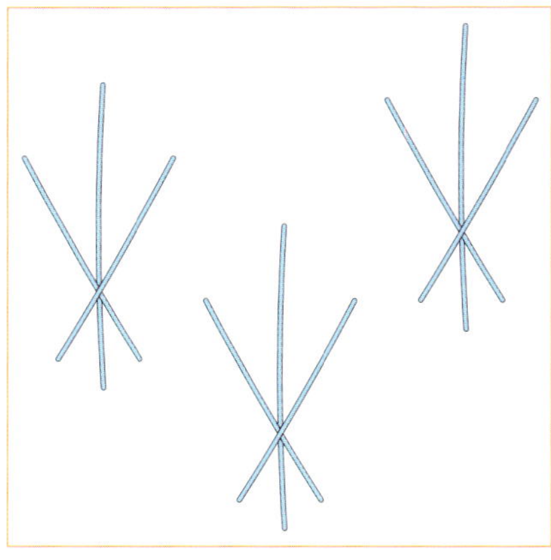

6 Repeat the stitch, filling the space as desired.

FLY STITCH FILLING

SURFACE.

Also known as Crossed fly stitch.

This surface stitch uses joined rows of fly stitches (see page 28) to form a trellis of diamond shapes.

It is similar to cloud filling stitch (see page 234), but its different structure normally gives a more angular effect.

METHOD

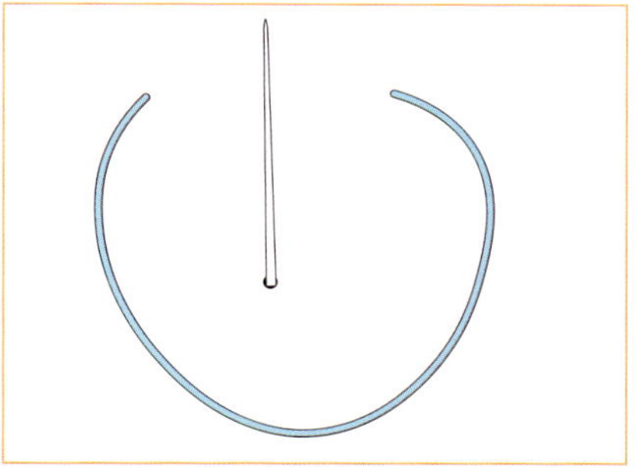

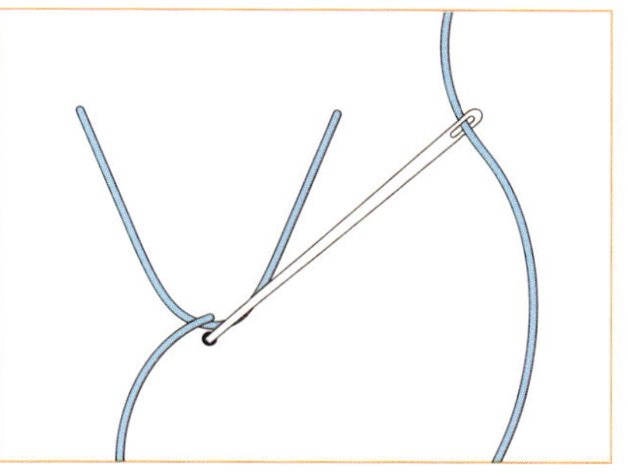

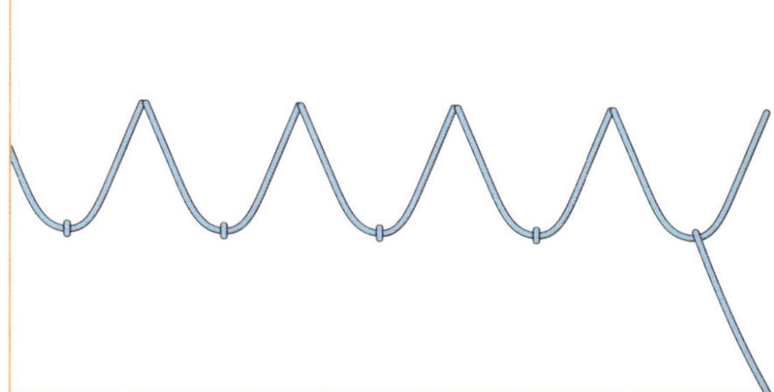

1 Bring the needle up through the fabric and back down short distance apart – this will be the width of your diamonds. Leaving a loop on the surface, bring the needle up again centrally below the two points to form a triangle.

2 Draw the excess thread to the underside tightening against the needle to create a 'V' shape. Draw the thread to the surface and use a small holding stitch over the thread to secure.

3 Repeat to complete a line of fly stitches; each stitch should start by sharing a hole with the previous stitch.

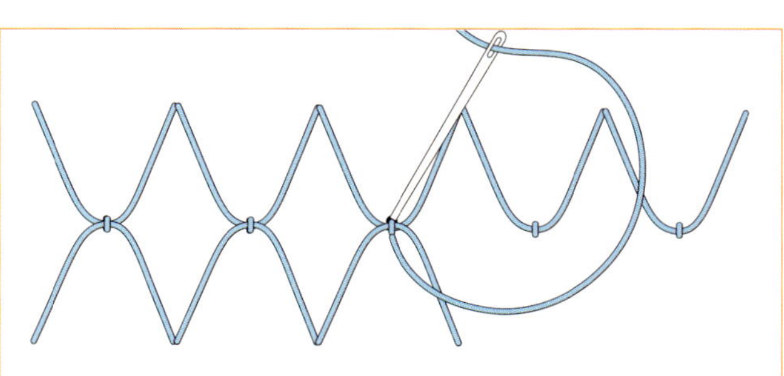

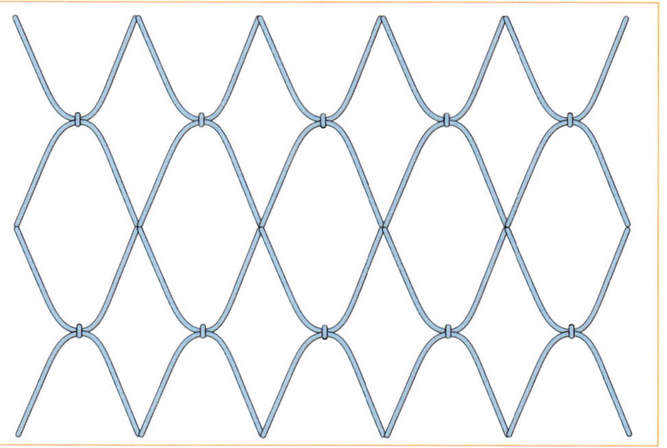

4 The line below should be worked as a mirror image; the holding stitch is positioned over the one from the previous row.

5 Continue to cover the area to produce a diamond trellis.

FOUR-SIDED STITCH

WHITEWORK; PULLED THREAD; HARDANGER.

Also known as Four-sided openwork stitch, Four-sided border stitch, or Square open hem stitch.

Four-sided stitch is a pulled thread stitch consisting of vertical and horizontal stitches which form a square pattern on the front of the fabric and crosses on the reverse side. This stitch can be worked with single wraps or double wraps.

If this stitch is worked diagonally, it is similar to multiple rows of single faggot stitch (see page 266), although the reverse is different.

Four-sided stitch dates at least to the 18th century as shown by a Turkish or Albanian embroidered cover held by the V&A South Kensington. According to the museum's website, Louisa Pesel called four-sided stitch 'square open hem stitch', as evidenced by her sampler, also held by the museum.

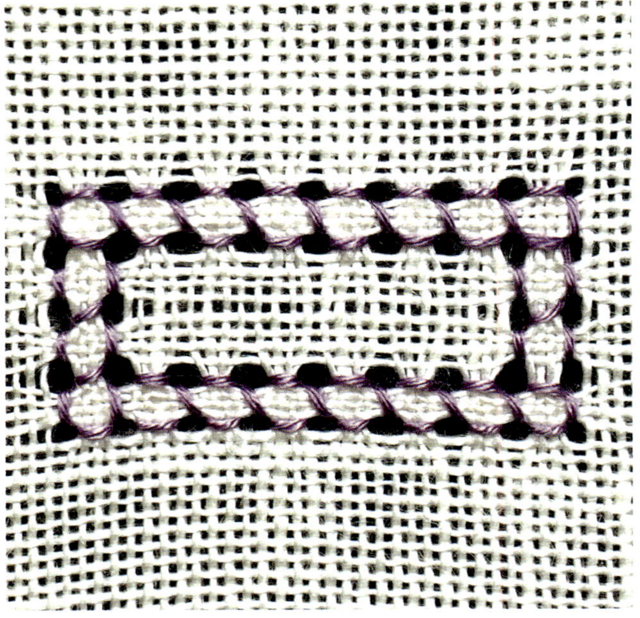

METHOD

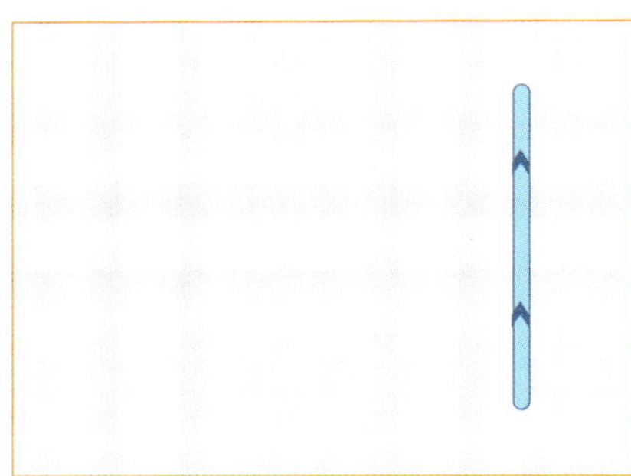

1 Bring the needle up at the bottom right corner of the stitch and make a vertical stitch up over four threads of the fabric.

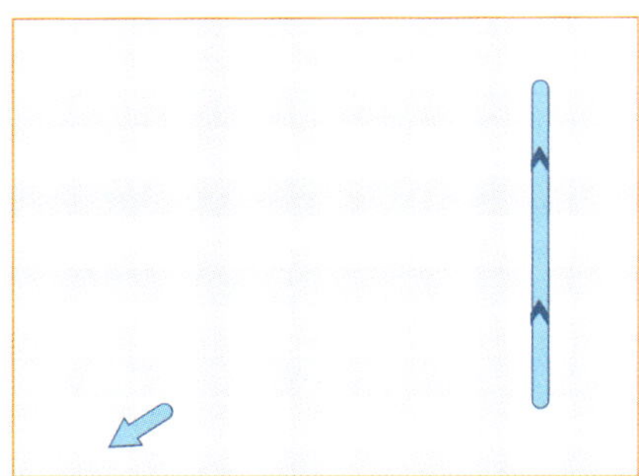

2 Count left four and down four and bring the needle up, making a diagonal stitch on the reverse side. Pull tight.

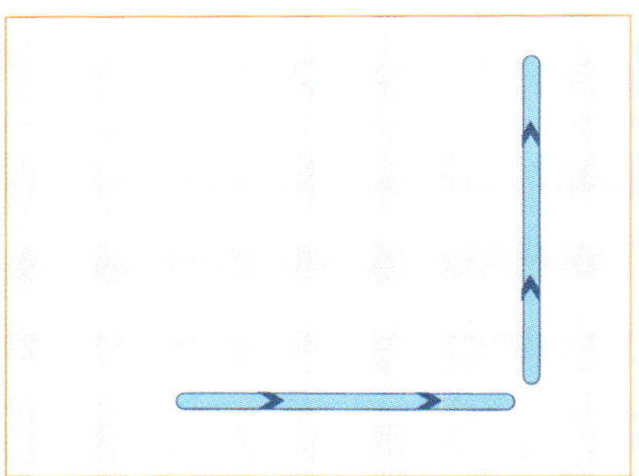

3 Make a horizontal stitch four to the right, taking the needle down in the first hole.

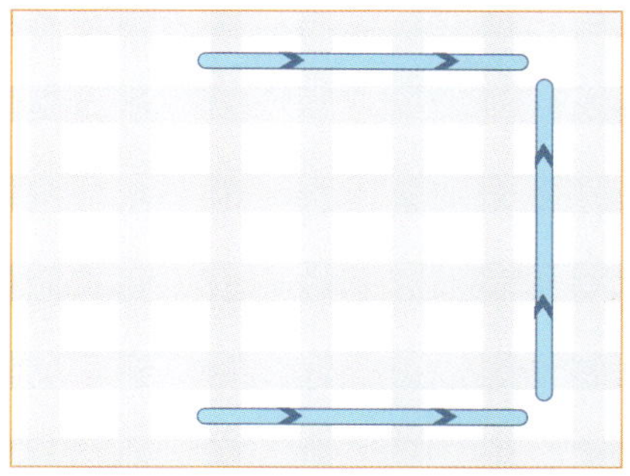

4 Count left four and up four and bring the needle up, making a diagonal stitch on the reverse, and pull. Make a horizontal stitch four to the right, taking the needle down in the top right hole.

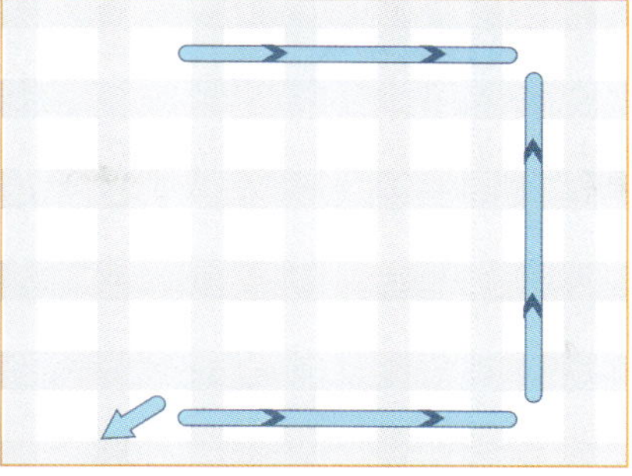

5 Count left four and down four, bring the needle up in the bottom left hole, and pull.

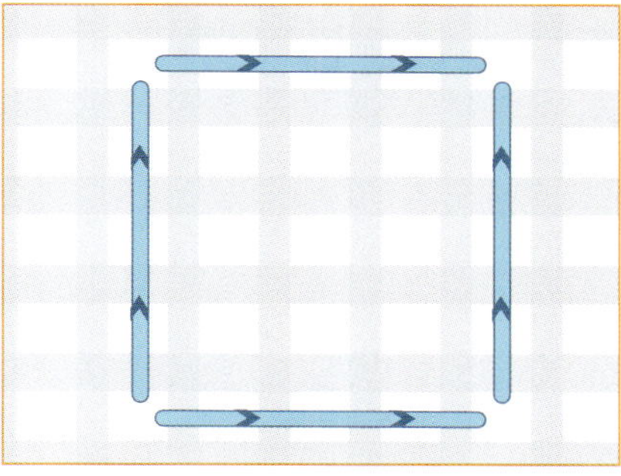

6 Make a vertical stitch up over four threads. This becomes the first stitch of the next square.

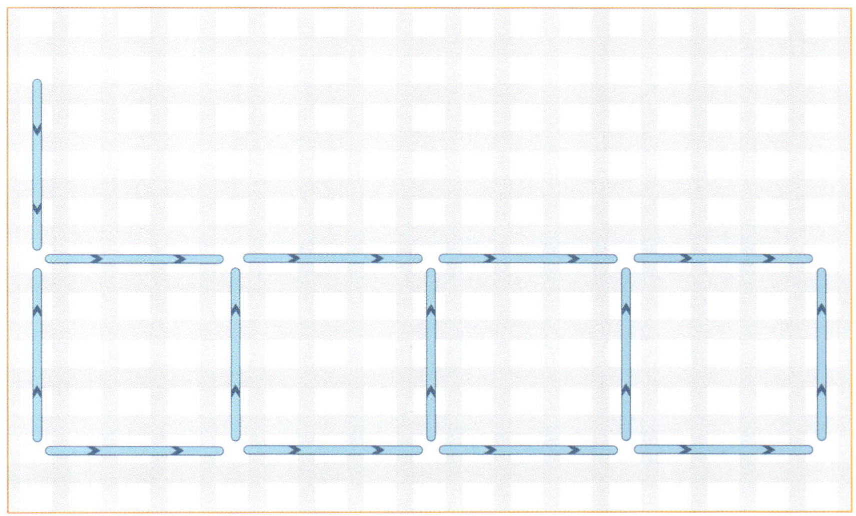

7 Repeat to complete the row. To begin the next row, make a holding stitch on the outline or in the border, which will will be covered later on.

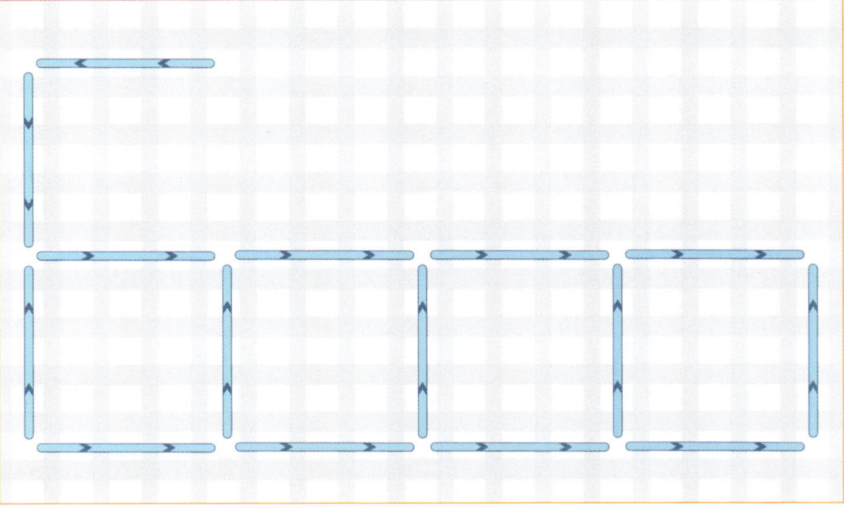

8 Work the next row in the same way as the first row, but in reverse. Continue to fill the design area.

FRAMED CROSS FILLING

Whitework; Pulled thread.

This pulled work stitch consists of a grid of regular square apertures, each with a cross in the centre. It has similarities with cobbler filling stitch, although the latter has two threads between each square, rather than one.

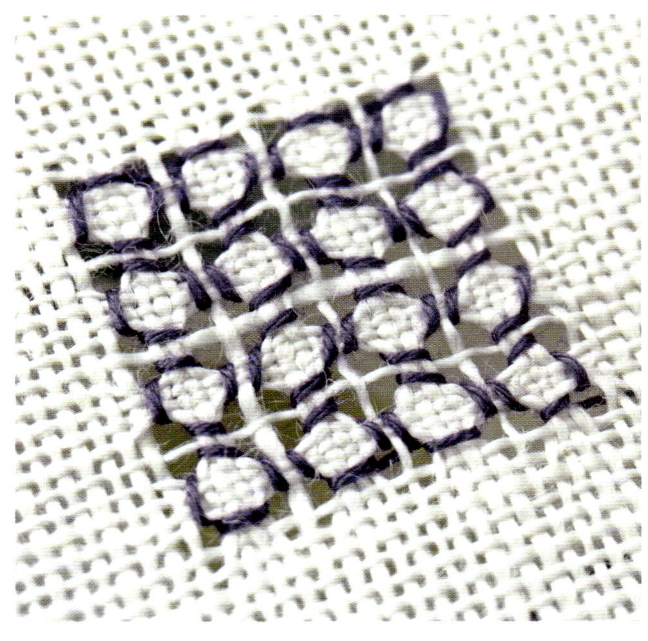

METHOD

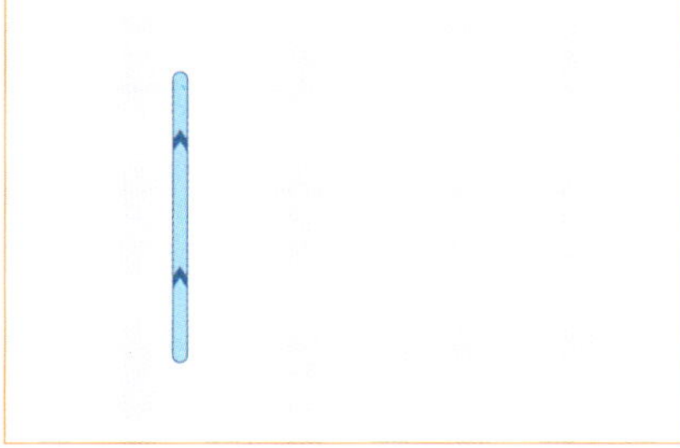

1 Bring the needle up to the surface and take it back down over four fabric threads. Pull the thread tight.

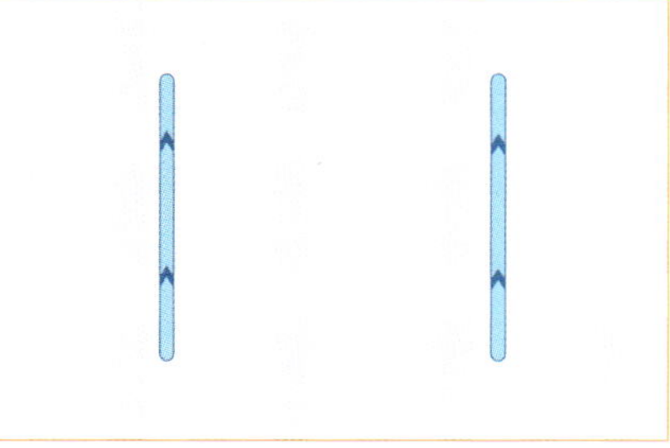

2 Bring the needle up at four threads to the right and four threads down, and insert it four threads above. Pull the thread tight.

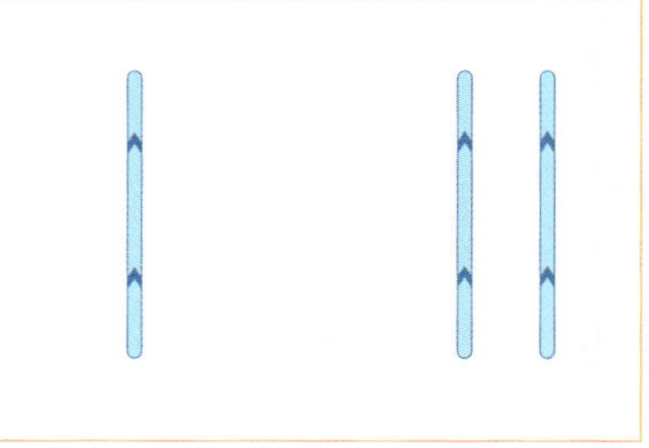

3 Bring the needle up at one thread to the right and four threads down, and insert it four threads above. Pull tight.

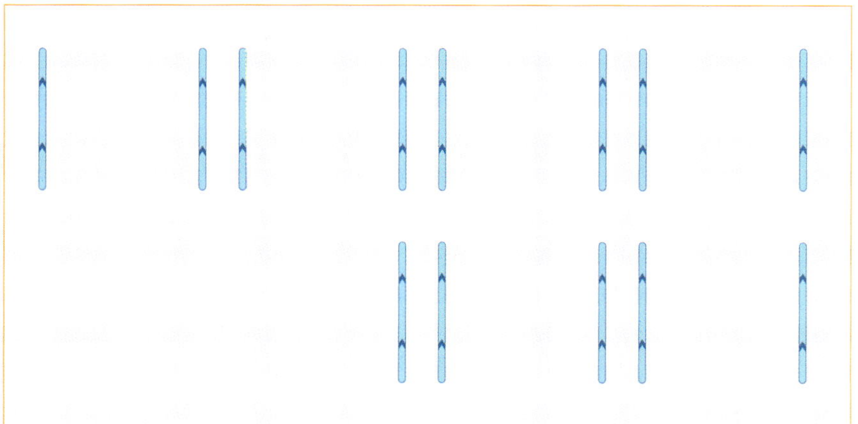

4 Repeat along the row until the end of the filling area, and work the second row directly below in the same way.

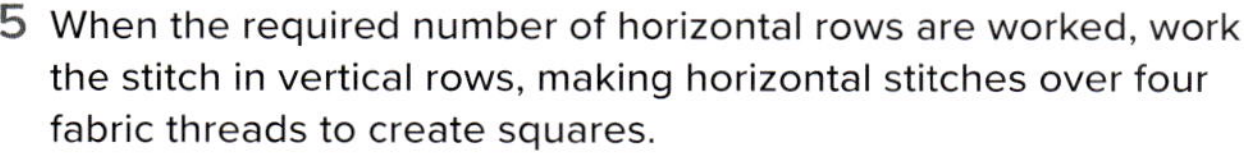

5 When the required number of horizontal rows are worked, work the stitch in vertical rows, making horizontal stitches over four fabric threads to create squares.

6 Move onto the next row, pulling the stitches tightly.

7 Continue until the area is filled.

GREEK CROSS FILLING STITCH

WHITEWORK; PULLED THREAD.

Also known as Greek four-sided stitch.

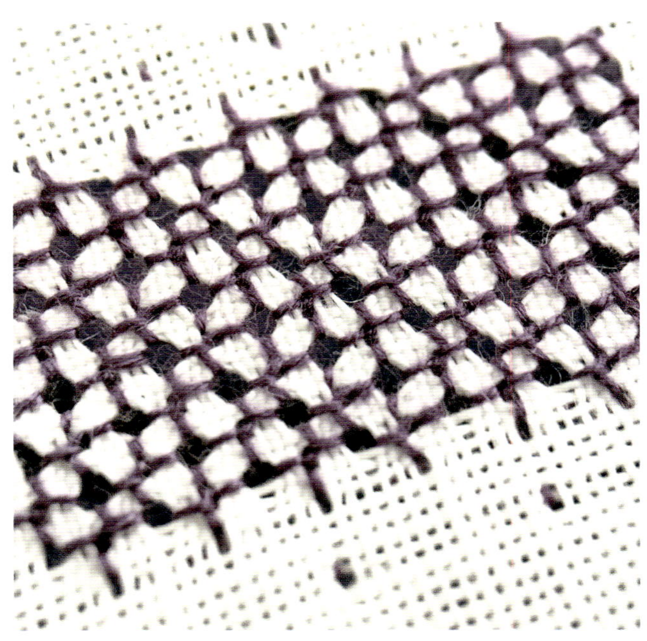

This pulled thread filling is formed of crosses worked in diagonal lines to form an open grid.

Each cross is composed of four stitches, all of which start in the centre of the cross. After working the fourth stitch, the needle comes up at the centre of the next cross.

A variation of Greek cross filling stitch where the cross is anchored in the centre will feature in a future release.

Greek cross filling, in common with many pulled thread stitches, has been in existence for centuries. It is used on a southern Italian whitework border from the late 17th century, currently held by the Art Institute of Chicago and a European fragment from a similar date held by the Indianapolis Museum of Art. It features on an 18th-century altar cloth border from Germany, and a 19th-century sampler from Sweden.

METHOD

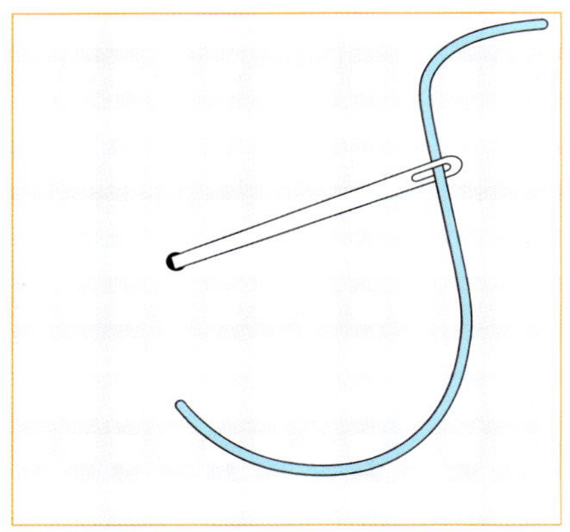

1 Bring the needle out at the centre of the cross, and insert it at three threads up.

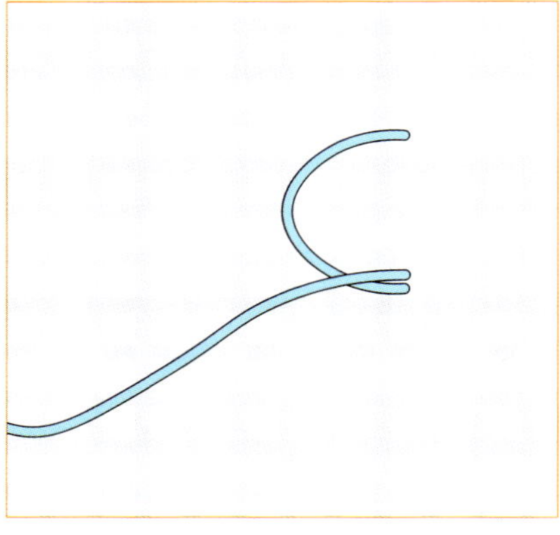

2 Bring the needle out at the centre again, and draw the needle out over the working thread, similar to a buttonhole stitch (see pages 20–21).

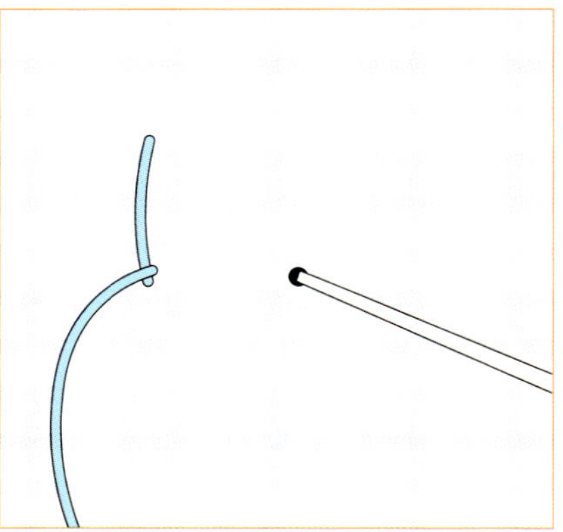

3 Pull the stitch tightly and insert the needle three threads to the right.

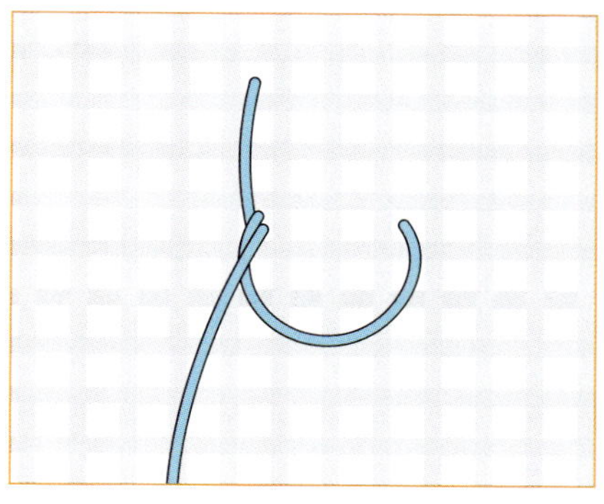

4 Bring it back at the centre again, drawing the needle out over the working thread like a buttonhole stitch.

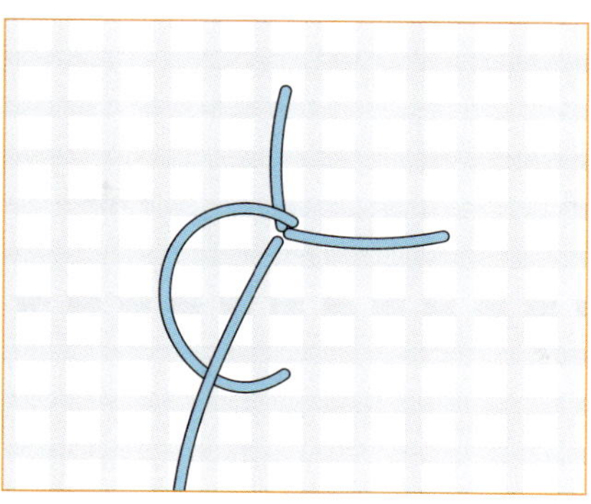

5 Insert the needle at three threads down and bring it up at the centre again to work the third stitch.

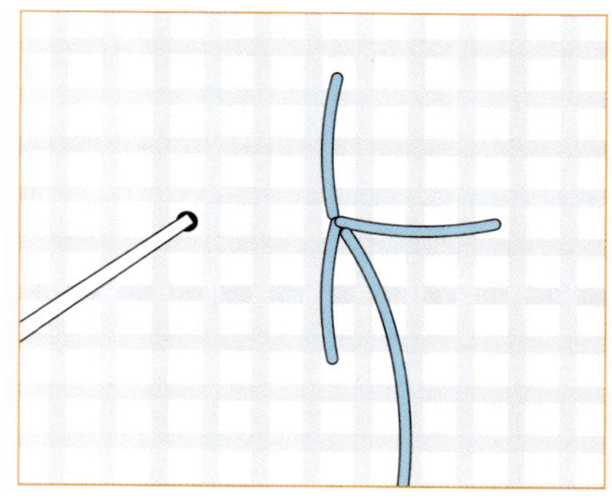

6 To form a cross, insert the needle at three threads to the left.

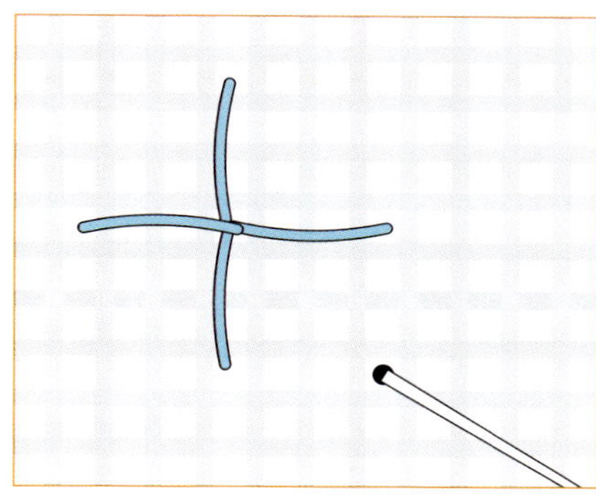

7 Do not come up at the centre as before, but instead, bring the needle out six threads to the right and three down, which will be the centre of the next cross.

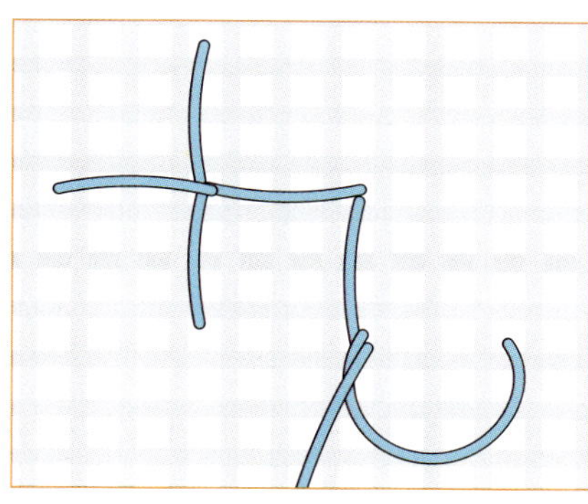

8 Repeat working the four stitches in this order – top, right, bottom and left. The crosses are worked in a diagonal line.

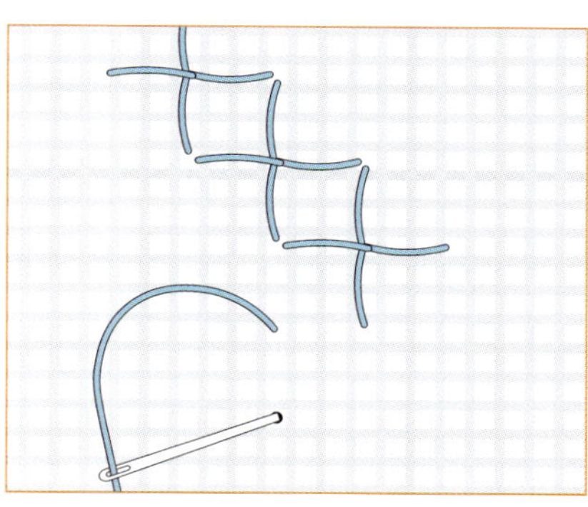

9 When you reach the end of the area to fill, make a tiny stitch to secure the thread at the edge of the area. For the second row, bring the needle up at the centre of the next cross and work four stitches again, this time working in the reverse order: bottom, left, top and right.

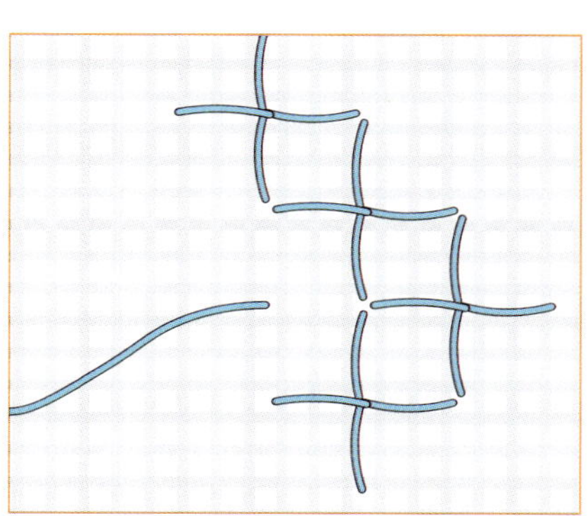

10 Continue to fill the area. If you prefer, at the end of each diagonal line, you can turn the fabric round and work in the same order as the first row – top, right, bottom and left.

11 Repeat the process, making sure you pull each stitch tightly.

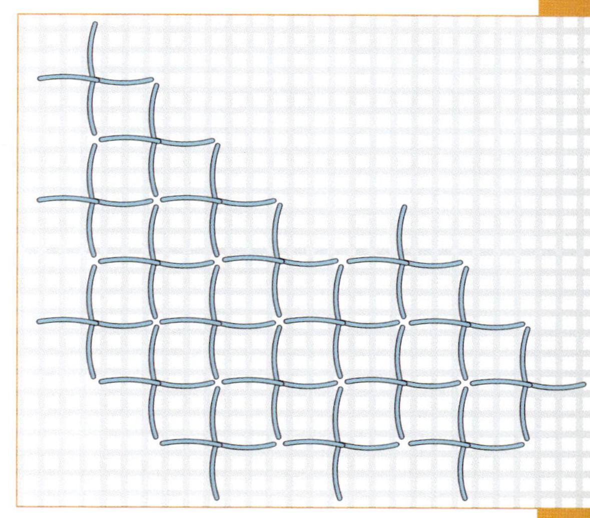

HONEYCOMB FILLING

Pulled thread; Whitework.

Also known as Pulled honeycomb stitch.

This pulled thread stitch provides a textured hexagonal pattern, hence the name 'honeycomb'. It is formed through the use of horizontal and vertical stitches which are then pulled tight to create the diagonal sides of the hexagons. The vertical stitches are worked twice into the same holes to keep sufficient tension on the working thread.

METHOD

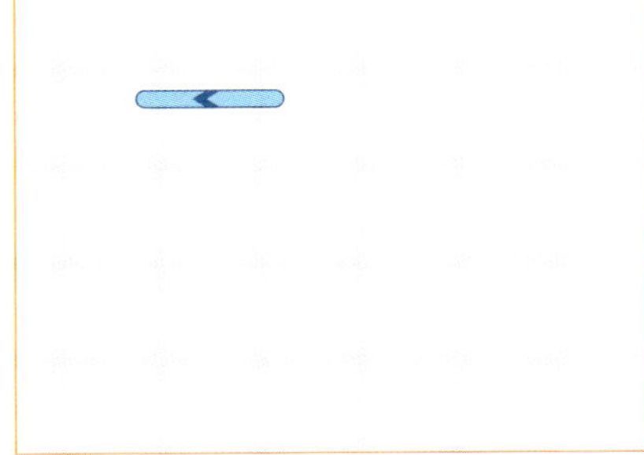

1 Using a tapestry needle, bring the thread up to the surface and then back down over three threads of the canvas creating a horizontal stitch from right to left.

2 Bring the needle up to the surface three threads below.

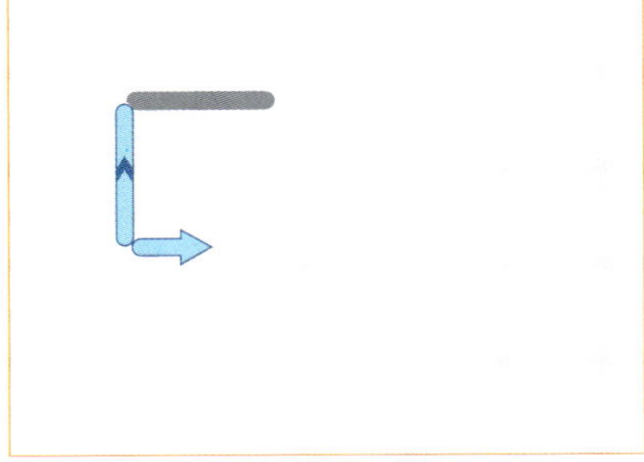

3 Count three threads up and take the needle into the previous hole to make a vertical stitch. Bring the needle up three threads below and pull the stitch tight to distort the fabric threads.

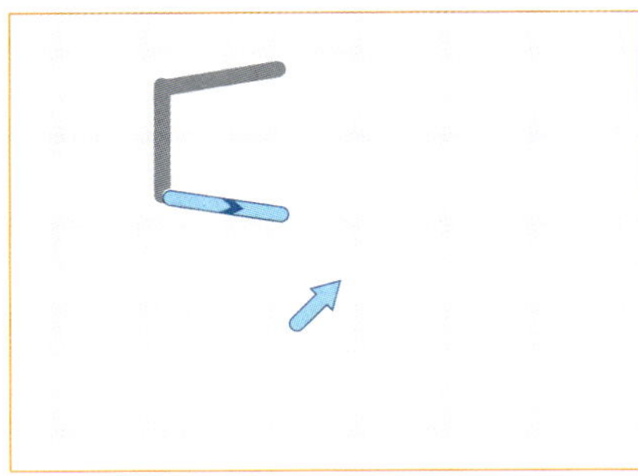

4 Create a horizontal stitch from left to right over three threads and bring the needle up to the surface three threads below.

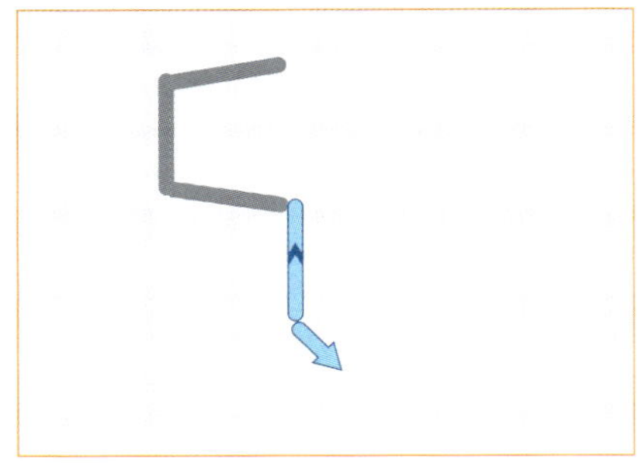

5 Repeat the vertical wrapping stitch from before: take the needle back vertically over the three threads and up into the same hole, effectively wrapping the canvas threads. Again, pull taut.

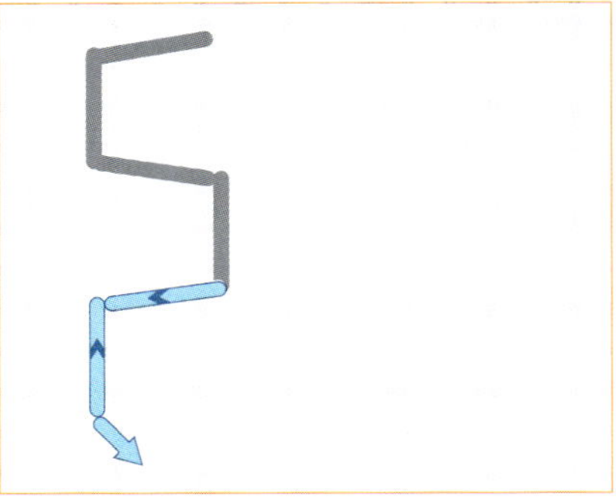

6 Create a horizontal stitch from right to left over three threads and bring the needle up to the surface three threads below and make another vertical wrap.

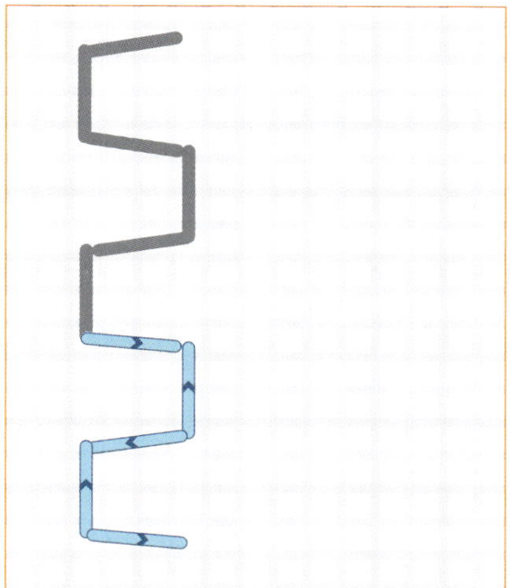

7 Repeat this sequence to the end of the row.

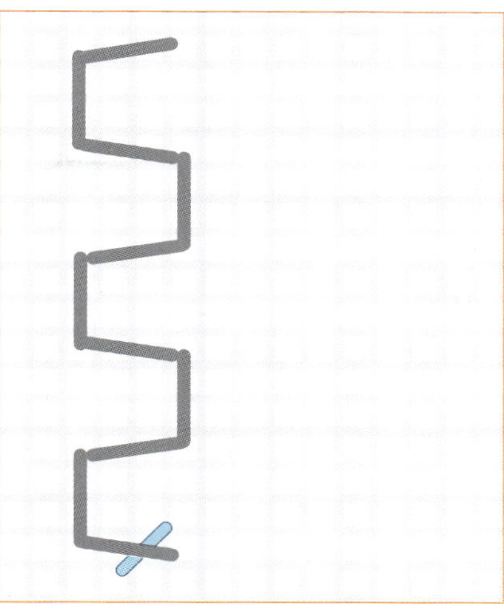

8 Before starting a horizontal stitch on the next row, secure on the underside by passing the needle through a stitch on the reverse.

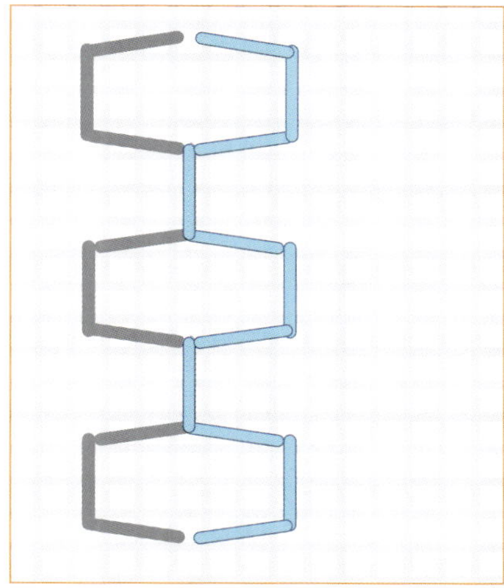

9 Repeat the sequence in the opposite direction.

TIP

The blue stitch here is on the underside of the fabric, passing under the last stitch.

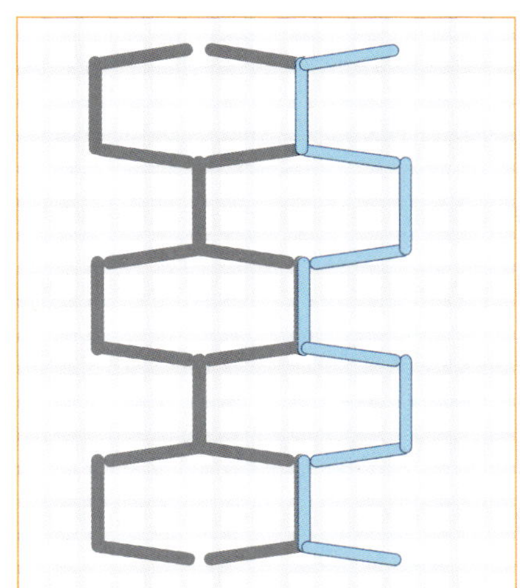

10 Work back down the next row by repeating the first row; there should be no need to secure the thread on the underside when working in this direction.

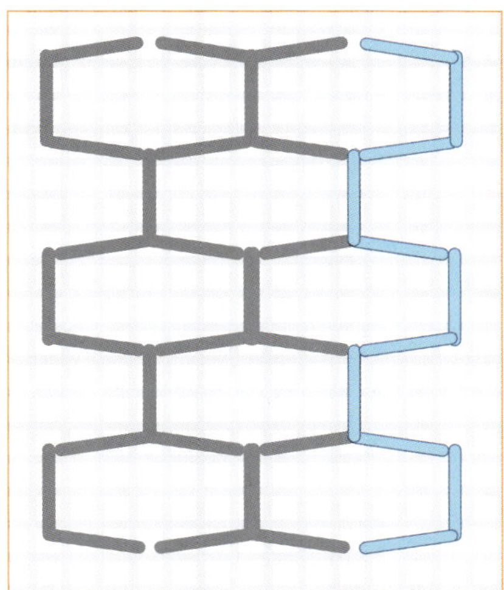

11 Repeat this sequence up and down to fill the space.

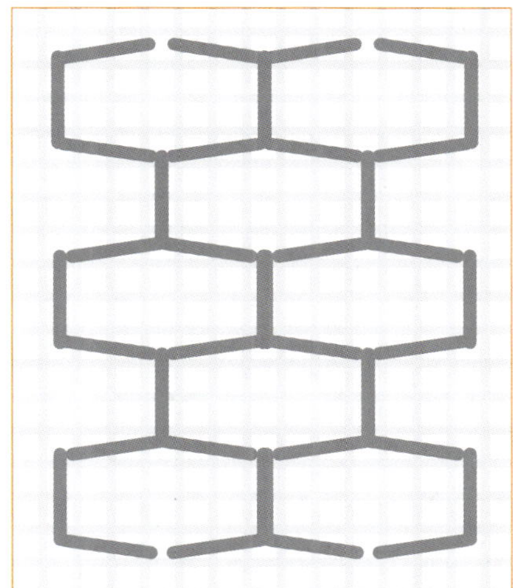

An area filled with honeycomb filling stitch.

LACE (PATTERN)

BLACKWORK.

A complex decorative blackwork pattern made up of an open cross shape and a lozenge. It is a large scale of pattern and is suitable for rounded shapes and for depicting the natural world.

METHOD

1 Study the pattern and divide it into areas that can be easily worked back and forth across the shape to be filled.

2 Systematically work across the shape using a combination of back stitch (see page 16) and double running stitch (see page 71).

LONG-TAILED DAISY STITCH

CREWELWORK; SURFACE.

Also known as Long-tailed chain stitch.

This stitch is a long-tailed version of detached chain stitch (see page 240), also known as lazy daisy stitch. It consists of a small, single chain stitch which is anchored with a long tail.

Usually found as a powdered filling in Jacobean embroidery, it may be arranged singly or in groups.

For more background, see the entry for chain stitch (see page 22).

METHOD

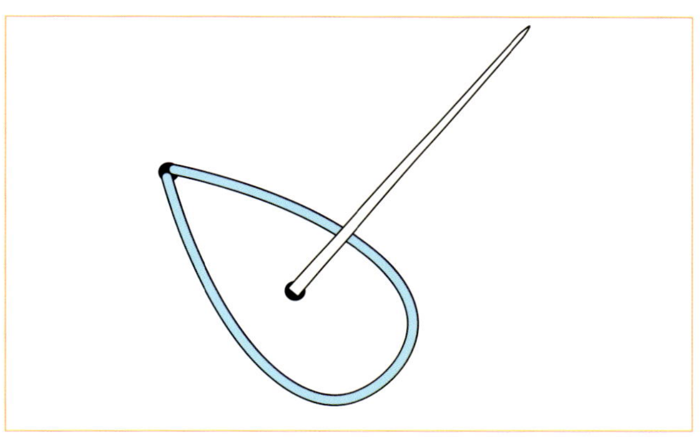

1 Bring the needle up and down in the same hole, leaving a loop on the surface. Bring the needle up in the loop.

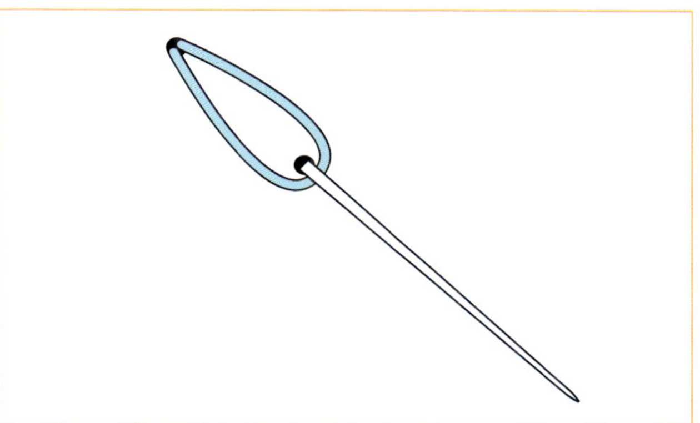

2 Pull the slack of the thread against the needle and then bring the needle through to the surface.

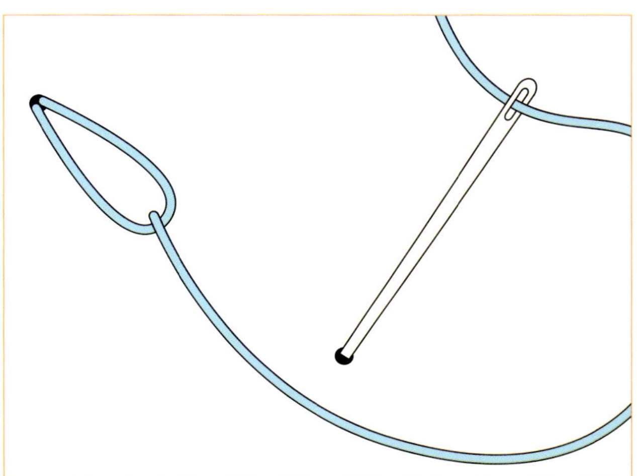

3 Decide how long the tail should be and take the needle and thread to the underside.

OCTAGON STAR (PATTERN)

Blackwork.

This blackwork pattern is made up of small squares and octagons with a star inside. It is a mid-scale pattern and is suitable for more rounded, organic shapes.

METHOD

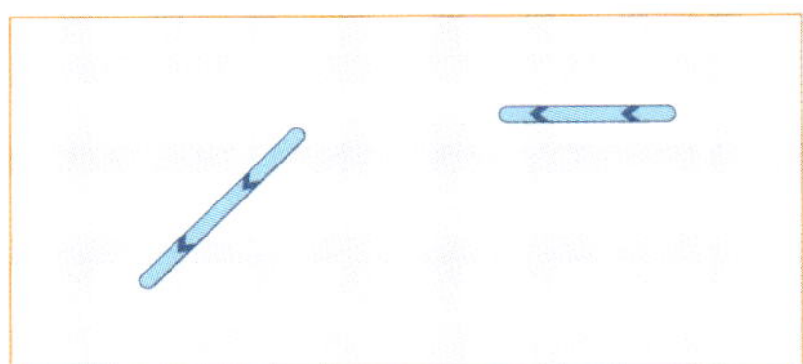

1 Stitch a horizontal stitch over two threads, miss two threads and then make a diagonal stitch over two intersections.

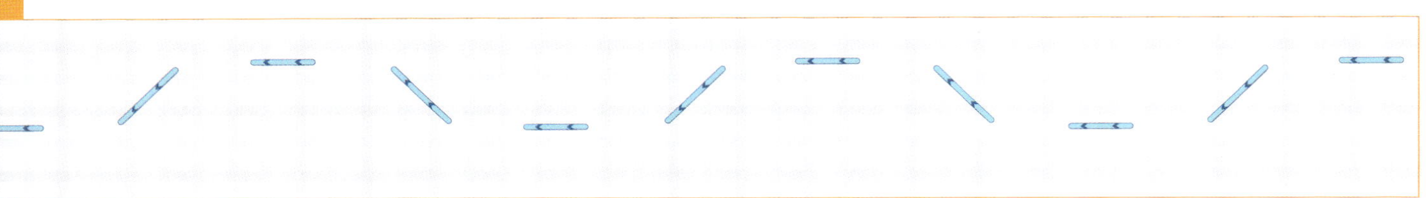

2 Continue across the width of the area to be filled with straight and diagonal stitches.

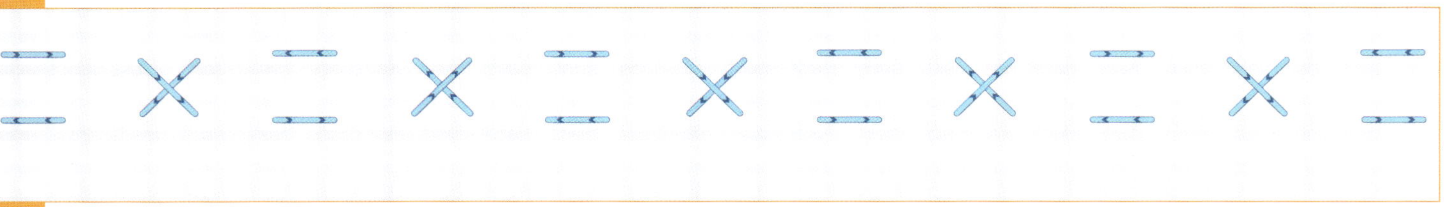

3 Return back across the area with a mirror image of the same stitches to produce a line of 'X' and '=' shapes).

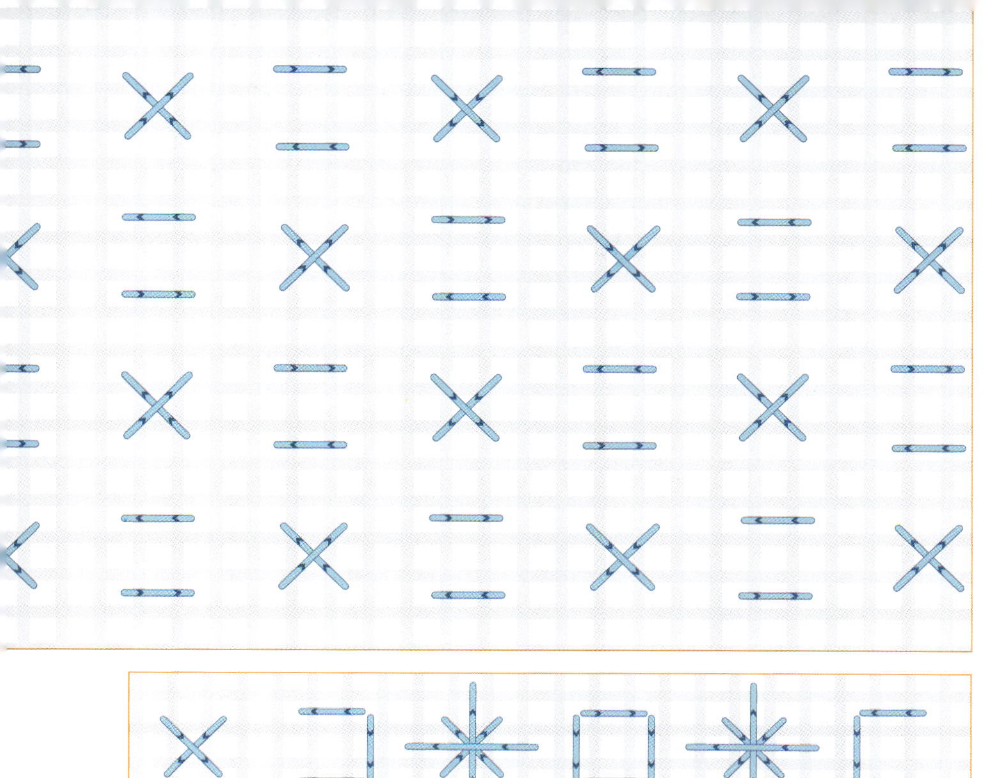

4 Continue to work horizontally to fill the shape.

5 Working up and down the shape, stitch a vertical stitch to complete the boxes, and a diagonal stitch to connect the boxes. Additionally stitch a vertical and a horizontal stitch over each cross to complete a star.

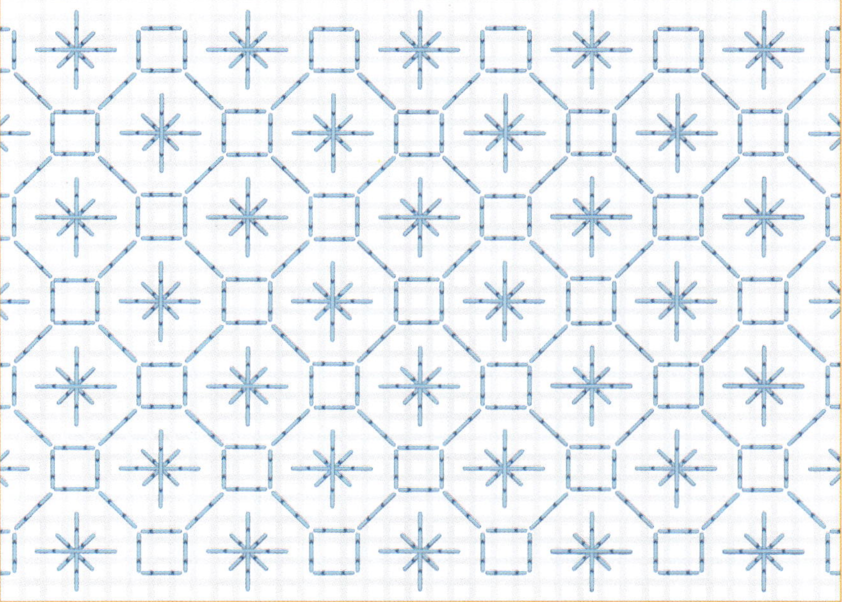

6 Continue to work up and down the shape.

PISTIL STITCH

Crewelwork; Silk shading; Surface; Stumpwork.

Also known as French knot on stalks stitch, or Long-armed French knot.

Pistil stitch consists of a straight stitch ending in a French knot (hence its alternate name of long-armed French knot).

The stitch is named for the part of a flower which sits in the very centre of the stamens and anthers and which it closely resembles. The origins of the stitch are obscure but predate the Arts and Crafts era, as it is listed as one of the range of historic stitches used by the embroiderers at Morris & Co. (William Morris' company).

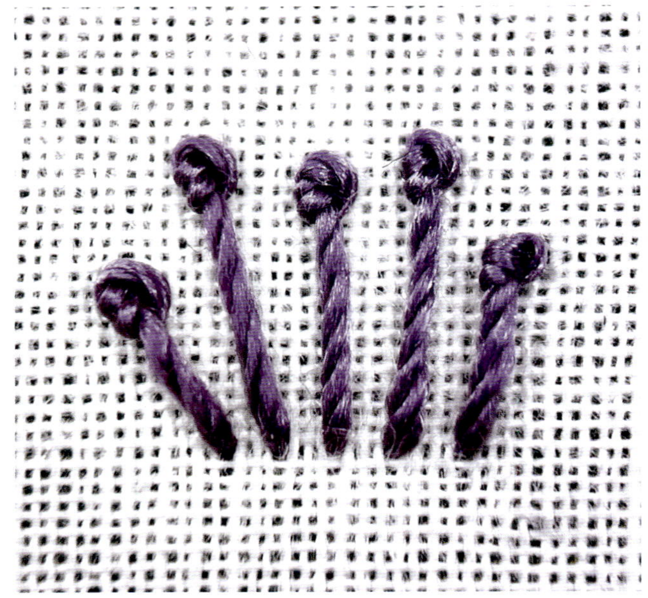

METHOD

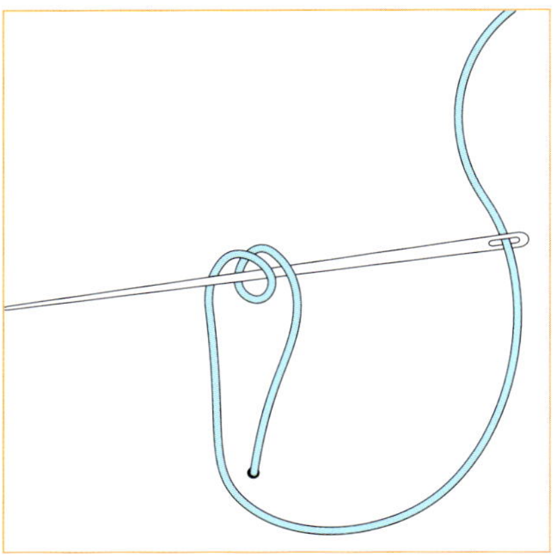

1 Bring the needle up through the fabric. Hold the needle near to where the thread emerges, then take the thread around the needle once or twice.

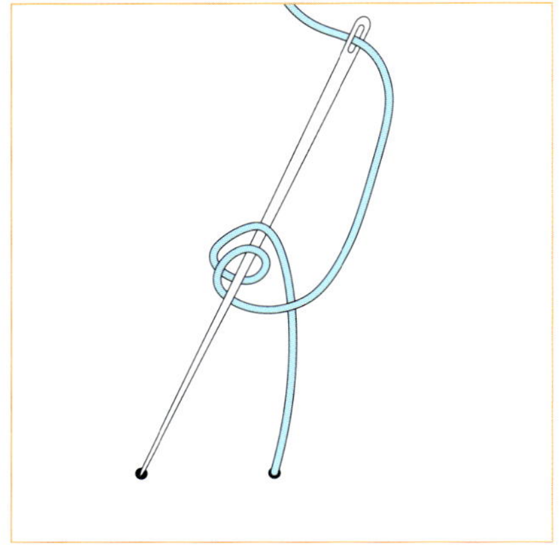

2 Place the needle part way into the fabric, a short distance from where the thread emerges.

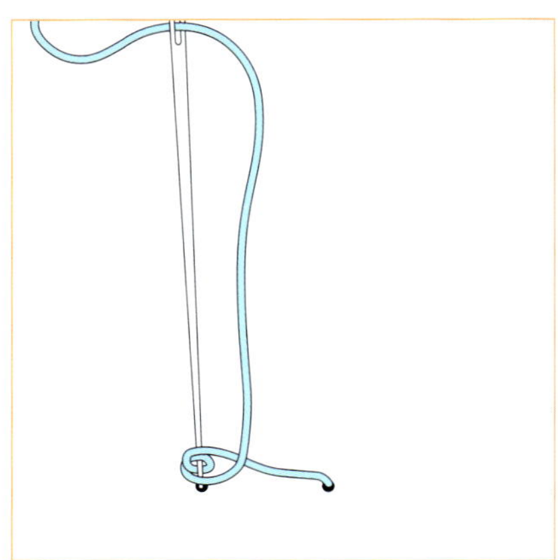

3 Holding the needle in place, draw the spiral down to the fabric surface.

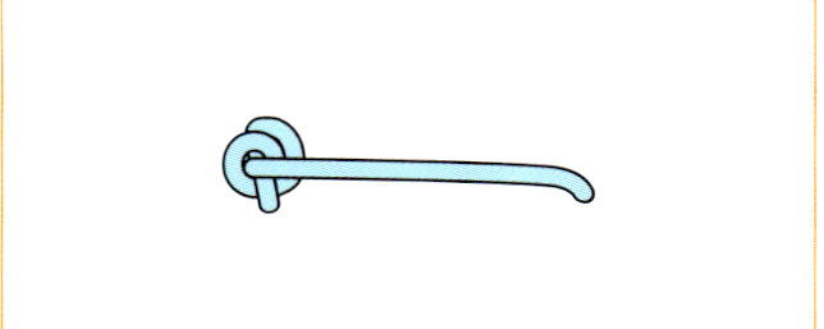

4 Keeping the thread taut, draw the needle and thread through the fabric to complete the pistil.

REVERSED FLY STITCH

SURFACE.

This stitch consists of two interlocking fly stitches: one is stitched as a 'V' or 'Y' shape, and the second is rotated 180 degrees and stitched over the top. This results in an intricate isolated stitch which can be used as an open filling or joined into lines.

METHOD

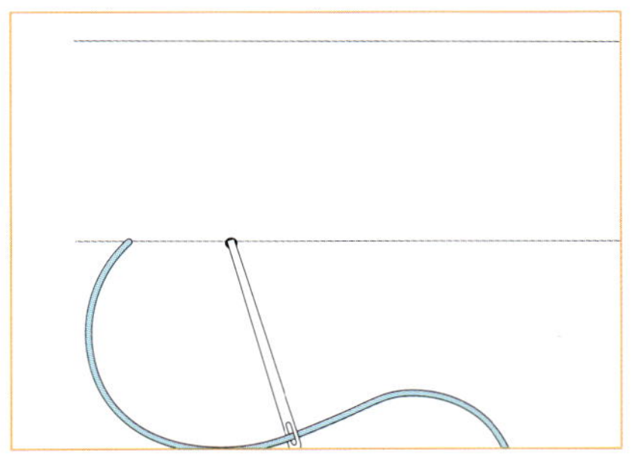

1 Bring the needle up at the left end of the bottom guide line, then take it down a short distance to the right.

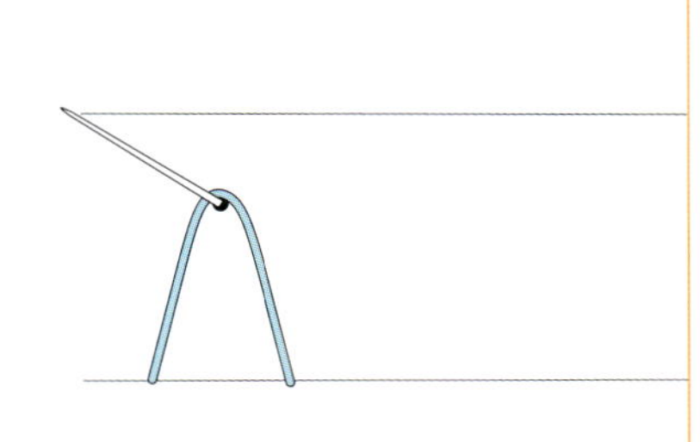

2 Leave a loop on the surface and bring up the needle inside it to form an upside-down 'V' shape. Tighten the loop against your needle.

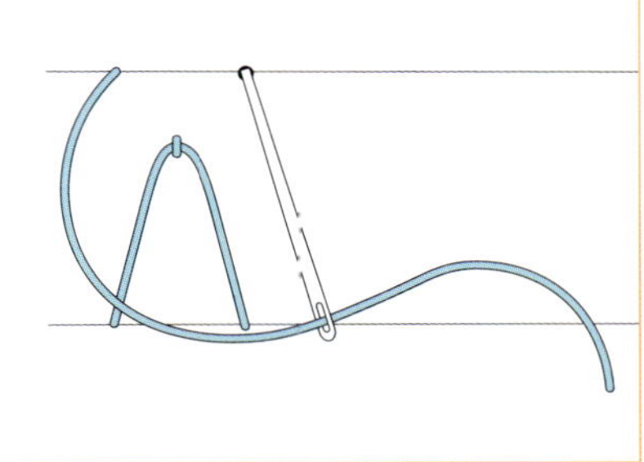

3 Take the needle down immediately outside of the 'V' to anchor the stitch. Bring the needle up on the top guide line, immediately above the start of your first stitch. Take it down on the same guide line, immediately above the end of your first stitch.

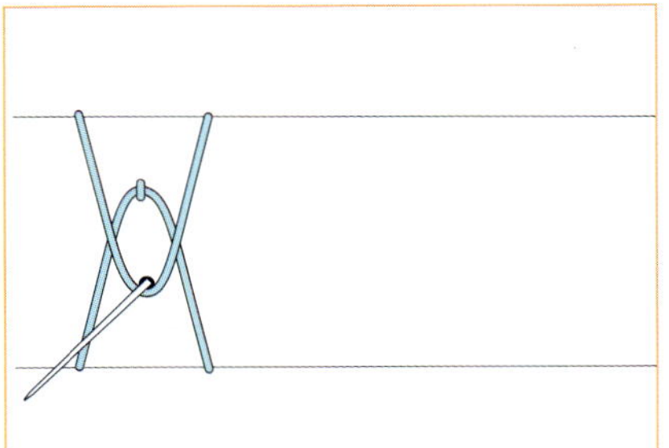

4 Leave a loop on the surface and bring up the needle inside it to form a 'V' shape. Tighten the loop against your needle.

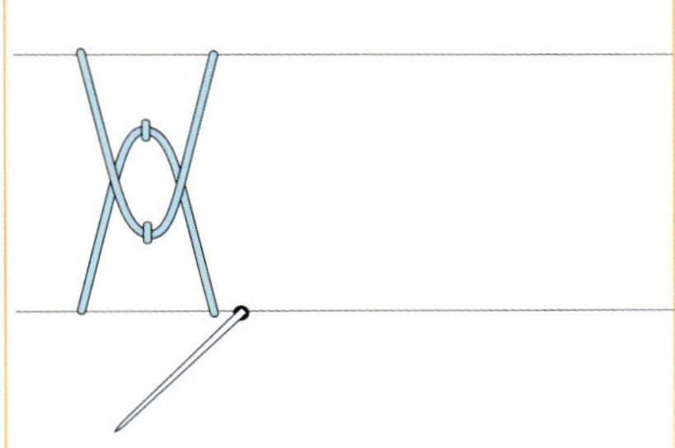

5 Take the needle down immediately outside of the 'V' to anchor your stitch. This completes your first reversed fly stitch. Bring the needle up on the bottom guide line, slightly to the right of your previous stitch.

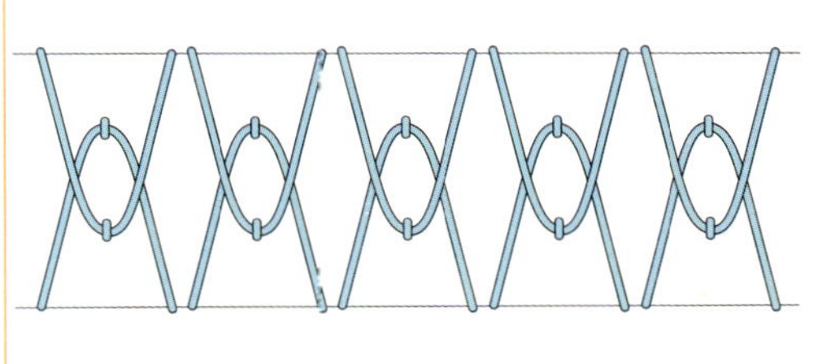

6 Repeat the steps above to form a row of stitches.

▲▲ Detail of Four-panel screen, RSN Collection

The full screen can be seen on pages 14–15.

This screen was worked by one lady in the 1920s. She combined fine shading with many different stitches, including French knots, bullion knots (see pages 29 and 299 respectively) and – shown here – seeding stitch, which has been used as an effective background covering.

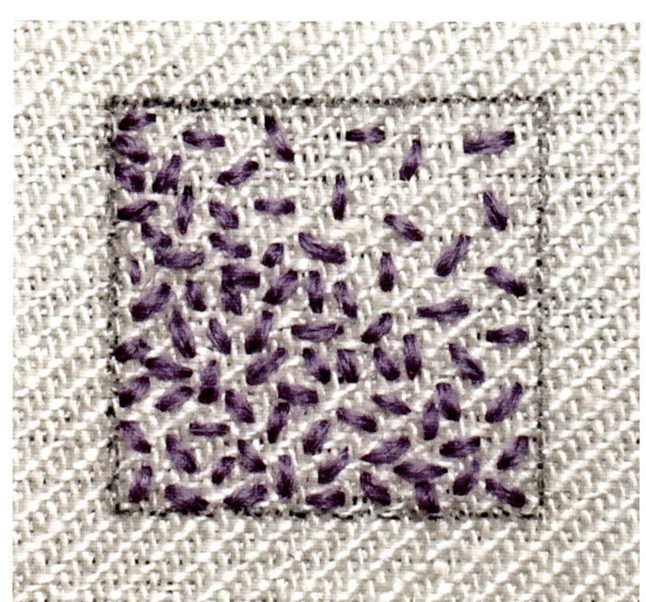

SEEDING STITCH

Crewelwork; Whitework; Mountmellick; Surface; Blackwork; Elizabethan.

Also known as Seed stitch, Speckling stitch, Isolated back stitch, or Powdering.

Small straight stitches are worked in random directions for this stitch, giving the appearance of scattered seeds. Varying the density of stitches you work over the area can produce effective shading – the more stitches, the darker the area. Working in parallel pairs makes the stitches easier to see from a distance which is perfect for larger scale embroideries.

Seeding stitch was one of those used by the ancient Egyptians and has featured in many embroidery traditions since then: a 16th-century sampler, a mid 17th-century embroidery picture of King Charles I and King Charles II (both pieces held by the V&A South Kensington); and a set of 18th-century crewel New England bed curtains all feature seeding stitch.

Seeding also features in Rabat embroidery, a technique dating back to 17th century Morocco; Guimarães embroidery, a 19th-century technique from northern Portugal; and Rice embroidery, a whitework tradition popular in North America and Western Europe.

METHOD

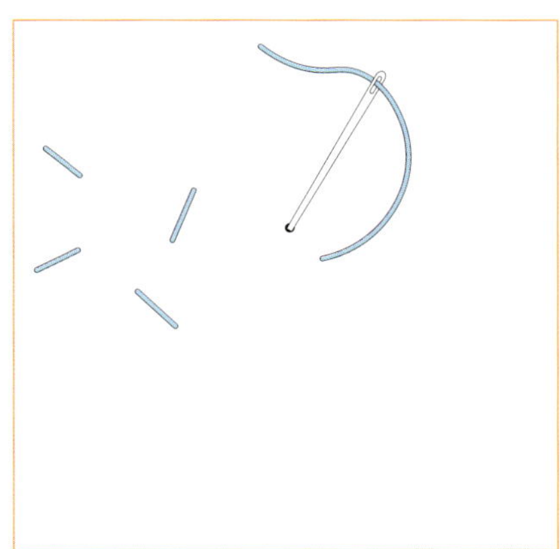

1 Working stitches in random directions, fill the area by making tiny straight stitches, each approximately 1–2mm ($\frac{1}{16}$–$\frac{1}{8}$in) long.

2 Pack the stitches closely together for a dense appearance.

3 Spread the stitches further away from each other to create lighter shading.

SINGLE FAGGOT STITCH

PULLED THREAD; WHITEWORK.

Also known as Diagonal line stitch, Diagonal square stitch, Four-sided stitch, or Square openwork stitch.

Single faggot stitch is a simple pulled thread stitch worked on the diagonal. It is the foundation for a variety of diagonal stitches.

Reversed faggot stitch, as the name suggests, is the same as the reverse of this stitch.

Multiple rows of this stitch have similarities with a diagonal version of four-sided stitch (see page 250–251), although the reverse is different. Some texts suggest they are the same stitch (hence the alternative name) but there are subtle differences in the direction of each component of the stitch.

In her *Encyclopedia of Needlework*, Thérèse de Dillmont calls this 'Third pattern'.

METHOD

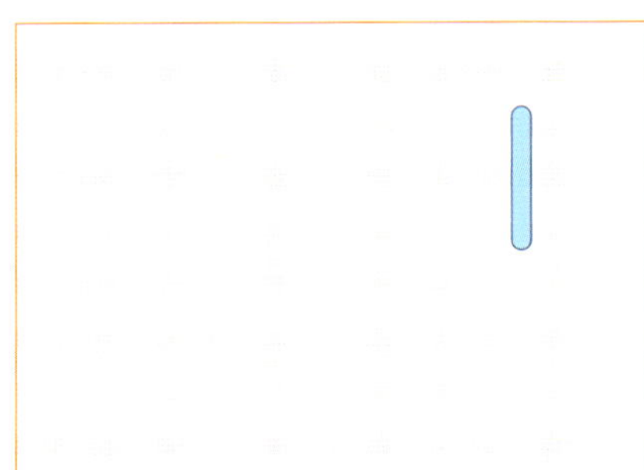

1 Bring the needle up just inside your outline. Make a vertical stitch up over three threads.

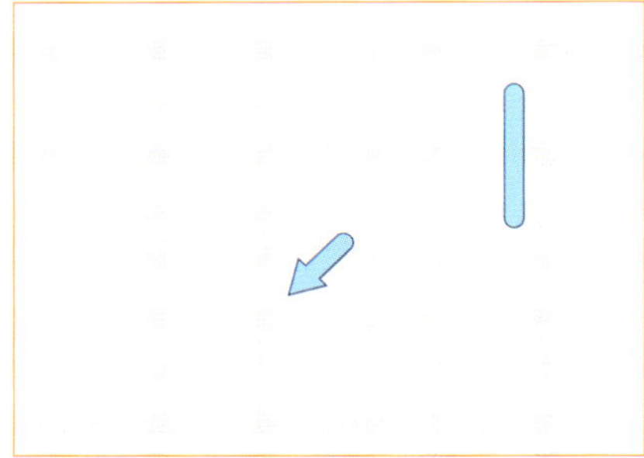

2 Count left three and down three, bring the needle up and pull.

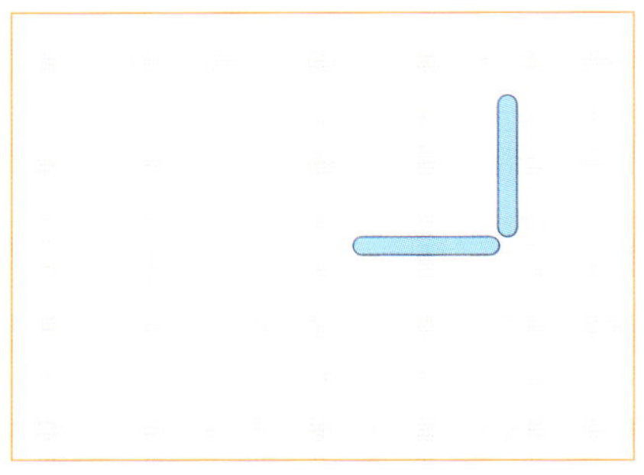

3 Make a horizontal stitch three to the right, back down into the first hole.

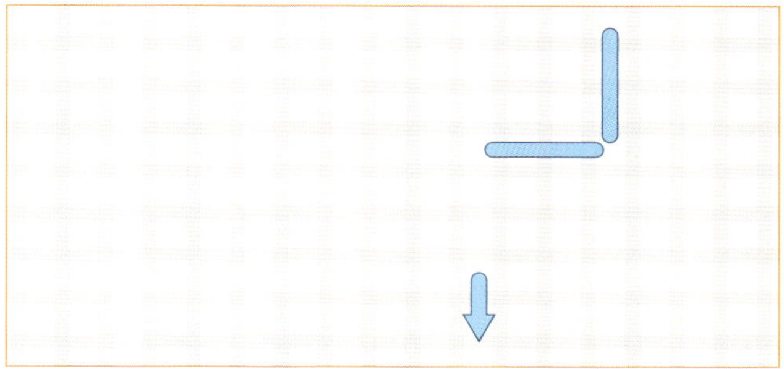

4 Count three left and three down, bring the needle up and pull.

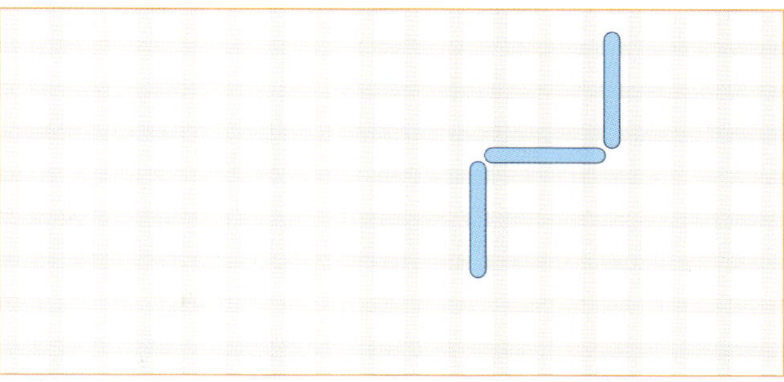

5 Make a vertical stitch up over three threads, into the previous hole. Repeat to complete the first row.

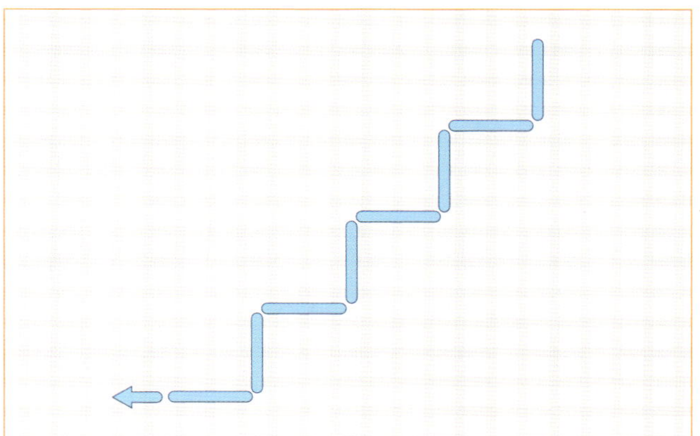

6 To begin the second row, bring the needle up through the last hole of the previous row and make a horizontal stitch over three threads to the left.

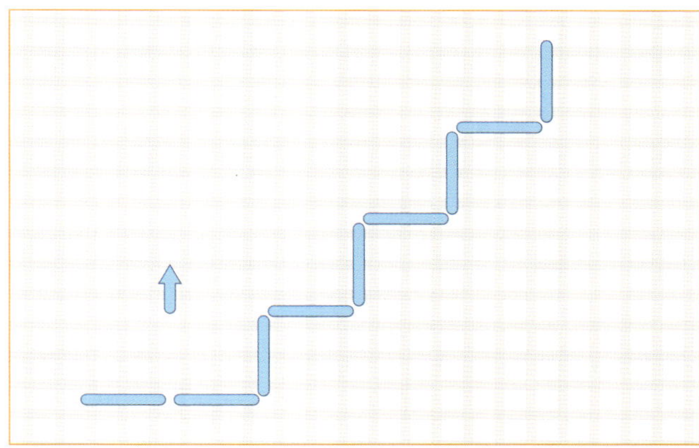

7 Count right three and up three, bring the needle up and pull.

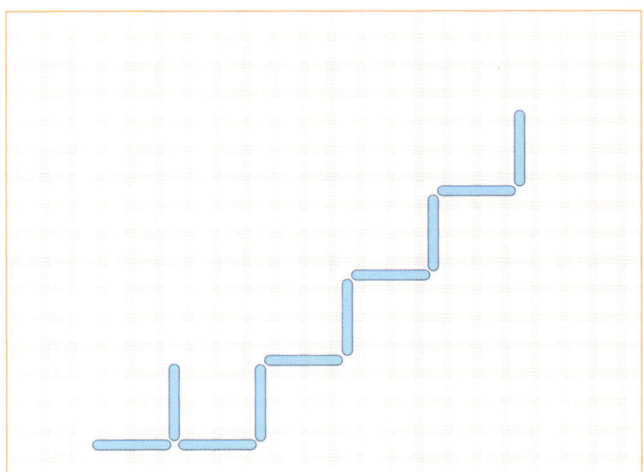

8 Make a vertical stitch down over three threads, into the hole of the previous row. Repeat to complete the row.

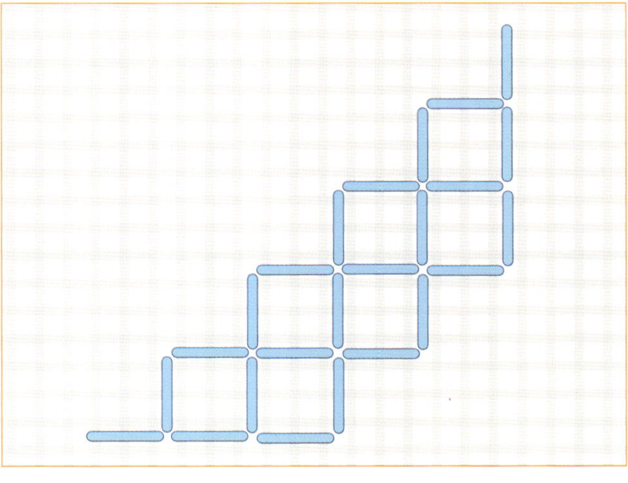

9 Continue creating more rows as above to complete single faggot stitch.

SPANGLES HELD ON WITH PURLS

Goldwork.

Spangles may be stitched down in a variety of decorative ways, either individually or in lines, with fancy stitching with coloured silk threads. Alternatively, they can be held down with chips, looped chips, beads or, invisibly, in fish-scale stitching which results in the overlapping spangles concealing the stitch that holds down the previous spangle.

Spangles have a long history across the world, with examples on Korean crowns having been dated to the 6th century. European clothing and artefacts decorated with spangles date back to the 16th century – initially for royalty, but eventually becoming used by nobility, in military uniforms, and beyond: they feature on a revolutionary cap from the French revolution now held by the Museum of Fine Arts, Boston.

METHOD

1 Cut a good number of small chips from a length of metal thread; this example shows Bright check.

2 Using a double waxed thread, bring the needle through to the surface of the fabric from underneath.

3 Thread on a single spangle ...

4 ... and gently manoeuvre it to the base of the thread, ideally without touching it with your fingers to prevent it tarnishing in the future.

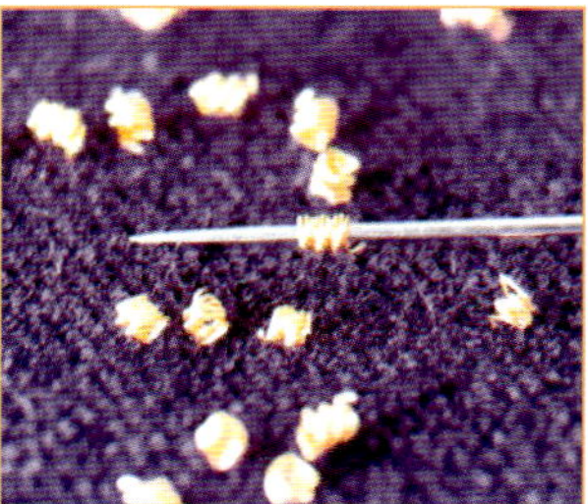

5 Thread a purl chip onto the needle ...

6 ... and gently manoeuvre it to the base of the thread on top of the spangle.

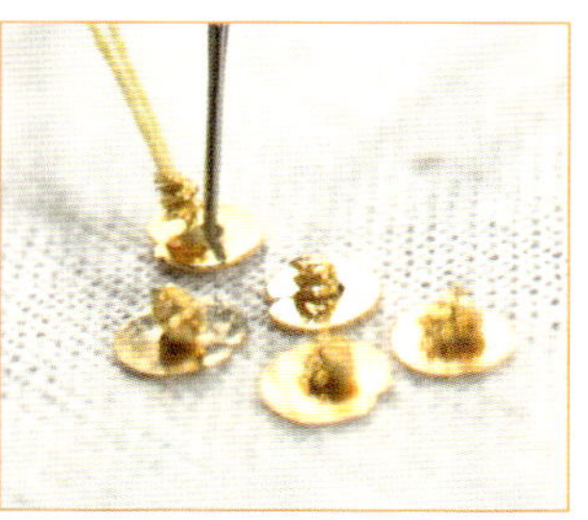

7 Stitch the purl chip in place by taking the needle back down through the spangle centre ...

8 ... leaving the purl chip on top to hold the spangle in place.

▲▲ Detail from letter heading, RSN Collection No. 4

The accompanying envelope can be seen on pages 296–297.

The text originally printed onto the silk has now faded, but the metal thread embroidery remains in splendid condition. It is an example of zardozi embroidery, a technique of using metal-bound threads that originated in Persia and developed in India, where this piece was made. Here amidst the fine filigree work, a lion and unicorn are subtly incorporated into the design, reflecting British Rule in India.

Spangles are used en masse to cover larger areas in the design, and also individually in the borders, where they are held on by beads.

SQUARE BOSS STITCH

SURFACE.

Also known as Raised knot, or Square boss.

This is a cross stitch with a diagonal stitch over each of its corners, which join to form a raised square. The stitch is normally used as an isolated stitch, although it can be worked in rows to form a border, or as a filling stitch either evenly spaced or randomly scattered.

Rice stitch (canvaswork) (see page 190) is a similar stitch which is used as a canvaswork filling stitch.

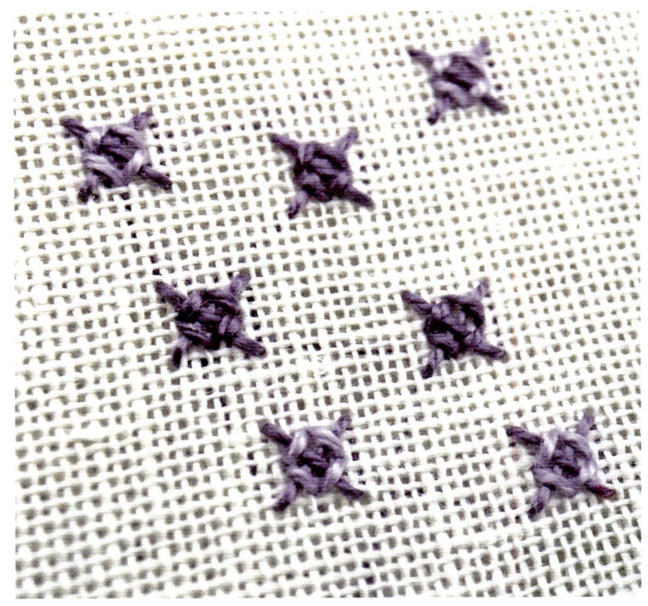

METHOD

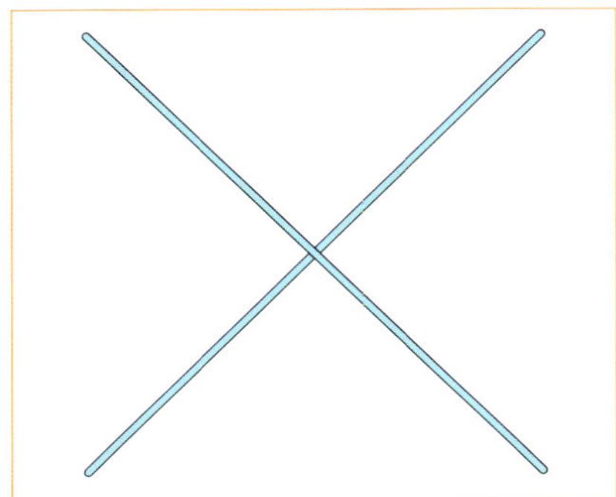

1 First, work a cross stitch.

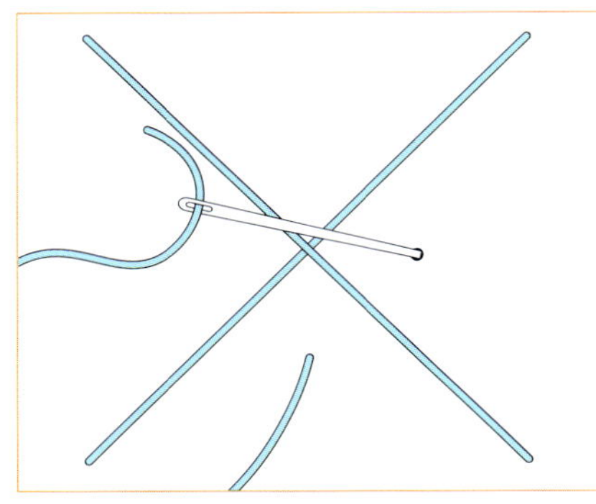

2 Then work a back stitch over the bottom right arm of the cross stitch.

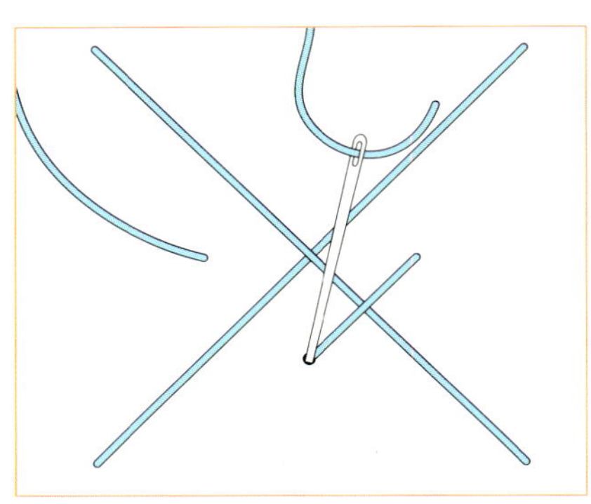

3 Next, cover the bottom left arm of the cross stitch with a back stitch – your stitch should end where the previous back stitch started.

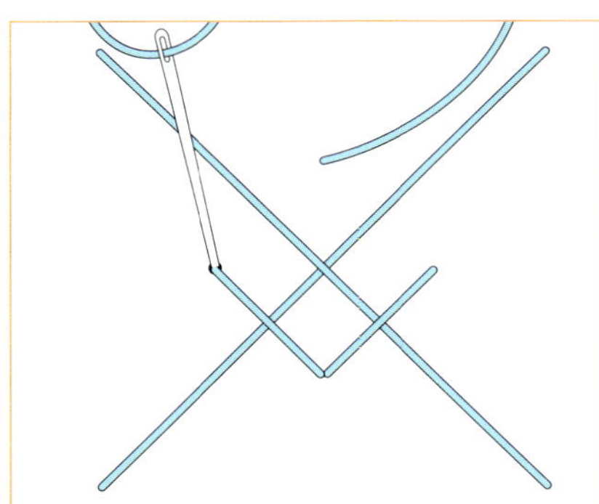

4 Work another back stitch, this time to cover the top left arm of the cross stitch, again sharing a hole with the previous stitch.

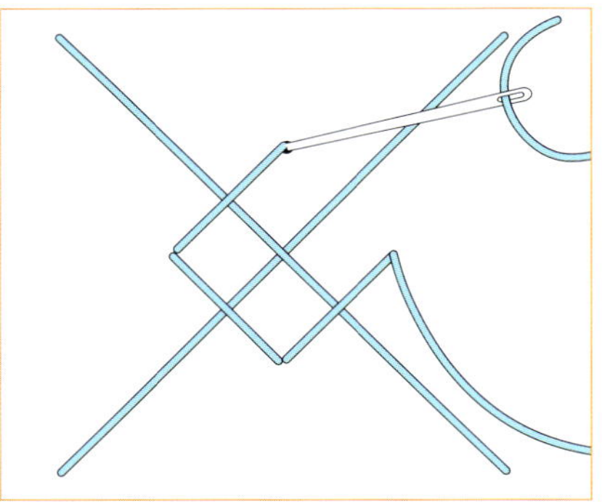

5 Finally, cover the top right arm of the cross stitch with a back stitch – this stitch should complete the square.

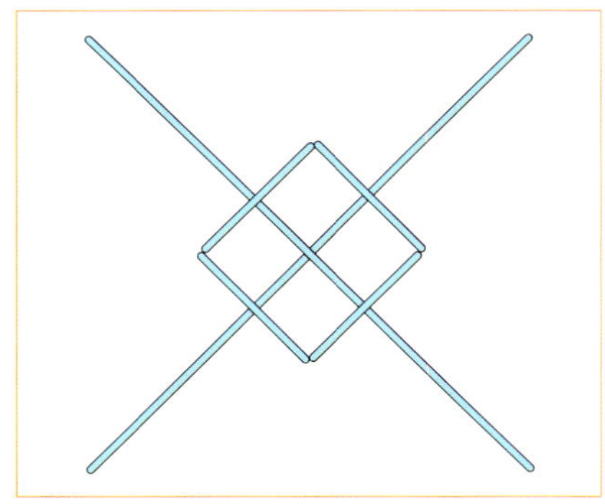

A completed square boss stitch.

TÊTE DE BOEUF STITCH

Surface; Crewelwork.

Also known as Ox head stitch, Ox-horn stitch, or Buffalo stitch.

Tête de boeuf stitch consists of a detached chain stitch with the addition of two slanting stitches above the chain stitch. The resulting stitch resembles the head and horns of a bull.

A charming decorative stitch that can be used in isolation or in a group as an open filling, tête de boeuf stitch was documented in use in the 1880s. Because both stitches consist of a detached chain stitch plus two extra small stitches, it has been confused with detached wheatear stitch (see page 241) and it is now not unusual for embroidery sources to swap the names of the stitches in error. However, the strong resemblance of the version illustrated here to the head of a bull suggests that this is the correct way to stitch it.

METHOD

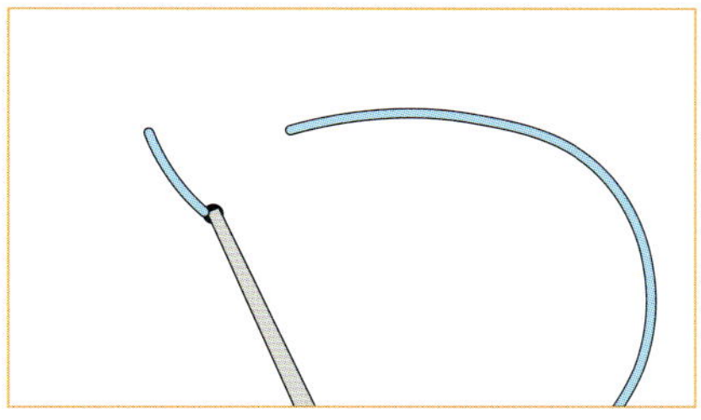

1 Make two slanting stitches, a short distance apart at the top and meeting at the bottom.

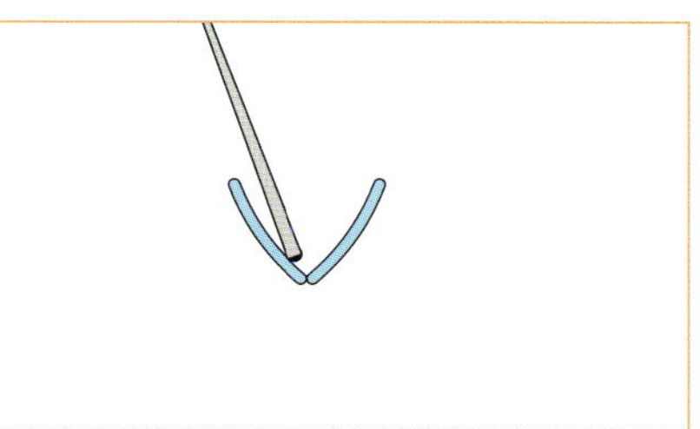

2 Bring the thread out a little above the bottom of the slanting stitches.

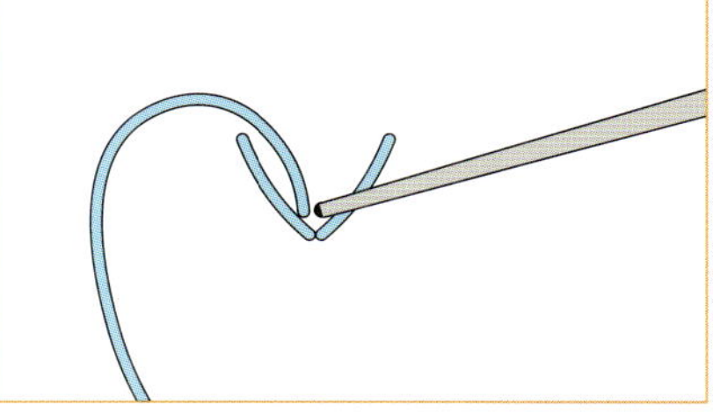

3 Insert the needle close to it and leave a loop on the surface.

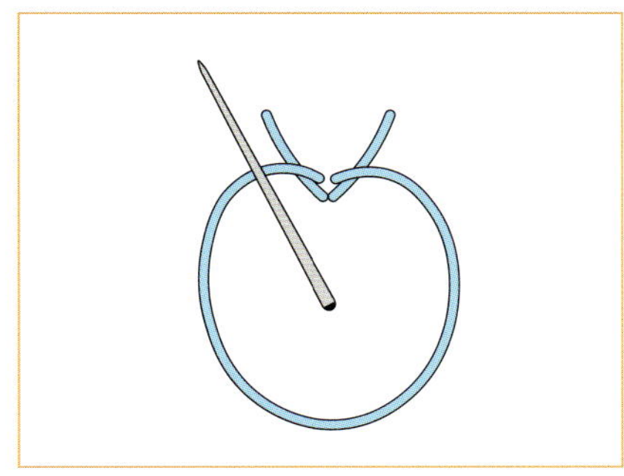

4 Bring the needle up from below, ensuring it comes up in the loop, central to the shape.

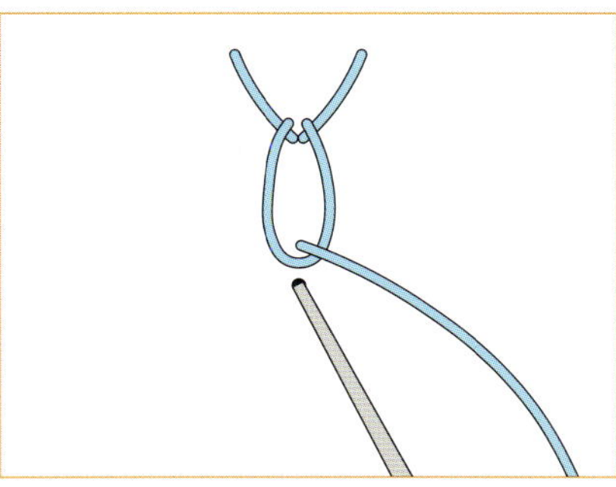

5 Tighten the loop against the needle and secure the loop into position.

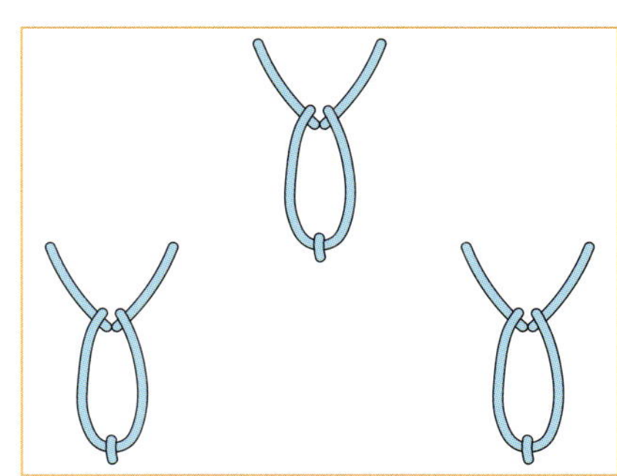

Completed tête de boeuf stitches.

THREE-SIDED STITCH

WHITEWORK; PULLED THREAD.

Also known as Bermuda faggoting, Lace stitch, Point Turc, Turkish stitch.

This pulled work stitch consists of two parallel lines connected by a pattern of zigzags which provide the triangle effect. The stitches are worked a second time over the original ones, which pulls the fabric slightly tighter and gives a heavier line. Each stitch is doubled on the right side of the fabric, but the diagonal stitches are single on the reverse side.

Three-sided stitch can be used as a border or as a filling by stitching multiple rows.

METHOD

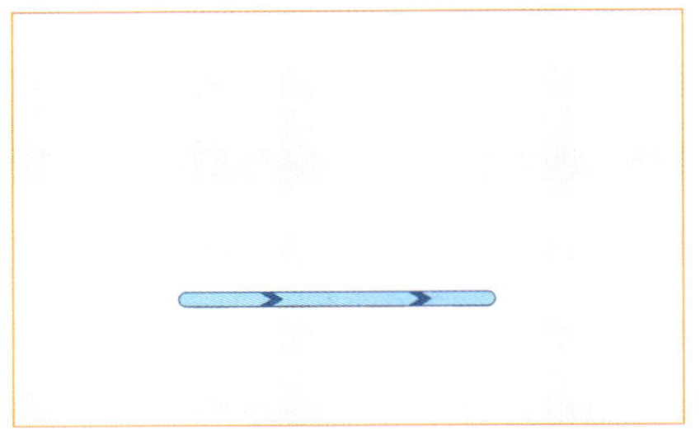

1 Bring the needle up four threads from the edge of the area to be filled, then take the needle down four threads to the right.

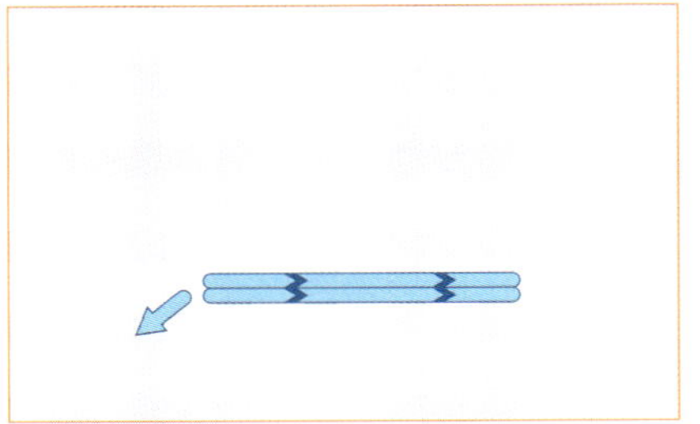

2 Come up again where it first emerged. Repeat this to make two stitches using the same holes.

TIP

Think of this as making a back stitch (see page 16) twice; one on top of the other.

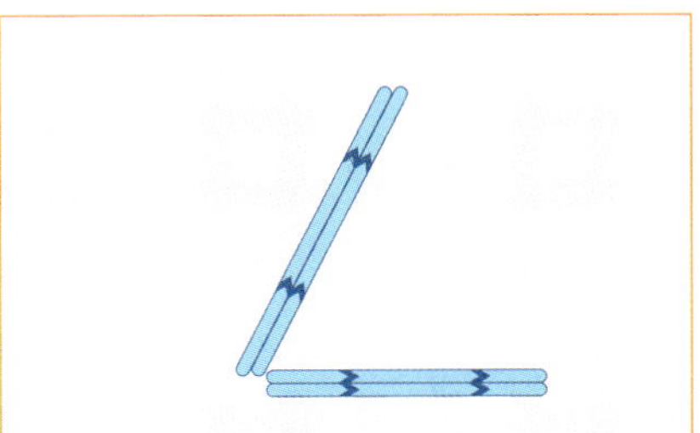

3 Make a pair of diagonal stitches: insert the needle four threads up and two threads to the right and then make a second stitch over this one.

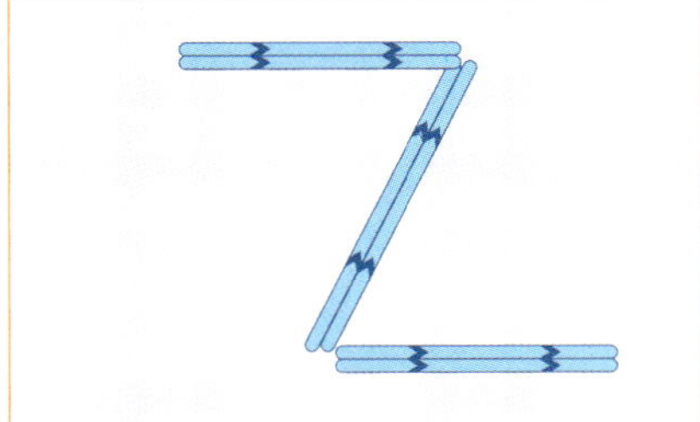

4 Make another pair of back stitches, bringing the needle up four threads to the left after the end of the diagonal stitches.

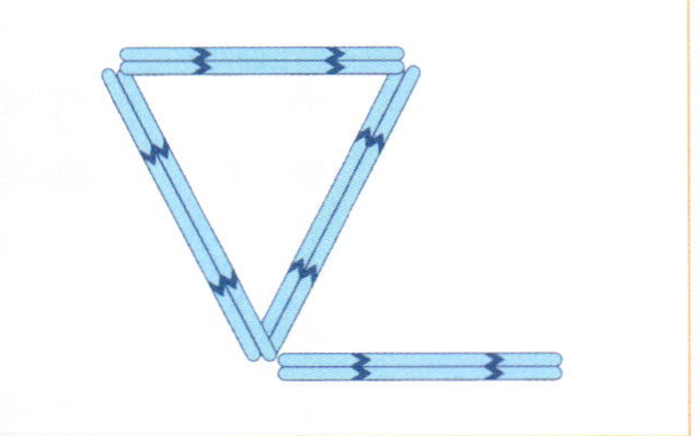

5 Make another pair of diagonal stitches, bringing the needle up four threads down and two threads to the right, which is where the first pair started.

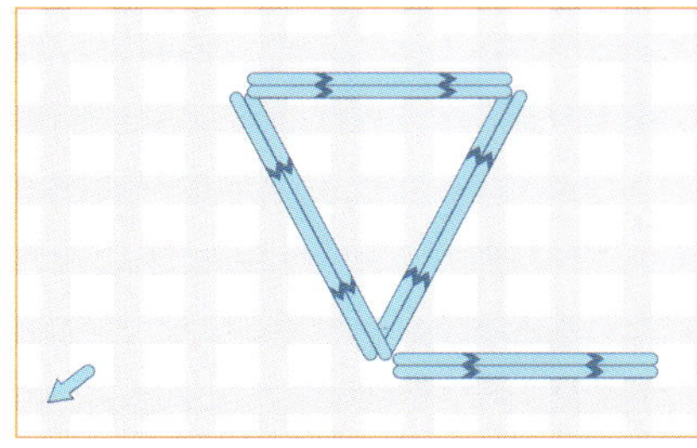

6 Make another pair of back stitches, bringing the needle up four threads to the left.

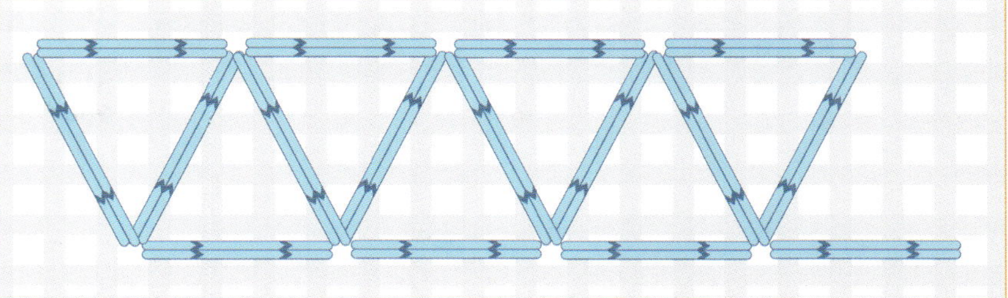

7 Repeat the process.

◂◂ 20th-century Jacobean sampler, RSN Collection No. 1222

Crewelwork enjoyed a revival in the 19th century thanks to the Arts and Crafts movement, which saw a resurgence of historic embroidery techniques. Frequently depicting animals or – as shown here – foliage, this style lent itself to the use of many different stitches, ranging from the complex to the very simple.

Trellis stitch (see overleaf) forms a filling for the petals of a blue flower, but even basic stitches like buttonhole (see pages 20–21), visible in the yellow part of the flower at the bottom right, are used to decorative effect in this style.

TRELLIS

CREWELWORK; SURFACE; MOUNTMELLICK.

Also known as Trellis filling, Square laid filling, Squared laid work, Couched filling stitch, or Jacobean couching.

A fast filling stitch useful in filling large areas quickly, it comprises of a grid framework, upon which other stitches may be worked to decorative effect.

This stitch consists of rows of long horizontal and vertical single stitches, perpendicular to each other, that cover the required area. A small stitch is then placed at each point where the two threads cross over one another to secure the trellis pattern.

Trellis dates from Jacobean crewelwork where it was used, alongside its variation cross bar filling trellis (see page 238), to fill large areas of designs.

METHOD

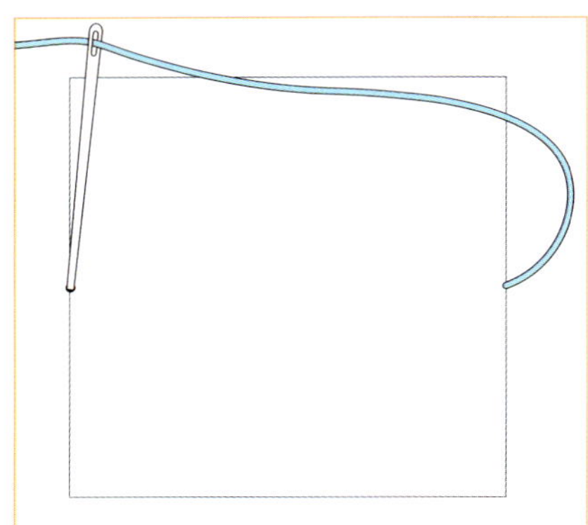

1 Bring the needle up at the edge of the area to be filled, and take it down on the edge directly opposite. It is advantageous to start in the centre or the widest part of the area to be filled.

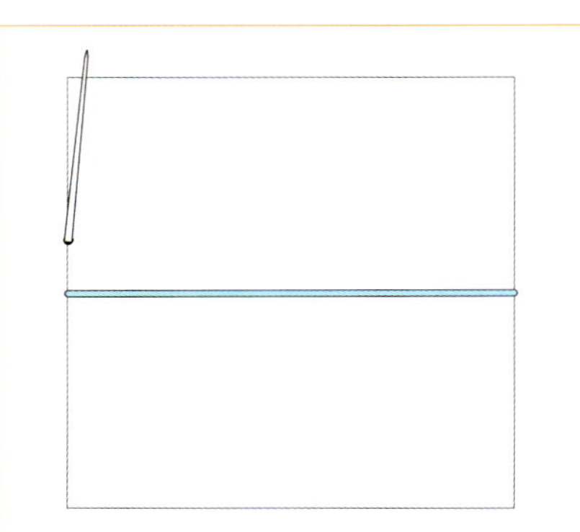

2 Pull the thread through so that the first stitch lies directly across the centre of the shape, then bring the needle up through the fabric further along the design.

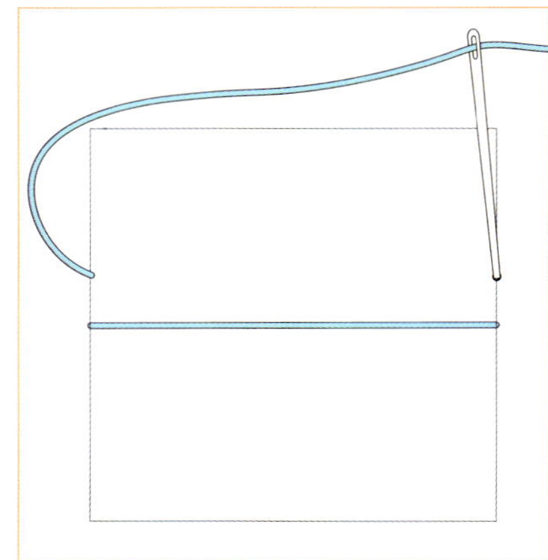

3 Take the needle down directly opposite, ensuring that the stitches lie parallel, to create a series of evenly spaced open laid stitches.

4 Continue to work one half of the shape in the same way, by building up parallel lines. Be careful to space them evenly.

5 Once you have completed this half of the shape, work the remainder in the same way, working away from the first stitch in the centre.

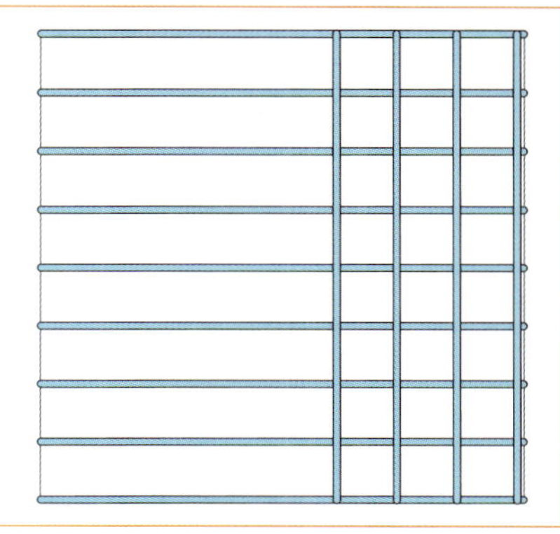

6 Again, starting in the centre or the widest part of the area to be filled, work perpendicular parallel stitches to cover one side.

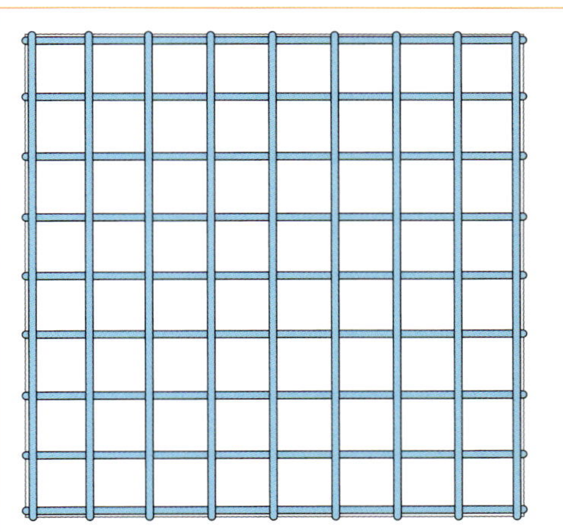

7 Work the other side in the same way and fasten off the thread on the paint line. You can hide the paint line later with an outline stitch.

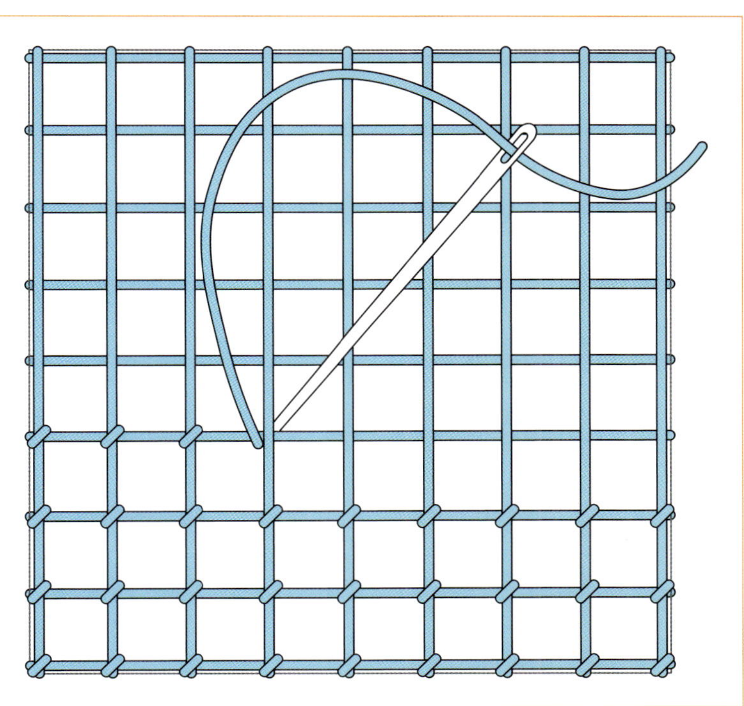

8 For a plain basic trellis, anchor each intersection with a small diagonal stitch.

TIP

This framework is the basis for a range of other open filling stitches. You can anchor the intersection using a variety of decorative stitches, such as battlement couching (see page 232) or cross bar filling trellis (see page 238).

WAVE STITCH FILLING (PULLED THREAD)

PULLED THREAD; WHITEWORK.

Wave stitch is a pulled whitework stitch that is very useful for filling small areas. It uses diagonal stitches in a 'V' format to give a wave effect.

Some modern authors call this wave stitch, but we have retained the original name of wave stitch filling to avoid confusion.

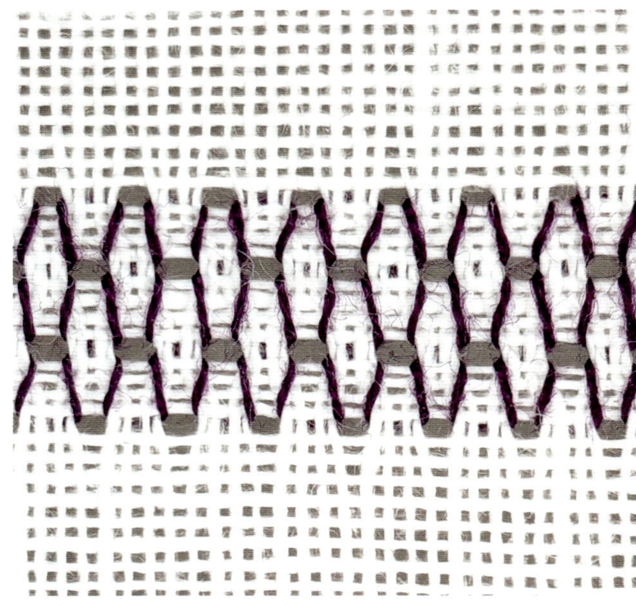

METHOD

1 Work from left to right to start with. Bring the needle up two threads inside your outline. Count left two and up four and take the needle down. Next, count right four, bring the needle up and pull tight.

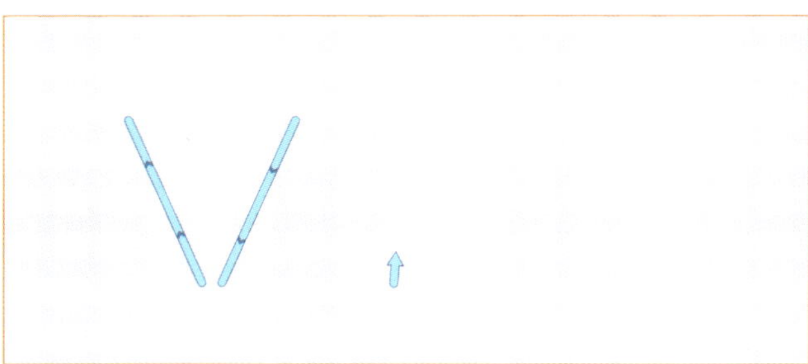

2 Take the needle back through the first hole (left two and down four). Next, count right four, bring the needle up and pull. Repeat to complete the first row.

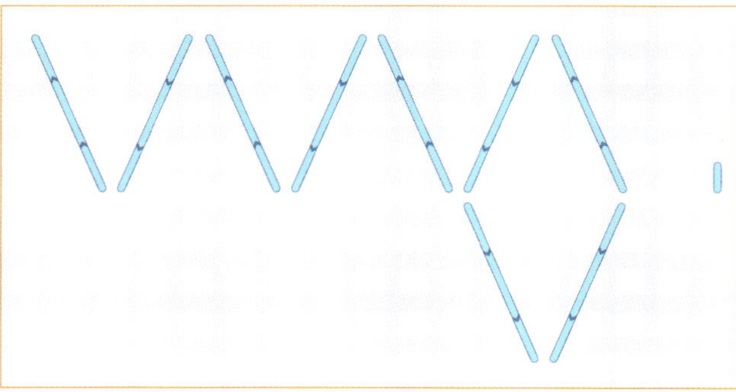

3 Make a holding stitch on the outline or in the border where this holding stitch will be covered later on. Then, count left two and down four from the last bottom hole of the previous row and bring the needle up. Take the needle down through the last bottom hole of the previous row.

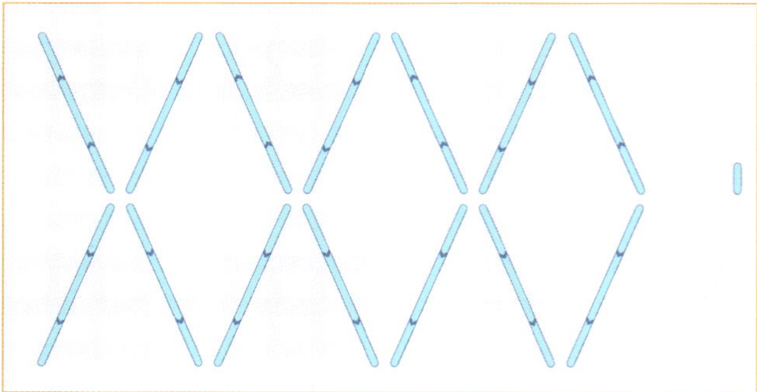

4 The second row is worked from right to left in the same manner. Continue until the design area is filled. Make sure to pull the thread tight each time.

ZIGZAG (PATTERN)

Blackwork.

A blackwork pattern where lines are formed by vertical rows of small zigzags, with each stitch worked diagonally over the fabric. It is quite a dense pattern, good for creating a linear effect.

METHOD

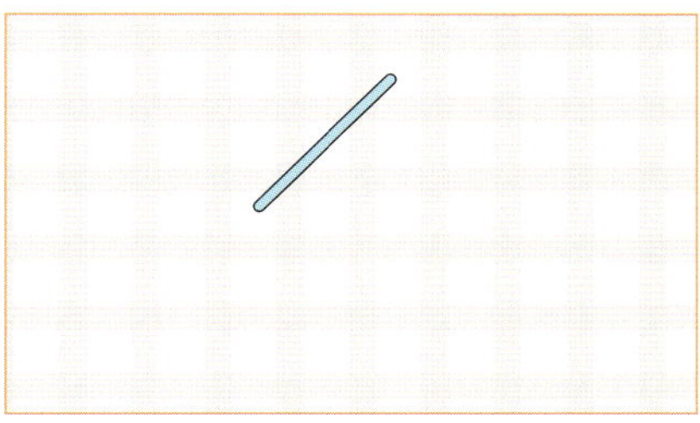

1 Make a diagonal stitch from top right to bottom left over two intersections.

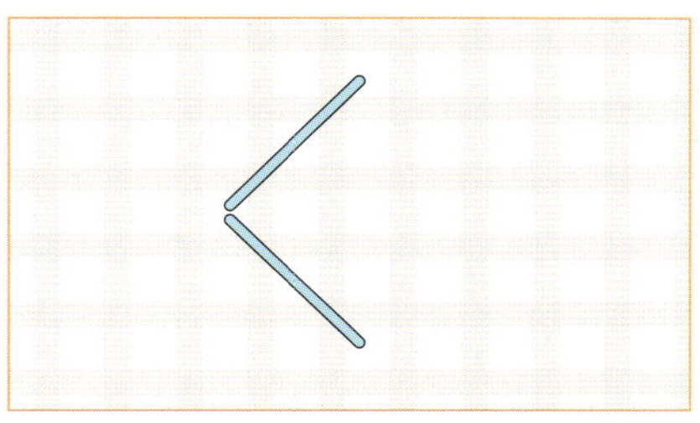

2 Bring the needle up two intersections down to the right and complete a diagonal stitch connected to the last.

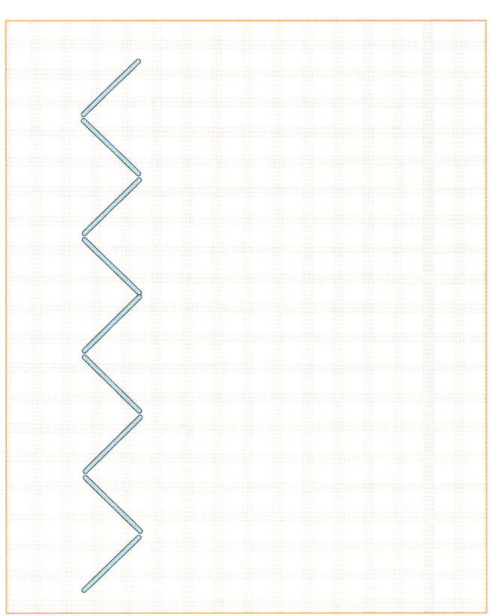

3 Repeat the last two steps and continue to work a zigzag column.

4 Working back up the shape, complete another identical column two threads away from the previous one.

5 Continue working columns across the shape, ensuring each stitch is in line with the stitches in the previous column.

EDGING STITCHES

As the name suggests, these are stitches which are used on the edges of fabric. They either bind the edge itself or are used to embellish it. You will have seen two of the most popular edging stitches (buttonhole and blanket) in the Basic stitches chapter (pages 12–43) and, as you can see from the names of the edging stitches, they form the basis of many of them.

Those stitches which bind a fabric edge form a dual function: they prevent the edge of the fabric from fraying and they also provide a decorative effect. Edging stitches can either be worked around the edge of a piece of fabric or to edge a hole which has been cut into it. There is a long tradition within various forms of whitework of cutting decorative holes into fabric and then binding those holes with an edge stitch. Sometimes picots (nodules made of wrapped or knotted threads) are added to embellish these edges (for a different type of picot which embellishes the surface rather than edge of the fabric, see embellishment stitches on pages 292–333).

Some of the stitches are depicted on an edge which has already been cut, as with overcast edging. Others, like buttonhole edging, are shown worked on a flat piece of fabric which is then trimmed up to the stitch. Both methods are widely used and depend on the required stitch, type of fabric and the stitcher's personal preference.

Some of the edging stitches can also be worked as a surface stitch rather than on the edge of fabric: long and short blanket stitch and up and down blanket stitch both fall into this category.

PAGE 283

PAGE 284

PAGE 285

PAGE 286

PAGE 287

PAGE 288

PAGE 290

▸▸ Pocket, RSN Collection No. 760

Early 19th-century pocket with surface embroidery on ecru silk, with floral and geometric motifs in green, brown and ecru silk thread and moralistic inscriptions in grey cross stitch. The pocket is edged with a dark pink silk fringe and features a horizontal opening slit edged with buttonhole stitch (see pages 20–21) in dark green thread.

This object was very likely made by a girl in an orphanage or charity school. Objects like pockets, samplers, hussifs, watch papers, and pillows were often embroidered by schoolgirls in orphan or charity schools and sold by the school to raise money. Many of these objects originally meant for sale lack names and dates. This pocket was probably meant to be hung on the wall and used to hold small items.

EMBROIDERY TECHNIQUE: WHITEWORK

Whitework is an overarching term used to describe white embroidery on white fabric. There are many different forms of whitework from across the world, but the absence of colour means that texture takes precedence in all of them.

Texture in whitework is achieved through a wide variety of methods: by raising stitches through padding or the use of needlelace; by creating holes in the fabric by the use of eyelets, cutwork or drawn thread work; by manipulating the ground fabric through pulled thread work; by stitching into net; or by the use of thread with a contrasting finish to the fabric.

Some whitework techniques use just one or two of these methods: e.g. Mountmellick uses a matt thread on a glazed fabric and also pads some stitches; other techniques use several methods, e.g. Ayrshire uses padded stitches, needlelace, cutwork, drawn work and pulled work.

Early forms of whitework are worked on linen as it can withstand bleaching and is strong enough to have threads removed or manipulated. Its strength also means it is sufficiently robust for functional items such as clothing and household items which require laundering. Over time cotton and silk have become popular for some techniques, but linen's strength means it is still widely used.

▸▸ Blouse, RSN Collection COL.1996.41

Unfinished silk crepe de chine blouse made in Madeira, Portugal in the 1950s. The blouse is white with floral cutwork panels at the chest, collar, and cuffs.

The front panels of this blouse are tacked together, the collar is not completely attached, and the cuffs (which also include chain stitches) have not been cut out. It is not known why this blouse was not completed, but its precise folding and tacking stitches suggest it was a sort of kit that was to be finished later.

Madeira blouses were very popular throughout Europe and the United States in the 1950s. Like this blouse, they are white and feature decorative cutwork and fine embroidery. Madeira embroidery, which emerged in the middle of the 19th century, is a form of Broderie Anglaise made by hand by the women on the island.

The letters on the blouse's stamp suggest this blouse may be associated with Imperial de Bordados, a company founded in 1926 to produce Madeira embroidery and still in business today.

▴▴ Detail of buttonhole edging – page 283

▴▴ Detail of satin stitch – page 37

BULLION PICOT

WHITEWORK; CUTWORK; NEEDLEPOINT LACE.

Also known as Point d'Espagne edging, or Picots in bullion stitch.

This edging stitch consists of a bullion knot which starts and ends at the same point to form a ring which protrudes from the edge of the fabric.

Bullion picots were evidently in use by the Victorian era as they appear in two publications from 1870: *Beeton's Book of Needlework* (in which it is called 'Point d'Espagne edging'), and Victor Touche's *The Handbook of Point Lace* (in which it is called 'Raleigh bars'). Evidence of their use prior to this date is hard to find, but much of the literature referring to picots doesn't specify their design and so it is likely that bullion picots had been in existence for a considerable time.

METHOD

1 Work buttonhole stitches along the edge. When you reach the point where you wish to make a picot, insert the needle back into the last buttonhole stitch.

2 Push through the needle more than halfway so that the needle is long enough to make a bullion knot (see page 299).

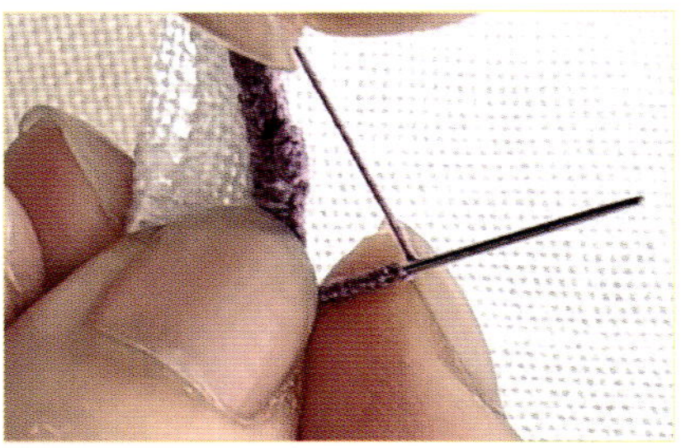

3 Holding the needle with your finger and thumb, wrap the thread anticlockwise 8–10 times, depending on the size of the bullion you wish to make.

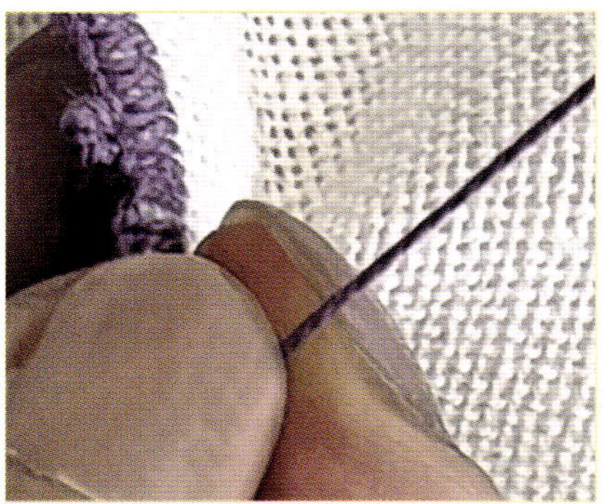

4 Push the wraps down to the buttonhole stitch. Holding the wraps gently, pull the needle through so the wraps lie evenly.

5 Bring the needle back up through the last buttonhole stitch and pull through so that the bullion wraps form a ring.

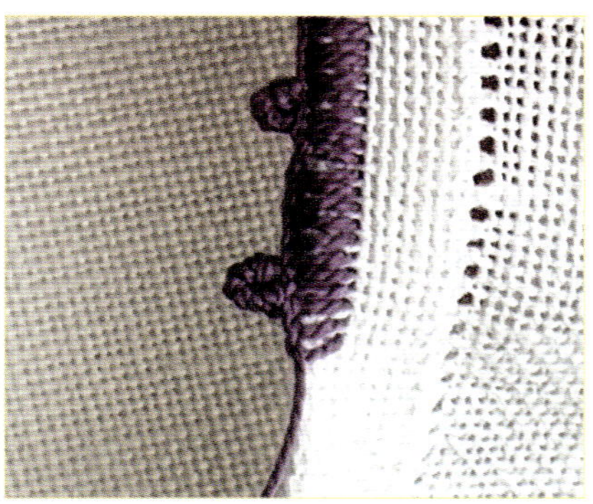

6 Continue working buttonhole stitch (see pages 20–21) until the next spot for another bullion picot.

BUTTONHOLE EDGING

WHITEWORK; CUTWORK; AYRSHIRE.

This version of buttonhole stitch, as its name suggests, is used to edge fabric. The stitch is completed before the fabric is trimmed and thus lends itself to creating decorative hems and large cutwork areas.

For an introduction to the basic stitch, see buttonhole stitch on pages 20–21. For an alternative method of working this stitch where the fabric is trimmed before the stitch is worked, see buttonhole edging (variation) overleaf.

METHOD

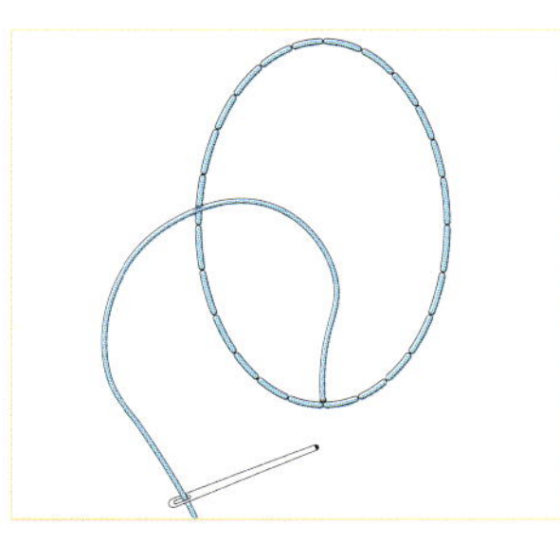

1 Work a line of double running stitch just outside the outline. To begin buttonhole stitch, bring the needle up just inside the line and take it down just outside the line, leaving a loop.

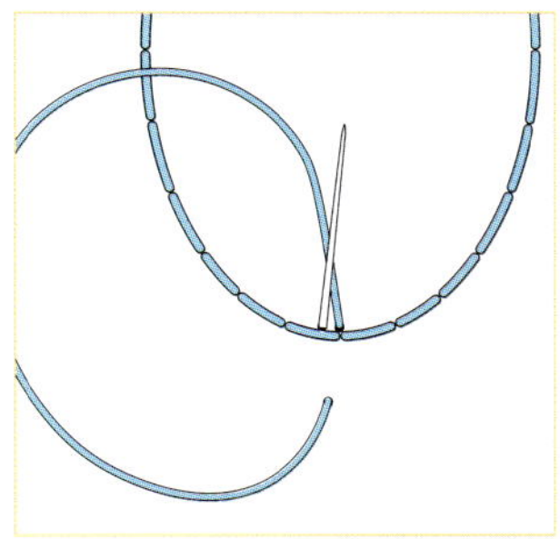

2 Bring the needle up just inside the line, right next to the first stitch, with the needle inside the loop.

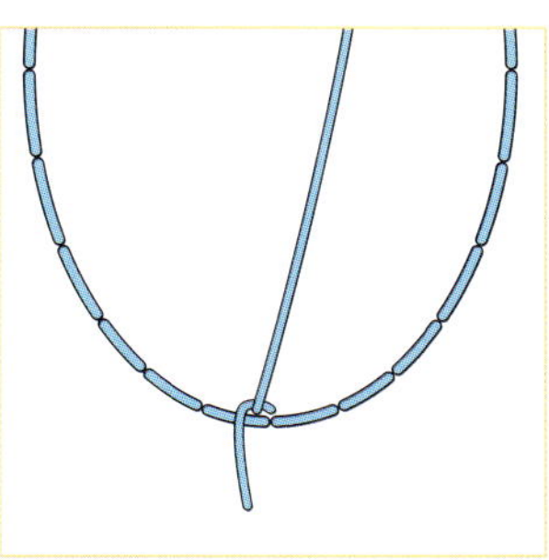

3 Pull the excess thread to the back and then bring the needle and thread through and pull taut to complete the stitch.

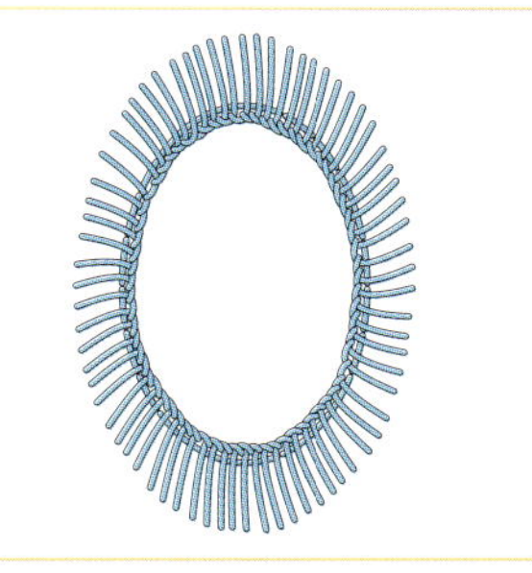

4 Working clockwise, repeat around the shape, placing the stitches as close together as you can. Make sure that the two ends match up neatly.

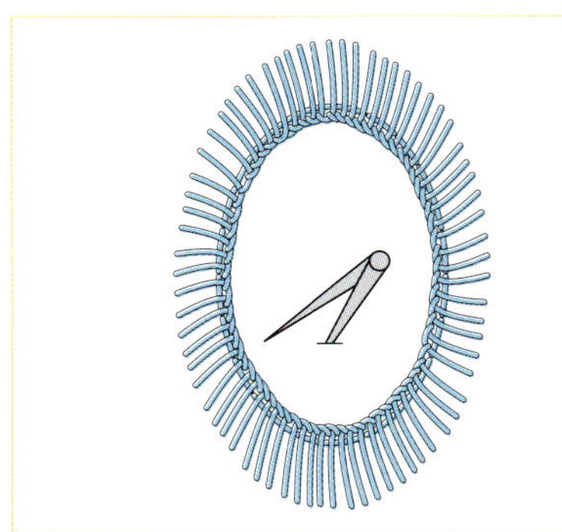

5 Begin trimming the fabric by cutting slits, first from the middle to the top, then to the bottom, and then to each side to make flaps.

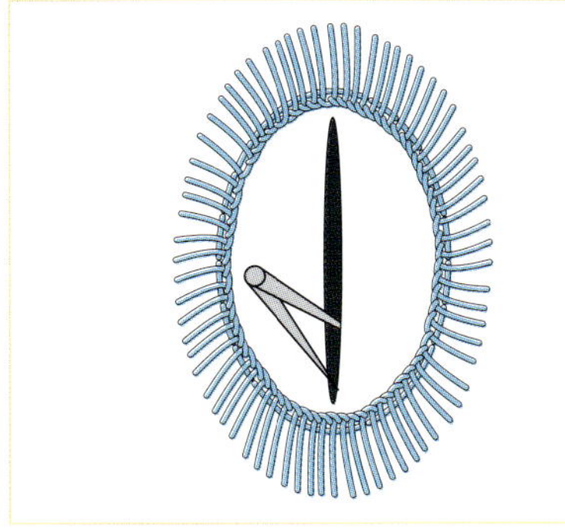

6 Fold the flaps to the reverse side. You can cut more slips to make smaller flaps in order to fold along the flaps more closely to the stitched line.

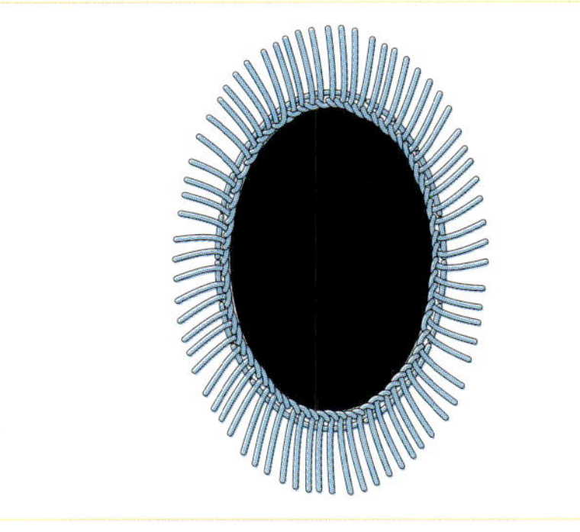

7 Take the embroidery out of the frame and turn it to the reverse side. Trim away the folded flaps up to the edge of the buttonhole stitch.

BUTTONHOLE EDGING (VARIATION)

Whitework; Cutwork.

This stitch uses buttonhole stitch (see pages 20–21) to edge a piece of fabric or a cutwork motif. In contrast with buttonhole edging on the previous page, this version is worked over an edge which has already been cut.

Some sources conflate buttonhole stitch with blanket stitch (see page 18) when it is used to edge a fabric: the crucial difference is the spacing of the stitches: there is no space between the 'legs' of buttonhole stitches, whereas blanket stitch has a small gap. This is due to practicalities: blanket stitch is normally used for more robust fabrics such as wool which doesn't fray very readily, whereas buttonhole stitch is normally used for finer, more delicate, fabrics.

In the 17th century, garments such as coifs were routinely edged with buttonhole stitch.

METHOD

1 First, outline the shape using evenly worked tiny running stitches (see page 36). Then cut away the fabric close to the running stitch outline.

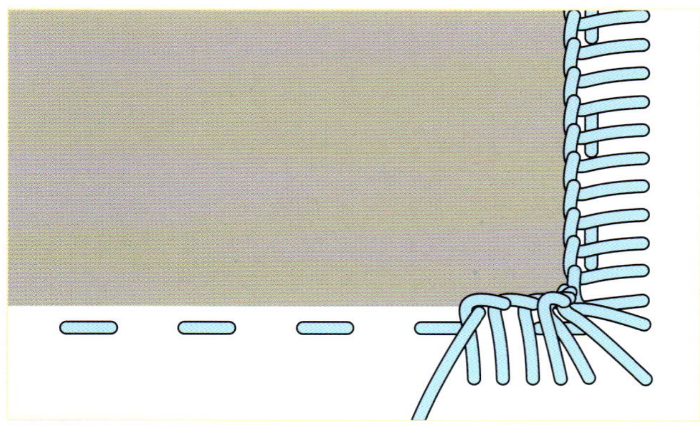

2 Start working buttonhole stitches (see pages 20–21) to cover both the running stitch and the raw edge. The distinctive edging of the buttonhole stitch sits on the edge of the fabric.

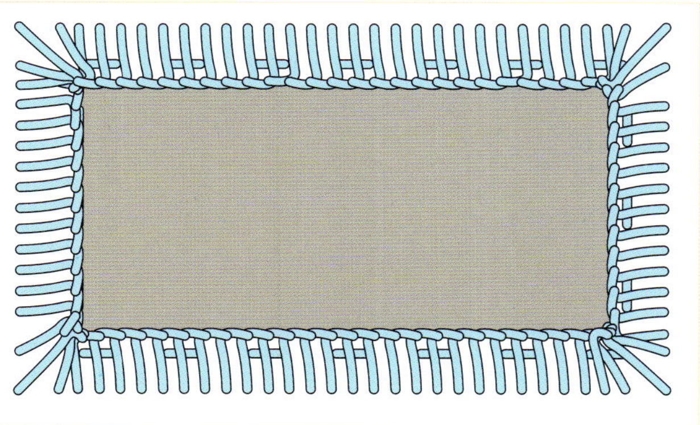

3 Make sure to work the buttonhole stitches closely together.

LONG AND SHORT BLANKET STITCH

SURFACE.

Long and short blanket stitch consists of a row of loops each anchored by the following stitch to form an 'L' shape. It is stitched in a similar way to blanket stitch (see page 18), the only difference is the assortment of stitch lengths. As the name suggests, it can be used to edge blankets, but it can also be worked as a surface stitch.

For more background, see blanket stitch.

METHOD

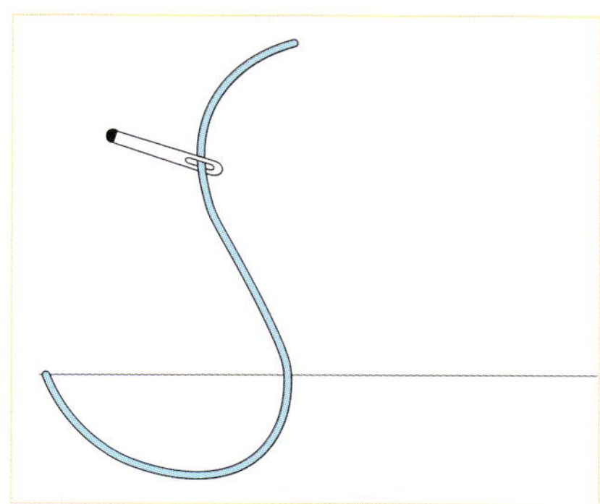

1 Bring the needle and thread up on the baseline and take the needle down a few millimetres along and in from the line, leaving a loop on the surface.

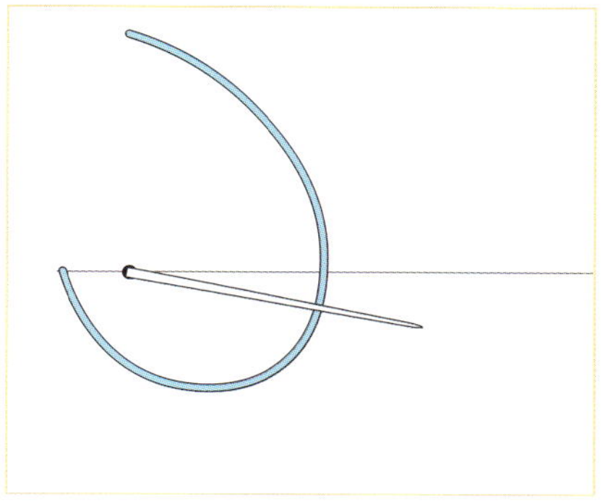

2 Bring the needle up inside the loop, on the baseline.

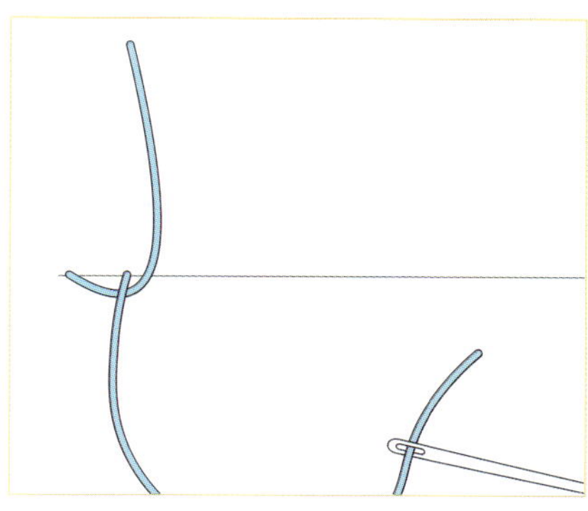

3 Tighten the loop to create a reverse L-shaped stitch on the surface and then pull the thread through.

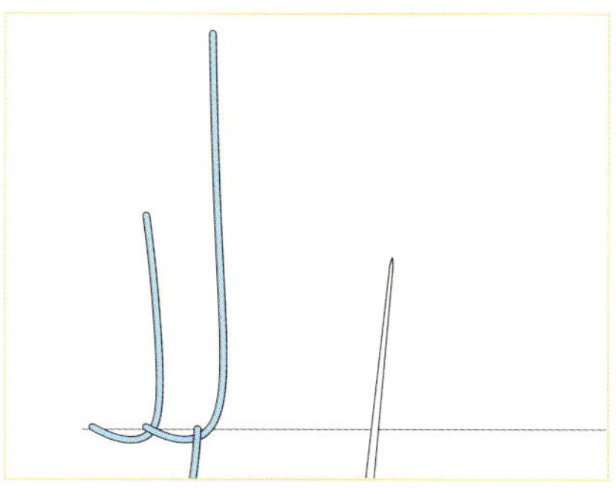

4 Continue to work along the baseline, varying the length of the vertical stitches.

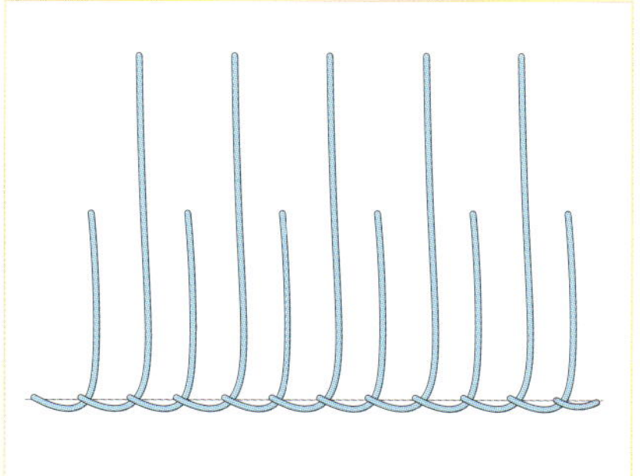

5 The length of the vertical stitches can be alternated to produce a long and short design (above left), or you can create interesting patterns and borders by creating stitches in repeated blocks of differing lengths (above right).

OVERCAST EDGING

WHITEWORK; CUTWORK; AYRSHIRE.

Also known as Overcasting.

Overcast edging uses simple parallel stitches to bind a cut edge; it gives a robust finish suitable for securing most types of fabric. The example shows a square with four sides cut away, but overcast edging can be used for any shape. The method is very similar to that used for working a large eyelet (see pages 312–313).

Overcast edging has been used to edge fabric for centuries: the Museum of Fine Arts in Boston has a Peruvian woven panel dating from 500–700AD which features an overcast edge.

METHOD

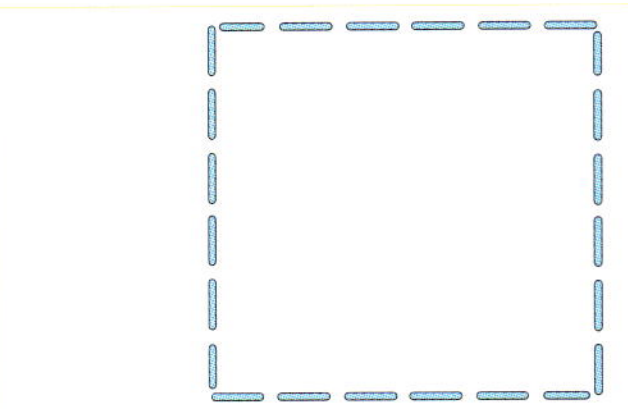

1 Starting with a waste knot, bring up the needle on the design line and work a running stitch around the shape. There is no need to do a starting stitch as the overcasting will hold your running stitches in place.

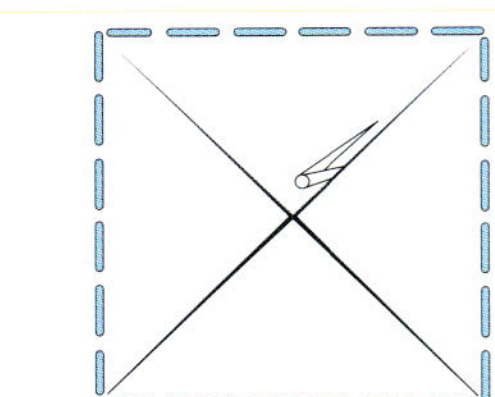

2 Insert the tip of some scissors in the centre of the shape and cut into the points/corners of the shape. Make sure your cut extends up to the stitching, but take care you don't accidentally cut it.

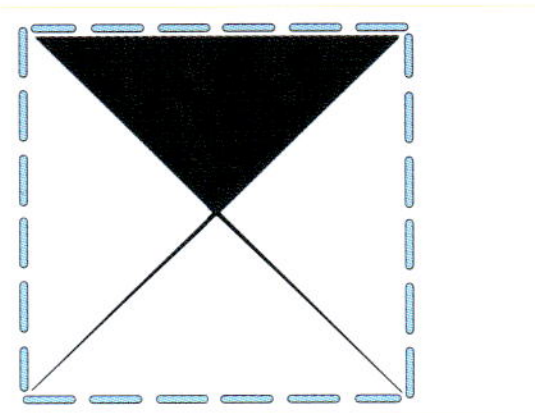

3 Fold the flaps underneath, and finger press the fold along the running stitch.

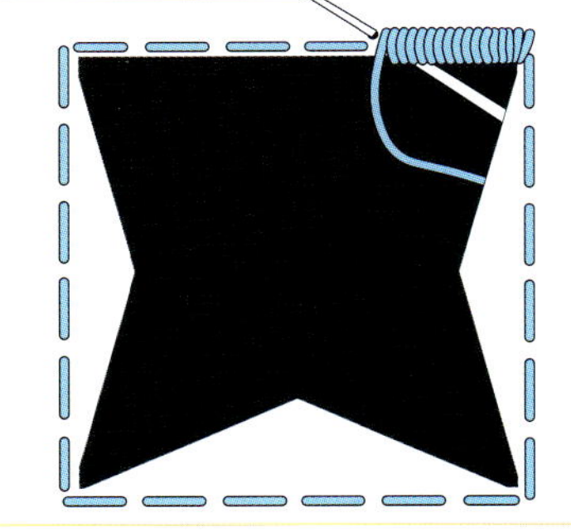

4 Overcast the edges by bringing the needle up through the fabric just outside of the running stitch, then drop it into the hole. Make these stitches at right angles to the edge of the fabric, and close enough to totally cover it. Repeat around the shape.

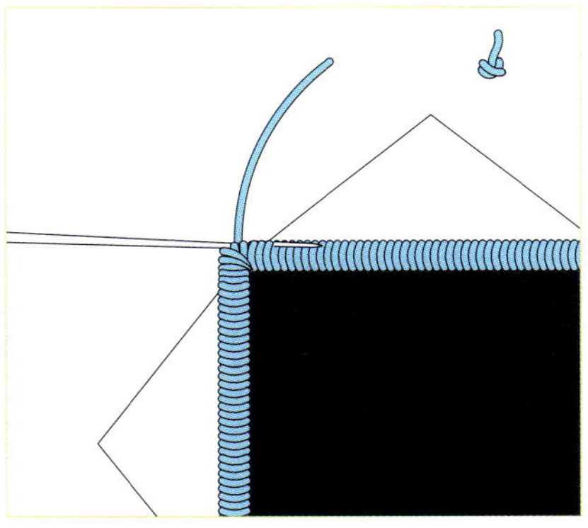

5 When you have finished, turn the fabric over and finish the thread by catching into the back of the work. Cut away the excess of the starting waste knot thread.

6 Cut the flaps away to finish.

PICOT 

Whitework; Hardanger; Needlepoint lace; Cutwork.

Also known as Simple picot.

This simple picot is formed by wrapping the thread around the needle three times and then taking the needle back into where it started. Its method uses a similar technique to the bullion knot (see page 299) and it therefore has similarities with the bullion picot (see page 282), but the result is much smaller and forms a nodule rather than a loop.

These tiny picots are often used to embellish both buttonhole bars and also other picots, especially ring picots (see pages 288–289).

METHOD

1 Work buttonhole stitches (see pages 20–21) along the edge. When you reach the point where you wish to make a picot, insert the needle back into the last buttonhole stitch.

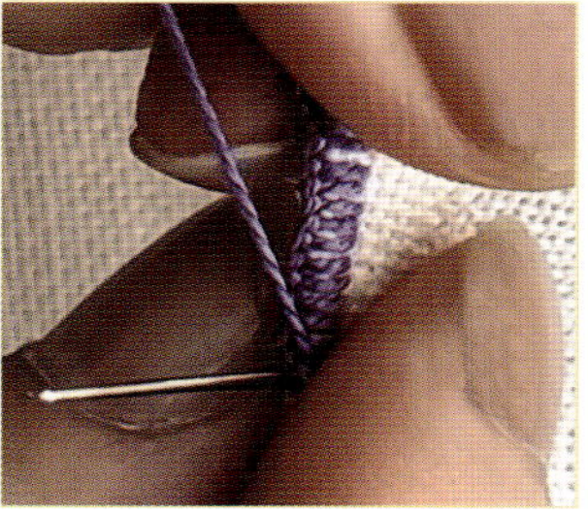

2 About halfway through, hold the needle with finger and thumb.

3 Wrap the thread three times anti-clockwise.

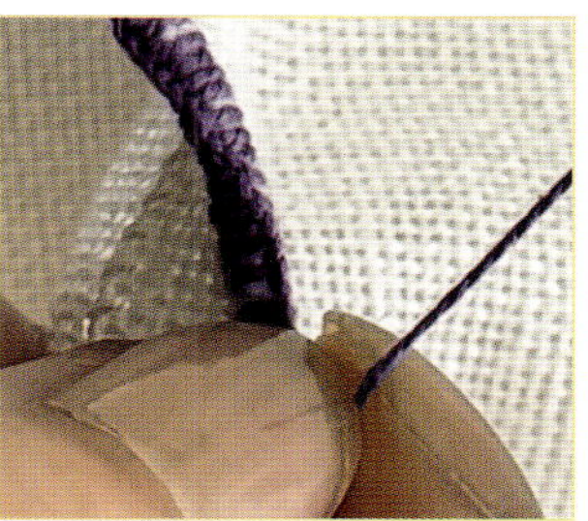

4 Push the wraps down towards the buttonhole stitch. Keep holding the wraps and then pull the needle through.

5 Now a simple picot is created.

6 Bring the needle back up through the last buttonhole stitch.

7 Continue working the buttonhole stitch (see pages 20–21) until the next spot for another picot.

RING PICOT

Whitework; Cutwork; Needlepoint lace.

Also known as Buttonhole ring picot, or Buttonhole ring.

A ring picot is a semi-circular loop, normally on the edge of a piece of fabric, covered in buttonhole stitches.

This picot can itself be embellished with a smaller picot, normally either a simple picot or a loop picot – as shown on the facing page.

Ring picots can be worked so that each semi-circle overlaps with the previous one to form a decorative edge.

The alternative name of buttonhole ring can also be used for buttonhole couronnes.

METHOD

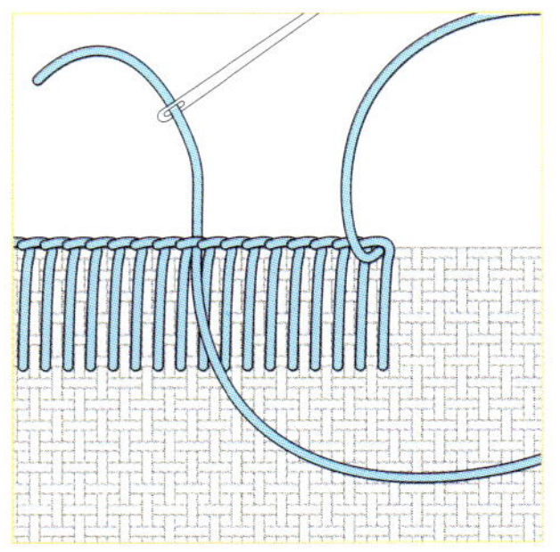

1 Work buttonhole stitches along the edge of your fabric. Count back 8 stitches and insert the needle into the top of the stitch. Always insert the needle from front to back.

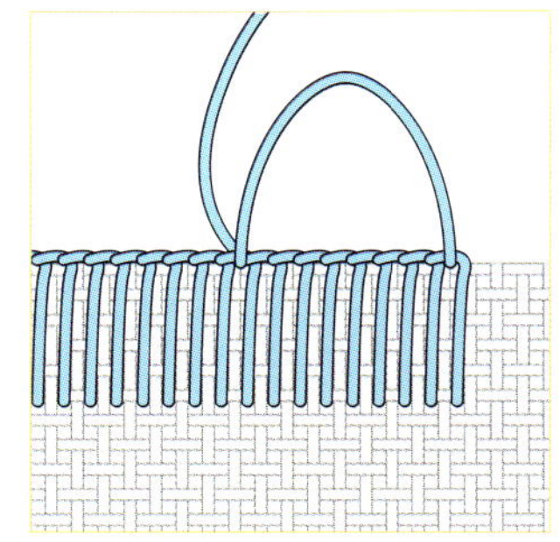

2 Pull the thread through to create a semi-circle.

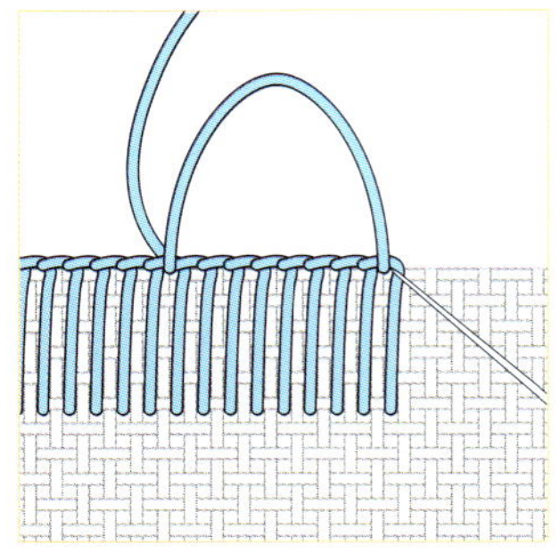

3 Insert the needle into the buttonhole stitch at the start of the semi-circle and pull through, leaving another semi-circle of thread.

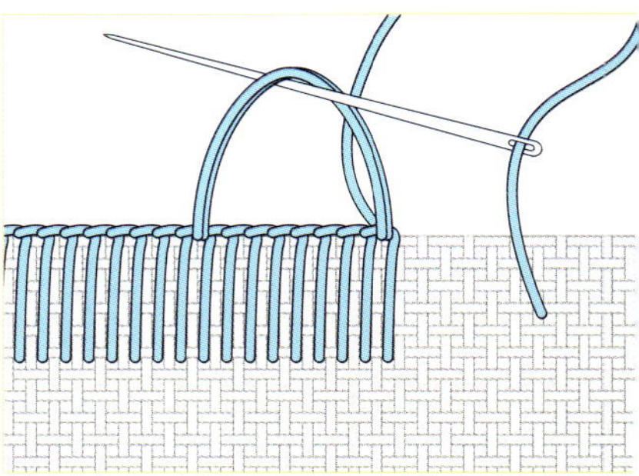

4 Use the needle to tension both semi-circles to the approximate size which you want.

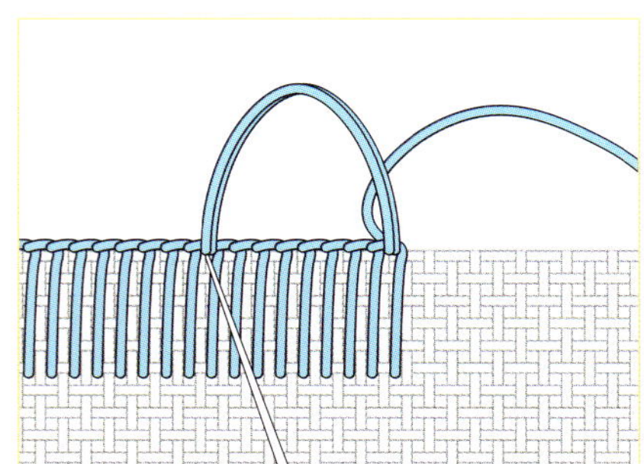

5 Insert the needle back into the top of the 8th buttonhole stitch. Try not to split your threads.

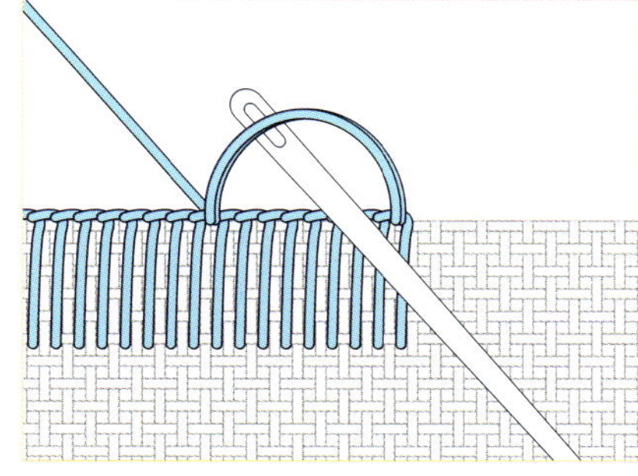

6 Use a large tapestry needle or similar implement to tighten all three threads to the required size.

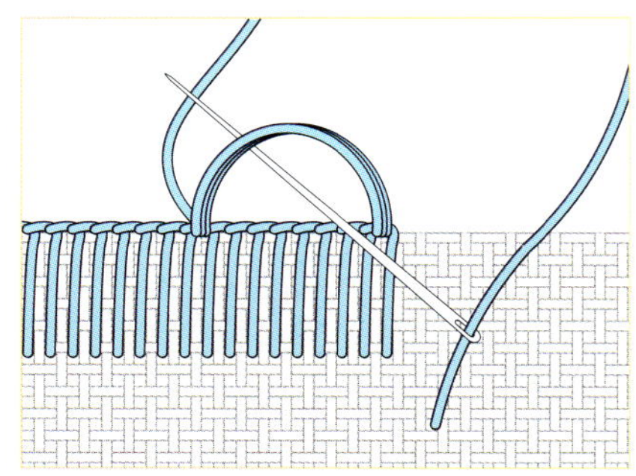

7 Insert the needle through the ring and over the working thread to work your first buttonhole.

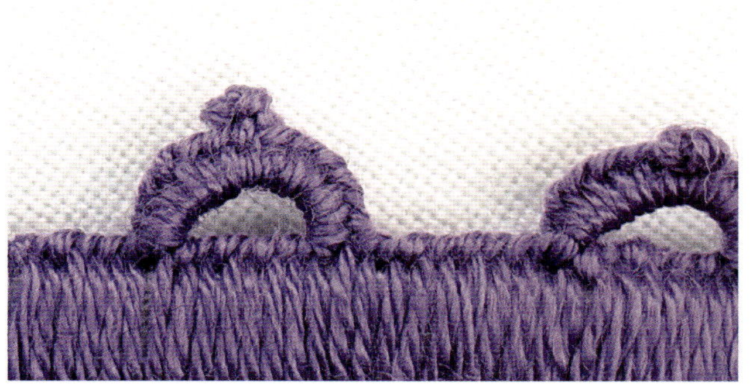

Ring picots with picots

A ring picot further embellished with a loop picot

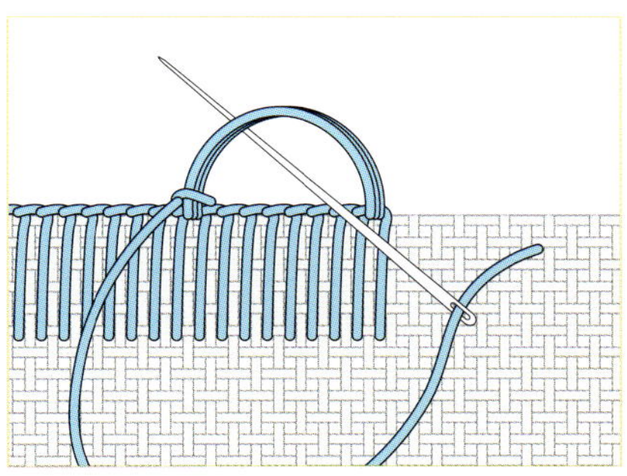

8 Pull the thread diagonally down so that the knot is at the very end of the ring.

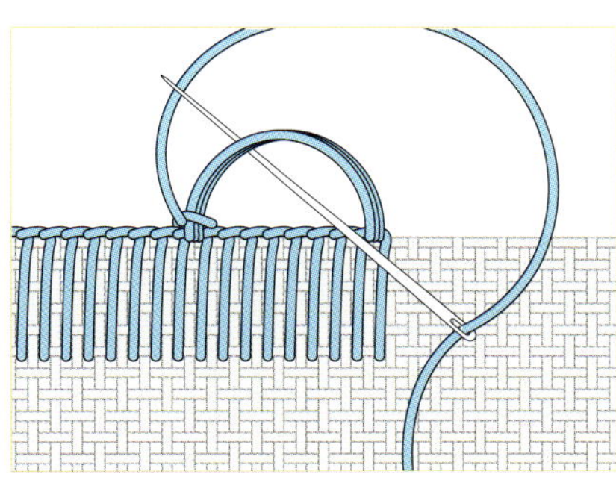

9 Work the next buttonhole stitch.

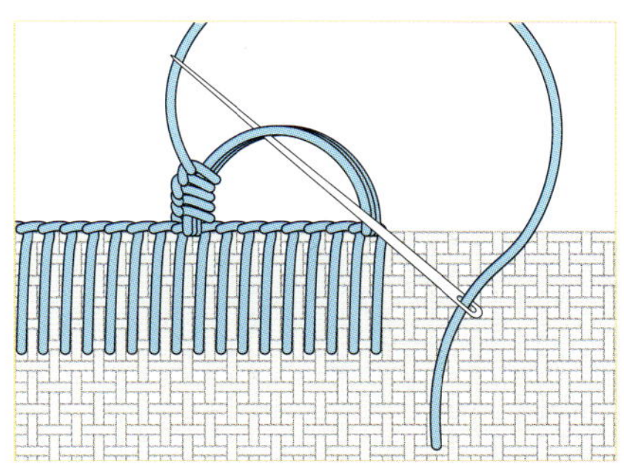

10 Continue working buttonhole stitches around the ring; the first few stitches may look uneven.

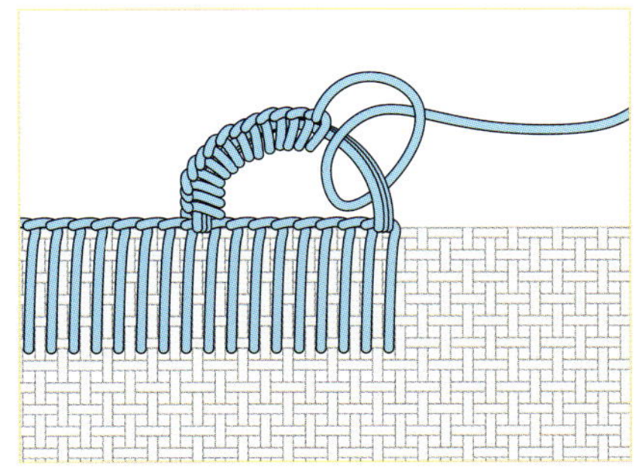

11 As you work around the ring, the buttonhole stitches will form a ridge around the edge.

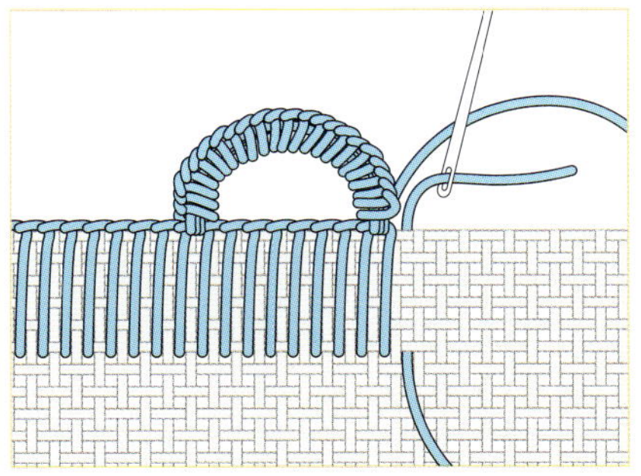

12 When you reach the end of the ring and can't fit in any more stitches, insert the needle into the fabric to work the next buttonhole edging stitch.

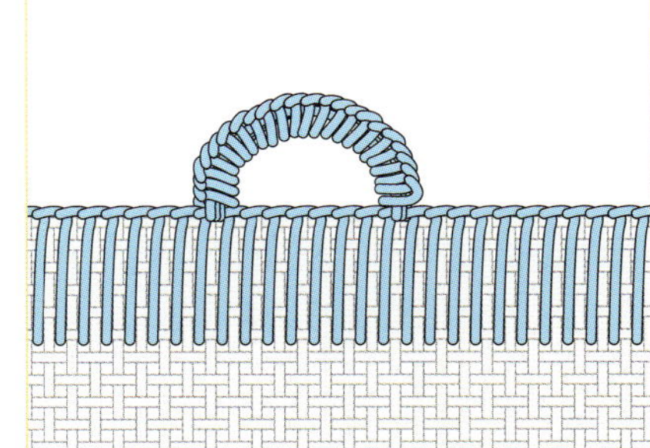

Finished ring picots.

UP AND DOWN BLANKET STITCH

Crewelwork; Surface.

A variation on regular buttonhole or blanket stitch, where alternate stitches are narrowly then widely spaced.

This is commonly used for borders, edgings, outlines and couching.

See also blanket stitch on page 18.

METHOD

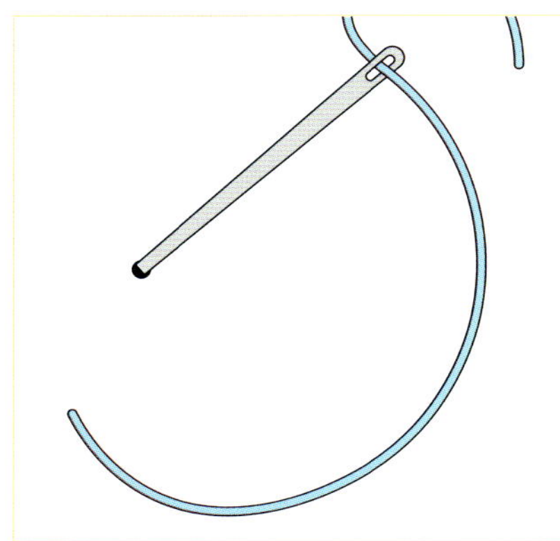

1 Working from left to right, bring the needle and thread up on the baseline and take it down on the top line, leaving a loop on the surface.

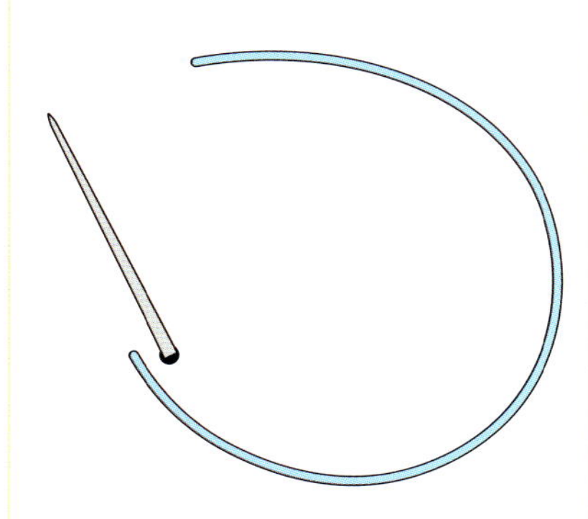

2 Bring the needle up in the loop on the baseline and tighten the loop against the working thread.

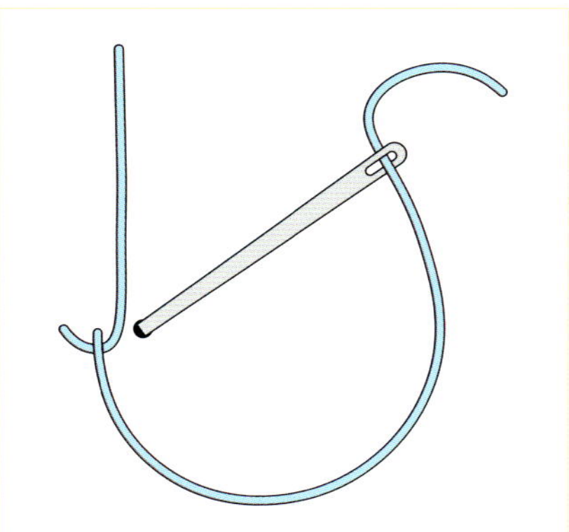

3 Take the needle down further along the baseline, ensuring you leave a gap of a thread's thickness, and draw the thread to the back to leave a loop on the surface.

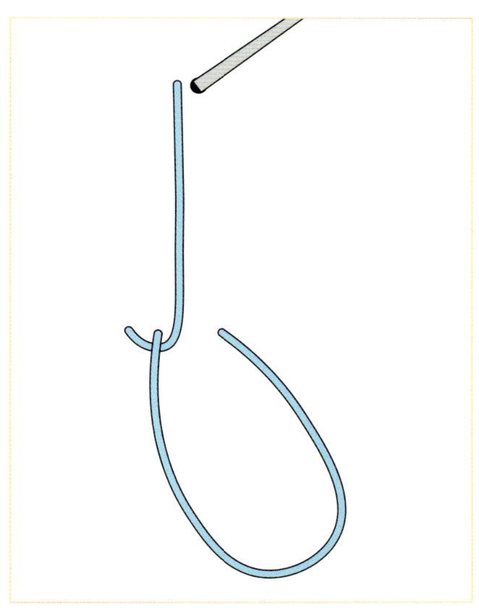

4 Bring the needle up on the top line very close to the previous stitch.

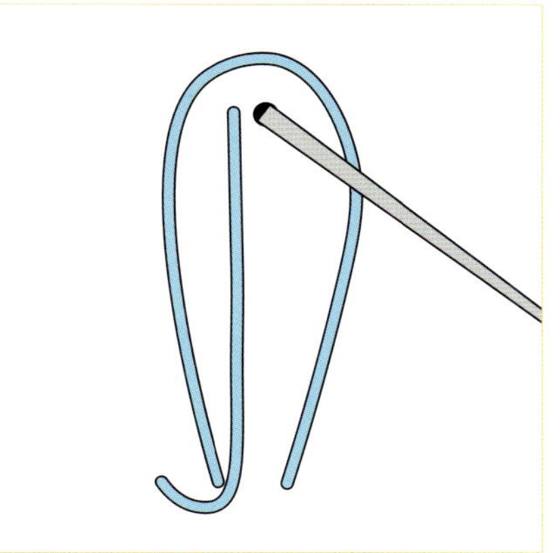

5 While the needle is still in the fabric, throw the surface loop over the needle.

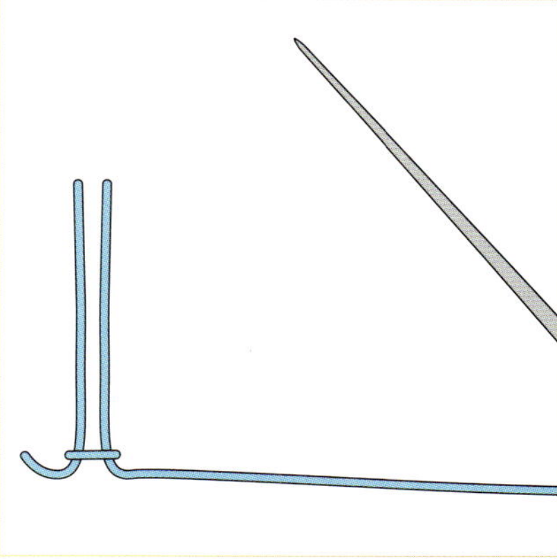

6 Draw the thread through to complete your first 'up and down' stitch.

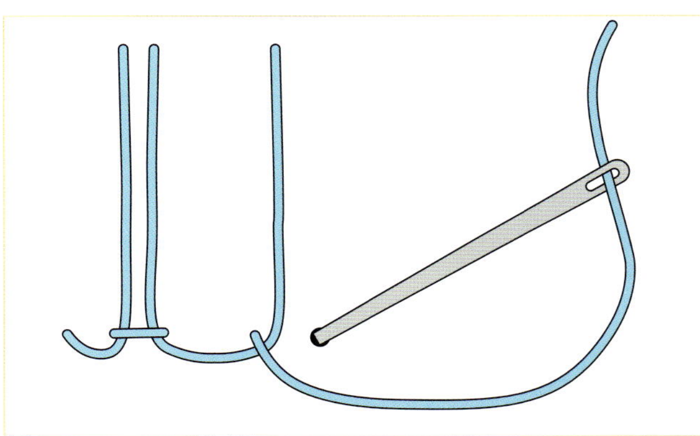

7 Repeat these steps to produce a series of 'up and down' stitches evenly spaced to achieve an up and down blanket stitch.

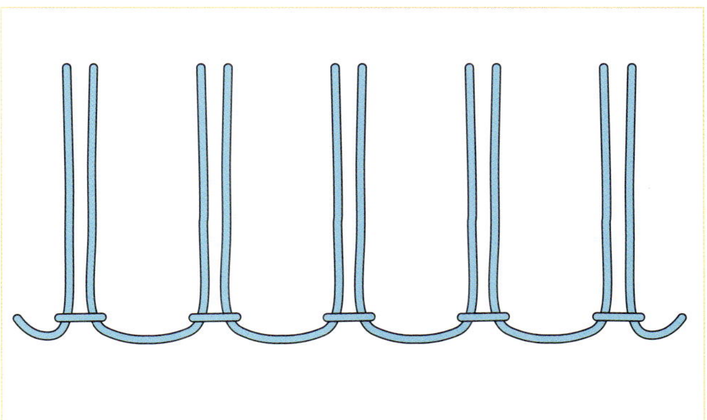

A completed row of up and down blanket stitch.

EMBELLISHMENT STITCHES

These stitches are used to form a decorative, textured effect. They are often used to form a standalone motif rather than as a repeating pattern to fill an area and are raised from the surface of the fabric.

Some embellishment stitches, such as detached woven picot and detached buttonhole bars, were minimally attached to the fabric; others, like woven wheel or buttonhole scallops, are firmly attached but still raised from the surface. We have included eyelets in this category – they form a distinctive texture through opening a hole in the fabric which is embellished around its edge.

Two forms of cross stitch which are both reversible feature in this category: the stitches are historically used to mark household linen with names or other identifying marks, hence the need for a stitch which is neat on both sides.

This category includes several circular stitches: buttonhole wheels, large eyelet, small eyelet, whipped wheel, woven wheel and shisha stitch.

▲▲ Firescreen, RSN Collection COL.2009.68

An embroidered firescreen behind glass in a carved wooden frame (not shown), probably made between 1890 and 1910 and gifted to the RSN Collection by Jean Panter in 2009. The embroidery depicts a peacock perching on a curved tree branch with a variety of floral images stemming from the main branch. While the floral imagery above the peacock blossoms naturalistically from curving stems, the floral imagery below is more ordered, blossoming from a wreath that frames the bottom of the tree branch.

On top of the padded body, rough purl has been couched in scallop shapes. The wing is padded and stitched with cutwork in rough purl, as well as S-ing. It has been edged in pearl purl. The feathers consist of couched silk twist thread with padded elements covered in satin stitch in silk thread.

PAGE 298

PAGE 299

PAGE 300

PAGE 302

PAGE 304

PAGE 306

PAGE 308

PAGE 310

PAGE 311

PAGE 312

PAGE 314

PAGE 316

PAGE 318

PAGE 320

PAGE 322

PAGE 323

PAGE 324

PAGE 326

PAGE 328

PAGE 330

PAGE 332

▲▲ Purificator, RSN Collection No. 2079

The ears of corn (see right) have been worked in bullion knot in a silk floss that is heavier than that used for the other elements in the work. This gives them additional weight and texture.

EMBROIDERY TECHNIQUE: GOLDWORK

Also known as metalwork, or metal thread embroidery.

Goldwork is the use of various types of metal threads and embellishments to adorn fabric. Threads include passing (a silk or synthetic core wrapped in very thin strips of metal), purls (hollow tubes of metal of various descriptions) and twists (multiple strands of very fine passing twisted together); embellishments include spangles (small circles of gold with a small break, similar to sequins) and kid leather covered with metal foil. Threads are normally couched down, threaded like a bead or applied.

Padding is used extensively in goldwork to maximize the effects of light on the metal; various materials are used to create different effects including string, felt, vellum and cardboard.

The majority of the metal thread remains on the surface of the fabric, partly because most of the threads are impractical to take through the fabric and partly for reasons of economy.

Goldwork formed part of Opus Anglicanum: most notably underside couching of gold file (like a very fine version of passing) but also regular couching, twist, purls and spangles.

Goldwork techniques can be worked in silver or other metal threads.

▲▲ Address case, RSN Collection No. 5

This is an envelope which contains a textile letter from India to King Edward VII on his coronation. It is an example of zardozi embroidery, a technique of using metal-bound threads. It originated in Persia and was developed in India, where this piece was made.

▲▲ Detail of s-ing (goldwork) – pages 318–319

▲▲Detail of pearl purl application – see page 97

ALGERIAN EYE STITCH

CANVASWORK; COUNTED THREAD; WHITEWORK; HARDANGER; WESSEX STITCHERY; PULLED THREAD; ELIZABETHAN.

Also known as Square daisy stitch or Star stitch.

A square shaped stitch with eight stitches radiating out from one central hole.

This stitch is similar to square eyelets: the difference is in the number of stitches radiating from the centre and how open the centre of the stitched is pulled.

The V&A South Kensington holds two 16th-century pieces which feature this stitch: an Italian linen cover and an English pillow cover. It also features on several samplers including one which dates from the 17th century, where the stitch is used to form the letters of the stitcher's name.

METHOD

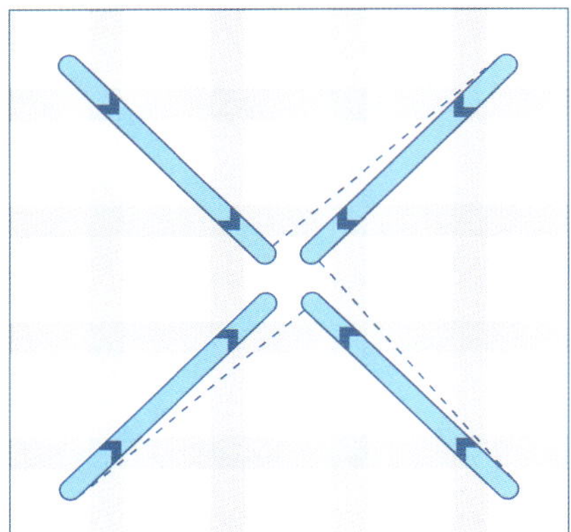

1 Work four stitches diagonally from four corners of the square into the central hole.

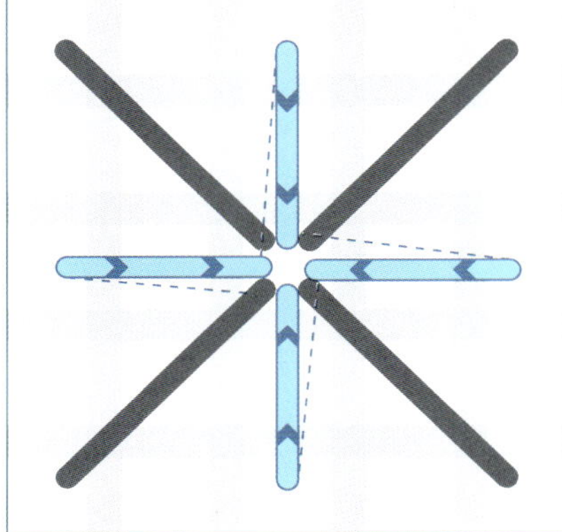

2 Work a second set of four stitches horizontally and vertically in between the first four diagonal stitches.

3 The Algerian eye stitch is worked with just eight stitches going into the central hole.

BULLION KNOT

CREWELWORK; SILK SHADING; MOUNTMELLICK; STUMPWORK; SURFACE.

Also known as Bullion stitch, Caterpillar stitch, Coil stitch, Knot stitch, Post stitch, Porto Rico rose, Roll stitch, Worm stitch, Grub stitch, Brazilian standard cast-on stitch, or Wound stitch.

A long wrapped knot used singly to embellish designs or in groups to produce a textural filling stitch.

The earliest evidence we have for bullion knots is from the 16th century, when they were used in both English embroidery and Italian cutwork. Guimarães embroidery from Portugal also used bullion knots as one of its signature stitches; the technique dates from the 10th century, but it is unknown at what point bullion knots started to be used.

METHOD

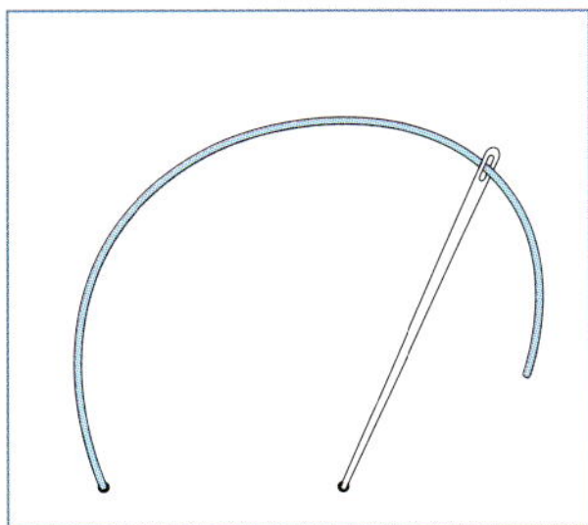

1 With the needle and thread on the surface, decide on the length of the knot and take the needle down at this point.

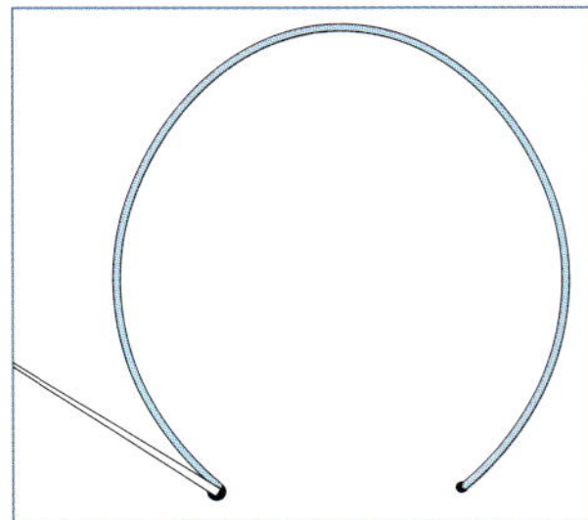

2 Leaving a large loop on the surface, bring the needle back up through the first hole.

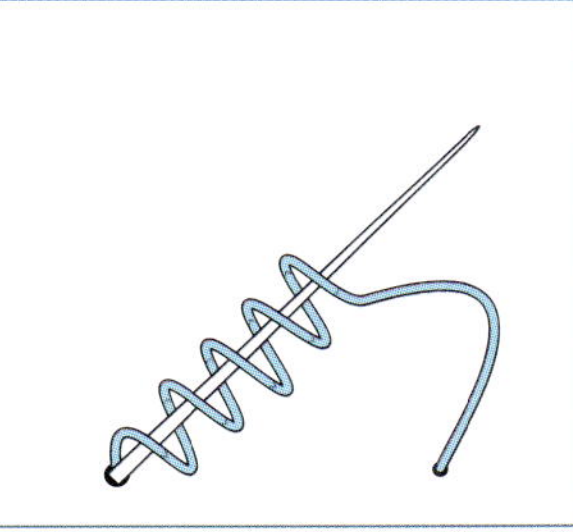

3 Wrap the loop of thread around the needle a number of times.

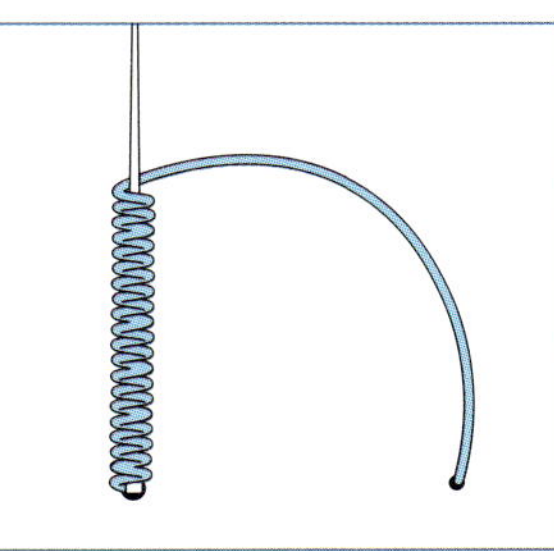

4 Condense the spiral down the shaft of the needle and lay it down to check the knot reaches the end hole. Wrap or unwrap the spiral of thread to adjust the length to fit.

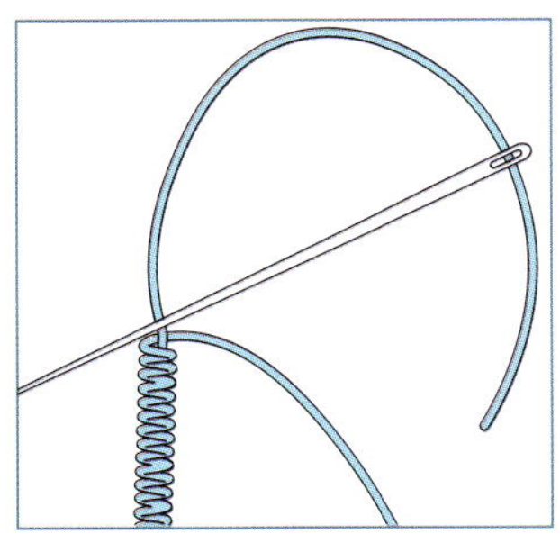

5 Pinch the spiral to hold it firm around the needle while you pull the excess thread to the back of the fabric, then gently pull the needle through the spiral.

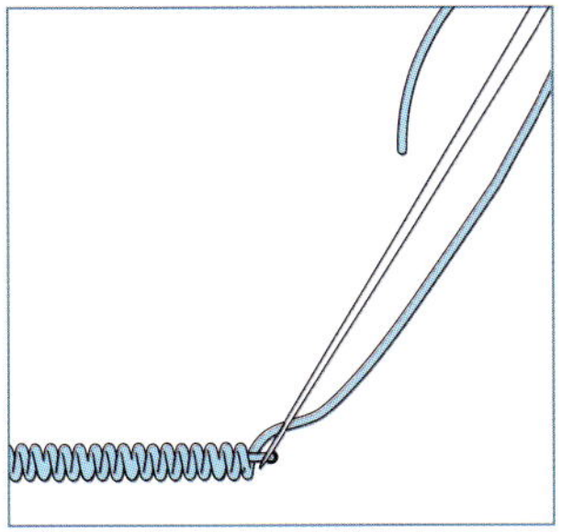

6 Pull the working thread in the direction the knot was worked to ease the loop smaller and pull the bullion knot into place.

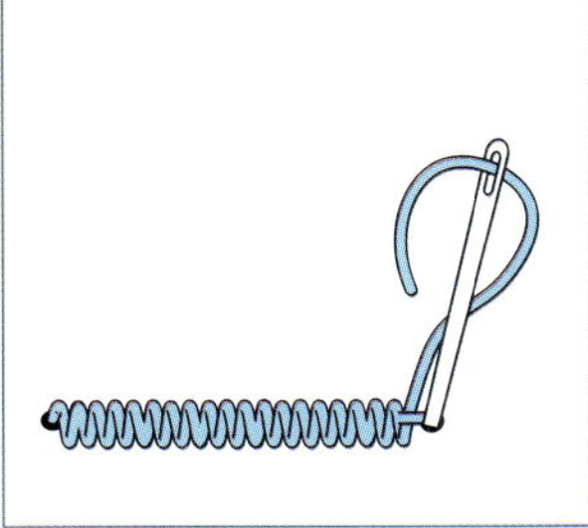

7 Take the needle down the second hole.

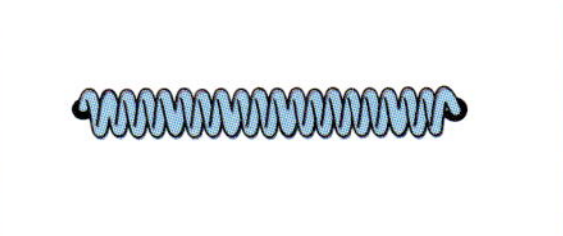

The finished bullion knot.

BUTTONHOLE BARS (CUTWORK)

WHITEWORK; CUTWORK; NEEDLEPOINT LACE.

Also known as Venetian bars, Festoon stitch, Brides bouclées, or Brides claires.

Cutwork buttonhole bars are buttonhole bars showcased by cutting away the fabric behind them. They allow you to cut away larger shapes by creating a network of supports.

Buttonhole bars have been used for centuries within the various European cutwork traditions: Renaissance work (dating from the 15th century); Reticella, from the 16th century onwards, popular for decorating Elizabethan ruffs; and Baldyring embroidery, in the 19th century. Buttonhole bars also feature on 17th-century European whitework samplers, as shown by several in the V&A collection.

METHOD

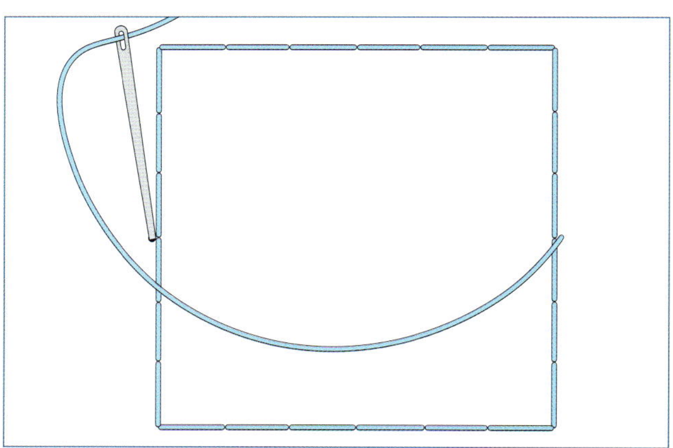

1 Bring the needle up on the right, just outside the double running stitch frame, and down on the left. Make two more stitches: left to right, then right to left. The three threads across the gap should be taut, even a little too tight.

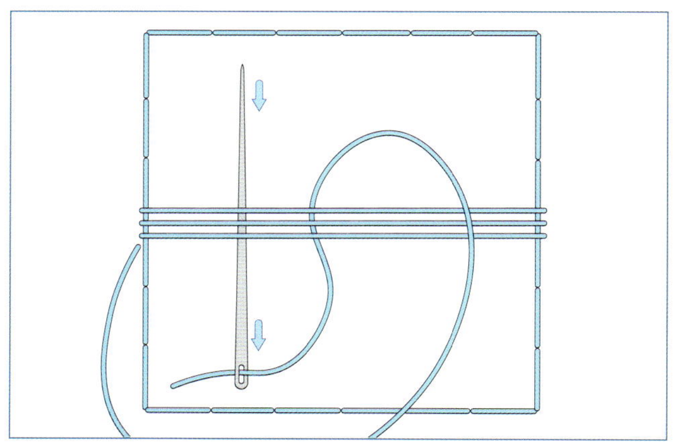

2 Bring the needle up on the left and begin to work buttonhole stitch across the three long stitches. Leading with the eye end of the needle, pass the needle under the threads from top to bottom, leaving a loop, then pass the needle through the loop.

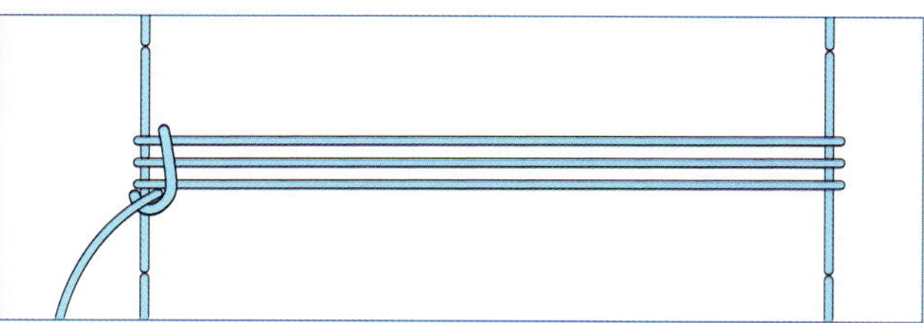

3 Pull the thread tight to complete the stitch.

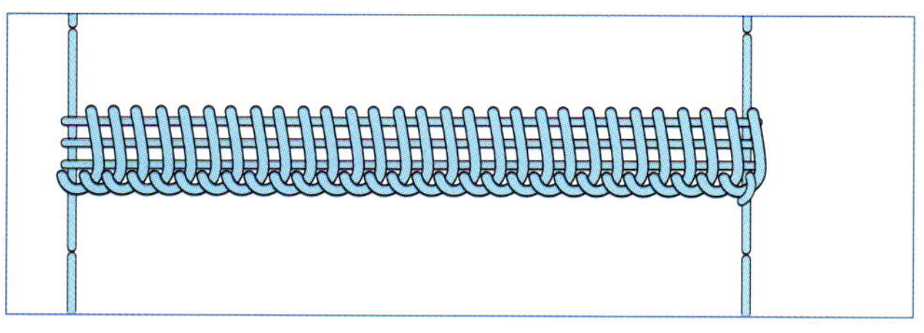

4 Repeat steps 2 and 3 across the bar, keeping the stitches close together and with an even tension. To finish the bar take the needle down outside the running stitch line.

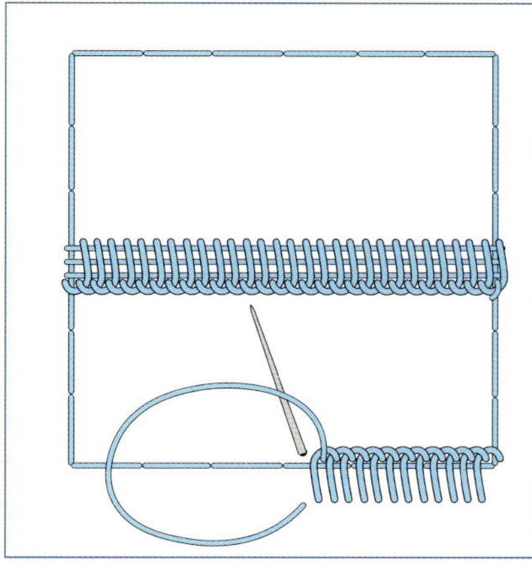

5 Repeat buttonhole stitch around the edges of the square, this time stitching through the fabric.

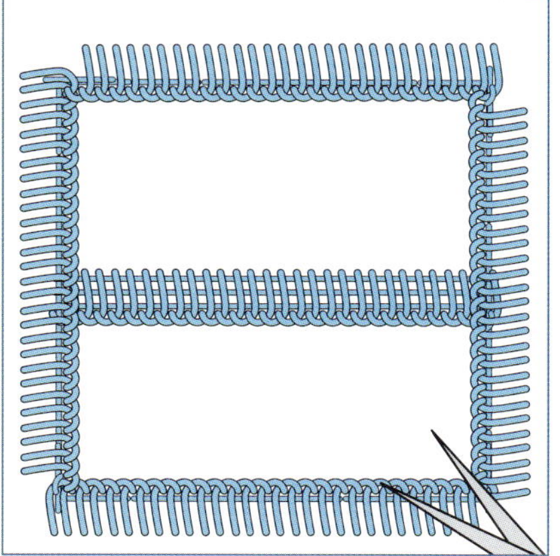

6 Insert the scissors so that the flat of the blade rests against the stitches (this helps avoid cutting the stitches). Begin to trim the fabric away by first cutting from the middle to each end, and then from the middle to each side.

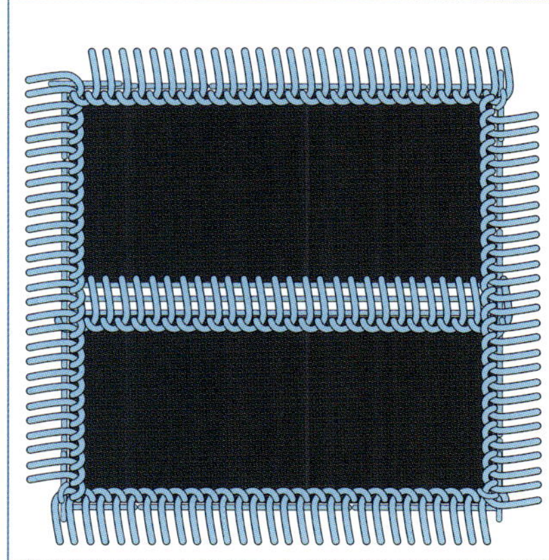

The finished sample of buttonhole bars.

TIPS

When cutting, use small snipping movements to gradually trim away the fabric. Sometimes it is useful to turn to the back.

◂◂ Detail from Broderie Anglaise and cutwork christening gown, RSN Collection No. 240

Reaching its height of popularity between 1840 and 1880, Broderie Anglaise is a specific form of whitework that makes extensive use of patterns formed through cutwork and trailing. Cutwork involves buttonhole edges for small and large eyelets. Trailing is satin stitch (see page 37) over a cluster of threads.

BUTTONHOLE COURONNE

Stumpwork; Whitework; Needlepoint Lace.

Also known as Hedebo ring, Ring, Couronne, Crown, or Buttonhole ring.

Buttonhole couronnes are small circles of buttonhole stitch which are detached from the fabric. They are worked around variously sized knitting needles or wooden dowels to produce rings of different size, which are then applied to the fabric or lace. They have similarities to buttonhole wheels (see pages 306–307), but the central hole is normally much larger and the ring is more raised.

Buttonhole couronnes are a traditional feature of Hedebo embroidery from Denmark, hence their alternative name of Hedebo rings (*hedeboringe* in Danish). Hedebo embroidery is a whitework tradition from Zealand in Denmark. It rose in popularity towards the end of the 18th century, when peasant reforms are credited with giving more free time for women to embroider.

Couronnes are used in other whitework and needlepoint lace techniques: Point de France from the late 17th century; sparingly in Point de Venice à reseau from the late 17th to the early 18th century; and in Carrickmacross from 19th century Ireland. More modern laces also use couronnes: Point de Colbert from France; Rosaline from Belgium; and Youghal from Ireland.

METHOD

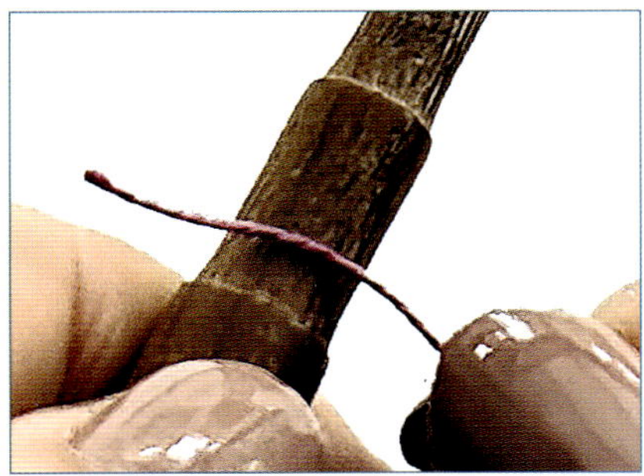

1 To make a buttonhole couronne, use a knitting needle or a hedebo stick if available. Hold the threads firmly in place on the stick.

2 Wrap the thread around the stick. This will be the core of the couronne.

3 Take the needle down behind the wrapped thread and bring it through the loop to make the first buttonhole stitch.

4 Tighten the buttonhole stitch firmly.

5 Make the second stitch just to the right of the first.

6 Continue around the stick, placing each buttonhole stitch firmly against the previous one to form a tight circle of stitches.

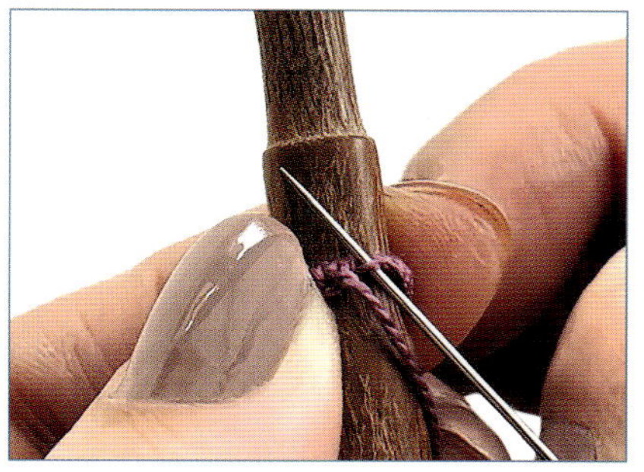

7 Complete the buttonhole couronne by taking the thread up through the first buttonhole stitch. Leave the tail thread for later use.

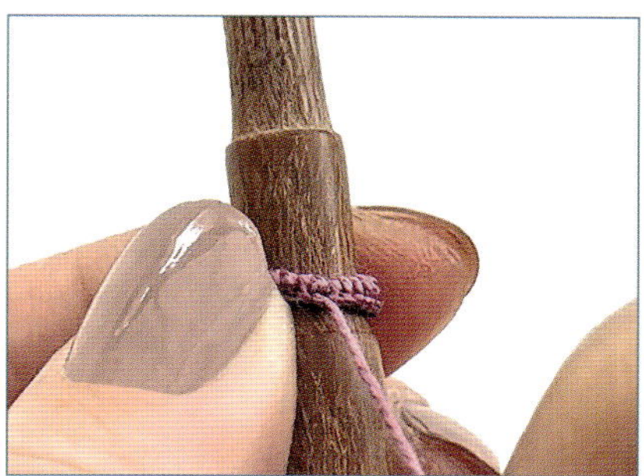

8 Remove the buttonhole couronne from the stick.

◂◂ Detail from sampler, RSN Collection COL.48

A sampler of stumpwork (raised work) made by Barbara and Roy Hirst in 1990, using historical techniques in a 20th century manner.

Between the figures and the stumpwork castle are four buttonhole couronnes with painted centres and colourful metal thread borders. The upper corners have three squares with different stitches, while the lower corners have two squares and a narrow rectangle, all with different stitches and materials, including leather.

BUTTONHOLE SCALLOPS

Stumpwork; Surface; Whitework.

Also known as Ring picot.

Buttonhole scallops are made of detached buttonhole stitches; the length and the thickness of the core thread determine the size of the scallop. The buttonhole scallops can be stitched singly or in lines, large or small. Sometimes they are used to decorate the edge of fabric: when pulled into a circular shape, rather than the semi-circle shown here, they are known as a ring picot.

This is a variant of buttonhole stitch; for more information see pages 20–21. In Italy, buttonhole stitch is called *punto a festone*, a name which comes from the garland shape formed by these scallops on the edges of lace ('*festone*' means garland).

METHOD

1 Insert a pin vertically into the fabric and make a stitch from left to right, taking the thread around the head of the pin. This will be the size of the scallop. Bring the needle back up just to the left of the start of the first stitch.

2 Form the first detached buttonhole stitch by taking the needle under the stitch and through the loop that has been formed.

3 Pull the thread to form a detached buttonhole stitch.

4 Continue making detached buttonhole stitches.

5 Remove the pin as you approach the centre of the scallop.

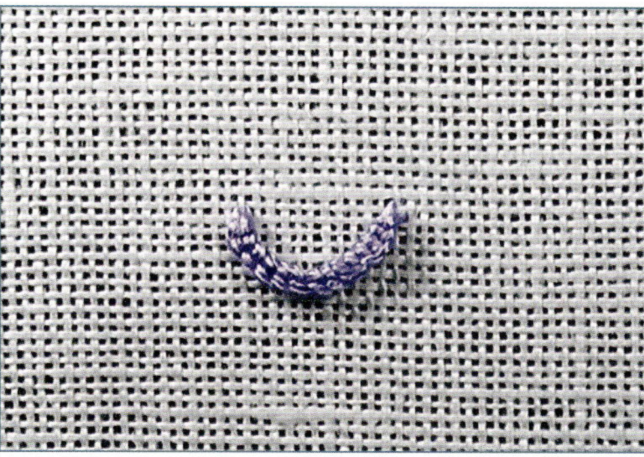

6 When the scallop is filled with the detached buttonhole stitches, take the needle through to the back of the work.

7 To make a row of scallops, insert a pin again, taking the thread around the pin as before. Bring the needle back up again to start the detached buttonhole stitches.

8 Work detached buttonhole stitches along the second scallop.

9 Repeat for the third scallop.

10 You can continue to make as many buttonhole scallops as you wish. Subsequent rows of scallops can be made to good effect.

BUTTONHOLE WHEELS

SURFACE; STUMPWORK.

Also known as Buttonhole stitch wheel, or Wheel stitch.

This stitch uses a standard buttonhole stitch to form a circle; each stitch is taken down into the same hole in the centre. The stitch tension creates a small central hole. The hole could be off-centre for a more informal look.

Buttonhole wheels have similarities with buttonhole couronnes (see pages 302–303) but there are two main differences: firstly, couronnes are worked independently from the fabric and then applied and so will normally be slightly raised, whereas wheels are stitched directly into the fabric; secondly, the central hole is normally smaller for a wheel than a couronne.

Buttonhole wheels were evidently in use during the 17th century, as they feature on a fragment found in Egypt which has been radiocarbon dated to 1599, +/− 37 years. The piece has several separate pieces of fabric joined together with scattered buttonhole wheels. It is currently held by the Ashmolean Museum, Oxford.

METHOD

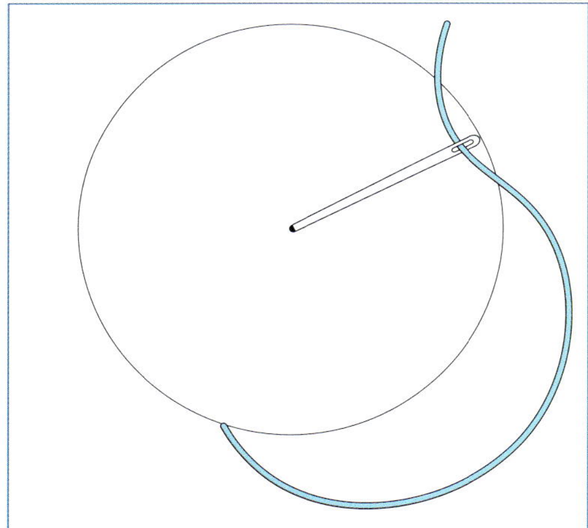

1 Bring the needle up on the edge of the circle, and then take the needle down in the centre.

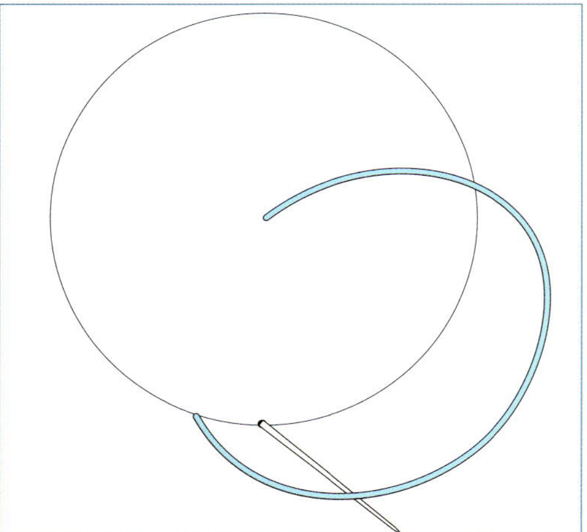

2 Leaving a loop at the front of the fabric, bring the needle up on the edge fairly close to the starting point, inside the loop.

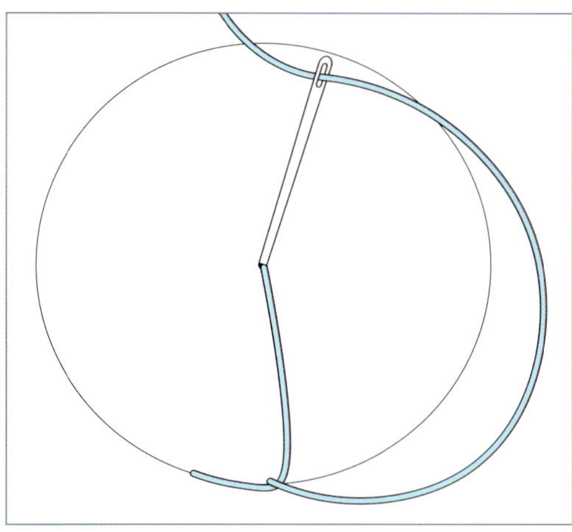

3 Pull the thread to make a buttonhole stitch. Take the needle down again at the same hole in the centre.

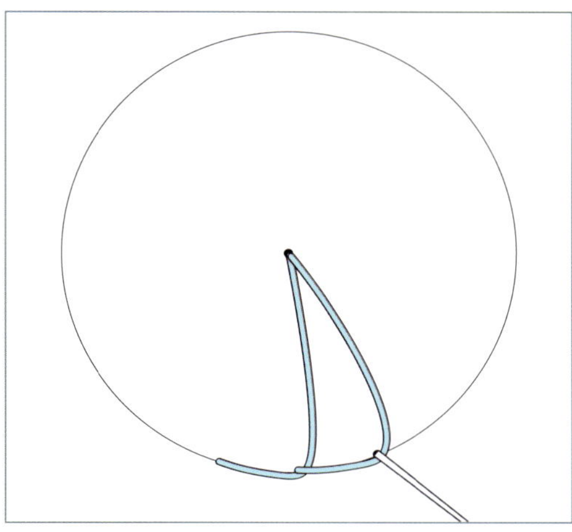

4 Come up on the edge again to work another buttonhole stitch.

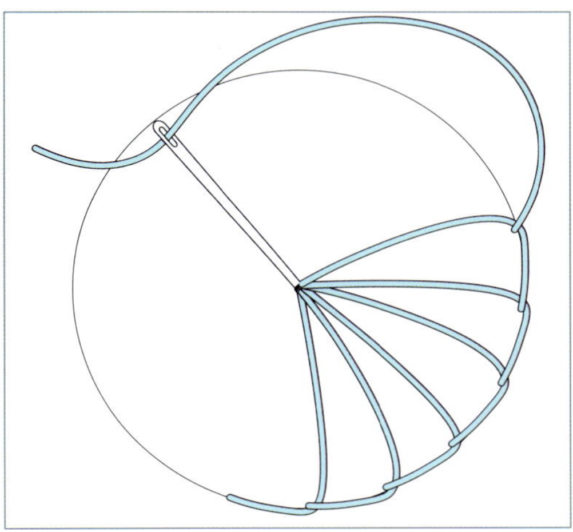

5 Continue working buttonhole stitches around the circle anticlockwise.

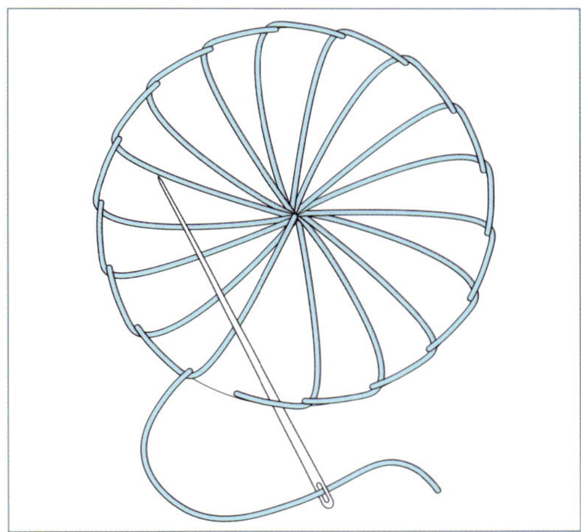

6 For the last stitch, pass the needle under the first buttonhole stitch and then take the needle down at the centre to complete the circle.

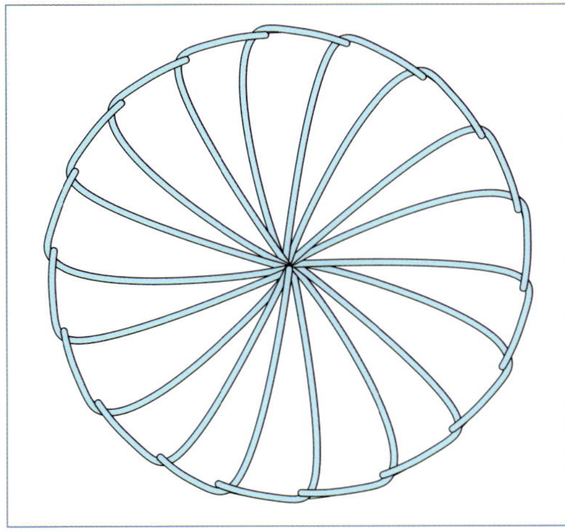

A complete buttonhole wheel.

DETACHED BUTTONHOLE BARS

STUMPWORK; WESSEX STITCHERY.

Also known as Detached buttonhole stitch.

Buttonhole bars can be attached to the fabric securely at both ends, or detached at one end to produce a stitch with movement and flexibility. In detached buttonhole bars the bar is attached at one end only, thus creating a raised length of buttonholes along a length of thread.

For more background see buttonhole stitch on pages 20–21.

METHOD

1 In this example, a detached buttonhole bar is used to create a tiny carrot. Insert a pin into the fabric and bring the green thread up just to one side of it.

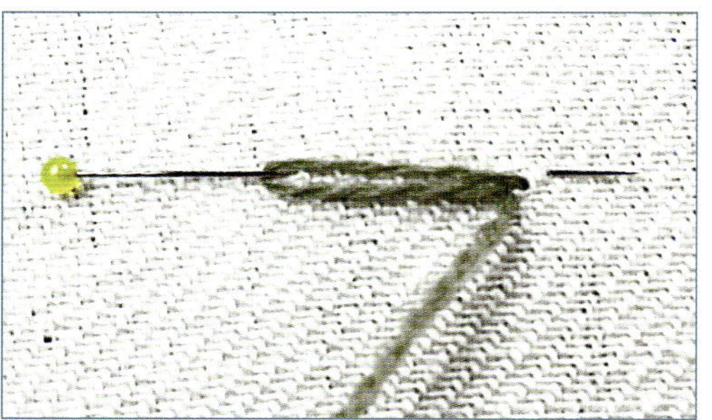

2 Wrap the thread around the top of the pin once and take the needle down the same hole. Bring the needle up very close to the starting point. Repeat two or three times and this will be the detached bar.

3 Cast off the green thread and change to the orange thread. Bring the thread up at the starting point.

4 Work a buttonhole stitch just a little down from the tip of the green thread bar.

5 Continue to form buttonhole stitches towards the end of the detached bar.

6 Try to make the buttonhole stitches as even as possible.

7 At the end of the bar, take the thread through to the back of the fabric and secure it.

8 Remove the pin and cut through the loop at the top of the green thread to make a carrot.

TIP

The detached buttonhole bars can, of course, be made with a single colour, working buttonhole stitches along the entire length of the bar.

▲▲ Border, RSN Collection COL.2018.52

Whitework baby shirt with hollie point, stitched by 14-year-old Eliza Amy Dod in 1761.

Drawn whitework techniques have been used across the shoulders, including hollie stitch (see pages 168–169), which involves creating knotted buttonhole stitches over horizontal stretched threads – a decorative approach more practical for clothing than detached buttonhole bars.

DETACHED WOVEN PICOT

Stumpwork; Surface.

Also known as Woven picot.

Woven picots can be worked large or small, thin or wide. Detached picots are attached to the supporting material only at the base and can only be worked with three or five prongs. You could use fine beading wire for the outside prongs of a detached picot to create shapes that you can bend and manipulate.

See also woven picots on pages 330–331.

METHOD

1 Place a pin in the fabric to mark the top of the picot. Bring the thread up, wrap it round the pin and take it down.

2 Bring the needle back through halfway at the bottom of the picot.

3 Wrap the thread around the pin again.

4 Do not take the thread through to the back of the fabric. Instead, weave the thread backwards and forwards across the shape's prongs, as in a normal woven picot.

5 Continue weaving the thread.

6 When reaching the bottom of the shape with your weaving, take the thread through to the back of the fabric on the side on which you finish weaving.

7 Remove the pin and bend the picot upwards, away from the fabric, with the end of the pin.

DIAMOND EYELET (SINGLE)

Pulled thread; Whitework.

This is a pulled thread stitch, where sixteen stitches radiate out from a central hole to form a diamond shape and are pulled tight to create a central opening.

For more information about eyelets generally, see small eyelet on page 322.

METHOD

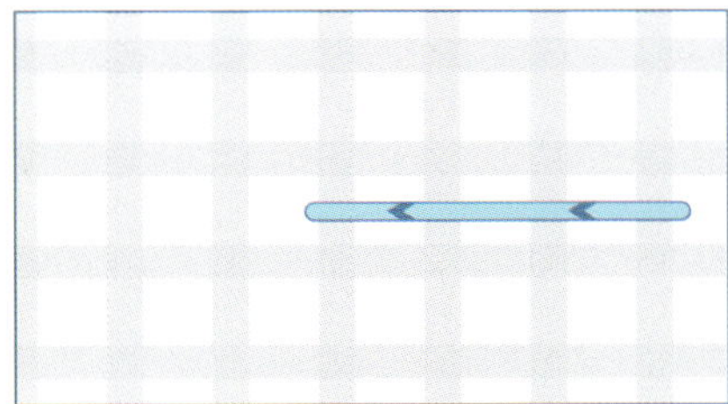

1 Bring the needle up and make a horizontal stitch four threads to the left (this is the position of the centre hole).

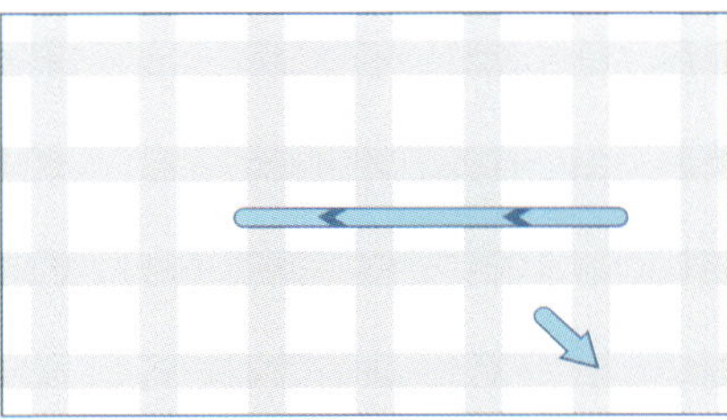

2 Bring the needle up one thread below and one thread to the left of the starting point and pull.

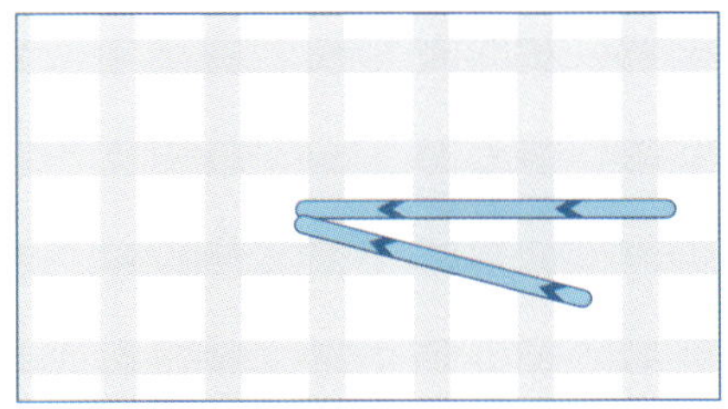

3 Take the needle down in the centre hole (three threads to the left and one thread up).

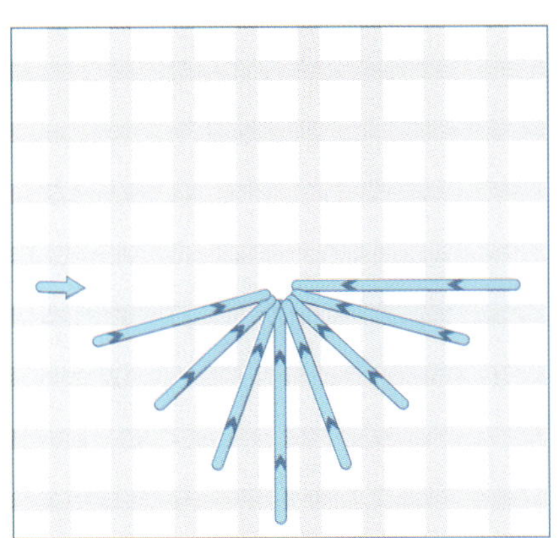

4 Follow the diagram for the placement of the stitches, and continue round the eyelet.

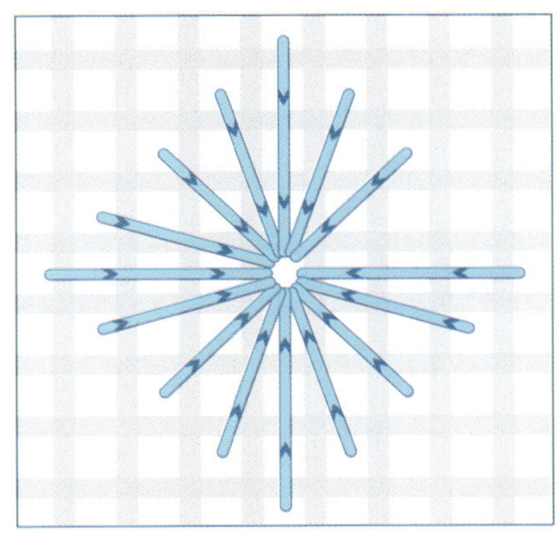

5 Pull the final stitch.

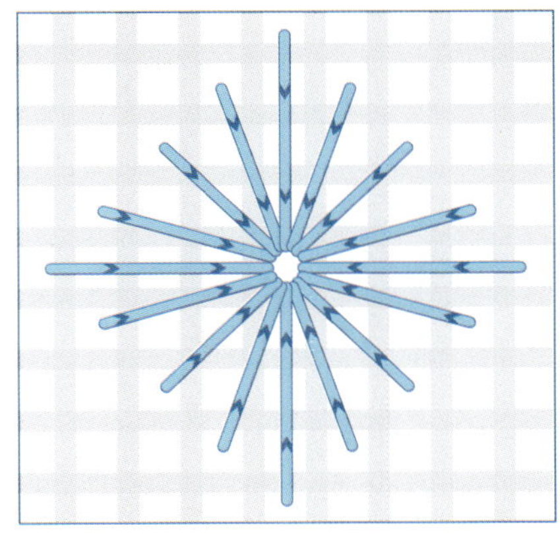

The finished eyelet.

LARGE EYELET

Whitework.

Also known as Shaped eyelet, Eyelet hole, Overcast eyelet, or Overcast edge.

A large eyelet is a large round hole in the fabric with stitched edges. The hole is made by cutting the threads of the fabric and then stitching over the edge of the eyelet to secure it.

Large eyelets have been a feature of Hedebo embroidery from the mid-19th century. They have also been used in various sizes and shapes in Broderie Anglaise since its inception in the later 19th century.

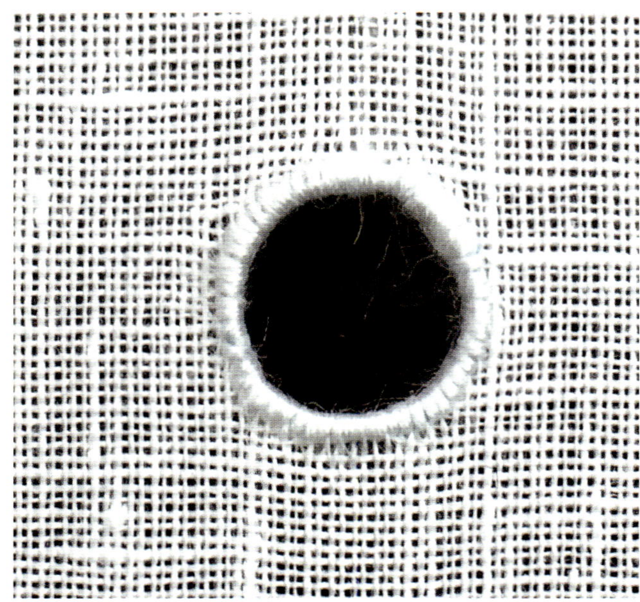

METHOD

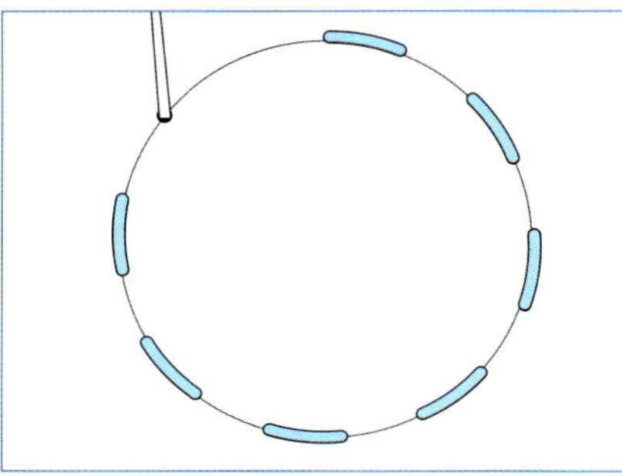

1 Work a line of running stitch (see page 36) around the shape (see tip, right). The stitches should be about 2mm (⅛in) long.

TIP

A single line of running stitch may be enough on fine fabric, but on coarse fabric double running stitch will provide more strength (reverse the stitch direction and stitch another circle of running stitch between the existing stitches).

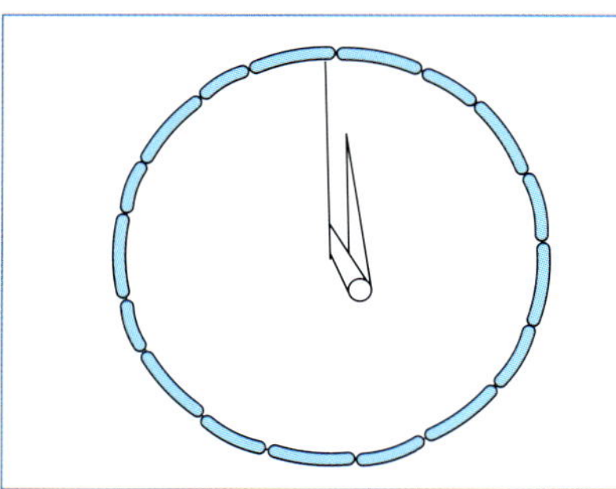

2 Insert the tip of a pair of very sharp embroidery scissors into the centre of the shape, and snip towards one end of the shape, being very careful not to cut your stitching.

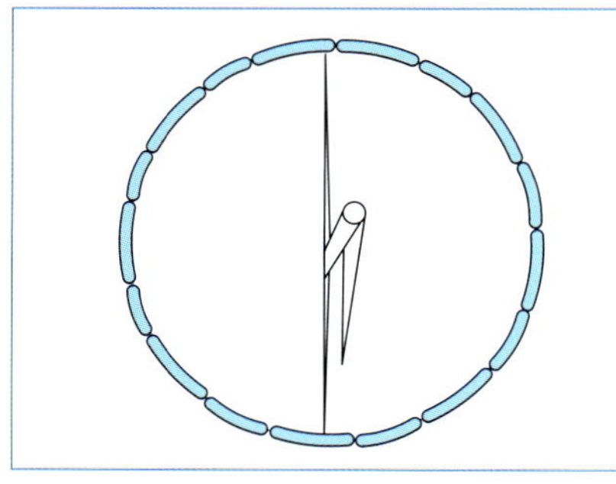

3 Turn the scissors around and snip to the other end of the shape.

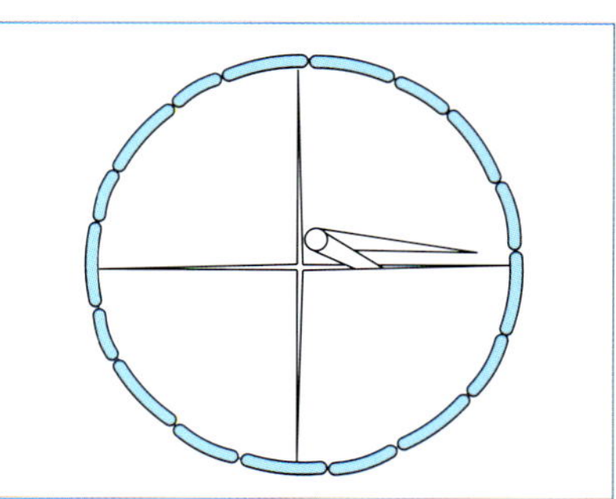

4 Carefully make two more cuts, from the middle to either side.

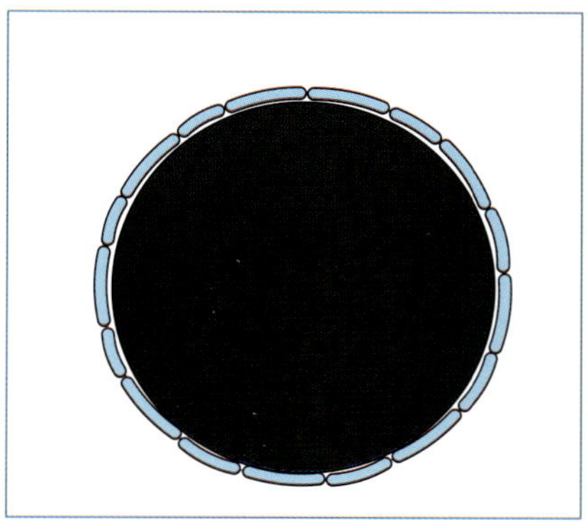

5 Gently fold each quarter of the fabric back underneath the surrounding fabric.

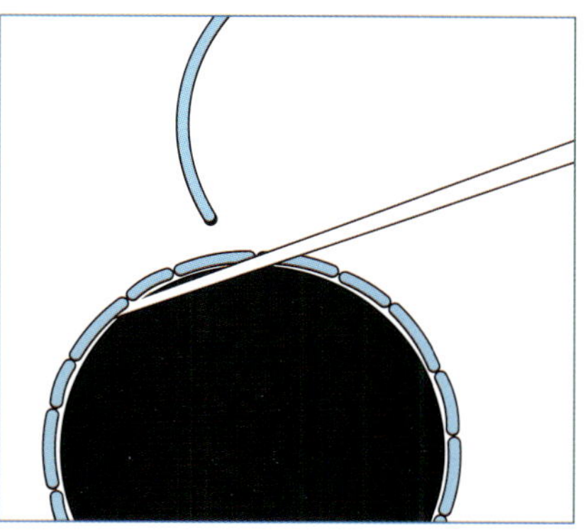

6 Bring the needle up about 2mm (⅛in) outside the running stitch line, and then pass the needle through the hole.

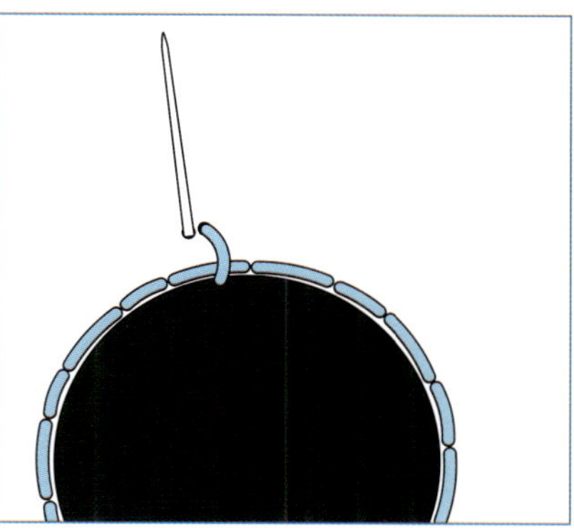

7 Bring the needle up again next to the first stitch and then back through the hole again.

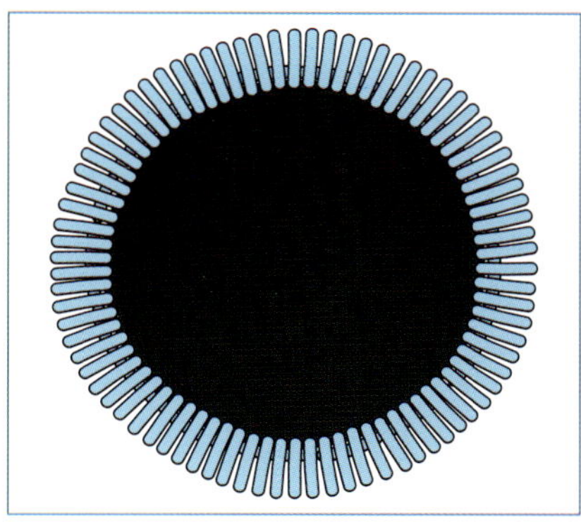

8 Continue all around the eyelet, trying to keep an even tension in the stitches and not distorting the fabric.

▲▲ Detail from handkerchief, RSN Collection COL.18

Early 20th-century monogrammed whitework handkerchief with Appenzell-style embroidery, most likely stitched in Switzerland or Hong Kong.

The large flower pictured is one of eight. Each has large eyelet stitches with Ayrshire needlelace fillings, while the smaller flowers have small eyelets (see page 322) at their centres.

MARKING CROSS STITCH

Surface; Counted thread.

Also known as Marking stitch, or Brave bred stitch.

This variation on cross stitch (see page 24) produces a square on the reverse of the fabric and one of the crossing stitches on the front is stitched twice. It can also be worked with the square side on the front and the cross on the reverse. See two-sided cross stitch (pages 326–327) for a way to work a cross stitch which appears identical on both sides. For a pulled work version of marking cross stitch, see four-sided stitch on pages 250–251.

Marking cross stitch is traditionally used to mark household linen with the owner's initials and other information. This could include the family's motif, or a coronet for a titled family (different styles of coronets were used for the different ranks of nobility), a number indicating which set of linen to which the item belonged and the date. Different alphabets were used, including both upper and lower case, and italic versions.

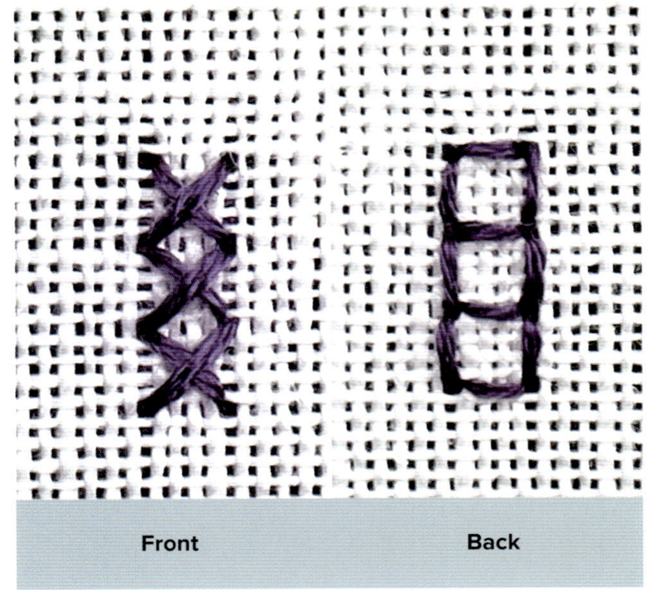

METHOD

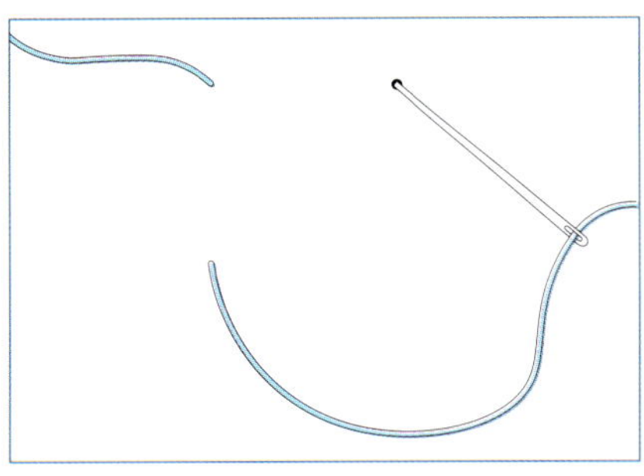

1 Start from the back with a waste knot. Take the needle down at the top left of the cross stitch, and bring it up at the bottom left (this also makes the first vertical stitch on the reverse). Make the first half cross from bottom left to top right.

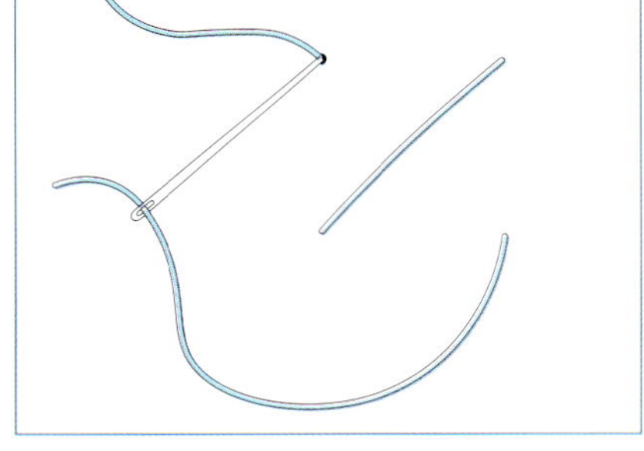

2 Now complete the cross from bottom right to top left. There will be two parallel vertical lines on the reverse side.

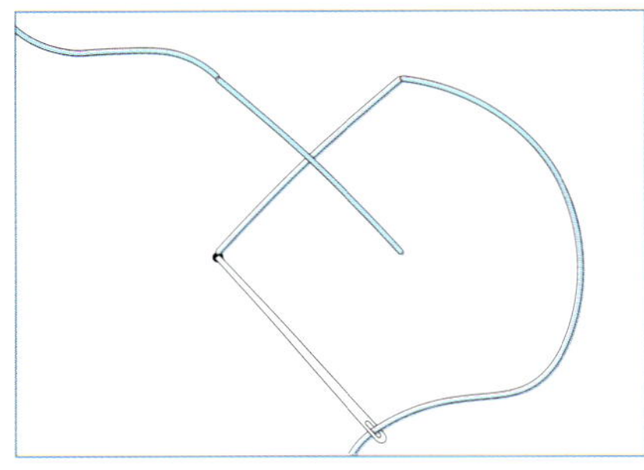

3 In order to make a square on the reverse, the first half cross needs to be stitched again: come up at the top right and go down at the bottom left.

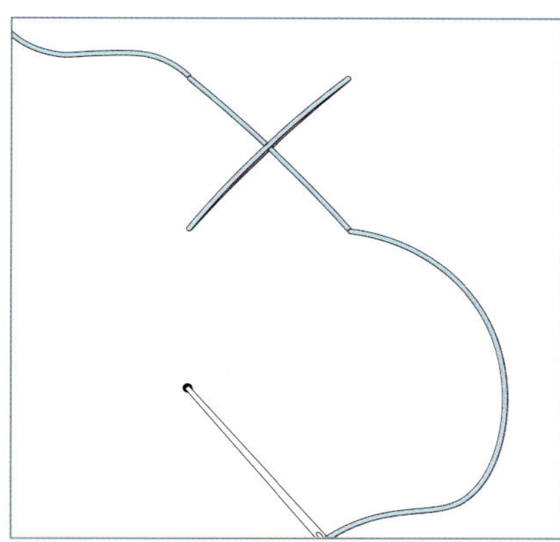

4 Come up at the bottom right in order to complete the square on the reverse. Work the next half cross stitch by going down at the bottom left.

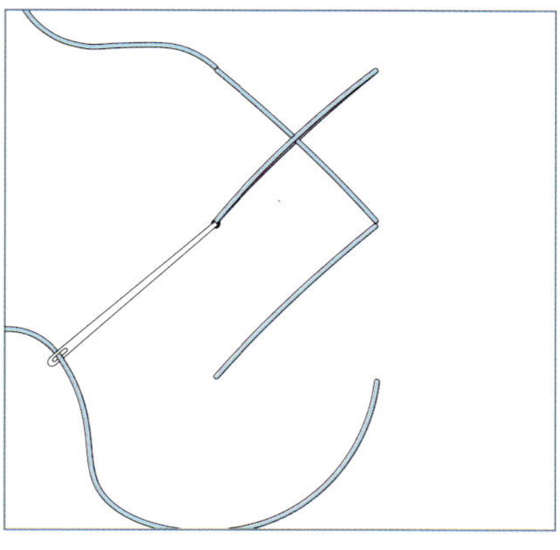

5 Complete the second cross from bottom right to top left, taking the needle down in the same hole as the bottom left of the first cross stitch.

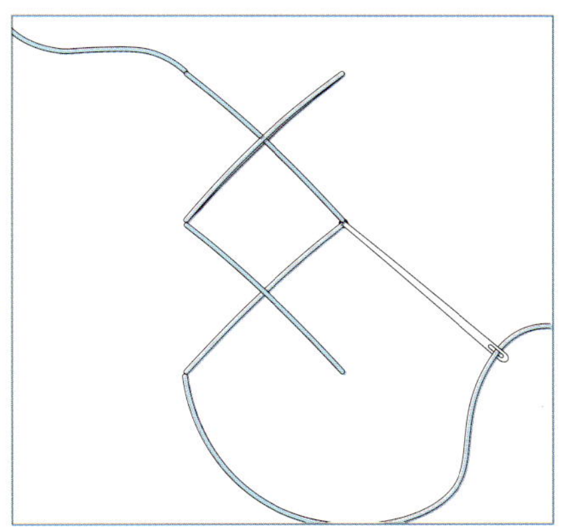

6 As before, in order to make a square on the reverse, the half cross needs to be stitched again: work the half cross from bottom left to top right.

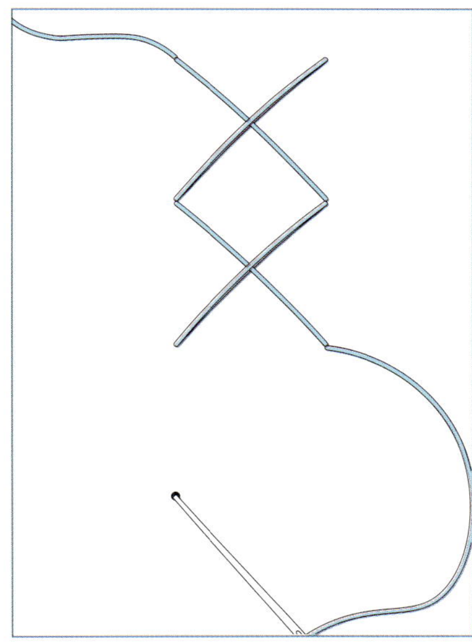

7 Come up at the bottom right of the second cross to complete the square on the reverse. Continue in the same way.

TIP

The waste knot can be woven through the stitch later on.

ROSETTE CHAIN STITCH

SURFACE.

Also known as Bead edging, Bead edging stitch, or Braid stitch.

This stitch is a more elaborate version of twisted chain stitch (see pages 118–119) where the stitches lie at a different angle from other chain stitches. If it is worked in a line, the stitches are parallel to each other; if it is worked in a circle, they radiate out from a central point.

Rosette chain stitch has been used under various names for several centuries. It features on a 16th century Italian embroidered border currently held by the Cooper Hewitt museum in New York, and on a 17th century embroidered panel currently held by the Art Institute of Chicago. Texts from the early 20th century and earlier tend to refer to the stitch as bead edging stitch or braid stitch whereas Mary Thomas' seminal 1934 *Dictionary of Stitches* features it as rosette chain stitch with an alternative name of bead edging stitch.

METHOD

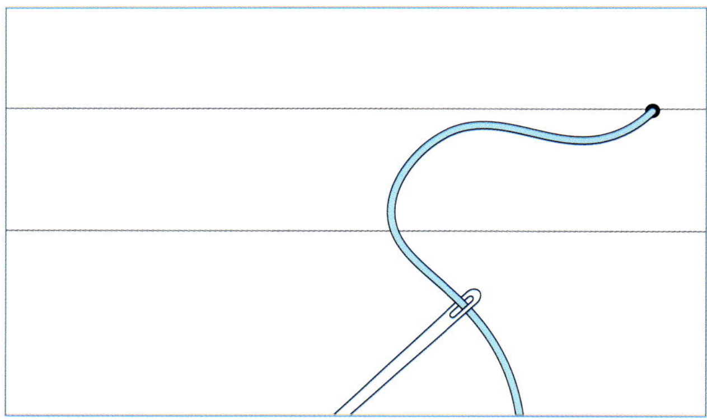

1 Draw or visualize two parallel guidelines and bring your thread up on the top line at the right-hand end.

2 Leaving a loop on the surface with the working thread uppermost, take the needle down slightly ahead along the same guideline.

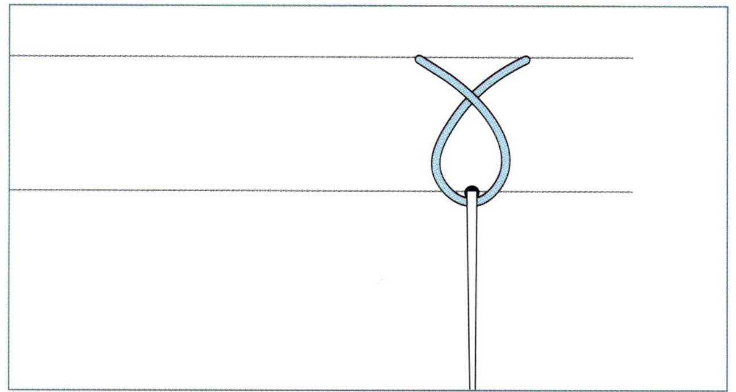

3 Bring the needle up on the bottom guideline, fractionally back from where it went down. Your needle should come up inside the loop of thread. Tighten the thread against the needle.

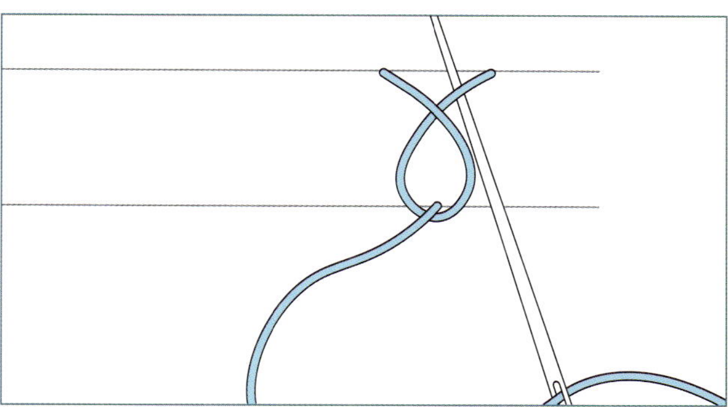

4 Pull the thread through but do not pull it too tight, then slide the needle under the first 'leg' of the chain stitch.

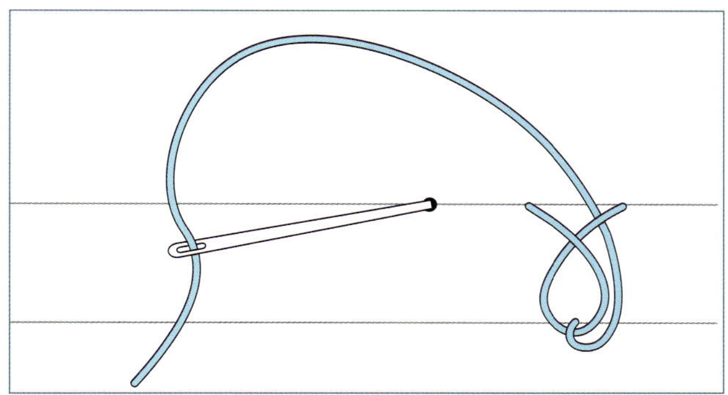

5 This completes your first rosette chain stitch.

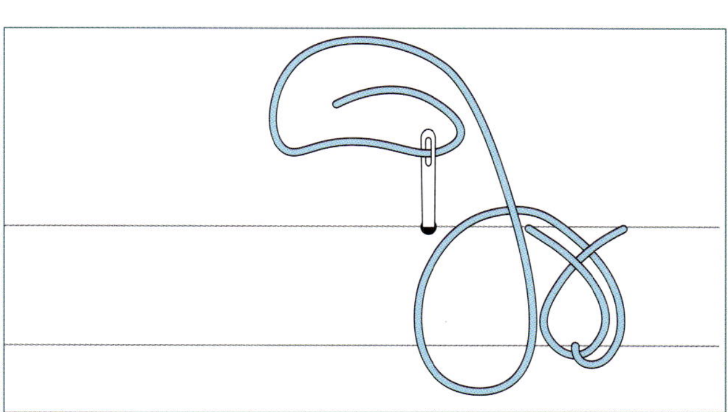

6 Leave a loop on the surface with the working thread uppermost. Take the needle down on the top guideline, a stitch's width along from where it came up.

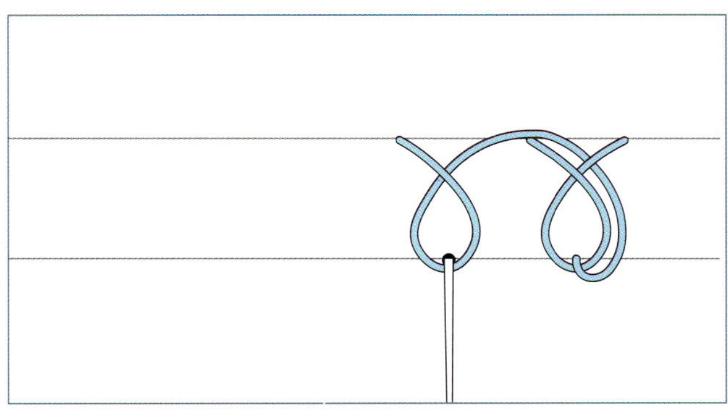

7 Bring the needle up on the bottom guideline, fractionally back from where it went down and slide the thread under the thread which links to the previous stitch. Continue in this way.

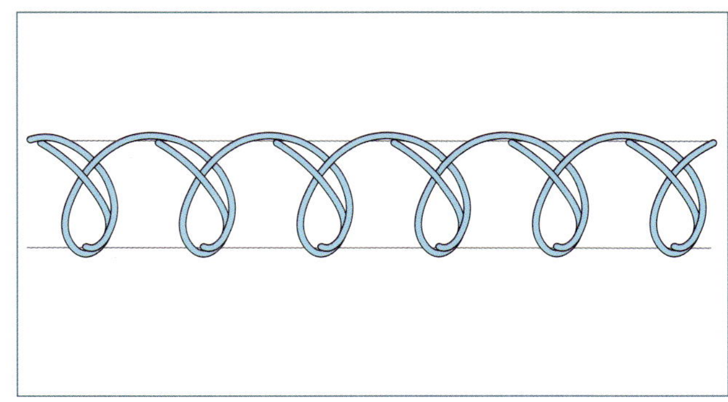

8 To finish, take the thread down on the top guideline.

S-ING (GOLDWORK)

GOLDWORK.

S-ing creates the look of a stem stitch worked in metal purl threads. Traditionally used to create stems or veins down the centre of leaves, it can also be used as an outline.

S-ing was evidently in use in the 17th century as it features on the reverse of a pocket book from that date, currently held by the V&A South Kensington.

METHOD

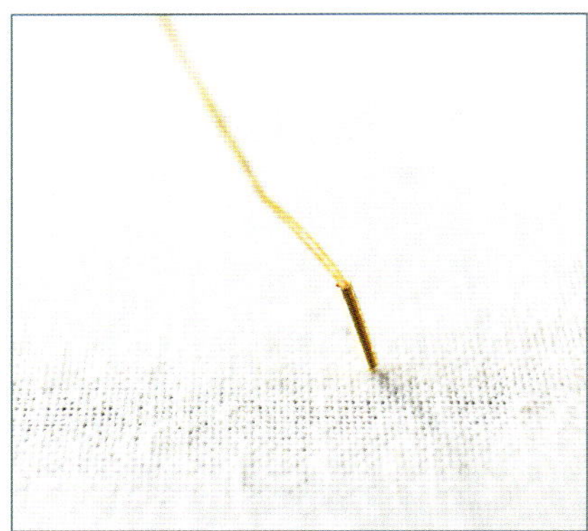

1 Cut several small equal lengths of purl. Using a waxed double thread, bring the needle and thread to the surface. Thread a purl onto the needle and gently manoeuvre it to the base of the thread. Avoid touching it with your fingers, as this causes tarnishing.

2 Secure the purl in position by taking the needle back down through the fabric just short of the purl length, so that the purl curves slightly.

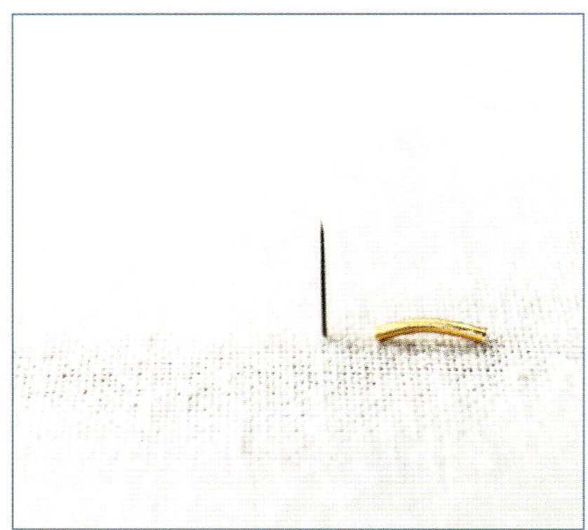

3 Bring the needle and thread to the surface half a purl's length ahead.

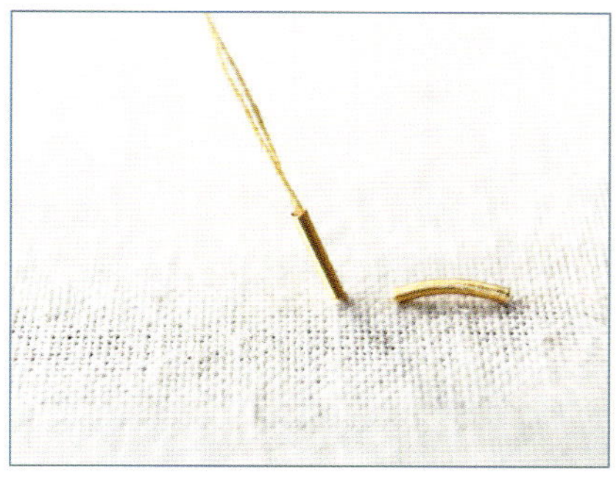

4 Thread a second purl onto the needle and gently manoeuvre it to the base of the thread.

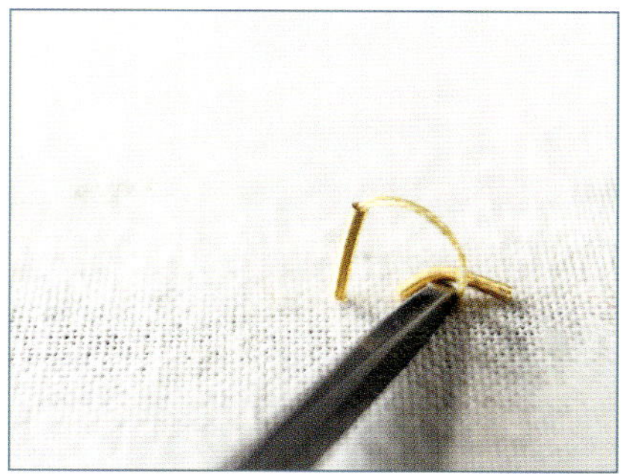

5 Secure the second purl into position by taking the needle down, halfway back under the left side of the previous purl.

6 Use a mellor or laying tool to gently lift the middle of the first purl, allowing the end of the second purl to slide into position.

7 Repeat the sequence by bringing the needle and thread to the surface half a purl's length ahead of the second stitch. Thread a third purl onto the needle and gently manoeuvre it to the base of the thread.

8 Secure the third purl in position by taking the needle down, halfway back under the left side of the previous purl and into the same hole as the end of the previous purl. Continue the sequence to create a stem stitch of metal threads.

◂◂ Goldwork crown detail from ecclesiastical piece, RSN Collection No. 590

For this early 20th century student diploma piece by Margaret Bartlett, s-ing has been worked around the jewels.

SHISHA STITCH (VARIATION 1)

APPLIQUÉ; SURFACE.

Shisha stitch is used to stitch small mirrors onto fabric. It has two stages: the functional element which anchors the mirror firmly and provides a framework for the second, decorative, stage. Two different methods of anchoring the mirror are shown in the picture on the right; the decorative element for this version consists of alternate buttonhole and chain stitches which form a decorative ring.

Shisha means 'glass' or 'mirror' in Persian and Hindi. Mirrors have been used in embroidery across the Islamic world although they are especially noted in embroidery from north-west India to Afghanistan and in central and eastern Europe. Pieces of mica (a shiny mineral) were used before the invention of glass and are still sometimes used, especially in western Sumatra.

METHOD

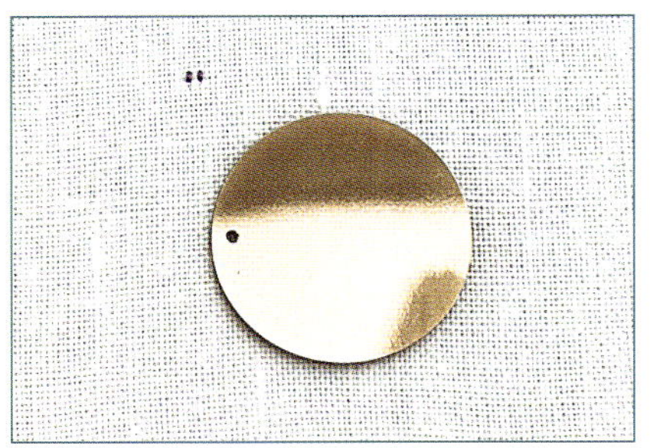

1 Start with a waste knot and make two tiny starting stitches, which will be covered with a circular disc or mirror.

2 Bring the needle up at the lower left-hand edge and make a horizontal stitch, pulling your thread taut.

3 Come up at the upper right-hand edge and make another horizontal stitch.

4 Come up at the upper left-hand edge to make a vertical stitch. Wrap the thread around the upper horizonal stitch first.

5 Then wrap it around the lower one. Take the needle down at the lower left-hand edge.

6 Repeat the process to work another vertical stitch on the right-hand side. This grid forms your foundation. Now bring the needle up at the lower left-hand edge.

7 Take the needle under the lower left intersection of the foundation, keeping the thread to the left.

8 Take the needle down where you first emerged, keeping the thread to the left to make a loop.

9 Bring the needle up inside the loop to make a chain stitch. The size of the chain stitch depends on how densely you wish to cover the mirror.

10 Repeat the process: take the needle under the grid foundation stitch, keeping the thread to the left.

11 Take the needle down inside the previous chain stitch and bring it up to make another chain stitch.

12 Continue working around the mirror.

13 To connect the last chain stitch to the beginning of the chain, take the needle under the first chain stitch. Then take the needle down inside the previous chain stitch.

14 Finish off the thread on the reverse, catching some stitches to secure the thread.

SMALL EYELET

Whitework; Ayrshire; Surface.

Also known as Round eyelet (Broderie Anglaise), Overcast eyelet, or Eyelet hole.

A small round hole is made by pushing the threads of the fabric apart (rather than by cutting it) and then stitching over the edge of the eyelet to secure it.

Eyelets are used in various embroidery traditions, the earliest of which is Guimarães embroidery from Portugal which dates from the 10th century. They became more widely used in the 19th century in various forms of whitework: Madeira embroidery, Wallachian embroidery, Ayrshire work, and most notably Broderie Anglaise which featured eyelets of varying sizes.

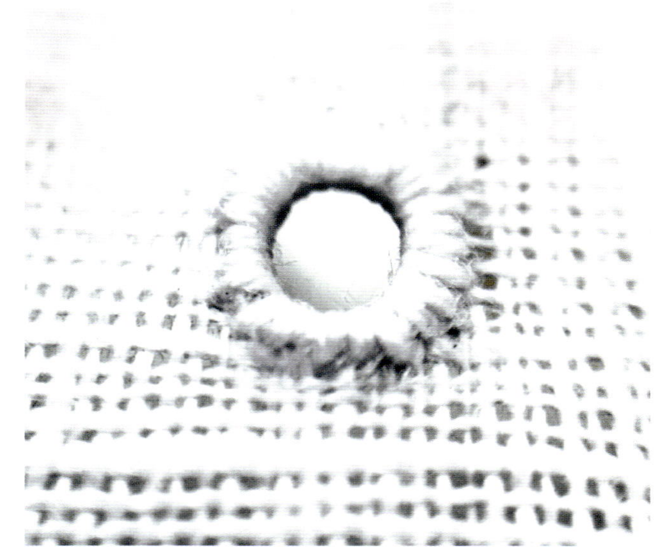

METHOD

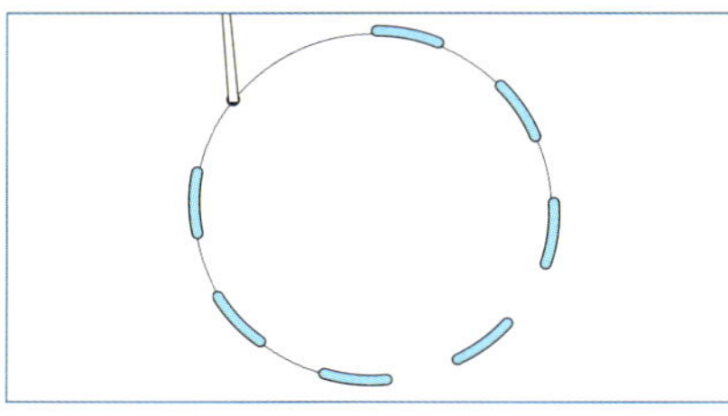

1 Start with a couple of holding stitches, then work a ring of running stitch the desired size of the eyelet. Each stitch should be about 2mm (⅛in) long.

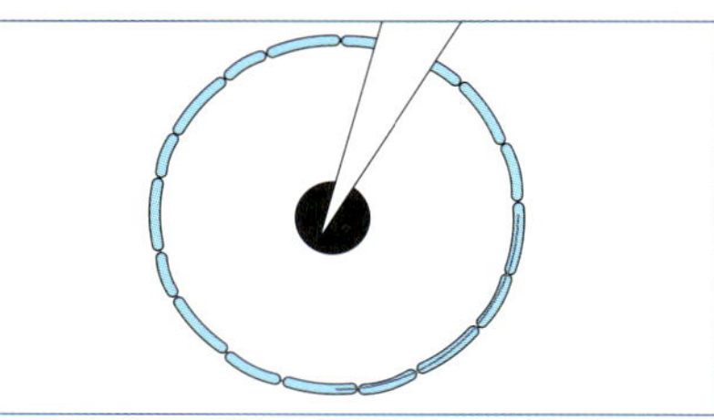

2 Push the tip of a stiletto into the centre of the ring, twisting the stiletto to increase the size of the hole gradually. Then remove the stiletto from the hole while you stitch.

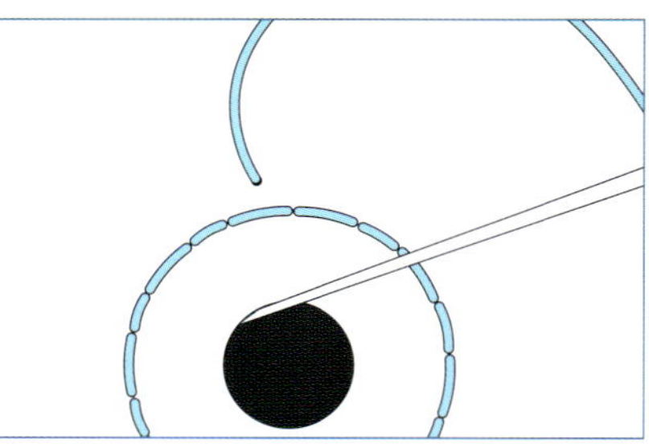

3 Bring the needle up about 2mm (⅛in) outside the ring, then pass the needle down through the hole. Bring the needle up again next to the first stitch and back through the hole again.

TIP

A single line of running stitch may be enough on fine fabric, but double running stitch is more secure; work back round to fill the gaps.

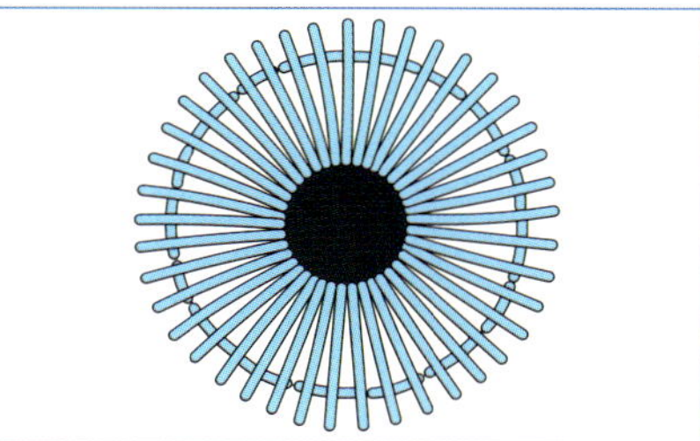

4 Repeat all the way around the eyelet, using the stiletto from time to time to neaten the hole.

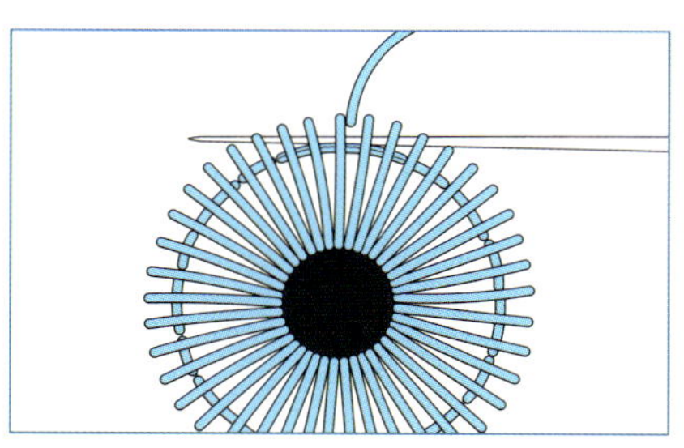

5 Once complete, run the needle under a few stitches on the back to finish it tidily.

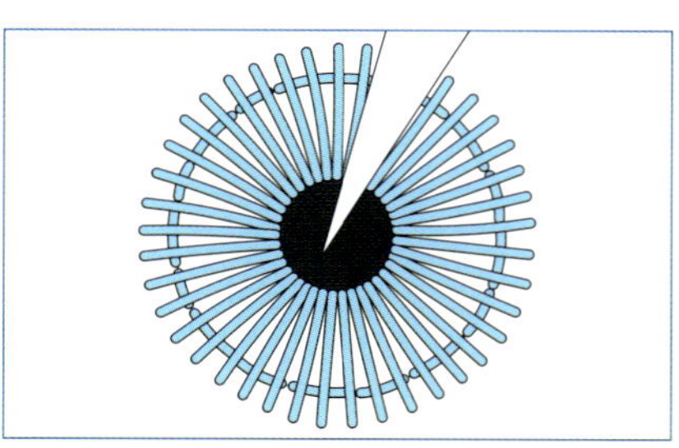

6 Use the stiletto to make sure the hole looks round.

SQUARE EYELET (PULLED THREAD)

PULLED THREAD; WHITEWORK.

Also known as Detached eyelet.

A square stitch consisting of an even number of stitches radiating out from a central hole. It can be worked individually or rows of square eyelet can be combined with other pulled work stitches to form a filling pattern.

Square eyelets date from at least the 17th century; they feature on a whitework swaddling band held by the V&A South Kensington. They also feature on 19th-century Turkish pieces currently held by the V&A, some of them using metal thread.

This stitch is similar to Algerian eye stitch on page 298: the difference is in the number of stitches radiating from the centre and how much tension is used to open the centre of the stitch.

METHOD

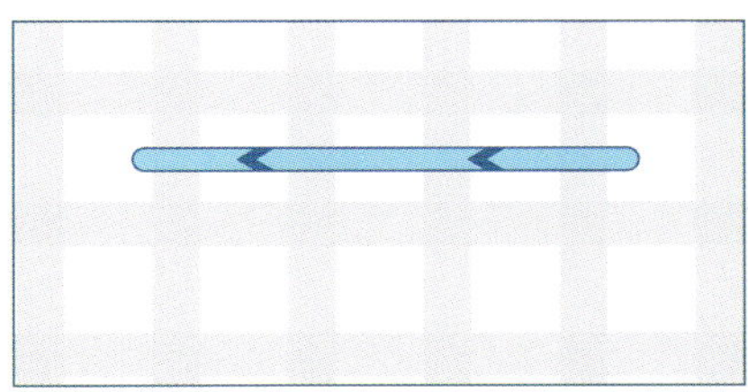

1 Bring the needle up and make a horizontal stitch four threads to the left (this is the position of the centre hole).

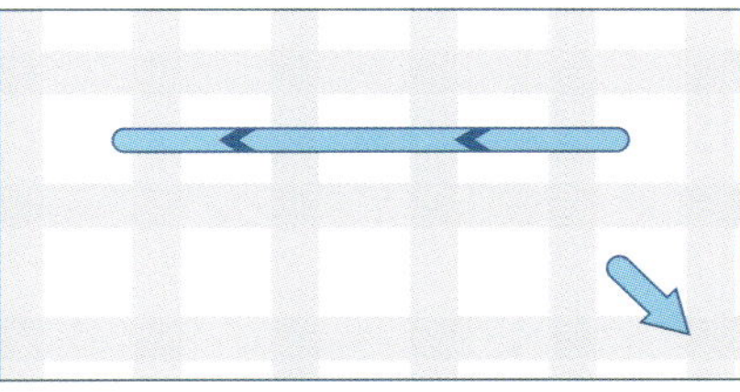

2 Bring the needle up one thread below the starting point and pull.

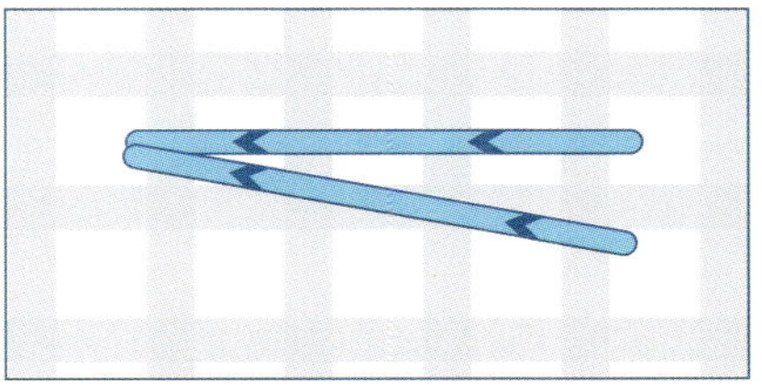

3 Take the needle down in the centre hole (four threads left and one up).

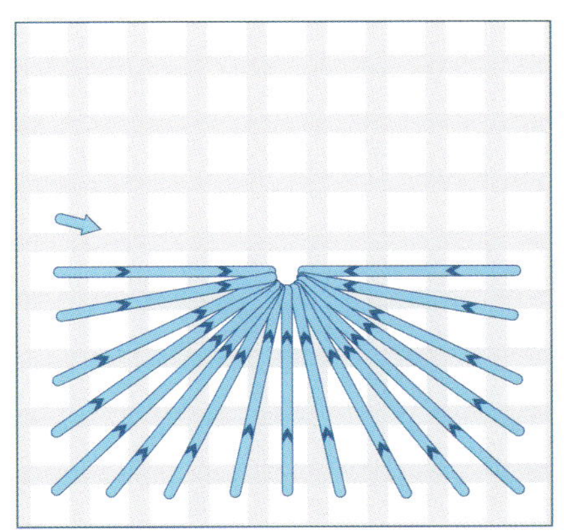

4 Follow the diagram for the placement of the stitches, and continue round the eyelet. Pull the thread each time you bring the needle up through the fabric, to maintain a neat hole.

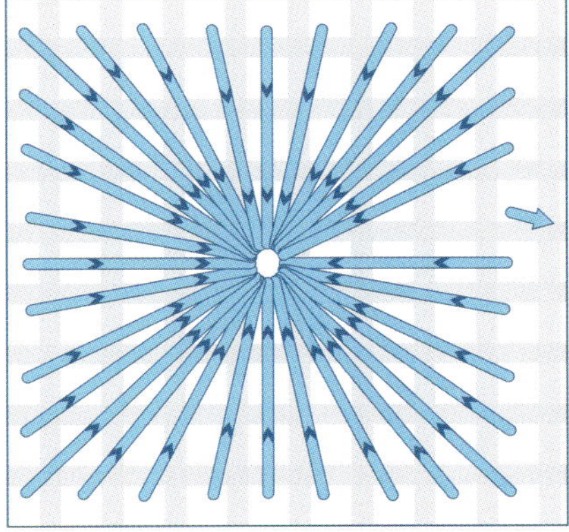

5 Pull the final stitch.

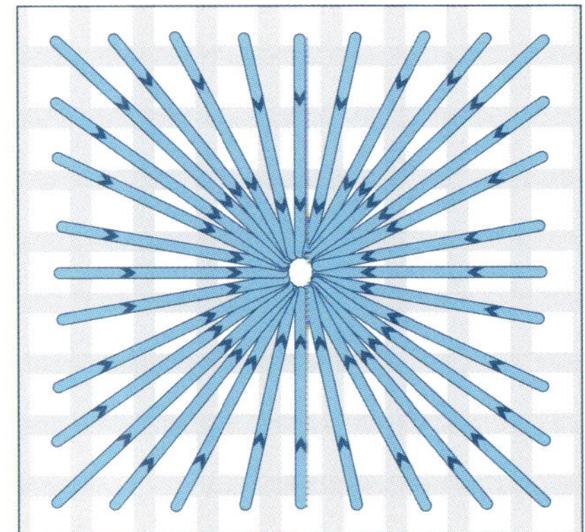

The finished eyelet.

STAR EYELET STITCH

Surface.

Also known as Spoke stitch, or Ray stitch.

This surface embroidery stitch consists of several straight stitches radiating out from a small central hole. The straight stitches can vary in number, length and spacing. The alternative names of ray and spoke stitch accurately describe the structure of the stitch.

Note that Algerian eye stitch (see page 298) is sometimes also known as a star eyelet.

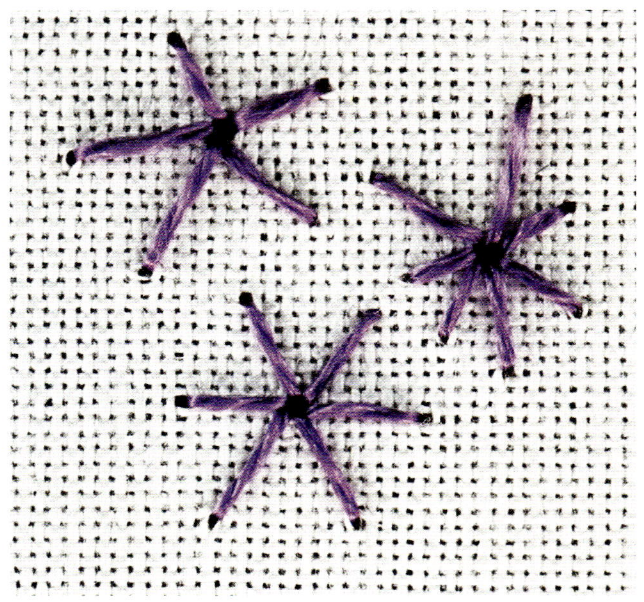

METHOD

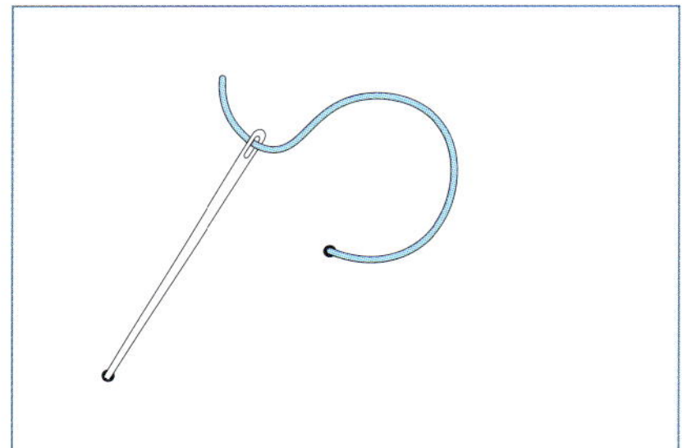

1 Decide where the centre of your eyelet is and how long you want the spokes of the eyelet to be, and bring your needle up that distance from the centre. Take your needle down in the centre of the eyelet.

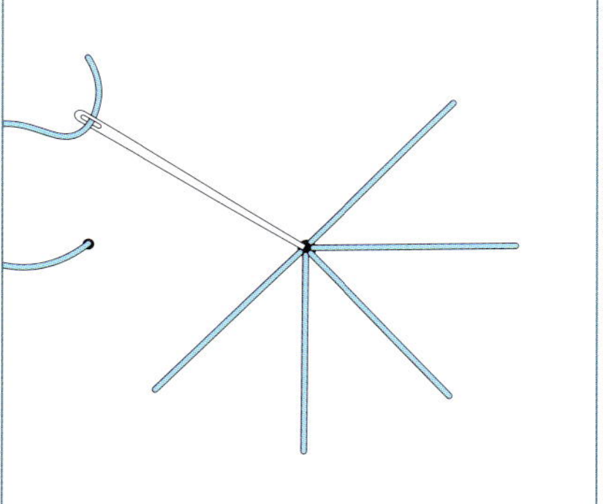

2 For subsequent spokes, bring your needle up a little further around the edge of the eyelet shape, then down again in the centre.

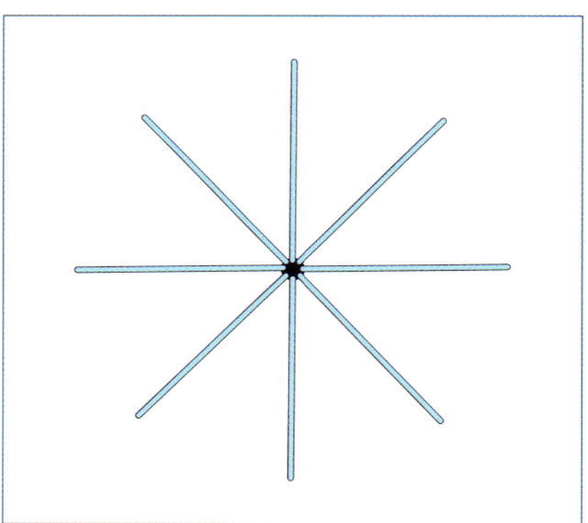

3 Repeat until you have completed the circle.

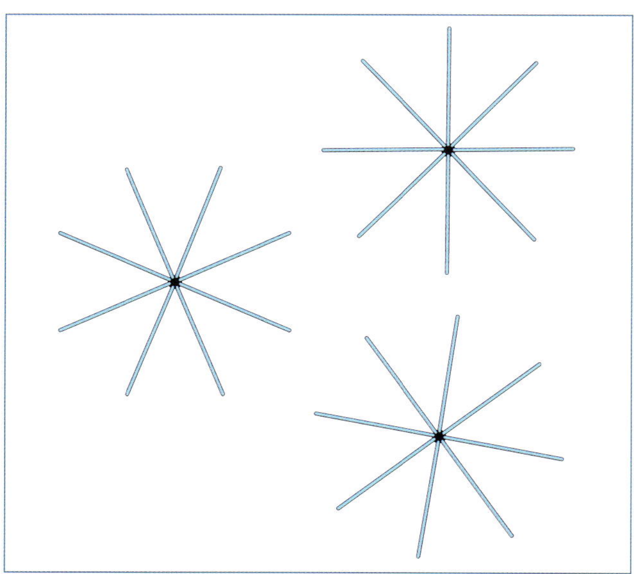

4 Further eyelet stitches can be added to fill an area or form a pattern.

▲▲ *Mater Amabalis*, RSN Collection No. 1211A

Part of the Litany of Loreto series, this piece features the delicate and simple use of straight stitches; some used to create cross hatching for the shading. Stem stitch (see pages 40–41) and split stitch (see page 39) are used; split stitch predominantly for the hair. Couching (see page 63) is used for the Japanese thread.

TWO-SIDED CROSS STITCH

SURFACE; COUNTED THREAD.

Also known as Double-sided cross stitch, Spanish stitch, or Double running stitch.

This version of cross stitch appears identical on both the front and reverse of the fabric. It is useful for embellishing garments or household items where both sides of the cloth are likely to be visible.

There are two methods of working this stitch: in these instructions the final cross in a row has the 'wrong' half cross stitch uppermost. For a slightly different version, where the final cross in a row is made up of quarter stitches which join in the centre of the cross, see RSN Stitch Bank online.

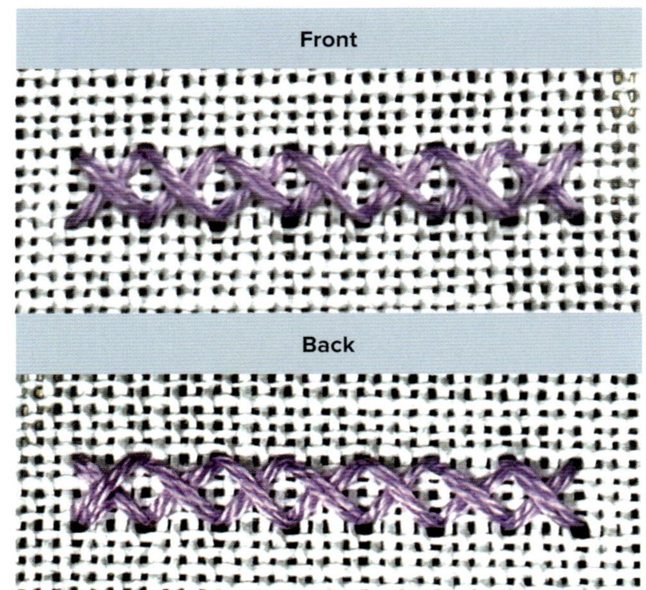

METHOD

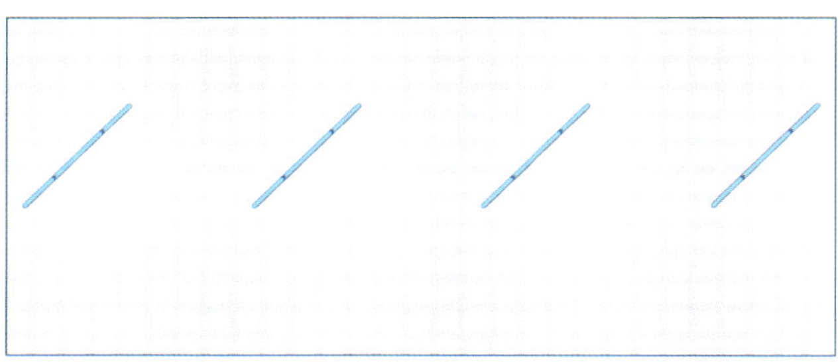

1 First journey: Work half crosses left to right as shown. The gaps between the stitches should be the same width as the half crosses.

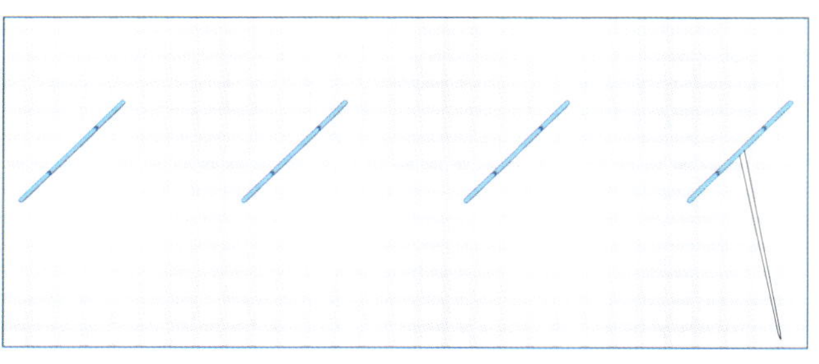

2 Second journey: At the end of the row, make an auxiliary stitch (¼ stitch) by coming up in the middle of the half cross.

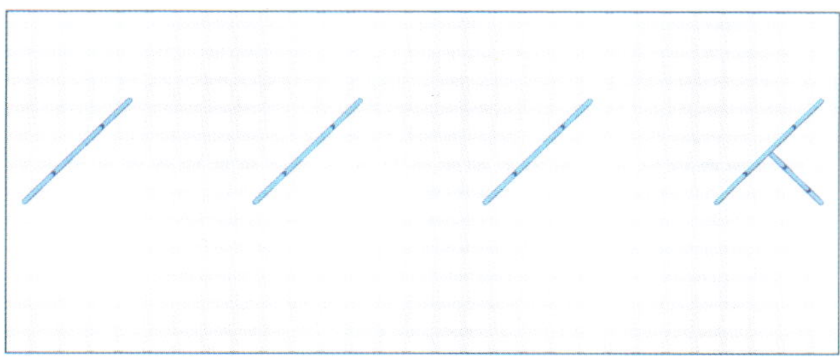

3 Go back down at the bottom right of the cross.

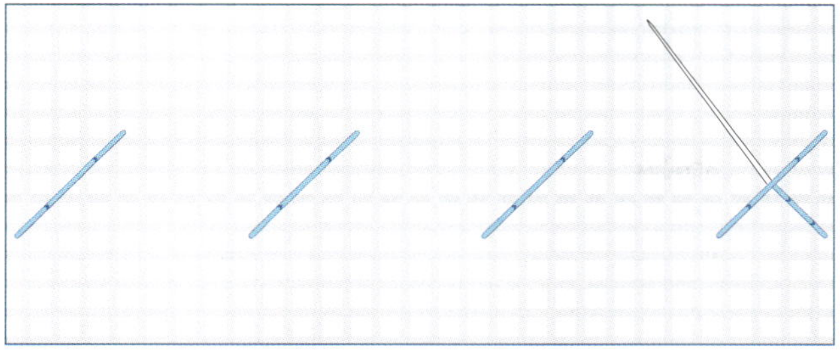

4 Make another auxiliary stitch (¼ stitch) by coming up in the middle of the half cross.

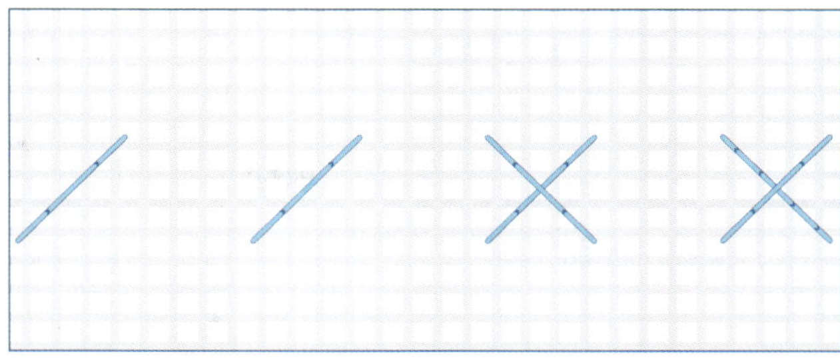

5 Go back down at the top left of the cross. Come up at the bottom right of the next cross and make a half cross to complete the cross.

6 Work the second journey from right to left.

7 Third journey: Come up at the bottom right of the first cross.

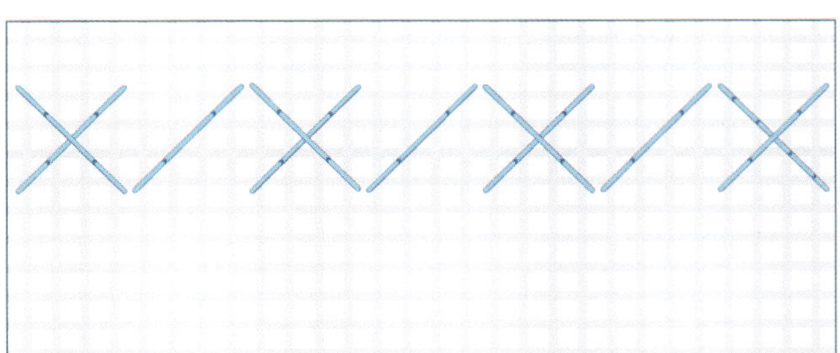

8 Work the third journey of half crosses from left to right as shown.

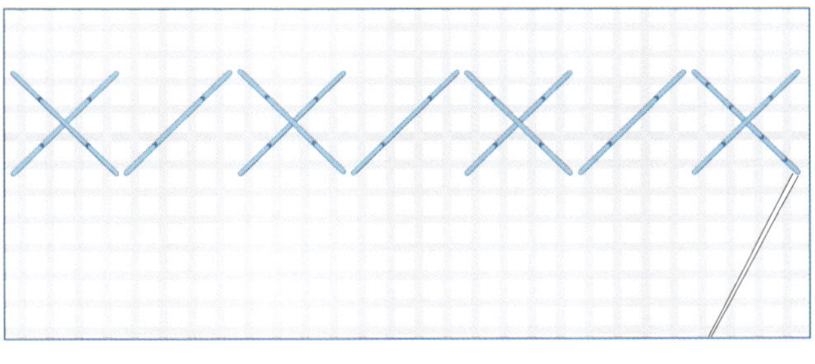

9 Fourth journey: At the end of the row, make an auxiliary stitch (¼ stitch) by coming up at the bottom right of the cross and going down in the middle of the cross.

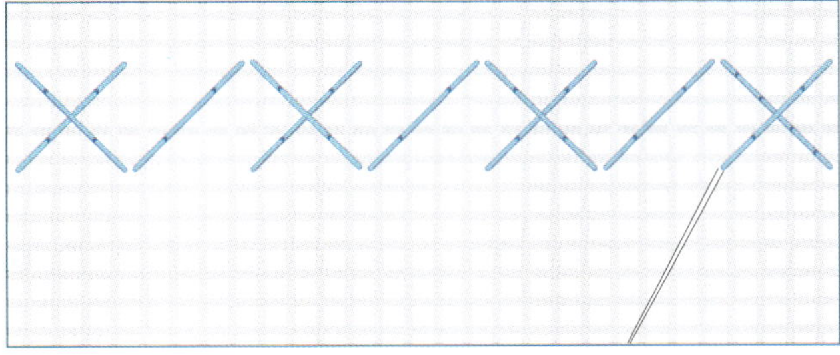

10 Come up at the bottom left of the cross to get ready to work half crosses.

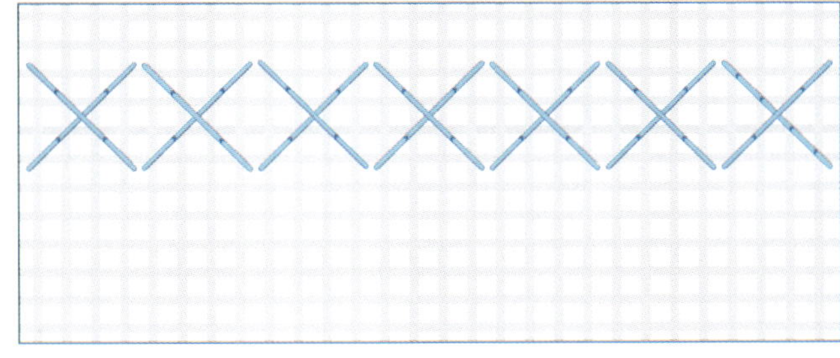

11 Work the half crosses from right to left to complete the four journeys. There should be crosses on the reverse as well.

WHIPPED WHEEL

Crewelwork; Ribbonwork; Surface; Stumpwork.

Also known as Spider's wheel stitch, Ribbed wheel, Ribbed spider's web, Back-stitched spider's web, Back stitch spider's web, English wheel, English rosette, or Rosette.

Whipped wheel can be worked over an odd or even number of spokes and produces quite a raised stitch that adds an interesting ribbed texture. Its origins are unclear, but it is referenced (as an English wheel) in *Mrs Beeton's Book of Needlework*, published in 1870.

METHOD

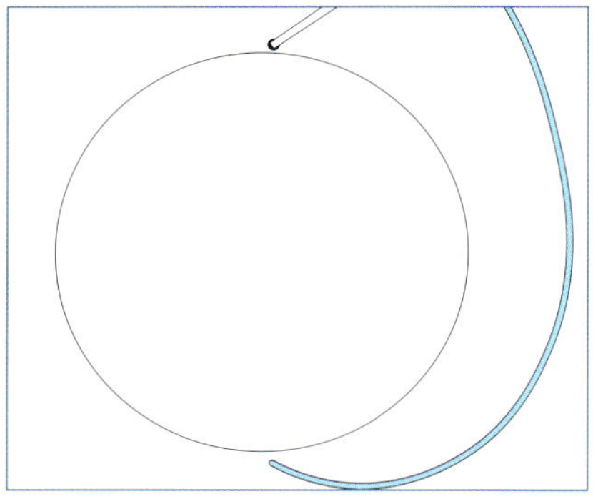

1 Bring your needle up just outside the edge of your circle, then take it down directly opposite.

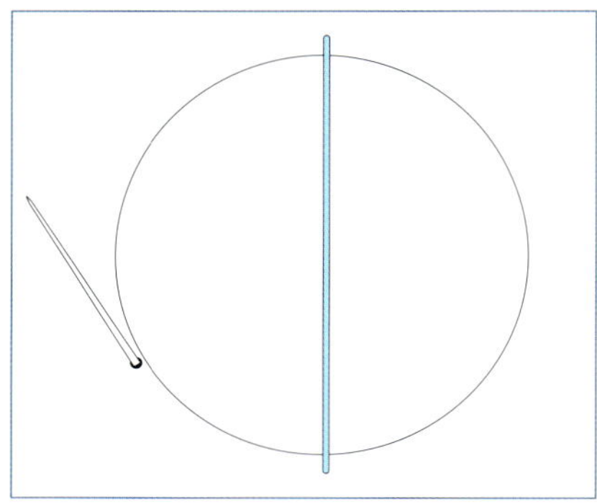

2 Take the needle down through the fabric and draw the thread through, then bring it back up two-thirds of the way around the circle.

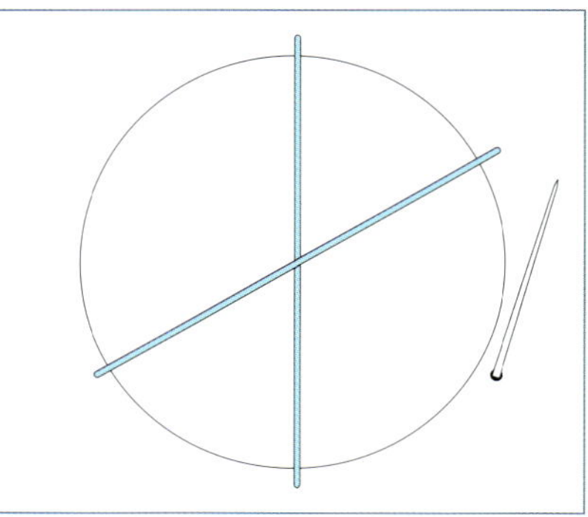

3 Take the needle down directly across, then bring it back up roughly a third of the way around the circle.

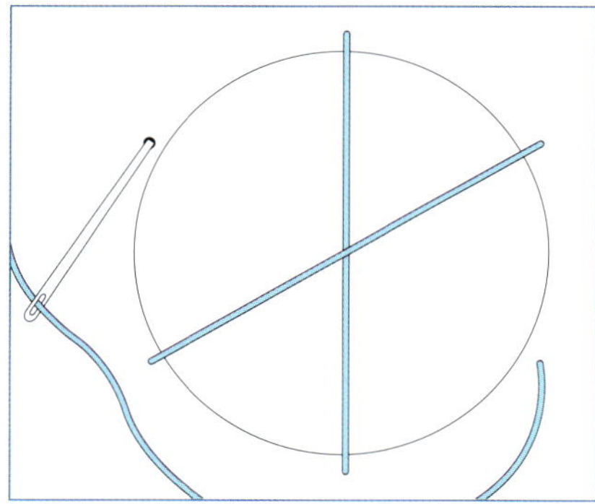

4 Draw the thread across and down opposite.

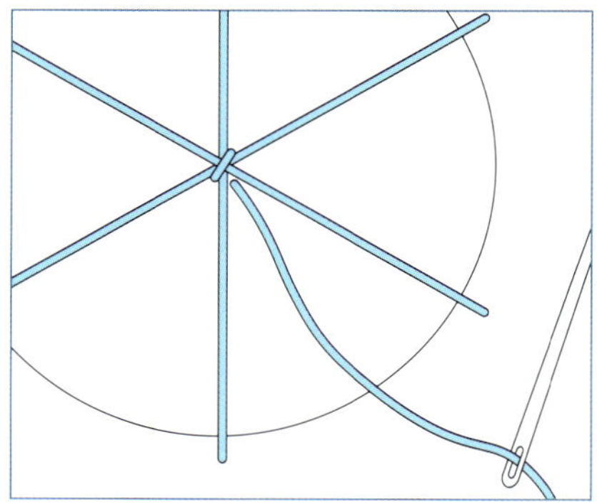

5 Make a small holding stitch in the centre. Bring the thread up between two of the spokes, then swap to a tapestry needle.

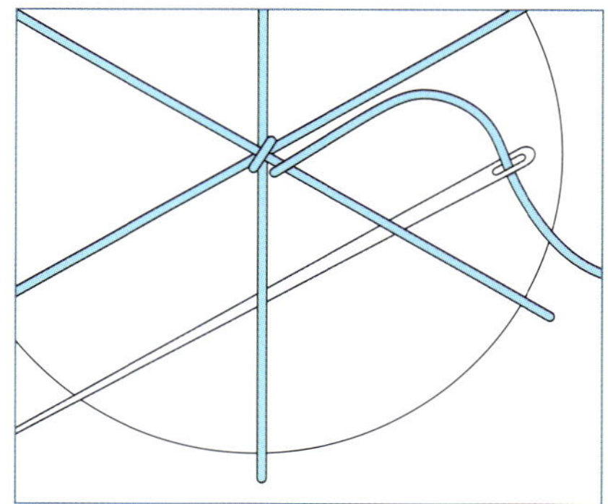

6 Bring the needle back up in the centre of the star. Take the needle anticlockwise, over the first spoke adjacent, then clockwise, under the first and second spokes.

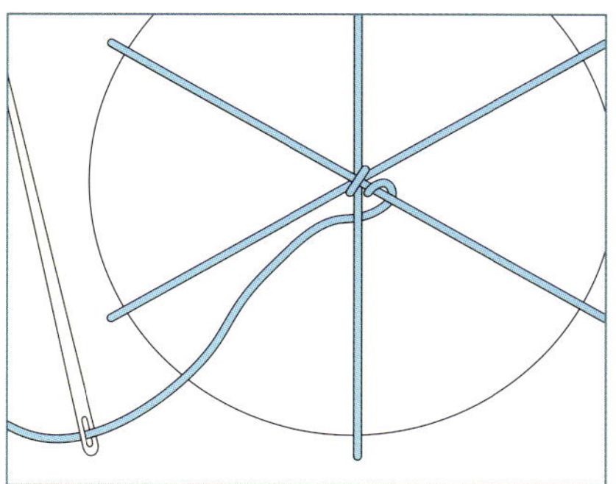

7 Draw the needle and thread through and pull the thread tight against the centre.

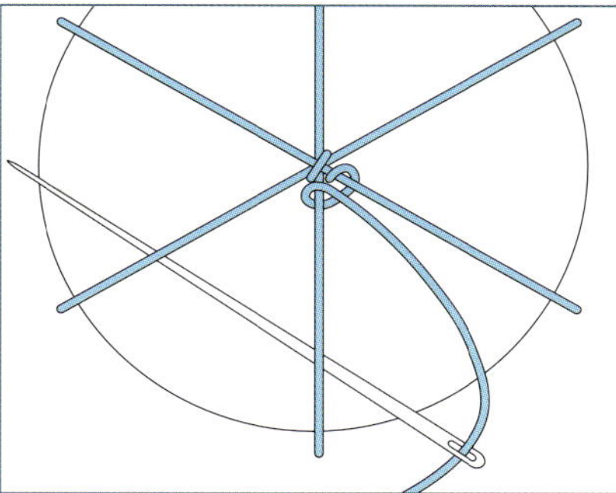

8 Take the needle over then under the second spoke, and also under the third spoke clockwise.

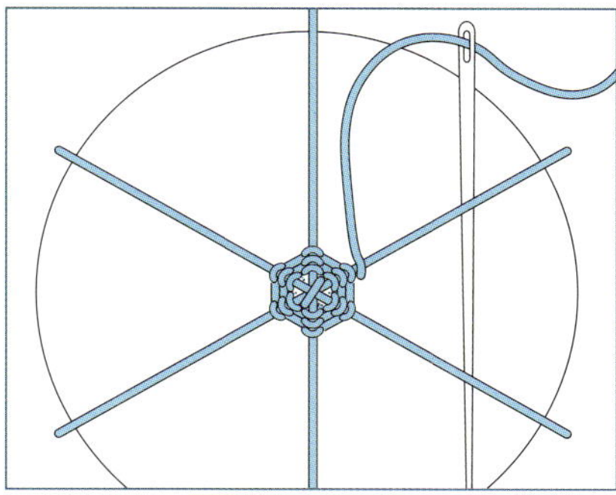

9 Continue this sequence, taking the needle back over the previous spoke, then under the next two.

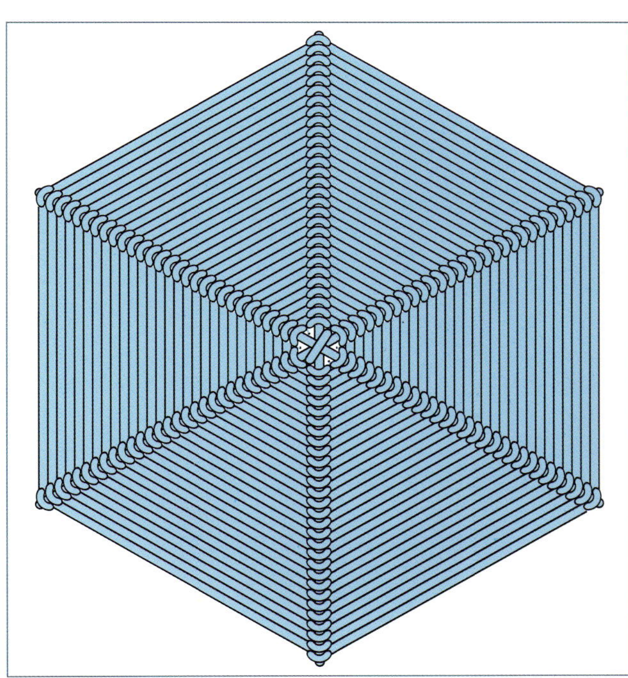

10 Work all the way around the wheel until the spokes are completely covered. Secure the thread as normal.

▲▲Detail from 20th century artwork, RSN Collection No. 1222

This piece has been worked in the Jacobean crewelwork style. Whipped wheel has been used here to form the basis of a flower. The full piece can be seen on page 273.

WOVEN PICOT

Stumpwork; Surface.

Also known as Brazilian needle weaving.

Woven picots can be worked large or small, thin or wide. Picots that are attached to the fabric at both the base and the point can be worked with two, three, four or five prongs.

Note that woven picots are distinct from both loop and ring picots (see pages 288–289). See also detached woven picot on page 310 for a detached version.

METHOD

1 For a two-pronged picot: Make two stitches form a point. This will be the size of the finished woven picot.

2 Bring the needle through to the front of the fabric just under the tip to the left.

3 To weave, take the needle over and under from left to right. Use a tapestry needle or the eye of the needle.

4 Then weave back by taking the needle over and under from right to left.

5 Weave back and forth across the shape, from top to bottom. Push the thread up with the needle as you work to ensure the rows are tightly packed.

6 Continue to the bottom of the shape, finishing the stitch in the centre of the base, tucking the thread up underneath the weave.

7 For a three-pronged picot, make the initial shape with two stitches as above, then work a third stitch halfway between them.

8 Bring the needle through to the front of the fabric just under the tip to the left.

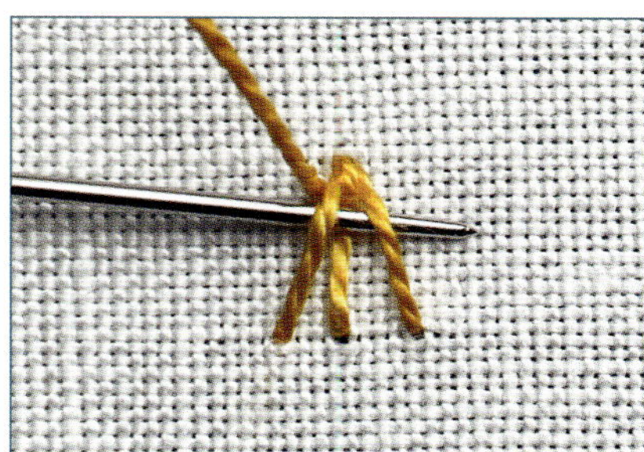

9 Start a three-pronged picot by going under the first thread, over the middle thread and under the third thread from left to right.

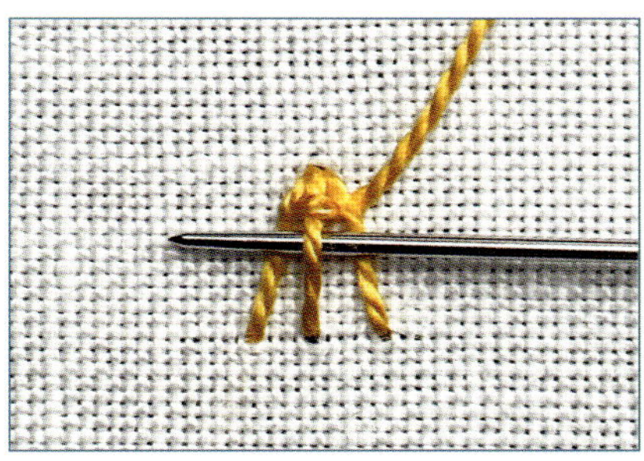

10 Then weave back by going over the first thread, under the middle thread and over the third thread from right to left.

11 Weave back and forth across the shape. Towards the end when it is hard to go under, over and under the three threads in one go, take the needle under the first thread.

12 Then go under the third thread.

13 Work down to the end of the shape and tuck the thread underneath the weave to finish it.

WOVEN WHEEL

Surface; Crewelwork; Ribbonwork; Wessex stitchery.

Also known as Wheel stitch, Spider's web, Spider web weaving, Whipped circle, Woven spot, Woven spoke, Berry stitch, or Sorrento wheel.

Woven wheel stitch is constructed from a wheel of an odd number of spokes with the same or a different thread woven around them. It produces a raised circle of thread which lends itself to portraying flowers.

Woven wheels feature in Elizabethan embroidery, as demonstrated by various textiles in the V&A South Kensington. The examples are typically stitched in metal thread, either silver or silver-gilt. They also feature in Hedebo work from Denmark, a whitework technique in which they embellish the centre of eyelets.

METHOD

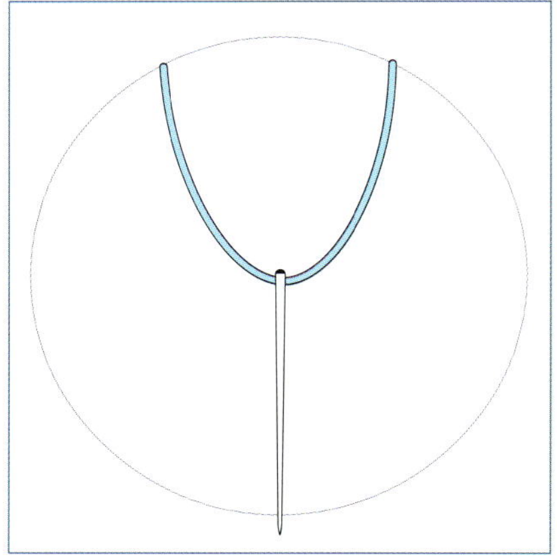

1 Bring your needle up at the edge of the circle, then take it down a little way around in a clockwise direction, still on the edge of the circle. Bring the needle up at the centre of the circle and tighten the loop against it.

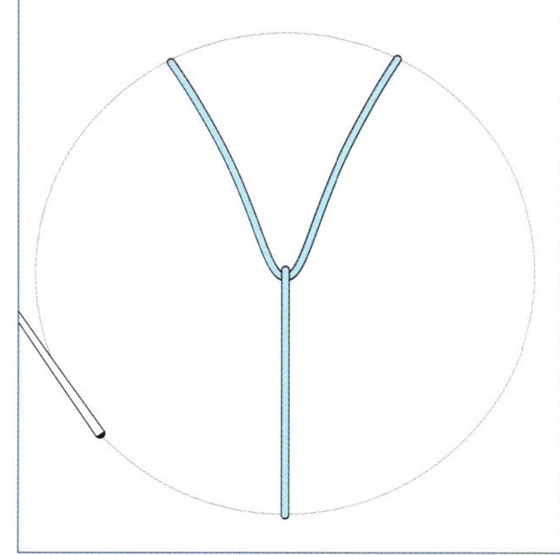

2 Take the needle down, as though finishing a fly stitch. Bring it up a little way clockwise around the circle (aim for the same distance as between the initial stitch's spacing).

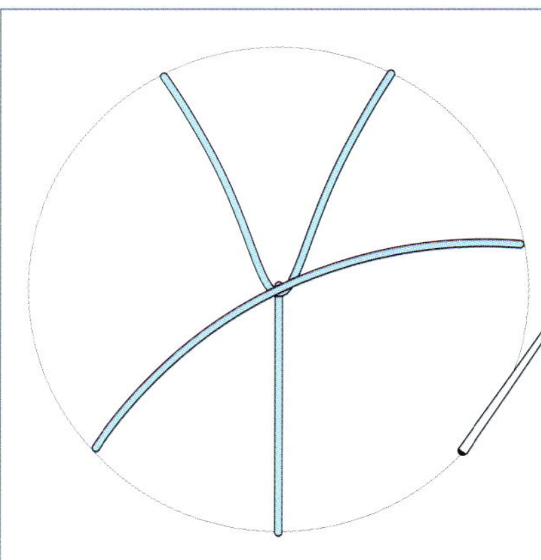

3 Take the needle directly across the centre, and down at the two o'clock position. Draw the thread through and bring it up a little way clockwise around the circle.

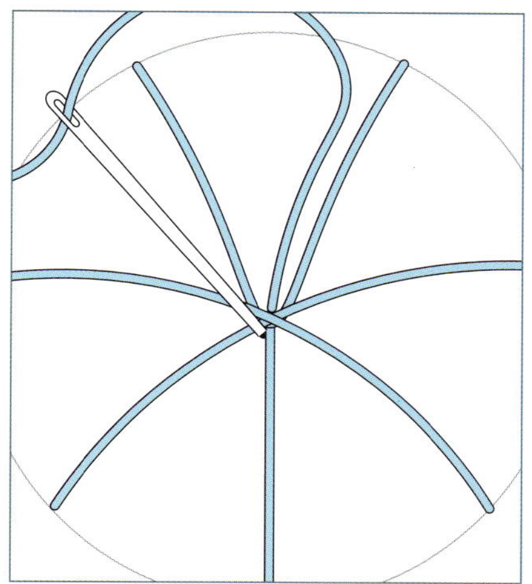

4 Take the needle across and down opposite, then make a small holding stitch in the centre of the spokes.

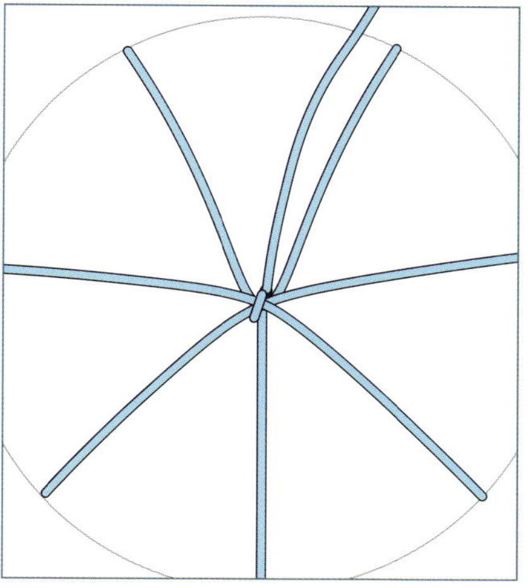

5 Bring the needle up slightly off-centre, between the spokes and close to the holding stitch.

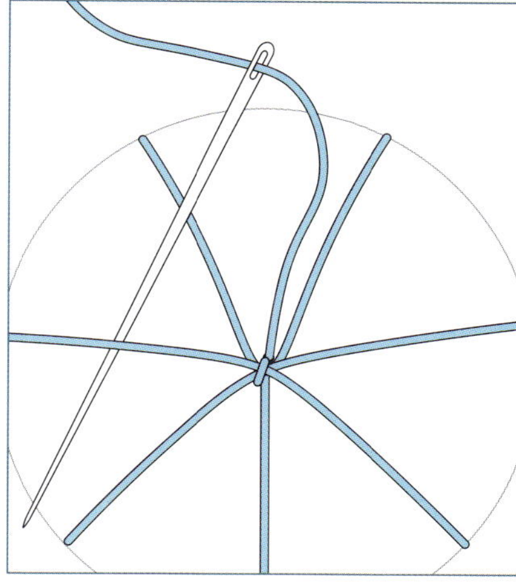

6 Change to a tapestry needle and, working anticlockwise, slip the thread over the adjacent spoke and under the next one.

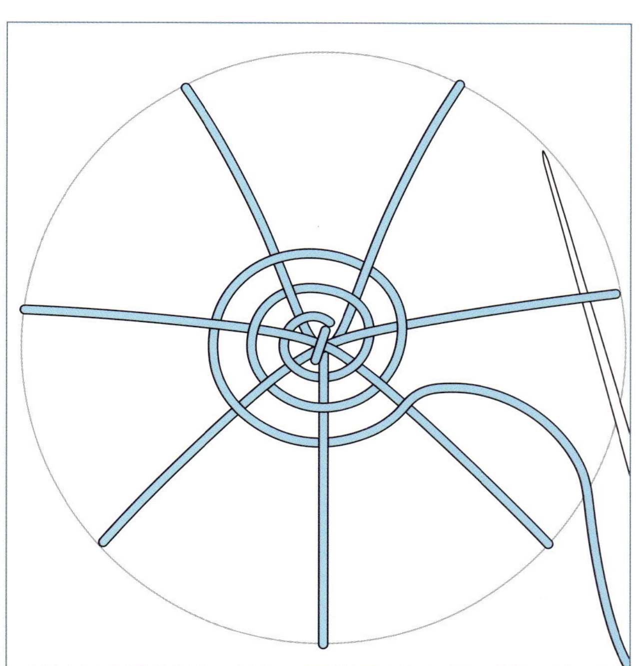

7 Continue working in this way, weaving the thread over then under alternate spokes. Work outwards from the wheel's centre.

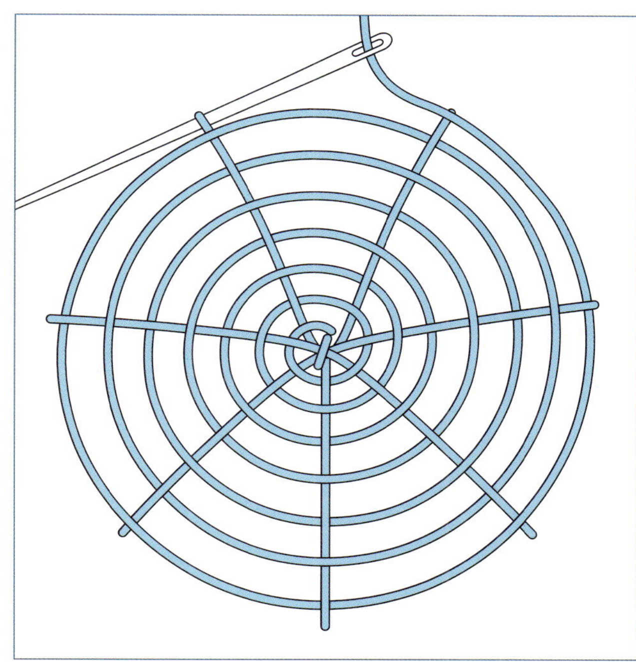

8 Continue working until the spokes are completely covered, then take the needle through to the back and secure the thread.

INDEX

STITCHES BY USE

STITCHES BY NAME

EMBROIDERY TECHNIQUES

First published in 2025

Search Press Limited
Wellwood, North Farm Road,
Tunbridge Wells, Kent TN2 3DR

4 5 6 7 8 9 10

ISBN: 978-1-80092 -286-0
ebook ISBN: 978-1-80093-278-4

Bookmarked Hub
For further ideas and inspiration, and to join our free online community, visit www.bookmarkedhub.com

Publishers' notes
The Publishers and author can accept no responsibility for any consequences arising from the information, advice or instructions given in this publication.

You are invited to visit the RSN's websites:
Royal School of Needlework: (www.royal-needlework.org.uk)
RSN Stitch Bank: (www. rsnstitchbank.org)
RSN Collection & Archive:
(www. collections.royal-needlework.org.uk)

For errata, please visit our website (www.searchpress.com) or the Bookmarked Hub (www.bookmarkedhub.com).

GPSR information can be found at www.searchpress.com
Printed in China, TT042026

▲▲ Detail from crest, RSN Collection COL.30

The lion's body was worked using turning metal thread couching. It is padded and worked in couched gold passing thread, and outlined in pearl purl.

Another detail of the crest can be seen on page 211.

RSN STITCHBANK

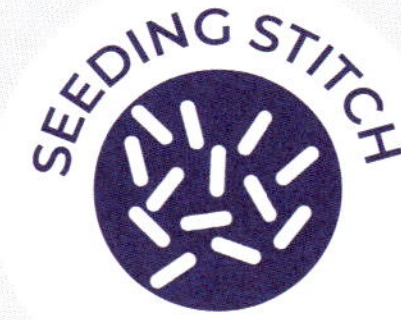